Twentieth-Century Britain

Twentieth-Century Britain

A Political History

WILLIAM D. RUBINSTEIN

First published 2003 by
PALGRAVE MACMILLAN
Houndmills, Basingstoke, Hampshire RG21 6XS and
175 Fifth Avenue, New York, N.Y. 10010
Companies and representatives throughout the world

PALGRAVE MACMILLAN is the global academic imprint of the Palgrave
Macmillan division of St. Martin's Press, LLC and of Palgrave Macmillan Ltd.
Macmillan® is a registered trademark in the United States, United Kingdom
and other countries. Palgrave is a registered trademark in the European
Union and other countries.

ISBN 0–333–77223–7 hardback
ISBN 0–333–77224–5 paperback

This book is printed on paper suitable for recycling and made from fully
managed and sustained forest sources.

A catalogue record for this book is available from the British Library.

A catalog record for this book is available from the Library of Congress.

10 9 8 7 6 5 4 3 2 1
12 11 10 09 08 07 06 05 04 03

Printed in China

Contents

1
Britain in 1900: Salisbury and Balfour, 1900–05

As the twentieth century opened, Britain and its Empire arguably remained the largest and most important geopolitical unit in the world. Britain had peacefully transformed itself, during the previous seventy years, into something like a democracy, and was free of much of the internal unrest present elsewhere in Europe; in particular (in contrast to Germany and France) it had no significant socialist party, and there were no domestic threats to the authority of the British government apart from Irish nationalism. Britain's political system consisted of a seemingly stable two-party system, with the Liberal party (frequently referred to in the press as the 'Radical party') and the Conservative party alternating in power after General Elections. Since 1886 the Conservative party had been allied with, and increasingly absorbed, a significant breakaway group from the Liberal party known as the Liberal Unionists. Officially, the Conservative party was, in 1900, known as the 'Unionists' in recognition of the end which had brought the Conservatives and the Liberal Unionists together: maintenance of the political union with Ireland and opposition to Irish Home Rule. Popularly, too, the Unionists were also known as the 'Tories' as the Conservative party still is.

The Liberal party traced its origins to the Whig opposition to Tory rule during the period of the French Revolutionary and Napoleonic wars. The sentiments which had animated Charles James Fox and his associates remained as significant and central forces in the Liberal party as the twentieth century opened: political and religious liberty, representative government, a friendly attitude towards democracy, and opposition (at least in theory) to hereditary privileges. The party stood for Free Trade and had always supported virtual 'laissez-faire' in the business sphere, although many younger 'New Liberals' and radicals now supported a much greater measure of government collectivism.

The party was responsible for the 1832 Reform Act and many other notable reforms of the nineteenth century, and had produced many of that century's leading British politicians, among them Lord Grey of the Reform Act, Lord John Russell, Lord Palmerston, and, above all, William Ewart Gladstone (1809–98), the 'Grand Old Man' of British Liberalism, four times Prime Minister. At the end of the nineteenth century, the Liberal party received much of its support from Nonconformists, especially in big cities and the industrialised

1

areas, many businessmen, especially outside London, and much of the working class. It was disproportionately strong in the Celtic areas: Wales and Scotland. It still included a small group of 'Whig' landowners, although since the 1880s most had left the party for the Unionists. Nonconformists, with their agenda of items such as temperance reform (legal limitations on the sale of alcohol and opening hours of pubs) were also very strong in the party, although most of the party's leaders were Anglicans from upper- and upper-middle-class backgrounds. The most important challenge facing the Liberal party as it entered the new century was how to accommodate the rising importance of the working classes, and whether to move further in the direction of collectivism and away from its laissez-faire roots. The party's policies towards Irish nationalism also needed clarification. In addition, the Liberals were deeply divided over the Empire and Britain's military and naval strength. While most of the leadership of the party differed surprisingly little from the Unionists over these issues, it also included a large segment of 'Little Englanders', often near-pacifists, who were very uncomfortable with Britain's imperial and Great Power role. By 1900, and despite its dominant position in British politics for much of the nineteenth century, the Liberal party was clearly the smaller and less successful of the two-party groupings.

In power were the Unionists, as the Conservatives were now known. From the 1760s until 1832 the Tories had been a consensual party of governance, embodying nearly all of the elements of the British 'Establishment', especially most of the landed aristocracy, the old mercantile classes, and the older professions. After 1832, with the ascendancy of the Whig–Liberal party in the wake of the Great Reform Act, the party had often seemed to consist of a rump of landowners, bereft of most business support, although the party still enjoyed close ties with the Church of England. In 1846, many remaining men of talent within the party had left during the split over Sir Robert Peel's famous plan to repeal the Corn Laws. This had allowed the previously little known Benjamin Disraeli (1804–81; created first earl of Beaconsfield in 1876) to rise to the leadership of the Conservative party. Under Disraeli and his successor as Tory leader, Lord Salisbury, the party expanded its bases of support in several ways. Disraeli became famous for enunciating a policy of 'Tory democracy', designed to woo working-class voters by instituting reforms and benefits for workers by curtailing some aspects of laissez-faire capitalism and by recognising the trade unions. Simultaneously, the Tories increasingly became the party of the 'Establishment', gradually uniting under their banner nearly all landowners and most businessmen and professionals in the south-east of England, especially those connected with the City of London, and particularly Anglicans. After the defection of the Liberal Unionists in 1886, the Tories became the normal majority party at late Victorian General Elections, enjoying the support as well of a considerable portion of the working class, especially those in areas like Lancashire where there was a popular Anglican tradition. The Tories also normally won most agricultural seats. In the late nineteenth century, the Unionists also did well in many big cities, especially Birmingham, where Joseph Chamberlain, the most important of the Liberal Unionists, ruled supreme.

What united all the elements of the Unionist party was opposition to Irish Home Rule. In 1886, Gladstone had proposed the creation of a separate parliament for the whole island of Ireland, with wide, but not unlimited powers. This was proposed as a solution to the hostility of most of Ireland's Catholic majority to British rule. Gladstone's proposal was rejected by the Liberal Unionists and by all Conservatives, who increasingly championed the right of Protestant Ulster not to be ruled by the Catholic south. In that age of imperialism, the Unionists also opposed Irish Home Rule because it appeared to foreshadow the break up of the British Empire.

In 1900, Britain ruled over about one-fifth of the earth's land surface, constituting the mightiest of all the colonial empires that had emerged in the centuries since the Age of Exploration. Granted increasing measures of self-government, Canada, Australia, New Zealand, and South Africa had been settled by Britons and other Europeans, while 400 million non-whites in India, Africa, and elsewhere comprised the majority of the British Empire's population. In 1900, it seemed evident to virtually all observers that the most salient single fact about Great Britain was its vast Empire. At a time before modern concepts of economic measurement like gross national product had yet been formulated, a country's strength was counted chiefly in such things as manpower and natural resources. By these criteria, Britain was very strong indeed, assuredly a world superpower possibly without equal. It also seemed as if the twentieth century was destined to be the age of mighty world-empires, while small nations were unlikely to last the course. Yet it also seemed to many that Britain was not doing as well as it might, and was in many areas lagging behind the United States and Germany. Many intellectuals and activists were loosely associated with a movement for 'national efficiency' aimed at improving the eugenic quality of the British race, enhancing Britain's military capacity, improving the economy, and exploiting the opportunities provided by the Empire. At the end of the nineteenth century, this movement was remarkably widespread, spanning the political spectrum from Fabian socialists on the Left to nationalistic Tories on the Right. There was a pervasive sense that Britain might well have passed its zenith and be heading downward, which surprisingly coexisted with the intense feeling of patriotism and national pride that existed at the same time.

The government that held office in 1900 had come to power in 1895. At its head was Robert Gascoyne-Cecil, third marquess of Salisbury (1830–1903), a remarkable aristocrat who had been the acknowledged leader of the Conservative party since the death of Disraeli in 1881. Salisbury was renowned for his pessimism about the future of Britain under democracy. He viewed the spread of socialism, and the confiscation of the property of the rich, especially the landed aristocracy, as virtually inevitable, the role of the Conservative party being to delay the inevitable as long as possible. Salisbury contrasted the unwritten British Constitution adversely with the written Constitution of the United States. There, the existence of a Senate, of state legislatures, and the deliberate separation of powers built into the American system of government made it very difficult for a popular-based socialist party to come to power. In Britain, no such explicit legal barriers existed to an extreme left-wing party achieving power and confiscating the wealth of the rich, and particularly the agricultural and urban estates of the great landowners. Given that Britain had had virtual manhood suffrage since 1884, sooner or later an extreme left-wing government would in fact win an election and enact a far-reaching programme of redistributive socialism. Britain's conservative forces might try to forestall this by changes in the Constitution, for example by transforming the hereditary House of Lords into an elected Senate. Essentially, however, Salisbury's main tactic in the war against the threat of the Left was to build as broad a coalition as possible of anti-radical forces. In this he was remarkably successful. He welcomed the dissident Liberal Unionists who broke away from Gladstone and the Liberal party in 1886. He won sweeping victories at the General Elections of 1886 and 1895, and was to win yet another General Election by a large majority in 1900. It can be argued that Salisbury was the most successful British political leader in the century following the Second Reform Act of 1867. This was a remarkable achievement for a man who feared that democracy would inevitably lead to the decline of civilisation, and may best be explained by Salisbury's utter cynicism about the uplifting qualities of democratic politics. Yet the political arena was not even Salisbury's primary field of endeavour: he was first and foremost a consummate diplomatist, a man who combined the offices of Prime Minister and Foreign Minister most of the time, a man recognised as the leading diplomat of Europe.

Salisbury's acknowledged heir apparent, and the second most important man in the government, was Arthur Balfour (1848–1930; later first earl of Balfour), who had made his name as a strong Secretary for Ireland from 1887–91 and served as First Lord of the Treasury (in effect, the associate Prime Minister) in 1891–92 and since 1895. Balfour, whose mother was Lord Salisbury's sister, was the son of a wealthy Scottish landowner. He was renowned both for his apparent dilettantism and his razor-sharp mind. Balfour was among the very best parliamentary debaters of his day and wrote works of philosophy that are still well regarded. His tendency to dilettantism caused many to underestimate him. Balfour could be a surprisingly hard and ruthless man, but one whose tendency to harshness was often compromised by his philosophical instincts, which often caused him to delay, prevaricate, and compromise. Unlike his uncle, Balfour had no clear-cut political philosophy apart from being a strong Conservative. He was a lifelong bachelor and a notable figure in Edwardian Society, and, many said, far less suited to be the head of a political party in the democratic age than his uncle. The Tory Cabinets of this period included a number of Salisbury's other relatives, causing them to be widely known (with less justification than many have assumed) as the 'Hotel Cecil', after a famous London hotel of the time that bore Salisbury's family name.

Salisbury's government also contained one other key leader, sociologically very different from members of the Cecil family, but a man arguably as important as the Prime Minister and his nephew. This was Joseph Chamberlain (1836–1914), a Unitarian screw manufacturer who had been closely associated with Birmingham for most of his adult life. Chamberlain had entered Parliament in 1876, after a dynamic period as the progressive Mayor of Birmingham. Originally the acknowledged leader of the advanced radical section of the Liberal party, an advocate of sweeping democratic reforms and heavier taxation of the rich to pay for public works, and greatly feared by all Tories, Chamberlain had in 1886 deserted Gladstone and the Liberal party over Home Rule for Ireland which he bitterly opposed. Chamberlain entered Salisbury's Cabinet in 1895 in the unlikely position of Colonial Secretary. By 1900, he had carved out a unique Cabinet niche for himself at the Colonial Office: this was perhaps the only time in Britain's modern history when arguably the most important man in the Cabinet, and certainly the most famous, held a relatively junior position. Temporarily at least, Chamberlain was more famous than the Prime Minister throughout Britain. He was generally regarded as the architect of the Boer War, which began in 1899 and lasted until 1902. Since the mid-1890s Chamberlain had emerged as the foremost champion of an expanding, world-straddling British Empire as the best way to ensure Britain's status as a great power in the twentieth century. He was regarded as the most dynamic member of the Salisbury Cabinet, the man most attuned to what clearly seemed to be the major trends of the new century.

The remainder of Lord Salisbury's Cabinet as it was constituted at the beginning of the twentieth century was thoroughly traditional in nature. To a surprising extent it failed, almost totally, to reflect the rise of the middle classes during the nineteenth century, and was not dissimilar, in its social composition, to any Cabinet of fifty years earlier. It contained 19 members, of whom 10 sat in the House of Lords. Of the Cabinet's 19 members, seven had attended Eton and four Harrow, while five had attended other well-known public schools. Ten had been students at Oxford, three at Cambridge, and one at Dublin University.

Despite its narrow base, to the majority of the electorate and informed opinion the Salisbury government appeared particularly able, and certainly better-suited to govern than the Liberal party, bitterly divided and containing a strong phalanx of impractical radicals and malcontents of every kind. In contrast, by vigorously adapting to the imperial ideal and by actively expanding the limits of the British Empire, the Salisbury government seemed to most informed observers at the time to be doing much of what was required to ensure Britain's continuing Great Power status in the twentieth century. The clearest evidence of the commitment of the Salisbury government to the expansion of the British Empire was the Boer War. This dispute had been brewing for some time, and its roots lay in the complex relationship of Britain to the states of South Africa. In the 1890s, the tip of southern Africa consisted of four states: the Cape of Good Hope (or Cape Colony), Natal, the Orange Free State, and the Transvaal. The first two of these had been British possessions for many years; the latter two were Boer-dominated areas, founded by Boer (Dutch settlers from the seventeenth century) cattlemen and their families who had migrated northwards from the Cape Colony in the 1830s. The two Boer states, whose culture was dominated by a bitter and narrow Calvinism and who fought constant wars with local tribesmen, found their fortunes transformed by the discovery of diamonds in 1867. In 1886, gold seams of unparalleled richness had been discovered at Witwatersrand in the southern Transvaal. In 1877, Britain had annexed the two Boer republics. They had again achieved semi-independence in 1881, but were loosely under British sovereignty. The discovery of diamonds and gold had brought thousands of British workmen and other immigrants to the Boer areas. Known as the 'Uitlanders' (foreigners), they may actually have outnumbered the Boers, but had no political rights. At least as importantly, from 1880 the diamond trade in South Africa had been organised from the Cape by two rival British concerns, the Barnato Diamond Mining Company, founded by Barney Barnato (1852–97), a London Jew, and the renowned DeBeers Mining Corporation, headed by the celebrated Cecil Rhodes (1853–1902), and Alfred Beit (1853–1906). The two groups merged in 1888. Increasingly, both the economic and political fate of British South Africa was in the hands of Cecil Rhodes, Prime Minister of the Cape Colony from 1890–96, who harboured a grandiose vision of a federal South Africa under British rule. In 1889, Rhodes had secured virtually unlimited economic and political rights from the British government for his British South Africa Company. Against Rhodes and his dreams of British expansion were the Boers of the Transvaal, headed by their President, 'Oom' Paul Kruger.

In December 1895, Rhodes authorised the administrator of the British South Africa Company, Dr Leander Starr Jameson, to launch a raid against the Transvaal with the aim of overthrowing the Boers and bringing the state under direct British rule. Jameson and 470 police then launched this raid across the border, but it was quickly put down. Events took a sinister international turn when Kaiser Wilhelm II of Germany cabled Kruger (the so-called 'Kruger Telegram') to congratulate him on destroying Rhodes' 'armed hordes'. In Britain, public opinion was both inflamed and polarised. A wave of anti-German, anti-Boer 'jingoism' swept the country, while much Liberal opinion attacked the Raid. Liberals were also fiercely hostile to Joseph Chamberlain, the newly appointed Colonial Secretary, who was widely accused of foreknowledge of or connivance in the Raid, and became the subject of a parliamentary inquiry. (His actual role in the Raid has never been satisfactorily resolved.) Queen Victoria's 1897 Jubilee celebrations, with its popular displays of imperial fervour, further increased patriotic sentiment.

Matters festered until November 1898, when an English workman was killed by a Boer policeman, deeply offending 'Uitlander' opinion. In May 1899, the British cabinet accepted a mass petition, signed by 21 000 British subjects on the Rand, demanding equal rights. It is clear that from mid-1899 Chamberlain and the Cabinet began actively to plan for war. The new High Commissioner for South Africa, Sir Alfred Milner (1854–1925), a German-born though British-educated barrister and civil servant, was an arch-imperialist who strongly sympathised with the 'Uitlanders'. In October 1899, Kruger demanded the withdrawal of British troops from the borders of the Transvaal. The British declined and war broke out between Britain and the two Boer republics the same month.

At first, the Boer War went remarkably badly for Britain. One might assume, given the lowly reputation enjoyed today by Britain's military leaders of that time, that this was not surprising. Nevertheless, it surprised most observers at the time. Britain enjoyed a universal reputation for having an extremely efficient and successful army (backed by the world's strongest navy), which had, in general, won colonial wars with admirable efficiency. Britain's problem, plainly, was the enormous distance involved in transporting vast amounts of men and material to South Africa by ship in a short period of time. The logistics of this – a difficult feat even today – were, in the 1890s, simply enormous. The Boers proved to be a formidable, flexible, ingenious, and brave military force, fighting on their home territories or nearby for a cause they believed was just. Rather like the South in the American Civil War, the Boers initially won a series of stunning victories until the overwhelming force that the British could potentially bring to bear from around the Empire was actually in place. At the beginning of the war, 50 000 British troops in South Africa faced 87 000 Boer soldiers. Initially, British forces were successfully besieged by the Boers in three fortified towns or areas: Mafeking on the Bechuanaland (now Botswana) border, and Ladysmith and Kimberley in the Orange Free State. In late 1899 and early 1900 the Boers won a series of impressive victories, especially at Magersfontein near Kimberley, during what became known as 'Black Week', 10–15 December 1899, when nearly 3000 British soldiers were killed, a number unparalleled since the Crimean War, and at Spion Kop where, on 25 January 1900, 1700 British soldiers were killed. (It was just after 'Black Week' that Queen Victoria made her celebrated comment to Arthur Balfour, 'we are not interested in the possibilities of defeat; they do not exist'.)

The original British commander in South Africa, Sir Redvers Buller, was then replaced by Field Marshal Lord Roberts (Sir Frederick Roberts, 1832–1914), a distinguished veteran of the Empire's wars, with the even more competent General Lord Kitchener (Horatio Herbert Kitchener, 1850–1916) serving as Chief of Staff. The tide now turned strongly in Britain's favour, with the relief of besieged Ladysmith taking place on 28 February and, in particular, the relief of Mafeking on 17 May, after a 217-day siege. In Britain, news of the relief of Mafeking resulted in an unparalleled outburst of wild, spontaneous, jingoistic street demonstrations, especially in London, the like of which had never been seen before. 'Mafeking Night' became legendary in the memory of everyone who lived through it, and arguably marked the high tide of imperialist senti-ment in Britain. Anti-war, pro-Boer 'Little Englanders' frequently became the object of popular hostility and violence, seen most famously in the near-lynching of David Lloyd George, then a 38-year-old radical Liberal MP, as he attempted to speak at Birmingham Town Hall in 1901. In May 1900, British forces overran and formally annexed the Orange Free State, renaming it the Orange River Colony; in September 1900, the Transvaal itself was formally annexed to Britain as the Transvaal Colony. The Boer War appeared to be over; Paul Kruger fled to Europe at the same time as the Transvaal fell.

In September 1900, euphoric from apparent military victory, Salisbury called a General Election, two years before one was legally necessary. It was the first of three so-called 'khaki' elections (from the colour of the British army uniform) held during the twentieth century at the conclusion of a war. The Tory gov-ernment, and Joseph Chamberlain in particular, were frank in their admitted desire to capitalise on the patriotic fervour released by the war; not surprisingly, the Liberals regarded this as unfair. The election, held over a four-week period from 28 September to 24 October 1900, showed virtually identi-cal results to those at the previous 1895 General Election, and a resounding victory for the Unionist coalition. The results of the 1900 General Election were as follows:

	Total votes ('000)	MPs elected	% share of total vote
Unionists	1 797 444	402	51.1
Liberals	1 568 141	184	44.6
Labour	63 304	2	1.8
Irish Nationalists	90 076	82	2.5
Others	544	–	0.0
Total	3 519 509	670	100.0

These statistics actually underestimate the scale of the Unionist victory to a very significant extent. Unionists were elected in no fewer than 163 seats where they stood without opposition by candidates from any other party, by far the highest total of unopposed parliamentary wins at any General Election between the third Reform Act and the present, while only 22 Liberals (and 58 Irish Nationalists) were unopposed. Such elections almost always occurred in a party's safest seats. If all such unopposed seats had actually been contested, the Unionist share of the vote would certainly have been far higher than the 51.1 per cent of the total with which they are credited. (No votes at all are recorded for candidates elected unopposed.) It is not unreasonable to assume that, had all parliamentary seats been contested by both parties in 1900, the Unionists would have won between 55 and 60 per cent of the vote, a higher percentage than at any General Election in the twentieth century except 1931 and possibly 1918. The Unionists won virtually every middle-class seat in the country, and were practically hegemonic in the south-east, winning 51 seats in the County of London to only eight for the Liberals, and almost every other seat in south-eastern England. The Unionists also won a majority of seats in Scotland (36 to the Liberals' 34) and did particularly well in the areas in western Scotland across from northern Ireland. Within the Unionist coalition, candidates elected as Conservatives won 334 seats and Liberal Unionists 68. The Liberals did not do quite as badly as these figures indicate, and actually elected seven more MPs than in 1895. They won the great majority of seats in Wales (26, compared with only six for the Unionists), and did quite well in the West Riding, eastern Scotland, and the north-east. In addition, they also did well in the two rural areas of surprising Liberal strength, north Norfolk and Cornwall and Devon. Nevertheless, the 1900 General Election certainly marked the zenith of the late Victorian Conservative party (crucially assisted by their Liberal Unionist allies). In the three further General Elections before the First World War, the Unionist vote declined markedly in relative terms. The Tory vote only recovered after the First World War, when the left-of-centre electorate was split between the Labour and Liberal parties.

Although the Boer War appeared to be virtually over when the election was held, it was to drag on for another eighteen months. Boer leaders organised a remarkably successful guerrilla campaign against the British, one of the first times guerrilla war had been waged in modern history. Kitchener,

Commander-in-Chief after November 1900, erected a line of fortified block-houses and caused more controversy by compelling 120 000 Boer women and children to move into what were officially termed 'concentration camps', where 20 000 died from disease. (Although the conditions in these camps were appalling, of course they had absolutely nothing to do with the infamous con-centration camps of the Nazi regime.) Britain's surprisingly ruthless actions were widely deplored by anti-war 'Little Englanders' and radicals. In June 1901, Sir Henry Campbell-Bannerman, leader of the Liberal party, made his celebrated remark, 'when was a war not a war? When it was carried on by methods of bar-barism in South Africa'. (Campbell-Bannerman's statement, meant to attack the 'concentration camps', was widely taken out of context and he became the sub-ject of widespread vilification.) Throughout the conflict a steady stream of left-wing anti-war tracts and pamphlets appeared, by such writers as J.A. Hobson, linking Britain's imperial expansion in South Africa with the needs of 'finance capitalism' for new markets to compensate for 'under-consumption' and under-investment at home. Some of these works had a disturbingly anti-semitic tone (something very rare in British political discourse), singling out South Africa's Jewish 'Randlords' for special attack, and frequently linking them to the landed aristocracy and the City of London in a vast conspiracy. (The view of imperial-ism as driven centrally by 'finance capitalism' became a major component of the Marxist view of imperialism, through the later writings of Hilferding and Lenin.)

Nevertheless, by bringing overwhelming power to bear in a ruthless way, the Boer guerrillas were eventually forced to submit, finally surrendering by the Treaty of Vereeniging on 31 May 1902. The British had performed prodigies of competent military organisation in fighting the war, something now often forgotten in light of the needless slaughter of the First World War. At the end of the hostilities, Britain had 300 000 troops in South Africa, double the total size of the British army in 1895. A total of 448 000 British soldiers and sailors were engaged in the Boer War, an enormous total for a country with no stand-ing army and no conscription. Tens of thousands of British troops and millions of tons of equipment had to be transported over vast distances even to get to South Africa. A total of 22 000 British troops (about 5 per cent of all military personnel engaged in the war) were killed in battle, or died of disease, or were taken as prisoners of war. The price of the war was, by the standards of the time, astronomical, with the cost of the war about £222 million, exactly dou-ble the total annual expenditure of the British government in 1898, the year before the war began. The physical unfitness of many would-be recruits, the incompetence of Britain's military leadership in the war's early stages, and the undue length of time required for the world's mightiest empire to defeat a community of impoverished farmers on horseback, all gave rise to searching national debates and were probably factors in the Unionist government's decline in popularity, leading to the debacle of 1906. Nevertheless, in the final analysis, and on any reasonable criteria of judgement, Britain acquitted itself fairly well in the Boer War, fought so far from home. Perhaps the worst conse-quence of that conflict was to give promotion and preference to cavalry officers who would be unsuitable to conducting the type of war that began in 1914. As usual, some lessons were learned but, also as usual, not enough.

In January 1901, Queen Victoria died after a reign of over 63 years. No one aged under about 70 could remember a time before she came to the throne, and she seemed as permanent a part of Britain's system of governance as Parliament itself. Unpopular after Prince Albert's death in 1861 during her lengthy withdrawal from public life, she lived to enjoy genuinely enormous popularity. Edward VII (1841–1910), who reigned from January 1901 until May 1910, had waited 40 years for a position of real responsibility and was nearly 60 when he became king. He was at once highly intelligent and a hero-ically active bon vivant – with women, as a gourmand, at the racetrack, and the cardtable. In politics, and in contrast to his mother's evident Toryism, Edward was something of a Liberal, a friend of Gladstone, who preferred the company of self-made men, especially (it seemed to many) Jews. Edward proved to be a good and competent king, and the Edwardian era – like his mother, he gave his name to a historical era – was remembered by many with great nostalgia decades later, the last period of genuine peace and prosperity, especially for the upper classes, before the catastrophe which began in August 1914. Edward's Coronation was set for June 1902, but had to be postponed until August because he became seriously ill with appendicitis. In July 1902, meanwhile, Lord Salisbury resigned and was succeeded by Arthur Balfour, who served as Prime Minister from 12 July 1902 until 4 December 1905. Balfour's succession was universally seen as inevitable. There was no election for the position, and no process of widespread consultation, although Balfour took pains to consult Joseph Chamberlain. Few Prime Ministers have ever come to office in a stronger position, with a large parliamentary majority, a weak and divided opposition, and a victorious war, recently concluded. Yet, Balfour's three and a half years' tenure as Prime Minister proved to be a political disaster virtually without parallel in modern British history, such that the Unionists were to lose nearly 250 seats at the 1906 General Election and remain in opposition for almost ten years. A good deal of the blame for this situation – though certainly not all of it – can be laid directly at the feet of Balfour. Although an adept and skilful politician, and surprisingly forceful when he had to be, he was also, as befits a philosopher, subtle to a degree and a considerable trimmer who, in one famous phrase, 'nailed his colours firmly to the fence'. Unlike Salisbury, he was unable to control the voices of division within his party.

Balfour made few changes to Salisbury's Cabinet. Perhaps the most impor-tant, made soon after becoming premier, was his appointment to the Cabinet of Joseph Chamberlain's elder son Austen (later Sir Austen, 1863–1937), as Postmaster General. Austen Chamberlain had been educated at Rugby and Cambridge, and was fully a part of the British 'Establishment'. Chamberlain attempted to look the very double of his father, always appearing with Joseph's famous trademarks, his monocle and the orchid in his buttonhole. Although Austen Chamberlain held a wide variety of offices, including the posts of Chancellor of the Exchequer and Foreign Minister, and served as leader of the Conservative party in 1921–22, he never became Prime Minister and, to cite a celebrated assessment, he 'always played the game and always lost it'. During the first decade of the century, however, Austen Chamberlain was actually often seen as an unscrupulous champion of tariff reform, his father's unprincipled lieutenant. This reputation, so different from Austen Chamberlain's later historical image, might well have cost him the succession to the Tory leadership in 1911. In contrast, the other new members of Balfour's Cabinet, until the government resigned late in 1905, were surprisingly lacklustre. Balfour himself had no obvious successor and failed successfully to identify and promote younger men of talent. Andrew Bonar Law, a future Prime Minister, and Sir Edward Carson, one of the party's best debaters, held ministerial but not Cabinet office; Lord Curzon was in India as Viceroy; Winston Churchill, then a young Tory MP, remained on the backbenches. Most of the new appointments made by Balfour came from the traditional aristocracy and he made little attempt to widen the social background of the Unionist Cabinet. When the Conservatives eventually returned to government a decade after the 1906 catastrophe, few of its parliamentary leaders had held senior positions under Balfour.

Nevertheless, the Unionist government that Balfour headed in 1902 was in a strong position, and few could have seen how quickly or seriously its strength deteriorated on many fronts. Trouble came from three unrelated areas: the alienation of trades unions and labour by the Taff Vale decision and other actions; hostility by Nonconformists to the Education Act of 1902; and the very deep splits within Unionist ranks generated by Joseph Chamberlain's scheme to enact Imperial Preference, a proposal which also had the effect of unifying the Liberal party and giving it an issue which it could successfully exploit throughout the whole electorate in 1906.

The first five years of the twentieth century saw renewed growth for the trades-union movement. During the 1890s, membership in the Trades Union Congress (TUC), the national federation of trade unions, had remained fairly stable at just over one million. By 1905, membership had reached 1.5 million. This represented only a small portion of the British labour force of 16 million (of whom 11.5 million were males), but organised labour was constantly growing in strength. Moreover, those industries which were most heavily unionised, like coalmining, shipbuilding, and engineering, were among the country's most vital and also tended to be concentrated in distinctive geographical locales (such as coalmining in south Wales) where a very large percentage of the population was employed directly or indirectly in that trade, or reflected its ambience. Unlike most continental countries, however, Britain had never had a socialist party or one based in the trade unions. By 1898–99, however, leaders of the old, unsuccessful Independent Labour Party were now successfully agitating for a broadly based Labour party that would champion the interests of the trade unions. The embryo of such a body was formed in a famous meeting of trade unions and socialist societies at the Memorial Hall in Faringdon Street, London, in February 1900. Delegates there established a 'Labour Representation Committee' (LRC) whose stated aim, as moved by Keir Hardie, was 'a distinct Labour Group in Parliament [with] their own Whips'. (James Keir Hardie, 1856–1915, formerly secretary of the Scottish Miners' Association, had been Independent Labour MP for South West Ham, 1892–95, and for Merthyr Burghs from 1900.) The secretary of the LRC was a young socialist activist, James Ramsay MacDonald (1866–1937) who became Labour's first

Prime Minister 24 years later. Members of the Fabian Society, the influential organisation of middle-class socialist intellectuals founded in 1884, were disproportionately prominent at this meeting, among them the playwright George Bernard Shaw (1856–1950) who had been a Fabian since its establishment. The new body was christened the 'Labour party', but it had elected only two MPs in 1900.

Nevertheless, the potential strength of the Labour party was clearly very great, even in the short term. Communities where the trade unions were already very strong were numerous, particularly in south Wales, Tyneside, Clydeside, and much of Lancashire. Such places typically had very small middle classes and little local elite leadership. Given the type of political system which emerged in the 1884 Reform Act, based chiefly upon single-member constituencies heavily class-based in the socio-economic makeup of their populations, it was seemingly only a matter of time before these strongly working-class seats, with their powerful trade unions, often centred in one or two industries, elected MPs who were explicitly associated with the new Labour party or close to it. It is difficult to say how many such seats there were of this type. In many heavily working-class seats (for instance in London's East End), the trade unions were not a significant factor; nor was it the case that only one industry always dominated the economy. In many other working-class seats, for a variety of historical reasons, the Liberal party (or, in parts of Lancashire, western Scotland, and northern Ireland, the Conservative party) had very deep roots that the new Labour party could not realistically displace in the short term, if ever. But it is probably fair to say that in upwards of, say, 100 parliamentary seats the new Labour party had, from soon after its foundation, a realistic chance of electing an MP. It should be stressed, however, that, equally, prior to the First World War, Labour had no realistic chance of electing an MP in the great majority of parliamentary seats. How Labour would actually perform depended, of course, upon many factors, especially the popularity of the Liberals and relations between that party and Labour.

After 1901, two specific issues further increased the influence of the fledgling Labour party. In South Africa the Balfour government, heavily influenced by unwise advice given by Lord Milner, allowed the introduction of nearly 50 000 Chinese coolie labourers to work in the mines of the Transvaal. They were paid virtually nothing and forced to live in closed compounds where drug addiction, prostitution, and homosexuality soon flourished. There was actually nothing new in the movement of cheap 'coloured' labour throughout the Empire: thousands of Indians had, for example, been brought to distant Fiji as labourers, where they comprised a major fraction of the population. Nevertheless, for some reason, the issue of so-called 'Chinese slavery' on the Rand became a burning issue on the British left. Trade unionists believed that Chinese 'slaves' had been introduced merely to undercut the pay of white Europeans, and that they might herald a limitless army of yellow 'slaves' being sent around the world to undercut workers' pay. Fears of the 'Yellow Peril', so common during this era of Social Darwinism, were also awakened. Remarkably, this absurd notion gained common currency in Liberal and left-wing circles, Lloyd George campaigning against the threat of 'Chinese slaves on the hills of

Wales' if the Tories were re-elected in 1906. As well, Nonconformists campaigned against the allegedly low moral standards of the Chinese coolies. The British left seized on this issue in the vacuum left by the end of the Boer War.

Trouble with the trade unions also grew from the famous Taff Vale legal decision of 1901. Prior to the judgement of the High Court in the case formally known as the *Taff Vale Railway Co. v. Amalgamated Society of Railway Servants*, trade unions had been afforded absolute protection for their own funds under the Trade Union Act of 1871. As a result of the Taff Vale decision, trade unions were no longer afforded this protection; a union could be sued by employers (or anyone else) and its funds confiscated as damages if the case went against it. The Amalgamated Society (a railway union) lost £32 000 in damages as a result of a lawsuit brought by a railway company. The Taff Vale decision greatly disturbed the trade union movement, especially in areas like south Wales where relations between management and labour were poor, and encouraged political activism and fund-raising on behalf of the Liberals at the 1906 General Election. Soon after the Liberals' election the Taff Vale decision was reversed by the Trade Disputes Act of 1906.

The Balfour government also managed to alienate the large and influential Nonconformist section of the community. Historically, Nonconformists had been among the backbones of the Liberal party, and the Liberals continued to rely on disproportionate Nonconformist support. As sociological differences between Anglicans and Dissenters narrowed, however, many Nonconformists had become more sympathetic to the Tories than in the past. The defection from the Liberals to the Unionists of Joseph Chamberlain, probably the best-known Dissenter in national politics, along with many of his Nonconformist allies, seemed to herald this shift, as did extreme Protestant fears of 'Rome rule' in Ireland.

The specific cause of Balfour's troubles with the Nonconformists lay in the important Education Act of 1902 (passed just before Balfour became Prime Minister), largely devised by Sir Robert Morant (1863–1920), a brilliant civil servant who was, at the time, assistant private secretary to the Duke of Devonshire, President of the Board of Education in the Tory Cabinet. The act was designed to ameliorate some legal flaws in the provision of state secondary schooling, and did so in a sweeping way, by giving greatly enlarged powers to local authorities to provide secondary education. It also abolished the school boards. However, it also brought the voluntary (i.e. religiously based) schools under the authority of local governments, paying their teachers with ratepayers' money for the first time. This pleased Anglicans and Catholics (most 'voluntary' schools were Anglican), but incensed Nonconformists, who objected to public funds being used to pay for denominational schools. Nonconformists were particularly angry at the fact that Anglican schools in country areas were given a lease of life. Typically, they were the only schools in the area, and Nonconformists were thus forced to pay to have their children attend schools whose religious lessons they found offensive. Balfour was fully aware of the distress caused to Nonconformists, but regarded the benefits of this bill, especially the greater provision of secondary education, as outweighing its faults. (The issue of the religious basis of state schooling proved to be contentious during much of the century.) However, he underestimated the response of the Nonconformists. Nonconformists, led by Dr John Clifford, a very prominent Baptist minister, launched a campaign of passive resistance against the payment of rates that undercut the purposes of the act. While the Education Act of 1902 greatly alienated Dissenting opinion, it is also, ironically, widely seen as perhaps the most important constructive piece of legislation adopted by the Unionist government, bringing considerable order to a haphazard system and increasing educational opportunities.

Nonconformist hostility to the 1902 Education Act was, however, only the tip of a great iceberg of Dissenting and Evangelical Anglican hostility to the religious trends of the day which did enormous harm to the Unionist government; this hostility has probably been underestimated by historians, especially those who are not sensitive to the continuing importance of religious issues in the twentieth century. Within the Church of England, the High Church wing of the church, which emphasised quasi-Catholic ritual and usage, was apparently winning the upper hand during the late nineteenth century. The number of Anglican churches in which eucharistic vestments (a leading quasi-Catholic usage) were worn increased from 336 in 1882 to 2158 in 1901, while the number of churches using incense (another, even more striking, pseudo-Catholic device) grew from only nine to 393 in the same period. In 1902, it was estimated that as many as 9200 Anglican clergymen out of 25 000 were 'ritualists', in sympathy with the quasi-Catholic wing of the Church. High Church Anglicanism was increasingly favoured by many Oxbridge graduates (who comprised most Anglican clergymen) and by an important component of the upper classes. Many Low Church (i.e. Evangelical and pro-Protestant) Anglicans and Nonconformists were deeply alarmed by this trend. For secular historians, it may seem difficult to believe that religious divisions of this kind could play a significant role in twentieth-century British politics outside of Ireland, which is why they have been downplayed or ignored. By this time, British politics 'should have been' chiefly about economic and class issues, not neo-medieval religious disputation. Nevertheless, it seems unquestionably true that religious divisions still had considerable political salience, as they have had even more recently. For Evangelical Anglicans and Nonconformists, the apparent success of High Church Anglicanism raised the spectre, so strong in the nineteenth century, of illegal 'Romanist' rituals, secretive clerical power, and (it was widely rumoured), thinly veiled homosexual and other deviant sexual practices allegedly associated with Catholicism and its English imitators. The fear of Roman Catholicism, so pervasive in Britain since the Reformation, remained extremely strong in Edwardian Britain. The period 1904–05 also coincided with a considerable religious revival in Wales and elsewhere. As a result of all this, there was a significant anti-ritualist and pro-Protestant backlash in Britain at this time, with a spate of works like Walter Walsh's *Secret History of the Oxford Movement* (1897) which had been reprinted five times in two years, and *England's Danger* (1898), a popular collection of anti-Catholic sermons by R.F. Horton, a Congregationalist minister. Numerous pro-Protestant and anti-ritual organisations also flourished at this time.

Even apart from this, many Nonconformists also felt a deep sense of continuing grievance at the fact that they were still excluded from the established institutions of England. Many had risen over the generations on the social scale, and were now eminently respectable and very wealthy, yet they were not included among the religious personnel or the symbols of the British 'Establishment', which in England was still limited to Anglicans. Few Dissenters had been ennobled and few sat in the Unionist Cabinet. Indeed, via the public schools, universities, and the network of imperial governance, Anglicans appeared to be as powerful as ever, with, by 1900, the nineteenth-century Dissenting challenge to Anglican establishment effectively checked. Nonconformists, in other words, felt a profound sense of 'relative deprivation', always an extremely potent source of grievance, which was an important factor in the Liberal victory in 1906. As well, Chamberlain's resurrection of Protection, especially the protection of agricultural products, seemed to many Nonconformists to comprise a subtle way of favouring the Anglican squirearchy and the Anglican church itself, at a time when the Church still relied extensively on rents for its income. The strength of Nonconformity, when added to the significant element of Low Church, Evangelical Anglicanism, was very considerable indeed, strong enough to prevent a categorical and unpopular swing to the 'right' by the Church and the British Establishment. This fact – that the non-political 'left' outnumbered the 'right' in modern Britain (although in the *political* sphere the British right was almost always more successful at winning elections) – is a very important factor whose ramifications can be seen many times.

The third source of trouble for Balfour, and, in political terms, the most important, came from Joseph Chamberlain and his scheme of 'Imperial Preference'. Chamberlain did not conceive of the Boer War or its additions to the British Empire merely in terms of greed and territorial expansion for their own sake, but always as part of a constructive vision of a united and progressive Empire. For years he had been flirting with overtly abandoning Free Trade in favour of a comprehensive and grandiose scheme for an imperial tariff, a tariff wall around the whole British Empire, leading to a much greater degree of imperial unity and eventually to imperial federation. In November 1902 he visited South Africa, making a point of touring the Boer colonies. He had previously proposed a system of reciprocal tariffs with the colonies, especially Canada, for corn (wheat), a kind of semi-revival of the old Corn Laws, repealed in 1846. On 15 May 1903, in Birmingham, he formally broke ranks with the entire Free Trade tradition of modern Britain, announcing in a major, much-heralded speech that he had been converted to a far-reaching plan of Imperial Preference, with systematic tariff retaliation against foreign governments that applied their own tariffs to British goods. 'No speech in British history has ever caused such a sensation', Chamberlain's biographer Julian Amery claimed, and it was often compared, at the time, to Martin Luther nailing his 95 Theses to the door at Wittenberg Church.

Chamberlain's plan was indeed a bold and far-reaching one. His long-term aim was to mould the whole British Empire into a single vast economic and military unit, able to meet the considerable threats posed by the obvious superpowers of the twentieth century, the United States, Germany, and Russia.

In a sense, Chamberlain's grand plan represented the strategy of what might be termed the battle for third place in twentieth-century geopolitics. Like many others, he realised that the United States was plainly destined to be one of the Great Powers of the new century. (Chamberlain had visited America several times and had recently married an American third wife.) Even in 1903, America probably already had the largest economy in the world and a population of around 80 million, twice that of Britain's. Chamberlain also probably envisioned that the great Russian Empire was destined to become the superpower of Eurasia, but only – which was far from certain – if it successfully modernised rather than disintegrated. The race for third place as a Great Power was therefore between Germany, then furiously industrialising behind a high tariff wall of its own, and Britain. In theory, with its worldwide Empire and virtually unlimited manpower and natural resources, there should have been no doubt of Britain's continuing ascendancy. But Britain had never fully realised the potential of its great Empire, and, as the last major country fully committed to Free Trade, lay at the mercy of foreign exporters and economic rivals against whom it could not retaliate. Chamberlain's scheme of 'Imperial Preference' would diminish unemployment and allow the British economy to grow. As well, the centrifugal forces working towards the disintegration of an Empire scattered all over the globe were very powerful, and had to be reversed.

Chamberlain's scheme also had a second, related outcome that was regarded by him and his supporters as of almost equal importance. Revenues generated by the tariffs would be used to fund measures of social reform such as old-age pensions. For many Conservatives who feared collectivist measures which entailed higher taxation to pay for social reforms, Imperial Preference represented a non-socialist method of achieving social reforms to benefit the working classes: 'making the foreigner pay', in the phrase of the day. Most of Chamberlain's supporters specifically linked social reform with the Empire and Imperial Preference as a package of progressive measures with which Britain could meet the new century and its challenges.

Chamberlain's programme was supported by many younger Tories and other right-wing figures, and he quickly gathered round him a 'brains trust' of economists and writers who made the intellectual case for Tariff Reform, and also many political activists who wished to win over the Unionist party or – many said – seize control of the party by any means. It is difficult today to convey the enthusiasm which Chamberlain's programme, with its vision of a mighty, unified world Empire, aroused among its strong supporters and continued to arouse for decades to come. Chamberlain's proposals also drew the support of many other disparate elements within the Conservative party and its associates, for instance landowners and farmers who had suffered during the previous twenty years from cheap imported grain, and the military and naval lobby and patriotic organisations associated with them. However, when Chamberlain first proposed Imperial Preference, it had catastrophic effects on the political fortunes of the Unionist party, and did so again in 1923 when Stanley Baldwin revived it as a means of dealing with Britain's post-war economic distress. Only in 1932, when the National government, with a huge Conservative majority during the Great Depression, enacted a form of Imperial Preference, was something like Chamberlain's programme put into action. In 1903, however, Chamberlain's proposal bitterly divided the Conservative party and was rejected by the whole of the Liberal party, for whom Free Trade was virtually a matter of religious faith. For Sir Henry Campbell-Bannerman, to dispute Free Trade was 'like disputing the law of gravitation'. Probably nothing else which emerged from the Unionists did more to lose them the 1906 General Election. Free Traders used all of the traditional arguments against tariffs that had been employed during the Corn Law agitation: tariffs hurt only those who enacted them, by raising prices and diminishing choice; tariffs would inevitably lead to local cartels and monopolies, augmenting inefficiency, while the political process (as in the United States) would inevitably come to revolve around lobbying by particular industries for special tariff protection, with all of the ample opportunities for corruption which this raised. Britain, according to Free Traders, had become the 'workshop of the world' under Free Trade, and if its position was declining (which was arguable), the solution lay in more efficient industries, not in tariffs. Left-wing Liberals and socialists wished social reforms to be paid for by taxation, while all Free Traders quickly pointed out the self-contradiction in Chamberlain's package: that if tariffs did exclude foreign goods there would be no revenue for social welfare, while if these tariffs raised significant revenue, they were not successfully excluding foreign goods. By far the most telling point made by Free Traders, and one which would be constantly reiterated by the Liberal party during the 1906 General Election, was that Chamberlain's programme would reverse the legacy of the repeal of the Corn Laws by enacting a tariff on bread and other foodstuffs. 'No tax on bread' became one of the most potent of political catchcries, with an especially potent effect upon working-class voters. As well, Free Traders pointed to the rather surprising reluctance of many colonial governments to support Imperial Preference, while Liberals pointed out that the Empire was unified by ties of history and tradition, and an Empire-wide tariff could well actually injure these ties, by interfering with the 'natural' economic growth of Dominions such as Canada and Australia.

Chamberlain's proposals thus had the unintended effect of unifying the hitherto disunited Liberal party, which almost to a man rallied around the Free Trade banner. But they also had the effect, just as serious politically, of bitterly dividing the Unionists, and, in particular, of making Balfour's position almost untenable. There is no parallel in modern political history to the holder of a relatively junior Cabinet post suddenly enunciating a major and novel political programme, entailing the most basic break with the accepted policy of several generations, and expecting the government to follow his lead. Few prime ministers would have tolerated such a thing for a moment; most modern prime ministers would have demanded Chamberlain's resignation on the spot. Chamberlain managed to survive only because of his unique position of strength within the Cabinet as a figure of national importance and the architect of the successful Boer War. Beyond the Cabinet, there were many in the Unionist party who were lukewarm to Imperial Preference, or actually hostile to it. Many traditional figures within the party believed that the central fight waged by the Conservatives should have been against the threat of collectivism from 'New Liberalism' and Labour, and that Imperial Preference was, if anything, another form of the same collectivism. In the House of Commons, there were about 50 so-called Unionist Free Traders, men who rejected tariffs on principle. (The best-known of these was Winston Churchill, who actually resigned from the Unionist party in 1904 and joined the Liberals, where he remained until 1922.) The leader of the Unionist Free Traders in the Cabinet was the eighth Duke of Devonshire (formerly known as Lord Hartington), an eminent Liberal Unionist politician who had, in the nineteenth century, three times declined requests from Queen Victoria to become Prime Minister. Unionist Free Traders argued that Chamberlain had no right to try to impose his revolutionary proposals on the Unionist government without the mandate of a General Election: tariffs had, plainly, not been mentioned at the previous General Election in 1900. Even within Parliament, it was notable that Chamberlain had few very senior enthusiasts for his programme, Andrew Bonar Law (1858–1923), an influential and rising junior minister but not a full Cabinet member, probably being the most notable. Strikingly, most of Chamberlain's supporters came from among intellectuals, writers, activists, and imperial figures outside the House of Commons. On the other hand, it was certainly the case that a majority of Unionist MPs were at least mildly sympathetic to Chamberlain's programme, while his overt opponents were clearly in a minority.

Arthur Balfour found himself in an extraordinarily difficult position, one that would have tested the mettle of the strongest of leaders. Balfour's initial response to Chamberlain's programme was to prevaricate, but in September 1903 he announced a policy of his own, a system of retaliatory tariffs against foreign governments that had enacted tariffs upon British exports. But Balfour explicitly ruled out either an imperial tariff of the comprehensive kind demanded by Chamberlain, or any tariff on foodstuffs. Balfour's programme pleased no one. It was, in fact, a last-minute response to a wave of poorly handled Cabinet dismissals and resignations earlier that month. By the end of September 1903 Joseph Chamberlain, the Duke of Devonshire, and three other Cabinet ministers had resigned. Neither Chamberlain nor Devonshire ever held office again. (Chamberlain resigned in order to head a national campaign on behalf of his programme.) Balfour then acted with apparent skill, appointing Joseph Chamberlain's son Austen as Chancellor of the Exchequer and Devonshire's nephew and heir Victor Cavendish (1868–1938) as Financial Secretary to the Treasury, Austen Chamberlain's deputy. Joseph Chamberlain now launched a national campaign on behalf of Imperial Preference, forming a Tariff Reform League and a Tariff Reform Commission, composed of sympathetic economists. Pro-Free Trade Unionists came under considerable and increasing pressure from Chamberlainite zealots. In response, Balfour made statements increasingly sympathetic to tariff reform, but was unable to unify the party. Balfour was himself moderately favourable to some form of tariff protection, but was too flexible to become committed to a dogmatic programme. By the time of the 1906 General Election, the Unionists appeared hopelessly divided over this key question. In mass democracies, a disunited party is a virtual guarantee of swiftly following electoral defeat, especially if the party leader appears weak and irresolute. Arthur Balfour was among the first, but by no means the last, modern British political leader to learn this lesson the hard way.

There were a number of other measures taken by the Balfour government that require comment. In 1904, Balfour upgraded the Committee of Imperial Defence (founded in 1902) to become a small, permanent advisory committee to the Prime Minister on defence matters (the Prime Minister served as its chairman). Composed of military leaders, civil servants, and Cabinet ministers, and manned by a permanent secretariat, it was the first such permanent intra-governmental defence committee in the modern sense. Two of Balfour's war ministers, attempted a comprehensive reform of the army that was to lean heavily on the rapid building of army corps in wartime. Neither minister could complete his task, although the antiquated post of Commander-in-Chief of the army (held for many years during the previous century by Queen Victoria's cousin the Duke of Cambridge) was abolished and replaced by an army council headed by a frequently rotating Chief of the General Staff, always a professional soldier. These changes did not fully modernise the British army, but possibly prevented complete disaster in 1914.

Like every modern government, Balfour's also attempted to pacify Ireland. His main effort was the Irish Land Purchase Act, 1903, sponsored by George Wyndham (1863–1913). Its aim, frequently attempted before, was to create a large class of Irish smallholders by providing funds to buy out the estates of large landowners. It worked well. Wyndham, however, attempted to go further and grant a kind of quasi-Home Rule by the back door, and tried to create a central Irish organ of government for some administrative purposes. Wyndham had been led on by his permanent undersecretary, Sir Anthony MacDonnell, an Irish Catholic, who enjoyed extraordinary powers for a civil servant. Opposition to anything that smacked of Home Rule was, almost by definition, at the heart of the Unionist government's *raison d'être*, and serious hostility to the proposal emerged from Irish Unionists in Parliament, forcing Wyndham's resignation. Walter Long took his place, and proved to be a forceful pro-Unionist minister who dropped the proposal. Nevertheless, Ireland was relatively quiet during the Balfour government, certainly so compared with that country's tortured centrality in British politics before and after.

The fourth measure of note passed at this time was the Aliens Act of 1905, which, for the first time in British history, imposed restrictions on immigration to the country. Large numbers of eastern European Jews had been arriving in the East End of London during the previous twenty-three years, as well as many Italians, Germans, and Chinese. This gave rise to some local anti-semitic and anti-foreigner sentiment, and the Balfour government, following on a royal commission, decided to act. Under the provisions of the Aliens Act, immigration officers had the right to exclude many would-be immigrants. In practice it would seem that Jewish immigration decreased by no more than about one-third over the next few years. The act applied only to migrants from outside the British Empire – an 'alien' is someone who is not a citizen of the British Empire – but did not apply to Empire citizens, who were still free to come. Self-evidently, no country in the twentieth century could allow absolutely unlimited immigration, and no government has ever thought of repealing the act, only of tightening it further, almost always to mass popular approval.

The Balfour government also initiated important changes in foreign policy. Wisely or not, Britain increasingly joined in the treaty alliances that divided Europe into two hostile camps. In January 1902, rather curiously, Britain entered into a formal alliance with Japan. Britain did this chiefly to forestall any Russian drive into Manchuria or Korea. Britain greatly feared that it would be the loser in any carve-up of China, the largest independent nation in the world outside Europe, and supported the continued independence of China after the Boxer Rebellion of 1900. Britain greatly benefited from the *status quo* in China, and was probably the predominant foreign economic power, owning Hong Kong and holding considerable trading interests in Shanghai and the 'Treaty Ports'. Britain became directly involved in Europe with the extremely important Anglo-French Entente of April 1904, which settled all differences in the colonial sphere between the two countries. This followed on the famous visit of King Edward VII to Paris in May 1903, a triumph that considerably improved relations between the two countries.

Although a close alliance between Britain and France may now seem natural, even inevitable, this was certainly not the case as recently as the 1890s. Indeed, in 1898 the two countries had nearly been involved in a war over the Fashoda Incident, a clash between rival, expanding colonial empires in central Africa. Many in Britain favoured what at the time seemed the most natural of alliances, between Britain, Germany, and the United States, which would have been anti-Russian and anti-French. The three Protestant 'Anglo-Saxon' powers seemed linked by a host of political and cultural ties, and seemed to most informed observers to be destined to dominate the twentieth century's geopolitics. Joseph Chamberlain had actually proposed such an alliance in a major speech at Birmingham in May 1898 (again, an extraordinary intrusion, for a Colonial Secretary, into the domain of the Prime Minister or Foreign Minister). The prospect of an Anglo-German alliance was again seriously discussed during the visit of Kaiser Wilhelm II and German Chancellor Count von Bülow to Britain in November 1899. What prevented it? Primarily the truculent hostility of Germany's ruling elite to Britain and the British Empire and, above all, Germany's bloody-minded determination to build a navy to rival Britain's. Although it lacked a compelling reason to do so, Germany decided to build a world-class ocean navy in two Navy Laws passed in 1897 and 1898 at the behest of Admiral Alfred von Tirpitz, Minister of the Marine. There were other causes as well; one was a fear of German economic rivalry. After 1870 Germany became the predominant industrial power on the continent, and, by the first decade of the twentieth century, was exporting considerable amounts of goods to Britain and to areas which Britain had long regarded as in her economic sphere, like Latin America. There were, as well, direct and increasing colonial rivalries between Germany and Britain, especially in the Ottoman Empire (where Germany hoped to build a 'Berlin to Baghdad' railway) and in southern Africa. Most basically, it had for centuries been the most fundamental principle of Britain's foreign policy to prevent the domination of Europe by one single power, and for that reason Britain had fought France in so many wars between 1689 and 1815. By the early 1900s, it seemed apparent to most British opinion-leaders that Germany now harboured dreams of continental hegemony, a vision which its dangerous combination of a mighty army, world-class modern industries, and a perverse, ultra-nationalistic ideology, might well make a reality. On top of that, Germany also seemed determined to challenge the traditional domination of the Royal Navy. For all of these reasons, an alliance between Britain and Germany, something which seemed quite possible in the late 1890s, had become equally impossible only ten years later. Both Balfour's Unionist government and his Liberal successors took part in this fundamental shift of opinion. Yet if Germany's ruling elite had not been so foolish, it is entirely possible that Britain and Germany might have emerged as allies, not enemies. France, not Germany, had been Britain's age-old rival, while most British opinion-makers regarded Czarist Russia, the 'prison of nations', with detestation.

Balfour's other problems were compounded by the economic difficulties he faced. Unemployment probably rose during his time as Prime Minister, although there are no reliable statistics. The output of Britain's leading products such as cotton, coal, and steel stagnated. Exports were steady, while imports rose. The government lost 26 by-elections between 1900 and 1905, an unusually large number. There were, however, no public opinion polls in the modern sense (these began only in the late 1930s), and the government had no way of anticipating the disaster that lay ahead. Indeed, despite all of his government's problems, Balfour also had good reason to believe that the Unionists enjoyed an advantageous political position. The Liberals had deep and continuing problems of their own. Their leader, Sir Henry Campbell-Bannerman (1836–1908), known as 'C-B', was widely regarded as a weak compromise figure; in 1905 he was already 69 years old. Many expected Lord Rosebery (Archibald Primrose, fifth earl of Rosebery, 1847–1929), Prime Minister in 1894–95, to return. For decades the party's petulant but brilliant 'golden boy', his absence from the Liberal front bench was regarded as a distinct weakness. Most observers perceived the Liberals as divided into hostile camps: the 'Liberal Imperialists' led by H.H. Asquith (later first earl of Oxford and Asquith, 1852–1928), Sir Edward Grey (1862–1933), and Richard Haldane (1856–1928), and radicals like David Lloyd George (1863–1945) and John Burns (1858–1943). Ireland and the unpopular goal of Irish Home Rule continued to haunt the party, as did very fundamental questions about its long-term evolution, especially its relations with Labour and the trade unions. The Liberals had not won a General Election outright since 1880 (they had formed a government in 1892–95 with the support of the Irish Nationalists), and had sustained serious defections during the Liberal Unionist split of 1886. Compared with the Unionists, they were chronically underfunded and supported by fewer national newspapers. The death of William E. Gladstone in 1898 had removed their most famous leader and political symbol. In this atmosphere, on 4 December 1905 Balfour took the unexpected step of resigning, two years before a General Election was actually required, and without calling an election. The Liberals, under Sir Henry Campbell-Bannerman, were then asked to form a minority government. Balfour's expectation was that Liberal divisions ran so deeply that they would be unable to form one at all, or that, if they did, its instability and unfitness to govern would soon become apparent. This instability, moreover, was likely to make the electorate forget all about the Unionists' own bitter divisions. It was a clever strategy and quite a reasonable expectation, however disastrous it seems in hindsight.

2
The Liberal Government, 1905–10

Balfour's expectations that the Liberals would be unable to form a stable government appeared to be firmly grounded in political reality. A few months earlier, in September 1905, Asquith, Grey, and Haldane, the three most prominent Liberal Imperialists, had met at Relugas, Sir Edward Grey's fishing lodge in Morayshire, and contrived what has become known as the 'Relugas Compact' under which none would serve in a future Liberal government unless Sir Henry Campbell-Bannerman, the party's leader, agreed to go to the House of Lords, becoming a figurehead leader with real power lying in the hands of the Liberal Imperialists in the Commons. There was also the question of whether the former Prime Minister Lord Rosebery, who had been increasingly estranged from the Liberal party, would serve. After being asked by the King to form a government, Campbell-Bannerman proceeded to do so with considerable skill. There was no question of his actually going to the Lords, and, despite the 'Relugas Compact', all the principal liberals agreed to join the government, the exception being Rosebery, who refused to serve but was not missed: he never held any office again. The Liberal Cabinet formed by Campbell-Bannerman in 1905 was acclaimed even at the time as a 'government of all the talents', and has assumed legendary status since, but it is important to note that many of its members, so famous now, were little known then, or had reputations very different from their historical ones. David Lloyd George, for instance, was known then chiefly as a troublemaking Welsh radical and 'Little Englander'. Although obviously articulate, his capacity for office was unknown as he had never before held any government position.

Campbell-Bannerman's Cabinet consisted of 19 men. Only six were members of the House of Lords, easily the smallest number ever to sit in the upper house in any full Cabinet. Sir Henry Campbell-Bannerman was Prime Minister. The background of 'C-B', was something like that of Peel and Gladstone, whose immediate ancestors were self-made businessmen who had successfully moved into the landed gentry. His father was a self-made Glasgow merchant who had married the daughter of another Scot who had prospered in Manchester as a manufacturer. C-B's father had served as Lord Provost (mayor) of Glasgow, had been knighted, and purchased an estate in Perthshire. He himself was educated at Glasgow High School (the equivalent of a minor public school), Glasgow University, and then, unusually, at Trinity College, Cambridge. Unlike Peel and

Gladstone, he then became a partner in his father's business (he was the first British Prime Minister with active business experience), married into the Scottish gentry, inherited another country estate in Kent, and entered the House of Commons in 1868, 37 years before becoming Prime Minister. In politics, he had been a typical Gladstonian. As a platform speaker, however, he was notoriously poor. As a parliamentarian, he was pedestrian, even mediocre, but performed quite competently as a government minister, especially as Secretary of State for War in 1892–95. C-B was chosen as the Liberals' leader because he was safe, inoffensive, and a competent administrator. His celebrated attack on the 'methods of barbarism' employed by Britain in South Africa gave him a reputation as a radical, which he was not. He was a solid, conscientious, Gladstonian liberal whose preference was to continue the traditional Gladstonian policies of Free Trade, retrenchment and reform.

C-B's Chancellor of the Exchequer, and the man generally seen as second in the new government, was Herbert Henry Asquith, a leading barrister, very clever and competent, brilliant at Oxford, and married into a family of great wealth. An MP for East Fife since 1886, he had previously served as Home Secretary from 1892–95. Sir Edward Grey was Foreign Secretary. Like Asquith he was a leading Liberal Imperialist. He came from a landed family in Northumberland and was a relative of Earl Grey of the Reform Act. The third of the prominent Liberal Unionists to be given high office was Richard Burdon Haldane (1856–1928), made Secretary of State for War. A Scottish barrister, he had studied at Gottingen University in Germany, and was (like Balfour) a considerable philosopher; he had translated Schopenhauer. His German affinities caused great difficulties from xenophobes during the First World War. Haldane had been an MP since 1885 but had not previously held office.

Two of the most publicised appointees to the Cabinet were highly visible because of their backgrounds. John Burns, made President of the Local Government Board, was both the first man of working-class origin ever appointed to a Cabinet and the first avowed socialist. Apprenticed as an engineer, he was an early member of the Social Democratic Federation and had been gaoled for six weeks in 1887 for assaulting a policeman during a labour demonstration. In 1889, he helped to organise the famous London dock strike. By the 1890s, however, he had moderated considerably and pointedly declined to join the new Labour party. Like many autodidacts Burns was cultured in surprising ways: his notable collection of old books on early London was purchased after his death by a newspaper baron and presented to the London County Council. On being appointed, Burns reportedly slapped the Prime Minister on the back and said 'Bravo, Sir Henry! This is the most popular thing you have yet done.' Burns proved to be an anti-progressive administrator of the Local Government Board, his lack of experience making him the tool of a particularly narrow group of civil servants. Finally there was David Lloyd George, a Welsh solicitor of meagre background, known at the time as a wild radical, even a demagogue, whose detestation of the aristocracy, the Church of England, and foreign wars was already well known. Appointed by C-B to be President of the Board of Trade, it seemed easy to imagine him as the 'scourge of the dukes' which he became a few years later, but very difficult indeed to foresee him at the head of a largely Tory government, victorious in a war after four years of bloody struggle.

In sociological terms, C-B's Cabinet was, as noted, more likely to be drawn from the middle classes than any previous one. According to one study of the social origin of Cabinet ministers, among the 19 members of the 1905 Cabinet, seven could be termed 'aristocrats' (in the sense of having at least one grandfather who held an hereditary title), while 11 were drawn from the middle classes and one (John Burns) from the working classes. Only 11 had attended a public school, and only three had been educated at Eton (the most ultra-exclusive of the great public schools), compared with, respectively, 16 and nine in Balfour's 1902 Cabinet. Twelve in C-B's Cabinet attended Oxbridge, with another two educated at other universities.

The new government was, of course, a minority one which still faced a huge Unionist majority in the Commons. Having successfully formed a Cabinet, C-B's next aim was to dissolve Parliament and call a General Election. Parliament was dissolved in early January, and the General Election was held with remarkable speed, over a four-week period between 12 January and 7 February 1906. In their campaigning, the Liberals strongly attacked Chamberlain's tariff reform proposals as their central plank. Their cry of a 'tax on bread' proved successful nearly everywhere. With their attractive, united government giving the lie to the Unionist supposition that they would be unfit to govern, the election produced one of the greatest routs in British political history. Indeed, no left-of-centre government (not even Labour in its great 1945 victory) experienced so devastating a General Election victory again until 1997, when Tony Blair's 'New Labour' party won in arguably similar circumstances. Completely reversing the results of the two previous General Elections, the Liberals won 400 seats and the Unionists only 157. The overall results were as follows:

	Total votes	MPs elected	% share of total vote
Conservatives	2 451 454	157	43.6
Liberals	2 757 883	400	49.0
Labour	329 748	20	5.9
Irish Nationalists	35 031	83	0.6
Others	52 387	–	0.9
Total	5 626 503	670	100.0

The turnout in this election was nearly 83 per cent of the enrolled electorate, up 8 per cent from 1900. There were also many fewer unopposed returns than in 1900 – only 13 Unionists and 27 Liberals. The ridiculously low Irish Nationalist vote was the result of the fact that 74 of its 87 candidates were elected unopposed.

It will be seen from these figures that the Liberal total of 400 MPs was greatly in excess of its actual share of the vote, the total Liberal vote exceeding the total Unionist vote by less than 5.5 per cent. If strict proportional representation had been in effect the Unionists would have elected 256 MPs outside of southern

Ireland, nearly 100 more than they actually did. Under the British system of 'first past the post' voting, far more MPs are elected by the victorious party than their actual due at virtually every election (normally held to be in proportion to the so-called 'law of cubes', by which the proportion of MPs elected by each party is roughly equal to the percentages of the cubes of the vote actually cast for them). The 1906 election was one where this inequality reached an extreme. The Liberals were also helped by the fact that the election took place over a period of weeks rather than in one day. The earliest returns were from Lancashire, where the strong vote in favour of Free Traders and against tariff reformers (Balfour himself was defeated in one of the Manchester constituencies) probably produced something of a snowball effect in subsequent constituency polls. Nevertheless, 1906 was one of the most striking electoral victories of all time. The Liberals were triumphant almost everywhere, particularly in their normal strongholds in the industrial and Celtic areas (the Unionists won only one seat out of 34 in Wales), but also in many normally safe Tory areas in the south of England. The Unionists did well only in the safest of their seats in the southeast, rural areas, and Ulster. Because of Joseph Chamberlain's influence, they did fairly well in the West Midlands, as well as on Merseyside and in a number of other industrial areas like Sheffield. The chief novelty of the election, however, and one remarked upon by every observer, was the striking increase in the number of Labour MPs. Candidates who stood either as 'Labour' or 'Liberal-Labour' won 54 seats (30 as straight 'Labour'), more than one-third of the total of Unionist MPs. They did well, particularly, in south Wales, Tyneside, and parts of industrial Lancashire, but less well than subsequently in other future areas of strength like Glasgow, Liverpool, and the East End of London, where Liberal candidates still were in the ascendancy. The year 1906 gave them a visible presence on the parliamentary stage, but the wilder outbursts of fearful Tories such as comparing this election result to the 1905 revolution in Russia, were clearly exaggerated. The Liberal contingent elected in 1906 mainly consisted of middle-class, often but not always self-made, businessmen and professionals, among them large numbers of barristers, solicitors, and writers (including Hilaire Belloc and A.E.W. Mason). About one-third had attended a public school or Oxbridge. Apart from the 'Lib-Labs', fewer than 10 were trade unionists. The Liberals differed from their Unionist counterparts in two ways: many fewer were traditional landowners or their close relatives, while many more, a very large minority of the whole party, were Nonconformists. It appears that about 180 among the 400 Liberal MPs were Nonconformists (63 of whom were Congregationalists and 27 Methodists), compared with only about 10 Unionist and 20 Labour Nonconformists elected at the same time. The great majority of the new Cabinet, however, was Anglicans (or members of the Church of Scotland).

Given a parliamentary majority without equal since just after the 1832 Reform Act, what did the Campbell-Bannerman government do? It cannot be stressed too strongly that it did remarkably little. In no sense was C-B's government a radical one; it did not initiate the Welfare State nor enact far-reaching constitutional reforms. In so far as the Liberal governments of the 1905–14 period were radically innovative, their far-reaching measures date, almost without exception, from the years after C-B's death in April 1908. Indeed, the Liberal government of 1905–08 may more reasonably be seen as the last of the Gladstonian administrations rather than the first of the twentieth-century political world. In some respects the new government was arguably more conservative than its late Victorian predecessors. Despite its huge majority, it did not enact Irish Home Rule, church disestablishment, strong measures of temperance reform, or any other of the nostrums of late Victorian radicalism. It enacted no significant social legislation whatever.

One reason for this was the position of Sir Henry Campbell-Bannerman. He quickly and decisively gained a large measure of parliamentary ascendancy when, during a major debate on tariff reform initiated by the Unionists, replying to an especially convoluted question by Arthur Balfour (who, following his defeat at Manchester, had been re-elected for the City of London), C-B compared the former Prime Minister to 'the old Bourbons – he has learned nothing … I say, enough of this foolery. Move your amendment and let us get to business.' With 'enough of this foolery!' C-B immediately became feted in Liberal circles for his robust commonsense. Nevertheless, this belied the true situation: his wife, to whom he was very close, died in August 1906, and he suffered two heart attacks soon afterwards, before dying at 72 in April 1908. At the Exchequer, Asquith also proved to be a very traditional Chancellor whose aims were strictly in the Gladstonian mould. Total government expenditure actually fell between 1905 and 1908 from £149.5 million to £143.4 million, while government income increased from only £153.2 million to £156.5 million. Revenues raised by the income tax actually declined in this period by about £100 000. For instance, a bachelor in employment earning £10 000 per annum (a colossal income at the time, one enjoyed by around one person in 500), had retained £9375 after taxes in 1903 during the aftermath of the Boer War whereas he kept £9500 in 1908. As Chancellor, Asquith cut the duty on tea by one penny and introduced a distinction in the income tax between earned and unearned income, slightly lowering the tax on the former. Apart from these, Asquith changed little or nothing.

During C-B's time as Prime Minister the government passed a number of pieces of legislation which are remembered, two of which were defeated in the House of Lords. A Trade Disputes Bill, designed to overturn the Taff Vale verdict (and other anti-union court decisions) was passed, but only after strenuous efforts by the unions to replace a much narrower, legalistic bill favoured by much of the Cabinet. The government's Education Bill, designed to remove Nonconformist complaints but also very narrow, was passed by the Commons but defeated in the House of Lords, as was a reforming bill to eliminate plural voting (at the time – and until 1948 – electors with homes or business premises in more than one constituency could vote in each; this obviously favoured the Unionists). Several minor acts to encourage smallholdings were passed, while Lloyd George, as President of the Board of Trade, enacted measures relating to merchant shipping and patents that strengthened the rights of British sailors and inventors. He also established, by legislation passed in 1908, the Port of London Authority, providing for the first time a unitary governing body for all the wharves and shipping facilities along London's docks. The government passed a bill, promoted by the Labour party, enabling local government authorities to help provide meals for children attending State elementary schools. A Court of Criminal Appeal was established, and a Deceased Wife's Sister Act was passed. The last was bizarrely contentious. The Bible seemingly forbade the marriage of a widower to his deceased wife's sister, and English law had long prohibited such a union. Given the number of women who died in childbirth, and the likelihood that the widower would look to her sister as her replacement, this prohibition seemed arbitrary and unfair, but it took until 1907 to be permitted under British law. The Liberal government of 1905–10 had a notable record in penal reform. In particular, in 1908 it established the first Borstal institutions for young offenders, named for the first such custodial school founded under the scheme, at Borstal in Kent. Nevertheless, it is also important to note that it made no basic changes in the administration of justice. There was, for instance, no question of it abolishing capital punishment. Mainstream radicalism had not yet fashioned an agenda on these matters.

This really does not amount to very much: nor was it. The most notable achievements of C-B's premiership were, somewhat surprisingly, in military and foreign affairs. Haldane's Territorial and Reserve Forces Act, 1907, and his creation of an Imperial General Staff in 1908–09, were among the most important acts of this government. Building on Arnold-Forster's ill-starred army reforms of the previous government, Haldane created an Expeditionary Force of seven divisions ready for rapid mobilisation overseas, and created a new non-regular force, the Territorial Army, professionally led and trained, and twice as large as the Standing Expeditionary Force. This replaced the old locally based, much more amateurish yeomanry and volunteer forces. Haldane also organised an Officers' Training Corps among public and secondary school boys. Although attacked by conservatives for interfering with the old local militia power structure and its leadership of local notables, Haldane's reforms actually reinforced the class basis of the British army, while also modernising it. Britain differed from all other major European countries in not having conscription, and in traditionally valuing its navy above its army. The Liberal reforms meant that Britain went into the war in 1914 with a much better-prepared army than would otherwise have been the case, but they did not cure the obvious deficiencies in Britain's military which became evident once the war began.

The Liberals strengthened the military links between Britain and France that had been initiated by the previous Unionist government. In January 1906, following consultation with C-B, Asquith, and Haldane, but no one else, Sir Edward Grey initiated a series of official conversations with France on mutual assistance in the event of a German attack. During the years preceding 1914, this unofficial but real alliance between Britain and France grew so that, to most of the influential members of the Cabinet, it was very likely that Britain would come to the assistance of France were it to be attacked by Germany. There was little discussion in Parliament, or even in the Cabinet, of the direction in which Grey and a few of his colleagues had taken British policy, in part because the Liberal contingent in Parliament consisted, especially among backbenchers, of old-fashioned radicals, often Nonconformists, who were opposed to 'secret treaties' when they were not overt pacifists. Nevertheless, by 1914 it had long been accepted by the Liberal Cabinet that Britain might well go to war with

Germany. Even more signally, in August 1907 Britain entered into a formal Entente with Russia, which (like the informal 1904 Entente with France) was intended to increase cooperation between the two states by removing all areas of diplomatic friction. Spheres of influence were carved out in Persia and mutually conflicting expansionist drives in Afghanistan and Tibet were checked. British policy towards Russia had long been ambiguous: since the Crimean War most Tories mistrusted Russian expansionism in India and Turkey, while most Liberals detested the Czarist government. On the other hand, since Gladstone's time many Liberals saw in Russia a beneficial, christianising influence in the Balkans. By the 1900s, however, growing mistrust of Germany brought about the embryo of a formal alliance.

Probably the most constructive move overseas by Campbell-Bannerman's government occurred in South Africa, where the Liberal government, building on very conciliatory steps taken by Balfour's government but greatly expanding them, extended complete internal self-government to the four South African republics, including the two Boer states with which Britain had recently fought. This was done in the teeth of fierce Tory opposition in Parliament, later readily admitted by them to have been misguided. The fact that it was Campbell-Bannerman, coiner of the phrase 'methods of barbarism' to describe the Boer War, who initiated this policy of reconciliation produced reciprocal measures of goodwill by the Boers, and more moderate Boer leaders emerged, such as the great statesman Jan Christian Smuts (1870–1950). In 1910 came the formation of the Union of South Africa, a self-governing Dominion like Australia and Canada, with a British Governor-General; it remained a loyal part of the Empire/Commonwealth until its resignation in 1961. Of course, most if not all of the black natives were almost wholly excluded from the political processes of the new state; this was, in the long term, to prove the Union's Achilles heel and shame. C-B's policies also highlighted both the similarities and differences between Liberal and Tory policies in the white Empire. To most Liberals, loyalty towards the vision of a larger British Empire grew, and could only grow, out of the voluntary consent of a free people whose loyalty was freely given. While Unionists acknowledged this, they were much more willing to use both compulsion and the continuing economic links which an Empire tariff would have provided to accomplish this end. But it is important to note that both Liberals and Unionists had virtually the same end in mind: a worldwide British Empire that remained a very great geopolitical unit, perhaps the world's greatest. Both parties saw the development of the Empire as central to Britain's role in the twentieth century.

Early in 1908, C-B suffered a serious illness and, after lingering on a sickbed at 10 Downing Street for several months, resigned on 3 April 1908 (he died less than three weeks later). Perceived as a weak compromise figure, he had presided over one of the greatest electoral triumphs in history and led a strong government but one which, chiefly because of his moderation, was losing direction. On 4 April 1908 King Edward VII, on holiday in Biarritz, summoned H.H. Asquith and appointed him Prime Minister. During C-B's illness he had served as Acting Prime Minister, and there was no other feasible successor.

Herbert Asquith was probably the first middle-class man, in the sense this is normally used, to become British Prime Minister. His father was a minor woollen manufacturer in the West Riding and a Congregationalist who died young, leaving only £500. His mother, widowed a second time, moved south and sent her son to the City of London School, a rather minor but academically excellent public school for day boys. Asquith excelled at school and, in particular, at Balliol College, Oxford, taking a first and later becoming known as 'the epitome of the Balliol man', marked by effortless, clever superiority. Asquith became a leading barrister and QC, married young, and entered Parliament, where he soon became a major Liberal star. After the early death of his first wife, he married Margot Tennant, the brilliant and striking (though not strikingly beautiful) daughter of Scotland's richest businessman, Sir Charles Tennant. In Parliament, Asquith was renowned for his command of any situation and his calm, intelligent leadership under fire. Yet he had some serious character faults: he drank too much and was too friendly with much younger women. As a political leader, and the head of one of the great reforming British governments, he was surprisingly lacking in radicalism and without long-term strategic plans. 'He is...not the man of visions... No great cause will ever owe anything to him in its inception', was the comment of one Liberal newspaper when he became Prime Minister. A prominent Tory politician noted that 'he was a great parliamentarian, one of the greatest since Robert Peel...But...I found myself increasingly disappointed...It was only at the end of the speech that one wondered what, beyond the immediate vote, he really intended. That sense of purposeful action which animated the speeches of Joseph Chamberlain or...Lloyd George, was in him entirely lacking.' These are probably fair comments, and go far to explain the successes and failures that he enjoyed in peace and war.

Asquith's Cabinet was essentially similar to that of C-B, although with some significant changes. Of the 20 members of Asquith's original Cabinet, 14 sat in the Commons, and only six in the Lords. Even this conceals a marked decline in the Cabinet's aristocratic nature, for only two of its members, Lords Ripon and Crewe, came from old landed families. Asquith's Cabinet was probably the first whose peers seem clearly to be a minor appendage to its commoners, and in which no politicians of the first rank sat in the Lords. Asquith also made some important changes in the Cabinet he had inherited from C-B. The most important was the promotion of David Lloyd George from the Board of Trade to become Chancellor of the Exchequer, a post he held, always at the centre of national attention, until he became Minister of Munitions in the first wartime Coalition in May 1915. Winston Churchill now entered the Cabinet for the first time, replacing Lloyd George at the Board of Trade, a post Churchill held until becoming Home Secretary in February 1910. Reginald McKenna (1863–1943), a barrister who had entered C-B's Cabinet the previous year as President of the Board of Education, became First Lord of the Admiralty, where he was prominent in obtaining construction of 18 Dreadnoughts, the most modern type of battleship, intended to keep Britain's naval supremacy intact. Many of the best-known Liberals of this period joined the Cabinet during Asquith's time as Prime Minister – Charles Hobhouse, Sir Rufus Isaacs, Herbert Samuel, and Sir John Simon.

Asquith's appointment thus seemed clearly, on the basis of the personnel in his government, to signal a move to the Left, and certainly to foreshadow a more active programme than the government had followed under Campbell-Bannerman. In particular, the promotion of Lloyd George and Churchill to key Cabinet ministries made a more advanced programme likelier. There were additional reasons for this change. After the previous election, the opposition Unionists had picked themselves up off the floor, albeit with considerable difficulty. Between 1906 and 1909 the Unionists had won 12 by-elections, while the Liberals had lost no fewer than 18 (the others were won by Labour or other parties), and there was a general recognition that the size of the Liberal victory in 1906 had been a fluke, and that whatever happened the Tories were likely to make many gains at the next General Election. Arthur Balfour still remained Tory leader while, increasingly, tariff reform enthusiasts gained the upper hand within the party, driving pro-Free Trade Unionists out of the party. Their great leader, however, was incapacitated: on 8 July 1906, a few days after enormous celebrations in Birmingham to mark his seventieth birthday, Joseph Chamberlain was struck down by a stroke, and lingered in semi-paralysis until he died in 1914. Austen Chamberlain, lacking his father's charisma but possessing some of his Machiavellian qualities, assumed the leadership of the tariff reform forces. Tariff reform actually regained much of the popularity it lost as a result of the 1906 election a year or two later, when Britain suffered a serious recession, with mounting unemployment. Promising younger Tories had meanwhile emerged, most notably F.E. Smith (1872–1930, later first earl of Birkenhead). Smith, one of the most colourful politicians of his day and another of the very great barristers in politics, came to widespread notice on the same day as C-B had demanded of Balfour 'enough of this foolery', when he gave the most famous parliamentary maiden speech in history, successfully baiting Lloyd George over the 'Chinese slavery' issue in an unforgettable way. Always sailing close to the wind and always brilliant (and often being mistrusted for these reasons), Smith nevertheless soon became personally close to Lloyd George and Churchill as one of the cleverest men in the House, but, strangely enough, made his mark as one of the best reforming Lord Chancellors of the century.

Balfour and the Unionist leader in the House of Lords, Lord Lansdowne, decided on an active strategy of using the in-built and automatic Tory majority in the House of Lords to defeat the more radical bills enacted by the Liberal majority in the Commons. In this, they were perfectly within their rights. The Lords existed as a revising and delaying chamber on which no restraints had been placed. All other second chambers in the democracies acted in the same way. The American Senate, to which each state sent two members regardless of its population, were then selected by the legislature of each state, not elected; at the time, the US Senate was often known as the 'millionaires' club', and regarded by progressives in America as a prime obstacle to 'progress'. The enormous majority which the Liberals enjoyed after the 1906 election was obviously a fluke, and the government enjoyed absolutely no electoral mandate for quasi-socialist or confiscatory legislation. Yet using a hereditary chamber, chiefly composed of very wealthy men, to defeat the popularly elected House of Commons was also a strategy fraught with danger. Many Unionists would have greatly preferred an elected upper house something like the American Senate, with the legitimacy provided by democratic election. Others increasingly flirted with the notion of advocating the holding of a national referendum on very controversial pieces of legislation. Nevertheless, it is easy to underestimate the position of the Unionists around the time Asquith became Prime Minister. If the Liberals moved sharply to the Left, the strategy of Unionists would be to depict the government as being in the hands of left-wing madmen, bent, like the socialists on the continent, upon the confiscation of the property of ordinary persons. Such an electoral strategy has generally been successful in twentieth-century Britain; before the First World War, when historians estimate that only 60 per cent of the male electorate had the vote, and the electoral system was still biased towards the rich, this kind of argument could easily produce victory at the polls. The Irish issue, deliberately kept on the backburner by the Liberals, so long as they enjoyed a huge parliamentary majority, might well again come to the fore. Home Rule had never been popular in Britain and there was no reason to suppose it would be in future. As of 1908, most of the electoral straws in the wind were quite favourable to the Tories. In April 1908, Winston Churchill was appointed President of the Board of Trade and, under the law as it existed at the time, had to fight a by-election in his constituency of North-West Manchester. Normally his re-election would be a foregone conclusion, but in the event he was defeated by William Joynson-Hicks, a truculent and very extreme pro-tariff reform Tory. (Churchill was then easily elected, a month later, at Dundee.) The previous year, the Tories had won a sweeping victory at the London County Council elections, reversing an 83-35 majority for Liberal councillors to a 79-38 Tory majority. (In London's municipal politics, the Liberals were known as the 'Progressives' and the Tories as the 'Municipal Reform Moderates'.) Without an energising force, and despite the Unionists' internal divisions, the Liberals in 1908 had less reason to be sanguine about the future than might seem the case in retrospect.

Moreover, the Liberals also faced a challenge, potentially even more important to their future, from the Left. The Labour party had regarded itself as essentially an appendage to the Liberals and certainly not their full-scale challenger. Yet, electorally, it became increasingly apparent that Labour was enormously popular in many predominantly working-class constituencies and could, if and when it wished, defeat the Liberals and win important elections. At the same time as the great Liberal majority was haemorrhaging to the Tories in the right, there were also very significant by-election losses to pro-Labour candidates running as independents, especially the remarkable victory of Victor Grayson, a young 'independent socialist' candidate at the Colne Valley by-election in July 1907. The Colne Valley was a typical grim area of mill towns in the West Riding adjacent to Lancashire. Sir James Kitson, a wealthy Liberal ironmaster, had been elected unopposed in 1906. When he was given a peerage in 1907, Grayson won a three-cornered by-election against a Liberal and a Tory, although Tom Mann, the famous Labour leader, had finished third when he stood as a Labour candidate in 1895. (Grayson, 1882–1920?, a middle class journalist, served in Parliament until 1910; in 1920 he literally disappeared, and the mystery of his whereabouts has never been solved, despite all manner of theories by historians.) There were, moreover, other straws in the wind. In 1908, the MPs from mining districts who had been sponsored by the Miners' Federation left the Liberal party (where they had been classified as 'Lib-Labs') and officially joined the Labour party, raising the number of Labour MPs to 45. Also, in 1908, Arthur Henderson (1863–1935) replaced Keir Hardie as chairman (i.e. leader) of the Parliamentary Labour party. Henderson, an official of the Iron Founders' Union, was an extremely astute moderate (and a devout Methodist) who proved a much more formidable leader of the Labour party than the more extreme Hardie. That the Liberals would, sooner or later, have to compete with Labour for many working-class votes (and the support of middle-class radicals) was evident to all by this time. On the other hand, there was as yet little or no reason to suppose that Labour would prove electorally successful outside heavily working-class seats, especially those in mining areas.

It was against this background that the radicalisation of the Liberal government after Asquith became Prime Minister ought to be viewed. Most of the credit for this radicalisation belongs to David Lloyd George, and his ascent to the very centre of British political life dates from his becoming Chancellor of the Exchequer in April 1908; he then remained at the political core continuously until he was forced to resign as Prime Minister in October 1922. More has been written about Lloyd George than any twentieth-century British politician except Churchill, and the past generation has seen an endless array of scholarly writing about his life and career. Nevertheless, it is probably fair to say that he remains essentially as elusive as ever, among the most difficult of twentieth-century political leaders to understand. Much of what is probably known to the average person about him is false: his surname, for instance, was 'George' (his father's name was William George), not 'Lloyd George'. ('Lloyd' was his mother's surname and his middle name.) Lloyd George was born in Manchester, not Wales (albeit to a Welsh-speaking family). He did not emerge from the working classes: his father was a school headmaster; Lloyd George himself was a solicitor. His Welsh associations were always with rural Wales, with Criccieth in north Wales and Pembroke in the south. Of the new industrial Wales, the mining valleys of Glamorgan and Monmouth, he was never a part. Lloyd George's radicalism was aimed primarily, if not wholly, at absentee Tory landowners allegedly oppressing the small farmer and the villager, and at the Anglican clergymen whose church was legally established in Wales despite the fact that three-quarters of Welshmen were Nonconformists. It was never aimed centrally at industrialists and manufacturers. Lloyd George was not a socialist, nor even, perhaps, a social democrat, but an old-fashioned radical who argued for the unity of industrialists, especially self-made men, and their workers in the manner of the Chartists and Anti-Corn Law Leaguers 70 years earlier. Lloyd George also emerged from the distinctive Welsh Nonconformist preaching tradition of vigorously outspoken and eloquent sermonising, and of simple dichotomies of right and wrong. This made him appear much more radical than he actually was, although to this Welsh tradition he added a good measure of overt demagoguery and an extremely clever sense of the direction which the Liberal party had to take if it was to continue to win elections. Together with these elements was another significant one, even more difficult to explain clearly: Lloyd George's British patriotism. Although he became nationally known in the late 1890s as an anti-Boer War 'Little Englander', in government he was always a strong patriot and, indeed, champion of the Empire. One is reminded here of the peculiarly French tradition of politicians who are both radical anti-aristocrats and anti-clericalists and yet intense patriots, indeed often super-nationalists. To make this element in Lloyd George's psyche even more complex, he was also a Welsh nationalist long before this became fashionable and a champion of small oppressed nations such as the Boers, Belgians, and Jews (Lloyd George's philo-semitic Zionism was also an important element in his intellectual moorings). He was also unbelievably energetic and unquestionably one of the best public speakers of his time – formidable qualities. Like Churchill, whom he resembled in some respects, he was also widely mistrusted, even by his political allies, and probably lacked the full greatness of Winston Churchill, which was rooted in a peculiar historical vision of British power within the English-speaking world community.

Lloyd George's sparking of the Liberal government's leftward move was probably not wholly deliberate but was in part the product of making a virtue of necessity. As Chancellor, Lloyd George attempted, almost simultaneously, to find the resources to pay for two very expensive innovations: old age pensions and Dreadnought battleships. Until 1908, Britain had no state system of old age pensions. Support in one's old age was purely a private matter, to be paid for from money set aside in one's working lifetime, often through the friendly societies, which were voluntary insurance companies. Anyone who did not save faced the prospect of private charity or the workhouse, the grim institutional system created by the New Poor Law of 1834 and universally feared. By the Edwardian period it was widely acknowledged that provision for old age was inadequate and would have to be considerably revised, almost certainly in the direction of much greater state input. Increasingly, many intellectuals and social commentators abandoned the Victorian view of poverty as caused by deficiencies of character and lack of foresight by the person concerned and came to view it instead as the product of deep faults within the British economic and social system over which the individual had virtually no control. By the Edwardian period it was widely accepted that many groups in society could simply not make adequate provision for their old age, especially working-class men, frequently unemployed and at the borderline of poverty, and most women. The example of Germany, where Bismarck and his successors had erected a far-reaching social welfare system, chiefly to ward off the threat provided by the Socialist party to Germany's conservative regime, was also well known. By the early 1900s, both the Unionists and the Liberals were divided on the question of state-provided old age pensions, with many Chamberlainite Tories having long advocated such welfare measures, to be paid for by the imperial tariff, while many Gladstonian Liberals continued to oppose them as an undue extension of state intervention, impossibly costly without greatly increased taxation, and sapping individual initiative.

Lloyd George's first venture into this field came in his 1908 budget, where the very modest sum of around £6 million (in a budget of roughly £157 million) was allocated towards a scheme of non-contributory old age pensions, to begin on 1 January 1909. The pension was tiny, ranging from one to five shillings a week, given to persons over 70 years of age with an income of no more than £31 per year. Married couples could receive no more than seven shillings and sixpence. As tiny as these sums were, they could not readily be paid within the constraints of the budget unless the number of persons who applied did not exceed 500 000. In reality, by 1910 nearly 700 000 persons applied for the pension (including 98.6 per cent of all persons aged 70 or older in Ireland, compared with only 44.7 per cent of Englishmen), its cost exceeding the original estimate by £2.5 million. Given the adamant refusal of the Liberals to enact tariffs, the only realistic means of paying for non-contributory pensions was via higher taxes. Higher taxes were even more necessary if the state welfare system was ever to be extended even further, as desired by many left-Liberals and intellectuals of the so-called 'New Liberalism'. In mid-1909, Lloyd George visited Germany and other central European countries specifically to study the advanced social welfare system provided there by the state, which convinced him of the necessity of similar initiatives in Britain.

At about this time, naval warfare was revolutionised by the building of the Dreadnought-class battleship, a super-warship, oil-fired and turbine-powered, armed with big guns capable of sinking an entire fleet. The first had been built by the British at Portsmouth in 1905, and it soon became clear that Britain would have to construct considerable numbers of these ships to keep pace with Germany's gratuitous naval armaments programme. The First Lord of the Admiralty, Reginald McKenna, had requested six new Dreadnoughts, compared with only four preferred by the Cabinet's economically minded members. A compromise was reached so that four would be built at once and another four later, if necessary. The Tories, in favour of British naval supremacy, whipped up an agitation with the slogan 'We want eight, and we won't wait'. As a result of Britain's shipbuilding expansion, expenditure on the Navy rose from £31.4 million in 1907 to £44.4 million by 1913. The Dreadnoughts were to cost £15 million, an extraordinary sum at the time.

Lloyd George also faced another political reality at this time, the fact that the House of Lords was likely to defeat any radical measures passed by the House of Commons, as they had with Liberal attempts to reform the licensing laws and amend the Education Act of 1902. At this time, and despite recent Liberal creations of new peers, the overwhelming majority of members of the House of Commons were Tories, mostly hereditary landowners. About 550 peers were entitled to sit in the House of Lords, of whom no more than 100 at most were Liberals or their supporters, compared with 300–400 Tories. The majority of the Tories had inherited their titles; they included a significant number, dubbed 'backwoodsmen' by the Liberals, who took little or no part in the proceeding of the Upper Chamber, although they were still entitled to vote, which they did in force whenever a radical measure was under consideration. As noted, the leadership of the Conservative party did not regard the House of Lords as an automatic rubber stamp for government legislation. What were the limits to which the Lords were prepared to go to resist radical legislation passed by the great Liberal majority in the Commons? Would it, for example, decline to pass a government's budget if this was seen as extremely radical, although the Lords had not interfered with government budgets for 250 years? If it did, would not the Liberal party have an ideal issue on which to fight the next election – 'the peers *vs* the people' – at a time when it appeared that they were tired and lacking in direction? The evidence suggests that Lloyd George did not necessarily have this aim in mind at the time, but seized on the opportunities provided to exploit this possibility to the full.

Lloyd George brought everything together in his celebrated 'People's Budget', delivered to Parliament at the end of April 1909. To pay for the old age pension, the Dreadnoughts, and other novelties (including the first attempt to improve Britain's road system in the age of the motor car), Lloyd George proposed a series of new taxes that seemed startling if not revolutionary. The most important was a Land Values tax, a duty on the unearned increment of land value, whenever land was sold. This in turn entailed producing a complete valuation of all land in Britain. As well, Lloyd George raised income taxes, and added a new so-called 'super-tax', an additional tax on all incomes over £5000. Although very small by later standards, this was the first time in British history that the very rich were taxed at a higher rate than others liable to pay income tax. Thirdly, death duties were raised by substantial amounts. (Lloyd George also raised taxes on alcohol and tobacco.)

While all of these taxes were odious to most Conservatives, the land tax seemed to signal a personal vendetta by Lloyd George against the landowning class, although one backed by the full force of the Liberals' great majority. There was, in truth, a large measure of accuracy in the Tories' views: Lloyd George's Welsh rural radicalism was probably highly significant in explaining his choice of targets. Since the 1880s, landowners had often been the focus of radical ideologues, spurred on by the writings of Lloyd George's unrelated American namesake, Henry George (1839–97), whose *Progress and Poverty* advocated a 'single tax' on land. According to George, unlike any other form of production the value of land increased purely by the bounty of nature, unaffected by entrepreneurship. This curious – and very misleading – theory had an enormous vogue throughout the English-speaking world in the late nineteenth century, such that by Edwardian times the Liberal party contained many advocates of the Georgian viewpoint. Even those radicals who were unable to accept all of Henry George's notions generally viewed the hereditary landed aristocracy as the very worst of the 'idle rich'. To this Lloyd George added a particularly Welsh hostility to 'absentee landlords', almost always English and Anglican, who took little or no interest in the welfare of their tenant farmers or, still less, their agricultural labourers.

It became increasingly clear that the House of Lords might well reject the Budget, a course increasingly threatened by the Tories' leaders. Lloyd George now turned wholly against the Lords, sensing a winning political tactic for the next election. He did this with no holds barred, in a number of celebrated speeches of unprecedented venom, at a mission hall in Limehouse, in the East End of London on 30 July 1909 and at the Palace Theatre, Newcastle, on 9 October 1909. In a fairly typical extract from the Limehouse speech, Lloyd George asked rhetorically:

Have you ever been down a coalmine? I went down the other day ... In the very next colliery to the one I descended, just a few years ago, 300 lost their lives ... and yet when the Prime Minister and I knock at the doors of [the] great landlords, and say to them: 'Here you know these poor fellows who have been digging up royalties at the risk of their lives ... Won't you give us towards keeping them out of the workhouse?' They scowl at us. We say 'Only a ha'penny, just a copper.' They retort, 'You thieves.' And they turn their dogs on us ...

At Newcastle he went even further, addressing the House of Lords and its threat to vote down his Budget:

Let them realize what they are doing. They are forcing a revolution, and they will get it. The Lords may decree a revolution, but the people will direct it. If they begin, issues will be raised that they little dream of. Questions will be asked which are now whispered in humble voices, and answers will be demanded then with authority. The question will be asked whether five hundred men, ordinary men chosen accidentally from the unemployed, should override the judgement ... of millions of people who are engaged in the industry which makes the wealth of the country ... Who made ten thousand people owners of the soil, and the rest of us trespassers on the land of our birth? Who is it who is responsible for the scheme of things whereby one man is engaged through his life in grinding labour to win a bare and precarious subsistence for himself, and when at the end of his days, he claims at the hands of the community he served a poor pension of 8d a day, he can get it only through a revolution ...?

There are two ways of viewing Lloyd George's extraordinary and unprecedented rhetorical extremism. On the one hand, it was clearly demagoguery of the most naked and palpable kind. Inevitably, in a democracy demagoguery eventually rebounds upon the demagogue. Lloyd George singled out 'the dukes' and 'the landlords' for his venom, but it would not take long for socialists to add 'the factory master' and 'the bankers' to the list, and the old-fashioned distinction between landowners and the rest of High Society drawn by Lloyd George would be swept away. As well, by legitimating demagogic extremism, Lloyd George virtually invited others to engage in the same thing, to debase the language of political debate still further, and, worst of all, to begin to link words with action. In the twentieth century, more bloodshed has been spilled because of race and ethnicity than because of class, and Lloyd George may be seen as opening the floodgates to the equally extremist rhetoric of the militant Ulster Protestants a few years later which nearly brought Britain to a state of civil war. Asquith was fond of terming the deliberately abrasive, insulting, and truculent tone adopted by Andrew Bonar Law in the House of Commons after he became Tory leader in 1911 'the new style', but its inventor was Asquith's own Chancellor of the Exchequer. Extremist language was a viciously circular game in which anyone could join.

On the other hand, in the short term Lloyd George appeared to give the Liberals the political upper hand and to place the Unionists very much on the back foot, and from this perspective his speeches were arguably brilliant tactics. The Tories were faced with the choice of acquiescing in a provocatively radical budget against the wishes of their core supporters, or resisting it by an unprecedented use of power in the hereditary Upper House. It also brought into the open the deep divisions between the Tariff Reformers among the Unionists, who often welcomed the provision of social welfare from the working classes (to be paid for from tariffs) and the party's anti-statist advocates of laissez-faire. In particular, it drew attention to Arthur Balfour's prevarication and lack of forceful leadership.

Most centrally, Lloyd George moved the party to the Left in order to forestall a challenge from Labour. On 3 May 1909 Labour won a dramatic by-election victory at Sheffield–Attercliffe, where Joseph Pointer, a local trade unionist, was victorious in a hitherto absolutely safe Liberal seat, pushing the Liberals into third place. Soon after, however, as the Budget reached the centre-stage of British politics, the Liberals won a series of dramatic by-elections (admittedly in their own safe seats). Because Lloyd George appeared to have revivified the Liberals, his violent rhetoric was not condemned by Asquith and other leaders of the Cabinet, who would normally have deplored such extremism. Asquith, in fact, gave the Budget all-out support. That the Liberal party would unanimously support the Budget was not automatic: many Liberal MPs believed that Lloyd George had moved too far to the Left, rejecting, in particular, the 'super-tax' on incomes. Everyone, however, recognised that a corner had been turned: the rhetoric of class conflict had now entered British political debate at the highest level, and was unlikely to disappear for many years. The word 'Limehouse' also entered the language as a generic term for political vituperation, taking its place alongside 'Mafeking' and similar terms to come later such as 'Jarrow'.

The Liberals had still to pass the Budget in Parliament, including the House of Lords, and the central question now became whether the Tories would use their majority in the upper house in such a dramatic way. Tory opinion now hardened in favour of rejecting the Budget and forcing a General Election over the issue, and both Balfour and Lord Lansdowne, the Unionist leader in the Lords, led on by their backbench opinion, also came round to this extreme and novel step. 'If we believe a thing to be bad, and if we have a right to prevent it,' said Lord Milner about the Budget, at Glasgow in November 1909, 'it is our duty to try to prevent it and to damn the consequences'. Milner here stated a view heard increasingly from the Tory far right that if the House of Lords was to be reformed and lose its powers to amend or negate Liberal legislation, it should do so in a blaze of glory. The 'last ditchers', as they became known, peers and their associates who would die in the last ditch rather than allow radicalism to triumph, increasingly set the tone for the Unionist response. King Edward VII now became directly involved in the dispute, attempting, without success, to reach a compromise resolution. On 30 November 1909, the Lords indeed carried out their threat, voting against a second reading for the Budget by a majority of 350-75. On 25 November 1909 Asquith had no choice but to dissolve Parliament, calling a General Election three years earlier than necessary, solely over the issue of the powers of the House of Lords. With the usual delays over the Christmas period, voting took place between 12 January and 7 February 1910.

3

The Liberal Government, 1910–14: A 'General Crisis'?

Two General Elections were fought in 1910. The second was held at the end of the year because the new King, George V, insisted that another General Election be held before he would agree to create the several hundred peers apparently necessary to reform the House of Lords. These elections are known respectively as those of January 1910 and December 1910. Both produced remarkably similar results, and their outcomes were partially responsible for the troubled political situation in the years immediately preceding the outbreak of the First World War. Both the Liberals and the Unionists were disappointed in the results of the January 1910 election. The Liberals expected their popular anti-House of Lords cry to be echoed by the electorate, while the Unionists expected to win back the ascendancy with the electorate that they had enjoyed before the abnormality of 1906. The results were as follows:

	Votes	Seats	% of votes
Unionists	3 127 887	273	46.9
Liberals	2 880 581	275	43.2
Labour	532 807	40	7.6
Nationalists	126 647	82	1.9
Others	26 693	0	0.4
Total	6 667 404	670	100.0

In other words, the two large parties were virtually equal in terms of seats. Nevertheless, the Liberals would definitely continue in power, but with the proviso that they were dependent for remaining in office on the parliamentary votes of the Irish Nationalists and of Labour. This was reminiscent of the situation during the period 1892–95, when the Liberals under Gladstone and Rosebery found themselves in a similar position. For both parties, the outcome was something of a disappointment: while the enormous Liberal majority of 1906 had been corrected, the Tories failed to put the electoral clock back to their halcyon days of 1895 or 1900; they not merely faced an indefinite period of continuing Liberal rule, but a Liberal government in a position to be blackmailed by the Irish or Labour. The election of January 1910 began a period of intense and increasing frustration and vexation for the Unionists, lasting until the outbreak of the war, in which they feared that a period of permanent Liberal rule might have begun. The Liberals, while they remained in power, knew that the populist appeal of Lloyd George had been, at best, only partially successful, and that they were the potential prisoners of minority parties and interests.

Ambiguity also surrounds the changes brought about by the election. The Unionists gained 108 seats compared with 1906, and secured over 150 000 more votes than the Liberals, but won seats only unevenly, chiefly in London and the south-east and in the Midlands and south Midlands. The Liberals and Labour were predominant in Lancashire and the West Riding, in remote rural areas like Cornwall and Norfolk, and, of course in Scotland (where they trounced the Unionists, winning 61 seats to the Tories' nine) and in Wales (32-2). Research has shown that voting was heavily along class lines, with the Unionists failing to win many working-class seats; tariff reform did not help them at all. On the other hand, the Liberals lost many of the seats, especially in the south-east, that they had won anomalously in 1906. Labour made no breakthrough, winning only 40 seats, while the impregnable Irish Nationalist contingent elected its usual 82 MPs (55 of whom were returned without opposition). The January 1910 election was also the first in which members of the House of Lords could legally campaign on behalf of candidates hoping to win seats in the Commons. Rather curiously, before then it was illegal for peers to take any part in a parliamentary election, for instance by delivering an election speech on behalf of a candidate. In the late nineteenth century this worked against the Conservative party, which had many more leading figures in the Lords than did the Liberals. Paradoxically, peers were allowed to participate in elections at the very time when the number of significant aristocrats among the Conservative party's top leaders was declining sharply.

The four years before the outbreak of the First World War are often seen as unusually troubled ones, so much so that the best-known history of this period (written in 1936) is entitled *The Strange Death of Liberal England*. Many historians have seen the Liberal government as facing an unusual number of unrelated but determined and even violent challenges to its authority, from the forces of labour and the trade unions, from extreme right-wing Tories, and their allies the Ulster Unionists, and from militant women campaigning for female suffrage, all set against the background of the darkening international situation and the outbreak of the world war in August 1914. Soon after the end of the war, the Liberal party was replaced by the Labour party as the major British left-of-centre party. With hindsight, Britain indeed appeared to have reached a crisis point, perhaps a 'general crisis'. Some Marxist historians have argued that Britain's imperialist phase had reached saturation point, and was no longer able to satisfy the increasingly militant workers and others at home: hence a period of marked class (and ethnic and gender) conflict at home and heightened international rivalry leading to catastrophe throughout Europe. Whether the years before the outbreak of the war should be viewed in this light, or whether the apparent validity of such a perception is merely based in hindsight, remains a hotly debated topic by historians to this day.

The first issues facing the Liberal government after the January 1910 election were the closely related ones of passing the Budget and reforming the powers of the House of Lords in order to prevent a recurrence of their rejection of this measure. The question of reforming the Lords had featured in the rhetoric of the left-wing of the Liberal party for the previous 30 years. Campbell-Bannerman had made it clear, in 1907, after the Lords had defeated a spate of Liberal bills passed by the Commons, that reform was actively on the government's agenda. Reform of the Lords comprised two separate components, not necessarily related: its composition and its powers. Perhaps curiously, the Liberal party consistently preferred to leave the composition of the Lords alone, in order to concentrate on amending and restricting its powers. For most Liberals, the main problem with the Lords was its inbuilt, automatic Tory majority. Lloyd George's famous retort (made on 26 June 1907) to a Tory frontbencher's claim that the Lords was 'the watchdog of the Constitution', summarised the Liberal's chief concern. He said: 'You mean it is Mr. Balfour's poodle! It fetches and carries for him. It barks for him. It bites anybody that he sets it on to.' Although the Liberals paid lip service to reforming the composition of the Lords, perhaps by replacing it by an upper chamber partially elected and partially appointed, in practice it was perfectly happy to use the Lords as it existed, so long as that body's powers were curtailed. The reason for this was that peerage creations provided a uniquely valuable and useful form of patronage and reward for the party's most important and wealthiest supporters. Throughout the twentieth century all left-of-centre governments, whatever their original intentions about reforming the Lords, have come to the same conclusion, that the ability to reward influential (or difficult) supporters by ennobling them was just too valuable a prerequisite to give up. As well, there were distinct limits, even after the death of C-B and the radicalisation of the Liberal government, to the reforms it was prepared to enact. The moderates who still led the party simply did not wish for so far-reaching a change as an elected upper house. Finally, there was another major difficulty that all proposed reforms of the House of Lords have encountered, namely that a reformed upper house, especially an elected one, would be more powerful than the largely hereditary House of Lords and might either comprise an elected majority of the party which was in the minority in the House of Commons or challenge any bill passed by the Commons with democratic legitimacy.

The predominant view of the Unionist opposition at this time was very nearly the opposite of the Liberals: they were quite prepared to scrap the hereditary House of Lords, or greatly diminish its hereditary element, provided that the elected or largely elected upper house thereafter had greater powers to defeat radical legislation passed by the Commons. In particular, the Tories desired an upper house that could defeat any proposal for Irish Home Rule; further down the track, an elected upper house would hopefully defeat, or greatly amend, any socialist or quasi-socialist taxation proposals emerging from a radical House of Commons. The model many Tories had in mind was the American Senate, whose members were elected for longer terms than those of the House of Representatives (the lower house of the American Congress) and on a different, narrower electoral basis. Of course, many traditionalist Tories wished to preserve the centuries-old aristocracy and its rights, but would readily have replaced them with an elected upper chamber if this was the only way of forestalling ever-more-left-leaning radical measures.

For Asquith and the Liberal government, reforming the Lords was a much more complex matter than it appeared. The House of Lords could simply not be reformed by fiat of the Commons alone: constitutionally, it would have to consent to reforming itself. Given the automatic Tory majority in the Lords this was extremely difficult. The most clear-cut way out of this dilemma was for the King, on the advice of the Prime Minister, to create new peers in sufficient numbers to pass the government's reforming legislation. Nothing like this had happened since the early eighteenth century, when the House of Lords was much smaller, and, to be successful, would, in 1910, require the creation of over 500 new peers. No such mass creation had ever occurred in modern times. Lord Salisbury had created 44 new peers in seven years, an average of just over six per year, Balfour 18 in three years, and Campbell-Bannerman 21 in two years. It was very doubtful that King Edward VII would have readily agreed to such a course, which would seemingly have made a mockery of the House of Lords. Asquith actually had held discussions with King Edward VII in December 1909 on just this matter, with the King declining to agree to create new peers in such numbers until after a *second* General Election. The King's model here was apparently the passing of the Great Reform Act of 1832, when King William IV had given similar assurances about the mass creation of pro-Reform peers sufficient to carry the Act in the House of Lords, but only after Whig electoral victories at the General Elections of 1830 and 1831. In February 1910, Asquith told the Commons that he had obtained no 'guarantees' from the King. Hostility to Asquith mounted from both Irish Nationalists and Ulstermen, with Asquith prevaricating on what course he actually intended to follow, repeatedly using the phrase 'wait and see' (which, apparently, he coined) in response to a question in Parliament in April 1910. Finally, the government produced a series of proposals defining and narrowing the powers of the House of Lords that were incorporated in the Parliament Bill, 1910. The Lords could henceforth neither amend nor reject a money bill (as defined by the speaker of the House of Commons); they could only delay other legislation for up to two years and one month. Any bill passed three times by the Commons would become law even if it were defeated by the Lords. Finally, and unrelated to the question of the Lords, the maximum term of Parliament before a General Election was reduced from seven years to five years. Shortly after the Commons passed Asquith's resolutions in late April 1910, the Lords approved through the 1909 Budget without a division.

At this stage, a *deus ex machina* intervened when, on 6 May 1910, King Edward VII died of throat cancer at the age of 69 and his eldest surviving son, George, Duke of York (1865–1936), succeeded to the throne as King George V. (George's elder brother Albert, Duke of Clarence, 1864–92, had died of pneumonia at the age of 28; had he lived, he would have succeeded to the throne. George V married his fiancé, Princess Victoria Mary of Teck (later Queen Mary). Some amateur historians, incidentally, have put forward the theory that the Duke of Clarence was actually 'Jack the Ripper', who brutally murdered five prostitutes in the East End of London in 1888. There is no actual evidence for this view.)

George V was to preside over one of the greatest periods of political and social change in modern history, witnessing the fall of time-honoured monarchies in Austria-Hungary, Germany, Russia, and Turkey. By the 1930s, he and Queen Mary stood out as rocks of stability and were genuinely and immensely popular. Many historians also believe that George V was the best modern monarch, who used his influence to bring Labour into the circle of governance and was at home among the working classes and throughout the Commonwealth. George regarded himself, and was regarded by others, as a simple sailor (he had spent a good deal of time at sea) of bluff common sense and often salty language. He was also an extreme conservative in his outlook on social behaviour and a martinet in bringing up his sons. Unlike most British monarchs, he had been shown all state papers by his father. He exercised a good deal of direct political influence at various times of national crisis, almost always intelligently.

The new King was at first heavily dependent upon the advice given by his Private Secretaries, Lord Knollys and Sir Arthur Bigge, and had, unusually, not been informed by his father of his promise to create new peers after a second General Election. Because of this situation, Asquith agreed to a temporary political truce in which serious discussions would be held with the Unionists aimed at seeking an agreed resolution of the Lords reform question, and possibly of other matters as well. This truce lasted from May until November 1910, and entailed the holding of 21 formal discussions by eight leading political figures (four Liberals and four Unionists) between June and early November. Remarkably, these discussions not only produced a measure of agreement on Lords' reform, but very nearly saw the formation, unique in peacetime since 1832, of a coalition Liberal–Conservative government. This proposal came from Lloyd George of all people, who viewed as potential allies the progressive and dynamic men of the Unionist party, especially the strong pro-tariff reformers such as Austen Chamberlain and younger, ambitious men such as F.E. Smith. This arrangement very nearly succeeded, and might well have led to agreed Lords' reform, a federal system of local government, some kind of conscription to meet the obvious threat of war on the continent, and even a measure of tariff reform, all of which were actively discussed. It might seem as if backbench Liberals had more to fear from such a coalition than did Tories, but in the end it was backbench Unionist opinion which made a coalition impossible while, indeed, it was also Unionist opinion which made an agreed reform of the Lords impossible. The stumbling block was Ireland and Home Rule. Here Lord Lansdowne, the leader of the Unionists in the House of Lords (and a great Irish landowner) was adamant that any proposal for Home Rule should be subject to a national referendum if passed by the Commons and defeated by the Lords. The Liberals could not accept this, and all of these negotiations came to an end in November 1910. Asquith decided to proceed with a Parliament Bill embodying the moderate principles of reform noted above. The Liberals did not pursue any wider measure of reform, either entailing a national referendum on vital issues (as desired by the Unionists) or a change in the composition of the Lords (as proposed by dissident Liberals such as Lord Rosebery and by many Unionists). Shortly after the breakdown of the constitutional discussions, with considerable difficulties, and after he had decided to call another General Election, Asquith secured from the new King a secret promise to create hundreds of new peers if necessary to pass the Parliament Bill in the Lords. Asquith actually drew up a list of over 250 men who would have received a peerage had this become necessary. Most were wealthy Liberal worthies and former MPs, little different in kind from the men whom the Liberal government had ennobled since taking office. A few names were more unusual, among them Bertrand Russell the philosopher, Thomas Hardy the novelist, and Baden Powell the founder of the Boy Scouts. In terms of ability, these men would certainly not have disgraced the Lords.

Asquith dissolved Parliament on 28 November 1910, and a second General Election in 1910 was held from 2 until 19 December. Asquith clearly had hoped for an increased majority by an electorate anxious for reform of the Lords, but was to be disappointed, since the results of the General Election, amidst considerable public apathy, were virtually identical to those earlier in the year:

	Votes	MPs elected	% of the votes
Unionists	2 420 566	272	46.2
Liberals	2 295 888	272	43.9
Labour	371 772	42	7.1
Nationalists	131 375	84	2.5
Others	8 768	0	0.2
Total	5 228 369	670	100.0

Compared with January, the Unionists won more seats in southern cities and agricultural seats, while the Liberals won more in the London slums, in Lancashire, and in parts of Scotland. Overall, however, there was remarkably little apparent change, with the government still being absolutely dependent upon Irish and Labour MPs to pass controversial legislation. One feature of the December 1910 election was apathy: over 1.4 million fewer votes were cast than in January, and there were many more uncontested returns: 163 compared with 75. In Great Britain, the majority of these were Unionists (72, compared with 35 Liberal and three Labour members), many more than in January (respectively, 19 and one). This meant that although the Unionist share of the total vote had declined very marginally (from 46.9 to 46.3 per cent), it had probably actually risen by a few per cent, since the uncontested Unionist seats were absolutely safe for the party. In reality, almost precisely the same electoral situation existed after the election as before it.

The results of the election also meant that it could reasonably be argued that the Liberals had no mandate to proceed with reform of the Lords. Many Tories said the two elections were 'a dead heat', and support by the Irish Nationalists, crucial to any outcome, was certainly not guaranteed unless the government committed itself to Home Rule, something it had notably failed to do at any time since it took office. A strong movement also grew up among right-wing Tories to resist parliamentary reform when the Liberals' bill came to the House of Lords for approval, necessitating the creation of hundreds of peers. The 'die-hards', as they were known, organised themselves into the 'Halsbury Club' (named in honour of the 87-year-old Tory former Lord Chancellor,

Lord Halsbury) and included many MPs, party activists, journalists, and intellectuals who had been prominent in the tariff reform campaign and virtually worshipped Joseph Chamberlain (who strongly supported them from his sick bed). Their leader in the Lords was the previously unknown Lord Willoughby de Broke, a typical landowning 'backwoodsman' who had, nonetheless, developed a coherent ideology of right-wing resistance to Liberal reforms similar to that found elsewhere on the Tory far right at this time. This ideology strongly emphasised British nationalism and Empire unity, social reform at home to be paid for by tariff reform, military preparedness based in a strong navy and, possibly, conscription in Britain, and opposition to Irish Home Rule and to socialism.

Asquith's Parliament Bill was passed in the House of Commons in May 1911 by a majority of 121 on its Third Reading, supported by the Irish and Labourites. After debating a series of alternative measures of reform, the Lords heavily amended Asquith's bill and returned it to the Commons. On 24 July 1911 came one of the more dramatic scenes in the House of Commons in modern times, when Asquith was repeatedly howled down and prevented from speaking by 'die-hard' Unionist MPs (led by Lord Salisbury's son Lord Hugh Cecil), something without precedent except from Irish 'obstructionists'. The 'die-hards' also had as their aim stiffening the backbone of Arthur Balfour, whose leadership of the Unionist party, after three General Election defeats, was obviously being questioned, and who was widely regarded by right-wing Tories as too soft and lacking in firm principles. The political atmosphere in Britain now became very bitter indeed, marring the celebratory atmosphere created by George V's coronation on 22 June 1911.

A major split also emerged among Unionist peers in the House of Lords, who would, once more, have to vote on the Parliament Bill when it was returned to them for reconsideration. An important group of moderate Tory peers, known as the 'hedgers', was headed by Lord Curzon (George Nathaniel Curzon, 1859–1925, Viceroy of India, 1899–1905, and later Foreign Secretary, 1919–24) who was frequently mentioned as a possible Conservative Prime Minister but was also renowned for his legendary *hauteur*. On 10 August 1911, after one of the most dramatic debates in its modern history, the House of Lords passed the Parliament Bill by a majority of 131 : 114. The result was swayed by the fact that 29 Tory peers joined with the Liberals, as did 13 out of 15 Anglican archbishops and bishops who voted. (At the time – and throughout the twentieth century – both Anglican archbishops and the 24 Anglican bishops are entitled to sit and vote in the House of Lords.) 'We were beaten by the bishops and the rats', was Tory frontbencher George Wyndham's famous verdict. Thus, the House of Lords reformed itself and the mass creation of new peers was never carried out. In reality, the Parliament Bill lacked the reforming effects its proponents expected and its opponents feared. The Lords seldom sought to challenge radical legislation passed by the Commons, and almost certainly would not often have done so, since the threat of far-reaching reform or even abolition of the upper house always hung over its head. Probably as a result, the Lords survived with no dramatic alterations to its composition until the end of the twentieth century, but was seldom more than a minor, if often useful, amending chamber.

At the same time as the Parliament Bill was passed, a separate, unrelated financial resolution was enacted by the Commons paying all backbench MPs a salary of £400 a year. Until that time, only government ministers had been paid a salary; backbench (and Opposition) MPs served for nothing. This state of affairs was very important in excluding working-class men from Parliament or, indeed, any one who was not independently wealthy or could earn a living (as a barrister could) without unduly affecting his parliamentary career. The lack of payment to members also unfairly benefited those with a London business or profession, who could realistically try to combine employment with a parliamentary career. Four hundred pounds a year was a pittance to most businessmen, but it was two or three times what even a skilled manual worker earned at the time, and its enactment was an important necessary precondition for the rise of the Labour party.

Within the Unionist party, discontent was now mounting sharply over the leadership of Arthur Balfour. He had just lost his third General Election in a row (albeit the number of Unionist and Liberal MPs was virtually identical). Later in the twentieth century, it would be almost inconceivable that a leader of a major political party could lose three elections in a row and still remain as head of the party, but in the Edwardian period politics still remained in the shadows of an earlier tradition when, for instance, Lord Derby and Disraeli headed a Conservative party which failed to win a General Election outright for 33 years, yet remained firmly in leadership positions. Moreover, there was no established procedure for a leader of the Conservative party to be removed: he was replaced only if he either resigned or died. Indeed, it was still not entirely clear that the choice of party leader, at least when the Tories were in office, did not lie with the Sovereign, who could, theoretically, call upon whomever he wished to attempt to form a government. Nevertheless, in an age of mass democracy, Balfour's losing ways, combined with his fence-sitting vagueness and ambiguity, proved intolerable to many desperate Tories.

From mid-1911 a very serious and widespread campaign among Tory MPs and sympathetic journalists got underway with the catchcry 'Balfour Must Go', which became so often reiterated that it was better known by its abbreviation, 'B.M.G.'. After serious splits in the Shadow Cabinet over the Parliament Bill, Balfour suddenly resigned on 8 November 1911. (A 'Shadow Cabinet' of frontbench Tory ex-ministers had met regularly after 1906; from 1910, new additions were made of men who had not previously held ministerial positions, including F.E. Smith.) There was no acknowledged procedure for choosing a new leader under these circumstances, and the Unionist party was sailing in the dark. Very basic questions about choosing a new leader were ambiguous: technically, the party was choosing a leader in the House of Commons; Lord Lansdowne remained leader in the House of Lords from 1903 until 1916. Were the Unionists to win the next election (due to be held before December 1915), it was an assumption, but not a foregone conclusion, that the leader of the party in the Commons would become Prime Minister. If this assumption had proved correct, this was a very modern innovation indeed, for when Lord Curzon failed to become Prime Minister in 1923 in part because he sat in the Lords, it was supposed that this was a recent, post-1918 innovation brought about because the Labour party was virtually unrepresented in the Lords. As well, technically speaking the Unionist party consisted of two separate groupings, the Conservatives (numbering 240 MPs after December 1910) and the Liberal Unionists (numbering 34 MPs), who had not yet formally merged. That Liberal Unionists could indeed participate in the election of what was, essentially, the Conservative leader was not self-evident, despite the fact that one of the two main candidates for the leadership, Austen Chamberlain, was a Liberal Unionist. (Liberal Unionists did participate in this process, and the two nominally separate party groupings merged the following year.)

There were two main candidates for the leadership: Austen Chamberlain and Walter Long. Chamberlain was closely identified above all with tariff reform, and his selection would have meant the ascendancy of the pro-tariff reform forces in the party. Many Tory MPs doubted that the party could ever win an election if it were too closely associated with tariff reform, and the movement's extreme, fanatical supporters. Chamberlain was also personally mistrusted, and many still found his Birmingham Nonconformist roots unpalatable and his Liberal Unionist background inappropriate. Walter Long (1854–1924) was clearly the less well-known contender but, despite a personally aggressive and unpleasing manner, as well as ill-health, enjoyed surprisingly wide support, and might well have won a contested election. Long was, from 1906–10, the Unionist MP for Dublin County South, the only Irish Unionist MP outside Ulster, and was thus closely associated with the leadership of the southern Irish Unionists (as opposed to the Ulster Protestant Unionists). Together with his background as a considerable landowner in England, this endeared him to the traditionalist elements in the Unionist party, especially those who wanted the Tories to engage in a broadly based anti-Liberal platform, centring on opposition to Home Rule – in 1911, the major controversial area on the government's agenda – rather than the more unpopular one of tariff reform. From 1910, Long was MP for the Strand division in central London, and was also very popular in London, having in 1902 secured the passing of the important Metropolitan Water Act.

In the event, with support for the two evenly matched, both candidates agreed to avoid a bitter party election campaign by withdrawing in favour of a third candidate, the relatively little-known, but very able Andrew Bonar Law. (The latter's surname was actually 'Law', Bonar being his middle name, but he is invariably known as 'Bonar Law'.) Born in New Brunswick, Canada in 1858, the son of an Ulster-born minister in the Free Church of Scotland, he was thus the first Nonconformist to lead the Conservative party. Returning to Britain as a small child, he attended Glasgow High School, a fee-paying day school for the middle classes, but left at 16 to enter the offices of cousins of the family named Kidston who were wealthy merchant bankers in Glasgow. Later, he became a successful iron merchant in that city. In personality, he was dour, frugal, and laconic. His hobby was chess (he played at nearly a master level) and was well known for having a pay telephone in his London house which family and guests were obliged to use. As leader of the Unionist party, he was certainly an extraordinary choice and as great a contrast to his predecessors, Salisbury and Balfour, as one can imagine. Although wealthy, Bonar Law was unrelated to any aristocratic family, had attended no exclusive school, and lived a puritanical lifestyle. He remains one of the only leaders of the Conservative party who had never held a Cabinet post prior to becoming head of the Tories. Yet he was also curiously representative of all of the main concerns of the Unionist party at the time: Ulster, tariff reform, the Empire, the business classes. In particular, his strong support for the Ulster Protestants and for tariff reform was able to bridge the gap between the supporters of Long and Chamberlain. Bonar Law probably owed his selection in part to the machinations of Sir Max Aitken (1879–1964; created baron Beaverbrook in 1917), a newly arrived Canadian stockbroking millionaire. Born, like Bonar Law, in New Brunswick, Aitken lost little time in acquiring a parliamentary seat, political influence, and a title. (He had not yet, however, acquired a newspaper, for it was in 1916 that he purchased the *Daily Express* from which time until his death he was primarily known as one of the greatest of the 'presslords'.) Aitken certainly stiffened Bonar Law's resolve to contest the leadership and was influential in securing support within the party's backbenchers. Bonar Law already had some support before Aitken's arrival. Although Aitken was Bonar Law's friend and financial advisor, he was in no sense his Svengali as some (especially Beaverbrook himself) have alleged. In personality they were virtual opposites, while their politics were already so similar that Bonar Law needed no instruction from the bumptious Canadian.

Bonar Law officially became leader of the Unionist party on 13 November 1911. As parliamentary leader, his style was in complete contrast to that of his predecessor, being utterly vigorous and direct rather than subtle and clever. 'Bonar Law's style was like the hammering of a skilled riveter, every blow hitting the nail on the head', one Tory MP later wrote. This self-made Scottish businessman also seemed strange to the aristocracy and landed gentry who still dominated so much of the party's hierarchy. One society lady gave a well-known description of the first time she heard him speak (in 1912): 'I am bound to say that his personality and his voice with his Glasgow accent were disconcerting at first (I felt rather as if I were being addressed by my highly educated carpenter)' but 'he inspired me with such confidence as he went on that I forgot that, and of course one has to recognise that a new era in political life has dawned for England.' Bonar Law was indeed strongly representative of where the Unionist party was moving: by 1914 there were more Unionist MPs who were businessmen than landowners.

The contrast between Bonar Law and Balfour was paralleled by the contrast, in Parliament, between Bonar Law and Asquith. Although coming from very different social backgrounds, Asquith and Balfour were both typical, but superior, products of the classical system of education at the public schools and Oxbridge, and Asquith the Balliol classics scholar and Balfour the Cambridge philosopher both spoke very much the same language. In contrast, Bonar Law was a blunt and truculent no-nonsense businessman with an amazing mental command of facts and figures but little culture. Many Liberals saw Bonar Law as introducing into the House of Commons a so-called 'new style' of personal insult. In a speech at Belfast in April 1912 he accused the government of having 'turned the House of Commons into an exchange where everything is bought and sold'. His remarks were quoted in the Commons with derision by Asquith, who said:

> 'This Mr. Speaker is the new style ... Am I to understand that the right honourable gentleman repeats that here, or is prepared to repeat it on the floor of the House of Commons?'
> Bonar Law: 'Yes.'
> Asquith: 'Let us see exactly what it is. It is that I and my colleagues are selling our convictions.'
> Bonar Law: 'You have not got any!'
> Asquith: 'We are getting on with the new style.'

Not surprisingly, Bonar Law found Lloyd George – the actual pioneer of the 'new style' – much more congenial than Asquith, despite the fact that their politics and personalities were, at least superficially, exact opposites. Bonar Law worked loyally and effectively under Lloyd George as the number two man in the Coalition government that existed from 1916 to 1922. Lloyd George recognised Bonar Law's political capability early, making the often quoted remark that 'the fools have found their best man by accident' when Law became Unionist leader.

It was clear that the central issue before the Parliament elected in December 1910 would be Ireland and the Home Rule question, as it had been in the 1880s and 1890s. The Irish Nationalist party, headed by John Redmond (1856–1918), now held the balance of power in the House of Commons, and Asquith's government could survive only by enacting Home Rule, something which it had shown no inclination to do before 1910. Redmond was a moderate who wished Ireland to remain in the United Kingdom and the British Empire and, by 1910, it appeared that the Irish Nationalist movement had moderated to a considerable extent. The violence associated with the nineteenth-century Fenian movement appeared to be in the past; Ireland was fairly prosperous; the British Empire seemed to be one of the dominant geopolitical units in the world. It should not be forgotten that although it existed since 1905, *Sinn Fein*, the extremist revolutionary movement that uncompromisingly demanded complete independence from the United Kingdom for the whole of Ireland, was very small, marginal, and unpopular, as were other similar ultra-nationalist groups. Moderate Liberal and neutral opinion was also probably more sympathetic to Irish Nationalist sentiment than in the past, with the example of the Boer republics, won over to loyalty within the British Empire by a deliberately conciliatory policy after their defeat in the Boer War, being offered many times as a successful precedent to a loyal post-Home Rule Ireland also won over by conciliation.

With the passage of the Parliament Bill in 1911, one crucial difference emerged between the situation then and previously, namely that the House of Lords would be powerless to negate the passage of Home Rule for any more than two years; Irish Home Rule thus seemed absolutely inevitable. Since the 1880s, resistance to Home Rule had emerged most strongly within Ireland itself from the Ulster Protestants, whose own nationalistic assertiveness was now at its absolute zenith. The great majority of Ulster Protestants regarded themselves as a separate nation with a distinctive national history. While Ulster was prosperous (the SS *Titanic* was built in Belfast's shipyards, among the most advanced in the world), Catholic southern Ireland languished, according to the Ulsterites, under Catholic neo-feudal backwardness. While Ulster was loyally and patriotically British, the Asquith government, like its Liberal predecessors, was perversely bent on appeasing the disloyal Irish Nationalists of the south. Most Ulster Protestants wanted no Home Rule of any kind, but in particular desired total exclusion from the semi-independent Home Rule Irish state which would emerge from the pending legislation. Many wanted the exclusion of all of Ulster, with others willing to settle for the Ulster provinces where Protestants were in the majority. The semi-secret Orange Order, with its permanent central remembrance of the Battle of the Boyne in 1690, was then at the peak of its influence among Protestant Ulstermen.

Protestant Ulster saw two leaders of very considerable ability, but also great fanaticism, emerge to head their movement at this time: Sir Edward Carson and James Craig. Carson (1854–1935) came from southern Ireland and was of partially Italian descent; he was a highly successful barrister in London who was known for hypochondria and melodrama. Craig (1871–1940), a wealthy distiller and stockbroker from Belfast, was one of the leaders of the Orange Order and the chief organiser of Ulster resistance. (After the establishment of the Irish Free State, Craig served as the first Prime Minister of Northern Ireland from 1921–40.) From 1910 onwards, the great majority of Protestant Ulstermen joined a popular movement of resistance to Home Rule, a popular movement arguably without parallel in modern British history, based upon monster rallies and public declarations of unity. The most dramatic example of this spirit occurred in September 1912, when Craig and the Ulster Protestants drew up a 'Solemn League and Covenant' (in conscious imitation of the agreement made by Scottish and English Protestants in 1643) pledging its signatories to use 'all means which may be found necessary to defeat the present conspiracy to set up a Home Rule Parliament in Ireland'. This document was signed by no fewer than 471 414 persons (with a nearly equal number of men and women), virtually the whole adult Protestant population of Northern Ireland. The signing of the Covenant was proceeded by a procession throughout Ulster of 40 000 Ulstermen in military order, headed by Carson. It ended in Belfast, where he was presented with the flag carried by William III at the Battle of the Boyne. Covenant Day (28 September 1912), when so many Ulstermen signed the document, was declared a national holiday throughout Ulster.

For many on the British right, the Ulster Covenanters presented the archetype of everything that a popular conservative movement should be in twentieth-century politics: the nation in arms, fighting in unity for a patriotic and historical cause rather than a radical one. On the other hand, many other Tories were somewhat disturbed by the movement. Unionists of southern Ireland and their supporters (including many great landowners) resented the implicit acquiescence in the abandonment of three-quarters of the island where Catholics were in the majority, while others thought that Ulster was a sideshow to the more central issues of tariff reform and military preparedness. Nevertheless, Bonar Law felt deeply about Ulster, heading many rallies in England on its behalf, especially another mammoth rally in the grounds of Blenheim Palace in July 1912 attended by 20 000. By 1914, resistance to Home Rule had become arguably the most central tenet in the Unionist party's agenda.

Asquith and the Liberals were of two minds on the Ulster question. As a rule, the Liberals had always regarded Ireland as a unity and consistently rejected any special provisions for Ulster. They also tended to downplay the force of Ulster nationalism, describing it as 'orangeade'. On the other hand, by 1912 even the Liberals realised that a failure to grant some accommodation to the Ulsterites would almost certainly lead to major trouble. Asquith and the Liberals recognised the justice of Irish Nationalism (chiefly when forced to do so to maintain their parliamentary majority), but perversely failed to recognise the historical reality of another nationalism and national identity on the island.

The third Home Rule Bill (the first two, in 1886 and 1893, were introduced by previous Liberal governments but failed to become law) was introduced in April 1912. It was a moderate document, and the degree of self-government it granted to Ireland was very similar to that accorded to northern Ireland when that province attained local self-government in the early 1920s. The Westminster parliament was to remain supreme, but the new Dublin parliament was to be given control over local affairs. The number of Irish MPs at Westminster was to be reduced from 101 to 42 when the act came into force, with about 32 from southern Ireland. While Asquith recognised that 'special treatment' had to be provided for Ulster, the proposed bill made no specific provision for any such 'special treatment'. After long discussions with Redmond, the furthest Asquith (or the Irish Nationalists) was willing to go was to grant a kind of 'parliament within a parliament' for Ulster, rather than exclusion from the act *per se*. In mid-1912, Asquith specifically refused to support a proposal from a backbench Liberal MP to exclude the four most clearly Protestant counties (Antrim, Armagh, Londonderry, and Down) from the bill. A long series of negotiations involving the King and the Tory leaders could not reach agreement. By September 1913, after a terrific struggle, the Home Rule bill had twice passed both the Commons and the Lords, but it was not until September 1914 that the bill actually became law. Unionist opposition had become so intense that Asquith was forced (in March 1914) to offer a compromise in which each of the nine Ulster counties (including those with Catholic majorities) could be excluded from the new arrangement for six years. In June, the Lords (who, under the 1911 Parliament Act, having defeated the bill twice, were powerless to prevent its passage thereafter) altered the bill to exclude the whole of Ulster without time limit. Matters had now become so serious that in July, King George convened a conference of eight leading politicians, including Asquith, Bonar Law, Carson, and Redmond, to reach a compromise. It failed to do so, but the outbreak of war intervened, and the Home Rule Act was suspended until its conclusion.

Within Ireland itself, things had gone from bad to worse. From 1912, ablebodied Ulstermen formed an Ulster Volunteer Force, headed by a retired Indian army general, Sir George Richardson, which grew to 90 000 men, specifically to resist Home Rule when it came. (In 1910, the entire British army, including those serving in the Empire, numbered around 440 000.) This whole procedure was extraordinary, if not overtly treasonable, but the Force then proceeded secretly to purchase arms from abroad, especially Germany. In April 1914, agents of the Force landed 35 000 rifles and five million rounds of ammunition. At the same time, in March 1914, came the so-called 'Curragh Mutiny'. Lord Willoughby de Broke, the leader of the 'Diehard' right-wing Tory peers, proposed that the House of Lords should refuse to pass the annual Army Act (which allowed an army to maintain discipline in its ranks; because of fears of a standing army, the act was required to be renewed annually by Parliament), thus making it impossible to use the army to enforce the Home Rule Act when it came into effect. Bonar Law and other leading Tories took up this extremist proposal and, as a result, the government ordered Major-General Sir Arthur Paget, the commander-in-chief in Ireland, to reinforce his troops in Ulster in preparation for any showdown with the Ulster Volunteer Force. Much of the British army was officered and manned by Anglo-Irish Protestants (not necessarily Ulster Presbyterians) or others with close connections to them, and Paget demurred. He obtained from John Seely (1868–1947), the Secretary of State for War (whom Asquith had appointed in 1912) a promise that army officers resident in Ulster could 'disappear' when Home Rule had to be enforced, provided that they solemnly promised not to join the Ulster Volunteers. Amazingly, Seely agreed, adding that like-minded officers not resident in Ulster could honourably resign from the army rather than be dismissed. In one cavalry brigade 57 of 70 officers indicated that they would prefer dismissal to enforcing Home Rule. In the end, after much negotiation, these officers (and their leader, Brigadier-General Hubert Gough, shortly afterwards a leading and very controversial commander on the Western Front) were assured by the government that they would not be required to enforce Home Rule. As a result of this demonstration of government weakness, Seely was forced to resign, with Asquith taking over the position of Secretary of State for War on 30 March 1914, not so much because of gathering war-clouds on the continent, but to enforce Home Rule in Ireland.

Most British Unionist leaders strongly backed the most extreme Ulster Protestants with open support and rhetoric which was if anything even more extreme. Bonar Law's most famous words about Ulster came at the July 1912 Unionist rally at Blenheim, when he declared that Ulstermen 'would be justified in resisting [Home Rule] ... by all means in their power, including force ... I can imagine no length of resistance to which Ulster can go in which I should not be prepared to support them', one of the few times in modern history that the leader of a major political party appeared to advocate violent resistance to laws passed by Parliament.

These extraordinary developments in Ulster naturally produced an equivalent movement among the Catholics of the south (and among the Catholics who lived in Ulster), although, since Home Rule obviously favoured them and was supported by their leaders, it was not as extreme or widespread as among the Ulstermen. In November 1913, an Irish Volunteer movement was founded in Dublin, headed by Professor John MacNeil, and Patrick Pearse (later the self-proclaimed 'President of the Irish Republic' during the Dublin Easter Uprising of 1916, when he was executed). Shadowy extremist movements led by subsequently renowned, but then little-known, Irish Nationalists such as Arthur Griffith, James Connolly, and James Larkin, began to grow in influence at this time. The Irish Secretary, the amazingly incompetent Augustine Birrell (1850–1933), a Cambridge-educated barrister and *belles lettres* essayist, who was utterly out of his depth during the Irish crisis, compounded matters further by imposing a ban on importing weapons into Ireland in response to the formation of the Nationalists' Irish Volunteers. Since he had not issued an equivalent ban in response to the formation of the Ulster Volunteers, a storm broke out among the Irish Catholics. When the First World War began, Ireland seemed assuredly poised for a civil war in which Protestant Ulster might well have declared some form of independence or semi-independence, with intercommunal bloodshed a strong likelihood. Many in the Cabinet indeed greeted the outbreak of war with relief that the Irish question would be put into deep freeze for the duration.

Asquith's government manifestly failed over Ireland. Historians have been debating the reasons ever since. There are two schools of thought on the matter. Sympathisers with Asquith point to the pervasive intractability of the Irish question, which had been festering throughout the nineteenth century, and in particular of the Ulster issue, which remains unresolved today. Asquith, they claim, did no worse than anyone else. It was not his fault that Ulster Protestants engaged in a dangerous, hysterical strategy bordering on open rebellion, egged on by Unionist leaders who were virtually advocating unconstitutional behaviour. Asquith always did his best to steer the Irish situation into a moderate direction. Nor should it be forgotten that three-quarters of the Irish people were Catholics, and the Home Rule Bill was aimed at providing justice for them. Critics of Asquith, however, contend that his policy of justice for Catholic Ireland came at the expense of Protestant Ulster, and that the crisis could have been avoided had the government been sensitive to the reality of Ulster nationalism. Throughout the twentieth century, whenever two peoples who occupy the same land detest each other, the only possible way to avoid a bloodbath of ethnic destruction has been partition of the land, as in British India, Cyprus, Palestine, or Yugoslavia. The Ulster situation was more amenable to resolution than many others because the Ulster Protestants occupy a geographically contiguous area of the island, although to be sure the precise boundaries of Protestant Ulster are ambiguous. Asquith stubbornly refused to consider the obvious solution of a separate Ulster, one that actually came into force in 1922, preventing significant bloodshed in Ireland for nearly 50 years. Like Gladstone, Asquith simply failed to understand the force of Ulster Protestantism; most of all, the electoral realities of the Liberal majority in the House of Commons after 1910 made appeasement of the Irish Nationalists necessary for the Liberals to continue in office.

The second great challenge allegedly facing the Liberal government after 1910 was the challenge of Labour and of socialism. The nature of this challenge is much less clear-cut than that emerging from Ireland; it is, indeed, arguable whether there was a crisis in the same sense. At any rate, there were separate components to the challenge of Labour which were not necessarily interconnected and which entailed very different types of opposition to the government and the institutions of the day. These include the evolution of the Labour party, the growth of the trades unions, the great increase in the number of strikes, and wider changes in the British economy. As well, the responses of the Liberal government must be considered, especially the set of important social welfare legislation it passed after 1908.

If the 'challenge of labour' in the years leading up to 1914 is meant to mean the challenge presented by the Labour party (rather than by the trade unions) it is very difficult to sustain the view that there was in fact a 'challenge'. As noted, Labour won 40 and 42 parliamentary seats in the two 1910 General Elections. It won few by-elections in the years preluding the outbreak of the war. It did not contest most by-elections, and when it did, it invariably finished third in a three-way contest. From June 1912 to June 1914, the two years immediately preceding the outbreak of the war, Labour or Socialist candidates contested 18 by-elections (out of 47 held), finishing last on every occasion, even in what subsequently became absolutely safe Labour seats. For instance at Tower Hamlets Poplar in February 1914 the Liberal candidate polled 3548 votes, the Tory 3270, and the Labourite only 893. On a number of occasions the intervention of a Labour candidate gave a close by-election result to the Tories, and the Liberals lost 13 seats to the Unionists between December 1910 and 1915, a slightly higher than average number, but on balance Labour had virtually no real impact on parliamentary by-election outcomes before the war, probably less than before 1910. While the number of Labour party constituency organisations increased significantly prior to 1914, in general Labour showed no signs of breaking out of the few geographical areas of strength it had established in 1906, chiefly in mining seats. At the local level, while the number of elected Labour councillors rose from about 56 in 1907 to 184 in 1913, this should be set in the context of the many thousands of local councillors throughout Britain. On the London County Council, the largest local government authority in Britain, Labour elected three councillors (out of 118) in 1910, but only one in 1913, the last election before the end of the war, compared with, respectively, 55 and 50 for the 'Progressives' (as the Liberals were known).

The small parliamentary Labour party, headed at this time by George Barnes (1910–11) and Ramsay MacDonald (1911–14), with Arthur Henderson playing a crucial role as its long-serving secretary (from 1911–34), was relatively successful in some important areas. The party evolved a distinctive ideology and style, emphasising the peaceful resolution of international disputes and opposition to militarism and 'secret diplomacy', and a woolly-minded, very vague, and idealistic commitment to socialism in Britain. This ideology (especially recognisable as MacDonald's) had a certain appeal, but while it differed from that of the frontbench of the Liberal party, it was very similar to that of an important segment of backbench opinion, especially among radical Nonconformists. It was also far too idealistic and imprecise for many doctrinaire socialists. As well, it dissented sharply from the dominant spirit of imperialism of the time. More concrete were a series of measures that the influence given to the 42 Labour MPs as a result of the 1910 elections was able to bring about. These included the payment of members in 1911 and the reversal of the Osborne Judgement of 1910 by the Trade Union Act of 1913. In the famous 1910 verdict, in the case of the *Amalgamated Society of Railway Servants vs Osborne*, it was ruled that trade unions could not legally collect and administer funds for political purposes. This verdict threatened to take away the chief funding source for the election and maintenance of Labour MPs, and, indeed, possibly to end the existence of the Labour party. In 1913 – in the long run, probably unwisely – the Liberal government passed an act allowing trade unions to establish separate funds for political purposes, provided that individual members of the union had the right to opt out of paying the special levy. It can be argued that no other parliamentary act gave more real political power to the trade unions.

The decade before the war was also one of solid gains for the trade union movement, with membership in the Trades Union Congress (TUC) increasing from 1 541 000 in 1905 to 2 332 000 in 1913 – still, to be sure, a small fraction of the British workforce, which numbered 18.4 million in 1911. By another set of statistics, the percentage of the labour force belonging to a trade union rose from 12.6 per cent in 1901 to 17.7 per cent in 1911 – again, still a very small fraction, much lower than in the post-1918 period. Unions increasingly entered the circles of governance, with some historians viewing Lloyd George as anxious to create a proto-corporatist vision of society, one in which capitalists, trade unions, and the government actively participated as partners. The TUC and the Labour party also remained close in this period, with a steady rise in unions officially affiliated to the Labour party. Nevertheless, there was simply no reason to suppose, even in 1914, that the overwhelming strength of the Liberal party compared with Labour would change in the near future, if ever.

Much more evidence for the oft-repeated view of a general 'Edwardian crisis' is provided by the very great rise in the number of strikes in the few years before the outbreak of the war, such that some historians have written of a 'worker's revolt' in this period. Between 1908 and the outbreak of the war in 1914 there were 23 major strikes in which more than 500 000 working days were lost (the equivalent of 10 000 persons striking for at least five days). This was certainly one of the most strike-prone periods in modern British history, exceeded perhaps only during the immediate post-1918 years. In the whole decade of the 1970s, for instance, there were only 19 strikes in which more than 500 000 working days were lost, despite the much greater size of the unionised work force and the reputation of the 1970s as a decade of endemic strike action. The very largest strikes of this period involved cotton operatives in the north (September 1908, 120 000 workers affected, 4.8 million days lost) and, in particular, a nationwide coalminers' strike in February 1912 in which one million workers lost 30.8 million working days. The total of working days lost was exceeded by only two other strikes in the twentieth century, one of which was the 1926 General Strike. A nationwide rail strike in August 1911 left the country without trains for two days. In the same summer, strikes also took place among seamen and dockers, and carters and dockers. Some areas of the country saw continuing strike action: London (in a variety of trades) was one; south Wales, especially the mining towns of the Rhondda, saw chronic strikes accompanied by violence, rioting, and near-insurrection such that many London newspapers freely compared the situation there to Russia in 1905. The strikes also spurred the growth of larger, more active, and militant unions, like the

Transport Workers' Federation, formed in 1910, and the National Union of Railwaymen three years later. In June 1914 came the formation of the so-called 'Triple Alliance' (an informal agreement between the railwaymen, transport workers, and coal miners), which seemed to portend future mass strike action on a grand scale.

It is not absolutely certain why this wave of strikes broke out in these years, although some main causal factors are clear. Many strikes were purely local in origin, or 'copycat' in nature, but the main cause was chiefly economic. This period saw a steady decline in unemployment, which paradoxically made workers more likely to strike (they knew that they would not join the 'reserve army of the unemployed') combined with a plateau in real wage rates and a rise in prices – a situation that would now be termed 'stagflation'. At the same time the Liberal taxation measures were beginning to affect the rich, albeit in a minor way, so that a bachelor earning £10 000 who had retained £9500 after taxes in 1909, kept only £9242 in 1911. Death duties on large estates also rose, with maximum rates (on millionaire estates) doubling in 1907 from 8 to 15 per cent. Capitalists attempted to keep their incomes intact by cutting costs wherever possible, while workers took industrial action to prevent this from happening. The spread of trade unionism made this clash much more widespread than previously.

As well, the pre-war period witnessed the growth of extreme left-wing unionist ideologies and activism, especially the Syndicalist movement, which advocated so-called 'industrial unionism' (all members in a specific industry to belong to a single union), with the eventual use of a general strike to overthrow capitalism. This type of union power, potentially uncontrollable by either government or even the established labour movement, may have played a role in the industrial unrest of the period (as it did elsewhere around the world), although it is doubtful that it was more important than the economic factors.

The Liberal government adopted a 'carrot and stick' approach to industrial unrest. It strongly favoured the creation of permanent conciliation boards to adjudicate industrial disputes, and in 1911 established an Industrial Council to achieve the same ends. Lloyd George (in particular) was personally involved in settling very serious strikes. On the other hand, the Liberal government was very prepared to use the mailed fist when necessary, and in a surprisingly forthright way. In November 1910, Winston Churchill (who had become Home Secretary in February of that year) authorised the use of troops and London police to quell a particularly violent outburst of strike and mob violence at Tonypandy in the south Welsh coalfields, Churchill thereby gaining a reputation for being anti-labour that he never lost. In 1911, gunboats and armoured cars were sent to Liverpool when a serious strike threat began. Many other examples of the determined use of force by the government to quell very serious labour unrest during this period occurred, with Asquith making it clear to railway unions in August 1911 that he would 'employ all the forces of the Crown' to stop a national rail strike which threatened to paralyse the country.

Nevertheless, the most important measures embarked upon by the Liberal government to deal with the grievances of the working classes were constructive, long-term ones, measures on which the reputation of the Asquith government as the progenitor of the Welfare State largely depended. The government's central piece of legislation in this field was the National Insurance Act of 1911, which greatly extended the provisions of the Old Age Pension Act of 1908, breaking new ground by entering the field of health insurance as well. This act was the brainchild of Lloyd George, but he was assisted by Winston Churchill, who was increasingly prominent as a progressive in this area. Lloyd George was heavily influenced by the German model of state-sponsored social security, but took Britain in a different direction. Germany had no state insurance against unemployment; this was included in the British model. Britain had evolved a fairly extensive voluntary sector of insurance companies and friendly societies which, by Edwardian times, had millions of subscribers including many in the working classes. Lloyd George did not abolish these, but brought them into the British scheme. Part I of the National Insurance Act dealt with health matters and also with unemployment. It covered everyone aged between 16 and 70 who were manual workers or who were earning less than £160 per year, regarded as the uppermost limit of working-class incomes. (The middle classes were not covered by the Act; nor were the self-employed, those already provided for by other schemes, or those outside the labour force.) There was no central, national fund as such: the scheme was administered through already existing 'approved societies', or local insurance committees. The act provided insurance for medical, sickness, and maternity needs, to be paid for by contributions from the employee, his employer, and the government. The basic weekly sickness benefit was 10 shillings for men and 7 shillings 6 pence for women. With difficulty, Lloyd George managed to secure the approval of the British Medical Association (initially opposed to it), chiefly because the ordinary doctor found himself much better off, especially those serving poorer areas. It did not establish a scheme of 'socialised medicine', but merely provided guaranteed payments for those insured, although it did adversely affect the poorer existing friendly societies. The weekly contribution of 9 pence per insured male (8 pence per insured female) was chiefly paid by government and employer contributions, so that the insured worker had to pay only 4 pence. 'Ninepence for fourpence' became a famous catchcry of Lloyd George and the government. Contributions were to be remitted by the employer by means of an elaborate system of revenue stamps affixed to a card belonging to each insured person. The licking of revenue stamps – something unknown until then – caused great resentment among the wealthy classes, especially the ordeal of aristocratic ladies having to lick stamps and affix them to the proper form for their servants.

Part II of the National Insurance Act covered unemployment insurance. It was even narrower in scope than the medical component of the Act, applying only to 2.3 million men employed in building, mechanical engineering, iron-founding, shipbuilding, vehicle construction, and saw-milling, trades which were deemed to be given to particularly high rates of periodic unemployment. An insured worker made unemployed was to be paid seven shillings per week (to a maximum of 15 weeks per year), paid for by a weekly levy of twopence halfpenny each from the man himself, his employer, and the government. This part of the act was obviously very limited, not applying to, for example, coal mining or the cotton industry. It was much less controversial than the health insurance component of the Act, and had accumulated a surplus of £3.2 million when the war began in August 1914, about two years after it came into effect. It was one of the first 'counter-cyclical' financial measures ever officially adopted in Britain, that is, where prudent saving during good times was to carry the needy through bad times and was, in a sense, a progenitor of the logic adopted much later by Keynesian counter-cyclical measures of government finance and expenditure.

The Liberal government also produced a number of other important measures in this field. 'Sweated labour' – the employment of workers, generally women and often immigrants in small factories and workshops paid by piece-rate – was dealt with by a Trade Boards Act of 1909, establishing trade boards consisting of employers, employees, and government officials in industries given to 'sweating' (such as tailoring), who were empowered to fix minimum wages; the Act was enforced by a body of factory inspectors. This Act was, in particular, associated with Winston Churchill. Churchill was also largely responsible for the Labour Exchange Bill of 1909 (drawn up with William Beveridge, the famous social reformer and academic), which empowered the Board of Trade to open 'labour exchanges', offices where the unemployed could find a central listing of available jobs. By the outbreak of the war, over 430 labour exchanges had been opened. Obviously, these could not create employment, only facilitate hiring where jobs were available.

Before Asquith became Prime Minister, Liberal acts had mandated the provision of school meals and of medical inspection in schools, and consolidated regulations relating to the welfare of children in the Children Act of 1908. A Shops' Act in 1911 introduced the principle of a legal weekly half-holiday (usually, Saturday afternoon), and laws around that time also dealt with coal mines, copyright, and the smallholding of land. A Housing and Town Planning Act, 1909 introduced provision for town planning schemes and strengthened the powers of county councils. There is general agreement that the pace of reform slowed notably just before the outbreak of the war, with the government preoccupied with Ireland and the foreign situation, and the effects of the 1911 National Insurance Act needing time to be felt.

The impetus for this new burst of legislation, but also the limitations in their scope and degree of effectiveness, came from a variety of sources. Astute Liberal politicians, especially Lloyd George, clearly viewed them as a means of thwarting both the rising socialism of the Labour party and also the tariff reform programme of many advanced Unionists, with its own agenda of social reform. As stated, Lloyd George was also positively influenced by the social policies of Germany and other countries that had adopted welfare schemes. Most historians traced the intellectual origins in Britain of these programmes in the so-called 'New Liberalism' to the writings of a disparate group of intellectuals and activists in the field of social policy who believed that laissez-faire was now obsolete, and that the enhancement of individual freedom in the real world could come about only by the diminution of the mass poverty of industrial society by active state measures. Many other intellectual underpinnings were apparent in the 'New Liberalism', ranging from the neo-Hegelian philosophy which was popular in Britain at the time (which viewed the whole of society as a single organism), to the growing revelations of the degree of primary poverty and want among the working classes revealed in surveys of urban areas carried out by Charles Booth (1840–1916) and Seebohm Rowntree (1871–1954). Booth's multi-volume *Life and Labour of the People of London*, produced in 1891–1903, and Rowntree's *Poverty: A Study of Town Life* (1901), which surveyed York, found that possibly one-third of town-dwellers lived in primary poverty, being unable to earn enough to enjoy even a minimally satisfactory standard of living. The Settlement House movement, which began in the 1880s in the East End with Toynbee Hall in Whitechapel, brought Oxbridge graduates to the London slums to do social work on behalf of the poor. As well, there was an important element of 'national efficiency' sentiment in the 'New Liberalism' (as there was in the Unionist party), with the Boer War having raised grave concern about the physical shortcomings of many recruits, leading to fears of national 'degeneracy' as the poor outbred the middle classes.

By the late Edwardian period, a new view of poverty and its causes was becoming widely held (although certainly not ubiquitous) in Liberal circles that were concerned with this issue. Probably the best-known expression of this view was the famous Minority Report of the Royal Commission on the Poor Laws and the Relief of Distress, which had actually been appointed by the Balfour government in November 1905, and which issued its 47 volume Report in February 1909. The Royal Commission, which consisted of 20 members headed by Lord George Hamilton (1845–1927), a former Conservative minister, was also significant for being the first truly important public document in modern British history to be in part the product of female authors. The most famous member of the Royal Commission was Beatrice Webb (*née* Potter, 1858–1943), the celebrated socialist organiser and writer; she was the author of the celebrated Minority Report. Other women members of this Royal Commission included Mrs Helen Bosanquet (1860–1928), the influential social theorist, and Octavia Hill (1838–1912), the famous philanthropist who was also one of the founders of the National Trust. Both the Majority and Minority Reports were critical of the existing system of poor relief, both recommending a radical overhaul of public assistance at the local level. The Minority Report, however, went much further, advocating the end of the New Poor Law that had determined the government's relief of poverty since 1834. The relief of unemployment for the 'able-bodied poor', it suggested, should be dealt with by a new Ministry of Labour using a wide variety of measures, including public works programmes during periods of high unemployment. Even the Minority Report, however, had little time for the wilfully idle and certainly did not advocate measures of socialism in the accepted sense. The new ideas of poverty associated with the Minority Report were to be found across the political spectrum. Progressive Unionism's tariff reform proposals also recognised that the State could and should take actions to diminish unemployment; within the Liberal government intellectual politicians such as Charles Masterman (1874–1927), who was Under-Secretary of State at the Home Office at the time, published *The Condition of England* in 1909, a wide-ranging and realistic study of poverty and inequality. On the Left, obviously the Labour party was deeply concerned with these issues. It should be stressed, however, that orthodox and neo-laissez-faire approaches to poverty were still dominant: the Minority Report by definition represented a minority viewpoint. In particular, no one yet conceptualised the British economy in now-familiar terms such as gross national product, annual growth rates, or even national unemployment rates, none of which were invented or compiled for another generation.

The third of the great so-called crises facing the Asquith government was the issue of women's suffrage. The situation at the time was that women ratepayers could both vote, and stand for office, in local elections, but could not vote in parliamentary elections or serve in Parliament. Women ratepayers were, in general, middle-class spinsters or widows who owned their own home, or other properties or businesses in their own right; it is reasonable to assume that most would have voted Tory in General Elections if they had the vote. Traditionally, arguments against women suffrage took two forms. Throughout the nineteenth century, the right to vote was regarded as a privilege, granted to those with a perceptible stake in the community such as the ownership of property. It was always deemed that the head of the household represented all members when he voted; the head of the household was the male breadwinner. By the Edwardian period, this rationale was clearly obsolete. While all adult males did not yet have the vote, almost no one continued to argue that the right to vote was a privilege to be restricted to the head of the household. In any case, single and widowed women, and the increasing number of career and well-educated women with a stake in the community, were obviously discriminated against by the arbitrary restriction against women voting. They remained unprotected electorally, and unable to function as a political lobby to further their interests. Secondly, opponents of women's suffrage made the familiar 'separate spheres' argument: women were simply unsuitable to pass judgement on the deadly serious business of warfare, national finance, and the Empire. They were 'emotional', and would either be swayed by demagogues, or would simply vote as directed by their husbands or fathers. There was also a fear that a women's lobby would attempt to 'purify' British life, acting against drink and other amusements. Frequently whispered, but seldom stated overtly, were fears that, during menstruation and the menopause, women were 'irrational' and 'hysterical'. No doubt, expressers of such views conceded, there were women who were exceptions to all of these fears, but they were likely to be in a small minority. As well, enfranchising women meant, potentially, doubling the size of the electorate, with incalculable political consequences. The obvious solution was to begin by enfranchising those women who could vote in local elections, perhaps adding those others who were obviously well-qualified to vote, such as female university graduates, making in all perhaps 10–15 per cent of all adult women in Britain. After a decade or two, when it had become clear that the skies had not fallen, the female franchise could be progressively broadened, just as had occurred among male voters during the nineteenth century.

It is difficult to see why this course was not adopted. Among Tories, inertia and conservatism are the likely explanations; among Liberals, these factors plus the additional one that most women initially enfranchised were likely to be Tory voters. By 1910, many western American states and several parts of the British Empire such as New Zealand and most Australian states, had granted women the right to vote, without any obvious effect on the local political culture or political outcomes. In particular, women simply did not form political parties in the manner of working-men and Labour parties.

Attempts by women to achieve the franchise suffered from a number of other handicaps as well. Although there had been organisations founded by women to secure the vote since 1867, there was, until the early part of the twentieth century, no well-known, continuing body that could coordinate these efforts. Many women's organisations were devoted to other aims, generally in some aspect of social or educational reform. During the struggle to expand the male franchise in the nineteenth century, it was unknown for middle-class or working-class men without the vote to oppose the granting of the franchise to themselves, yet there was in the late Victorian and Edwardian periods a significant body of women who opposed the extension of the vote to women, generally arguing that politics was inherently corrupt, and participating in it would make women as corrupt as men, while women could already exert considerable indirect influence. Female opponents of women's suffrage ranged from Queen Victoria to rather surprising sources, such as Beatrice Webb the socialist. It was also the case that most men simply did not take the issue of women's suffrage very seriously or, if they did, seldom considered it to be central to the political agenda. Very few men (and possibly only a minority of women) regarded the arbitrary denial of the vote to half the British population as a glaring, central injustice. In November 1912, George Lansbury (1859–1940), the Labour MP for Bow and Bromley, in the East End of London (and much later leader of the Labour party, 1931–35) resigned from his seat in order to contest a by-election in the same seat purely on the issue of women's suffrage, one of the few times in British history that a sitting MP has unnecessarily resigned in order to secure re-election on a specific issue. Whereas Lansbury had been elected in December 1910 with 56 per cent of the vote, at the November 1912 by-election he was defeated by his Tory opponent by an almost identical percentage, his support for female suffrage (in a London slum seat) having cost him the election. The general lack of centrality given by most politicians to the issue of women's suffrage was fully reflected by Asquith and his government, which most certainly did not view it as a fundamental issue of justice.

The most famous of the organisations of Edwardian England whose chief aim was to agitate for female suffrage was the Women's Social and Political Union (WSPU), founded in 1903 by Mrs Emmeline Pankhurst (*née* Goulden, 1858–1928). Mrs Pankhurst and her famous daughters Christabel (1880–1958) and Sylvia (1882–1960) were chiefly responsible for increasing both the militancy and the visibility of the 'suffragettes', as campaigners for women's suffrage became known. Mrs Pankhurst, the daughter of a wealthy Manchester cotton manufacturer, and the wife of a barrister, who was herself employed as a civil servant, represented middle-class radical feminism of the time, yet became celebrated for engaging in extreme militant action. (The term 'suffragette' was coined to contrast with the more moderate 'suffragist' – a name that never caught on.) From the 1906 General Election until the outbreak of the war, Mrs Pankhurst and the suffragettes engaged in a series of disruptive, often violent demonstrations and interruptions of public meetings that became universally known and remain one of the most famous images of Edwardian England. Frequently arrested – the government did not know how to deal with them and often overreacted, with heavy sentences imposed for trivial offences – the suffragettes turned to hunger strikes in prison, leading to the forcible feeding of women prisoners in order to keep them alive. After the seeming failure of agreed parliamentary legislation to enfranchise women, the suffragette movement became even more militant in the two years immediately preceding the war, engaging in widespread arson, the breaking of plate-glass windows in Regent Street, and the slashing of paintings in museums. The most extreme action taken by the suffragettes took place on Derby Day in June 1913, when Emily Davison, a militant suffragette, threw herself under King George V's horse and was killed. Demonstrations staged by the WSPU drew up to a quarter of a million people. In 1913, the government was forced to pass the so-called 'Cat and Mouse' Act, officially known as the Prisoners (Temporary Discharge for Ill Health) Act, which empowered the government to release imprisoned suffragettes on hunger strike until their health improved, and then to re-arrest them.

Although the campaign for women's suffrage enjoyed the support of most Labourites, many Liberal backbenchers, and many of the frontbench leaders of the Unionist party, it was always received coolly by the Liberal government, as well as by most Tory backbenchers. As a result, legislation to enfranchise women was never passed and never received the support of the government. Legislation to enfranchise women was introduced and voted on during this period, but always by backbenchers without official support. In May 1908, a Liberal backbencher introduced such a bill, which was passed on its second reading by a 179 majority, but died when Asquith refused to support it. In 1910, after a cross-party parliamentary committee recommended enfranchising women ratepayers, a bill to this effect introduced by Labour MP David Shackleton was passed by a 109-vote majority, but died when the Liberal Cabinet declined to support it. Precisely the same thing happened in 1912 and 1913. It seems clear that Asquith's adamant opposition to female suffrage was the primary reason why it was not enacted until the later stages of the First World War. Plainly, women's suffrage in some form was inevitable and it has been argued by some historians that Asquith was moderating on this issue when the war broke out. To many historians, admittedly writing with hindsight many decades later, the refusal of the Asquith government to enact women's suffrage was its greatest single failure, both of conscience and of imagination. It certainly demonstrated the very distinct limits to the Liberal government's radical credentials.

The Asquith government also ran into controversy in other unrelated areas. Religious matters (outside Ireland, of course) appeared to be virtually buried and forgotten during this period, and certainly they occupied a much less central place in the national political agenda than a generation before. Yet they were still extremely important and often not far from the centre of political life. The most important manifestation of this was the Welsh Disestablishment Bill, passed by the House of Commons in 1912 but decisively defeated in the Lords in February 1913 and again in July of that year. Wales was 72 per cent

Nonconformist, but the Anglican church was the established church in Wales, as it was in England. The Anglican church of Ireland, in a country which was nearly 80 per cent Catholic, had been disestablished in 1869, and Welsh Liberal MPs had long sought the same course for Wales. The two situations were by no means parallel, however: the Anglican church (or rather, its predecessor before the Reformation) had entered Welsh life in the Middle Ages and represented the majority faith until the late eighteenth century. It was thus the authentically Welsh church that, by translating the Bible into Welsh, probably saved the Welsh language from extinction. Through its own undoubted many failings, it had ceded the position of majority religion to the Nonconformists during the eighteenth century, yet ironically these sects – Wesleyanism, Congregationalism, the Baptists, and others – were English imports. They were, moreover, divided among themselves and were often rivals rather than allies.

In 1912, however, and due in part to the efforts of Lloyd George, the House of Commons passed a bill disestablishing the Anglican church in Wales and also disendowing it, that is, removing the subsidies it received from the state. These changes were furiously resisted by the Tories, especially the church's disendowment, which was regarded as an unfair attack on property rights. The Lords twice defeated the Welsh Disestablishment Bill. When war was declared, the act was placed in abeyance and it did not become law until 31 March 1920. There is general agreement that the Anglican church in Wales was strengthened by disestablishment, removing its privileged position which had been a source of resentment to most Nonconformists.

While the period just before the outbreak of the war is often regarded by historians as a time of crises if not of general crisis in British life, it seems perfectly clear from this that this description is an exaggeration. To be sure, the near-simultaneous occurrence of several unrelated sources of grave political unrest, even violence, was unusual, while the highly organised nature of the protest movements of this time – through the trade unions, the Orange order, and feminist groups – was also novel. Yet, even over Ulster, the government always remained master of the situation.

Asquith's government had, in fact, reached the time of the outbreak of the war in reasonably good order. It had survived one of the most famous political scandals of that period, the Marconi scandal of 1912–13. In that year the British government signed a contract to link the Empire by wireless with the British Marconi Company. This was a separate company from the American Marconi Company, although both companies had the same chairman, Godfrey Isaacs, who was the brother of Sir Rufus Isaacs (1860–1935; later marquess of Reading), the Attorney-General, and the British company owned most of its American counterpart's shares. The scandal arose because in April 1912 three prominent Liberal ministers, Isaacs, Lloyd George, and Alexander Murray (1870–1920) – the Liberal Chief Whip who was known by his courtesy title of Master of Elibank (he was the eldest son of Viscount Elibank) – each purchased 1000 shares in the American company, later selling them at a profit. The scandal also affected a fourth minister, Herbert Samuel, who had signed the contract but did not own any shares. These proceedings, when they became known at the end of 1912, led to a great scandal. Although the four ministers were officially absolved of blame, this affair nearly ended the career of all, including Lloyd George. Tory newspapers had a field day attacking 'radical plutocrats', while extreme right-wing sources tried to give the scandal an anti-semitic flavour (Isaacs and Samuel were Jewish), although the Tory front-bench had no truck with either line of pursuit and, indeed, did its best not to extend the scandal unduly, perhaps because the behaviour of the Tory party's own plutocrats would not bear too close an inspection.

By the outbreak of the war, Asquith had introduced much new and talented blood into the Cabinet, men who would have led the Liberals in the 1920s and 1930s had the war not initiated their downfall as a governing party. Such men as Sir John Simon (1873–1954), Herbert Samuel (1870–1963), Sir Rufus Isaacs, Walter Runciman (1870–1949), and Edwin Montagu (1879–1924), all held significant Cabinet positions by 1914, as did Winston Churchill, who was First Lord of the Admiralty at the outbreak of the war. Not only were such men as these extremely talented but, significantly, all continued to play a role in politics following the decline of the Liberal party, with Churchill, needless to say, emerging as Britain's greatest modern leader. Not only did the Liberal party thus appear to be suffering no loss of talent in 1914, it seemed to be literally awash with rising men of the highest ability.

Additionally, while our image of the Edwardian Liberal government is that it introduced the beginnings of the Welfare State and curbed the powers of the House of Lords, it is important to realise how traditional that government was in many respects and how easily it fitted into the pattern of confident governance. From 1832 until 1886 Whig–Liberal governments were predominant in British politics, and many Tories feared that this situation had returned. The Liberal government, despite its attack on the House of Lords, made skilful use of its patronage powers, ennobling many businessmen, and granting baronetcies and knighthoods to many more. A good many of these titles went to successful Nonconformists, which did much to diminish the sense of 'relative deprivation' felt by many Dissenters at the opening of the century. The government also took the first steps towards bringing Labour and working-men into the circle of governance. It did this without altering any of the traditional, ceremonial bases of the British state and, indeed, invented a few new 'traditions' of its own, most notably the investiture ceremony of the Prince of Wales in 1911 (literally invented by Lloyd George) and the grand tour of the Empire by King George V in the same year, shortly after his coronation.

Yet, the ultimate health of the Liberal government and the Liberal party at this time has been among the most hotly debated of all topics of modern British political history. This is because within ten years of the outbreak of the war in 1914 the Labour party had replaced the Liberal party as the normal left-of-centre British political party, and the Liberals never again won a General Election. Historians have asked whether the seeds of the Liberals' decline were evident by 1914, or whether this occurred owing to the events of the war and the post-war years. It is very easy to view the decline of the Liberals as inevitable: the middle classes increasingly voted Tory, leaving the Liberals with a largely working-class electoral base. This situation made the Liberals highly vulnerable to the Labour party, specifically founded to advantage the working classes, especially as class and class loyalties became more salient than religion, geographical locale, and other non-class based modes of voting allegiance. The position of dominant left-of-centre party was thus, according to this critique, ripe for picking by the Labour party essentially whenever it chose to do so and organised itself as a national party. The Liberals in effect bought time for themselves with their social welfare legislation, but this also had the effect of alienating middle-class support without really satisfying the working classes. By, say, 1925, according to this critique, Labour would almost certainly have replaced the Liberals even without the war and its social and economic effects. By 1914, the Liberals were living on borrowed time.

Although this view is superficially attractive, there is surprisingly little evidence from before the First World War to support it, and its accuracy is unknowable, depending upon counter-factual claims about what might have occurred. Essentially, the only real evidence for this view is that Labour was gaining seats in local elections, although at a snail's pace. Labour made no gains at all in the two 1910 General Elections, nor, by and large in by-elections thereafter. Even Labour's limited success at the 1910 General Elections was crucially dependent upon an arrangement between Arthur Henderson and Herbert Gladstone, the Home Secretary, not to nominate Liberal candidates in a number of safe Labour seats. That Labour certainly did not appear automatically destined to displace the Liberals was a view held, apparently, by most Labour leaders as well. Philip Snowden (1864–1937), then an influential Labour MP who was widely regarded as a radical (he was subsequently Labour's first Chancellor of the Exchequer and as such totally orthodox) wrote in his *Autobiography* (1934) that in 1914

> It looked as if the [Labour] Party was destined to remain a mere group, depending for what representation it had upon the goodwill of the Liberals in a number of constituencies. As far back as 1903 Mr. Sidney Webb, whose political prophecies were usually very accurate, had expressed the belief that the British Labour Party was not likely ever to become so strong as to be a successful competitor with the Liberals and Conservatives for office. Even up to 1914 it looked as though Mr. Webb's forecast would prove to be true.

'But,' Snowden continues, 'the War completely changed the situation.'

Some historians, noting that the Liberals were not declining by 1914, have offered explanations as to how the party achieved its success. Probably the best-known such view is that of Professor Peter Clarke, who has contended that the Liberals were successfully transforming themselves from a party led by businessmen (especially Nonconformists and Celts) to one led increasingly by socially conscious professionals who welcomed the Welfare State and whose 'New Liberalism' attempted to deal directly with the problems of poverty and the working classes. In the short term at least, this proved successful in keeping the working classes loyal to the Liberals, at least where they had been loyal to them before. Naturally, this view has also been disputed by historians, and the short answer to this question is that no one knows, or will ever know, what would have occurred had not war intervened. A useful comparison, however, might be drawn with the situation in the United States, bearing in mind of course that America's history, constitution, and political culture were obviously different in many respects from Britain's. In the United States, no socialist or Labour party ever emerged to challenge the Democrats and Republicans, although there was an American Socialist party whose Presidential candidate, Eugene V. Debs, received 897 000 votes (out of 15 029 000 cast, or 6 per cent of the total vote) in 1912. The Democratic party, headed, under President Woodrow Wilson from 1912–20, by 'Progressives' with an agenda similar to Britain's 'New Liberalism', moved successfully to meet the demand for moderate social reforms, a demand which, if unmet, might have led to the growth of a stronger socialist party. Under Franklin Roosevelt from 1932–45 the Democrats emerged triumphantly as the normal majority party on a programme of social democratic reforms which, nevertheless, was never anti-capitalist or overtly socialistic. Similarly, in Canada no successful socialist party ever emerged, while in Australia and New Zealand moderate Labour parties had emerged as the normal parties of the Left chiefly because they were formed earlier than their non-Labour equivalents. There is really no reason to suppose that the British Liberal party could not have continued indefinitely as the normal party of the Left.

The Liberals' position posed many difficulties. Asquith had no obvious heir apparent, and much of the Liberals' success had been occasioned by the esteem he enjoyed and his great command of Parliament. While we automatically assume that Lloyd George would have succeeded Asquith, he was widely mistrusted within the party and, had Asquith retired in the normal course of events around 1920, the leadership might have gone to a younger man such as Simon, Samuel, or even Churchill, although the latter was, like Lloyd George, also widely mistrusted. At some stage, too, the balancing act successfully pursued by the Liberals between capitalism and socialism might have come unstuck, although this chiefly depended on Labour asserting itself far more than it had before 1914.

The Unionists have also been the subject of considerable historical debate along the same lines. Most historians, including Michael Kinnear and John Ramsden, who have closely investigated the Edwardian Conservative party in recent decades, have been impressed by its strength, especially by Bonar Law's reforms of the party's organisation and finances after he became leader in 1911. The Tories were doing well in by-elections; the number of Irish MPs, whose presence at Westminster had so often given the Liberals a parliamentary majority, was due to decline sharply; in the years immediately preceding before the war, Liberals appeared very tired and had alienated many women (not voters, yet influential behind the scenes) and working men, as well as most of the middle classes. When these factors are added to the normal swing of the pendulum against a party in power for ten years, it seems very likely that the Tories would have won the General Election due to take place in 1915. This view has recently been challenged by E.H.H. Green, who has pointed to deep divisions within the Unionist party, especially between tariff reform activists and extremists, with their positive programme of imperialism and social reform, and the party's moderates, more concerned with opposing the Liberal's 'socialism' and its

Home Rule. Green may, however, exaggerate the internal divisions within the Unionist ranks, which were certainly no greater than those within the Liberal party during its years in the wilderness from 1895 to 1905. All parties, without exception, appear more divided when they are in opposition than when they are in power. On balance, then, it seems likely, though far from certain, that the Tories would have won the 1915 General Election with Bonar Law becoming Prime Minister. It would then have been up to them to deal with the range of issues, from social welfare to military preparedness, inherited from the Liberals. The Tories would have faced very difficult choices indeed, especially over Ireland and tariff reform, as well as over even more extreme measures advocated by many of its supporters, such as peacetime conscription. The Liberals would then have been in opposition, with all the tendencies to internal division this brings, and might have faced a serious challenge from Labour, although it is likely that its considerable strength would have carried it through.

4

The First World War, 1914–18

It might be that more has been written on the origins of the First World War than on any event in modern history apart from those connected with the Nazis and their regime. While it is seemingly possible to arrive at any number of different views as to how the conflict began, the reasons for Britain's entry into hostilities seem fairly straightforward. From the 1890s onwards, Germany appeared to challenge, in an increasingly provocative way, two of the cardinal principles on which British foreign policy had rested for the previous century. Germany appeared to desire continental hegemony in Europe and her policy appeared to be to build up a navy to rival Britain's. As well, Germany's rulers seemed to wish to make trouble for Britain wherever they could, anywhere in the world, especially in the Ottoman Empire. The most important area of dispute between Britain and Germany was their naval rivalry: freedom of the seas, guaranteed by the Royal Navy, had been the very foundation of British foreign policy since Trafalgar if not since the Armada; Germany's very threatening and unnecessary programme of naval building appeared to be chiefly designed to undermine Britain's superiority at sea. Probably no other single factor did more to alienate British opinion from Germany, or to confirm that the understandings entered into between Britain, France, and Russia would determine British policy if war broke out. There were many other factors as well which caused Britain to be increasingly suspicious of Germany, from long-standing economic rivalry to the popular spy and adventure novels of the day, which often centred on what would happen in a war between Britain and Germany. These were sufficient to outweigh the important commonalities and links between Britain and Germany – the close relationship of the two reigning families, important cultural and financial linkages, and the widespread sense (discussed in a previous chapter) that the governance of the world in the twentieth century would be divided among the Protestant great powers of Britain, Germany, and the United States. Had the German ruling elite showed any cleverness at all, their country might well have formed an alliance with Britain rather than against her, with incalculable consequences for the world. Yet, time and again, Germany chose to oppose Britain; German elites often viewed her as an ageing but formidable power which obstinately stood in the way of Germany taking its rightful place in the world.

These were the long-term factors that increased the likelihood of war between Britain and Germany; there were short-term factors as well. A number of international crises emerged in the years prior to 1914 that repeatedly brought Europe to the brink of a general war, but never over the brink. In 1905–06, there occurred the first Moroccan Crisis, in which France and Britain came close to war with Germany, settling this dispute over Moroccan independence at the Algeciras Crisis. In 1908, Austria-Hungary formally annexed Bosnia and Herzegovina in the Balkans, Slavic areas which viewed incorporation into the Hapsburg domain with detestation. Russia, viewing itself as the protector of the Slavs, was increasingly incensed by the apparent expansionism of the Germanic powers into this area. In 1911, war very nearly broke out again between France and Germany over Morocco, with Germany sending a gunboat to Agadir on the Moroccan coast to frighten France. In July 1911, Lloyd George, hitherto regarded as a near-pacifist, gave a speech at the Mansion House apparently threatening Germany, and Britain actually began preparations for war. Happily, the crisis was peacefully settled by a compromise between France and Germany. In 1912 and 1913 came several Balkan wars, enormously complex struggles between Turkey and the Balkan states that resulted in the strengthening of the Slavic states in the region, but with Austria and Serbia nearly coming to war over their respective territorial designs.

The net result of all of these crises – and there were others as well – was to inure the major European states to the realistic likelihood of a general war breaking out. In each crisis, Europe's major powers pulled back from the brink of a European war before it was too late. These crises, however, failed to resolve the causes which led to war in 1914, especially the alliance system dividing the Central Powers (Germany, Austria-Hungary, and, at the time, Italy) and the Allies (France, Russia, and, semi-officially, Britain) into mutually hostile blocks. Europe's statesmen never properly realised that they were playing with dynamite on a cosmic scale which could wreck European civilisation as they knew it: things never got out of hand before, and there was no reason to suppose that they ever would. As late as 15 June 1914, Britain and Germany amicably concluded an agreement on the future of the Baghdad Railway (a link long desired by Germany to strengthen her influence in what was then the Ottoman Empire) which seemingly heralded the peaceful resolution of unresolved questions between the two states rather than war.

There was thus no necessary reason why the assassination of the Archduke Francis Ferdinand, heir to the Austro-Hungarian throne, on 28 June 1914 should have led to the outbreak of the war. Francis Ferdinand was killed in Sarajevo, part of Austria-Hungary, by Bosnian nationalists whose plans were known to the Serbian government. Austria unwisely decided to make the assassination a basic issue of war and peace with Serbia. Serbia was supported by Russia and France, Austria by Germany. Germany's rulers apparently believed that if war came it was better to fight in 1914 than later, since the Allies appeared to be growing more powerful each day, especially Russia. Russia's population of 150 million (compared with 65 million for Germany, 45 million for Britain, and 40 million for France) put her in an enormously powerful position if she could modernise her military and industrial base, something she was seemingly in the process of doing. Because of the chain reaction nature of the alliance systems, between 28 July 1914, when Austria declared war on Serbia, and

12 August 1914, when France and Britain declared war on Austria, nearly all of Europe found itself at war. It goes without saying that no power would have declared war if their rulers had possessed a crystal ball. The rulers of Germany, Austria-Hungary, Russia, and Turkey (which entered the war in November 1914) would have seen the overthrow of their dynasties and millions dead; France, though victorious, would have seen 1.4 million French dead; Britain, though victorious, would have seen 723 000 dead British soldiers and another 200 000 Empire soldiers dead. Both sides imagined a quick war, or at least not one that dragged out, inconclusively but destructively, for over four years.

Britain formally went to war because the neutrality of Belgium, which had been guaranteed by treaty in 1839, was violated by Germany. This decision was not a straightforward one, and, until the last minute (Britain declared war on Germany at 11 pm on 4 August 1914), the issue was far from settled. Initially, only a small minority of the Cabinet (chiefly Sir Edward Grey, the Foreign Secretary and Churchill, the First Lord of the Admiralty) had been definitely in favour of declaring war, and it seemed that an extremely serious split in the Cabinet was imminent, possibly forcing its resignation and the formation of a Unionist government. In order to accomplish the so-called Schlieffen Plan (the German blueprint for the invasion of France, drawn up in 1905), the German army had to invade and pass through Belgium in order to accomplish its 'wheeling movement' to encircle Paris and force a French surrender. On 2 August 1914, Germany issued an ultimatum to Belgium demanding free passage through the country for German troops invading France. The Belgian government rejected the ultimatum and appealed to France and Britain for assistance. Britain declared war as a result of the actual German invasion of Belgium on 4 August. (It was on the previous day that Grey, the Foreign Secretary, in his rooms in the Foreign Office, while watching the lamp-lighters dim the gaslights in the adjacent street, allegedly made his world-famous remark that 'the lamps are going out all over Europe. We shall not see them lit again in our lifetime.' Grey quoted those words in his autobiography, *Twenty-Five Years*, written in 1925. As nearly everyone expected a rapid end to the war, it is difficult to believe that they are authentic.) Germany actually conquered Brussels on 20 August, and held most of Belgium until the Armistice in November 1918. (One result of the German conquest of Belgium was that over 100 000 Belgian refugees – a remarkable number – came to Britain for the duration of the war; the most famous of these was a fictional character, Agatha Christie's detective Hercule Poirot who, of course, remained.)

Germany's invasion and conquest of Belgium in a particularly brutal way, which entailed considerable destruction to cities like Amiens, united British opinion. Instead of the many resignations one might have expected only shortly before, only two Cabinet ministers resigned: Viscount Morley and John Burns. Several days later, Charles Trevelyan, a junior minister, followed suit. The German invasion of Belgium allowed both Tories and Liberals to support the war with enthusiasm: Tories in order to thwart the German threat of continental and naval superiority, Liberals (and radicals) to support the independence of a small country which had been minding its own business. (Of course many Liberals also supported the war for reasons of *realpolitik* and to thwart German expansionism; indeed, most of the Cabinet did so.) This combination of right-wing patriotic and left-liberal idealistic motives for entering the war proved to be enduringly popular throughout the war, meaning that the broad coalition which supported the war when it began continued, despite much unrest and criticism, until the Armistice. The German invasion of Belgium made it much more difficult for a genuinely widespread anti-war front to emerge, even on the British left. Most Englishmen genuinely believed that they were fighting a war which was both just and necessary, however much opinion since the 1920s has strenuously denied both assertions. Many British leaders, including Asquith, also welcomed the outbreak of the war (which they thought would be short) as a way out of the Irish troubles and the other domestic crises discussed in the previous chapter. Since the 1920s, a familiar theory of the outbreak of the war (first posited, apparently, by Elie Halévy, the great French historian) is that the elites of the belligerent states joyfully turned to war to dampen unrest at home, especially the ever-growing challenge of militant socialism. If there is an element of truth in this view regarding the rest of Europe, it is difficult to credit it for the situation in Britain, where the foremost challenge to constitutional rule came from right-wing Ulster Protestants.

Although often challenged by historians, the prevalent view of Britain's conduct of the war is that it was hopelessly incompetent, Britain's commanders being 'butchers' who were plainly unfit to lead a modern army and who needlessly slaughtered a generation of British youth. While this opinion may well be true, there are a number of crucial points which must be kept in mind when considering Britain's performance in the war. The first is that of all the major combatant powers Britain was least well-equipped to fight a land war of endless attrition contested by mass armies, yet of all the major combatants Britain probably emerged as the most successful. Britain's military prowess had always revolved centrally around the Royal Navy and around very small colonial armies. Alone of the great powers it had no conscription and no centralised army officer elite. Until the latter part of 1914, no one in Britain expected the kind of war which was actually fought. Yet the British army, despite the slaughterhouse of the trenches, experienced no mutinies and always conducted itself in good order. The second point is very easy for historians of Britain's role in the First World War to overlook, namely that Britain was a relatively small part of a very big picture. The combatant powers (including the minor European states and Japan, but excluding distant nations such as those in Latin America which were officially at war with Germany) mobilised, in all, 65 039 000 men during the First World War. Of this vast number, 8 905 000 represented the military forces of the British Empire, or only 13.7 per cent of the total number of mobilised soldiers. The British Empire actually lost an even lower percentage of men estimated to have been killed in the war – by one common estimate (there are others) 908 000 of 8 544 000 men killed among all the combatants, or 10.6 per cent. It requires an effort of will to remember that the conflict was not primarily a British war. Even on the Allied side, the British Empire mobilised fewer men than did Russia (no less than 12 million) and suffered considerably fewer deaths than France, which suffered 1 363 000 casualties. (The gap among the wounded was even greater: France saw 4 266 000 men wounded, compared with 2 090 000 among the British Empire's troops; the figures for Germany were 1 774 000 killed and 4 216 000 wounded.) While the Western Front was, of course, central to the outcome of the war, it is also important to that the war was fought elsewhere with results quite as deadly. Possibly over two million men (including perhaps 1.7 million Russians) were killed on the Eastern Front. Up to one million men, including about 650 000 Italians, were killed in the conflict, largely fought in the Alps, between Italy and Austria, a campaign of which many people in the English-speaking world have literally never heard.

The third point is the most basic of all, but the easiest to forget amid the tidal wave of criticism of Britain's military leadership made during the past 80 years. Britain won the war; it was Germany, the mighty military behemoth, which lost. Indeed, with the exception of the United States, no major combatant emerged from the war more advantageously, or with less damage done to its institutions and infrastructure, than Britain.

What, then, was Britain's role in the First World War? Britain played a central, even crucial part in four or five unrelated facets of the conflict. Most obviously, she was one of the major provider of troops on the Western Front and, in 1918, was of great importance in securing Germany's defeat. It is important, however, to recall that Britain never provided as many troops as France or suffered as many casualties; the war on the Western Front occurred almost entirely on French soil. France was always regarded as the senior partner in the war, with British generals continuously deferring to French generals as their seniors. Second, the Royal Navy blockaded the northern coasts of Germany, crucially interrupting the supply of war material and, especially, food to the Central powers (as Germany and her allies Austria-Hungary and Turkey were known). While historians have debated the real effect of the blockade, it seems clear that the near-starvation experienced by many Germans in the later phases of the war contributed greatly to the willingness of Germany to end the war without actually being conquered by the Allies, and to the revolutions which closely followed. Third, Britain was a major provider of finance and war materiel to the other allies, allowing the war to be carried on through its darkest times. Fourth, Britain was of fundamental importance – although not always successful – at the war's peripheries, seizing Germany's colonies, taking Palestine and Mesopotamia from Turkey, and attempting, in a celebrated wartime failure, to conquer Gallipoli and then to advance to Constantinople. Finally (and certainly not the least), Britain was the main conduit to and from the United States, whose entry into the war in 1917 was arguably the chief reason why the Allies won. Cultural, political, and economic ties between Britain and the United States, especially with the United States' anglophile eastern elite, were crucial to drawing America into the war rather than remaining neutral.

When hostilities broke out, Britain had a home army of about 248 000 men, with another 190 000 in colonial armies stationed literally around the world from Central America to South Africa. Britain had six standing infantry divisions and one cavalry division. Britain was thus probably the very weakest of Europe's military powers. Among Britain's allies in 1914, France had 823 000 active soldiers and 2.9 million more reservists who were mobilised within two weeks of the outbreak of the war, in 80 infantry divisions and ten cavalry divisions, while Russia had 1 445 000 soldiers, which expanded to 3.4 million on the war's outbreak, arrayed in 115 infantry and 36 cavalry divisions. On the other side, Germany had a standing army of 700 000, which grew to no less than 3.8 million men within one week, thanks to the efficiency of the German reservist system. Germany had 87.5 infantry and 11 cavalry divisions at the outbreak of the war. Austria-Hungary had a peacetime army of 478 000 which quickly expanded to approximately 1.3 million, consisting of 50 infantry and 11 cavalry divisions. Britain's ability to mount an army on the outbreak of the war, or to grow with sufficient rapidity to make a difference to the outcome of the conflict's initial phases, was thus very limited indeed. Apart from a standing army of 247 000, Britain had about 499 000 other army reservists and territorials, who were immediately summoned, but she lacked a vast network of trained reservists on the continental scale. Moreover, a large proportion of the British army was stationed in India or elsewhere in the colonial Empire, and would take many weeks or months to reach the European battlefields, as would the potentially very large contingent from the Dominions and colonies.

Britain did, however, possess a formidable navy, which had always been regarded as the 'senior service' and the likely key to Britain's success in any future war. The navy had been built, and navy planning predicated upon, the so-called 'two power standard': that Britain's naval fleet should be the equal of any other two nations combined. With Germany constructing an enormous ocean-going navy, and with countries like the United States and Japan also increasing the size of their navies, this rule-of-thumb became increasingly difficult to maintain, especially given the vast costs of modern naval shipbuilding (which, of course, fell on all naval powers). Nevertheless, Britain still maintained something like the 'two-power standard' during the Edwardian period. In 1910, for instance, Britain had 65 battleships compared with Germany's 41, America's 34, and France's 23. The last years before the outbreak of the war saw, if anything, a substantial augmentation to Britain's naval lead, with no fewer than 15 Dreadnought battleships built or recommissioned between 1910 and 1914, to add to the four in existence at the time. The new Dreadnoughts were substantially bigger, heavier, and better-equipped than any of their predecessors.

The outbreak of the war led at once to changes in the Cabinet. Asquith replaced the pacifists with a number of relatively minor appointments (although Walter Runciman's succession to John Burns at the Board of Trade was significant), and one major and unusual new addition to the Cabinet, earl Kitchener of Khartoum at the War Office. This post had been held since 30 March 1914 by Asquith himself, in the wake of the 'Curragh mutiny'; on 5 August 1914, the day after Britain declared war on Germany, Kitchener was appointed, a spectacular gesture as Kitchener had no previous political experience. Field-Marshal Horatio Herbert Kitchener, first earl Kitchener of Khartoum (1850–1916), had defeated the dervishes at Omdurman in 1898 and had been a controversial, but ultimately successful, second-in-command to Lord Roberts in the Boer War, and then served as Commander-in-Chief in India and Consul-General in Egypt. He was probably Britain's most distinguished living soldier. In 1914, Kitchener became particularly famous for several things. The first was his conviction that the war would not 'be over by Christmas', as many believed, but would drag on for years, a war of attrition unprecedented in modern times. This unwelcome but accurate news helped to reorientate Britain's policy-makers to thinking in terms of a long, extremely costly war. Second, Kitchener proposed to raise a vast 'citizen's army', the so-called 'New Army' of millions of volunteers which would still be able to intervene decisively in the war several years hence when the other combatants had fought to a standstill. Kitchener was among the chief architects of the unprecedented increase in the size of the British army which soon followed, his face, pointed finger, and hortatory 'I want you' staring out (to potential volunteers) from the most famous of all war posters. Kitchener's touch was much less sure during the war itself, and his habitual secretiveness and power-seeking caused him to be increasingly marginalised as the war progressed, before his death by drowning when the ship carrying him on a mission to Russia, HMS *Hampshire*, struck a German mine in June 1916.

In 1914, Britain initially sent one cavalry and six infantry divisions to France, organised into three army corps. These consisted of Britain's regular army plus reserves and territorials. Within several years the British Expeditionary Force (BEF) in France consisted of 74 divisions organised into five armies and a cavalry corps. This vast recruitment of men consisted solely of volunteers until conscription was introduced in 1916: by February 1916, 2.6 million men had volunteered, slightly more than the total (2.3 million) conscripted in the final years of the war. Most enlisted voluntarily with a patriotic fervour difficult to imagine today. Command of Britain's forces in the war came, for the most part, to promoted cavalry officers who often lacked imagination and had no real idea of how to lead the mass armies assembled in France. Initially, command of the BEF was in the hands of Sir John French (1852–1925), a former cavalry officer, Inspector-General of the Forces, and Chief of Staff, who was closely connected with the 'Curragh mutiny'. French was a lamentable choice, an excellent leader of men in the old-fashioned sense, but plainly out of his depth in modern warfare. Apart from his inadequacies as a modern field commander, he lacked diplomatic skills perhaps to an even greater degree. He was removed from his post in December 1915. The three initial army corps were commanded by, respectively, Sir Douglas Haig, Sir Horace Smith-Dorrien, and Sir William Pulteney, while the cavalry division was led by Edmund Allenby. Haig (1861–1928; later first Earl Haig) is, of course, one of the most controversial figures in modern British history. A conspicuously successful staff officer to French in South Africa and Kitchener in India, Haig was original and forceful until the outbreak of the war. In the war – Haig succeeded French as commander-in-chief in December 1915 – Haig was, to very many, the very epitome of the First World War 'butcher', launching innumerable poorly conceived and executed offensives on the Western Front against well-prepared German lines which achieved limited, often short-lived gains at an appalling human cost. To his critics, Haig had a satisfactory knowledge of strategy but little of tactics or logistics, was woefully over-optimistic, chose poor advisors who were afraid to speak frankly, and possessed a horizontal learning curve. That Haig won the war was an accident. To his defenders, Haig was a surprisingly imaginative leader and his tactics were the only ones which could realistically be brought to bear in the horrifying and unique circumstances of trench warfare.

Despite the obvious mistakes he made, Haig did much to destroy the fighting ability of the German armies, remained imperturbable in adversity, increasingly employed modern methods of war, and, from August 1918 until the Armistice, secured Allied victory. Haig also suffered, according to his defenders, from the fact that Britain's army was always subordinate to France's, from contradictory strategies pursued by distant politicians, and from the necessity of raising an untrained, underfinanced army of millions of civilians out of the blue. Despite the sincerity of Haig's defenders, there is little doubt that the consensual opinion among military historians has been that he was barely competent and remained in command chiefly because there was no one obviously better and because he always retained many powerful friends. In contrast to Haig, Sir Horace Smith-Dorrien (1858–1930) was an extraordinarily able general who refused to waste soldiers' lives; as a reward for his competence he was sacked by Sir John French in May 1915. He or perhaps Herbert Plumer was the commander-in-chief whom the British should have had. Allenby (1861–1936) was yet another senior cavalry officer; he proved mediocre on the Western Front but turned into an outstanding commander in the Middle East after being made Commander-in-Chief in Egypt in June 1917. He secured Palestine, Syria, and Iraq from the Turks, with momentous consequences for the future and was thus the midwife of modern Jewish and Arab nationalism. Other notable senior British generals included Julian Byng (1862–1935); Sir Hubert Gough (1870–1963); Sir Ian Hamilton (1853–1947); Sir Henry Rawlinson (1864–1925); Sir William Robertson (1860–1933); and Sir Henry Wilson (1864–1922). Most were mini-Haigs, barely competent in the conditions of the war. Herbert Plumer (1857–1932), one of the few who understood modern 'siege' warfare, was the exception: ingenious and sparing of life. Robertson had risen from the ranks, the only senior British commander to do so; this did not necessarily make him better than those who had not. There is agreement among many military historians that the military abilities of the leaders of the Dominions armies were distinctly higher than those of Britain's leaders, especially Australia's Sir John Monash (1865–1931), and Canada's Arthur Currie (1875–1933). Monash, a civil engineer before the war, of German Jewish descent, applied scientific thought to his commands, avoided pointless bloodbaths, and was close to his men. He is often regarded as the best Empire general of the war. Currie employed very similar methods: some military historians rank him even above Monash. Sir William Birdwood (1865–1951), British by birth, was the commander of the Australian and New Zealand forces at Gallipoli, where he also proved to be more competent than most others.

British troops arrived in France in time to participate in the halting of the German drive to Paris and in the First Battle of the Maine in September 1914 which, at enormous cost in lives, saved France from German conquest. The six weeks between the middle of October and the end of November 1914 saw the First Ypres campaign, another concerted attempt by the Germans to smash through the Allied lines and seize the Channel ports. The Allies managed to hold a line stretching from the Belgian coast to the Swiss border which became the prime battlefield of the Western Front over the next four years. Britain lost 58 000 men at First Ypres. By the end of 1914, much of the pre-war British regular army had been decimated, with consequent loss of experienced men who might have trained others. By the end of the year, too, the war in the Western Front had settled into the pattern which was to continue until mid-1918: a bloody stalemate in France, with regular, periodical attempts by one side or another to break through, all doomed to failure at a human cost previously unknown in history. Trench warfare virtually guaranteed a murderous stalemate of this kind, unless one or another side was exhausted, or fresh men or new weaponry could be brought to bear in sufficient numbers. By itself, Germany was clearly the superior fighting force and would certainly have defeated France or Russia in a one-to-one conflict. But even with Austria-Hungary (and, from 31 October 1914, Turkey) on its side, Germany was just not strong enough to defeat the Allies – France, Britain, Russia, and, from May 1915, Italy. The gap between the two sides was not large, and one must keep squarely in mind the fact that, by late 1917 or early 1918, it appeared that the Central Powers were very close indeed to winning the war. It was the similarity in the strength of the two sides which caused the war to drag on so long and so destructively. Britain's eventual victory was plainly not a foregone conclusion, although the Allies would not have won the war without British participation, both on the battlefield and in other ways.

Asquith had brought a virtually united nation into the war. Nearly all of the anti-war sentiment which one might have expected to develop, and which had emerged less than 15 years before during the Boer War, evaporated once Germany invaded Belgium. Effectively, opposition to the war came only from some members of the Labour party, but even here a majority supported the war and continued to do so. On 5 August 1914 the Parliamentary Labour Party decided not to oppose the extra expenditure necessary for the war. Ramsay MacDonald, the party's leader, resigned, and Arthur Henderson, practical and pro-war, took his place. Even MacDonald's attitude was ambiguous, since he thought that once Britain entered the war it would have to fight till the end, although taking every opportunity to seek peace. Many Irish Nationalists also supported the war. Outside Parliament, opposition to the war came from small groups of convinced pacifists and also extreme leftists, to whom the war was an evil clash of rival imperialisms. Throughout the war, even in the conflict's darkest days, no more than a small percentage of the population vigorously opposed hostilities and (as will be discussed) it became impossible to construct a broad cross-party anti-war movement such as one might have expected to find once the casualty lists mounted apparently without end. The British situation replicated that almost everywhere else in Europe: once war came, patriotism and chauvinism proved immeasurably stronger than any ideology which opposed the war. International socialists became extreme nationalists; pacifists became warmongers; believers in rational progress reverted to primitive xenophobia.

Perhaps the most important vocal champion of the war to emerge in 1914 was David Lloyd George. Lloyd George had been one of the most visible 'pro-Boers' in the South African war, and, with his radical politics, one might well have expected him to lead the British opposition to the war. The precise reverse occurred. To be sure, for some years Lloyd George had been among the most enthusiastic advocates of large-scale expenditure on the Dreadnoughts, and even flirted at times with advocating conscription. In August 1914, with the invasion of Belgium, the process of Lloyd George's redefinition as a super-patriot was complete. On 19 September 1914 at Queen's Hall, London, Lloyd George made what was probably the most important speech of his life, and one of the best speeches delivered by anyone during the First World War, a conflict (unlike the Second World War) not notable for its inspired oratory. Here, Lloyd George was perhaps the first to employ a theme used over and over again during the war, that its sacrifices were necessary to produce the better, kinder nation which would emerge after the victory.

> May I tell you in a simple parable what I think this war is doing for us? I know a valley in North Wales, between the mountains and the sea. It is a beautiful valley, snug, comfortable, sheltered by the mountains from all the bitter blasts. But it is very enervating, and I remember how the boys were in the habit of climbing the hill above the village to have a glimpse of the great mountains in the distance, and to be stimulated and freshened by the breezes which came from the hilltops, and by the great spectacle of their grandeur. We have been living in a sheltered valley for generations. We have been too comfortable and too indulgent, many, perhaps, too selfish, and the stern hand of Fate has scourged us to an elevation where we can see the great everlasting things that matter for a nation – the great peaks we had forgotten, of Honour, Duty, Patriotism, and clad in glittering white, the great pinnacle of Sacrifice pointing like a rugged finger to Heaven.

This speech had a profound effect. Many claimed when they read it they had tears in their eyes. Tories, in particular, forgave the 'scourge of the dukes' everything that had gone before. Without this speech, it is unlikely that Lloyd George would have become Prime Minister two years later.

The war naturally brought with it many changes in the life of the country, all of which increased the role of the state or sharply deviated from the ideal of progressive rationality which underlay pre-war Liberalism. In November 1914, the government passed the Defence of the Realm Act (widely known as 'DORA'), which gave the government authority to bypass Parliament in order to prosecute the war by issuing Orders in Council and authorised trials by court martial or magistrates for their violators. The government was also authorised to requisition most factory output for the war effort. In effect, the government gave itself virtually unlimited, and certainly unprecedented, powers to prosecute the war, although many legal safeguards were built into the system and the conscription of civilians for military and civilian service did not come until much later in the war. Britain established agencies for the dissemination of propaganda about its war effort and the evils of the enemy, which also controlled the flow of information about the war. (Every combatant nation, without exception, did the same thing.) A wide variety of such bodies were established early in the war, haphazardly organised. These were centralised in a Department of Information in 1916 and in a Ministry of Information under Lord Beaverbrook in February 1918. The so-called 'presslords' like Beaverbrook and Lord Northcliffe (Alfred Harmsworth, 1865–1922), then at the peak of their influence, were often used for these ends; Northcliffe officially became Director of Propaganda in Enemy Countries in 1918. Films and rallies were also used by the government to drum up support for its policies at home and abroad, as were the talents of many writers and intellectuals. Arnold Bennett, the novelist, served as Director of Propaganda in the Ministry of Information in the latter phases of the war, while Rudyard Kipling headed efforts to present Britain's case in the best light in America and other Allied countries. Although early in the war the press remained relatively free (allowing populist rabble-rousers like Horatio Bottomley to flourish), by the latter phases of the war a Press Bureau became extremely influential in controlling the newspapers. In the preliminary phases of the war, too, a variety of incredible rumours about the conflict were to be found in the British press, such as reports of the 'Angel of Mons', a vision of St George and attendant angels allegedly seen by British troops over the Mons battlefield in late August 1914. (The 'vision' was invented by an imaginative journalist.) Another equally ludicrous rumour which appeared in dozens of newspapers at the same time (August–September 1914) was news that thousands of Russian troops had disembarked in Scotland and were taken by train to the Channel ports to fight in France. These Russian troops were allegedly known by 'the snow on their boots', although why their snow failed to melt in southern England even in an English summer was not explained. Although this tale of Russian troops was entirely false (and regarded as nonsense from the first by many level-headed journalists) it was actually reported in the *New York Times* in elaborate detail.

By the later phases of the war this kind of mass hysteria was, rather surprisingly, to be found less often, although rioting and violence against Germans and alleged pro-Germans continued throughout the war. Nevertheless, even here there was less than one might expect. Instead, most British civilians demonstrated a grim determination to get on with what they regarded as a just war. There was enough seemingly compelling evidence for German evil to justify this attitude. The Germans were the first (but not the last) combatant power to use poison gas on the battlefield, at Ypres in 1914, and used far more of it than the Allies. Germany's unrestricted submarine warfare, entailing the sinking of merchant ships, was a feature of the latter phases of the war. The Germans used zeppelins to bomb English cities, of course the first time that this had happened. Edith Cavell (1865–1915), a British nurse in Belgium, confessed to assisting Allied prisoners of war to escape and, after a court martial, was shot on 12 October 1915. The Germans were regularly their own worst enemies, creating needless hostility and opprobrium. Nothing the Germans did in the First World War could conceivably be compared to their atrocities in the Second, although many reasonable Britons believed that they were fighting a nation embodying similar evil. This unquestionably prevented effective opposition to the war from growing in Britain, and contributed to Germany's defeat.

Although the Liberal government was united when it took Britain into the war, it did not take long for tensions to emerge in government ranks. As the British death toll mounted, seemingly without end, and an apparently permanent stalemate emerged on the Western Front, the search began for an alternative strategy which would assist the Allies' war efforts, perhaps decisively, without killing so many of its sons. While some favoured the landing of a British army in the Baltic area, the favoured plan became an invasion of the Dardanelles, in European Turkey, which would lead quickly – on paper – to the conquest of Constantinople, Turkey's capital. At relatively little cost the Allies could thus eliminate Turkey from the war, probably take pro-German Bulgaria as well, crucially assist Serbia, and send war materiel to Russia, receiving grain from Russia in exchange. There was nothing wrong with this plan, which was enthusiastically backed by Winston Churchill, First Lord of the Admiralty, and much of the Cabinet. It was, however, opposed by Kitchener, who did not support a diversion of men from the Western Front, and by Admiral John 'Jackie' Fisher, first baron Fisher (1841–1920), the famous First Sea Lord (Commander-in-Chief of the Navy). As a result, the Gallipoli campaign, as it became known, was undertaken but horribly botched. In February and March 1915 two attempts by the Navy to seize the Dardanelles went badly wrong, although the Turks mounted little resistance. The main attempts to land substantial numbers of British and French troops on the Dardanelles, at the Gallipoli Peninsula in April and at Sulva Bay in August 1915, went even more askew, chiefly due to horribly inadequate planning and tactics and to much fiercer Turkish resistance. The Gallipoli campaign had many long-term consequences. Mustapha Kemal (later Kemal Ataturk, 1880–1938), the founder of modern Turkey, first became prominent in the successful Turkish defence of Gallipoli. Australia and New Zealand commonly date their true birth as independent nations from the bravery of the 'ANZAC' troops at Gallipoli, where they comprised a major part of the fighting force. Most unfairly, for his plans were sound and far-sighted, Churchill was blamed for the Gallipoli debacle, and gained a reputation for reckless impetuosity, especially among Tories, which it took him many years to overcome. Gallipoli ended any real attempt at 'sideshows' – as efforts to circumvent the Western Front stalemate became known – leading to an even greater concentration on the slaughterhouse of the Western Front. If Gallipoli had succeeded and Constantinople been conquered it is also just possible that the Russian Revolutions might not have occurred. On the other hand (as critics of Gallipoli said then, and since) Germany herself remained to be defeated, and it is very difficult to see how this could have been done except on the Western Front.

'Jackie' Fisher dramatically resigned as well at this time, refusing to serve under Churchill. The Tory opposition, which at first patriotically supported the government, now turned on Churchill (who, as a turncoat former Tory, many regarded as a traitor), and resolved to attack the government if Churchill remained at the Admiralty. Tensions were also beginning to be felt over the shortage of shells on the Western Front, which the Tories could also have exploited. (In late 1915 British factories were producing only 22 000 shells per day, compared with 100 000 in France and 250 000 in Germany and Austria.) The existence of a single-party government in a world war was itself an anomaly, and, in May 1915, heavily influenced by Lloyd George as well as by Bonar Law, Asquith agreed to form a Coalition government with the Unionists and also with pro-war Labourites. Asquith resigned as Prime Minister of a purely Liberal government on 25 May 1915, forming a Coalition government at the same time; 25 May 1915 was the last day on which a purely Liberal government ever held office in Britain.

By May 1915, owing to by-election gains, there were more Unionists than Liberal MPs in the House of Commons, and a Coalition should presumably have provided the Tories with at least an equal number of Cabinet seats to the Liberals. There was no question of the General Election due in 1915 being held: this was delayed until the end of the war. (Parliament has the power to do this, unlike the situation in the United States, where, according to the American Constitution, elections must be held at two- or four-yearly intervals.) Furthermore, the Unionist leaders should have been offered a reasonable share of the most important offices. In forming the Coalition government which lasted from May 1915 until December 1916, Asquith did neither of these things. Instead, he formed a Cabinet of 23 men of whom 12 were Liberals, nine Unionists, one, Arthur Henderson, a Labour member, and one, Lord Kitchener (who remained as Secretary for War) was non-party. The Liberals, moreover, continued to hold nearly all of the top posts. Besides Asquith, Reginald McKenna became Chancellor of the Exchequer, replacing Lloyd George, who moved to the crucial, newly created Ministry of Munitions to oversee the manufacture of war materiel. Grey continued as Foreign Minister while Sir John Simon held the Home Office. Winston Churchill was demoted from the Admiralty to the unimportant Duchy of Lancaster. Churchill was a victim of the failure at Gallipoli and of Tory insistence that he not be placed in a more crucial office. Given that Asquith was compelled to cut the number of Liberals in the Cabinet in half, some of his choices were curious. For instance, he retained Augustine Birrell as Chief Secretary for Ireland, with disastrous results.

What did the Unionists receive? Remarkably little. Bonar Law was given the Colonial Office, an insultingly junior position for the Leader of the Opposition, and could only be induced to accept this position after considerable exhortation by Lloyd George, to whom the Tory leader was drawing increasingly close. The only Tory given an important position was Arthur Balfour, who became First Lord of the Admiralty. Balfour was the only leading Tory whom Asquith admired, and had been appointed a member of the War Council by him in November 1914, the sole Tory member. The War Council was formed to give advice to the Cabinet on the war, which it normally accepted. Balfour was thus a kind of *de facto* member of the inner Cabinet already. Other Tories who received Cabinet positions included Curzon (Lord Privy Seal), Carson (Attorney-General) – a curious appointment in view of his flirtation with illegal activity over Ulster although Carson was, of course, a leading barrister – Lord Robert Cecil (Minister of Blockade), Austen Chamberlain (India), Long (Health and Local Government), and Lansdowne (Minister Without Portfolio). These were, clearly, the second half of the Cabinet in view of importance. As the Tories had not held office for ten years, Asquith had some excuse for this, and some historians have argued that his treatment of Bonar Law was clever, in that many leading Tories – Curzon, Chamberlain, even Balfour – regarded him as a stopgap leader, promoted above his merits, and giving him a junior office would both confirm their opinion and sharpen their knives. Nevertheless, it is also difficult not to believe that Asquith made a great mistake here, which resulted, 18 months later, in Bonar Law securing the premiership for Lloyd George. The natural position for Bonar Law was as Chancellor of the Exchequer; this was denied to him, it is believed, because of his protectionist views. By giving him a minor position Asquith gratuitously made an enemy of

Bonar Law. This was the first, but not the last, occasion in which Asquith played a strong hand very ineptly indeed. Asquith also made the first appointment of Labour MPs to any Cabinet, making Arthur Henderson, the leader of the party, President of the Board of Education and giving junior ministries to two other Labour MPs, William Brace and George Roberts. This move improved relations with the trade unions and working-class voters they represented; it also showed how much Labour was moving to the centre of political life and, above all, that most Labour members supported the war. Asquith was rapidly losing confidence in Kitchener, and would have been happy to replace him. But Kitchener's support among the public and in the press made this difficult to do, so he was retained as Secretary for War. Asquith's brother-in-law, Harold J. Tennant, was appointed Kitchener's Under-Secretary, doubtless to keep an eye on him.

The precise details of the new Cabinet would not have mattered very much if the war was going well. Unfortunately, the war was not going well, and both the stalemate and the endless series of bloody, pointless battles continued as before. In September and October 1915 came the campaigns of Artois and Champagne. Britain's shortage of manpower led to 60 000 casualties for little or no gains and to the replacement of Sir John French as British Commander-in-Chief by Sir Douglas Haig (who had opposed the offensive). The Sulva Bay débâcle came in December 1915. Yet neither could the Germans break through. They made extensive gains at Verdun in February–May 1916, but the Allies, led by French General Henri Philippe Pétain, managed to prevent a rout. Elsewhere, there was also some good news, but also much cause for concern. Italy was engaged in a difficult struggle with Austria, draining men on both sides. Serbia was largely conquered by the Central Powers. At sea, German submarines sank almost one million tons of Allied shipping in 1915.

The year 1916 was to be no better; if anything, worse. The Russian army under Alexei Brusilov broke through into eastern Austria-Hungary in June 1916, but its gains were comprehensively reversed by September, with losses of up to a million Russian soldiers. Romania, previously neutral, declared war on the Allied side in August 1916, but was then conquered in December by a brilliant German offensive under General August von Mackensen, one of the most successful German generals of the war. Italy emerged slightly better than Austria in that theatre of the war.

For Britain, however, 1916 will always be remembered for two great events, the Battle of the Somme and the naval engagement at Jutland. The Allies had long planned a major offensive for the summer of 1916. The BEF, under Haig, was given the primary task of leading this attack. Haig decided on a five-day campaign of unprecedented intensive bombardment of the German lines near the River Somme, a bombardment so powerful that British troops would literally walk across 'no man's land' to seize the German strongholds. As is well known, the bombardment, despite its strength, did not destroy Germany's deep emplacements, and Germany's machine gunners made mincemeat of wave after wave of British infantry when this incredibly foolish offensive began on 1 July 1916. About 19 290 British soldiers were killed on the first day of the Somme (not 60 000 as is often claimed: that figure includes the wounded, some of whom died later). This was, nevertheless, the greatest loss suffered by the British army on any day of its history. Although the Germans were worn down, virtually nothing was accomplished; nevertheless Haig pressed on with this attack in July and periodically until November 1916. By the end of July, Haig had gained about two and a half miles of territory. In September, the Germans turned the tide and threatened the British with disaster. Haig then employed tanks, a new invention, with good effect, but these proved insufficient to break through the German lines. The British lost 420 000 men, killed and wounded, the French 195 000, the Germans an unknown figure estimated by them at 400 000 and by the Allies at 650 000 or more. The French partially made up for the indecisiveness of the Somme by a fairly successful counter-attack at Verdun in the second half of the year in which the British were only marginally involved.

For the first two years of the war virtually everyone in Britain asked the question, 'where is the navy?' Before the war, nearly everyone expected the Royal Navy to play a crucial part in any great war with Germany, presumably by smashing its fleet, as had been accomplished against the French at Trafalgar. Nearly two years into the war, however, the Royal Navy had apparently done virtually nothing. The long-expected direct engagement between the British and German navies – or something like it – did at last eventuate at Jutland in the North Sea off the coast of Denmark in May 1916. Command of the British Grand Fleet was divided between Admiral Sir David Beatty (1871–1936) and Admiral Sir John Jellicoe (1859–1935). The Royal Navy knew the German secret naval codebook thanks to being given a copy taken by the Russians in the Baltic, and were able to forestall plans of the German High Sea Fleet to lure Beatty's fleet to its doom. Both Beatty and Jellicoe were able to engage the German fleet on the same day. Beatty earlier engaged the Germans, losing two battlecruisers before turning the tide. Jellicoe's fleet then made contact and gained the upper hand, although without the crushing victory many expected. While Jutland was not Trafalgar, it did mark a turning-point as the German High Seas Fleet never challenged the British Grand Fleet again. The Royal Navy certainly acquitted itself better, relatively speaking, than the army, although not in the way many foresaw.

The most important role of the British Navy, however, lay in enforcing the blockade of Germany. Historians have long debated the effectiveness of this blockade. Germany often developed substitute (*ersatz*) goods for those denied by the blockade, and obtained foodstuffs from the Scandinavian countries and, after 1917, Russia. Nevertheless, starvation and near-starvation became features of life in Germany and Austria from the middle of the war onwards, in a way which was never the case in the major Allied nations. By 1918, death rates were appreciably higher among civilians in Germany than among Allied civilians. The Central Powers had fewer resources to begin with; their agricultural base was more primitive and they had no access to the granaries of America, Canada, Australia, and elsewhere among the Allies. By 1918, hunger and destitution among ordinary Germans and Austrians led, as much as anything else, to a refusal to carry on the war although the Central Powers had not really been defeated. Indeed, these factors were probably the fundamental causes of the revolutions which swept away the old order and which briefly appeared likely to bring Bolshevism to central Europe.

The Allies also seized all of Germany's overseas colonies. Britain and France took her west African territories; Japan and Australia those in the Pacific; South Africa conquered German South-west Africa. All of these took place with little effort. Germany put up much stiffer resistance in German east Africa (Tanganyika), where resistance lasted until 1917 and guerrilla raids, organised by Paul von Lettow-Vorbeck from Mozambique, lasted until the Armistice. Surrender of Germany's colonies thus occurred during the course of the war itself, and was not imposed upon Germany by the victorious Allies.

The First World War also brought with it the first significant use of air power. Aircraft were used for the purposes of reconnaissance, for bombing raids, and for fighting other aircraft. Perhaps the most dramatic use of air power was in the zeppelin (dirigible) bombing raids by Germany on Britain and France. Germany manufactured 73 enormous airships which carried out 51 bombing raids against Britain during the war, as well as primitive biplane bombers which carried out another 57. Over 1500 British civilian lives were lost in these attacks, chiefly in London and the south-east. One raid on London, carried out by bombers in June 1917, killed 162 civilians, among them many children in a school in the East End. Later in the war, Britain responded with bombing raids of their own, against German factories rather than civilian targets. These raids are surprisingly little known today, overshadowed by the vastly greater air war in the Second World War. Better-remembered, however, is the plane-to-plane combat by legendary 'air aces' such as Germany's Manfred von Richthofen, 'the Red Baron' (the brother-in-law of D.H. Lawrence, as strange as this may seem), and America's Eddie Rickenbacker. Britain's best air aces were nearly as successful as their foreign counterparts, but are strangely little known. Britain's two best pilots, Major Edward Mannock and Lt.-Colonel William A. Bishop, shot down, respectively, 73 and 72 enemy planes, only slightly fewer than von Richthofen's 80 and 75 by France's best pilot, René Fonck.

The lack of progress in the war effort also led to major crises within the British government, notwithstanding the formation of the Coalition. The first was over conscription. As noted, Britain alone of major combatants had no conscription and raised her armies solely from volunteers. As the requirements for fresh soldiers became ever greater, it became apparent that purely voluntary enlistment could not be maintained. Conscription, however, was contrary to an extremely deep-seated and influential strand in Liberal thought. There was also a real question of who should be conscripted and who exempted – men were also needed in factories and mines; presumably unmarried men should go before married men, and so on. A scheme offered by Lord Derby under which both unmarried and married men were voluntarily to offer to serve contained too many ambiguities to work and in January 1916 a Military Service Act introduced conscription for unmarried men aged between 18 and 41. Sir John Simon, the Home Secretary, resigned, but after some initially strong Labour opposition the bill received wide support. An important feature of this bill was the legal enactment of the category of conscientious objectors, who could receive exemption from the draft on religious (but not other) grounds. About 10 000 men (out of approximately 16 000 who applied) were granted conscientious objector status. Another 1500 'absolutists' who refused any form of alternative service were drafted into military units until the government intervened; many, however, were imprisoned. Although the local committees which adjudicated the claims of would-be conscientious objectors sometimes acted unfairly, apart from the United States no other combatant nation recognised the status of objectors at all. In May 1916, a second Military Service law applied conscription to married men up to the age of 41. Neither of these two Acts was applied to Ireland, presumably owing to fears that it would spark a rebellion there. Nevertheless, very large numbers of Irishmen, from both the north and the south, volunteered for the war and Britain's war efforts were generally supported by the Irish Nationalists in Parliament. Exemptions from conscription were also applied liberally to men in industries necessary to the war; well over two million men of military age remained behind in 'starred' occupations which were exempt from the draft. Britain's economy, and the economic foundations necessary for carrying on the war, required British industry to produce at fever pitch.

In late April 1916 came the so-called Dublin Easter Uprising. Sir Roger Casement (1864–1916) was a British consular official who before the war had devoted himself to reporting on atrocities committed by the European colonial powers against the natives of the Congo and Latin America. He retired to Ireland in 1912 and became a passionate Irish Nationalist although (like Parnell) he was a Protestant. During the war he travelled to Germany to organise an invasion of Ireland, and was landed at Tralee by a German submarine (ironically, with advice to postpone the coming uprising). He was arrested, his diary as a homosexual was privately circulated, and he was hanged for treason. Casement's failure to procure German cooperation meant that a large-scale uprising by the Irish Volunteers did not occur. Nevertheless, on 24 April 1916 (the Monday after Easter Sunday 1916) a smaller group of extremists seized the Dublin Post Office and proclaimed the Irish Republic. Led by Patrick Pearse (the self-proclaimed President of the Republic), James Connolly, and Eoin MacNeill, the 'Uprising' was suppressed within a week, although not before several other groups of rebels, led by persons later renowned in modern Irish history such as Eamon de Valera and the Countess Markiewicz, also staged uprisings. About 1500 persons took part in the 'revolt', of whom about 220 were killed, along with 134 on the British side. The British authorities were at the point of arresting some of the leaders of the 'Uprising' on Easter Sunday, but had to await approval from the Chief Secretary for Ireland, Augustine Birrell, who was in London where he was reading a book (according to a letter he wrote to the Permanent Under-Secretary of State for Ireland) 'about the Chevalier de Boufflers and his enchanting lady-mistress and wife'. While permanent harm was done by the revolt, the manner in which the British exacted justice led to even more trouble. Fifteen of the rebel leaders were condemned by court martial (rather than civil trial) and shot, and other sentences were handed down with brutal capriciousness, even to those who had virtually nothing to do with the 'Uprising'. This combination of brutality and irrationality handed out by the British military authorities permanently alienated most Catholic Irish opinion, moved Sinn Fein from the fringes to the centre of political life, and made a peaceful resolution of the Irish situation impossible.

This was assuredly the worst mishandling of any situation in the United Kingdom ever made by Asquith as Prime Minister. Birrell immediately resigned, his political career mercifully at an end, as did other senior British officials. Into this vacuum Asquith sent Lloyd George who, remarkably, secured a far-reaching agreement by mid-June 1916 with the Nationalists and Ulsterites concerning the future of Ireland. Under this agreement, Home Rule would come into effect for the 26 counties of the south while the six counties of Ulster were excluded; Ireland's MPs at Westminster were not to be reduced. Tory objections to Home Rule and Asquith's failure to treat the agreement as fundamental to the future of the government led to Lloyd George's settlement being defeated in Parliament. Although quiescent for the remainder of the war, Ireland remained in limbo. At the 1918 General Election, held just after the end of the war, Sinn Fein swept everything in the Catholic south.

While Lloyd George did not shower himself with glory in Ireland, compared with Asquith he seemed the essence of dynamism, and he now began to move closer to supreme power. The steps by which he became Prime Minister in December 1916 are, however, rather complex. On 5 June 1916, Kitchener, the Secretary for War, drowned in the North Sea and, after a week's delay, Asquith offered the vacant post to Lloyd George. The other obvious candidate was Bonar Law; Lloyd George and Bonar Law negotiated closely together to reach a common front with Asquith, the beginnings of their successful partnership. Asquith was reluctant to offer the post to either one, since either man would obviously be seen as the 'prime minister-in-waiting' in such a central role. In the end he gave the post to Lloyd George after Bonar Law declined, but without any increased powers. (Kitchener's enormous powers had actually been whittled down by Lloyd George himself.) Lloyd George formally became War Secretary on 6 July 1916. Between then and December 1916 the war continued to go badly, with the failure of the Somme and German gains in the Balkans. Lloyd George proved a useful War Secretary, improving transport lines in France and visiting the troops at the Front. He initially established good working relations with Haig, although he soon realised the latter's inadequacies. In late September 1916, Lloyd George gave an interview to an American journalist, quoted around the world, pledging Britain to 'a fight ... to [the] finish ... to a knock-out', and rejecting any hint of a compromise peace. Britain would continue to engage 'until the Prussian military despotism is broken beyond repair'. That Lloyd George aimed at 'the knock-out blow' against Germany soon became the universal shorthand to describe his approach to the war. By saying this, Lloyd George was not merely signalling Germany and the United States (which was tentatively trying to arrange a peace conference) but anyone in the British government who might be tempted to view a compromise peace with favour, including Asquith. He was also clearly signalling the Unionists that he was as extreme an anti-German as any of them. As well, in this interview, Lloyd George gave the clearest indication given by any senior Cabinet minister of just why Britain was fighting: not merely to free Belgium, but, in a great extension of the war's original aims, to rid the world of 'Prussian military despotism'. Strangely enough, this had never been made absolutely clear before. Unlike the Second World War, when the Allies explicitly sought the 'unconditional surrender' of Germany and Japan, the war aims of Britain and France had remained very ambiguous.

Asquith thus came to the end of 1916 in a weakened position: his party was divided over conscription, his leadership was humiliated over Ireland, the war was going badly, and he faced an ever more formidable rival in Lloyd George. Yet his position was not critical and his replacement by Lloyd George was not inevitable. According to most contemporaries, he retained the confidence of most Liberals, as well as all the patronage powers of the Prime Minister. He did not have to worry about an election, and Lloyd George was still feared by many Tories for his radicalism. However, Asquith made a series of tactical mistakes in the last months of his premiership, which weakened his leadership. He allowed Parliament to conduct enquiries into the Mesopotamia and Dardanelles campaigns; MPs were only too eager to discover mismanagement. Asquith's eldest and brightest son was killed on the Western Front; this greatly aggravated his very apparent personal deterioration. In early November 1916 came the so-called Nigerian debate. Sir Edward Carson had become Attorney-General in the Coalition but had resigned in November 1915 over the Allies' failure to assist Serbia. He had become a bitter critic of Asquith and the government's conduct of the war. The Nigerian debate concerned the sale of enemy properties in that colony: the government proposed to sell them to the highest bidder; Carson submitted a resolution to sell them only to British subjects or British companies. A large number of Protectionist Tory MPs, as well as backbench super-patriots, supported Carson's resolution (although the government narrowly won). The Nigerian debate crystallised festering backbench Unionist discontent with the Coalition. The mover of the government's measure was, ironically, the arch-Protectionist Colonial Secretary Bonar Law, and it thus also became apparent that the latter's own position as leader of the Unionist party was itself potentially threatened by his backbench so long as he remained so closely linked with Asquith and the Liberals.

To all of these reasons for the undermining of Asquith's position there must be added others. Possibly the most important was the position enjoyed by the British press, especially the main daily London newspapers. At this time, with general literacy and a cheap mass circulation press, but before radio and newsreels, newspapers were at the peak of their influence, often headed by the great buccaneering proprietors like Alfred Harmsworth, Viscount Northcliffe (1865–1922) and his brother Harold, baron Rothermere (1868–1920) of the *Daily Mail* and, since, 1908, chief owner of *The Times*, the Levy-Lawson family of the *Daily Telegraph*, the Lloyd family of the *Daily Chronicle*, the Hulton family of the *Daily Sketch*, and Davison Dalziel of the *Standard*, and after 1916–18, Sir Max Aitken (Lord Beaverbrook) of the *Daily Express*. This was also a period of legendary editors, such as J.L. Garvin of the *Observer* and H.A. Gwynn of the *Morning Post*. The provincial press was also at the peak of its influence, with a range of local titles almost unimaginable today. Additionally, there were weekly and fortnightly journals of opinion – the *Economist*, the *Fortnightly Review*, the *Spectator*, and so on – with, again, legendary, iconoclastic editors such as Leopold Maxse of the *National Review*. While the importance of the press had been great before the war, it became greater still during the war. Since there was no effective Opposition during the war, and especially after the formation of the Coalition in May 1915, newspapers became a kind of unofficial opposition, although never questioning the war itself. Parliament was muted during the war, seldom holding debates on the fundamentals of the conflict. The newspapers were also better-informed than most MPs, and acted as conduits for the leaking of information by discontented civilians and soldiers. The most dynamic press barons of the day, especially Northcliffe, considered it their duty to criticise the failures of the war, indeed to make and unmake governments. In late 1916, the press turned increasingly against Asquith, generally to advocate greater vigour and central direction in the conduct of the war. Some came out explicitly for Lloyd George as Prime Minister. They saw in him the embodiment of energy seemingly lacking in Asquith, who was (with other leading politicians) at all times aware that the press was turning against him. Lloyd George himself at this stage advocated only the creation of a small inner War Committee consisting of about three members, to have total control of the war effort. Asquith was to remain as Prime Minister, but without membership in the War Committee. Lloyd George (who obviously intended to become chairman of the War Committee) then secured the full backing and support of Bonar Law. Asquith himself had been moving some way towards Lloyd George's proposals, perhaps to create two inner committees, one dealing with military affairs and the other the home front, but insisted on 1 December 1916, that he, as Prime Minister, must be their chairman. Owing in large part to Sir Max Aitken, who increasingly acted as an interlocutor to and intermediary between Lloyd George and Bonar Law, the latter now moved wholeheartedly behind the former's proposals. (On 2 December 1916, Lloyd George sent a famous letter to Bonar Law stating 'the life of the country depends on resolute action by you now'.) Bonar Law was renowned for being indecisive yet incredibly firm and stubborn once he had made up his mind; he now backed Lloyd George to the hilt. At first Asquith and Lloyd George appeared to reach a compromise to constitute a War Committee, but events were now moving swiftly. *The Times* (owned by Northcliffe) attacked Asquith insultingly on 4 December. Asquith assumed that Lloyd George and Northcliffe were in collusion, and determined on strong action. He submitted the resignation of all members of the Cabinet except himself to the King, and wrote a letter to Lloyd George stating that he, Asquith, had to remain its head. Unionist Cabinet ministers made it clear that they would not remain in any government without Lloyd George and Bonar Law. On 5 December 1916, Asquith resigned, having been Prime Minister for over eight years. It seems clear that he continued to enjoy the confidence of most Liberals, plus many of the Irish and Labour members who still held the balance of power. Had a direct vote in Parliament been held to choose between Asquith and Lloyd George, Asquith still might well have won. In a vigorous letter to Asquith, Lloyd George, who was still nominally War Secretary, also resigned on the same day.

King George then asked Bonar Law to form a government, but the latter demurred until after a conference at the Palace consisting of himself, Asquith, Lloyd George, Balfour, and Henderson. The possibility of Balfour becoming Prime Minister was discussed. Asquith left the Conference certain that he would not serve in a Cabinet except as Prime Minister. It is clear that this was a grave mistake; Asquith never held office again and the split between him and Lloyd George helped substantially to bring about the downfall of the Liberal party. Bonar Law now declined to form a government and, on the evening of 6 December 1916, Lloyd George was commissioned by the King to be Prime Minister and form a government. He was to remain as Prime Minister for nearly six years and to be remembered as one of the five or six most famous premiers since 1832. His government also won the war, although not without more catastrophic losses.

With the accession of Lloyd George there were two major changes in the composition of the Cabinet. Asquith's Cabinet had been mainly Liberal, with Unionists clearly in subordinate positions. Lloyd George reversed this order, and his Ministry was mainly a Tory one with Liberal additions. Second, from 6 December 1916 until 31 October 1919 there was an inner War Cabinet consisting of between five and seven members. It had central direction of the war, but existed side-by-side with a normal Cabinet, consisting of the usual number of members. The inner Cabinet was a constitutional innovation of great importance, which was obviously based in the idea of a small War Committee with executive functions, although it was designed to enhance Lloyd George's authority as Prime Minister, not to diminish the Premier's powers as his proposals to Asquith would have done.

Lloyd George's War Cabinet always contained, throughout the nearly three years it operated, himself, Lord Curzon, and Bonar Law. Lord Milner, the Conservative peer and champion of Empire, was a member from its formation until 18 April 1918, when he was replaced by Austen Chamberlain, who served for the remainder of the War Cabinet's existence. Arthur Henderson, the leader of the Labour party served from its formation until August 1917. Its other members were the famous South African statesman Jan Christian Smuts (22 June 1917 until 10 January 1919), whose appointment was remarkable as he was not a member of the British Parliament, and the businessman and Conservative MP Sir Eric Geddes (1875–1937), who had served as First Lord of the Admiralty in 1917–18 before being appointed to the War Cabinet in its final stages, from January to October 1919. The War Cabinet thus lacked some men whom one might have expected to find in it, such as Balfour, Carson, and Churchill (a pariah to the Tories). On the other hand, it contained two Tory peers, Curzon and Milner, presumably chosen because of their experience at command – Curzon as Viceroy of India, Milner as High Commissioner for South Africa – a quality useful in a wartime supreme executive. (Curzon, often seen as preciously useless in practical terms, turned out to be a very capable and businesslike administrator.) Henderson was chosen to further consolidate the support of Labour and the trade unions for the conduct of the war, Smuts, a capable lawyer, to speak for the Dominions. It might also be noted that only Curzon came from the old governing classes (although Milner and Chamberlain were university men), and Lloyd George's Coalition ministry saw a definite diminution in the importance of the old aristocracy and gentry to governing Britain, to be replaced, very largely, by self-made businessmen and professionals. The War Cabinet met numerous times, usually on a daily basis. It had its flaws, chiefly the overload of work it experienced. Nevertheless, as none of its members except Bonar Law (who was Chancellor of the Exchequer and *de facto* leader of the House of Commons) headed an administrative position but were ministers without portfolio, it was generally regarded as a great innovation.

The normal Cabinet appointed by Lloyd George in December 1916 consisted of 23 men. Fourteen were Tories, only seven Liberals, and two (Arthur Henderson and John Hodge, 1855–1937) represented Labour. As noted, the Tories held nearly all the major departmental positions. Apart from Bonar Law at the Exchequer, Balfour was Foreign Minister, while Austen Chamberlain went to the India Office. Lloyd George was very happy to appoint Tories like Walter Long (who became Colonial Secretary) who had been sympathetic to Asquith, hoping to isolate the latter further and diminish any chance of him making a comeback. Among leading Tories, only Lord Lansdowne – who was increasingly turning against the war – was not included in the new government. Indeed, Lloyd George's chief problem was finding well-known Liberals to serve under him. Apart from Asquith, Grey, Simon, Runciman, Samuel, McKenna and many other leading Liberals declined to serve; in some cases their careers came to an abrupt end, although others re-emerged in other guises. Churchill, who would have been extremely happy to serve, was excluded for the time being owing to the hostility felt towards him by the Tories, especially Bonar Law. (Churchill finally returned to the Cabinet as Minister of Munitions in July 1917, beginning a long-term move to the far right.) The Liberals appointed to the Cabinet in December 1916 were, in general, little-known: Sir Frederick Cawley (1850–1918), Lord Rhondda (David Alfred Thomas, 1856–1918), and Sir Albert Stanley (1874–1948; later first baron Ashfield), three leading industrialists (but fairly obscure as politicians) were typical. Christopher Addison (1869–1951; later first viscount Addison), a professor of anatomy and a leading radical social reformer, who hero-worshipped Lloyd George, was made Minister of Munitions. (Later he joined the Labour party and became an influential member of Attlee's post-war Labour Cabinet.) Lloyd George was widely supposed to enjoy the support of about 175 of 260 Liberal MPs. Initially he was given a free run by Asquith's supporters in the conditions of the war, but the split between Asquith and Lloyd George became increasingly bitter. Lloyd George received the support of the Labour party by the narrowest of margins, after a personal appeal to the party's National Executive. It should be noted, however, that the majority of Labourites supported the new government and the war.

Lloyd George also made two other important constitutional innovations upon becoming Prime Minister. He gave the War Cabinet a dedicated, fulltime secretariat under Sir Maurice Hankey (1877–1963), the enigmatic, perpetually energetic 'man of secrets', who became perhaps the most visible *éminence grise* in history. Hankey (who was distantly connected to a wealthy City family, although his father was an Australian sheep farmer) had been Secretary of the Committee of Imperial Defence. He attended hundreds of meetings, took efficient minutes, and bullied ministers into acting on decisions they had taken and then forgotten. The Cabinet had previously had neither secretary nor minutes, and in a sense the modern Cabinet, professional and political, dates from Hankey's appointment. He certainly freed Lloyd George and the other War Cabinet ministers from endless chores: for instance, the King was automatically sent Cabinet minutes, ending the necessity of the Prime Minister writing him a nightly letter. Under Hankey were four or five assistant secretaries as talented as himself, including Sir Mark Sykes (1879–1919), Leopold Amery (1873–1955), later a prominent Tory Cabinet minister, G.M. Young (1883–1959) the historian, and Thomas Jones (1870–1955). In addition, Lloyd George maintained his own private secretariat headed by W.G.S. Adams, Professor of Political Theory at Oxford, which included Philip Kerr (1882–1940; later eleventh marquess of Lothian), formerly a prominent South African administrator, David Davies (1850–1944; later first baron Davies), and others. Based in huts in the garden of 10 Downing Street, which became known as the 'Garden Suburb', they drafted Lloyd George's speeches, collected detailed information on specific topics, wrote position papers, and gathered material to be used against Lloyd George's enemies. Nothing like this had ever been seen in Britain before, and is surprisingly modern, very reminiscent of today's party research staffers and 'spin doctors'. Lloyd George also retained his own private secretaries, J.T. Davies (1882–1938) and Frances Stevenson (1888–1972), who was also Lloyd George's long-time mistress and who became countess Lloyd-George in 1943 after the death of his first wife.

David Lloyd George thus became Prime Minister with great energy and a genuinely reforming approach in Britain's great hour of peril. To many, even now, he was 'the man who won the war'. Yet what he actually did to win the war is much less clear. Lloyd George was, in fact, caught in a very considerable quandary. By proclaiming that Britain was fighting to deliver the 'knock-out blow' against Germany, and by vowing to rid the world of 'Prussian military despotism', Lloyd George was clearly signalling that 'side shows' like Gallipoli were definitely at an end, as was any compromise peace, and that Britain and France would chiefly continue to engage Germany directly on the Western Front. This appeared to be an endorsement of the policies of the BEF commanders such as Haig. Yet Lloyd George was perfectly well aware of how disastrous and inept were the Western Front commanders and their wasteful, pointless attacks. Lloyd George was in a real sense a victim of his own strategy and rhetoric, and under him Britain would continue to fight, albeit more efficiently and perhaps intelligently. One solution might have been to relieve Haig and replace him with an abler commander. Lloyd George always drew back from this course, although he would have very much liked to have taken it. Haig had very powerful friends and supporters, including the King, Northcliffe, and most leading Tories. There was no obvious candidate to replace him, and Lloyd George recognised that Haig, for all his manifest deficiencies, was probably the best commander available: certainly Lloyd George was not strongly drawn to any other figure. In the final analysis, however, it must be realised that in strategy Lloyd George and Haig were not so far apart, however appallingly wasteful in lives that strategy actually was.

Nevertheless, within the context of endorsing the Western Front strategy, Lloyd George was from the first searching for more vigorous and successful approaches to the war, for instance by introducing more and more tanks, probably the most important innovation in military hardware to come out of the Great War. His first real opportunity to show whether this would turn the tide for the Allies, however, proved to be a disaster. In December 1916, Robert Nivelle replaced General Joseph Joffre as French Commander-in-Chief. Nivelle, who had been a successful army commander for the French, convinced both the French and the British to attempt a great breakthrough, the 'Nivelle Offensive', which he argued could win the war in two days. Nivelle's plans entailed a surprise breakthrough aimed at Germany's strong but exposed salient near the Somme, chiefly undertaken by the French. Nivelle spoke fluent English, and charmed Lloyd George into accepting his proposals. Lloyd George also saw this as an opportunity to subordinate Haig the incompetent to the superior French.

As many military historians have noted, everything which could go wrong with Nivelle's offensive did go wrong. The Germans had withdrawn their exposed salient to the heavily fortified Hindenburg Line; the offensive started late; the French infantry was slaughtered by German machine guns. French gains were meagre if not non-existent, and Nivelle was replaced by Pétain as French Commander-in-Chief. Serious mutinies broke out in the French army, which were severely, but successfully repressed. In order to prevent a German breakthrough during the French mutinies, Haig was given permission to attack Arras and Vimy Ridge, in the Ypres salient. Plumer had dug deep tunnels under the Messines Ridge, held by the Germans, packing it with one million pounds of explosives in 20 mines. On 6–7 June 1917 the mines were detonated, probably the greatest man-made explosion in history up to that time. The noise was clearly heard in London. The explosion and its follow-up attack were a complete success for the Allies, one of their few striking victories at this stage. (Lloyd George was so impressed by Plumer that he nearly replaced Haig with him as commander of the BEF, and was prevented from doing so only by mistrust caused by the 'Maurice Debate' in May 1918, described below.) Unfortunately, the over-optimistic Haig followed this up, between July and November 1917, by yet another major, full scale attack around Ypres.

Rain had fallen on these battlefields for three weeks, meaning that the entire campaign was fought in a sea of mud. The campaign is known to us as Passchendaele; for Britain, next to the Somme, the most tragic and costly of all the battles of the war. About 300 000 British troops were casualties (including the wounded), of whom 90 000 were 'missing'. Many had literally sunk into the mud and drowned. Yet, amazingly, Passchendaele and its accompanying battles were, by and large, a success for the Allies, with Plumer and Currie, the Canadian commander, being notably successful. One victim of this campaign was Sir Herbert Gough, who was, perhaps unfairly, replaced as commander of the Fifth Army by Sir Henry Rawlinson. The dark year 1917 came to an end with the last of Britain's costly, inconclusive campaigns, at Cambrai. Here, tanks were initially used to good effect by Haig, in a campaign which took place in November and December 1917, and six miles – a significant total, in the stalemate of the Western Front – were taken. Then came an equally successful German counter-attack, by which they recovered almost the whole of the territory initially gained by the British.

For Britain, the situation on the Western Front at the end of 1917 was frustrating and indecisive. In late 1917, Germany knocked Russia out of the war, the Bolshevik regime suing for peace and, in March 1918, conceding the whole of western Russia to Germany. On the other hand, in April 1917 the United States entered the conflict, the British blockade of Germany was producing real hardship, and the resources of the Central Powers were more limited than those of the Allies. It would really be a race to see which side fell first from sheer exhaustion. It seems perfectly clear, however, that Lloyd George had no magic weapon for winning the war on the Western Front, and his ascent to power did not alter British strategy there in any fundamental way.

Britain, however, had much better luck in 1917 in other spheres of the war beyond the Western Front. The most important, surely, was the campaign against the U-boat threat to Allied shipping. In February 1917, the German navy resumed unrestricted submarine warfare against all shipping in British waters or bound for Britain. (Unrestricted submarine warfare had been suspended in August 1915 after American lives were lost when one British ship was torpedoed; it was feared by Germany that killing more Americans would bring the United States into the war.) Germany's aim was to bring Britain to her knees through starvation before America could effectively enter the war. Initially, Germany's 148 torpedo submarines scored great success. In April 1917 alone, when the campaign was at its peak, the Germans sank 550 000 tons of Allied shipping – 140 ships, two-thirds of which were British. Britain faced the real prospect of being starved of both food and imported war materiel, and would probably have lost the war as a direct result. Now came what was assuredly Lloyd George's finest hour as Britain's war leader, the institution of the convoy system. This was set in place directly by Lloyd George, against strenuous Admiralty objections, on 10 May 1917. (The Admiralty argued that such a system would require the diversion of most of the light ships of the Grand Fleet.) Henceforth, merchant ships to and from Britain were to travel in convoys of 40 or more vessels, accompanied by destroyer escort ships equipped with antisubmarine depth charges. Immediately a sea-change occurred (literally) in the fate of Allied shipping: by the latter part of 1917, losses at sea were around the same as before Germany resumed unrestricted submarine warfare, despite the greatly increased amount of transatlantic shipping following America's entry into the war in April 1917. Lloyd George's decision to institute convoys comprises his primary claim to being a great war leader.

Britain also made important gains in 1917 in the Near East. In October and November, the British (together with Australian troops) conquered the Holy Land, Allen by entering Jerusalem on 8 December 1917. At about the same time, the British under Sir Frederick Maude conquered Baghdad and Mesopotamia. In the Arab lands held by Turkey, Colonel T.E. Lawrence ('Lawrence of Arabia', 1888–1935), the celebrated leader of Arab irregulars, was simultaneously stirring up, and taking advantage of, resurgent Arab nationalism. In November 1917, Britain, having conquered Palestine, remarkably promised it to the Jews as a 'national home', in the renowned Balfour Declaration, a letter addressed by Britain's Foreign Minister Arthur Balfour to Lord Rothschild. (The text was actually written by Leopold Amery.) The motives behind this extraordinary move were varied. The Lloyd George government contained many convinced philosemitic pro-Zionists, such as Milner, Smuts, Churchill, and Lloyd George himself, as well as pro-Zionists among its administrative staff, especially Amery and Sykes. It was also attempting to woo the world's Jewish communities, especially in America, regarding them as especially influential. Lloyd George was repaying a particular debt to Chaim Weizmann (1874–1952), the British head of the international Zionist movement, a chemist whose wartime discoveries were important for the Allies. As a result, the path which led, 31 years later, to the creation of the State of Israel began to be laid. The Zionist venture was almost stymied at the outset by Edwin Montagu, the Secretary of State for India, a Jewish Cabinet minister who was resolutely anti-Zionist; he believed that the Jews were a religious group and that to assign them a special ethnic identity would create anti-semitism.

It was also in 1917 that some significant anti-war sentiment began to be heard for the first time. The unprecedented human and financial costs of the war, and the fact that it seemed destined to drag on for years meant that some began to question whether the losses of the war could conceivably be justified. It is, indeed, surprising that such dissent had not occurred before. This emerged, late in the day, from several different sources. In the political mainstream, the best-known explicit expression of the sentiment that the war was so wasteful that it should be ended on a compromise basis came from Lord Lansdowne, the former leader of the Unionists in the House of Lords, in a celebrated letter which appeared in the *Daily Telegraph* on 29 November 1917. Claiming that the war's 'prolongation will spell ruin for the civilised world', it recommended the beginning of a negotiated peace by Britain making it clear that it did not desire 'the destruction of Germany' or her post-war ostracism, but that it desired 'a pact for the settlement of international disputes without having recourse to war'. Lansdowne – who had been out of power since Lloyd George became Prime Minister – did not go beyond this. An immediate storm broke around his head, with most of the London press (especially the *Times*, owned by Northcliffe) denouncing him in vicious terms. But Lansdowne also had a great deal of support from much of the provincial and Liberal press. A 'Lansdowne Committee' was formed to advance his views, and Ramsay MacDonald said that he would welcome a Lansdowne government if it ended the war. Lansdowne's letter was, however, inopportunely timed, coming just before the Germans' March offensive, which was followed quickly by the Allies' final counter-attack and the Armistice. Had it come the year before, it might well have had some broader effect. Yet there were always great difficulties in the way of any moves towards a compromise peace. The Germans, effectively controlled by Ludendorff and the military, invariably vetoed even a hint of compromise. On the British side, xenophobia was the order of the day. Politically, it was impossible to find a significant leader for such a movement. The most obvious one was Asquith, but there was no sense in which he opposed the war or was prepared to lead an anti-war movement, even in conjunction with a Unionist like Lansdowne. An effective anti-war movement would have had to construct the unlikeliest of coalitions, from dissident Tories such as Lansdowne to revolutionary Marxists. Not only was this inherently implausible, but it would inevitably have been led by the extreme left, as well as by old-fashioned radicals, and achieved little success among Tories. Only if the war had gone catastrophically badly could such a coalition emerge.

Asquith finally made a move against Lloyd George, but it was too little and too late, and ensured another nail in his political coffin. On 7 May 1918 Major-General Sir Frederick Maurice (1871–1951), who was Director of Military Operations on the Imperial General Staff, wrote a letter, published in four different newspapers, accusing the government of making a series of inaccurate statements in Parliament about troop strength in France and the Near East. According to Maurice, these statements were 'known to a large number of soldiers to be incorrect'. After toying with the idea that Maurice's alleged breach of discipline in publicly criticising the government should be dealt with by the Army Council or a Select Committee, Lloyd George decided to have a full debate in the Commons on the matter. He strongly suspected that Asquith was somehow behind Maurice's letter, and decided to turn the debate into what was in effect a vote of confidence on the government's war policy. The 'Maurice Debate', held on 9 May 1918, was one of the most important of its time, for it drove a permanent wedge between Lloyd George and Asquith, and ended any chance of the emergence of a mainstream movement, critical of the war, headed by Asquith. Asquith had moved for a select committee on Maurice's claims. Lloyd George vigorously refuted the charges, in such a manner as to make it certain that Asquith's motion would be roundly defeated, which it was, by a vote of 293-106. In Asquith's camp were 98 Liberals, nine Labourites, and one Tory, while 71 Liberals voted for Lloyd George. Maurice was dismissed from the Army. Most historians believe that Maurice was actually accurate in his allegations, and Lloyd George knowingly disingenuous (a fact of which Milner and other members of the War Cabinet were aware). The Maurice Debate also caused Lloyd George to organise his own component of the Liberal party in coalition with the Unionists and to abandon any plans for reunion with Asquith and those Liberals like McKenna and Runciman who remained loyal to him.

Anti-war sentiment was also heard on the Left. In August 1917 Arthur Henderson was forced to resign from the Cabinet when he endorsed proposals to send delegates to Stockholm (in neutral Sweden) to meet at a conference of socialist parties, including Germany's, to discuss how to end the war. British seamen refused to carry delegates to Stockholm, and no British delegate attended. In June 1917, 1100 socialists (including Ramsay MacDonald) attended a conference in Leeds to bring the war to an end (and also to bring about a Marxist-style government in Britain). All such left-wing attempts to end the war foundered on the fact that a majority of workers and trade unionists continued to support the war. Once again, only if the war had gone horribly wrong was left-inspired anti-war sentiment likely to grow. As well, extreme right-wing ultra-xenophobic movements were to be found which, had the war gone badly, might well have increased in strength. In September 1917, Henry Page Croft (1881–1947), an extreme right-wing pro-tariff reform Tory MP, founded the National Party, with a programme of ultra-nationalism, anti-Germanism, and a corporate economy. It initially attracted over 20 MPs, and continued to have a separate existence, and some appeal, for several years.

Similar extreme right-wing parties and groupings were established at the time. The populist rabble-rousers N. Pemberton Billing (1881–1948), who claimed to have a list of 47 000 pro-German homosexuals in high places, and Horatio Bottomley (1860–1933) both won seats in Parliament in by-elections in the last year of the war. In June 1917, anti-German xenophobia caused the King to alter the family name of the Royal House from Saxe-Coburg-Gotha to Windsor. Had the war gone very badly or been lost, one might speculate as to whether some kind of significant British proto-fascism might have developed, especially in response to the militant left. Britain's institutions, and the British 'Establishment', were probably sufficiently strong to prevent any truly unconstitutional development, although no one can say what direction extremist movements might have taken, or how successful they might have been, in other circumstances.

The year 1918 proved to be the last year of the war, and that of Allied victory. Both these developments were unexpected up until almost the last minute. The situation in early 1918 appeared to be as bleak for Britain as ever, with the October 1917 revolution in Russia, knocking Russia out of the war and installing an explicitly Marxist Soviet government unlike any previously known, great German gains in Russia, and a continuing, seemingly unchangeable stalemate on the Western Front. Essentially, the Allies had only one new favourable development, but one of the greatest importance: the fact that America had finally entered the war on the side of Britain and France in April 1917. With a fresh and vigorous population of 100 million and the most advanced and wealthiest economy in the world, the United States and its entry into the war would certainly tip the balance to give the Allies their victory at last – if American troops could arrive in Europe, with sufficient weaponry and ammunition, in time. This was not a foregone conclusion. In the Second World War, the United States required two years and six months of preparation between Pearl Harbour and the D-Day landings. In 1917–18, she had to gear up for war, and train and transport over a million men across the Atlantic. It was, in fact, an extremely close-run thing as to whether American troops and equipment would reach the Western Front before the Germans, newly released from fighting in Russia, could defeat the Western Allies.

The Germans were able to move substantial numbers of troops from Russia to the Western Front by the spring of 1918, and, in late March of that year General Ludendorff launched the so-called 'Michael Offensive' in the Somme area. The attack was, initially, a complete success, and in ten days the Germans had gained 40 miles. On 23 March German long-range artillery began shelling Paris, 65 miles away. This was, for the Allies, probably the low point of the war. Gough, commander of the Fifth Army (which had virtually collapsed), was relieved of his command and his Army merged with Rawlinson's Fourth. Foch became Allied Supreme Commander on 3 April.

Sentiment for a settlement of the war by negotiation now grew sharply, often emanating from unexpected sources. The Germans were in control of vast areas of Russia, and were in the process of organising satellite kingdoms, under German princelings, throughout the area. Lord Milner confidentially proposed settling the war on the basis of Germany keeping these areas – and, by inference, gaining hegemony on the European continent – in exchange for the evacuation of Belgium and the Allies keeping Germany's overseas colonies. This was not at all a bad idea, especially if Germany could also have ceded Alsace-Lorraine to France: everyone would have gained something. The Germans fighting in eastern Europe in the First World War must be carefully distinguished from Hitler's invading force two decades later. Imperial Germany was not genocidal and her troops were often greeted as liberators – or, at least, tolerated – by the groups which suffered for 'racial' reasons, under Hitler's dark barbarism. Jews and Poles often greeted the relatively civilised Germans as preferable to Czarist autocracy, as did most of the other nationalities – Finns, Balts, Ukrainians – oppressed in the Czarist 'prison of nations'. Imperial German hegemony throughout central and eastern Europe, bringing a measure of constitutional rule and economic progress to that region would, in hindsight, have been infinitely preferable to rule by the Nazis and Communists. Had Germany won the First World War, it is virtually inconceivable that a Nazi regime would have emerged; it seems as certain as any counterfactual can be that Hitler would never have come to power, which he did on the back of Germany's defeat and the collapse of its old elites. It also seems very likely that a victorious Germany would have quickly overthrown the shaky Bolshevist regime in the Russian heartland, presumably replacing Lenin with some pro-German relative of the Czar. German hegemony in central and eastern Europe was, of course, directly contrary to Britain's age-old strategic aim of preventing the domination of the continent by any single power (to say nothing of France's strategic aims), but a satiated Germany, taking decades to absorb eastern Europe in its economic orbit, might well have been less of a threat to Britain's chief interests in the Empire and 'unofficial Empire' like Latin America and China than it had been before 1914. In any case, Germany would have found itself dealing with the now-vigorous nationalistic movements of these conquered areas, and would not necessarily have had an easy time of it there.

On 12 April, even Haig was almost desperate, and issued a famous proclamation stating – with amazing honesty – that the BEF was fighting with 'our backs to the wall', and, at this time, was seriously considering the evacuation of Britain's troops from the Western Front to the Channel ports. Haig himself seems – almost incredibly, in view of his intellectual rigidity – to have been won over at this point to supporting a compromise peace with Germany along the lines proposed by Lansdowne and supported, covertly but increasingly, by many leading British figures.

Yet the old cliché that the night is darkest just before the dawn was borne out with a vengeance in this case. Foch's appointment as Allied Commander-in-Chief proved to be something of a turning-point. Lloyd George easily defeated the criticism of the 'Maurice Debate' in Parliament, and stood absolutely firm against negotiations. American troops and materiel began to pour into Britain and France in ever-increasing supply, while the peace plans of American President Woodrow Wilson, the famous 'Fourteen Points' outlined by him before the United States' Congress on 8 January 1918, lent an idealistic purpose to the Allied cause. Wilson advocated the independence or autonomy of continental Europe based on nationality and democracy, the creation of an independent

Poland, freedom of the seas, a reduction in armaments, and the formation of an international body to guarantee peace and independence; this body, the League of Nations, came into existence in 1919 but, ironically, without American participation.

By June 1918 the German advance had been halted: Germany simply had insufficient manpower and weaponry to defeat the Allies. Austria-Hungary's last attempt to defeat Italy, the Piave offensive of June–July 1918, also narrowly failed. In August came the great Allied counter-attack. Eighth August 1918 was known to the Germans as 'the "Black Day" of the German army', when an extremely successful Allied attack, headed by 456 tanks and led by British and colonial troops, gained eight miles in one day. The Americans, under General John Pershing, also now entered the attack in force at Meuse-Argonne. The Allies now went all-out for victory in 1918, while Germany steadily collapsed. The Allied gains from September until November 1918 were among the most impressive of the war. The Germans, racked by mutinies and starvation at home and a lack of reserves at the Front, sued for peace at the end of October 1918. The Kaiser abdicated and fled to Holland; a German republic was declared. Austria-Hungary disintegrated into successor states at the same time, the age-old Hapsburg Empire at an end (although Hungary nominally continued as a Hapsburg monarchy without a king until 1945). Turkey also signed a peace Treaty with the Allies at the end of November. Direct negotiations between the Germans and the Allies took place between 7 and 11 November, when an Armistice took effect at 11 am.

The war placed unprecedented strains on the economy and made previously unparalleled demands on public finance. Britain had three Chancellors of the Exchequer during the war: David Lloyd George (1908–25 May 1915), Reginald McKenna (25 May 1915–5 December 1916), and Andrew Bonar Law (10 December 1916–10 January 1919). Each attempted to finance the war in a different way. Lloyd George stopped a panic in the City, chiefly by declaring a bank holiday and temporarily raising interest rates. There is general agreement that he did this well. His two wartime budgets, however, have often been criticised for failing to raise taxes sufficiently and by beginning the trend of extensive borrowing to pay for the war. He also took steps towards government control of the liquor trade. McKenna, a Free Trade Liberal, raised income taxes to unprecedented levels, introduced a new 'excess profits tax', and also greatly raised indirect taxes on ordinary commodities. More controversially, despite his Free Trade views, he introduced a 33.3 per cent tariff on a range of imported goods, the first time these had been introduced since the mid-nineteenth century. These changes proved insufficient to raise the colossal amounts required for the war, and the government issued a series of war loans and Treasury bills to pay for the difference. The war loans, repaid over many years at reasonably high rates of interest, were patriotically subscribed to by millions of people. Britain also liquidated much of its vast overseas portfolio, especially in America. Bonar Law continued these general financial tactics, further increasing taxes. The government never attempted to raise money by a 'capital levy' (the confiscation of wealth-producing assets) advocated by many leftists. Britain's war efforts produced many consequential problems as well: inflation was rampant as the incomes of ordinary persons rose while the volume of consumer goods produced declined; trade unions were far more powerful; Britain had been financing many of the war expenses of its allies, with little chance of recovering them (in the case of post-1917 Russia, a nil chance); the delicate pre-war financial equilibrium of the world, centred in the City of London and the Gold Standard, was forever shattered. Total gross government expenditure rose from £192 million in 1914 to £559 million (1915), £1559 million (1916), £2692 million (1918) and £2579 million (1919), while the aggregate national debt rose from £650 million in 1914 to the incredible sum of £7829 million by 1920. As a result of the necessity to repay this debt, government expenditure after 1918 could never decline to what it had been before the war, regardless of how greatly right-wing governments wished it might do so, and taxes had to remain considerably higher. While expenditure on welfare measures rose considerably, repayment of the debt always had the first claim on government expenditure.

Virtually no one had expected the war to end in 1918 or, given the strength of the German advance in March, to end so quickly. All of the top Allied leaders and generals, almost without exception, expected the war to continue until 1919 or even 1920. America was preparing to send another two million soldiers to Europe, increasing its strength from 1.2 million to 3.2 million men. Many Allied leaders would, in fact, have preferred an invasion and occupation of Germany, something which did not occur; it might, indeed, have been better for the future course of history if a total defeat and reconstruction of German society had occurred, as happened in 1945. While it was perfectly clear that Germany lost the war, no such total defeat and occupation took place in 1918. Under the Armistice agreement, Germany evacuated all occupied territory in France and Belgium and also surrendered Alsace-Lorraine to France, and allowed Allied troops to occupy, for the time being, her own territory west of the Rhine. The Armistice also annulled the Brest-Litovsk Treaty with Russia, under which Germany had occupied much former Russian territory, and Germany virtually disarmed. Nevertheless, the Allies never occupied German territory east of the Rhine, and there was a sense in which the Allies had not really won the war with a completeness commensurate with the sacrifices they had made.

Even apart from Germany, the war had many winners and losers. The United States henceforth became the most formidable nation in the world, although, because of the political triumph of leaders associated with 'isolationism', it failed to play a role in Europe commensurate with her power for several decades. In many respects, Britain was also advantaged by the war, and must be seen as one of the chief winners, however catastrophic the war's human and economic costs. Her institutions remained intact; her Empire was larger than ever; her arch-rival, Germany, was at least temporarily weakened. Within Britain, there were also distinct gainers and losers: women, and the residuum of 40 per cent of men previously lacking a vote gained this right (this is discussed in the next chapter); trade unions and the Labour party were gainers as were – perhaps – the middle classes, especially in London. Southern Ireland gained her independence. Pre-war Liberalism and its underpinnings – Evangelical Protestantism, the northern factory bourgeoisie, idealistic assumptions about human progress – were the chief losers. Commemoration of the war became a solemn annual event, symbolised by the unveiling, on the same day, 11 November 1920, of the Cenotaph in Whitehall and the Tomb of the Unknown Warrior in Westminster Abbey, amidst ceremonials as genuinely moving as any in modern British history. The tradition of commemorating the war dead on Remembrance Sunday or Armistice Day continued and, indeed, over 80 years later appears, if anything, to have risen in genuine mass popularity and solemnity, especially among young people who have never directly known a military conflict and presumably never will. As a general rule, it can be said that Evangelical forms of worship and modes of thought, with their emphasis on individual guilt, repentance, and reward, emerged the loser from the war, while communal modes of worship and modes of thought were the gainers – the Catholic or Anglo-Catholic as opposed to the Protestant, although there was a secular dimension to this as well, the triumph of collectivism over individualism. Because so many were killed, every extended family and every street in Britain knew its bereavements. German machine guns drew no distinction between the pious and upright and the reprobate, killing them impartially. Paradoxically, this probably made the losses easier to bear, since there were no agonising questions for the survivors to ask of why a life was tragically cut short, as there would in the case of an individual youth untimely cut down. While grief was universal, losses were not: young men died, not women. Ironically this probably assisted the emancipation of women, since in many thousands of cases the daughters of the household were left to carry on and to inherit, for which they needed the rights of men. Probably about 20 per cent of young men aged 18–25, the most 'at-risk' group, were killed in the war. Death came as no respecter of social class for, as is well-known, public school and university men, the backbone of the junior officer class, were killed in numbers as large as among the working classes. (At Clifton College, a typical public school, 3100 boys went to war and 578 died, about 18 per cent.) So, too, regularly, were men from the same town or factory, allowed to enlist together under the so-called 'Pals' system, who had the misfortune to be caught in a particularly gruesome slaughter. Probably another third of this age-cohort were wounded. Nevertheless, this is not quite a 'lost generation' (as the wartime losses became known) as horrifying and unbearably tragic as the slaughter obviously was. Of 9 669 000 British and Empire troops who served in the war, 8 722 000, or 90.2 per cent, survived. In June 1918, in a world physically weakened by the war, there broke out the Great Spanish Influenza Pandemic of 1918–19, the last (so far) great plague in the old sense. This epidemic killed an estimated 22 million people around the world, including perhaps 500 000 in Britain (more than half the number killed in the war), before it disappeared almost overnight in February 1919. Its origins are a complete mystery: one theory, put in all seriousness by Fred Hoyle, is that it was caused by micro-organisms carried to earth in a meteor shower; Hoyle points out that the Pandemic was first reported on the same day in Warsaw and San Francisco, something impossible at the time if the plague was spread by human contact, but explicable if the earth had been fatally bombarded from outer space.

For Britain, was the First World War 'worth it'? The only honest or accurate answer is no. Britain was never faced with the prospect of invasion, occupation, and enslavement, as it was during the Second World War. It had not been attacked: indeed, it had declared war on Germany, not the reverse. Britain was fighting Imperial Germany, an authoritarian but constitutional and civilised nation. It was not fighting against a murderous tyranny headed by psychopathic serial-killers like Hitler and Stalin, which simply had to be stopped, regardless of cost, for the sake of the survival of Western civilisation. The First World War, its aims and achievements, were simply not worth the deaths of 723 000 British and 200 000 Empire soldiers in scenes of slaughter closely approaching Dante's Inferno. While all this is clear enough to us, however, it was much less clear during the war itself. The German invasion of Belgium, and the arrogance of German militarism, brought a relatively united nation into the war. To the great majority of Englishmen, until 1917 the First World War seemed to be 'worth it', a just war fought for a noble purpose. Many, perhaps most, British soldiers went to their graves believing this, and posterity ought to respect this fact.

5
Lloyd George's Post-War Coalition, 1918–22

The First World War had also brought with it great political changes, of which four stand out as especially notable. The first and most important was that the basis of the franchise and the electoral system was altered very considerably by the Representation of the People Act 1918, passed in June of that year while the war was still raging. Its origins were to be found during the war, in a concerted drive launched in 1916 to enfranchise all soldiers. The debate on the bill led to a continuous enlargement of its provisions, so that the final act went well beyond any franchise bill which would have been acceptable to a Conservative-dominated government prior to 1914. Its most famous provision, of course, was the enfranchisement of every woman over 30 years of age, provided that she or her husband was a qualified voter on the local franchise. Despite this provision's limitations, at a stroke over eight million women became voters. The Act also had almost equally far-reaching effects upon male voters. All men over 21 (apart from prisoners, peers of the realm, and lunatics) now received the vote after living for six months in a constituency. Soldiers received the vote at 19, although, in a display of wartime spite, conscientious objectors were disenfranchised for five years. The 1918 Act added far more voters to the electorate than any of the previous Reform Acts. In 1910, the British electorate comprised 7 710 000 voters, about 28 per cent of the 26.1 million adults in Britain (and 58 per cent of adult males). In 1919, the electorate had nearly tripled, to 21 756 000, or 78 per cent of the adult population of 27.4 million. None of the nineteenth-century Reform Acts had added even a remotely similar number of new voters.

The Act also greatly affected parliamentary constituencies, dividing the country into equal single-member constituencies consisting of, in England, about 70 000 persons each. (Constituencies were smaller in Scotland and northern Ireland, and a number of two-membered constituencies survived.) Plural voting was limited to two votes (if a voter was qualified to vote in more than one constituency) and even that right was diminished by the fact that General Elections were henceforth to be held on a single day, rather than take place over a period of two or three weeks. All candidates for Parliament were required to put up a deposit of £500 – about £15 000 in today's currency – which was automatically forfeited if the candidate failed to win at least one-eighth of the votes cast in a constituency. The aim of this provision was to deter crank candidates from standing for Parliament. Its result was considerably to increase the power of the political parties, which had the means to put up deposits on a large scale. On the other hand, more extreme changes to the British electoral system, frequently discussed during the war, were rejected. In particular, proportional representation was spurned, and parliament has continued to be elected, as before 1918, under a 'first past the post' system which usually provides strong, one-party rule, but which weighs heavily against smaller parties, especially those without a geographical area of strength.

Second, chiefly as a result of the Dublin Easter Uprising of 1916, Sinn Fein became, within a year or so, nearly the predominant party among Irish Catholics. Between February 1917 and the 1918 General Election Sinn Fein scored five Irish by-election victories, while losing three such contests to the formerly predominant Irish Nationalists (one to the son of John Redmond, the Nationalist's leader). As a result, during the later years of the First World War, such celebrated leaders of post-1918 Ireland as Arthur Griffith, William Cosgrave, and Eamon de Valera were elected to the British Parliament. Sinn Fein, however, had a strict policy whereby none of its returned candidates would take their seats at the Westminster Parliament so long as they were required to swear the oath of allegiance to the British Crown. This meant that as Sinn Fein became completely dominant in Irish politics, southern Ireland would, after the next General Election, be largely unrepresented in the House of Commons, since none of its MPs would take their seats.

Third, the war had brought enormous changes in the nature of the Labour party. In September 1917 Arthur Henderson, leader of the Labour party, who had resigned from the Cabinet the previous month, took the initiative in reorganising the Labour party as a broadly based mass national party with the explicit aim of contesting the next General Election as an independent party similar to the Conservatives and Liberals. Labour would thus cease to be an appendage to the Liberal party, a role it had played since its members first entered Parliament. Henderson had a variety of motives in leading the way to a national Labour party. Rather curiously, as a moderate he regarded such a party as a left-centre social democratic alternative to the more extreme Marxist, syndicalist, and revolutionary parties which were growing in strength around the world as the war dragged disastrously on. Henderson had visited Russia in mid-1917, at a time when the Kerensky regime was collapsing and the Bolsheviks, who had attempted to seize power in July, were growing in popularity among the workers. He quite explicitly saw Labour as a non-revolutionary alternative to the extreme left in Britain. As well, Henderson realised that the Representation of the People Act 1918, by creating a fluid and unprecedented political situation with its vast expansion of the electorate, would create major opportunities for a new party; in Labour's case these opportunities were increased by the enhanced role of the trades unions brought about by the war. Henderson persuaded a rather unwilling Labour leadership that the party needed a new constitution and a wholly independent position. (Indeed, it was seriously proposed that the name of the Labour party be altered to the 'People's Party'.)

What emerged, in late 1917, was a reformulated Labour party very different from its predecessor. Membership in the party was expanded to include pro-socialist groups and individual membership, and a new national executive was formed. Trades unions remained the predominant element within the party (delivering 'block votes' at annual conferences: i.e. all votes were cast by a union as an undivided whole), but were to share power with other constituent elements, especially Fabian socialists and intellectuals. Early in 1918 the celebrated 'Clause IV' was added to Labour's constitution as its long-term objective. In words apparently written by Sidney Webb, Labour declared that it existed 'to secure for the producers by hand or brain the full fruits of their industry ... upon the basis of the common ownership of the means of production'. In 1928, the words 'distribution and exchange' were added to the end of the original clause. Labour was thus committed, at least on paper, to an extremely sweeping form of socialism. The wording of Labour's constitution was to give rise to endless trouble until it was finally repealed in 1995. Only a minority on the extreme left of the party ever believed in the full and complete nationalisation of the means of production, distribution, and exchange. Most Labour adherents never did, but their apparent commitment to drastic socialism could obviously be – and constantly was – exploited by Tories and pro-Tory newspapers to paint them as full-blooded and dangerous revolutionaries: paradoxically, as the party was re-fashioned in 1918 partly to keep Bolsheviks and other extreme socialists at bay. While Labour thus took its most important steps, in 1917–18, towards becoming a potential party of government, and the number of constituency Labour branches grew rapidly, most of its real growth came a few years after the war. By the time of the 1918 General Election it had yet not evolved a political organisation sufficient to mount a really successful election campaign, and, while its electoral vote increased markedly, the party did not do especially well in terms of parliamentary seats won.

Additionally, the war brought about a disastrous split in the Liberal party between Asquith and Lloyd George. It is important to note, however, that the long-term decline of the Liberal party and its replacement by Labour could not readily be foreseen at the time. The extent to which the split between Asquith and Lloyd George contributed to this, as obviously significant as it was, has been endlessly debated by historians. After the 'Maurice debate' in May 1918, the two leaders moved even further apart than before, although Lloyd George offered to bring Asquith into the Cabinet, perhaps as Lord Chancellor. Increasingly, however, Lloyd George came to head his own party or semi-party, the Lloyd George Liberals, which formed its own party machinery, had its own supporters and party funding. Although its scale may be exaggerated, funding was acquired, in particular, by the notorious sale of honours (a peerage allegedly cost £50 000, a knighthood, £10 000), the proceeds of which went into the Lloyd George party fund. Lloyd George's followers had characteristics somewhat distinct from those loyal to Asquith, probably including more industrialists and certainly more strongly pro-war Liberals, while Asquith's supporters comprised more old fashioned Whigs and, ironically, more strong radicals. By September 1918, Lloyd George had clearly decided on a General Election being held as soon as possible. Even as Prime Minister, he was, however, in a politically weak position, representing, numerically, the much smaller component of a coalition government formed with the Conservatives. By the end of the war, it became clear that Lloyd George would be fighting the forthcoming General Election in tandem with the Tories, with pro-Asquith Liberals and Labourites comprising the opposition. How the Conservatives and Lloyd George Liberals would jointly contest the election was a matter of much dispute. At the end of October 1918, just before the Armistice, an agreement was reached between Lloyd George and the Tories whereby 150 pro-Lloyd George Liberals and 450 Tories would receive 'coupons' of endorsement. (For this reason the 1918 General Election is often known as the 'coupon election'.) No 'couponed' candidate would oppose another 'couponed' candidate, meaning that Tory and pro-Lloyd George Liberal voters would be very likely to vote for the 'couponed' candidate regardless of party. Asquith and his supporters in Parliament – defined by the Coalition's leaders as those MPs (106 in number) who had voted for Asquith in the 'Maurice debate' – received no 'coupon'. Nor did most Labourites, apart from a handful who supported the Coalition. On the other hand, a number of Tories and other right-wing MPs did not receive the 'coupon', but stood (and often won) nonetheless.

Many Tories were perfectly happy with this arrangement in the long term as well as the short term, and hoped that a Lloyd George-led Coalition would continue indefinitely. They saw in Lloyd George the reincarnation of Joseph Chamberlain, the fiery radical Liberal who became the arch-imperialist Unionist and a supreme Tory icon. (Lloyd George was acutely conscious of the parallel.) They also saw in Lloyd George one of the few men in politics who could stem the tide of Bolshevism and socialism then sweeping across Europe. This would, they feared, inevitably reach Britain, where only Lloyd George possessed either the charisma or the credibility among the working classes to stem the extreme left-wing flow. Lloyd George, for his part, had worked extremely well with Bonar Law and, indeed, with the Tories as a whole during the war (much better than with Asquith). As noted, Lloyd George had flirted with a grand coalition as early as 1910, despite his radical rhetoric. Only a few major issues now squarely separated the Unionists and Lloyd George's Liberals, the most important being tariff reform. In particular (as will be discussed below) the previously central question which divided the parties, that of Ireland, was in the process of being resolved, albeit with difficulty. Most leading Unionists and Lloyd George Liberals – the 'first eleven' as they were increasingly dubbed (from cricket terminology) – knew and respected one another. Men like Balfour, Curzon, Austen Chamberlain, and F.E. Smith on the Tory side, and Churchill, Addison, Isaacs, and Montagu on the Liberal side saw a mutuality of talent and, increasingly, of interest and outlook which generally went beyond the wishes of their backbenchers. Nevertheless, for both sides this arrangement was also one fraught with potential difficulties. Lloyd George and his supporters were clearly the minority faction of this coalition, whose radical tendencies would inevitably be curtailed by the Tory majority, while many Tory backbenchers (and some frontbenchers) deeply mistrusted Lloyd George and his entourage, even apart from memories of his pre-war career as the 'scourge of the dukes'.

Nevertheless, the electoral arrangement based on the 'coupon' was all-powerful in the General Election held at the very end of 1918. Lloyd George dissolved Parliament in early November – actually informing the King a few days before the end of the war – and announced that a General Election would be held on Saturday, 14 December 1918, the first time that all votes were cast on the same day. The Parliament dissolved at this time had been elected in December 1910; owing to the war no election had been held for eight years. It was regarded as a foregone conclusion that the Coalition would be returned, and the only serious question was the size of its majority. There was no real Opposition: although Labour nominated 388 candidates (over 300 more than in December 1910), it was not really regarded as a possible alternative government. Asquith and his Liberal followers initially gave general support to the government, while only 253 non-Coalition Liberals stood, not enough to form a majority government even if every single candidate was elected. To his credit, Lloyd George (and, indeed, his Tory allies) did not fully join in with the 'Hang the Kaiser!' (meant literally) electoral theme espoused in Northcliffe's *Daily Mail* and in other popular newspapers. Instead, the Coalition Manifesto (issued on 22 November) consistently took the high road, emphasising the need for a just and lasting peace and equitable national reconstruction. It was, indeed, a remarkably radical document, calling for the removal of all legal barriers based on gender, the reconstruction of the House of Lords as an elected second chamber, and responsible government in India. It advocated some protection for key industries and a compromise peace in Ireland. It is very difficult to believe that the Tories, the predominant element in the Coalition, would in normal times have issued a Manifesto containing many of these promises. At first, Lloyd George continued to do his best to point to a brighter future for the ordinary person. On 24 November at a speech in Wolverhampton he made arguably the most famous single remark of his entire political career when he asked 'What is our task?' to which he gave the reply 'To make Britain a fit country for heroes to live in.' Later in the campaign he called for improvements in health, education, welfare, aid for returned servicemen, and similar progressive measures.

Increasingly, however, the campaign was swept along by a tidal wave of popular xenophobia, and again and again Lloyd George (and everyone else) was interrupted by repeated popular demands to hang the Kaiser and extract the maximum of reparations from Germany. As the campaign proceeded, Lloyd George himself went along with these demands, agreeing by early December that the Kaiser would be prosecuted and all enemy aliens expelled from Britain (as was demanded by xenophobes). The popular mood of the day was best summarised by Sir Eric Geddes, Tory First Lord of the Admiralty, who promised on 9 December 1918 that 'We will get everything out of [Germany] that you can squeeze out of a lemon and a bit more ... I will squeeze her until you can hear the pips squeak.'

Everything in 1918 thus favoured the right-wing forces in politics. There was a genuine, popular move to the Right because of the war, one which was also echoed in the other victorious democracies. In the United States, Warren G. Harding and the isolationist Republicans were elected in 1920 with a record majority. In France, the so-called 'sky blue' Parliament, elected in 1919, gave the centre-right *Bloc National* a great majority, one which denied the atheistic radical Georges Clemenceau the French Presidency despite his inspiring leadership in the war. In terms of the political institutions of Britain, the enfranchisement of women, the success of Sinn Fein in Ireland, the splitting of the Liberal party, and the other consequences of the 1918 Representation of the People Act all differentially benefited the Tories, despite the personal status as a national hero enjoyed by Lloyd George. In particular, the creation of single-member constituencies throughout Britain greatly advantaged the Conservatives, with some historians estimating that the number of absolutely safe Tory seats may have risen from fewer than 50 in 1910 to 200–300 after 1918.

The results of the 1918 General Election were delayed until 28 December to allow soldiers to vote (641 000 out of 2.7 million issued postal votes did so). While everyone expected a huge swing to the Right, no one was prepared for what occurred:

	Votes	MPs elected	% of total vote
Coalition Unionist	3 504 198	335	32.6
Coalition Liberal	1 455 640	133	13.5
Coalition Labour	161 521	10	1.5
Total Coalition	(5 121 359)	(478)	(47.6)
Other Conservative	370 375	3	3.4
Irish Unionist	293 722	25	2.5
Liberal	1 298 808	28	12.1
Labour	2 385 472	63	22.2
Irish Nationalist	238 477	7	2.2
Sinn Fein	486 864	73	4.5
Others	572 503	10	5.3
Total	10 766 583	707	100.0

The Coalition candidates thus won 478 seats. This was itself one of the very largest government majorities in modern history. In the 1906 landslide the Liberals won 400 seats (with another 30 going to Labourites, at the time close allies of the government). In 1945 Labour obtained 393 seats. Nevertheless, this figure in 1918 considerably understates the strength of the government, for the 23 'uncouponed' Tories, 25 Irish Unionists, and many of the ten candidates elected from other parties (generally small extreme right-wing groups such as the National Party) were supporters of the government, or, more specifically, of its right-wing Conservative majority faction. Indeed, the Opposition was smaller than at any time since 1832, consisting only of 63 Labour members and 23 pro-Asquith Liberals (termed the 'Wee Frees' after the minority sect which remained after the reunification of the Free Church of Scotland with the United Presbyterian Church in 1900). As noted, the 73 Sinn Feiners refused to take their seats. More than half were actually in prison. Early in 1919, 29 Sinn Fein MPs met in Dublin to proclaim the Irish Republic. They established themselves as an Irish Parliament (the *Dail Eireann*) and named Eamon De Valera as President, Arthur Griffith as Minister of Home Affairs, and Michael Collins as Minister of Finance.

Together, the Unionists had elected nearly 385 MPs, over 150 more than the combined total of the two Liberal factions and Labour. Although the two branches of the Liberal party still possessed, between them, 161 MPs, they had been reduced to an ineffectual rump and would remain as such even if Lloyd George and Asquith came together. In terms of actual votes cast, the Coalition parties had apparently done less well, winning only 47.6 per cent of the total of 10.8 million votes cast. Nevertheless, this underestimates their actual performance. Another 6.5 per cent or so of the vote went to uncouponed Tories, Irish Unionists, and minor right-wing parties, while 67 Coalition candidates had been elected unopposed. In all likelihood the Coalition and its allies received the support of over 60 per cent of the electorate, the Asquith Liberals and Labour together receiving only 33.3 per cent of the vote. The most notable single result of the vote, indeed, was Asquith's defeat in his East Fife constituency, by an uncouponed Tory, after 32 years in the seat. Herbert Samuel, Runciman, Simon, McKenna, and most other of Asquith's loyal supporters were defeated. So were many prominent Labourites who appeared to have opposed the war, including Ramsay MacDonald, Arthur Henderson, and Philip Snowden.

Superficially, Lloyd George appeared, at the end of 1918, to be in a stronger political position than any Prime Minister since 1832. Many believed that he would remain Prime Minister for life, and certainly for 15 or 20 years. Yet his position was also much more vulnerable than it seemed at first glance. He was, in a real sense, a prisoner of the Tories, many of whom remembered Lloyd George the pre-war radical far more vividly than Lloyd George the great war leader. To continue in office after the dust had begun to settle on the war, Lloyd George would also have to win the peace. He would have to win the peace on terms set down by the Tories, which was arguably more difficult for him than winning the war against terms set by the Germans. Lloyd George's future was thus far from secure in the long run.

Although the small inner War Cabinet continued until 31 October 1919 (and was frequently convened by Lloyd George, who preferred it to the larger Cabinet), on 10 January 1919 the Prime Minister reorganised a normal, peace-time Cabinet. Only barely did it reflect the political realities of the new Parliament, for nine Cabinet Ministers were Lloyd George Liberals compared with ten Conservatives and one pro-Lloyd George Labourite. While Tories held most of the senior offices, the Liberals clearly received far more posts than the number to which they were entitled. Among the Tories, Bonar Law became in effect, but not in name, Deputy Prime Minister, as well as Leader of the House of Commons with the title of Lord Privy Seal, acting as Lloyd George's deputy in fact as well as in an *ex officio* capacity. Most historians who have studied this period agree that this was among the most harmonious and successful of such double acts in modern history, with Bonar Law's dour Scottish realism the perfect foil to Lloyd George's exuberant Welsh hyperactivity. Many historians also date the real decline of the Lloyd George Coalition from Bonar Law's temporary retirement on health grounds in March 1921. Bonar Law had been Chancellor of the Exchequer. He now relinquished this post to Austen Chamberlain (who had previously been Chancellor many years earlier, in 1903–05). Chamberlain, like Bonar Law, was of course a tariff reformer, but was unable, given the nature of the Coalition, to erect tariff walls to protect British industry. Balfour remained Foreign Minister until October 1919, when he was succeeded by Lord Curzon, the Lord President of the Council. The remaining Tory Cabinet ministers (Long, Milner, Sir Robert Home) were unremarkable, although there were some exceptions. F.E. Smith was promoted from Attorney-General to the Lord Chancellorship, with the title of Lord Birkenhead, at the age of only 46. With his well-deserved reputation for irresponsible brilliance and fast living, Smith's promotion to the leading position in the British judiciary at an incredibly young age for the office was greeted with universal amazement. The celebrated comment of a provincial newspaper on this occasion (often incorrectly attributed to the *Times*) that his appointment was 'carrying a joke too far' was typical. Smith proved to be a superior, reforming Lord Chancellor, but one whose reputation for ill-considered public statements and sailing close to the wind made him, throughout the 1920s, into the one Tory whom the Tory press (and most others) loved to hate. In November 1923, in a Rectorial Address at the University of Glasgow, Birkenhead noted that 'the world continues to offer glittering prizes to those who have stout hearts and sharp swords'. Normally, such a remark, little more than the stuff of *The Boy's Own Paper*, would be regarded as unexceptional, but in the atmosphere following the fall of Lloyd George, and with a Labour government a strong probability, Birkenhead's words, suggestive of the cutthroat buccaneer (and taken out of context), were regarded as scandalous, and became notorious. Also in the Cabinet was Sir Eric Geddes, a businessman of middle-class Scottish background, originally brought into the government during the war. Geddes was notable for showing how far the Tories had become largely a party of middle-class men keenly averse to state spending, attitudes formerly associated with Gladstonian liberalism. In particular, his chairmanship (when Minister of Transport) of the Committee on National Economy in 1921–22 led to sharp cuts in spending, totalling £75 million, a procedure known as the 'Geddes Axe'. The Liberals in Lloyd George's 1919 Cabinet lacked most of the heavyweight names in the party. Apart from Lloyd George, only Winston Churchill, appointed Secretary of State for War and Air Minister, was indisputably of the first rank, although Edwin Montagu, who remained at the India Office, and Christopher Addison, at the Local Government Board (renamed the Ministry of Health in June 1919), were also important figures. H.A.L. Fisher (1865–1940), a well-known historian who was Vice-Chancellor of Sheffield University, had been brought into the ministry as Secretary for Education in 1916, and continued until 1922. He proved to be an outstanding choice, one of the very greatest educational reformers of recent times. But Edward Shortt (1862–1935), a Sunderland barrister, who had been Chief Secretary for Ireland in 1918–19, became surely one of the least-known Home Secretaries of the century. In addition, one Labour man remained from the wartime Coalition: George Barnes (1859–1940) who continued as Minister Without Portfolio until January 1920.

Although the Cabinet was dominated by Tories, its composition showed how far the traditional aristocracy and landed gentry had been replaced by the upper middle classes as the dominant element in British society. Only Curzon was actually a traditional landed aristocrat in the meaning of the act, although Balfour and Churchill were closely related to great aristocratic families, while

Walter Long, the First Lord of the Admiralty, belonged to the *bona-fide* greater landed gentry. All of the other members of Lloyd George's 1919 Cabinet were drawn from middle-class backgrounds, with a sprinkling of 'self-made men'. Indeed, since it contained only two old Etonians (Balfour and Curzon) and two old Harrovians (Churchill and Long) among its 18 members, Lloyd George's Cabinet had fewer pretensions to high status origins, as this is usually defined, than any Cabinet ever appointed until that time. In this it reflected the trends characterising the Parliament elected in 1918 as a whole. In the new House of Commons, 260 members had been elected for the first time, an unusually large number. They were somewhat older, as a rule, than most newly elected MPs. Most were certainly too old to have served in the war and many were Tory businessmen; it was these facts which caused one Conservative MP (usually thought to be Stanley Baldwin) to describe the new Parliament as composed of 'hard-faced men who look as if they have done very well out of the war'. In the nineteenth century, virtually every heir to an important peerage almost automatically sat for a time in the House of Commons. At the 1918 General Election, despite the enormous right-wing majority, only 12 heirs to peerages were elected. Significantly, not one heir to a dukedom, the highest rank in the aristocracy, was elected to Parliament, although 30 or 40 years earlier nearly all such men were likely to be sitting in the Commons. That it consisted of 'hard-faced men', which first appeared in print in John Maynard Keynes' *Economic Consequences of the Peace* (1919), has become the most familiar way of describing the 1918 Parliament ever since.

The first item of business faced by Lloyd George's post-war government was the conclusion of a peace treaty at the Versailles Conference, held between January and May 1919. While all of the Allied nations sent representatives to this famous gathering, it soon became clear that most important decisions would be made by the United States, represented by President Woodrow Wilson, France, represented by Premier Georges Clemenceau, and Britain, represented by Lloyd George and a delegation additionally consisting of Balfour, Bonar Law, and George Barnes. The self-governing Dominions (and India) were also represented at Versailles by their prominent leaders, the first time that nations like Australia and Canada had played a separate role on the world stage.

The Versailles Conference had to decide three interconnected issues: the amount of reparations which the Allies would exact from Germany, the fate of the former German colonies, and the nature of the international organisation, known as the League of Nations, which would come into existence to prevent another war and to adjudicate disputes between nations. Fairly consistently, Lloyd George and the British took a midway position between the high-minded leniency and internationalism of Woodrow Wilson and the attitude of France, which sought draconian punishments for Germany. Thus, although France wanted to detach the western Rhineland from Germany and form it into an independent pro-French republic, a compromise was adopted which left it part of Germany, but demilitarised, subject to Allied occupation for 15 years. Germany's former colonies were ceded to their occupying powers (Britain, France, Australia, South Africa, and Japan), but technically as 'Mandates' of the League of Nations rather than as outright colonies, legally subject to League supervision (although this soon became a dead letter). Large-scale reparations were to be exacted from Germany, but their amount was to be decided by an international commission.

The outcome of the Versailles Conference pleased almost no one: before the end of deliberations, Lloyd George received a telegram orchestrated by Lord Northcliffe and signed by no fewer than 233 Tory MPs, criticising the Prime Minister for not presenting a full bill for reparations to Germany on the spot. This dissent by so many right-wing Tory MPs was the earliest evidence of disillusionment by more extreme Conservatives with an aspect of Lloyd George's policies. Over the next three years criticism from this quarter grew apace, until it eventually brought down Lloyd George and his government. Criticism came from elsewhere on the political spectrum, too, for precisely opposite reasons. Later, in 1919, John Maynard Keynes (1883–1946), who had been the official Treasury representative to the Versailles Conference, published his book *The Economic Consequences of the Peace*. (For many years Keynes was more renowned for writing this work than for inventing 'Keynesian' economics in the 1930s.) Drawing on a well-established neo-liberal tradition which, in 1910, had produced Norman Angell's equally famous work *The Great Illusion*, Keynes argued that the Versailles settlement was too harsh; in particular, making Germany pay vast reparations would simply injure her ability to purchase British goods and thus harm the international economy, contributing to world instability rather than the reverse. Keynes's work may be seen as the first evidence of disillusionment with Versailles and with harsh treatment of Germany. By the mid-1920s, the mood among mainstream opinion-leaders in Britain had clearly changed from one keen to punish Germany to one which sought international reconciliation and the normalisation of relations with the former enemy. Bad conscience over alleged harshness towards Germany has often been blamed (especially in France) with creating the mood which led, 15 years later, to appeasing Hitler rather than resisting him. The Germans themselves were appalled by the Versailles Treaty. The reparations and loss of colonies was bad enough, but worse still was the so-called 'war guilt' clause (Clause 231) of the final Versailles Treaty, under which Germany's signatories to the treaty had to admit the 'guilt' of Germany for starting the war. Few historians would accept such a sweeping claim about a very ambiguous series of events (even if, indeed, Germany bears a disproportionate share of the blame for starting the war); it led, in Germany, to enormous hostility towards the Treaty and was skilfully exploited by the Nazis in their rise to power. Finally, although the League of Nations came into being in 1919 as a well-intentioned predecessor body to what is now the United Nations, its ability to cope with international aggression and crises was vitiated by the fact that the United States Senate, dominated by 'isolationist' Republicans, refused to ratify the Treaty of Versailles or to join the League of Nations. Virtually everything about the Versailles Treaty and its underlying mood came unstuck within a few years.

The greatest problem facing the Lloyd George government, central to all the others, was economic in nature. Initially, for the first 18 months or so immediately following the war, there had been an extraordinary boom, with an unprecedented round of speculations and mergers. Excess profits made during the war went into domestic financing and it seemed, initially, as if the good times would last indefinitely, although price inflation had made almost every commodity twice as expensive as before the war. The first year or two after the war also greatly influenced the development of the British economy, with large-scale corporations and combines replacing, in large measure, the residuum of smaller-scale family capitalism prevalent before the war. The 'Big Five' high street clearing banks emerged in the form they took until 1970 (when the National Provincial and Westminster banks merged to form NatWest, thus initiating the 'Big Four'). A substantial fraction of the agricultural land owned by the aristocracy and gentry was also sold off at this time, sometimes to the new rich, sometimes to farmers, as the traditional bases of landed society changed greatly. The post-war boom lasted until the spring of 1920. In April 1920, the government raised the bank rate from 6 to 7 per cent, triggering the end of the boom and the beginning of a period of deflation and unemployment. During the interwar period, Western governments consistently misused the interest rate weapon (one of the few at their disposal), fearing inflation far more than unemployment. Soon after the start of the Great Depression of 1929, the American Federal Reserve Board raised interest rates for this reason. Most economists believe that this illogical action tipped a severe, but containable, recession into a worldwide economic catastrophe.

The next two years, 1921 and 1922, were a time of economic recession in most of the basic industries. Unemployment rose inexorably, doubling from 691 000 (5.8 per cent of insured workers, probably an underestimate) to 1 355 000 in March 1921 and then to 2 171 000 (17.8 per cent) in June 1921, only three months later. It then declined significantly, to 1 503 000 in June 1922 and to 1 432 000 (12.2 per cent) in December 1922. Throughout the interwar period unemployment remained at roughly this figure even in the best of times, declining only to 10.6 per cent of insured workers in 1927 and 11.0 per cent in 1929, the height of the 1920s boom. Thereafter, the Great Depression again played havoc with these figures: unemployment reached 22.5 per cent in 1932 before declining after 1933. But at no time before the outbreak of the Second World War was unemployment less than about 11.3 per cent, more than twice the level generally associated with full employment. During the 1920s there was never a time when fewer than about 1 059 000 workers were unemployed (a level reached in May 1927). The early 1920s also ushered in perhaps the major feature of the British economy in the interwar years, the sharp divide between the relatively prosperous south-east (especially Greater London) and the West Midlands on one hand, and the chronically appalling conditions in most of the old industrial areas of the north of England, south Wales and Scotland. In general, while the services and newer manufacturing industries such as automobiles and the production of consumer durables did well, the old industrial staple industries experienced a consistent, catastrophic slump, with trades such as shipbuilding, engineering, iron and steel, and many textiles experiencing extremely heavy unemployment. Since the opportunities for coal export disappeared as petrol, oil, and electricity replaced 'King Coal', the coal mining industry was similarly affected.

The government approached this chronically unfortunate situation in a fairly consistent way, by attempting to deflate the economy, reduce the national debt, reduce taxation (but only when possible), and restore the British economy to the normality it had enjoyed in the 'golden age' before 1914. British governments favoured the City of London over northern, industrial Britain, hoping to restore the City to its former pinnacle at the centre of the world economic system. Britain's return to the Gold Standard in 1926 was, of course, the best-known such tactic.

As Chancellor of the Exchequer from January 1919 until April 1921, Austen Chamberlain unpopularly raised taxes in order to reduce the national debt and eliminate a budget deficit. There was no question (as there would certainly have been after the 'Keynesian revolution' of the late 1930s) of deliberate deficit spending in order to increase employment, with the newly employed workers themselves in turn generating government revenue through the higher amounts of taxation and lower welfare benefits that their employment created. At that time, no one thought in Keynesian terms. Instead, nearly everyone viewed as central the extraordinary rise in the levels of the national debt, which had risen eleven-fold from 1914 to 1920. As a result of the increase in the national debt, even right-wing governments had to finance a level of expenditure far greater than in the pre-war years through levels of taxation much higher than in the pre-war period, despite the fact that virtually all Tories (and many Liberals) regarded tax rates as confiscatory and counterproductive. In 1914, the British government had raised £59 million in revenue through income tax, £10 million through the 'super-tax' on very high incomes, and £28 million through death duties. In 1920 these three figures were, respectively, £339 million, £55 million, and £48 million. A bachelor earning £10 000 retained £9242 in 1914 after paying income tax and super-tax. In 1920 he retained only £5813, although the pound had lost half of its value during the intervening years. Even in 1928, after three years of Tory rule, the same bachelor retained only £6968. The level of estate duty payable on a probated estate of £100 000 was 8 per cent in 1914, but 14 per cent in 1920 and 19 per cent in 1928, while the very top level of estate duty, payable on estates of £1 million or more, rose from 15 per cent in 1914 to not less than 40 per cent by 1928, and then rose even further, to 50 per cent throughout the 1930s. There was thus no full return to the 'good old days' for the rich and the upper middle classes, a reality which most opinion-leaders at the time thought central to Britain's economic malaise. Instead, Tory-dominated governments had apparently introduced 'Bolshevism' by the back door. Of course this mood of nostalgia should not be exaggerated: middle-class Britain for the most part was extremely well-off in the interwar years, while (unlike elsewhere in Europe) most of the familiar landmarks of British society and government survived the war intact. Nevertheless, the economic consequences of the war for the well-off were significant and lasting.

Because of the permanently higher levels of state expenditure and national debt, most opinion-leaders on the centre and right of politics saw sweeping reductions in government spending as the only justifiable response, in order to take the burden of taxation from the shoulders of the 'productive classes'. The most important manifestation of this was probably the so-called 'Geddes Axe', mentioned briefly above, named for Sir Eric Geddes (Minister of Transport until November 1921), the chairman of a Committee on Public Expenditure which was appointed in August 1921 and which reported in February 1922. Geddes' committee recommended savage cuts in all government departments. Its axe was swung impartially, recommending £41 million in cuts (equivalent to around £1.5 billion today) for the army and navy, the reduction of the salaries of teachers and policemen, cuts in public health spending, the merger of ministries. An enormous storm ensued, most loudly from the military. The government accepted cuts of £64 million compared with £75 million from the entire government recommended by Geddes. As a result, the government was indeed able to reduce the income tax from six to five shillings in the pound (i.e. from 30 to 25 per cent), while the size of the budget also declined significantly, from £1136 million in 1921 to £910 million in 1922 , but was still nearly five times higher than in 1914.

One solution to Britain's economic problems which was not tried in a comprehensive way was tariff reform. This was rather curious: the Tories, committed to tariff reform as a virtual panacea, had an enormous majority in the House of Commons, while the slump affected precisely those industries most threatened by foreign imports. Reginald McKenna's 1915 budget had imposed some tariffs, which were retained after the war. With Austen Chamberlain, the son of the father of 'tariff reform', at the Exchequer, a more wide-ranging scheme seemed very likely, even inevitable. Chamberlain did indeed make a move towards a fuller tariff scheme in his budgets, while the Board of Trade (headed after April 1921 by Stanley Baldwin, the future Prime Minister) pushed through the Safeguarding of Industries Act of 1921. While this measure was, at first glance, encompassing (over 6000 imported items were affected), it was extremely haphazard, seemingly offering protection for items (dolls' glass eyes were one) on which the economy did not depend. (Many such items were produced mainly in Germany; it was widely felt that tariffs aimed at German goods were morally justified.) The Act entirely lacked the imperial dimension which had been at the heart of all tariff reform proposals since 1903, and satisfied no one. Why, then, did the government not adopt a comprehensive programme of tariff reform and Imperial Preference of the kind which the National government enacted, with considerable success, in 1932? The main reason, of course, was the fact that half the Cabinet were Liberals, as were about 28 per cent of the Coalition's MPs. So long as Lloyd George was Prime Minister, it was impossible to contemplate a comprehensive tariff programme. As discontent with Lloyd George escalated among Tories, the failure of the government to abandon Free Trade in a wholehearted way was one of the main reasons for the revolt which ended the Coalition in October 1922, although one often overlooked by historians.

Two other issues, however, dominated the period in which Lloyd George was the peacetime Prime Minister. The first was the rise of the Labour party and of trade union militancy and the second was Ireland. The war had greatly strengthened the British Labour movement and also pushed it towards the Left. For the political left around the world, the seminal event of the contemporary period was the Bolshevik Revolution of 1917 and the establishment, in Russia, of the world's first overtly Communistic regime. Henceforth, all left-wing and trade union movements found it necessary to define their identities and orientations in relationship to Soviet Communism. For the first few years after 1917, and particularly in the deeply troubled period immediately after the war, open revolution and the possibility of establishing Soviet-style governments outside Russia loomed as real possibilities. Short-lived Bolshevik-style regimes were established in Bavaria and Hungary, and it briefly appeared that similar regimes might be established in Germany as a whole and elsewhere. Communist parties, loyal and, eventually, blindly loyal to Moscow, were formed throughout Europe, gaining considerable electoral support on the continent. A small Communist party was also established in Britain in mid-1920. Seemingly, however, Britain was impervious to these wider trends. The fact that Britain won the war, her institutions and Empire intact, her economy in good shape for the first few years thereafter, her constitutional habits very deeply rooted, made the prospect of revolution remote. In 1920, the Labour party rebuffed all attempts by the British Communist party to affiliate to it, initiating a policy of non-cooperation by Labour which remained until the demise of Communism. Nevertheless, for the first year or two following the Armistice, violent revolution appeared to some to be a possibility, and it was fortunate that the economic downturn did not begin until several years later. There was considerable rioting early in 1919 by soldiers over the snail-like pace of demobilisation, which the government was accordingly forced to hasten. More serious, however, was the spectre of 'Red Clydeside', also in 1919, a year famous among extreme left circles around the world as one in which high expectations of international revolution were dashed by the forces of established society and of reaction. A mass strike of all significant factories on the Clyde in January 1919 led to an enormous crowd marching on George Square in central Glasgow, where the red flag of revolution was hoisted at Glasgow City Chambers. The government in London took this move with the utmost seriousness, convinced that it might be replicated elsewhere. Troops with tanks and machine guns were sent to the outskirts of Glasgow. While these were never used, the Glasgow police baton-charged a crowd gathered at George Square on 31 January 1919, a mêlée broke out, the Riot Act was read, and troops occupied the city. The strike collapsed by mid-February. The radical upsurge had been led by Clydeside shop stewards, who had become a force to be reckoned with, and by three notable left-wing radicals, Willie Gallacher (1881–1965), Emanuel Shinwell (1884–1986), and David Kirkwood (1872–1955). While Gallacher became the long-time head of the British Communist party, Kirkwood and Shinwell remained in the Labour party and, in the time-honoured British way of doing things, were both eventually given peerages, ending their days sitting in the House of Lords beside the dukes and earls.

Although the wave of near-insurrectionary militancy associated with 'Red Clydeside' did not spread, Lloyd George was extremely fortunate that full employment continued until 1920. The reality of crippling strike action did, however, continue throughout his period of office. Indeed, the three years between early 1919 and mid-1921 were among the most troubled, in terms of labour disputes, in modern history. During this period there were nine strikes in which more than one million working days were lost (the equivalent of 100 000 workers each striking for ten days), headed by the national miners' strike of October 1921 in which 1.1 million workers participated and no less than 72 million working days were lost. There were, in addition, three other extremely serious miners' strikes in these years: in Yorkshire in January and July 1919, and throughout Britain in October 1920. A national railway workers' strike in September 1919 crippled British transport; there were also serious strikes among shipyard workers, cotton operatives, shipyard carpenters, and engineers in these years. During this period the trade union movement appeared to many to assume the form of a giant behemoth, for it was arguably the most powerful interest group in the country. Unions affiliated with the Trades Union Congress (TUC) represented 2.2 million members in 1913; this figure had grown, chiefly as a result of the war, to 6.5 million by mid-1920. Many of the most powerful and familiar trade unions were formed or consolidated at this time, including the Amalgamated Union of Engineering Workers (AUEW) in 1920; the Transport and General Workers' Union (TGWU) in 1922; the General Municipal Boilermakers and Allied Trades Union (GMBATU) in 1924; and two important unions outside traditional heavy industry, the Union of Post Office Workers (UPW) in 1921 and the National Union of Distributive and Allied Workers (NUDAW) in 1921. The largest individual unions now had vast memberships – for instance, the Miners' Federation of Great Britain had 800 000 members in 1921, the National Union of Railwaymen (NUR), formed in 1913, had 341 000, the TGWU 300 000 – and were the most powerful single institution in many industrial towns, especially those whose economy was based on one or two heavily unionised trades. In areas such as South Wales, Clydeside, Tyneside, and mining regions up and down the country the trade union of the dominant industry quickly came to be the best-organised public group of any kind, the power behind local politics. After 1918, the traditional landed and middle classes looked upon such areas as virtually alien nations, while class bitterness and hostility aimed at the erstwhile rich and powerful of the region escalated as the economy deteriorated and socialist or quasi-socialist ideological undercurrents became the common staple of many workers and their families.

Given the power of the unions, much depended upon their ultimate aims for Britain's industry. Although Labour was committed to nationalising the basic industries, this was clearly meant to apply more forcefully to some industries than to others. In particular, coal mining and the railways were generally seen as the prime candidates for passage into public ownership. Coal mining was probably the most dangerous and back-breaking occupation in Britain: if a mine explosion or cave-in did not kill its workers quickly, a more drawn-out death awaited many by some horrifying lung disease. Colliery owners were, typically, absentee and remote, wealthy magnates, while coal mining communities were close-knit and self-sufficient, ready material for class war. The railway represented the type of natural monopoly which most socialists thought ripest for state ownership. Another industry seen as a good candidate for nationalisation, or at least state control, was the drink trade. Public house opening hours were heavily restricted during the war and remained tightly controlled until the 1990s.

Lloyd George dealt with demands for nationalisation by appointing various high level commissions to study the questions of nationalisation and workers' benefits. Most historians see these as delaying tactics which did the trick: after the first unsettled post-war years, the most militant aims of the unions were moderated. In 1919 a Coal Industry Commission, headed by Sir John Sankey (1868–1948), a high court judge (and Lord Chancellor in the 1929–31 Labour government and in the National government from 1931–35), was appointed to study the future of the mines. Unusually, half of its members were trade unionists or were pro-Labour, among them Sidney Webb (1859–1947, later first baron Passfield), the celebrated Fabian and husband of Beatrice Webb, and R.H. Tawney (1880–1962), the famous socialist theorist and academic. When the commission reported, it was sharply divided, but Sankey recommended 'either nationalization [of the mines] or a method of unification by national purchase and/or joint control'. It also recommended, rather curiously, the 'nationalization of royalties' and the establishment of a minister of mines. These findings were bitterly contested by its members who represented the industry's owners. Lloyd George took the opportunity of a miners' strike in mid-1919 to reject outright nationalisation, but a Coal Mines Act of 1919 gave miners a seven-hour day. Although the unions felt betrayed by Lloyd George, there was little else that he could do: it seems inconceivable that a Parliament with an enormous right-wing majority would have nationalised the coal mines, even in the very troubled conditions of 1919.

Lloyd George's main policy towards labour increasingly became one of attempts at reconciliation through the creation of joint labour–capital councils and prevarication at any far-reaching or radical steps. The so-called Whitley Councils were continued after the war. Named for J.H. Whitley, a Liberal politician who chaired the commission which recommended them, they were established in 1917 as joint employer/trade union councils, chiefly in smaller industries, with an aim of adjudicating disputes. Lloyd George also passed the Industrial Courts Act of 1919, which set up a court, headed by a leading judge, to decide on matters of dispute, including pay claims, between owners and trade unions. These had limited success, most notably in 1920 when Ernest Bevin (1881–1951), later a leading Labour minister, secured pay increases for the dockers' union. Nevertheless, strife continued. The government dealt with a national railway strike, also in 1919, by calling in troops and organising an emergency road transport network, presaging its actions in the General Strike of 1926. Many in the government would have preferred the nationalisation of the railways (which had been operated by the government since the beginning of the war). Instead, by the Railways Act of 1921 the 120 private railway companies were amalgamated into four large groups: the Great Western; the London, Midland, and Scottish; the London and North Eastern; and the Southern railways. A Railway Rates Tribunal was also created, and companies were limited in the revenues they could earn. The period of railway amalgamation, which lasted until nationalisation in 1948, proved to be one of the most successful in the history of Britain's railroads, with a good deal of modernisation and investment in new infrastructure.

The climax of this period of intense labour unrest, but one dominated by the large unions rather than by extreme left-wing shop stewards or militants, came with two other disputes over coal miners' wages in mid-1920 and again in early

1921. In 1920, it appeared that the three biggest and most powerful unions, the miners, railwaymen, and transport workers, would cooperate in a massive strike. The three unions, known as the 'Triple Alliance', planned for a strike to begin in late October. The government passed an Emergency Powers Act to take control of basic industries, and the unions backed down, signalling this by an agreement over miners' wages due to expire on 31 March 1921. The next day, another coal miners' strike began. This strike, however, came at a time of worsening economic conditions and the miners were offered not increases in pay but substantial cuts. Once again, a general strike headed by the 'Triple Alliance' appeared almost certain. In retaliation, the government recalled all members of the armed forces on leave, requisitioned motor vehicles, and created a special Defence Force with 75 000 volunteers. On Friday, 15 April, after intense negotiations between the government, Coalition MPs, and trade union leaders, the 'general strike' was called off. In Labour and socialist memory, 15 April 1921 is known as 'Black Friday'. It may well indeed have been the last possible date on which the preconditions for a class-based 'civil war' existed in Britain. Thereafter, the steady decline of manufacturing industry, and the heavy growth in unemployment, caused the union movement to lose both members and influence. Between September 1921 and September 1923 the total membership of unions affiliated to the TUC declined from 6.4 million to 4.4 million, a drop of 32 per cent. Working days lost through strikes, which totalled 26.6 million in 1920 and 85.9 million in 1921, declined to 19.9 million in 1922, 10.7 million in 1923, and to only 8.4 million in 1924. 'Normality' was returning to British society and both Labour and the trade union movement were being integrated into Britain's structure of governance, but under relatively unfavourable circumstances. Thus the General Strike of 1926, although it involved a far greater number of striking workers than the disputes of five or six years before, took place at a time when there was little or no possibility of it becoming a socialist insurrection against established society, but instead showed a surprising degree of goodwill on both sides.

Even more than the threat to the established order seemingly posed by militant trade unions was the threat to the political and economic bases of society represented by the apparently relentless rise of the Labour party after about mid-1919. Between July 1919 and July 1922 Labour candidates won 14 by-elections from other parties, far more than either the Unionists or Liberals did (although these began, of course, with many more seats). Most of Labour's by-election gains came at the expense of the Liberals, especially the Coalition Liberal supporters of Lloyd George. Among Labour's key by-election victories at this time were those at Spen Valley (in the West Riding) in January 1920, where Thomas Myers (an unsuccessful candidate in 1918) narrowly defeated Liberal and Coalition Liberal candidates, who split the anti-socialist vote; and at Dudley in March 1921, where the Labour candidate, James Wilson, narrowly defeated a Tory junior minister (Sir Arthur Griffith-Boscawen) who had been legally obliged to contest the seat upon appointment to the Cabinet. Labour moreover won by-elections in all parts of the country – in London (Southwark South-East in December 1921 and Camberwell North in February 1922), in the industrial north (Heywood and Radcliffe in June 1921 and Manchester

Clayton in February 1922) and even, more disturbingly still, in rural areas (South Norfolk in August 1920, and Bodmin in February 1922). Often, although not always, these successes occurred because the non-Labour parties were split, especially when both the Coalition Liberals and pro-Asquith Liberals contested the seat simultaneously. Even when Labour did not win, it usually increased its vote considerably compared with the 1918 General Election. Again, the rise in the Labour vote occurred almost everywhere, even in the unlikeliest places. At Taunton (in Somerset), the victorious Unionist candidate received nearly 13 000 votes at both the 1918 General Election and a by-election which took place in April 1921, but the Labour candidates increased their votes from 4800 to 8300.

This steady, seemingly relentless rise of the Labour party terrified all Tories and many Liberals, such that it is hardly an exaggeration to say that British politics increasingly revolved, in the five years or so after 1919, around the response to the rise of Labour by the non-Labour parties. In view of the fact that there was now virtual universal adult suffrage, that the poor outnumbered the rich, and that a strong Labour party, representing the working classes, had now emerged, it seemed to many observers only a matter of time before it would win a General Election. This state of affairs was accentuated by the fact, although it had elected only 63 MPs to the 1918 Parliament, that Labour was now effectively the Opposition. For the Liberals to resume their former position of being the left-of-centre major British party, at the very least reunion of the two wings of the party was a *sine qua non*. Asquith, indeed, re-entered the House of Commons at a by-election at Paisley in February 1920, triumphantly defeating a Labour candidate (whose total vote, however, rose considerably compared with what it had been at the General Election) and a Unionist. It seemed for a time as if Asquithian Liberalism was indeed about to rise from the ashes. Yet all attempts to secure some kind of reunion between Asquith and his former supporters and Lloyd George came to nothing. Meetings in mid-1921 between Asquith, Grey, and other Liberals, plus the dissident Tory Lord Robert Cecil, to lay the basis of a centre-left opposition which would also include left-wing Tories and moderate Labourites, went nowhere. The great stumbling block was the total opposition of Lloyd George, at this stage, to reunion with Asquith. This would have meant the dissolution of the Coalition, with its Tory majority, and possibly the end of Lloyd George's career.

In addition, the Liberals, irrespective of who led them, appeared to many to be truly yesterday's men, fighting on a programme of old-fashioned radicalism which had been made obsolete by the war. Only Labour, with its avowedly socialist agenda (at least on paper), appeared to advocate a radical solution consistent with post-war realities. Above all, only Labour could win the allegiance of the majority of the working class, and especially of the trade unions which the party largely existed to represent.

For these reasons, a real sense of desperation overtook the non-Labour forces in British politics at this time, based on fear that the established orders were living on borrowed time; this sense of desperation probably exceeded the mood of extremism among the 'die hard' Tory right in Edwardian politics. Some intellectuals and activists on the right of British politics were convinced that an international revolutionary conspiracy, a 'hidden hand', existed, directed from Moscow, of which the Labour party, Sinn Fein, and Lloyd George's soft-skinned Liberal supporters were the advance guard. For one of the few times in modern British history, something like overt anti-semitism was expressed by figures on the extreme right, linking 'foreign Jews' to Moscow's plans for 'world revolution'. There was also a surprising amount of anti-Americanism, and resentment at the United States' new-found position of world economic supremacy. Talk of arming a 'citizen's army' to resist Labour whenever it came to power was also occasionally found on the Right at this time. By the time Lloyd George fell in 1922, deep hostility towards him personally, towards his entourage, and towards his policies in Ireland and India, were widespread on the far right of the Tory party.

On the other hand, many centre-right Tories (and many pro-Lloyd George Liberals) drew the opposite conclusion: that the only way to halt the inevitable growth of Labour was for the anti-Labour forces to combine, probably leading to a formal merger between the Tories and the Coalition Liberals. This course was favoured by many (not all) frontbench Tories, especially Austen Chamberlain and F.E. Smith. Lloyd George himself often appeared to support a broad anti-socialist front, although he continued to maintain a separate, well-funded Coalition Liberal party apparatus and also sometimes gave the impression that he himself would like to become leader of a broad radical coalition, encompassing Labour members and Liberals. He was, after all, the foremost pre-1914 radical, and had certainly not accepted the Tory viewpoint on every issue. While some Labourites might well have welcomed Lloyd George's adhesion to their cause, possibly as its leader, most others mistrusted him as much as right-wing Tories did, seeing in him a chameleon-like demagogue with few fixed principles. Lloyd George himself did little or nothing at this time to destroy the existing Coalition or his position of leadership in it. Ironically, the Prime Minister, a man with an unrivalled reputation at the end of the First World War, quickly became dependent for his political survival on the attitudes of other men. This unsatisfactory state of affairs eventually led to his downfall.

The most central concern of the Coalition government for most of its peacetime history, however, concerned Ireland. Irish affairs had been at the forefront of British politics for over a century; from the 1880s, they often appeared to dominate most political debate. Few other issues so sharply separated pre-war Liberals from Tories, with Liberals favouring Home Rule for Ireland, Tories opposing it and championing the rights of the Protestant minority in Ulster. Between 1919 and 1922 Ireland experienced both a bloody series of internecine wars and a settlement of the Irish question which remains fundamentally in place today, based upon the division of Ireland into an independent Catholic South and largely Protestant Ulster, which has remained within the United Kingdom. This settlement was, in many respects, the most notable achievement of the Coalition government, although it was accompanied by unparalleled bloodshed and the long-term mutual animosity of the two Irish communities.

The sequence of events in Ireland between 1918 and 1922 was also extremely complicated, and can be explained here only skeletally. At the 1918 General Election, 73 Sinn Fein candidates were returned, winning virtually every seat in southern Ireland. As explained, they refused to take their seats in the Westminster Parliament but met in Dublin and, in January 1919, declared themselves to be the *Dail* (Parliament) of *Saorstat Eireann*, the Irish Republic, which had been proclaimed in the Dublin Easter Uprising in 1916. Sinn Fein then led a campaign to oust Britain from Ireland which comprised boycotting and also increasing violence with 18 murders recorded in the second half of 1919.

The British government of course did not recognise the *Dail* and in August and September 1919 'proclaimed' (declared illegal) both Sinn Fein and the *Dail*. It decided to crack down on the rebels by reinforcing the Royal Irish Constabulary (RIC) with ex-soldiers, the so-called 'Black and Tans', so named because they initially wore surplus khaki uniforms together with black belts and dark green hats. Another force, the Auxiliary Division of the RIC (known as the 'Auxis'), manned chiefly by English ex-officers, was also recruited. The Black and Tans and Auxis were given virtual *carte blanche* to destroy Ireland's militants, and in particular the Irish Republican Army (IRA), which was formed in 1919 from the pre-war Irish Volunteers. Sinn Fein and the IRA actively recruited from Catholic Ireland, and were heavily funded by Irish-American groups, often far more extreme than the Irish themselves. Throughout 1920 and into 1921 Ireland saw a bloody guerrilla war, one of the earliest such wars ever fought, let alone in the United Kingdom, in which shadow armies of Irish rebels and 'Black and Tan' official forces gave no quarter to one another. There were perhaps 50 000 British troops in Ireland in 1920, and about 15 000 IRA supporters. It is believed that between January 1919 and July 1921, 752 Irish persons and 230 British police and soldiers were killed. Innumerable atrocities took place, such as the 'massacre' at Croke Park, Dublin on 21 November 1920 (known as 'Bloody Sunday') when 12 persons watching a hurley match were killed by the Black and Tans, in retaliation for the murder by the IRA earlier that morning of 14 British officers and civilians. The Irish Nationalists employed tactics to gain publicity which they would continue to employ many decades later. In October 1920 Terence MacSwiney, the Lord Mayor of Cork, died in London's Brixton Prison after a hunger strike lasting no less than 74 days. The IRA turned his death and funeral into an international event, beginning with his body lying in state at St George's Roman Catholic Cathedral in Southwark. Although the British forces eventually got the upper hand, they were fighting under the handicap of having to show some restraint, for fear of liberal opinion in Britain and of being court-martialled in extreme cases of brutal behaviour. The British never attempted to execute the leaders of the IRA, and, indeed, showed less ruthlessness in this respect than the Irish generally showed to their own dissidents. Of course, in a democracy, it is virtually impossible in the long run to govern by force against the will of a large section of the population.

Simultaneously with all of this bloodshed major political changes in the status of Ireland were taking place. The Home Rule Act of 1914, which would have created an Irish Parliament, from which Ulster would be excluded for six years, had been suspended during the war. In September 1919, a new Home Rule Act was drawn up by the Tory-dominated Cabinet, and became law in December 1920. Its provisions were a mixture of pre-war Home Rule and

Ulster loyalist demands. Ireland was to have Home Rule, but remain a part of the United Kingdom. There were to be two Parliaments, at Dublin and Belfast, the one in Belfast to govern the six most heavily Protestant counties of the north rather than the nine counties that historically comprised Ulster. A Council of Ireland, its members drawn from the two parliaments, was to have powers over such matters as railways common to both parts of the country. Partition was to continue indefinitely until both parliaments voted to end it: as far as Ulster was concerned, that time would presumably never come.

The Protestants of Ulster accepted this new Parliament, although without much enthusiasm. The IRA had frequently (and counterproductively) targeted Protestants and their property in Ulster, and Protestant opinion in Ulster became, if anything, even more extreme. What can reasonably be described as anti-Catholic pogroms took place throughout Ulster at this time. Hundreds of Catholic families were driven out of their villages, and Catholic workers were sacked from many Belfast shipyards if they refused to 'curse the Pope'. Sixty-two persons were killed. The Ulster Volunteer Force formed the basis of the Ulster Special Constabulary, founded to keep order. Southern Ireland completely rejected the 1920 Home Rule Act, boycotting the British machinery of government. An election throughout Ireland under the Act, held in May 1920, was treated by Sinn Fein as an election to the *Dail*, their Irish Parliament. Sinn Fein won 124 of 128 seats outside Ulster, and refused to take part in the Southern Home Rule Parliament. In Ulster, the Unionists won 40 of the 52 seats, with Sir James Craig, the pre-war leader of the Ulster Protestants, becoming Prime Minister of Northern Ireland, a position he held until his death in 1940. Relations between southern and northern Ireland became even more frigid than before.

In mid-1921 the British government decided that something had to be done to secure a workable settlement in Ireland. Extensive negotiations had been conducted behind the scenes, with King George V playing a conciliatory role for which he has been given insufficient credit. Lloyd George decided to meet Eamon de Valera, the leader of the *Dail* Cabinet. Amazingly, a truce came into effect on 11 July 1921. After a good deal of delay, de Valera met Lloyd George, who, sitting in front of a giant map of the British Empire in order to impress him, invited Ireland to become a Dominion. De Valera remained unmoved, but agreed to attend a conference to work out a settlement. This conference, held in London, began in mid-October. The most extreme Sinn Fein opponents of a settlement were left at home. The British position was to offer southern Ireland Dominion status, with recognition of the King as Head of State and Ireland continuing as part of the Empire being Lloyd George's non-negotiable demands. Sinn Fein was (rather curiously, in retrospect) willing to go a certain way to meeting the demand, with de Valera agreeing to recommend a 'treaty of free association with the British Commonwealth' which recognised the King as head of the Commonwealth. At the conference, Sinn Fein's position became even more moderate when Britain promised to redraw northern Ireland's boundaries so that it would, sooner or later, have to rejoin the south. Lloyd George exercised all his magical gifts of persuasion, and there is general agreement that this was the outstanding achievement of his peacetime government.

In the end, he got almost everything he desired. A treaty was agreed to on 6 December 1921. Britain recognised the *Dail* as the law-making body of southern Ireland. That country, to be known as the Irish Free State, became a Dominion, with all members of the *Dail* required to swear allegiance to the British Crown. The Royal Navy would retain the use of four 'treaty ports' in the new state. On the key question of Ulster, northern Ireland could continue as a separate entity if it wished, but a Boundary Commission was to readjust the borders 'in accordance with the wishes of the inhabitants'.

A great split then occurred in southern Ireland between the supporters and opponents of the Treaty. Most southern Irish, it would seem, supported the Treaty. It passed through the *Dail* by a small majority, 64 : 57. The British Lord-Lieutenant formally handed over powers to the new government on 16 January 1922. Instead of peace, however, there now ensued what is generally known as the Irish Civil War, which lasted from March 1922 until May 1923. The Anti-Treaty component of the IRA, known as the 'Irregulars' conducted a war of terror and destruction in which over 100 country houses (belonging to Irish Unionists or Treaty supporters) were burned and hundreds of deaths occurred. The Four Courts, major government premises in Dublin, were seized by the rebels but recaptured in July 1922. In the process, the building was burned down. The Four Courts housed the Irish Public Record Office; as a result, most of Ireland's historical archives were destroyed. The previous month, Sir Henry Wilson (an Ulsterman), formerly Chief of the Imperial General Staff, was assassinated by two Irishmen on his London doorstep. Kidnappings and the destruction of property occurred on a large scale. The new *Dail* government of the Irish Free State responded to the Civil War with a firmness – indeed, brutality – which went far beyond Britain's past actions. Some 77 rebels were executed by the *Dail* government, among them Rory O'Connor, the leader of the Irregulars and also, for the crime of possessing firearms, Erskine Childers, the famous novelist of British background who had become an extremist Irish patriot.

Timothy Healey, a long-serving Nationalist MP, became the first Governor-General of the Irish Free State in December 1922, and affairs in the south gradually settled down. Northern Ireland, it soon became clear, would refuse any change to its boundaries (and had no intention of ever accepting them). In 1925, the proposals of the Boundary Commission, which recommended changes in the borders between Ulster and the Irish Free State, were rejected by both sides and the boundaries of Ireland became permanent. In the late 1930s, the IRA again turned to violence, and Irish neutrality emerged as an issue, though a minor one, during the Second World War. Nevertheless, the Irish settlement of 1921–22 ensured that, for nearly 50 years, Ireland would no longer be a problem for British politics, until the 'troubles' began again in 1969. Lloyd George's settlement was approved by most moderate opinion in Britain. On the right of the Conservative party, however, it caused considerable bitterness, with the creation of the Irish Free State viewed widely as cowardly surrender to terrorists and betrayal of the significant body of Unionists and landowners in the south. Many right-wing Tories believed that Lloyd George hoped to force Ulster into the Irish Free State. Among Tory 'die-hards' (numbering about 50 MPs) the Irish settlement was a potent element in the deep and increasing mistrust of Lloyd George which eventually ended his premiership.

The Lloyd George government also enacted major policy departures in the social field. Here, too, however, a combination of economic constraints and irresistible political pressures to modify these policies exerted by the Coalition's Tory majority worked to curtail the more progressive instincts of Lloyd George's closer supporters. In three fields, in particular, was this pattern seen: housing, unemployment relief, and education. As well, a somewhat similar trend, but one not directly linked to the others, can be seen in the status of women.

Lloyd George had won the 1918 election promising a Britain of 'homes fit for heroes', a pledge which was seen as applying most centrally and literally to housing. The demands of the wartime economy necessarily meant that home-building and construction had been almost non-existent for five years, while millions of British people continued to live in urban slums of the worst kind. To meet this demand, the government enacted the Housing and Town Planning Act of 1919, commonly known as the 'Addison Act' in honour of its author, Dr Christopher Addison, at the time a loyal Lloyd George Liberal MP of advanced views who served as President of the Local Government Board from January–June 1919 and then as the first Minister of Health, with a newly enlarged portfolio, from June 1919 until April 1921. Under the Act, local government units were given the power to build houses for rental in their areas, with the central government providing generous subsidies for construction. (These subsidies proved far too expensive and were cut back after 1922.) The Act did greatly increase the number of houses built in Britain. In 1920–21 the private sector built 23 000 new houses nationwide, with the public sector building 17 000 (total 40 000). In 1921–22 the relative totals of the two sectors was 32 000 and 110 000 (total 142 000) and in 1922–23, 45 000 and 67 000 (total 112 000). In all, nearly 214 000 new houses were built under the Addison Act. Most were 'council houses', built in large estates on vacant land at the edge of towns. While these were obviously better than the inner-city slums they replaced, they perhaps began the trend to suburban alienation in place of the older urban face-to-face communities. During the interwar period home building became one of the greatest, and most typical of British industries, with private builders responsible for about two-thirds of houses built, the public sector for one-third. As a result, the number of houses in England and Wales rose from 7 550 000 in 1911 to 7 979 000 in 1921, but then to 9 400 000 in 1931 and 11 263 000 in 1939, while the percentage of the population living in owner-occupied homes (those which were owned outright or being purchased) rose from an estimated 10 per cent of all households in 1914 to 25 per cent in 1939. Whatever its drawbacks, the Addison Act was one of the more important pieces of legislation of the Lloyd George government.

Additionally, the government passed a series of measures which increased the scope of unemployment relief. The Unemployment Insurance Act of 1920 offered insurance to most wage-earners earning less than £250 a year (domestic servants, agricultural labourers, and low-paid civil servants were excluded), greatly extending the scope of pre-war welfare legislation. Insurance (15 shillings per week for men, 12 shillings for women), paid to unemployed workers, made it extremely difficult to continue the fiction that 'outdoor relief' (i.e. payment to the unemployed) apart from the workhouse was immoral or counterproductive. As unemployment increased from 1921 onwards, the government doubled the 16-week period in which benefits could be paid, but with a gap between the periods. An array of committees was also established to ascertain whether recipients were genuinely seeking work. This greatly increased resentment towards the whole system, especially when articulate middle-class men and women found themselves unemployed. Wives and dependent children of unemployed men were covered by a separate act in 1921. For those not covered by any scheme, the local Poor Law Guardians were able to provide additional relief, increasingly known as the 'dole'. Some Boards of Guardians were more generous than others, especially the Poplar Council in the East End, which paid up to 43 shillings per week to each local unemployed family. This was financed by the rates and by borrowing. Excessive borrowing by councils was precluded by Parliament in 1921. George Lansbury (1859–1940), the then Labour Mayor of Poplar (and later leader of the Labour party in the House of Commons, 1931–35) and other local councillors refused to pay any local rates to the London County Council, claiming that the money was needed in Poplar and that the wealthier districts of west London should pay more. They were jailed for over a month. 'Poplarism', as their stance became known, seemed to herald a mutiny by poorer urban boroughs which the government was anxious to avoid, and legislation lightening their burden was rushed through Parliament. The government also initially attempted an ambitious programme in education. Under the Education Act of 1918, the leaving age for compulsory attendance at schools was raised to 14, and provision was made for part-time education for all children between 14 and 18.

All of the Lloyd George government's social legislation was passed with remarkably little opposition, the Tory majority in Parliament agreeing to legislation, often virtually without demurral, which nearly all would surely have opposed as near-revolutionary before the war. Most Tories were genuinely anxious to reward those who fought the war, or bore its burdens at home, and were well aware that adamant right-wing opposition to social reform would simply make the rise to power of Labour, even perhaps the extreme left, more likely. So long as Britain's economy was prosperous, there was little opposition to these provisions. As soon as the economy started to decline, however, most right-wing MPs threw their weight behind the 'Geddes Axe' and similar measures of retrenchment, and most of the generous social expenditure passed in the first post-war years was greatly modified.

Another, very important, area of social policy which perhaps demonstrated a similar pattern was that of women's affairs. During the war, hundreds of thousands of women took over, at least temporarily, the occupations previously reserved for men. Their reward came with the 1918 Reform Act which gave women over 30 the right to vote. This was followed, in 1919, by the remarkable Sex Disqualification (Removal) Act, which abolished, at a stroke, all barriers to entry to the professions, universities, and the exercise of any public function based upon sex or marriage. Professions such as the law were now open to women, and, within a few years, Britain had its first female barristers and solicitors. However, while theoretically far-reaching in the extreme, the effects of the Act were diluted because barriers of the type which one might assume that it explicitly precluded were allowed to remain, especially restrictions on married women entering higher administrative positions or receiving equal pay to men. As well, some professions remained completely closed to women, such as the Anglican clergy. Nor could the Act compel any employer to appoint or promote a woman. The senior ranks of business, and most professional activities, remained almost entirely all-male preserves for many decades to come. Nevertheless, however tiny, a phalanx of women began to enter many areas of occupational life previously closed to them. As before, such fields as writing, art, and the stage were open to women, and many of the most renowned and typical cultural figures of the interwar years were female – Virginia Woolf, Agatha Christie, Dorothy L. Sayers, Daphne Du Maurier – to mention only some of the most obvious authors.

More widely, however, after the war many women who had temporarily entered an all-male trade left it (or were compelled to leave), and most, one assumes, eventually married and became housewives, despite the numerical excess of women over men among the age-cohorts affected by the war. It has been widely observed that pre-war feminism declined greatly in visibility and drive after 1918, although some historians have seen it as changing direction rather than disappearing. Why the militant suffragette movement became so much less visible after 1918 than it was previously, and why the feminist movement had to wait for more than 50 years to produce a new wave of women's rights activists equally committed, have also been endlessly discussed. One might offer three reasons for these facts: the striking achievement of most suffragette goals in 1918–19; the growth of the Labour party, where radical feminists were now offered a potentially powerful home but in the short term achieved little influence; and the fact that the so-called 'Second Wave feminism' which arose in the 1960s revolved centrally around a sexual agenda (such as abortion reform) which was politically impossible to advocate, much less achieve, in the 1920s, or around 'equal opportunities' legislation which was also far in the future.

After 1919 the Lloyd George government did little or nothing specifically to ameliorate the condition of women, although the extension of the non-contributory 'dole' advantaged those, especially women, outside the traditional workforce. A Maternity and Child Welfare Act, 1918, empowered authorities to establish 'home help' clinics and schemes: this was really the only major piece of legislation directly affecting women passed between 1919 and 1922. In the mid-1920s came some further legal advances for women, but only after Lloyd George's fall, ironically under right-wing Tory governments.

The whittling down of advanced social programmes and expenditure perfectly illustrated the dilemma that Lloyd George increasingly found himself in: dependent upon the Tory Coalition majority, but separate from it. Lloyd George could never decide whether he was really still a radical or had now become a Tory and, as a result, was widely mistrusted. From 1921 onwards, he entered into the decline phase of his premiership, with most of the high hopes of 1918 increasingly dashed. There were structural reasons for this decline: his Coalition Liberals had no clear-cut policies, while many of their senior leaders, appointed during the war, began to retire in numbers. In March 1921, Bonar Law suddenly resigned from politics for health reasons (severe high blood pressure). Bonar Law's retirement was widely seen as an extremely grave blow to the prospects of Lloyd George remaining in power; since December 1916 the two had acted together as a uniquely harmonious team. Austen Chamberlain, Bonar Law's successor as leader of the Conservative party, who officially became leader on 21 March 1921, was also a strong supporter of continuing the Coalition – if anything, even stronger than Bonar Law – but lacked the authority among backbench MPs which Bonar Law had attained.

In the end, however, it was a series of events in 1922 which brought an end to the Lloyd George government. The first was the so-called 'Honours Scandal', which erupted that year. In order to build up the funding required to maintain an independent Coalitionist Liberal party machine, Lloyd George more or less openly sold titles – peerages, baronetcies, knighthoods. There was really nothing new in this: throughout modern British history, anyone who contributed generously to party coffers could expect an honour of some kind. Nor did this practice cease with Lloyd George, but has continued under every subsequent Prime Minister (including Labour Prime Ministers). Moreover, contrary to popular belief, the scale of titles awarded by Lloyd George was not really lavish. During his six years as Prime Minister, he created 91 new peerages and advanced in rank 25 existing peers. This compares, for instance, to 84 and 15 under Asquith, who served as Prime Minister for eight years, and to 44 and six under Ramsay MacDonald during his four years (1931–35) as National Prime Minister. Lloyd George had, moreover, to honour all the victorious generals and admirals of the war, and to reward an unusually large number of senior MPs in 1918, who retired after a Parliament which lasted for eight years instead of five. Where Lloyd George differed from others was that he was quite willing to sell for cash a title to literally anyone regardless of merit, even men who had rendered no public service whatever. (The Prime Minister normally recommended all such titles to the king.) The money – a peerage allegedly cost £50 000 – went into the Lloyd George fund, which was used for such political causes as the Prime Minister favoured. The alleged misuse of the honours system became well known at the time – Cardiff, in particular, became known as the 'city of dreadful knights' – and remains one of the few things which the layman remembers today about Lloyd George's peacetime government. Of course, a rich man who wished to purchase a title had no guarantee that he would be successful. One hopeful, Sir James Buchanan, a Scottish whisky millionaire who wished to become Lord Woolavington in the New Years Honours list of 1922, allegedly gave Lloyd George a cheque for £50 000, but signed it 'Woolavington' and dated it '2 January 1922': the cheque would be worthless unless a peerage was forthcoming. Buchanan was indeed created Lord Woolavington on 1 January 1922.

Lloyd George ran into real trouble over this issue early in 1922. He made several particularly controversial recommendations for peerages early that year, especially Sir William Vestey (created Lord Vestey), a meat-importing multimillionaire notorious for his large-scale tax evasion, and, Sir Joseph Robinson, a South African 'Randlord' who had been fined no less than £500 000 for fraudulent practices in South Africa only a few months earlier. After Robinson's peerage had been announced, but before it was officially 'gazetted', he had in fact to 'return' it, one of only two men in modern times who have had to do this. In June 1922, the House of Lords held an extremely damaging debate on the awarding of honours, which did much to alienate right-wing Tory opinion from the government.

Considerable opposition greeted aspects of Lloyd George's imperial and foreign policies. Perhaps the most extreme example of this occurred in India, and especially in opposition to the policies of Edwin Montagu, the Coalition Unionist who was Secretary of State for India from July 1917 until March 1922. In August 1917, in response to the beginnings of Indian nationalism, Montagu, on behalf of the government, declared that the long-term aims of Britain towards India was 'the progressive realisation of responsible government in India as an integral part of the British Empire'. In theory, this was a revolutionary step, the first time that Britain had promised something like self-government to a non-white part of the Empire. No one really expected anything of the sort for generations to come, if ever, and even with the best will in the world, there were manifold problems to its achievements. India was divided into innumerable separate units of administration, with a significant share of the country, the princely states, nominally ruled by independent potentates. The deep animosity between Hindus and Muslims was already a reality. The overwhelming majority of the population were illiterate peasants, with the caste system all pervasive. India had not been a truly unified nation for centuries. Very powerful economic and military interests in Britain were opposed to making any concessions whatever to native Indian nationalism. Both the progressive intent of Montagu's statement, and the stringent limitations on what Britain was actually prepared to do, were evident in the document that the government issued in response to an inquiry into India's future. Known as the Montagu–Chelmsford Report of 1918 (Lord Chelmsford was Viceroy of India, 1916–21), its recommendations were, in turn, embodied in the Government of India Act, 1919. The aim of this act was to create a 'dyarchy' (joint rule), with certain powers delegated to native-dominated legislative councils, but with the most important powers reserved to the respective local British Governors. A bicameral legislature was also to be established for the whole country, but it too would be subject to the ultimate control of the Viceroy and his Executive Council.

The 1919 Act came amidst unprecedented unrest sparked by nationalist forces. One incident, in particular, stood out as marking a turning-point in Indian opinion: the so-called Massacre at Amritsar. After four Europeans had been murdered by a mob, a large but unarmed crowd assembled in an enclosed space in Amritsar, a town in the Punjab near Lahore, close to what is today the border with Pakistan. The crowd was ordered, by Brigadier-General R.E.H. Dyer (1864–1927), commander of the Punjab, to disperse. It failed to do so, whereupon Dyer ordered his soldiers to fire upon the crowd. This resulted in 379 persons killed and 1208 injured. Amritsar is often seen as the point at which nationalistic demands for independence became strident and eventually inevitable. Dyer was relieved of his command in 1920 following an official investigation. In the debate in Parliament on the massacre, Dyer's actions were (not surprisingly) condemned by the government, especially by Edwin Montagu, the Secretary of State for India. Most right-wing Tories, however, strongly supported Dyer as the 'man on the spot' who had to deal with the realities of the situation as he found them. The attitude of the government was seen as supine, of a piece with its later 'surrender' to Sinn Fein. Montagu (who was Jewish) became a particular *bête-noir* of the Tory far right, attacked with malice often tinged with anti-semitism. When Montagu was sacked by Lloyd George in March 1922 after he leaked a Cabinet document concerning the Turkish situation, right-wing Tories erupted with a torrent of cheering and shouting. The tentative steps the government had taken down the road to Indian self-determination were bitterly resented by many Tories, although once in power their power continued down much the same path.

It was another aspect of foreign policy which was instrumental in bringing about Lloyd George's fall. The early 1920s had witnessed many moves towards international reconciliation throughout Europe, especially the Genoa conference of April–May 1922, the first at which Weimar Germany and the Soviet Union were represented. Yet the conference proved a failure, hallmarked by France's refusal to contemplate any reduction in German reparations, and the Treaty of Rapallo signed between Russia and Germany, which signalled a *de facto* alliance between the two outcast states. In south-eastern Europe, another crisis loomed. Turkey, under her great leader Mustapha Kemal Ataturk, had gradually been reasserting herself against Greece and against the treaties which had delimited her territories. Chanak, in the Dardanelles, had been declared a neutral area and was held by British troops. In September 1915 the Turks advanced on this area intending to take it. The Cabinet decided on resolute action, with Lloyd George's key supporters, especially Churchill, Balfour, Birkenhead, and Austen Chamberlain, being especially outspoken. Britain tried to summon support from the Dominions and from France. For a variety of reasons, support from most of the Dominions was not forthcoming, nor was it from France or other former allies such as Italy. War with Turkey was only narrowly averted by a last-minute compromise.

The Tories in the Cabinet were, rather surprisingly, cool towards resolute action; one might have assumed that they would be enthusiastic for 'gunboat diplomacy' and a 'whiff of grapeshot' against a minor power like Turkey, especially as Turkey was the aggressor and directly threatened the post-war settlement. Apparently, most Tories decided that adventurism in the Near East was less desirable than normality. It was at this stage that many backbench Tories decided that Lloyd George would have to go and the Coalition would have to end.

Although the Conservative party had always included a 'die-hard' minority which detested Lloyd George, his supporters, and the Coalition, those in the party who backed the continuation of the Coalition, and the eventual 'fusion' of the Tories and Coalition Liberals were even stronger. Virtually every front-bench Tory of repute took the view that Labour was almost certain to make major gains at the next General Election (due before December 1923), perhaps even to win it outright, and that accordingly all non-socialist forces had to unite to survive.

As usual, a great deal of debate and negotiation, public and private, ensued. On 15 October 1922, Lord Curzon, the Foreign Secretary, resigned in protest at Lloyd George's Chanak policies. Austen Chamberlain, the leader of the Conservative party, then decided to call a meeting of all Conservative MPs to decide on their attitude towards the Coalition. This meeting, held on 18 October 1922 at the Carlton Club (the Conservative party's London head-quarters, then on Pall Mall) was one of the most celebrated and momentous in modern British political history. While the right-wing MPs in favour of ending the Coalition were given little chance of winning, two things happened to alter the outcome. First, Bonar Law was rather miraculously restored to health and, more amazingly, and after a great deal of hesitation and advice, decided to do his best to end the Coalition which he had done so much to create. Bonar Law had, moreover, now decided that he was not merely ready to end the Coalition, but to head a purely Tory government. At the Carlton Club meet-ing, he was received with great enthusiasm, while Chamberlain and the other pro-Coalitionists were heard quietly.

Second, a new potential leader of the Conservatives emerged almost out of the blue. This was Stanley Baldwin (1867–1947; later first earl Baldwin of Bewdley). Baldwin, the son of a wealthy ironmaster who was chairman of the Great Western Railway, had been a little-noted backbench MP until a few years previously. In 1921 he had entered the Cabinet for the first time as President of the Board of Trade. In the Cabinet he hardly spoke, had virtually no influence, and was widely regarded as a nonentity. Nevertheless, he had many hidden resources. These included, especially, a foot in both the old and new Tory parties owing to his status as an industrialist (he was a steel manufacturer and ironmaster in Worcestershire) who had been educated at Harrow and Cambridge and loved the English countryside. He also had an unexpected literary bent and an inherited flair for words; Rudyard Kipling was his cousin. At the Carlton Club meeting Baldwin gave a memorable speech describing Lloyd George as a 'dynamic force but a dynamic force was a very terrible thing'. Lloyd George had destroyed the Liberals 'and would destroy the Tories as well if given a chance'. This speech had a great effect and significantly increased Baldwin's prestige. Yet no one could have known that Stanley Baldwin would prove to be Britain's most important political leader during the next 15 years.

Bonar Law then spoke in favour of ending the Coalition, and the Carlton Club meeting decided by 187 votes to 87 to leave the Coalition, Chamberlain and nine other ministers siding with the minority. Chamberlain and the Tory ministers were then compelled to resign from the government. Lloyd George resigned an hour later, ceasing to be Prime Minister on 19 October 1922. The King then sent for Bonar Law to form a purely Conservative government. This was highly unusual, since Austen Chamberlain was still nominally leader of the party while Bonar Law was technically only a backbench MP. Bonar Law at first demurred, but gave way and, on 23 October 1922, was officially elected as leader of the Conservative party and was also officially appointed Prime Minister. He had come back, almost literally, from the political dead.

Few foresaw it at the time, but Lloyd George would never hold any government office again and both he, and his style of government, were finished. It seems clear that Lloyd George's post-war government was a severe disappointment, although the great expectations of the war years could not readily be fulfilled and it was not Lloyd George's fault that 20 years of economic crisis had begun. Yet Lloyd George's ideological ambiguity was surely also the cause of much mistrust. Clearly, the government's resolution of the Irish question, however marked by bloodshed, was its greatest achievement, and it had many other positive achievements as well. But the legacy of corruption, 'kitchen cabinets', adventurism, and the generally fevered and hothouse atmosphere of the post-war years meant that, in the end, most members of the majority Conservative faction in the Coalition were only too ready to see the back of Lloyd George.

6
Britain in the 1920s: Bonar Law, MacDonald, and Baldwin

Bonar Law was faced with the prospect of forming his Cabinet without the support of most of the heavyweight Tory members of Lloyd George's government. Thirteen Conservative ministers in the former government declined to support the new government. The most important of these were Austen Chamberlain, Birkenhead, Balfour, and Sir Robert Horne (1871–1940). Indeed, only four Cabinet ministers in the former government were willing to join the Bonar Law Cabinet – Curzon, Baldwin, Viscount Peel, and Sir Arthur Griffith-Boscawen. Curzon decided at the last minute to desert Lloyd George. This probably cost him the dukedom which he apparently expected as a reward, whenever Lloyd George left office. (He would probably have become Duke of Scarsdale, one of his family titles.) It did, however, gain him reappointment to the Foreign Office, an important source of continuity between the two governments. Curzon was (it was universally conceded) a good Foreign Minister, one of the strongest and most experienced of the century. Deserting Lloyd George did, however, enhance Curzon's reputation for untrustworthiness, which may have cost him the Prime Ministership less than a year later. Bonar Law gave the Exchequer to the then little-known Stanley Baldwin, President of the Board of Trade in the previous government, and one of the principal speakers in favour of ending the Coalition at the Carlton Club debate. Baldwin was a successful businessman, and the appointment was perfectly sensible, although Bonar Law's first choice had been the Liberal businessman Reginald McKenna, whose lucrative appointment as Chairman of the Midland Bank prevented him from taking up the offer.

The other members of Bonar Law's Cabinet were, for the most part, then little-known Tory figures, who were, from the first, derided by their opponents as lightweights. 'A government of the second eleven' was Churchill's famous description. (It might be necessary to explain that this term means the substitute side in a cricket match: an American equivalent term would be the 'B team' or 'minor leaguers'.) A 'government of under-secretaries' was another oft-repeated description, a reference to the fact that many in Bonar Law's Cabinet (for instance Leopold Amery (1873–1955), the new First Lord of the

Admiralty) had been junior ministers under Lloyd George. There is some truth to these characterisations: Bonar Law's government certainly had some peculiar features. It contained more peers than any post-1914 government, no fewer than seven out of 16 Cabinet ministers, including a duke (Victor Cavendish, ninth Duke of Devonshire), the last duke to sit in a Cabinet, two marquesses (Curzon and Salisbury), an earl (Derby), and three viscounts (Cave, the Lord Chancellor; Peel; and Novar, the Scottish Secretary). In addition, two other Cabinet ministers, William Bridgeman (1864–1935), and Edward Wood (later second viscount and first earl of Halifax, 1881–1959), were the sons of aristocrats. With three other knights (all of whom – Sir Arthur Griffith-Boscawen, Sir Clement Montague-Barlow, and Sir Philip Lloyd-Graeme – had double-barrelled surnames) the government certainly had an upmarket appearance which many saw as clashing with the dominant spirit of the post-war age. (In 1924 Sir Philip Lloyd-Graeme (1884–1972) rather confusingly changed his name, upon inheriting a legacy, to Sir Philip Cunliffe-Lister, by which name he is better-known. More confusingly still, in 1935, he was created Viscount Swinton and, in 1955, earl of Swinton, by which name he is better known still.) As well, only a minority of the new government had held cabinet rank previously – seven out of 16 – which was curious among a group of ministers who had, after all, been part of Coalition governments for the previous seven and a half years.

Nevertheless, the government clearly did not deserve the derisory label it attracted (chiefly from the pique of those who refused to join). Baldwin was to prove one of the greatest politicians of the first half of the twentieth century; Wood (Halifax), Amery, and perhaps Cave were men of great ability. At the junior ministerial level the government introduced Neville Chamberlain (1869–1940), Sir Samuel Hoare (1880–1959), and Sir Douglas Hogg (1872–1950; later first Viscount Hailsham) into the circles of governance for the first time. While not sparkling, it was perfectly competent, even talented, just as was the government with which it is sometimes compared, the so-called (for its alleged obscurity) 'Who? Who?' Tory government headed by Lord Derby and Benjamin Disraeli, which briefly held office in 1852, formed from the rump of Protectionist Conservatives who did not follow Sir Robert Peel and most of the other brilliant men of the party into endorsing Free Trade.

Having formed a right-wing Tory government, Bonar Law then proceeded to call a General Election. Bonar Law had taken office on 23 October 1922. Four days later he dissolved Parliament, and called an election for 15 November 1922. The General Election campaign was one of the most confused in modern history. The Liberals were still divided into two very hostile camps, led by Lloyd George and Asquith, who detested each other. Everyone knew that Labour would gain many seats, but no one knew how many, or how far the Labour tide would roll before it was halted. The Tories, although in power, notably lacked many of their most senior leaders, including Austen Chamberlain, who had actually been leader of the party until four days before the General Election was called. For the first time since 1800, southern Ireland sent no MPs to Westminster, a factor whose significance could not be gauged in advance. Nor could the likely effects of the women's or the war veterans' vote be calculated.

In the election campaign which followed, Bonar Law made his central theme that of a return to normality. 'The crying need of the nation at this moment ... is that we should have tranquillity and stability both at home and abroad ...' Throughout the interwar period, this seemingly uninspiring election theme almost always proved to be a potent vote-winner. In America, Warren G. Harding was elected President in 1920 by a record majority when he promised 'not nostrums but normalcy' following the social experimentation of Woodrow Wilson and the turmoil of the war. After Bonar Law, Stanley Baldwin became synonymous with advancing a policy of 'tranquillity', also with great electoral success. Bonar Law was, clearly, trying to differentiate the Conservatives from both Lloyd George and his Liberals, with their frenetic and possibly corrupt policies, and from the doctrinaire extremists of the Labour party. This appeal was especially successful, it would seem, among women and with middle-class former Liberals who could no longer support that party. It also represented a marked contrast with the radical Toryism of the Edwardian Conservative party, which came so close to advocating insurrection over the Ulster question.

It was not a foregone conclusion that the Tories would win and indeed Bonar Law might well have completely misjudged the mood of the electorate. The opaqueness of the election was further compounded by the fact that, there were many candidates who described themselves as Independent Conservatives, as Lloyd George Liberals, Asquith Liberals, or simply as Liberals, or as candidates of the Cooperative movement or as Socialists, most of whom might or might not attach themselves to one or another of the larger parties. In the end, how-ever, Bonar Law and the Tories won a substantial victory, at least in terms of numbers of MPs if not of votes cast. The overall results of the election held on 15 November 1922 were as follows:

	Total votes	MPs elected	% share of total vote
Conservative	5 500 382	345	38.2
National Liberal (i.e. pro-Lloyd George)	1 673 240	62	11.6
Liberal (i.e. pro-Asquith or independent)	2 516 287	54	17.5
(Total Liberal)	(4 189 527)	(116)	(29.1)
Labour	4 241 383	142	29.5
Others	462 340	12	3.2
Total	14 393 632	615	100.0

The main results of the election are clear from this table: the Tories won a clear victory. Their win in 1922 was, in fact, their first outright triumph, without the benefit of coalition partners, since 1900. (Although the Tories had not won since 1900, they were actually in government for twelve of 22 years, in 1900–05 and 1915–22.) Nevertheless, the Conservatives victory was far less comprehensive than it seemed. Sixteen of the elected Tory MPs described themselves as 'Independent Conservatives' and the like, while the Tory contingent included the remaining pro-Coalitionists, like Austen Chamberlain. Much more seriously and strikingly, the Conservatives won only 38.2 per cent of the total vote, meaning that the Liberals, Labour, and smaller party candidates took nearly 62 per cent of the vote. Should the two left-of-centre parties ever unite, the Tories faced potential electoral annihilation. (Forty-two Tory MPs were elected unopposed, compared with 15 for all other parties. Since they were in safe seats, this meant that the Conservative vote would have been higher than 38.2 per cent had all been opposed – probably around 42–43 per cent – although still well short of a majority of the votes.)

The biggest gainer at the 1922 election was, clearly, the Labour party, which became the official opposition with 142 MPs. Labour nominated 411 candidates and won 4.2 million votes, 29.5 per cent of the total vote. There are (as is so often the case) two ways of looking at Labour's results. Compared with 1918, when it won 2.4 million votes but elected only 63 MPs (out of 388 candidates nominated) it had come very far indeed. Yet it was also clear that Labour was not, in the near future at least, going to sweep all before it. While perhaps 75 per cent of Britain's population could be termed working-class, less than half of that number voted Labour. In many regions of the country, especially the south-east of England apart from London's slums, Labour won almost no seats. It was now almost all-powerful in such areas as south Wales, the industrial West Riding, Tyneside, and Clydeside, but did surprisingly poorly in places where it should, arguably, have done better, such as south London, Liverpool, Manchester, and Birmingham. Labour's 142 seats were 15 fewer than the Unionists won in 1906, regarded as the greatest major party electoral debacle in modern history.

The Liberals won a very respectable total of votes, nearly 4.2 million, only 52 000 fewer than Labour, or 0.4 per cent of the total vote cast. Yet they elected only 116 MPs, 26 less than Labour. The main reason for this, and the major reason for the Liberals' weakness in the post-1918 period, was their lack of contiguous geographical areas where they continued to secure a plurality of the vote. In 1922, only northern Scotland, Wales, parts of Devon and Cornwall, and of the East Midlands remained fairly solidly Liberal, although they managed to elect the odd MP or two almost everywhere. In a 'first past the post' electoral system without proportional representation, the Liberals were seriously disadvantaged compared to the Tories, with their stranglehold on the south-east and in most rural areas, and Labour, with their grip on mining and engineering seats. In addition, in 1922 the Liberals were bitterly divided, lacking either a single leader or a coherent policy. Lloyd George Liberals won slightly more seats than those won by Asquith supporters, but gained considerably fewer votes.

The election of 1922 was the first to feature a pattern which recurred periodically throughout the twentieth century: a split (very roughly) of 40 : 30 : 30 as between the Conservatives, Labour, and the Liberals. Given the nature of the British electoral system, this strongly advantaged the Tories, who were very likely to win handsomely even without a majority of the votes cast. As well, the turnout in the 1922 General Election, 71.3 per cent, was much higher than the turnout in 1918 (58.9 per cent) and about what it would be at most subsequent elections (except those of the 1950–66 period, when it was higher), possibly showing that women now voted more readily than in 1918. It might also be noted that two Communists were elected to Parliament in 1922: J.T. Walton Newbold, a teacher, at Motherwell, and a Parsee (one of the few non-Europeans elected to Parliament before the 1980s), Shapurji Saklatvala, at Battersea North.

During the election campaign Bonar Law had made few promises, apart from commitments to rigorous economy. He did, however, make some which were noteworthy. He promised to implement the Irish Free State Bill. This promise effectively buried the Irish question in British politics, given Bonar Law's unimpeachable credentials as a Unionist. Perhaps more importantly, he promised not to implement any programme of tariff reform before holding a second General Election on this issue. Balfour had given a similar pledge in 1910; Bonar Law evidently felt that former Liberals had to be brought into the Tory camp at all costs. This pledge cost Bonar Law's successor Stanley Baldwin dear only a year later. The only other notable feature of the election was a pledge given by Labour for a capital levy (a once-only tax on wealth) to pay off the war debt. This proved so unpopular that Labour was forced to drop it during the campaign, one of the first real hints that Labour was withdrawing from a full-scale commitment to anything like socialism. Bonar Law's own personal character, as a transparently honest, blunt, and down-to-earth 'ordinary' businessman, also had a strongly positive effect on the election outcome and ought not to be minimised. In this, he also paved a path which Stanley Baldwin exploited with finesse and much greater renown.

Although brief, Bonar Law's term of nine months (23 October 1922–20 May 1923) as Prime Minister was not without incident. A major controversy emerged early in 1923 over the issue of the international resettlement of the war debt. Britain owed the United States £900 million for munitions and other wartime supplies, but was itself owed much more by France and other European powers. Britain protested strongly to America that what was required was an all-around settlement aimed, hopefully, at a general cancellation of the debt. This wish, expressed by Arthur Balfour to the American government in August, 1922, met with a chilly American response. In January 1923, Stanley Baldwin, the Chancellor of the Exchequer, and Montagu Norman, Governor of the Bank of England, travelled to America for high-level talks on the issue, regarded at the time as crucial to Britain's recovery. As things stood, Britain was obliged to pay £46 million per year in interest to the United States. Bonar Law and the British government wished this to be reduced to £25 million. The Americans were willing to reduce the demand to £34 million for ten years, but not to go any further to meet the British position. Despite very strong pressure from Bonar Law not to compromise, Baldwin and Norman acceded to the American proposal as the best they could get, given the resolute isolationism of the Republican administration in the United States and, in particular, of the American Congress. Baldwin compounded his handling of the negotiations by making a series of ill-considered remarks upon his return to England, and was widely but inaccurately reported in the press as describing the American Congress as composed of 'hicks from way back'. Bonar Law was furious at being presented with a *fait accompli* by Baldwin, and in late January 1923 threatened to resign. Everyone in the Cabinet felt that this would have been a disaster for the Tory government. There was no obvious successor. Baldwin, hitherto almost unknown, had caused the crisis, while it was notable that even then there was no great enthusiasm for Curzon, widely assumed, in the press, to be Bonar Law's heir apparent. Most of the Cabinet reluctantly supported Baldwin's deal with the Americans, and successfully prevailed upon Bonar Law to continue in office. This incident is noteworthy for not only showing that the prospect of Curzon as Prime Minister pleased few, but that Baldwin had already established a kind of ascendancy over the Cabinet.

Bonar Law also had considerable trouble with by-elections during his brief premiership. Sir Arthur Griffith-Boscawen, the Minister of Health, had lost his seat at the 1922 General Election and proceeded, after much delay, to lose a by-election in a seat which seemed absolutely safe for the Tories. As a result, in his place Bonar Law appointed Austen Chamberlain's half-brother Neville (1869–1940) to the Health ministry, a position he filled with considerable distinction for most of the 1920s. Neville Chamberlain, who had never sat in a Cabinet before his appointment by Bonar Law, became even more influential in the Tory hierarchy and in 1937 became one of the most controversial (many would say disastrous) of all modern Prime Ministers. The Conservatives' loss of safe by-election seats was due to intervention by pro-Coalition Conservatives. Throughout his term as Prime Minister, Bonar Law was handicapped by the fact that the 'heavyweight' Tory Coalitionists, especially Austen Chamberlain, refused to join the government, regarding the Tory government as hopelessly incompetent and likely to collapse completely once Bonar Law, already known as an ill man, eventually retired. Bonar Law's government was also notable for having no specific plans to deal with unemployment (which, although extremely high, was admittedly beginning to fall). It rejected all proposals made by the trade unions for employment creating schemes, pinning its hopes on the restoration of prosperity and normal trading through rigorous deflation. The one positive option endorsed by most Tories to deal with unemployment, tariff reform, had been ruled out in advance by Bonar Law's election commitment. Although 'normal times' did appear to be returning in some measure, the Conservatives had no positive plans to deal with unemployment, in contrast to Labour's more activist philosophy.

Bonar Law had increasingly suffered from a throat ailment which had impeded his ability to speak in public. Early in 1923 this condition worsened, and in May, inoperable throat cancer, likely to kill Bonar Law within six months, was diagnosed. On 20 May 1923 he resigned as Prime Minister, a very sick man, and died that October. Certainly the most unlikely man to head the Conservative party since Disraeli, he was an outstanding political tactician and an ideal number two man. His term as Prime Minister was too brief to form a clear verdict, but many of the interwar Conservative party's underlying trends and philosophies, often attributed to Baldwin, were actually Bonar Law's. If he was indeed 'the unknown Prime Minister' (as Asquith reputedly whispered at his funeral) this does not mean that he was without influence and impact.

Bonar Law's sudden resignation created a political vacuum almost unique in twentieth-century British politics. There was no such post as 'deputy Prime

Minister' in 1923, and no procedure, within the Conservative party, for electing a successor to Bonar Law. Bonar Law pointedly did not directly recommend a successor. There is no clear-cut explanation for this inaction other than that he was very ill. Until a few months before his resignation, Bonar Law clearly assumed that Curzon would succeed him, and spoke at some length to Baldwin about leading the House of Commons when the next Prime Minister, Curzon, sat in the Lords. Shortly before his death, however, Bonar Law had cooled very considerably on Curzon, being offended (as many others also were) at his arrogance. Thus, while Curzon was certainly the most likely successor, there was no heir apparent. Bonar Law had tried to woo Austen Chamberlain back into the government with a promise to relinquish the Prime Ministership in his favour within a year, but had been turned down.

The choice of Bonar Law's successor now fell to King George, one of the last times that this decision has been that of the Sovereign. As is well known, after taking soundings, chiefly through his Private Secretary Lord Stamfordham (Sir Arthur Bigge, 1849–1931), the King sent for Baldwin to form a government. Historians have endlessly debated the reasons for this. The King was heavily influenced by an unsigned memorandum, now known to have been written by J.C.C. Davidson (who had been Parliamentary Private Secretary to both Bonar Law and Baldwin) leaning heavily towards the choice of Baldwin. Curzon's membership of the Lords, at a time when the Labour party had no representation at all in the upper house, certainly weighed heavily against him. Curzon was, as noted, also surprisingly unpopular within the Conservative party, being seen as arrogant; he was widely mistrusted as a partisan of Lloyd George who had deserted the Coalition at the last possible moment for personal advantage. In contrast, although Baldwin was new to the front ranks, he was already well regarded, even widely popular, in a way which was the mirror-image of Curzon. Curzon was, of course, bitterly disappointed, actually crying when he heard the news, describing Baldwin as 'a man…of the utmost insignificance'. The choice of Baldwin was also extremely important in constitutional terms, making it all but impossible for a peer ever to become Prime Minister again. Such a possibility arose twice more in the twentieth century. In 1940, at a moment of supreme national peril, King George VI agreed that Winston Churchill should succeed Neville Chamberlain instead of Lord Halifax, whose presence in the Lords was a factor (although not the major one) in this decision. In 1963 a peer, Lord Home, actually became Prime Minister, but (under the provisions of a recently enacted legislation) disclaimed his peerage and was immediately elected to the Commons as Sir Alec Douglas-Home.

Baldwin's lasting reputation among people of his time (if not necessarily to historians) as a plain-spoken, decent Englishman, slightly naive and putting his faith in the time-honoured verities, was in the process of becoming established even before he became Prime Minister. In a well-known speech in Parliament in February 1923 he contrasted the Soviet system with what was necessary to bring 'salvation to this country and for the whole world': 'four words of one syllable … "faith", "hope", "love", and "work".' This very typical exposition of Baldwin's style endeared him to a generation of Englishmen looking for stability and honesty in a world of change. In the age of television rhetoric of this kind would be greeted with deep cynicism. In the 1920s, it was enormously popular. As well, throughout his career Baldwin went out of his way to depict himself as a simple country squire, even a simple farmer (in reality he was an ironmaster and steel manufacturer who had been educated at Harrow and Cambridge), happiest when walking through the mud to round up his pigs. Although Baldwin was sincere enough in this self-portrayal, it also contained a strong element of deliberate artifice, hearkening back to a simpler, more honourable lifestyle in keeping with Britain's most emotive myths. (In the same vein, at this time American President Calvin Coolidge, who lived in Boston, Massachusetts, used to be popularly photographed in American Indian headdress.)

Baldwin's first job as Prime Minister was to form a Cabinet. Plainly, most of the existing ministers would remain in place. His primary tasks were to find a replacement for himself as Chancellor of the Exchequer and, if possible, to bring the leading Coalitionist Tories into the government. There was also the problem of Curzon, who reluctantly agreed to stay on as Foreign Minister (where everyone agreed he was doing a good job). Baldwin could not persuade either Robert Horne or Reginald McKenna to become Chancellor of the Exchequer, and from May until August 1923 combined the two offices of Prime Minister and Chancellor. Since this entailed an enormous workload, he appointed Sir William Joynson-Hicks (1865–1932), an extreme right-wing 'die-hard' Tory MP, to the Cabinet as Financial Secretary to the Treasury to do the Chancellor's routine work. In August 1923, Neville Chamberlain was appointed Chancellor, serving until the government left office five months later. At the same time he also brought Sir Samuel Hoare, Lord Robert Cecil (1864–1958), the brother of Lord Salisbury, and Sir Laming Worthington-Evans (1868–1931), three other prominent Tories, into the Cabinet, and gave a ministerial post, Chancellor of the Duchy of Lancaster, to his Private Secretary and confidant J.C.C. Davidson (1889–1970). In other respects the Cabinet remained the same. Baldwin was not able to convince any of the leading Coalitionist Tories to join the government, with the exception of Worthington-Evans, and the rift between the two factions remained unhealed. Baldwin's initial period of six and a half months as Prime Minister between his appointment and the General Election of December 1923 contained few achievements. The Housing Act of 1923, generally seen as the government's most important measure, put through by Neville Chamberlain as Minister of Health, offered subsidies for the building of housing by private builders or local authorities. This act led to much house-building by private builders but little by local governments, who could simply not afford the costs. Despite this meagre record, and despite a slight rise in unemployment, in the latter half of 1923 (to 1 350 000 in October, or 11.7 per cent of the workforce), the new government seemed in reasonably good shape. It lost only one by-election (to the Liberals at Tiverton in June) between May, when Stanley Baldwin became Prime Minister, and December. On 25 October 1923, however, Baldwin dropped one of the greatest bombshells in twentieth-century British politics when he announced, in a speech at Plymouth, that he wished to revive Imperial Preference and a high tariff wall in order to reduce unemployment, but, in view of Bonar Law's pledge in 1922, could not do so without holding an election, and therefore had

decided to call one. It is difficult to think of any parallel in modern British politics to Baldwin's actions in holding a General Election nearly four years earlier
than necessary while enjoying a large, unthreatened Parliamentary majority, for
no compelling reason and out of the blue. Given the seminal outcome of the
General Election which Baldwin called, historians have vigorously debated his
motivations.

Baldwin's announcement was quickly termed 'insanity' by many Tories, while
other commentators highlighted the curious dichotomy in his personal character, in which a cautious, sensible half existed side-by-side with an unpredictable
and illogical component. (This was widely attributed at the time to Baldwin's
genealogical mixture of down-to-earth 'Saxon' ancestors and wildly romantic
Scottish forebears.) Most historians who believe that Baldwin had a deliberate
plan in mind point to two or three advantages for the Conservatives. First, it
gave the Tories a positive programme to deal with unemployment and economic
distress which could compete electorally with Labour for the working-class
vote (and which, since it did not entail a rise in taxation, was likely to appeal to
conservative-minded Liberals). There is little doubt that Baldwin was genuinely
appalled at the intractable nature of post-1918 unemployment, and wished
to find a way to reduce it. Secondly, an election revolving around the tariff
issue was almost certain to bring Austen Chamberlain back into the Tory fold,
moving him away from any residual notion of a coalition with Lloyd George.
As the heir to the instigator of tariff reform, Joseph Chamberlain, Austen could
hardly continue to stand aloof. It was also likely to have the same effect on Lord
Birkenhead, a keen tariff reformer, and on many businessmen among the pro-
Coalition Tories. Baldwin was also probably motivated by rumours that Lloyd
George would soon turn to his own programme of tariff reform in an attempt
to re-enter the centre of political life. Baldwin, a keen student of electoral
politics, may have realised that, whatever happened, neither the Liberals nor
Labour could win a parliamentary majority in their own right.

While Baldwin was able to carry his Cabinet colleagues with him to an imme-
diate dissolution of Parliament, and a General Election in early December 1923,
he also secured the support of Austen Chamberlain and Lord Birkenhead.
Nevertheless, a political backlash quickly ensued, with pro-Free Trade Tories
(strong in Lancashire) opposing both the election and tariff reform, and many
Conservatives opposing the possible re-entry of Lord Birkenhead into the
Cabinet, given his reputation for fast living and ill-considered remarks.
Although the campaign went well and the Tories expected to win, both the
Liberals and Labour campaigned strongly on the old Achilles heel of previous
tariff reform proposals, the apparent 'tax on food', especially imported grains,
which any programme of tariffs seemed to portend. With the inflation and
unemployment of the post-1918 world, any gratuitous increase in the cost of
necessities remained an almost automatic vote-loser. As well, the Liberals were
temporarily reunited under the pro-Free Trade banner which, after all, was one
of their most fundamental rallying-cries between 1903 and 1914. Finally,
Labour was also better organised in working-class constituencies it was likely
to win, while high unemployment under a Tory government obviously worked
in its favour. The attitude of Labour to tariff reform was more ambiguous.
There was no *a priori* reason for Labour, with its calls for sweeping government

controls over the economy, to oppose intelligently considered tariffs as a way of benefiting the British working classes. On the other hand Labour shared the same deep roots in Nonconformist Victorian Britain, where Free Trade was a virtual religious doctrine, as did the Liberals. As well, by late 1923, five years after the war ended, Labour could no longer be depicted as an anti-patriotic, subversive force, but had to be taken seriously and on its own terms.

The results of the General Election held on 6 December 1923 surprised everyone. The Conservatives managed to lose 87 seats. Although they remained the largest single party, with 258 seats, the two pro-Free Trade parties between them had a large majority in the new Parliament, ensuring that tariff reform could not be enacted.

	Total votes	MPs elected	% share of the vote
Conservative	5 538 824	258	38.1
Liberal	4 311 147	159	29.6
Labour	4 438 508	191	30.5
Others	260 042	7	1.8
Total	14 548 521	615	100.0

The great sensation of the election was the increase in the number of Labour MPs. With 191 MPs they were now in a strong position to form a minority government should the Tories be unable to continue in power (as seemed likely). Almost equally impressive was the recovery of the Liberals, now reunified under Asquith, who received only fractionally fewer votes than did Labour. (The gap between Labour and the Liberals was even less than is suggested by the voting figures, since 11 Liberal MPs were returned unopposed, compared with three Labourites and 35 Tories.) Because of the vagaries of the British electoral system, however, the Liberals only managed to elect 159 MPs, 32 less than Labour.

Although the Conservatives elected a majority of MPs, as usual, in the south of England apart from London and in northern Ireland, everywhere else they failed to elect more MPs than the two opposition parties. Labour made deep inroads in the East End of London, West Yorkshire, the north-east and, in particular, in Scotland, where it elected 34 MPs compared with 22 Liberals and only 14 Tories. In Wales, it also (as in 1922) elected the majority of MPs, 19 out of 35. The most remarkable gains, however, were made by the Liberals, who managed to elect members in seats (for instance Basingstoke, Blackpool, Finchley, and Shrewsbury) they had failed to win in 1906. In particular, the Liberals did especially well in agricultural seats – normally an ironclad Tory preserve – winning 43 of 86 seats so described by electoral analysts, to the Tories' 38 and Labour's five. Farm prices had declined very sharply since the end of the post-war boom, and there was considerable rural distress. While the urban working classes responded to the disturbed post-war economic conditions by voting Labour, in rural areas the electorate turned to the Liberals. The Liberals won a swath of seats in south-west England (including nearly every seat in Cornwall and Devon), all of the rural seats in Wales, and many in the east Midlands. They did less well, however, in greater London while, of course, they had lost the industrial working-class seats to Labour.

Needless to say, Stanley Baldwin received almost universal condemnation from Tory sources for gambling so pointlessly and losing. Today, it is very unlikely that a party leader who gambled and lost in this manner could survive, and in today's conditions Baldwin would almost certainly have had to resign the leadership. Nevertheless, Baldwin was not forced to resign. Tory MPs resented the attempts by the 'presslords' Rothermere and Beaverbrook to dictate to the party and actually rallied round him. In fact, the political situation was deeply confused and not necessarily disadvantageous to the Conservatives, who were still the largest single party. The political situation which resulted from the 1923 General Election had never been seen before in British history, one in which there were three large party groupings in Parliament rather than two. As a result, there were no clear-cut precedents to cover the 1923 outcome, and many different possibilities were discussed. In particular, many right-wingers who were appalled at the prospect of even a minority Labour government looked forward to a Tory–Liberal alliance, under Balfour, Austen Chamberlain, Asquith, or even Lord Grey, in retirement for nearly a decade. Winston Churchill, who had almost completed his transformation from a left-wing radical Liberal to a right-wing Tory, and who was passionately anti-socialist, stated during the campaign that 'The enthronement in office of a Socialist [i.e. Labour] Government will be a serious national misfortune such as has usually befallen great States only on the morrow of defeat in war.'

However, Labour had a surprisingly easy time in being given the opportunity to form a minority government. There was a genuine realisation that, as Asquith put it, sooner or later there would be a Labour government and it could 'hardly be tried under safer condition' than as a minority government. As Neville Chamberlain noted privately, Labour 'would be too weak to do much harm but not too weak to get discredited'. Some far-sighted Tories actually preferred a Labour to a Liberal government, realising that many Labour supporters were actually Tories of a kind who had the misfortune to be born poor; they were patriots rather than committed radicals. Given the vague and utopian nature of Labour's policies and their inexperience, in practice they were likely to take their advice from conservative-minded civil servants. Some Tories also realised that the Liberals were obviously on the way out, that the Tories were already the largest single party and that any further diminution of Liberal strength could only bring more moderate Liberals into the Tory camp, probably giving them a winning majority for decades to come. These far-sighted Tories proved remarkably astute. By 1924, too, the deep sense of panic and impending catastrophe which animated right-wing thought just after the war, in the wake of the Russian Revolution, had largely dissipated as 'normality' returned. There was a widespread sense that a minority Labour government, in the mid-1920s, did not mean the end of the world and could not possibly do so. Furthermore, a parliamentary coalition between the Tories and the Liberals, specifically in order to keep Labour out, was almost certainly politically impossible because of the sharp differences between the two parties over tariffs.

Baldwin decided to take the constitutionally correct course, despite very great pressure from right-wing sources, and to continue in office until Parliament met. This it did on 8 January 1924. The Tories were then defeated over a 'no-confidence' vote on the King's speech (which promised increased public spending to alleviate unemployment) on 21 January, by a vote of 328 to 256. Baldwin resigned the next day. The King then sent for the leader of the next largest party, Ramsay MacDonald, the leader of the Labour party, to attempt to form a minority government. This he did on the day that Baldwin resigned, 22 January 1924, thus becoming the first Labour Prime Minister. Historians have long pointed to the exemplary role of King George V in bringing Labour into the inner circle of governance. The King personally detested all socialists and radicals. Nevertheless, as a salty and blunt-spoken former naval sailor, he discovered that he actually had a good deal in common with Labour's working-class leaders, and developed a genuine friendship with them. In some respects he preferred their earthy honesty to the normal flattery of courtiers. Historians have also pointed to the very self-defeating actions of Asquith and the Liberals in allowing Labour in for the first time with no guarantees at all as to a working arrangement between the two left-of-centre parties to preserve the Liberals as a party of governance. In today's political climate, it is very difficult indeed to see one large minority party which had been one of the normal parties of government only a few years earlier allowing in an upstart rival without a long list of concessions. A Labour–Liberal coalition was an obvious one; another was a working arrangement not to oppose each other in significant number of seats at forthcoming elections. Some kind of close electoral pact between Labour and the Liberals might have kept the Tories out indefinitely and changed the course of British politics for generations. Instead, Asquith demanded nothing and received nothing. This must be seen as the last in a series of fatal, curiously incompetent serious mistakes he had been making during the previous 15 years, and arguably the worst of all. Asquith apparently believed (correctly) that a minority Labour government would not last a year and (incorrectly) that he would then be asked to form a minority Liberal government. He still greatly mistrusted Lloyd George, and it is perfectly true that many Liberal MPs would not have welcomed an alliance with the collectivists of the Labour party, especially if this gave Labour the parliamentary numbers to enact far-reaching social legislation. By supinely acquiescing in a Labour government, however, Asquith ensured that the Liberals would not play a serious role as a party of governance for many years.

One might also consider at this point who supported the Labour party and what it actually wanted. Support for Labour tended to be heavily based in particular communities, especially mining, engineering, and, later, factory communities. It was, of course, heavily class-based, but was also differentially based among the working classes of different types of seats and in different parts of Britain. Since up to 75 per cent of the British people could be defined as 'working class', but Labour never, down to 1945, received more than 38 per cent of the vote (and generally much less), it was not ubiquitously popular among the social class to whom it directly appealed. Labour was strongest in the Celtic areas and in very heavily industrialised regions like Tyneside, but was weaker elsewhere, even in large cities like Birmingham and Liverpool with different traditions. Its strength was greatest, by and large, in former Liberal areas of strength, but it never had the appeal which the Liberals had had in rural areas and small towns. There is no compelling evidence that it was supported by more than, at most, about 40 per cent of the electorate before the Second World War.

While many intellectuals and other middle-class men and women associated with Labour favoured far-reaching programmes of the political and social reorganisation of British society, most of the trade unionists and working-class backbone of Labour's support were far more limited in their goals. Essentially, most of them wanted an appropriate slice of the cake of governance for the trade unions and the working classes such as the middle classes had apparently achieved in 1832 and 1846. There is little or no evidence that they wished for a fundamental reorganisation of British society and, on issues like the monarchy, they were almost as invariably conservative as any Tory. Many, indeed, were just as right-wing as any Tory but could not readily identify with the Conservative party. In the 1923 General Election campaign, too, it is notable that Labour quietly ditched its demands for a 'capital levy' on the rich in favour of greater social welfare spending: in other words, a reformist rather than revolutionary agenda. Even among its middle-class radicals, who were often committed to sweeping left-wing solutions, the Fabian Society, the most important association of middle-class Labour intellectuals, if anything made a fetish of its programme of gradual rather than sudden change: 'the inevitable gradualness of our scheme of change', in Sidney Webb's famous phrase (made at the June 1923 Labour party conference). Perhaps the greatest difference between Labour and the conservative forces in British society was in foreign and colonial policy, where Labour opposed 'secret treaties' and international military alliances, and sought eventual independence for the colonies much earlier than the Tories. In particular, Labour's opposition to *realpolitik* in international affairs brought many middle-class idealists into the party (and was perfectly understandable, given the alliances which produced the catastrophe of the war). But Labour was perfectly capable of ditching any quasi-pacifism when Britain was confronted by the Nazi threat. Most real revolutionaries and pro-Bolshevists in Britain were well aware of the conservatism of Labour, and, as well, as of Labour's desire to distance itself from left-wing extremists.

James Ramsay MacDonald (1866–1937), the new Prime Minister, was the illegitimate son of a Scottish servant girl in a remote fishing village. His father was probably a farm labourer, although during his lifetime MacDonald did nothing to dampen speculation that his father was a duke or an earl. After growing up in dire poverty, he drifted to London where he became an invoice clerk: he was never a manual labourer and was never associated with a trade union. He was, however, closely connected with the Fabian Society, with radical Liberal politics, and with a number of proto-'New Age' movements. MacDonald, a very handsome and articulate man with a commanding presence, married well, the daughter of a wealthy chemistry professor named Gladstone (but not, apparently, a relative of the G.O.M.). He was one of the leaders of the Labour party from its earliest days, entering Parliament in 1906. Great controversy came to him during the war, when his apparent anti-war stance brought him much obloquy and cost him his seat in 1918. Returned to Parliament in 1922, he was narrowly elected leader of the Labour party over J.R. Clynes.

MacDonald's political viewpoint was and is somewhat difficult precisely to define. MacDonald was a utopian social democrat, committed in an undoctrinaire way to socialism and 'social justice'. But throughout his career he was extraordinarily vague, a characteristic which became more marked as he grew older. He led mainly through charisma, although his contributions to making Labour the main left-of-centre party were central. MacDonald was also a very lonely man, especially after his wife died in 1911 (he never remarried), had few close friends, and was very much a lone wolf in politics, being closely associated neither with the trade unions nor with high-powered socialist intellectuals like the Webbs. He was also increasingly susceptible to the influence of aristocrats, especially aristocratic women, which many in the Labour party saw as instrumental to his formation of the National government in 1931.

MacDonald insisted on a free hand in picking his Cabinet, and refused to let the Labour party have any role in it. He had a good deal of trouble fitting men to offices. MacDonald's Chancellor of the Exchequer was Philip Snowden (1864–1937; later first viscount Snowden of Ickornshaw), whose biography is something like that of MacDonald's. Although his father worked in a mill in Yorkshire, Snowden became a pupil teacher and then entered the Inland Revenue as an excise official. Like MacDonald, Snowden was never a manual worker. Also like MacDonald, he married a woman, Ethel Annikan Snowden, who was fairly well-off, as well as a socialist lecturer and activist of note. (It was Ethel Snowden who actually coined the phrase, later made world-famous by Winston Churchill, that the Soviet Union was surrounded by 'an iron curtain'. She invented the phrase upon returning to England from Soviet Russia in 1920.) In 1891, Snowden contracted a crippling spinal infection which made it difficult for him to walk without crutches. At about the same time he discovered socialism, to him a moral creed influenced by Methodism, Chartism, and utopian writings, and became a nationally known socialist orator, although totally lacking in any deep theoretical basis. His socialism was also highly evolutionary in nature, allowing implementation of socialism in practice to be, if necessary, indefinitely postponed. During the war he was an outspoken pacifist and was widely seen as an extreme radical. Like MacDonald he lost his seat in 1918 and regained it in 1922. Even more than MacDonald, he was, in government, an old-fashioned orthodox Gladstonian liberal, actually one of the most conservative, pro-retrenchment Chancellors in modern history who (like MacDonald) became even more conservative, almost a Tory, and openly supported the Lloyd George Liberals at the 1935 General Election. The ambiguities in Snowden's outlook well illustrated the ambiguities in the Labour party as a whole.

MacDonald did not quite know what to do with Arthur Henderson (1863–1935), who probably did more than anyone apart from MacDonald to bring Labour to power, and whom MacDonald may have seen as a dangerous rival. In the end he made Henderson Home Secretary. J.R. Clynes (1869–1949), whom MacDonald had defeated for the party leadership, and J.H. Thomas (1874–1949) were two prominent trade union leaders (associated with, respectively, the General and Municipal Workers and the National Union of Railwaymen) also given senior posts as Lord Privy Seal and Secretary for the Colonies. For the key post of Foreign Secretary, Ramsay MacDonald, most unusually, appointed himself, a combination unknown since Lord Salisbury's days.

One notable feature of the first Labour government was the fact that no fewer than eight of its 20 members were of upper or upper-middle-class background. MacDonald went out of his way to seek men of 'Establishment' background willing to work with Labour. The most prominent such appointee was Lord Haldane, the former key Liberal who became Lord Chancellor. Haldane had by far the most experience in government of any member of the new Cabinet, another obvious advantage. Other men of this stamp included Lord Parmoor, the Lord President of the Council (Charles Alfred Cripps, 1852–1941), a wealthy High Church Anglican barrister of impeccable 'Establishment' background who had been Attorney-General to the Prince of Wales and a Tory MP until 1914 (Parmoor was the father of Sir Stafford Cripps, the famous Labour leader of the 1940s and brother-in-law of Beatrice Webb); Lord Olivier, Secretary for India (Sydney Haldane Olivier, 1859–1941), a former Colonial governor and permanent under-secretary in the civil service (and uncle of Sir Laurence Olivier, the world-famous actor); Lord Chelmsford, First Lord of the Admiralty (Frederick Thesiger, 1868–1933), a former Viceroy of India, no less; and Josiah Wedgwood, Chancellor of the Duchy of Lancaster (1872–1943), of the famous pottery family and a former Liberal MP (who was closely related to Charles Darwin, Thomas Huxley, and Ralph Vaughan Williams, and was the uncle of Dame C.V. Wedgwood, the renowned historian). Such men – and there were others as well – would have been seen as rather up-market in a post-1918 Tory government; in a Labour government their presence was simply extraordinary (and extremely bewildering to Marxists), evidence of the lengths which MacDonald went to make Labour into a fully accepted party of governance. Labour went to great lengths to prove this in other ways, too, for instance by adopting formal court dress whenever required. Their presence also showed the extent to which Labour had begun to attract influential converts from outside the working classes. Most such 'Establishment' figures joined Labour because of its stance on foreign policy, and the party's commitment to a new, peaceful international order, although some shared the evolutionary view of socialism held by most of Labour's leaders. The new government also contained the famous Fabian socialist intellectual and founder of the London School of Economics Sidney Webb as President of the Board of Trade, and two (but only two) avowed radicals, John Wheatley (1869–1930) as Minister of Health and Fred Jowett (1864–1944) at the Ministry of Works. (Wheatley was one of the few Roman Catholics to hold a Cabinet post in this period.) MacDonald's junior ministers (including the legal officials) were even less plebeian, and these appointees were notable as well for including the first women to hold any office in a British government (unless the highly political office of Mistress of the Robes under Queen Victoria be described as a government position, which is quite arguable), Margaret Bondfield (1873–1953) as Parliamentary Secretary to the Ministry of Labour, and for giving Clement Attlee (1883–1967; later first earl Attlee) his first official position, as Under-Secretary at the War Office. Nevertheless, the novelty behind the new government ought not to be understated. Eleven of the 18 members of the new Cabinet were of working-class background. None of these had more than an elementary education, and most had known poverty and unemployment in their youth, or even later. While the MacDonald government did contain an aristocratic and upper middle-class minority, only eight had attended a public school (with none at all at Eton), and six Oxbridge. In Bonar Law's 1912 Cabinet, in contrast, 14 of 16 had attended a public school (eight at Eton alone) while 13 had been educated at Oxbridge. Even in Lloyd George's wartime Coalition nothing like a Cabinet with a plebeian majority had ever been seen before. MacDonald had, however, apparently done the impossible, rewarding the hopes of millions of British workers that some of their own would at last sit in the inner counsels of governance, while reassuring the upper and middle classes that they were still largely in control.

Labour's minority position in Parliament ensured that it could make no radical innovations. Nevertheless, within strict limits it did embark on a number of innovations. Wheatley's Housing Act, which increased the state subsidy for houses built for rental purposes, was very successful in increasing new housebuilding in this sector of the market. Snowden's budget was an expansionist one, which cut duties on tea, coffee, sugar, and other items, and also, unexpectedly for a Labour Chancellor, repealed the corporation profits tax. His Free Trade orthodoxy did him no harm with Liberal voters. There was also a minor, but proto-Keynesian expenditure (£28 million) for road-building and public works. In education, the government increased the number of free places in secondary schools and university scholarships. In all this was a useful and constructive programme. Labour's main failing was its inability to make more than a dent in unemployment, which stood at an average of 11.6 per cent of the insured workforce in 1923, 10.9 per cent in 1924, and 11.2 per cent in 1925. The number of unemployed persons, 1 374 000 in January 1924, declined somewhat to 1 087 000 before rising again to 1 281 000 when the government fell in October. It is paradoxical indeed that the economic problem the Labour party had come into being centrally to cure proved its most obvious failure, and evidence that Labour had no panaceas in this area.

Labour's record in foreign policy was much more successful, even distinguished. The party brought what was in many ways a genuinely novel approach to foreign policy questions. Labour's ministers had no experience in the traditional conduct of foreign policy, and its trades unionists were unconnected with the aristocratic circles which had conducted diplomacy for many centuries. Some middle-class converts to Labourism had joined specifically in disgust at the 'secret diplomacy' and treaty alliances which had led to the catastrophe of the war, and were determined to find a better and more constructive way to conduct foreign policy with the aim of achieving international peace and disarmament. By 1924, too, most of the Western world had put wartime feelings of vengeance behind it, and were ready for major steps towards international reconciliation. Labour also looked upon itself as the successor to the Cobdenite Liberal tradition of Britain leading the way to international peace and peaceful commerce between nations.

The major issue facing Europe at this time was international agreement on the reparations question, which would satisfy the Allies while bringing Germany peacefully into the community of nations again. After preliminary discussions with France, MacDonald headed an international conference in London in July–August 1924 which went a considerable way to producing something of a reconciliation between France and Weimar Germany. Labour also placed great faith in the League of Nations and was on the point of pushing through, and ratifying, a Protocol for the Pacific Settlement of International Disputes which made all international disputes subject to adjudication by the International Court of Justice, and also made international sanctions mandatory against any aggressor. As well, Labour attempted to normalise relations with the Soviet Union, an international outlaw since its foundation but, by 1924, in a relatively moderate period of leadership (by its normal standards), prior to the ascendancy of Stalin to power some years later. The left wing of the Labour party was exceptionally keen to establish normal relations with Soviet Russia, which many regarded as the 'workers paradise', while, in contrast, virtually all Tories and most of the right-wing press regarded the Bolshevik state as more or less the satanic kingdom come to earth, with Lenin and Trotsky as Satan and Beelzebub. MacDonald and the mainstream of the Labour party were not especially sympathetic to Bolshevism, but admired some of its achievements, and argued that international reconciliation in Europe was impossible unless Russia (like Weimar Germany) was brought fully into the world of normal diplomatic relations. Russia was still governed in large measure by fanatical international Communists who regarded Britain as one of the worst bulwarks of capitalist imperialism and MacDonald and the Labour party as lackeys of the ruling class of international predators. The Soviet attitude, though softening, did not make reconciliation any easier. Britain had signed a trade agreement with the Soviet Union in 1921, but had never recognised the Soviet government, and relations between the two were frigid. Upon taking office, on 1 February 1924, the new Labour government recognised the Soviet Union as the *de jure* government of Russia, and instituted a conference in London to settle any disputes between the two. This began in April, but remained deadlocked until early August when a wide-ranging series of treaties was agreed to between Britain and Russia. The most-favoured-nation status was given to the Soviet Union in exchange for concessions to British holders of Czarist bonds, and Britain agreed to recommend a loan to the Soviet government. Labour's overall foreign policy successes were notable, and were appropriate to the mood of international reconciliation which prevailed during the middle and later 1920s. When, however, an unappeaseable aggressor did appear on the world scene, as Hitler did after 1933, Labour's faith in rationalism and the settlement of disputes through adjudication was increasingly inappropriate, requiring a fundamental readjustment by Labour to world realities which was psychologically difficult.

These accords seem moderate enough, and inevitable, but they set off an hysterical series of attacks upon Labour not only in the right-wing press, but among many Liberals, including Lloyd George, who attacked them. These agreements were the first 'socialist' measures undertaken by the Labour government, and began a change in mood towards Labour by the Tories, the Liberals, and the 'Establishment' which was to bring about its sudden downfall and yet another General Election. In September, MacDonald admitted that he had been given a Daimler car and £30 000 of shares in the McVitie and Price biscuit company by Sir Alexander Grant, its proprietor, who had been MacDonald's childhood friend, and who shortly afterwards received a baronetcy from the Prime Minister. The affair was somewhat more complex than this it seemed (Grant, a famous industrialist, was already on the 'waiting list' to receive such an honour), but such an apparently blatant example of old-fashioned naked corruption involving a 'socialist' Prime Minister severely shook the government.

Shortly afterwards, in late September, came the event which was to bring about the government's downfall, the so-called 'Campbell case'. In July, J.R. Campbell, the acting editor of a Communist periodical in London, the *Worker's Weekly*, published an article urging British soldiers not to fire on their fellow-workers, either in the course of a strike or in a war. Copies of this article were distributed by Communists near a military base in Hampshire. Both the publication of the article and its distribution were illegal under the Incitement to Mutiny Act of 1797. In August, the offices of the party were raided and Campbell arrested. Shortly afterward, after intense pressure from influential Labourites, the Attorney-General Sir Patrick Hastings (1880–1952) ordered the prosecution against Campbell dropped. Although it first seemed as if the matter would blow over, both the Tories and Liberals decided to make a major issue of the government's behaviour, with the Conservatives moving a vote of censure on the government and the Cabinet deciding to make this into a vote of confidence on the government's future. On 8 October 1924, both the Tories and Liberals joined together (technically, on an amendment to the Tories' motion moved by the Liberals) to defeat the government by a large majority in the House of Commons, 364-198. This crisis came to a head very suddenly and unexpectedly, ending abruptly what had been a rather promising term of office for Labour. The next day (9 October 1924), MacDonald saw the King and recommended that a General Election be held. This was not an automatic outcome to the crisis – the Tories, by far the largest party, might have been commissioned to form another minority government, or the Liberals under Asquith given a chance – but the King reluctantly accepted MacDonald's logic that no party could form a stable government. A General Election was called for 29 October 1924, although MacDonald technically remained as caretaker Prime Minister until 3 November 1924, some days after the 1924 election. Labour's period of office in 1924 was instrumental in making it into the normal left-of-centre party in Britain. As a government, it should probably be ranked as slightly above average, but as a watershed in British politics it was a clear triumph. Had Labour not held office even briefly in 1924 it might well never have had any experience of government until the Second World War (if then), and been both far more radical and more incompetent when it actually did form a government. Ramsay MacDonald deserves the highest praise for his accomplishments in 1924.

The General Election of 1924 was one of the most bitter of the century. For reasons which are not self-evident, the very moderation of Labour in office drove the two older parties to try and prove the harder that Labour was in league with Bolshevism and Moscow, and most of the early phases of the campaign revolved around the Russian treaties and the Campbell case. In late October, only four days before voting, came one of the great election sensations in history when the *Daily Mail* newspaper published a banner headline story alleging that the Soviet leadership in Russia wished the British Communist party and left-wing elements in the Labour party to bring pressure to bear on the Labour Cabinet to ratify the Russian treaties and to set up subversive cells in the British army and in munitions factories, leading to eventual revolution.

These orders from Moscow allegedly took the form of a secret letter, written in September, from Grigori Zinoviev, the head of the Communist International, to Arthur McManus, a leading British Communist, and quickly became known as the 'Zinoviev letter'. When the letter was published in the press, it was accompanied by another letter, from a Foreign Office official, protesting to Moscow at Zinoviev's epistle, which gave it the appearance of an actual document. In fact, the Zinoviev letter has long been known to be a fraud, almost certainly concocted by anti-Bolshevik Russian exiles in order to embarrass the government. MacDonald mishandled the affair, ordering the letter of protest to be drawn up before its authenticity was known, and then not commenting on the letter for several days after its release. The right-wing Tory press had a field day, accusing Labour of virtually being Soviet stooges.

It is often said that the election outcome turned largely on the 'Zinoviev letter', but other factors were also important. Baldwin had used his period in opposition to good purpose, reforming the Conservative Central office and, at last, restoring unity by bringing Austen Chamberlain, Balfour, and Birkenhead into the Shadow Cabinet. As well, Winston Churchill was well on his way to rejoining the Conservative party, although he narrowly lost (by 43 votes) a by-election in the Westminster-Abbey seat to an endorsed Conservative, while standing as an Independent with wide Conservative support. In contrast, the Liberals did poorly in by-elections (both Labour and the Tories did well), appearing virtually leaderless and bereft of ideas. Asquith continued to be the official leader of the Liberal party, although he was 72 years old in 1924 and had held senior Cabinet posts for over thirty years. Labour now definitely appeared to the party of progress and of the future, winning, in particular, the support of many scientists and progressive intellectuals for a technological, rational future something like that depicted in *Things to Come*, the famous 1936 film, while securing the loyalties of increasing numbers of Nonconformists and former Liberals. The Tories were clearly the party of both moderates and immoderates who supported the old values of Empire, patriotism, and 'normality'. In contrast, the Liberals appeared to look backward to a past which had vanished in 1914, advocating Free Trade but little else. One should not exaggerate this failure, given the remarkable Liberal success in popular votes at the 1923 General Election, if not in seats. Nevertheless, there was little in the Liberals' performance in 1923–24 to be sanguine about a revival.

In spite of the reasonable success enjoyed by Labour in office, the 1924 General Election was a triumph for the Conservatives, who secured the largest parliamentary majority they had ever achieved in their entire history since 1832:

	Total votes	MPs elected	% share of the vote
Conservative	8 039 598	419	48.3
Liberal	2 928 747	40	17.6
Labour	5 489 077	151	33.0
Communist	55 346	1	0.3
Others	126 511	4	0.8
Total	16 639 279	615	100.0

As usual, the British electoral system exaggerated the number of seats won by the dominant party. The Tories actually secured fewer than half of the total vote, but elected 68 per cent of all MPs in the new Parliament. Labour's total vote had increased by over one million, although the number of Labour MPs elected declined by 40. Since Labour had nominated 90 more candidates than the previous year, its total share of votes per candidate declined slightly. Nevertheless, Labour was now plainly the larger left-wing party, the main sensation of the 1924 General Election being the collapse of the Liberals, whose vote declined by nearly 1.5 million and worse, elected only 40 MPs (118 fewer than in 1923), a derisory total and a catastrophe for the party. Turnout in the 1924 election, 76.6 per cent, was the highest since the war and evidence that many more women were now voting.

The Tories were predominant almost (but not quite) everywhere, and the south of England produced virtually unbroken Conservative triumphs everywhere except in the slums of London. Labour still had a solid grip on its primary areas of strength, especially in South Wales, the West Riding, and the north-east, but the Tories actually won a majority of seats in Scotland, 36, compared with 26 for Labour and eight for the Liberals. The Liberals retained only two notable areas of strength, in northern Scotland and rural Wales, plus a number of odd pockets here and there.

Rather unusually, MacDonald took four or five days to resign, with Baldwin not officially taking office as Prime Minister until 4 November 1924, a day after Labour's resignation. Within the Labour party, there was a good deal of resentment against MacDonald's alleged incompetence, especially his making the Campbell affair into a vote of confidence, and resentment as well that the seemingly inevitable growth of Labour at successive General Elections had been halted. Nevertheless, there was no obvious successor to MacDonald as leader, with his most likely challengers such as Snowden and Thomas being seen as even less acceptable to the party's left-wing than he was, and MacDonald was re-elected leader of the Labour party with little opposition.

Stanley Baldwin formed his second Cabinet, being now in an impregnable position within the party. Most of the ministers in Baldwin's previous Tory government were retained, in an enlarged Cabinet of 21 men (compared with 16 in Bonar Law's Cabinet, formed in 1922). There were, however, some notable changes. The most spectacular, and probably the most important, was the completely unexpected appointment of Winston Churchill to be Chancellor of the Exchequer. Churchill's appointment was extraordinary. A 'traitor' who defected from the Tories to the Liberals in 1904, he was the *bête-noire* of the Tory far right, whom they bitterly mistrusted. He was a confirmed Free Trader whose position seemingly ruled out tariff reform, despite the Conservatives' vast majority. Churchill knew nothing of finance, had no commercial or business experience, and had held no relevant office in his long career apart from two years as President of the Board of Trade 15 years (1908–10) earlier. What was Baldwin thinking? Clearly, he was impressed by Churchill's commanding intelligence and unique oratorical gifts. Chiefly as a result of the Russian Revolution and the rise of Labour, Churchill had moved, during the previous seven years, from the left of the political spectrum to the extreme right, and was, by 1924, to be classified as arguably to the right of many 'die-hard' Tories. Indeed, from the early 1920s until he became Prime Minister in 1940, Churchill was regarded by most British leftists as one of the worst reactionaries in England. However, the main reason for Baldwin's offer to Churchill was apparently to show, in the most visible way possible, that former Liberals would be very welcome in Baldwin's Conservative party. Short of appointing Lloyd George or Asquith to his Cabinet (obvious impossibilities), Baldwin could not have made clearer that high-profile ex-Liberals had a place in the Conservative party, as a balance to the many ex-Liberals who were said to be joining the Labour party. Baldwin, a superb political strategist, might also have seen Churchill as the possible leader of a revivified Liberal party and attempted to forestall this outcome. It is also possible that the intellectually flexible Churchill could be converted to tariff reform, taking many ex-Liberals with him. There is a famous story that when Baldwin offered him the position of 'Chancellor', Churchill assumed that he meant the minor position of Chancellor of the Duchy of Lancaster, and burst into tears when it dawned on him that he was being given the second-highest position in the Cabinet, which his father (Lord Randolph Churchill) had held nearly 40 years earlier.

Baldwin also had to find places for the leading Coalitionists who had, until then, steadfastly remained out of Tory Cabinets. Austen Chamberlain, briefly the party's leader in 1921–22, was made Foreign Secretary, an appointment which entailed moving Curzon (the holder of this post in the last Tory government) to the largely honorary position of Lord President of the Council. Birkenhead was given the curious position of Secretary of State for India rather than the obvious post of Lord Chancellor (which went to Lord Cave, its holder in 1922–24), possibly because his staunch views on India would be acceptable to the party's right wing, and because a heavyweight politician was needed in a region marked by internal unrest. Baldwin also thought that the post 'will keep him pretty well occupied' and out of mischief. Initially, no post was offered to the 76-year-old Lord Balfour (as Arthur Balfour had become in 1922) but he later joined the Cabinet as Lord President of the Council upon Curzon's death in April 1925. Balfour provided a unique link with the Conservative's remote past, having known Disraeli well and served as the Private Secretary to his uncle, Lord Salisbury, in 1878–80, nearly half a century before.

Baldwin also made a number of other controversial appointments, some more successful than others. To the Home Office he appointed Sir William Joynson-Hicks who had briefly sat in Baldwin's 1923–24 Cabinet as Financial Secretary to the Treasury. Joynson-Hicks, a solicitor who was universally known as 'Jix', was an ultra-conservative Evangelical Low Church Anglican who deplored all modern innovations, especially socialism and nightclubs. As Home Secretary he carried on a well-publicised campaign of vigilance against tawdry London nightlife, foreign agitators, and unorthodox approaches to morality, and represented a concerted attempt to respond to the moral standards of the 'Roaring Twenties' with renewed Victorianism. As such, he was a stock figure of fun to most enlightened intellectuals, and was regarded as extreme, even slightly ridiculous, by most of his Cabinet colleagues. Efforts by recent historians to depict Jix as an anti-semite, proto-fascist, or 'Mussolini Minor' (as he was known in some circles) are, however great exaggerations. Jix's greatest passion was the preservation of the Low Church Evangelical tradition in the Church of England in the face of High Church attempts to increase the quasi-Catholic usages in the Anglican church, and he took a leading part in the Prayer Book debate of 1927.

Another unusual, probably much more successful appointment by Baldwin was that of Neville Chamberlain to the Ministry of Health, a post he had previously held for a few months in 1923–24. Chamberlain (who had apparently declined the Exchequer before Churchill's appointment) proved to be one of the most successful and constructive Health ministers of the century, and increasingly joined with Baldwin at the innermost circles of the Tory party, by the end of the decade probably surpassing the influence of his half-brother Austen. Another notable appointment was that of Sir Douglas Hogg (Hogg was the father of Quintin Hogg, Lord Hailsham, 1907–2001, the senior Tory leader of the 1955–85 period), as Attorney-General with, unusually, a seat in the Cabinet. Hogg, an outstanding barrister, almost overnight became one of the Conservatives' most articulate debaters in Parliament. (There is a famous anecdote of one Tory politician noting to another, early in the 1920s, of the remarkable but hitherto unknown platform speaker he had discovered, 'Douglas Pigg'.)

In other respects the 1924 Baldwin Cabinet was a normal Tory one as this had evolved after the war. There were fewer peers than in the 1922 Cabinet – six, compared with 15 in the Commons – but it was a distinctly upper-class Cabinet by the standards of the time, with every single member of the Cabinet having attended a public school (seven to Eton alone), and 16 having attended Oxbridge. It was noted at the time that Birmingham was especially well-represented in the Cabinet compared with Lancashire, with Lord Derby being excluded from the new Cabinet for no obvious reason. This was interpreted at the time as a tilt to tariff reform and against Free Trade (Lancashire was regarded as a bastion of Free Trade sympathy), yet this was belied by Baldwin's appointment of Churchill to the Exchequer. The government also contained the first woman to be given a ministerial appointment by the Tories, the Duchess of Atholl (1874–1960), Parliamentary secretary to the Board of Education. With Churchill, Birkenhead, Curzon, Austen and Neville Chamberlain, Leo Amery (Colonial Secretary 1924–29 and Dominion Secretary 1925–29), and others, the Cabinet was one of the more talented in some time, and many continued to note the contrast between the ability of many in the Cabinet and the apparent insignificance of Baldwin as head of the government. Baldwin was still only grudgingly conceded to be more than a nonentity, although most now respected his political skills. Over the next five years, his original and conciliatory approach to politics alienated many of the more extreme members of his party, who wanted an all-out war against socialism. Yet, the consensual view of Baldwin is that his conciliatory tone succeeded, in the short-term and long-term, both in making the Conservatives the normal party of government in Britain for the next 70 years, and in further moderating Labour and weakening its left-wing extremists. Baldwin believed that there was a natural anti-socialist majority in Britain which could normally be tapped by the Tories *if* they did not appear too extreme. He also believed that Labour itself would move towards the political centre unless compelled to take a more left-wing position by the unnecessary extremism of the Conservatives. He also believed that tranquillity and stability were necessary preconditions for the full economic recovery of Britain.

Most of the great issues faced by the second Baldwin government were economic, and most of what is now remembered about public affairs in the 1924–29 period revolved around economic and trade union questions and conflicts. There were in Britain in the 1920s several interrelated problems whose solutions were exceedingly difficult. The pre-1914 international economy had been largely shattered by the war. Prior to 1914, the City of London was recognised as the world's financial centre, with the gold standard (gold being used to determine the value of all international currencies and paper money bank notes being automatically convertible to gold equivalent to the value of the bank note) giving an automatic and extra-national objective determinant of the value of currencies. After 1914, most countries withdrew from the old system, while New York took over many of the functions formerly held by the City of London. After 1918, America was obviously wealthier than Britain, and while Britain was owed very substantial amounts of money by its allies in the war, it in turn owed vast amounts to the United States. It was less able to pay for these than in the past, having liquidated much of its foreign holdings to pay for the war.

At the same time, British industry was often antiquated and badly in need of modernisation. The staple products – coal, cotton and woollen textiles, engineering equipment, ships – which had sustained the British economy prior to 1914 now no longer found foreign markets or, indeed, as much demand at home. For instance, 755 steamships with a total of 950 000 tons had been constructed in Britain in 1913, but only 438 steamships, totalling 564 000 tons, in 1925. Similar declines were often found in other staple industries. The best solution to the decline of the old industries lay in creating vibrant new ones, but here there were many difficulties. During the interwar years numerous observers pointed to the emergence of what J.B. Priestley called 'the third England' – in contrast to rural and industrial Britain – the England of suburbs and relatively affluent consumers. Especially in London and the West Midlands, this 'third England' was plainly growing by the 1930s, often resembling, at least in part, the relatively affluent world of the United States. Yet Britain was not the United States. It still contained a vast working class in the old sense, one with few obvious means of upward intergenerational social mobility, which still remained totally outside of the 'affluent society' of post-1945 Britain even in embryonic form. Although many Tories welcomed the creation of a 'property-owning democracy' in place of class war and an impoverished working class (the phrase was coined by Archibald Skelton, a Scottish Conservative MP, in a book published in 1924, and was made familiar by post-1945 Tory leaders), there was a vicious circle of mass unemployment and the lack of any reforms broadening the educational system which greatly hindered its achievement in the short run. Labour's solution, at least in theory, was nationalisation and socialism, but this offered no obvious solution to the immediate problem of mass unemployment or the backwardness of British industry. In the latter 1920s, Lloyd George and the Liberals began to advocate a proto-Keynesian programme of deficit spending to cure unemployment, but this was seen by most orthodox economists at the time as wishful thinking and had surprisingly little mass support. There were, as well, many other difficulties in the way of curing Britain's economic woes. Tariffs were ruled out, at least in a comprehensive form, by the results of the 1923 General Election, while government spending was so high that direct taxes could not return to pre-war levels. During the interwar years, unemployment never fell below 10 per cent, even during the highly affluent (for the middle classes) later 1920s. Of course not everything was black: British net national income per head had grown slightly during this period, from about £44 per head (in 1900 prices) in 1913 to £51 per head (in 1900 prices) in 1929. Britain's upper and upper-middle classes remained largely very well off, while the middle and lower-middle classes did increase in size. By the end of the interwar years, all observers agreed that the desperate, grinding poverty of the nineteenth-century unskilled working classes had greatly diminished, in part as a result of the growth of the economy, in part because population growth no longer occurred at the same rate as in the past, so that Britain managed to avoid the 'Malthusian trap' of population growth outstripping economic growth.

As Chancellor of the Exchequer, Winston Churchill attempted to deal with these problems as best as he could, but, in the process, made one of the most controversial economic decisions of the twentieth century. Although Churchill in 1925 reintroduced the so-called McKenna duties on a range of foreign luxury goods abolished by the Labour government in 1924, and extended provisions for 'safeguarding' industries which applied for protection with a $33\frac{1}{3}$ per cent duty if they could show they were threatened by foreign competition, he neither could nor would introduce a general tariff such as many Tories wished to see. In April 1925, however, Churchill announced that Britain would return to the pre-war Gold Standard, abandoned when Britain entered the war. Henceforth, one pound was deemed to be worth $4.86 (usually abbreviated as $5.00), redeemable in gold. The return to Gold was furiously debated by economists and civil servants. There were several advantages to restoring the Standard. The City of London, and Britain in general, would again be seen (as before 1914) as the safe and secure centre of world finance, while an independent standard (gold) for assessing the value of the pound forced British industries to cut both costs and prices. As well, some observers believed that, as British and American prices were – in their view – similar, the return to Gold would not disadvantage British industry. The objections to the return to Gold were even more formidable. Pegging the value of one pound at $4.86 was much too high, and would price British goods out of many export markets, while the cost-cuttings necessitated at home would accentuate unemployment and greatly exacerbate labour unrest. The opposition to the return to Gold was argued most strenuously by John Maynard Keynes, then an extremely influential economic advisor who was in the process of developing – but had not fully developed – his seminal economic theories of deficit spending and full employment. Keynes was actively involved in the discussions over Gold, and, after the decision was taken, attacked the decision in a famous 1925 pamphlet, *The Economic Consequences of Mr. Churchill.*

Most historians would agree that the negative case against the return to the Gold Standard was proved true by events, at least in a limited way. Interest rates in Britain were raised from 4 to 5 per cent in December 1925, in order to attract foreign currency which would otherwise have gone elsewhere as Britain's adverse balance of payments resulted in gold shipped elsewhere. The return to Gold, however, probably handicapped Britain less than many have thought, except in a minority of industries, while the City of London did achieve something of its old supremacy again.

One key industry, however, where the return to Gold probably caused trauma was in coalmining. It is important, however, not to attribute too much to the 1925 decision. Coalmining in Britain was relatively backward and old-fashioned compared with foreign mines (especially in Europe). Productivity had risen by little compared with the pre-war era. The method of dealing with these problems preferred by the coalmine owners was not greater investment and modernisation, but cutting wages and lengthening hours, in order better to compete with foreign coal. Relations between owners and the unions in coal were always notoriously bad in any case, while the first few years after the war saw a rash of strikes in the coal industry. By the mid-1920s the situation in the coal industry was bad once again, so bad that it led to the General Strike of 1926. That there was a General Strike in 1926 was rather surprising, as both the trade unions and the Labour movement on one hand and the Conservative government on the other appeared, by and large, to strongly favour moderation. The Conservative government, in particular, seemed keen to reject pointed anti-union legislation, despite its enormous parliamentary majority. The most famous example of Tory moderation on this issue occurred in March 1925, when a backbencher introduced a bill to abolish the unions' political levy, that is, its contribution to the Labour party, mandatory for all union members, which greatly added to the Labour party's finances and political strength. Most Conservative leaders would, surely, have been only too happy to abolish the political levy, which conscripted money from all unionists, including those who voted for other parties besides Labour. Baldwin, however, rejected the proposed bill out of hand, in what was perhaps the most moving speech he ever made. Stating that the Tories in power were not going to use their majority for purely partisan ends, Baldwin concluded (echoing the *Book of Common Prayer*) 'Give peace in our time, O Lord.' Baldwin was obviously sincere in this, and his unexpected magnanimity in the national interest won universal approval, except on the far right. On the trade union side, and despite a sharp increase in extreme leftist rhetoric at trade union and Labour conferences, it was widely noted that moderates now controlled the TUC and many of the big unions, while the Labour party also voted pointedly, once again, to exclude Communists from membership.

Nevertheless, despite these apparent moves to moderation, the most extreme example of labour unrest in British history was about to occur, the General Strike of 4–13 May 1926. The cause of the strike was a wages settlement in the coalmining industry, arrived at in May 1924, which was extremely favourable to the workers. Unfortunately, coal exports declined sharply in 1924–25, causing the mine owners to announce, in June 1925, that the agreement would be terminated and wages drastically cut. The Miners' Federation quickly enlisted the support of the TUC, which decided to make a clear stand on the issue. The government intervened but, on 31 July 1925, was forced to concede an enquiry into the mining industry and a significant subsidy which permitted normal wages to be paid. The Miners' Federation and the TUC then backed down from their strike threat. (The day of the government concession, 31 July 1925, became known as 'Red Friday'.) Many viewed the government's move as the buying of time to prepare for a successful confrontation with the miners at a later date.

A Royal Commission into the Coal Industry, under the chairmanship of the former Liberal Cabinet minister Sir Herbert Samuel, was indeed appointed in September 1925. (It consisted only of four members, the others being Sir William Beveridge, the famous director of the London School of Economics, and two industrialists; no trade unionists or explicitly pro-Labour figures served on it.) The Royal Commission reported in March 1926, after very extensive hearings. Its recommendations pleased few. Rejecting the demands of both owners and workers, it rejected the nationalisation of the coal industry but advocated its reorganisation in a more efficient form in private hands, more industry research, and better employer–labour relations through better housing and conditions. In the short-term, however, it clearly recommended that wages be cut, although not the length of the working day. While the government reluctantly accepted the Royal Commission's recommendations, both the owners and the Miners Federation rejected them. Objective opinion was almost unanimous in viewing both sides as incredibly foolish, with Lord Birkenhead making, at this juncture, his oft-repeated remark that he would have readily thought that 'the miners' leaders were the stupidest men in England' if he had not met the owners. The deadlock between the two sides could not be broken, and matters moved relentlessly to a climax. The period of the subsidy granted by the government came to an end in April 1926. In the meantime Baldwin's position itself hardened, and it became obvious that the government opposed the miners' claims. Even more seriously, the trade union movement collectively decided to give all-out support for strike action by the miners, in what might well become a General Strike which could bring Britain to a virtual standstill. The mine owners responded by a 'lock-out' of workers. On 1 May 1926 the General Council of the TUC decided almost unanimously to call a General Strike in support of the miners from midnight on 3 May 1926. The miners, led by their head A.J. Cook, had formulated a well-known slogan, 'Not a penny off the pay; not a minute on the day', which summarised their position.

After further intense negotiations, marred by misperceptions and increasing bitterness, the government announced that it had broken off negotiations on 3 May 1926. There is general agreement that this decision, taken over a triviality (the refusal of the Printers Union to print an anti-strike editorial in the *Daily Mail* newspaper) was unjustified. Baldwin, a natural peacemaker, had given way to the anti-union views of more extreme members of the Cabinet like Churchill and Joynson-Hicks. There is widespread agreement that the General Strike could have been avoided by wiser leadership by the government, and that most of the TUC was also not keen to see events escalate.

From 4 May until 12 May 1926 Britain was gripped by an unprecedented General Strike. When the Strike began, the Government issued a Royal Proclamation declaring a State of Emergency. For most of the Strike, there were virtually no trains or buses, newspapers, or transport of goods. Because of the lack of newspapers, the government, headed by Churchill, issued its own daily newspaper, the *British Gazette*, which produced pro-government, anti-strike propaganda. The government also recruited large numbers of middle-class men and women and university undergraduates to provide essential services, and used military and naval men for the same purpose. University and middle-class men often responded with gusto to the once-in-a-lifetime opportunity to be bus conductors and lorry drivers for a few days. As a result (and also because not every union was on strike) electricity and gas continued to be produced, and a skeleton service of public transport continued. It is well known that there was little or no violence, and one of the best-known images of the General Strike is that of policemen and strikers playing football. Like most popular images, although it contains a strong element of truth, it is also an exaggeration. The government stationed warships in most significant ports, and moved large numbers of troops to London, attracting much attention, in readiness for violence. The government recruited nearly 250 000 special constables for use in emergency. Strikers frequently clashed with police, and buses and trucks were overturned in Glasgow and other industrial cities. Baldwin and the Cabinet were genuinely expecting violence, fanned by Marxists, to occur as the strike dragged on and were determined to resist it. The BBC, the only radio station in existence at the time, toed the government line, even refusing to allow the Archbishop of Canterbury to broadcast an appeal for a settlement of the strike. As well, the government considered confiscating the funds of the striking trade unions and perhaps arresting its leaders.

In the end, cooler heads prevailed. Baldwin (whatever his more extreme colleagues thought) was anxious to settle the Strike, and neither the TUC nor the Labour party wished to procrastinate the situation and allow genuine extremists within the ranks of labour to gain the upper hand. Sir Herbert Samuel, head of the Royal Commission on the Coal Industry, who had been abroad when the Strike began, now returned to England and, convening a series of conferences with government agreement, worked out a series of measures (known as the 'Samuel Memorandum') for ending the dispute. This Memorandum was very vague, and indeed put off the difficult questions concerning miners' pay and hours to future negotiations. Nevertheless, the TUC and, with some reluctance, the government accepted it in order to end the General Strike, the government insisting that it represented a complete backdown by the unions. The General Strike thus ended on 12 May 1926.

Most right-wingers gloated over this apparent total victory by the government, while many unionists and radicals were appalled at the actions of the TUC taken without their consent. As a result, a second General Strike began on 13 May. Though not a 'general' strike it was particularly bitter, involving (in particular) railwaymen outside of London. The government replied with even greater firmness, sending an armoured food convoy on trucks through London in a show of force, but also promising no 'victimisation' of the strikers.

This second General Strike ended on 21 May. Nevertheless, the central cause of the turmoil, the unrest in coalmining, still continued, with the miners' strike continuing until December 1926. There is general agreement that the miners lost everything they had tried to gain, with lower wages and higher unemployment being the result. In economic terms, the strikes were a disaster for the British economy, with 1 580 000 non-miners ceasing to work as a result of the General Strike (15 000 000 working days lost), and 1 050 000 miners affected, losing no less than 145.2 million working days during their strike. The total of working days lost through strikes in 1926 was 162.2 million, compared with only 7.9 million in 1925, 1.1 million in 1927, and 1.4 million in 128. Britain lost valuable overseas markets for its coal to cheaper countries like Poland, and the total value of British coal produced declined by about 20 per cent between 1923–24 and 1927–28. Employment in coalmining also declined markedly, from 1 240 000 in 1924 to only 939 000 in 1929, and then kept declining, to only 792 000 in 1937. The coal strike left a legacy of bitterness and 'class war' in that industry which persisted for two generations.

Some right-wing response to the government's apparent victory in the Strike was to be expected, as 'die-hards' got the upper hand in the Cabinet from a position of strength. This in fact happened, with the passing of the Trade Disputes and Trade Union Act, 1927, which enacted much of the anti-union legislation that Baldwin had rejected in his 'Peace in our time' speech two years earlier. It banned 'sympathetic strikes' (i.e. those carried out in sympathy with another unrelated strike) and strikes 'designed ... to coerce the government', and, more importantly, made 'contracting in' the rule, not 'contracting out' (i.e. union members who wished to contribute to the Labour party had specifically to ask to do so, not ask not to do what was automatic). Finally, it banned civil servants from belonging to a trade union. A mandatory 'sixty-day "cooling off" period' before any strike could be called (similar to provisions enacted in the United States after the Second World War) was narrowly excluded from the bill. The Labour party lost about one-quarter of its income from the 'contracting in' provision, and there was, of course, no repetition of the general strike. Indeed, the remainder of the 1920s was, for the most part, unusually peaceful. The boom of the 1920s gradually reduced unemployment (although never below ten per cent) and the militant unions were cowed by the failure of the General Strike.

A few other explicitly right-wing measures also followed. Many members of the Cabinet (although not Sir Austen Chamberlain, the Foreign Minister) had been dissatisfied with the normalisation of relations with the Soviet Union, while backbench Tory opinion, often reflecting a far-right extremist viewpoint, was livid. In May 1927, the Home Secretary Sir William Joynson-Hicks ordered 200 policemen to carry out a raid on the London offices of Arcos Ltd, a British company engaged in trading with Russia, and the Russian Trade Delegation in the same building. The aim was to secure a government document which it argued had been stolen by an employee working in the building. No such document was found. Amazingly, the government decided to break off diplomatic relations with the Soviet Union, citing as well alleged anti-British Soviet influence in China. Baldwin rather confusingly allowed a vote to be taken in

Parliament on his actions, which, despite vigorous Labour and Liberal protests, it won by 367 votes to 118. No diplomatic relations existed between Britain and the Soviet Union from June 1927 until the Labour's return to power in late 1929. This pointless action, seemingly so far removed from the international spirit of peace of the 1920s, occurred just as Stalin was seizing absolute power in Russia.

Where the government had most claims to a sweeping domestic programme was in the area of social welfare legislation. This was strongly associated with Neville Chamberlain, whose long career in local government in Birmingham before coming to Westminster had given him wide experience in this area. Neville Chamberlain's success came in two areas, in pension legislation and in local government reform. The Widows', Orphans' and Old Age Contributory Pension Act of 1925 provided for a contributory scheme of old age and other pensions for almost everyone covered by the 1911 National Insurance Act. Pensions were payable to widows of insured persons for the first time, and to insured persons and their wives over the age of 70 (reduced in 1928 to 65). The weekly rate payable was ten shillings for widows and old age pensioners, and lesser amounts for orphans and children. Chamberlain followed this up with an even more sweeping Local Government Act of 1929. This abolished the old Poor Law Guardians, transferring their responsibility for poor laws to the county councils and county borough councils. With Churchill's budgets, taxes had been cut and, in particular, agricultural land, most industries, and railways had been 'de-rated', that is, freed from paying most or all rates or local taxes. This was done to encourage entrepreneurial activity and the hiring of labour. To compensate, the government made 'block grants' to local government areas for the money they lost. Chamberlain was, however, less successful in dealing with long-term unemployment. In 1927 a departmental committee headed by a law lord, Lord Blanesburgh, recommended lower benefits to the unemployed in exchange for a statutory right to extended unemployment benefits. This, and the resulting Unemployment Insurance Bill of 1927 provoked considerable Labour hostility. Even more controversial were the government's powers, enacted after the General Strike, to remove local Poor Law Guardians who paid excessively generous benefits to the unemployed ('Poplarism', named for the borough of Poplar in East London whose Poor Law Guardians had attempted to do this), a common feature of some councils in areas of high unemployment especially in London. Essentially, however, Chamberlain (and, to a lesser but perceptible extent, Churchill as Chancellor of the Exchequer) pursued a constructive policy of 'Tory Socialism' (of course the term is an exaggeration) in keeping with the spirit of Disraeli and Joseph Chamberlain and very consistent with the 'One Nation' moderate Toryism of Stanley Baldwin, despite the government's rather unwonted right-wing militancy during the General Strike.

There were notable and constructive measures in other fields. These included the Electricity (Supply) Act and the granting of a charter to the BBC, both at the end of 1926. The first of these established a state-owned Central Electricity Board, which took over the distribution of electrical power throughout Britain. It was empowered to buy electricity from any local generator and sell it either to private concerns or local governments for retail sale. More importantly, it had the power to create a 'national grid' throughout Britain to transfer electrical power from one region to another, which it did by the mid-1930s. This remarkable exercise in semi-socialism did much to modernise Britain's industrial base and consumer expectations, and was probably a *sine qua non* for successfully fighting the Second World War.

The British Broadcasting Company (the BBC) had been established in 1922 and quickly became the most important national broadcast venue. A committee of inquiry under Lord Crawford, a former Tory Cabinet minister, recommended in 1925 that the BBC be given a monopoly of all radio broadcasting in Britain and be reorganised as a public corporation, which was brought about by the 1926 Act. Britain thus took a path in radio (and later television) broadcasting which was diametrically opposed to that in the United States, where hundreds of privately owned local radio stations (which became organised into private national networks) were quickly established in the 1920s, and where there was no national, government-owned broadcaster. British opinion was strongly of the view that American radio stations demeaned culture and that nothing of the kind should occur in Britain. From 1923 until he retired in 1938 the Director-General of the BBC was Sir John Reith (1889–1971), a Scottish engineer and industrialist who was known both for his severe, old-fashioned moral views and his strict impartiality. During the interwar years Reith was certainly one of the most important men in Britain. In an age when Orwellian propaganda was the norm in Europe's dictatorships, the BBC acquired an enviable worldwide reputation for accurate and truthful broadcasting which it still retains; millions of oppressed peoples in the totalitarian regimes turned to the BBC to learn the truth about international affairs. By and large, the BBC also remained neutral in British politics, although both the Right and the Left complained that it discriminated against them. It introduced classical music, educational shows, and high-minded, intelligent discussions of serious issues to millions of ordinary British people for the first time. On the other hand, the broadcasting monopoly it enjoyed is hard to square with any concept of pluralistic democracy (although it did not disappear until the late 1950s or even later), the BBC being the sole and arbitrary determinant of who should broadcast on it to the British nation. It is often said that down to the 1960s, the BBC largely and deliberately reflected the viewpoint of the South of England Oxbridge-educated elite, although this may well have been no bad thing and certainly served to unify the British nation.

The questions of national culture raised by the form taken by the BBC also occurred in many other ways throughout the 1920s. Throughout the world, there was a strong sense that the Great War had ended 'Victorianism' in all its guises, especially concerning sexual behaviour. Throughout the English-speaking world the 1920s produced a rash of celebrated 'experimental' writers who introduced new modes of literary expression or dwelled on subject-matters which would have been considered taboo only a decade or two before, such as James Joyce, T.S. Eliot, Ezra Pound, and D.H. Lawrence in Britain and Ireland. These writers found close parallels in other art forms, including music, painting, and sculpture, and indeed in such apparently unrelated areas as science, with the new theories of Einstein and his contemporaries, and in the psychoanalytic practice of Freud, Jung, and others. While now widely seen as artefacts of one of the most important eras of cultural innovation in modern history, many conservatives viewed these trends as very disturbing, often linking them with 'Bolshevism' and socialism in politics and keenly wishing that the old certainties of the pre-war era could return. (In the early 1920s the term 'Bolshevist' [or 'Bolshy'] came to be popularly applied to any new or disturbing trend, from Picasso's paintings to American jazz music, where it had no relevance whatever.) Worse still, in the eyes of many conservatives, these disturbing new trends were also reflected in the behaviour and appearance of youth, especially well-off, well-educated youth who should have known better, but also more widely in nearly all British youth. Women's short skirts, bobbed hair, smoking in public, and loose sexual morals, and the mannered effeminacy of many Oxbridge men, were regarded as particularly offensive. On the other hand, the widespread image of the 'roaring twenties' is often formed in large measure by American examples, many of which had no parallel whatever in Britain. For instance, the Prohibition Amendment in the United States, in force between 1918 and 1933, which prohibited the manufacture or sale of any alcoholic beverage and which led directly to the rise of organised crime lords like Al Capone, obviously had no parallel in Britain. Nor were the license and 'vice' of Paris of the 'Lost Generation' or Weimar Berlin really like anything at all in Britain. London in the 1920s was extraordinarily sedate compared with other world metropolitan centres.

Nevertheless, the Home Secretary Sir William Joynson-Hicks was determined to clean up whatever low living there was in London, and launched a great campaign, among other things, against nightclubs frequented by the rich then flourishing in London. He also strictly enforced the laws against male homosexuality, prosecuted Radclyffe Hall's lesbian novel *The Well of Loneliness*, and raided exhibitions of 'pornographic' art. While England's sophisticates were shocked by his actions, as were its liberals, he unquestionably enjoyed widespread support in many quarters. It is important, too, to note that 'Jix' did not introduce any new restrictive legislation, only enforced laws already on the books. Many working-class persons and Labour supporters unquestionably supported the Tory government's Puritanism, which may also be seen as another aspect of its attempt to restore the pre-1914 world in so far as it could. (Although, ironically, Victorian England was notorious for its sexual underworld of prostitution and vice, which the state at the time made absolutely no attempt to curb.)

'Jix' was, essentially, a frightened conservative Evangelical Anglican rather than the quasi-fascist as he is sometimes depicted. He could work harmoniously with other religious conservatives, including Liberals and Labourites. This is best evidenced by one of the most extraordinary and perhaps significant events of the 1920s, the debate and vote in Parliament over the revision of the Church of England Prayer Book. During the years prior to the Prayer Book debate, a number of important trends had occurred within the Church of England. It had gradually been given greater powers over its own affairs, allowing it to make changes in its organisation with approval by Parliament only as a last step, and with the expectation that Parliament would acquiesce in anything the Church really wanted. (As the established church, the Church of England, was always subject to the final approval by Parliament of any significant changes it made.) This was seemingly enacted into law by the Enabling Act of 1919, which established the Church Assembly, a kind of Parliament of the church. Second, during the previous 40 years the 'High Church' wing of Anglicanism had gradually grown more powerful, especially in affluent parishes in London and the southeast. High Church Anglicans viewed the Church of England as, essentially, a reformed Catholic church rather than a Protestant one, and wished to introduce innovations into the Church of England's practice to correspond as closely as possible with the usages of the Roman Catholic church. A variety of pseudo-Catholic innovations had gradually been introduced into High Church parishes, such as the use of incense, confessions, and the reintroduction of celibate orders. All of this was extraordinarily offensive to the 'Low Church', Evangelical wing of the Church, which emphasised Anglicanism's Protestant, Reformation heritage and often drew upon the very strong tradition of popular anti-Catholicism which existed throughout Britain, especially in Scotland, Wales, and parts of the north of England like Liverpool.

These competing trends came to a head in 1927 when the Church attempted to gain Parliament's approval for a 'Revised' Prayer Book which seemed to embody many of the worst changes in a High Church direction that Evangelicals most feared. In particular, it seemed to sanction the Reservation of the Sacrament in Anglican Holy Communion (where the Sacrament was not shared among all members of the congregation), a pseudo-Catholic alteration which Evangelicals found particularly disturbing, implying the superiority of the priest over the congregation as a whole.

It may seem well-nigh incredible that matters such as the Reservation of the Sacrament in Anglican Holy Communion could become a burning issue in twentieth-century British politics, but it led to one of the most remarkable, and deeply felt, parliamentary debates of modern times. An extraordinary coalition of right-wing Evangelical Anglican Tories, led by Sir William Joynson-Hicks and Sir Thomas Inskip (1876–1947; later first viscount Caldecote; Inskip was then Solicitor-General and later served as Lord Chancellor) and left-wing pro-Protestant, anti-Catholic Labourites and Liberals, led by Rosslyn Mitchell (1879–1965), a Glasgow solicitor and Labour MP, combined to defeat the Revised Prayer Book by 238 votes to 205 on 15 December 1927. Few other issues which came before Parliament in the 1920s attracted more public discussion and debate. Supporters of the Revised Prayer Book complained, with some justice, that non-Anglicans (including a Parsee MP, Shapurji Saklatvala) voted on a matter wholly internal to the Church of England, but this was a necessary outcome of the Anglicans' status as the Established church.

Until very recently, the 'Prayer Book debate' has not received the attention by historians that it obviously deserves. Most historians have conceptualised twentieth-century British history purely in terms of secular ideology, social class, and economic change; that a purely religious question redolent of the more obscure theological debates of 300 years earlier could become a central issue in Parliament in the 1920s is seemingly so bizarre as to be outside serious notice. Yet from the 'Prayer Book debate' one might draw several important conclusions about British politics at the time. Religion still mattered enormously, both at the 'elite' and mass level, and non-economic, non-secular issues must simply not be dismissed as antique relics. These religious distinctions tended to cut across party lines, indeed across the apparently basic lines of ideology, and may have represented a fundamental fault-line in British consciousness essentially distinctive from that of the political parties. As well, the importance of grass roots Labour opinion shows that the party's MPs were sensitive to non-economic, non-trade union issues, even most unusual ones, and that they were often the direct successors, in this area, of the radical Liberal MPs of the previous generation. In a curious way, too, the vote against the Revised Prayer Book paralleled the elections on tariff reform in 1906 and 1923: although in Britain the Conservative party might be the normal majority party, in contrast there was a normal popular majority for the 'Left', which prevented a marked move to the Right when this was put to the electoral test. In religious terms, a coalition of Nonconformists and Evangelical Anglicans proved stronger than the Anglican's High Church wing, and prevented a determined attempt at swinging to the theological 'Right'.

The 1920s were a decade of peace between two terrible storms, and the attitude to foreign policy of the Tory government of the time reflected this fact. Indeed, in foreign policy there is little to report but growing efforts at achieving peace and reconciliation in Europe. Part of the reason for this lay in the fact that Sir Austen Chamberlain served as Foreign Minister during the whole of the period from 1924–29. Building on the foundations for reconciliation laid by Curzon and, more specifically, MacDonald, he was also fortunate in holding office at the same time as France's Foreign Minister Aristide Briand and Germany's Gustav Stresemann, both of whom were determined to pursue a policy of mutual reconciliation, and also simultaneously with American politician and Vice-President Charles Gates Dawes, who worked to limit excessive payments of reparations and more generally for peace. (All four of these men, including Austen Chamberlain, were awarded the Nobel Peace Prize. Dawes had another, rather extraordinary claim to fame: he was a talented songwriter, who wrote 'It's All in the Game', a standard popular song.) The 'Period of Fulfilment', as the mid and later 1920s are often known, saw the Locarno Conference and Treaties of 1925, which guaranteed the existing boundaries in Europe, pledged mutual arbitration and support in case of war, and led (March 1926) to the admission of Germany to the League of Nations. In 1927 came a darker cloud: the three-power naval conference in Geneva, where Britain, the United States, and Japan tried, and failed, to reach an agreement on the limitation of warships in the Pacific. But August 1928 saw the signing of the Kellogg–Briand Pact (named for Frank Kellogg, America's Secretary of State, and France's Foreign Minister Briand) which pledged its signatories, including Britain and the Dominions, to outlaw war and employ international means of conciliation and arbitration in cases of foreign disputes. By 1929, it seemed to most observers that perhaps the First World War was a 'war to end wars' after all, and that the millions had not died in vain. Even Britain's Conservatives, usually advocates of *realpolitik* and very suspicious of utopian schemes of international arbitration, seemed swept along by the worldwide mood of peace. It seemed literally inconceivable that a second worldwide general war, far deadlier than the last, could break out only 10 years later. The sudden and wholly unforeseen descent of Europe into preparations for another war is one important reason why the response to the rise of Hitler was so weak for so long: no one could believe that the situation could deteriorate so quickly and decisively.

For most Britons, possibly the most important aspect of overseas policy in the 1920s revolved around the constitutional changes which were occurring in the Empire, and the unrest in several of Britain's colonies. It had long been apparent that the self-governing Dominions – Canada, Australia, New Zealand, South Africa, and Newfoundland – were, in reality, separate sovereign nations, although they retained many crucial ties to Britain, especially the ceremonial and constitutional links to the Crown. (The Irish Free State, which nominally was in the same constitutional position as Canada and Australia, was, of course, in reality an entirely separate matter.) After the war, the question of the precise status of the self-governing Dominions became of greater significance. The war had greatly heightened the 'imperial idea' and imperial unity. It is perhaps not fully understood that the Empire reached its greatest extent after 1918, not before, taking in many of Germany's former colonies and Palestine, Transjordan, and Iraq in the Middle East. In 1924, a kind of 'world's fair', the British Empire Exhibition at Wembley in London, focused exclusively on the Empire and its achievements, attracting no less than 17 million visitors. In 1926, an Imperial Conference in London wrestled with the best method of ensuring something like legal equality for Britain and the Dominions (but not, of course, the colonies) within the Empire. A report, drafted by Lord Balfour (as Arthur Balfour, given an earldom in 1922, had become) devised the famous formula that Britain and the Dominions were 'autonomous Communities within the British Empire, equal in status... united by a common allegiance to the Crown, and freely associated as members of the British Commonwealth of Nations'. Thus, in 1926, the Commonwealth was officially born, although not until the passage of the Statute of Westminster in 1931 was this change given legal effect.

While internal affairs in the colonies and dependencies of the British Empire were relatively tranquil in this period, there was some unrest, in Mesopotamia and, especially, in India, where seething inter-communal violence between Hindus and Muslims (in which over 500 people died) and growing Indian nationalism, headed by Mohandas K. Gandhi (1869–1948) a London-educated barrister, committed to non-violent resistance, who had lived in South Africa for many years, and the Indian National Congress, made governing the country increasingly difficult, although it must also be said that for the most part British rule went on much as before. The Viceroy between 1926 and 1931, Lord Irwin (Edward Wood, who inherited the title of Viscount Halifax in 1934, and served as the extremely controversial Foreign Minister from 1938–40) was increasingly committed to granting eventual dominion status to India, a policy change which infuriated Britain's conservatives.

The period of the 1920s also saw one other very significant piece of basic legislation, the Equal Franchise Act of 1928, which voted the minimum voting age for women from 30 to 21, thus putting female suffrage on the same footing as male suffrage for the first time, and actually giving women a majority of the electorate. The unlikely father of the Act was Sir William Joynson-Hicks, who, in a parliamentary debate, offhandedly promised to pass such an act before the next General Election. Joynson-Hicks was, however, a genuine supporter of this reform who then piloted the act through a dubious Cabinet and Parliament. Many Tories feared that the so-called 'flapper vote' of young, irresponsible women would go heavily for Labour or the Liberals, and it is unlikely that this reform would have become law without Joynson Hicks' support. One result of this Act was that the British electorate was vastly larger than it had been less than twenty years before. In 1910, about 7.7 million men were enrolled to vote. In 1919, the electorate had grown to 21.8 million, and in 1929 to 28.9 million. The twentieth-century world of mass media politics became a necessity as a result of the obvious impossibility, under these conditions, of any kind of personal, face-to-face relationship with most voters in a constituency. This in turn gave the party leaders a greatly enhanced role, as media performers attempting, via radio, newsreels, and the press, to reach millions of voters in a short period of time.

By law, a General Election had to be held by October 1929, five years after the 1924 General Election. For the ruling Conservative party, the timing of the election was far from ideal. With the General Strike three years in the past, it was difficult to run a campaign on the issue of 'trade union subversion' or the like. Although there were boom conditions in the United States until the Stock Market crash of October 1929, economic conditions in Britain had not really improved and in early 1929 started to worsen, with unemployment beginning to rise again. The Tories appeared to have no issues to run on, and no really successful record of legislation or achievements in office. By-elections began to go very badly for the government, with the Tories losing a string of by-elections to both Labour and the Liberals in 1928–29 in all parts of the country by ever-increasing majorities, so that the swing against the Tories at by-elections rose from 5.8 per cent in 1927 to 12.9 per cent in 1929.

Labour had also done little to take a commanding place in the political world, MacDonald concentrating on foreign policy issues and the party issuing moderate declarations on policy. Most attention, however, came to the Liberals, who were determined to try for a strong comeback one more time. In October 1926 Asquith at long last retired as leader of the party (he had officially been leader since 1908, except for the 15 months in 1918–20 when he was out of Parliament; Sir Donad MacLean [1864–1932] was officially leader during this period, notwithstanding the fact that Lloyd George was Prime Minister). At long last, David Lloyd George officially became leader of the Liberal party as a whole, holding this position until November 1931. While there was still considerable grumbling at Lloyd George's ascendancy from pro-Asquith Liberals who had never forgiven him for splitting the party, it was recognised that Lloyd George was infinitely the most famous figure among the Liberals. In addition, Lloyd George still had in his personal possession the 'Lloyd George fund' of perhaps millions which he had collected from the sale of honours when he was Prime Minister. Reinvigorated, Lloyd George was determined to make an all-out attempt to regain their old place in the political hierarchy. To this end, he launched a series of policy statements which became well known. Some, like

Land and the Nation (1925) reiterated the old radical programme of independent smallholders. Two, however, *Britain's Industrial Future* (1928), known as the 'yellow book' and *We Can Conquer Unemployment* (1929) were seen as political landmarks. Heavily influenced by John Maynard Keynes and his newly emerging theories of deficit spending, they advocated a far-reaching programme of public works, to cost hundreds of millions of pounds, simultaneously to end mass unemployment and modernise Britain's infrastructure, especially through a huge scheme of road building, as well as the greater provision of public utilities like electricity and telephones. This programme was to be paid for by deficit spending, with the government deliberately spending more than it received in tax revenues in order to 'prime the pump' of consumer spending. Universally adopted as 'Keynesianism' throughout the Western world after 1945, such ideas had never been seriously proposed before, and seemed to many to represent a viable, progressive 'middle way' between laissez faire capitalism and state socialism. These ideas, however, ran directly contrary to the accepted economic wisdom of the time, in which unemployment could only be ameliorated by cutting the cost of wages, that is, reducing salaries. The Treasury and the government launched a major campaign to refute Lloyd George's proposals as impractical. This was the rather unsatisfactory political mood as Britain drifted towards another General Election.

7

The Second Labour Administration and the National Government, 1929–35

The 1929 election campaign was a rather unsatisfactory affair. The Conservatives, who, despite their unpopularity at by-elections, were favoured to win, campaigned under the rather curious slogan of 'Safety First'. This was an echo of a successful road safety campaign (and hence already well known as a slogan to the public) and also of previous appeals to the electorate portraying the Tories as the sensible policy of moderation. Labour had produced a gradualist, but in the British context, recognisably socialist programme (written by R.H. Tawney and Ramsay MacDonald) pledging to nationalise land, coal, power, transport, and life insurance, to extend social services, and cut expenditure on armaments. On the crucial issue of unemployment the programme was extremely vague, offering some generalities such as suggestions that waste and inefficiency in industry would be attacked and that there would be 'a direct increase of purchasing power in the hands of the workers', a goal obviously impossible to achieve. This last point may have represented an indirect bow to the proposals already offered privately to MacDonald by Sir Oswald Mosley. Mosley (1896–1980), a brilliant aristocrat who joined the Labour party in 1924, tried repeatedly to win MacDonald over to a programme of proto-Keynesian reflation of the economy to cure unemployment, but without much obvious success. As noted, the Liberal party, still led by Lloyd George, campaigned in 1929 on a very similar policy, and held high expectations of winning many seats.

The results of the election, held on 30 May 1929, were unsatisfactory for all the parties. The Tories suffered a catastrophic loss of seats, from 419 in 1924 to only 260, as well as a considerable reduction in their total vote. While Labour won more seats than any other party, it was still in a minority and actually polled fewer votes than the Tories. The hopes of the Liberals were almost wholly dashed. The results were as follows:

	Total votes	MPs elected	% of total vote
Conservative	8 656 473	260	38.2
Liberal	5 308 510	59	23.4
Labour	8 389 512	288	37.1
Communist	50 614	0	0.3
Others	243 266	8	1.0

A total of 22 648 375 votes were cast, 76.1 per cent of the electorate of 28.9 million. The electorate had grown by over seven million since the 1924 election, thanks in large measure to the enfranchisement of women aged from 21 to 30.

In 1929, Labour won most of the industrial and urban slum seats, scoring notable gains in east and south London and, in particular, in the west Midlands. In the County of London area, Labour won 36 of 58 seats, compared with only 19 in 1924. In Birmingham, hitherto a Chamberlainite Tory bastion, Labour won half the seats. Labour won most of the urban working-class seats throughout Britain, but was still virtually unrepresented in rural areas and the southeast outside of London. The Conservatives actually won nearly 300 000 more votes than Labour but secured 27 fewer seats. They won nearly as many seats in England as did Labour (221 compared with 226), especially in the south-east, but only one seat in Wales and only 20 of 71 seats in Scotland. The Liberals were terribly disappointed by the results, which were plainly unfair, since the 5.3 million votes they polled should have given them 144 seats rather than only 59. The Liberal areas of strength remained as before: Gaelic Scotland and Welsh Wales, Cornwall and Devon, parts of Norfolk and the east Midlands. The Liberals lost virtually all of their seats in the big cities, holding only two in London and two in Manchester.

Baldwin had, however, to resign and Ramsay MacDonald, it was equally clear, was entitled to form a Labour government although he was 48 seats short of even a majority of one in the House of Commons. This he did on 5 June 1929, six days after the General Election. The formation of the second Labour government in British history proved surprisingly difficult, with the distribution of the key offices among Labour's top men leading to much acrimony. In particular, it proved almost impossible to satisfy Arthur Henderson, who keenly wanted the Foreign Office, a well-deserved appointment. But MacDonald also wanted to continue jointly as Prime Minister and Foreign Minister or, failing that, appoint someone in his shadow like J.H. Thomas. MacDonald wished Henderson to become Lord Privy Seal with special responsibility for unemployment. There were also more than the usual number of disputes over appointments to the House of Lords, to legal offices, and the representation of avowed radicals in the government.

In the end the government did not look too different from Labour's administration five years before. Henderson finally got his wish and became Foreign

Minister; Snowden returned to the Exchequer; Thomas was given the office of Lord Privy Seal with responsibility for bringing down unemployment; and J.R. Clynes, the fifth of Labour's 'Big Five', became Home Secretary. Probably the greatest single novelty of the government was the appointment of a woman to a British Cabinet for the first time in history, with the selection of Margret Bondfield (1873–1953) as Minister of Labour. A trade unionist long active in women's affairs, she was on the right-wing of the party and a MacDonald loyalist. The Cabinet contained four peers – Lord Parmoor became Lord President of the Council and Lord Sankey, a pro-Labour judge, Lord Chancellor. Sidney Webb returned to the Cabinet as Colonial and Dominions Secretary with a peerage, became Lord Passfield. (As is well known his celebrated wife Beatrice Webb refused to be known as Lady Passfield.) Lord Thomson also returned to his old post as Air Minister, holding office until he was killed in the R101 airship disaster in France in October 1930. The rest of the Cabinet combined former Liberals, often of upper-class background, like Noel Buxton at the Agriculture Ministry and Sir Charles Trevelyan at the Department of Education, with Fabian lecturers like Arthur Greenwood (1880–1954) at the Ministry of Health, and leading members of the Co-operative movement like A.V. Alexander (1885–1965) at the Admiralty. As in 1924, only one recognised member of the party's Left was appointed to the Cabinet, George Lansbury (1859–1940; the actress Angela Lansbury is his granddaughter). Lansbury, a Christian socialist pacifist from the East End and former editor of the *Daily Herald* in 1912–22, became First Commissioner of Works. Although 37 members of the semi-separate Independent Labour Party were elected to the 1929 Parliament, often spirited critics of the government, its actual influence was slight. Much more important was the growing influence of the TUC under the potent leadership of Ernest Bevin (1881–1951), general secretary of the Transport and General Workers' Union, and Walter Citrine (1887–1983), general secretary of the TUC, whose aim was to maximise the influence of the trade unions on a Labour government. They were largely successful – even more successful than in the past – so that, especially after the formation of the National government in 1931, for many decades the TUC was unquestionably the most important single influence on the Labour party in and out of Parliament. Paradoxically, this helped keep Labour on the centre-left and prevented a takeover by the extreme left, the TUC being fiercely anti-Communist and anxious to avoid extreme militant action, such as the General Strike, whenever possible. All in all, the 1929 Labour Cabinet appeared more workmanlike than its predecessor, and was probably closer to the trade union movement and its centre-leftist ideology.

The new Labour government also contained many interesting figures at the junior ministerial level, including several figures of great import in later years, like Clement Attlee, Herbert Morrison, Emanuel Shinwell, and Hugh Dalton. Sir Oswald Mosley was appointed Chancellor of the Duchy of Lancaster, with special responsibilities for alleviating unemployment. Another controversial appointment was that of Sir William Jowitt (1885–1957) as Attorney-General. Jowitt had been elected as a Liberal and had to seek re-election as a Labourite. No seat could be found in Parliament for nearly two years for the Solicitor-General appointed in 1930, Sir Stafford Cripps (1889–1952), a maverick left-wing, well-born Anglican Christian Socialist, who was the son of Lord Parmoor and the nephew of Beatrice Webb. MacDonald also added another woman to his government at the junior ministerial level, Susan Lawrence (1871–1947), Parliamentary Secretary at the Ministry of Health.

The new government was, of course, dependent, as in 1924, upon the good-will of the other parties to remain in office. Rather remarkably, some sort of working partnership with the Tories was considered but rejected on the grounds that the two parties differed fundamentally on the tariff question, with Labour continuing to carry the Free Trade banner. This left the Liberals, with Lloyd George in the same unfortunate position as Asquith five years earlier, of having to support Labour from the outside in preference to the Tories. MacDonald began moderately enough, with vague schemes of economic development promised in the King's speech, but no socialistic measures. MacDonald was actually already making very clear noises about functioning as a 'Council of State' in which 'cooperation will be welcomed' with the other parties; this might be seen, perhaps, as presaging the extraordinary events of two years later.

Labour took office at the height of the worldwide boom of the 1920s, although there were already many signs of an impending downturn while, of course, the whole interwar period in Britain was marked by extraordinarily high levels of unemployment. On 29 October 1929 came the Wall Street crash, when American stocks lost nearly $16 billion in value in one week, the equivalent of over $400 billion, or £250 billion, in today's money. The American Federal Reserve and the American government mismanaged the situation in an extraordinarily incompetent way, raising interest rates and doing nothing to restore investment confidence. The Crash had direct effects throughout Europe, still in a fragile state after the war, but fewer direct effects in Britain, although the conviction on fraud charges of Clarence Hatry, a fabulously wealthy self-made City financier, in September 1929, caused a panic of its own in the City. As a result of all of these things, unemployment in Britain began to mount up inexorably, although not perhaps in the spectacularly catastrophic manner as in the United States or Germany, where it seemed by 1932 as if the end of capitalism was nigh, if not the end of civilisation. There were 1 164 000 persons unemployed in Britain in June 1929, 1 520 000 by January 1930, but then 1 761 000 in April, 2 319 000 in October, and 2 500 000 in December 1930. The number of unemployed still kept rising thereafter, but at a slower rate, reaching a peak of 2 955 000 in January 1932 after the formation of the National government, before beginning to decline. As a percentage of the workforce, unemployment (on average, for the year as a whole) was 11.0 per cent in 1929, 14.6 per cent in 1930, and 21.5 per cent in 1932. The rate dropped below 20 per cent only in 1934, and below 15 per cent only in 1937. As horrifying as these figures seem to be, they were probably significantly lower than in the United States or Germany, where unemployment may have touched 35–40 per cent in 1933 (before, respectively, Franklin Roosevelt and Adolf Hitler came to power).

As always in interwar Britain, too, unemployment was far worse in the staple industries and in the old northern and Celtic industrial heartland than in London, the south-east, or the west Midlands. In the staple industries of the old industrial areas, unemployment was truly appalling and its human cost can hardly be exaggerated, or even imagined. In 1932, the worst year of the Great Depression in Britain, unemployment had reached an incredible 62.0 per cent among all workers in shipbuilding and repairing throughout the United Kingdom. Among all workers in iron and steel founding, unemployment averaged 47.9 per cent; among pig iron workers, 43.8 per cent. Unemployment was also over 30 per cent in the crucial industries of coalmining and cotton textiles, as well as in pottery and earthenware and among dock workers. In contrast, in newer trades and the service industries the picture was distinctly brighter, at least relatively: unemployment stood at 16.8 per cent in electrical engineering and 12.6 per cent among workers in the distributive trades. In regional terms, the unemployment rate was just as unequally distributed, standing, in 1932, at 36.5 per cent in Wales, and at just over 27 per cent in Scotland, Northern Ireland, and Northern England, in contrast to only 13.7 per cent in London and south-east England. The very symbol of the mass unemployment of the 1930s was Jarrow, a shipbuilding town on Tyneside near Newcastle. Palmer's shipyards, formerly the largest employer in the town, closed and unemployment reached 80 per cent (some sources say 60 per cent). Jarrow became nationally renowned in 1936 when a 'hunger march', organised by the local MP, fiery left-wing Labourite Ellen Wilkinson (1891–1947), saw 200 unemployed march the 274 miles to London to present a petition to the House of Commons; Wilkinson's famous book on Jarrow, *The Town That Was Murdered*, also did much to make its plight known to all. In the colliery areas of South Wales, the situation was almost as grim, and was constantly highlighted by the famous Labour MP for Ebbw Vale, Aneurin Bevan (1897–1960). It must be realised, however, that the upper and middle classes based in and around London, and, indeed, the lower middle classes in these areas, were shielded from the very worst effects of the Great Depression. Indeed, if anything they were in a better position than they had been for some decades, as the cost of living declined and a good deal of growth occurred, especially after 1932, in the service sector. The relative prosperity of the middle classes (combined with such pre-existing factors as Britain's victory in the Great War and the continued existence of the Empire) itself had profound political consequences: unlike Germany, whose middle classes were heavily affected by the Depression, in Britain the middle classes never turned to fascism or the extreme Right, and never left the political centre-right. Similarly, despite all the unemployment, with rare exceptions the working classes never embraced Communism and never moved to the Left of the Labour party.

MacDonald's government thus came into office facing, almost immediately, an economic situation of arguably unprecedented seriousness verging on the catastrophic for whose amelioration it was responsible. There is universal agreement among historians that it failed to alleviate the Depression and there has been considerable debate among historians as to why it failed. It might help, however, to clarify exactly what was demanded. Above all, Britain's economy failed in the area of export-oriented industries. But the success of exports depended upon the willingness of other countries to buy British goods, and no British government had any control over this except possibly in the Empire. In any case all other countries were suffering in the Depression and many, most notably the United States, were erecting higher and ever higher tariff barriers to protect their own goods.

Essentially, too, Labour could opt for one of four different approaches to alleviating mass unemployment. It might introduce far-reaching socialist measures such as nationalising the banks and the basic industries; it could introduce a tariff wall protecting Britain and the Empire; it could attempt proto-Keynesian measures of 'pump-priming' and deficit spending; or it could remain with the traditional neo-orthodox approach of waiting out the worst of the Depression as labour costs declined in the wake of unemployment. Among these possibilities, Labour was least likely to pursue far-reaching measures of socialism, despite its doctrines and rhetoric. Lacking a majority in Parliament, it could not pass any measures of nationalisation even if it wished to. None of Labour's leaders were genuinely committed to nationalisation, except in the very long term, and certainly did not wish to affect business confidence adversely. Increasingly, too, MacDonald was frankly abandoning any pretence to socialism, even in theory and was already moving in a quasi-Tory direction.

The solution of a tariff barrier around the Empire had been a panacea urged by many Tories for nearly thirty years; whenever put to the electoral test, however, it had proven (perhaps surprisingly) an automatic vote-loser, chiefly because it entailed a 'tax on bread' harmful to the working classes. MacDonald himself, however, was, from early 1930, moving in the direction of advocating a revenue tariff to pay for social services. Yet, most Labourites remained self-consciously the inheritors of the nineteenth-century 'religion' of Free Trade and opposed a general tariff as adamantly as most Liberals – somewhat incongruously, since (as many Tories pointed out) for Labour to advocate intervention in the economy everywhere except imposing tariffs was highly inconsistent. In particular, however, Philip Snowden, the Chancellor of the Exchequer, remained a absolutist opponent of tariffs under any circumstances.

The third option, an expansionist fiscal policy aimed at decreasing unemployment, was the one which all Western governments since 1945 would have automatically adopted in similar circumstances. In 1929, however, and despite the efforts of Lloyd George to popularise such a programme, it seemed to defy every accepted economic law and lacked the theoretical basis which Keynes would give it in the mid-1930s. Despite Sir Oswald Mosley's urging of such a policy, the Labour government never embraced it in a wholehearted way, although it did enact a number of public works policies aimed at job creation.

This left the orthodox approach of balancing the budget, reducing expenditure wherever possible, deflating the economy, and hoping for the inevitable upswing in the business cycle which had always come after previous recessions. In general, Labour pursued this policy in its two years in office, although sometimes making attempts at a more expansionist programme.

Policy-making on the question of unemployment was delegated to J.H. Thomas and three assistants, George Lansbury, Thomas Johnston (1882–1965), a Scottish journalist and MP and Sir Oswald Mosley. Thomas seemed initially to favour an expansionist policy based on road and railway improvements and development in the Empire. But most such proposals were, in effect, vetoed by civil servants in charge of spending departments and by the Chancellor of the Exchequer,

Philip Snowden, a rigorous Gladstonian, and Treasury officials. In January 1930 MacDonald created an Economic Advisory Council, which included an amazingly distinguished group of economists, trade unionists, and businessmen, among them Keynes, G.D.H. Cole, Sir Josiah Stamp, R.H. Tawney, and Ernest Bevin. Rather sadly, it accomplished little despite its pioneering attempt to arrive at fresh ideas from a disparate body of experts. In its attempts to produce cooperation across the ideological spectrum, however, one can perhaps see some glimpses of the motivation for the National government formed the following year. The government also attempted to reorganise the coalmining industry. Although it cut the miners' hours of work, it certainly did not attempt nationalisation but instead subsidised coal exports. Both the Tories and the Liberals criticised the government's coalmining act, which narrowly passed. Throughout the period of the second Labour government, MacDonald was kept in office by the Liberals (who held the balance of power) on the understanding that the government would agree to enact a reform of the British voting system in the direction of electoral reform such as proportional representation, which would increase the Liberals' representation in the Commons. It became increasingly clear that Labour had no intention of doing this, not least of all because MacDonald and Lloyd George detested one another, but also because many backbench Liberals opposed any working arrangement with Labour. Paradoxically, both MacDonald on one hand and many Liberals on the other were moving closer to the Conservatives' position, with their emphasis on a tariff to revive British trade.

The most concerted attempt to move the Labour government towards a proto-Keynesian programme of mass public works expenditure came from Oswald Mosley, who, acting independently, submitted to the Cabinet what became known as the 'Mosley Memorandum' in February 1930. (Although a minister, Mosley – who was only 33 years old – did not have a seat in the Cabinet.) He recommended public spending increases, the rationalisation of industry by the state, public control of banking, and an imperial tariff and the bulk buying of goods throughout the Empire. The proposals were formally rejected in May, although after considerable debate. J.H. Thomas, Mosley's minister, also resigned the following month (becoming Dominions Secretary); Vernon Hartshorn (1872–1931), a former miners' union executive, took his place, while Clement Attlee took the place of Mosley. MacDonald also announced that he himself would take general control of unemployment policy. While Mosley persisted, at special Labour party conferences, in advancing his radical programme, he was consistently rebuffed by Labour delegates, still very loyal to MacDonald. In December 1930, he began the formation of a separate, radical party, which was officially formed in February 1931 as the New Party. Initially he was supported by 17 radical Labour MPs, including Aneurin Bevan, but in the end only six Labour MPs (among them Oliver Baldwin, Stanley's left-wing son, who was a Labour MP) joined Mosley's new group, a number which then dwindled to three. After the 1930 election Mosley's pro-fascist proclivities, evident before, became clear, and in 1932, severing all ties with Labour, Mosley formed the British Union of Fascists (BUF) in imitation of Benito Mussolini's blackshirts. (One should be very clear, however, on one or two points: prior to 1933 or 1934 Mosley was not a follower of Hitler – whose Nazi party did not even come to power until January 1933 – and nor was it anti-semitic; indeed, initially the BUF had Jewish members.) From 1934 Mosley increasingly turned to Hitler as his role model, becoming overtly anti-semitic, actively recruiting thugs from the slums, and responding to his opponents and hecklers with violence.

Labour was thus forced back on a traditional neo-orthodox policy to deal with unemployment, modified by some attempts at increased public spending. This was, in effect, a confession of bankruptcy at how to deal with the worst economic downturn in modern history, especially for a Labour government which existed to represent the workers and build the 'New Jerusalem'. MacDonald was under no illusions whatever about his plight, noting in his diary in December 1929, 'Unemployment is baffling us ... I sit in my room in Downing Street alone and in silence. The cup has been put to my lips – and it is empty.' Labour did pass a number of significant measures, including an Unemployment Insurance Bill in November 1929, which put the onus on wel-fare officials to prove that an applicant for unemployment insurance had refused reasonable offers of work, rather than the applicant prove that he was genuinely seeking work. On the other hand it also considerably tightened eligibility for benefits as the Depression deepened, in particular for married women. The gov-ernment, lacking a majority, had no luck with its other proposals. An Education Bill to raise the mandatory school leaving age from 14 to 15 was defeated by the Lords and had been heavily opposed by Roman Catholics, who viewed it as an attempt to secularise Catholic education. Other controversial measures, such as an attempt at electoral reform, also failed to pass. The government did increase expenditure on public works projects, but to a limited extent and insufficient to make any impact on unemployment, which mounted relentlessly.

In foreign and colonial affairs the record of the Labour government was also very mixed. The European mood, which in the mid-1920s very strongly favoured international reconciliation and unity, turned sour with the Depression. Nevertheless, the government had a number of triumphs, especially the London Naval Conference of 1930 (presided over by MacDonald), which led to an agree-ment among America, Britain, and Japan to restrict their naval tonnage to the ratio 5:5:3. Britain also strengthened its commitment to the international adju-dication of disputes, slowed down work on the Singapore naval base, and re-established diplomatic relations with the Soviet Union. It also made some progress on the perpetually vexed question of German war reparations, extend-ing the time-period under which Germany had to pay in exchange for a guaran-teed payment of £2 million per year. Already, however, the dark clouds of the 1930s were gathering: Japanese aggression in Manchuria, Mussolini making increasingly xenophobic speeches, Germany moving more and more in the direction of ultra-nationalist rule.

Even more trouble occurred in the British colonies. Arthur Henderson forced the resignation of Lord Lloyd (George Lloyd, 1879–1949), the High Commissioner for Egypt, for being too firm with the Egyptian government and too slow in putting Anglo-Egyptian relations on a friendlier footing in the face of growing Arab nationalism. A new Arab treaty with Egypt in August 1929,

following Lloyd's resignation, ended British occupation of the country except
for the Suez canal and turned the Sudan into an Anglo-Egyptian condominium.
Negotiations over this treaty broke down, however, and no treaty was promul-
gated until 1936. In Palestine, the British government had done its best during
the 1920s to foster a Zionist infrastructure in that backward area; during the
1920s, British policy in Palestine seemed to favour the Jews and was certainly
not pro-Arab. In August 1929, a few months after Labour took office, occurred
the 'Wailing Wall' incident, an outburst of militant Arab hostility at the growing Jewish presence in which 133 Jews and 116 Arabs were killed in Jerusalem
and elsewhere. The new Colonial Secretary, Lord Passfield, issued a White Paper
in October 1930 which restricted future Jewish immigration to lands already
in Zionist possession. This began a decade of the steady erosion of the British
commitment to the Balfour Declaration and the continuing appeasement of the
Arabs, culminating in the MacDonald White Paper of May 1939. By restricting
the areas of Jewish settlement, it also foreshadowed eventual partition of the
Mandate as a solution to the Palestine question.

It was in India, however, that the most controversy developed. Throughout
the 1920s, India saw an endemic and seething feeling of mutiny approaching
insurrection, led by the Congress Party of Mohandas Gandhi and Jawarharlal
Nehru, and the growing tide of Muslim Indian nationalism headed by
Mohammed Ali Jinnah, although it must also be stressed that British colonial
administration, trade, and internal development went on much as before. An
Indian Statutory Commission, headed by the former Liberal minister Sir John
Simon, was appointed in 1927 to examine India's future. It included a number
of Labour party nominees, among them Clement Attlee and Vernon Hartshorn.
In October 1929 (before the Simon Commission reported), the Viceroy Lord
Irwin issued a seemingly momentous statement that the 'natural issue of India's
constitutional progress is the attainment of dominion status'. On paper, this was
a truly revolutionary alteration of British policy, and led to vehement criticism
from the Conservative party's right wing, although no one really believed it
was likely in the foreseeable future, least of all India's nationalists. The
Simon Report itself, issued in June 1930, was not nearly as radical, calling for
an enlarged electorate and responsible government in the British provinces (as
opposed to the princely states). Because high expectations had been dashed,
a widespread campaign of civil disobedience broke out throughout India,
headed by Gandhi and his associates. In response, MacDonald summoned a so-
called Round Table conference in London in November 1930. Boycotted by
the Congress Party, it did include many of India's leading princes, who agreed
to join in any Indian federation which eventually emerged (and thus signed their
own death warrants as local rulers). The fury of the Tory right was greater than
ever. Opposition to any hint at Indian independence became increasingly
headed by Winston Churchill, who now lost any remaining pretence to his old
Liberalism and headed the 'Die-hard' right, at least over this issue. In 1931, he
resigned from the Conservative Shadow Cabinet, a step which kept him in the
political wilderness for the next eight years. In February 1931, Churchill
renownedly described Gandhi as 'a seditious Middle Temple lawyer, now
posing as a Fakir of a type well known in the East, striding half-naked up the

steps of the Viceregal Palace to parley on equal terms with the representative of the King-Emperor'. He also stated many times in after-dinner speeches that he hoped that Gandhi would be bound hand and foot and trampled by an elephant ridden by the Viceroy. Baldwin and the party's moderates were much more sanguine and seemed to accept the likelihood of a greater degree of self-government for India with surprisingly little discord: Irwin (later Lord Halifax, the Foreign Minister) the Viceroy, was one of the pillars of the Tory party.

By early 1930, it was clear that the Labour government was in serious electoral difficulties, losing a string of by-elections. According to historians who have investigated this in detail, there was a swing to the Conservatives at by-elections of 6.9 per cent in 1930 and 10.1 per cent in 1931. Clearly, the government's inability to make even a dent in unemployment was the main reason for this electoral slump; this led to a mood of apathy among Labour activists, who declined to work for the party. Although the party promoted some younger men of talent like Herbert Morrison (1888–1965), who reached the Cabinet in March 1931 as Minister of Transport, MacDonald's was an unusually old government. While MacDonald was still very popular, widely seen as arguably the ablest politician in the country at this time, relations between members of the Cabinet were unusually acrimonious. Relations between MacDonald and Arthur Henderson, in particular, were notably bad. The government had also alienated many in the trades unions and most of the far left. Because of the government's unpopularity, MacDonald could not dare to call a General Election, at which Labour would certainly be defeated, but continued to limp along dependent upon Liberal and Tory goodwill.

The electoral collapse of Labour came about at the same time as the other two parties were both in the midst of great internal turmoil, especially the Conservatives. Stanley Baldwin, the leader of the Tories since 1923, was still widely regarded as, to a surprising extent, a political nonentity. Having lost the 1929 General Election it was obvious that a movement to replace him as leader would gain force; in a similar situation in Britain today, it is very difficult to see him surviving as party leader. The specific movement to replace Baldwin as leader began in July 1929, when Lord Beaverbrook, proprietor of *The Daily Express*, launched a campaign for 'Empire Free Trade', another revival of the old Chamberlainite tariff reform programme. At this time *The Daily Express* had an average daily circulation of 1.6 million, second among Fleet Street newspapers, and Beaverbrook's influence was enormous. The tariff reform cry had been heard many times before, always proving electorally disastrous, but with unemployment worsening by the week and British manufacturing industry in a seemingly terminal state, 'Empire Free Trade' was likely to prove more popular than in the past. Beaverbrook joined forces with Lord Rothermere, the owner of the *Daily Mail*, the newspaper with the largest circulation of all (1 968 000) to form a United Empire Party. Baldwin moved some way towards the presslords' position, advocating the 'safeguarding' of threatened industries but shying away from any 'tax on food' without a referendum. Baldwin's position came under threat at this time from a variety of other sources. Churchill (who remained opposed to 'food taxes'), now strongly influential on the Tory right, split with Baldwin over India; Neville Chamberlain, who had just (in June 1930) become head of the Conservative Party's organisation, the powerful Central Office machine, was being seen more and more as a likely successor to Baldwin.

In March 1931, things came to a head at the by-election in St George's, Westminster, the constituency in London's West End which included many of the wealthiest areas in Britain, including Mayfair and Belgravia. There Alfred Duff Cooper (1890–1954), a rising Tory MP who had lost his seat in 1929, stood as the pro-Baldwin candidate against Sir Ernest Petter, a right-wing engineer, who stood as an anti-Baldwin, pro-'Empire Free Trade' Independent Conservative (there were no other candidates). In one of the most spirited and closely watched by-elections in history, Duff Cooper won handily. Two days before the by-election, Baldwin made one of the most famous political speeches of the twentieth century, furiously denouncing Beaverbrook and Rothermere, and concluding memorably, 'What the proprietorship of these papers is aiming at is power, but power without responsibility – the prerogative of the harlot throughout the ages.' (These famous words were apparently written by Rudyard Kipling, Baldwin's cousin.) This by-election triumph certainly saved Baldwin, who continued to lead the Conservative party for another six years. Paradoxically, however, the results did little to weaken the growing strength of the pro-tariff reform lobby. Not only among businessmen, but from quarters which were deeply hostile to tariffs and strongly supportive of Free Trade often for generations, a virtual consensus was now growing up that the unique severity of the Great Depression required the erection of new safeguards for British industry and for British workers. Many economists (including Keynes), City of London magnates, the TUC, and even voices within the Liberal party, were now willing to rethink their previously sacred doctrines.

The Liberal party, too, was plagued by internal dispute. Mistrust between former supporters of Asquith (who had died in 1928) and Lloyd George meant that meetings of party members were often extremely divisive. The party was disunited over virtually the whole range of issues from support for the Labour government to tariffs and economic policy. As well, Lloyd George still had his large personal fund, which he was free to use as he wished for the party's benefits, while the party itself was virtually insolvent. Electorally, the party seemed to be dying on its feet after 1929, losing support at most by-elections, almost always to the Tories. Many lifelong Liberals, too, had come to the view that the shibboleth of Free Trade was now obsolete, and were ready to consider tariffs to deal with the economic emergency. After 1929, the Liberals seemed to have lost almost all sense of purpose.

By the middle of 1931 a full-scale national economic crisis, arguably without any peacetime precedent in history, was in the process of unfolding. The Labour government had appointed two high-powered and distinguished committees to make recommendations on the economy, the Macmillan Committee, appointed in 1929, headed by H.P. MacMillan, a Scottish barrister, officially known as the Committee on Finance and Industry; and a Committee on National Expenditure, appointed early in 1931, and headed by Sir George May (1871–1946), the secretary of the Prudential Assurance Company, and chiefly comprised of businessmen and accountants. It was widely expected that both, especially the May Committee, would recommend significant government expenditure cuts. In the middle of 1931 the world's international banking system had virtually collapsed, especially in Germany, Austria, and elsewhere in central Europe. The City of London, although relatively strong, was certain to be adversely affected by these developments.

The crisis broke in the summer of 1931. Against a background of 2.7 million unemployed and a catastrophic decline in British exports, gold deposits in the Bank of England were recalled by foreign governments at the rate of £2.5 million per day (about £60 million in today's money). While interest rates were raised sharply, the situation deteriorated still further so that, by late August, there was agreement among key City bankers that the British financial system was about to collapse. At virtually the same time, the May Committee issued its report, which turned out to be far more radical than anyone had foreseen. It recommended new taxation (totalling £24 million) but also cuts in government spending amounting to £96 million, most of which was to come, in its view, from reducing unemployment benefits. The gloomy prognostications it made of the state of the British economy further aggravated the financial crisis, as remaining foreign confidence in sterling dwindled.

The recommendations of the May Committee were precisely the opposite of what any similar group would have recommended in post-1945 Britain. It proposed to reduce economic demand for goods and services still further, while the crying need of the hour was for 'pump-priming' and greater consumer expenditure to stimulate the economy. In this, the May Committee reflected the neo-orthodox position that wage cuts and reductions in government expenses would reduce the cost of labour and other inputs in the cost of production, and hence make British goods more competitive internationally. Politically, the May Committee also alienated, in the most basic way, the bedrock of Labour and its supporters who would be the primary sufferers in any reduction of expenditure on the unemployed.

At this time, in August 1931, newspapers and opinion-leaders began to enunciate the idea of a 'National government' to meet the unprecedented emergency. MacDonald was also advised, by bankers and others with whom he met, to open official negotiations with the other two parties. A series of preliminary meetings did occur in mid-August, but with no effect. MacDonald and Snowden, who had both accepted the main findings of the May Committee, now began lengthy discussions in Cabinet about the extent and nature of the substantial spending cuts which were envisioned. Meetings between MacDonald and the leaders of the Opposition parties – which, of course still held a majority in Parliament – also increased. Essentially, the government was willing to cut expenditure by about £56 million, but the two opposition parties insisted that cuts of the order of £78 million or more were necessary. Snowden believed that the next budget was likely to be in deficit by £170 million, far higher than even the May Committee foresaw. It was also necessary to raise a large emergency loan from Wall Street bankers in America, and their view of the crisis became crucial.

The Labour Cabinet, meeting all day for a crucial session on 19 August 1931, moved a long way towards accepting substantial cuts and even came close to ratifying the imposition of a tariff. A serious and, in the end irrevocable, split emerged in the Cabinet over accepting in full all of the cuts in unemployment benefits. In the end, it deferred a decision. New rounds of party meetings followed, while attitudes in the full Cabinet hardened against accepting all of the proposed cuts. As well, the leaders of the TUC came out against further cuts in unemployment benefits or in the pay of public sector workers like teachers. In contrast, the opposition party leaders made it clear that they would oppose in Parliament anything less than the full round of cuts. Defeat in Parliament would have meant the end of the Labour government, but, as well, an uncertain future thereafter as leading politicians turned over all of the unpalatable possibilities, such as a General Election, against the background of impending financial crisis.

The idea for an emergency National government apparently came from Sir Herbert Samuel, the acting leader of the Liberal party (Lloyd George was ill) in conversation with King George V on 23 August 1931. The King was holding discussions with the three party leaders after MacDonald made clear that the Labour government might well have to resign. Soon after, Baldwin agreed to serve in such an emergency National government under MacDonald, or alternatively to form a Conservative or Tory–Liberal government. The King increasingly looked to MacDonald as the national leader in the emergency situation, and prevailed upon him to remain as Prime Minister even if other Labour Cabinet ministers resigned. The role of King George V in the 1931 crisis was certainly important, even crucial, and harkened back to the politically active monarchy of the previous century. While King George was certainly an anti-socialist in his personal views, he had good, even genuinely friendly relations with MacDonald and other Labour ministers, and was obviously anxious not to foment class-based hostilities.

The final crisis within the Labour Cabinet came over the key decision to cut unemployment benefits by 10 per cent, with the Cabinet deeply and irrevocably split, at its final meeting on 23 August 1931, between a majority of 11 who were in favour of accepting the cuts and a minority of nine who were not. It was now clear that the government would be compelled to resign; this MacDonald attempted to do the next night at a meeting with King George. Instead, the King called for a crucial meeting of the three party leaders on Monday, 24 August 1931. As a result, provisional agreement was reached on the formation of an all-party National government. The Labour Cabinet, however, knew little or nothing of this development. Each member had handed his letter of resignation to MacDonald, but was not aware that the government was actually at an end. At a stunned final Labour Cabinet meeting on 25 August 1931, MacDonald informed them that the Labour government elected in 1929 was at an end, and that he was heading a temporary emergency Cabinet composed of selected individuals, rather than a Cabinet in the normal sense; MacDonald thus in effect dismissed most of his amazed colleagues. MacDonald asked a few Cabinet loyalists – Snowden, Thomas, and Sankey – to join the emergency National government and they agreed. He did not at this stage ask any other ministerial colleagues to join: MacDonald simply washed his hands of the Labour Cabinet.

Ramsay MacDonald's actions in the summer of 1931 are among the most controversial in modern British political history. For decades thereafter, MacDonald was invariably depicted as a traitor, if not a class traitor, to the

Labour movement, and occupied the place of unique odium always reserved for traitors. MacDonald's alleged treason became the subject of a novel well known in its day, Howard Spring's *Fame is the Spur*, made into a famous British movie 15 years later, in 1946. Until the 1970s it was almost impossible to mention MacDonald's name in Labour circles without venom. There is probably some truth, perhaps a good deal of truth, to a part of this critique. It had been fairly clear for years that MacDonald was uneasy with his Labour roots, and, as a lonely widower, was cultivating the close friendship of well-born women, especially Lady Londonderry, a relationship which (though, apparently, platonic) became so close as to cause considerable scandal. MacDonald, a loner with only a vague political ideology, was also clearly becoming uneasy with most of his Labour colleagues and, perhaps, with the Labour party. It seemed to many that he was moving markedly to the political right; indeed, moving along the well-trodden and familiar path previously taken by Joseph Chamberlain, David Lloyd George (at least from 1915 to 1922), and Winston Churchill from the left to the right of British politics. There is certainly an element of substance in this critique of Ramsay MacDonald. On the other hand, it seems equally clear that, however brusque and high-handed his treatment of his Labour colleagues in 1931, he genuinely regretted the breach which had grown up between them.

In August 1931, the second Labour government thus abruptly passed into history. It was surely one of the least successful governments of the twentieth century and among the most obscure. Because Labour would not form a government in its own right for another 14 years, the leadership careers of many of its members came to a sudden end while, because so many lost their seats in the General Election held a few months later, many were quickly forgotten. Such members of the Cabinet as William Adamson, Tom Johnston, H.B. Lees Smith, and Thomas Shaw, are among the least known senior politicians in twentieth-century British politics. Many were already old, and only five lived to serve in the Labour Cabinet elected in 1945. For whatever reason, few received peerages and their careers at Westminster ended decisively in 1931.

MacDonald's task then became the formation of a National government. Its formation was announced on the evening of 24 August 1931, a few hours after the Labour government resigned. It included four Conservatives, two Liberals, and three other Labourites whom MacDonald persuaded to stay on. The Tories, Stanley Baldwin (Lord President of the Council), Neville Chamberlain (Minister of Health), Sir Samuel Hoare (Secretary for India), and Sir Philip Cunliffe-Lister (President of the Board of Trade), were somewhat curiously chosen but naturally held what in the final analysis was a whip hand over the other coalition partners, being much the largest party in the new government. Almost equally important were the Liberals, who still held the balance of power in the new government. This was given recognition by the key offices they were given, Sir Herbert Samuel at the Home Office and Lord Reading (Sir Rufus Isaacs, 1860–1935) at the Foreign Office. No more than 15 or 20 Labour MPs followed MacDonald into supporting the National government; some estimates put the number as low as eight. While this number included some senior figures, MacDonald's choice of appointees was very limited. By far the two most senior figures to remain with MacDonald were Philip Snowden, who stayed as

Chancellor of the Exchequer, and J.H. Thomas, who was given the Dominions Office. Lord Sankey, the former Liberal Lord Chancellor, also kept his old job. Below the Cabinet often were the ministers and junior ministers. The bulk of these were Conservatives (including the former leader of the party, Sir Austen Chamberlain, who was given the post of First Lord of the Admiralty, but outside of the Cabinet), with Liberals also strongly represented: among 18 ministers not in the Cabinet, eight were Tories, six Liberals, one non-party, but only two were Labourites (Lord Amulree and Sir William Jowitt). Among the 35 junior ministers (who included such future notables as Anthony Eden and Duff Cooper), 19 were Tories, 10 Liberals, six non-party (mainly Royal Household appointments), but only two were Labourites, one being Malcolm MacDonald, the Prime Minister's son. The great majority of sitting Labour MPs refused to join the coalition government, leaving MacDonald with only a tiny rump.

The new government was also notable for whom it excluded. Most obviously, despite claims to being an emergency National government, it was without David Lloyd George (although his son Gwilym held a junior post) and Winston Churchill. Lloyd George was ill (although he served in the Commons for another 13 years). Churchill, increasingly at odds with the Tories' leadership, now began a period of eight years of intense alienation from the policies of the National government, eventually becoming the embodiment of opposition to its Appeasement policies and, in due course, the saviour of the nation. Also excluded were many well-known right-wing Tories, especially the very talented Leopold Amery (vetoed by MacDonald as too extreme), Lord Salisbury and the other still-important Cecils, Lord Brentford (Sir William Joynson-Hicks), Lord Hailsham (added to the Cabinet in November), and other stalwarts of Baldwin's former Cabinet. Despite these omissions, however, this rather strange collection of disparate individuals held office as the first National government from 24 August until 5 November 1931.

The new government's tasks were enormous and even its continued existence uncertain. Because so few Labour MPs joined MacDonald, Labour still remained the largest single party in the House of Commons: in other words, the so-called 'National Government' did not include Parliament's largest party. However, soon after Parliament met in early September, it did win a vote of confidence by 311-251, suggesting that it had a working majority of about 30 seats or so. Philip Snowden then put forward his latest Budget proposal, increasing both direct and indirect taxes, and cutting expenditure all around. Benefits to the unemployed were cut by 10 per cent and all public employees suffered salary cuts, with teachers losing 15 per cent. By these means the Budget was, at last, balanced. The next step was much more unexpected. The Bank of England's gold supply had been steadily draining away to overseas creditors. In mid-September came word of the so-called 'Mutiny at Invergordon', in fact a strike of naval lower-deck able seamen at the Royal Naval port in northern Scotland against the proposed pay cuts which struck able seamen, especially unmarried men, especially hard, particularly compared with officers. Talk of a 'strike' was led, as it happened, by active Communists. To many foreigners (and, indeed, many in Britain), for the Royal Navy to 'mutiny' was a trumpet blast that the end of the world was at hand, and something like international financial panic ensued. In mid-September the majority of gold in the Bank of England was withdrawn by overseas creditors. This led directly to a major change in British financial policy; on 19 September the Governor of the Bank of England, Montagu Norman, advised the British government to abandon the Gold Standard which had been controversially reinstated by Churchill in 1925. While in previous times this would have been regarded as a revolutionary step, virtually no one in Britain objected. The value of the pound against the American dollar fell from its traditional level of $4.86 to around $3.40 (where it remained until the late 1940s). This helped British exports. The National government, in part as a result of the 'Invergordon Mutiny', moderated its most severe wage cuts, which, under the revised policy, in no case could now exceed 10 per cent. Combined with a continuation of the dole, and slight rises in interest rates, some semblance of confidence was restored to the British economy. For Britain the nadir of the Great Depression, if is probably fair to say, was reached in September 1931 and things began to look up, however slightly, from that point onwards. This chronology was in marked contrast to the course of the Depression in the United States and Germany, where the economy deteriorated still further in 1931, 1932, and into 1933. This led directly to the radical political responses adopted by America and Germany, Franklin Roosevelt's quasi-social democratic 'New Deal' and Hitler's National Socialism. In contrast, Britain responded to the Depression with a more orthodox mixture of neo-classical deflationary cuts, some 'pump priming', marked flexibility in the international exchange rates, and, from 1932, the imposition of tariffs. In practice, Britain's emergence from the Depression was not dissimilar to America's in terms of the timing of falls in unemployment and new investment. More than America, however, Britain retained a seemingly intractable pool of the permanently unemployed in the old staple industry areas. Unlike America (and, obviously, Nazi Germany), Britain did not initiate any constitutional innovations or sweeping social reforms, and its government structure was almost identical in 1939 to what it had been ten years before. In contrast, the 'New Deal' in the United States resulted in a vast, unprecedented increase in the powers of the federal government and the beginnings of a 'Welfare State', previously absent.

Over the next few months, two cries were increasingly heard from the Conservative majority in the National government, for a speedy General Election to give the administration a fresh mandate, and for the introduction of tariffs as a response to unemployment. As the predominant element in the coalition, the Tories were increasingly adamant on both points. Both MacDonald and his Labour allies (especially Snowden) and the Liberals were opposed to both. Samuel and the Liberals were in an especially invidious position, with a commitment to Free Trade virtually the only thing which continued to distinguish them from the other parties. On the other hand, there was now an ever-growing consensus among opinion-leaders that Free Trade was simply inappropriate to the present crisis, and would have to be abandoned. An influential section of the Liberal party led by Sir John Simon now openly called for the imposition of tariffs. If the National government did hold a General Election with a commitment to introduce tariffs, both Philip Snowden (an ardent Free Trader) and Herbert Samuel and the bulk of the Liberals would certainly have to resign. Great pressure (including pressure from King George) was exercised to have them remain in place if a General Election were held. At the last moment, an unprecedented formula was found by which the parties and individuals comprising the National government would 'agree to differ' over the tariff issue, with each party returning to its pre-existing position after a General Election. This formula was unique in British electoral history and appeared to run entirely contrary to the Westminster system of government, which is based upon the assumption that a Cabinet will always present a united front once a policy has been agreed upon. In view of the decisive outcome of the 1931 General Election, it is strange that the opposition Labour party did not make more of this curious policy, with more successful results.

By the end of September 1931 Tory pressure for an immediate General Election had become irresistible, and MacDonald formally dissolved Parliament on 7 October 1931, with the General Election to take place on 27 October. The three-week political campaign which ensued was one of the best-remembered and most strident of the twentieth century. Although MacDonald was moving in the direction of supporting tariffs, he explicitly stated that he went into the campaign stating only that he had an 'open mind' on the subject. He asked instead for what he memorably termed a 'doctor's mandate' to do whatever was best to help the British economy recover, thus putting the best face on the divisions in the coalition partners. Baldwin was also vague, seeming to endorse a tariff but only following a careful examination of the subject following the election. The Conservatives had been penalised for openly advocating a tariff at a General Election so often that they were not going to throw away this opportunity with reckless promises. The highlight of the campaign, however, came with a celebrated radio broadcast made by Philip Snowden (who, ironically, was not standing for re-election and did not support tariffs) on 17 October. Snowden described the Labour party's General Election manifesto as 'The most fantastic and impracticable programme ever put before the electors ... . This is not socialism. It is Bolshevism run mad.' Labour's election would 'plunge the country into irretrievable ruin'. That the speaker was not a right-wing fanatic, but, until two months before one of the most senior figures in the Labour party, was lost on neither his friends or foes.

In this atmosphere, the Labour party attempted to re-adjust as best it could. Even without MacDonald, the party was still the largest in Parliament. Arthur Henderson was elected its leader, not without some hostility by the trade unions, which demanded loyalty. (William Graham and J.R. Clynes became joint Deputy leaders.) Labour's General Election manifesto was indeed rather radical (although not 'Bolshevism run mad'), advocating the nationalisation of foreign investments and of the banks, taxation of unearned incomes, and condemning all government cuts. MacDonald and Snowden were rightly angry that Labour could now oppose spending cuts when its own Cabinet had made very severe cuts shortly before. Labour tried to portray the National government as a 'bankers ramp' which was inherently anti-working class. There was still very considerable regret that MacDonald (and, before his broadcast, Snowden) had left the party and a real hope that, once the emergency was over, they would be back. There was, as yet, no real sense that the break would be permanent.

The campaign was heavily weighted in favour of the National government and against Labour, with the whole of the 'Establishment' obviously in strong support of the coalition government. With the exception of the *Daily Herald* (owned in part by the TUC) and the Sunday paper *Reynold's Illustrated News* (owned by the Co-operative Society), the whole of the national press strongly supported the return of the National government, even normally pro-Liberal papers. Among the important provincial press, only the *Manchester Guardian* supported Labour. Remarkably, even the Archbishop of Canterbury, Cosmo Gordon Lang, praised the 'courage' of Ramsay MacDonald, while the Bishop of Winchester explicitly called for the re-election of the government with a large majority. Late in the campaign, Labour was accused of having taken money from the assets of the Post Office Savings Bank, clearly implying that the deposits of millions of its small savers would be confiscated if Labour was re-elected.

There was a universal expectation that the National government would be re-elected with an increased majority, but no one was prepared for the actual outcome. Many Labour voters abandoned the party and there seems no doubt that Ramsay MacDonald's presence at the head of the government won over countless Labour supporters. Virtually the whole of the middle classes supported the government, as did virtually all former Liberals. Support for the National government was almost universally depicted as a patriotic duty in a time of national emergency, while Labour was portrayed by most opinion leaders as a party which put class loyalty before the national interest, advocating a wild programme of extreme socialism. In addition, the National government presented candidates under a variety of party labels. Its MacDonaldite supporters were known as 'National Labour', while its Liberal supporters were split between 'National Liberals', pro-tariff backers of Sir John Simon, now virtually indistinguishable from the Tories, and the residuum of the Liberals under Sir Herbert Samuel, who remained adamantly in favour of Free Trade. By and large, all candidates supporting the government were given an uncontested run by the other coalition parties, although there was no 'couponing' as in 1918.

Nevertheless the results, when they were reported, exceeded anything which the most sanguine supporters of the National government had expected. Indeed, the results were without parallel in British electoral history, even in previous landslide years like 1906 and 1918.

	Total votes	MPs elected	% of total vote	
National Government				
Conservative	11 978 745	473	55.3	
National Labour	341 370	13	1.6	60.6
National Liberal	809 302	35	3.7	
Liberal	1 403 102	33	6.5	
Total National Government	14 532 519	554	67.1	
Opposition				
Labour	6 649 630	52	30.6	
Independent Liberals	106 106	4	0.5	
Communist	74 824	0	0.3	
New Party	36 377	0	0.2	
Others	256 917	5	1.2	
Total	21 656 373	615	100.0	

The supporters of the National government received over two-thirds of the votes cast, easily the highest share by any grouping at any General Election in history. In 1906, for instance, the Liberals achieved their enormous parliamentary majority on the basis of only 49.0 per cent of all votes cast and, even adding in their Labour and Irish allies, just over 55 per cent of the total vote. In 1924, the Tories had elected 419 MPs on 48.3 per cent of all votes cast. Even in 1918, remarkably, the Coalition parties received only 47.6 per cent of the total vote (53.7 per cent if non-Coalition Unionists are included). The National government was triumphant everywhere, especially its Conservative majority component. The Tories won 399 seats in England alone, 24 more than the Liberals won in the whole United Kingdom in 1931. They won 471 in the United Kingdom as a whole, including 48 of 71 seats in Scotland, compared with only 20 seats there in 1929. In already heavily Tory areas their strength was simply overwhelming, with their popular majority in Brighton being the largest in electoral history. At Hornsey in suburban London, the first result to be declared on election night, the Conservatives increased their majority from 9511 (19 per cent) to 33 609 (69 per cent), and seat after seat showed the same trend. The sweep, and the transferral of so many Labour and Liberal votes to the Nationals, also brought in, very much as junior partners, 13 National Labour followers of MacDonald, plus 68 Liberals, divided almost equally between the anti-tariff Samuelites and the pro-tariff Simonites. (There were, in addition, four so-called 'Independent Liberals', a group which consisted of Lloyd George and his family, all elected from Welsh seats. Together, the three components of the old Liberal party elected 72 MPs, 20 more than Labour, and were, technically at least, the second largest party in Parliament.)

There are two ways of viewing the performance of the Labour party in 1931. Superficially, of course, it was virtually annihilated as a parliamentary force. Only one Cabinet member in the 1929–31 government who remained loyal to it was elected, George Lansbury; only two ministers (Clement Attlee and Stafford Cripps); and only five junior ministers. In only five areas of the country did Labour do even moderately well: in the East End slums of London, parts of Glasgow, and the mining seats of South Wales, west Lancashire, and the West Riding. Even here, however, for the most part the number of elected Labour MPs shrank dramatically. In London, for instance, the number of Labour MPs declined from 36 to only five. Only in Wales was there even a hint of former strength, with 16 Labour MPs elected, all in the South. On the other hand, the nature of the British electoral system, as always, greatly exaggerated the scale of the swing in popular terms. Labour's share of the total vote, nearly 31 per cent, was actually slightly higher than its share at the 1923 General Election, when it elected 191 MPs and formed a minority government. Its 1931 vote represented, indeed, only about 6.5 per cent less of the total vote than it secured in 1929, when 287 Labour MPs were elected. The crucial difference between 1931 and previous post-1918 General Elections was that in 1931 the non-Labour parties were united, not divided, while most Liberals (and many Labourites) voted for a Tory candidate.

The performance of minor parties at the 1931 General Election is also noteworthy. Both the British Communist Party and Mosley's proto-fascist

New Party polled only derisory number of votes, the Communists just 74824 among 26 candidates and the Mosleyites only 36377 among 24. Wracked by internal disputes and slavishly following the Moscow line which branded even the Independent Labour Party as 'social fascists', the Communists had little support outside of some Scottish and Welsh mining seats, while the esteem it enjoyed among some left-wing intellectuals because of its anti-fascist stand later in the 1930s was not yet evident. Mosley's New Party, at this stage a broadly based party of radicals of the far right and left dissatisfied with the National government's economic orthodoxy, failed to make a breakthrough of any kind. In contrast to many other countries in Europe, both the middle classes and working classes failed to desert the political centre for extremist parties, one of the main reasons why the British system of government survived the 1930s intact.

The composition of the Conservative majority in the National government elected in 1931 illustrates how the social background of the party had changed over the past two generations. Even in the late nineteenth century the majority of Conservative MPs in any Parliament would have been great landowners or their close relatives, with many related to the titled aristocracy. Although nearly 500 Tory MPs were elected in 1931, only 25 were the heirs to peerages (24 of whom were Conservatives), a fraction of the number in any nineteenth-century Parliament. About 26 per cent of all Conservative MPs appear to have come from the old landed aristocracy or gentry (although others married into it). This apparent democratisation of the Conservative party was, however, fully disguised by the fact that about two-thirds of Tory MPs attended a major public school, about 27 per cent to Eton alone, with smaller percentages attending Harrow, Rugby, Charterhouse, Winchester, Marlborough, Wellington, and 20 or so of their rivals. Though ill-understood by many historians (who wrongly take attendance at a major public school to indicate gentry status), this differential demonstrated how a new form of status had replaced the old. Most of those who had attended a well-known public school, but did *not* emerge from the aristocracy or gentry, were the scions of businessmen or professionals, sometimes wealthy, usually successful, but almost always representing a new and different stratum of success than the old landed aristocracy and gentry. By the 1930s, these two groupings appear to the outside world to have merged, and were, indeed, often indistinguishable by accent, lifestyle, and political beliefs. A new upper class had replaced the old, although the new upper class kept most of the forms and titles of the old. The Conservative party proved the beneficiary of this change, and now had many claims to being regarded as the only party of the British 'Establishment', without rivals or many exceptions.

Shortly after the sweeping General Election victory, MacDonald replaced the smaller emergency Cabinet with a normal one of 20 members, which took office on 5 November 1931. It consisted of 11 Tories, four MacDonald Labourites, and five Liberals, still representing both the pro- and anti-Free Trade wings of the party. While the new Cabinet brought in some important figures who had been excluded from the first National government's Cabinet, it still excluded such men as Churchill, Lloyd George, Amery, and Salisbury. Since Sir Austen Chamberlain voluntarily retired it was, indeed, somewhat less representative than before of major figures. It patently over-represented the non-Tory elements in the coalition to a marked extent. The most important change was that Snowden (who retired from the Commons and was given a peerage and the honorary position of Lord Privy Seal) was replaced at the Exchequer by Neville Chamberlain. Neville Chamberlain now became evidently the number two man in the Conservative party (Baldwin, the leader, held the post of Lord President of the Council). As the son of the great Joseph Chamberlain, the progenitor of Imperial Preference, had become Chancellor, some kind of tariff now became almost inevitable. Lord Hailsham, the very talented former Lord Chancellor, became War Minister. Liberals still did very well from the new arrangement, with Sir Herbert Samuel as Home Secretary, Sir John Simon at the Foreign Office, Walter Runciman at the Board of Trade, and Sir Donald Maclean at the Education Ministry. The traditional aristocracy and its associates did less well. Although four members of the Cabinet were peers, only Lord Londonderry at the Air Ministry came from the old titled aristocracy, and only one or two others (such as Wiliam Ormsby-Gore, later fourth baron Harlech, 1885–1964, at the Ministry of Works) were *bona fide* significant landowners. Despite the enormous Tory parliamentary majorities of the decade, the 1930s are often seen as a time when national leadership passed, even in the Conservative party into the hands of the upper middle class, often Dissenters or the children of Dissenters. This is often said to be an important reason for the failure of the British government to respond vigorously to the threat of fascism: while the old aristocracy would never have accepted the insults, threats, and aggression of Hitler and Mussolini, the middle classes, unused to international power politics and naive to a self-destructive degree, prevaricated and pretended that Appeasement could work. This frequently held viewpoint also sees the return to national leadership of old-line aristocrats or their close relatives like Churchill, Eden, and Salisbury as a major reason for abandoning Appeasement and fighting Hitler. Like most such theories, there is an element of truth in this view, although among the leaders of Appeasement were many old aristocrats like Lord Halifax. Nevertheless, it is probably true that middle-class men like Baldwin and Neville Chamberlain were uncomfortable in the exercise of international power politics, and certainly failed to appreciate the true depravity of Hitler and his allies.

The first and perhaps most important measures of the new government brought in protection and the abandonment of Free Trade, first in a limited way and then wholeheartedly. As soon as Parliament reconvened, Walter Runciman, President of the Board of Trade and formerly a very typical Liberal frontbencher, introduced the Abnormal Importations Bill. This gave the Board of Trade the power, for a six month period, to impose duties of up to 100 per cent on imported manufactured goods which were entering Britain in 'abnormal' quantities, a poorly defined term which soon became conflated to the even more ambiguous term of goods which were 'dumped' in Britain. Only the Labour opposition voted against this bill, and duties of 50 per cent were imposed on a wide range of such products, ranging from cotton goods to typewriters to gloves.

An even more wideranging measure was to follow. The government had promised a careful inquiry into the tariff question before imposing any. This was cheerfully disregarded with the Abnormal Importations Bill, but the Cabinet now appointed a so-called Balance of Trade Committee, with Neville Chamberlain as chairman and a protectionist majority. The Committee recommended the imposition of a general tariff. Free Trade Liberals and Philip Snowden in the Cabinet threatened to resign, and a continuation of the election situation ensued, with freetraders 'agreeing to differ' and remain in the Cabinet. This presented an immediate breach among the Coalition partners, although the Tories, with their enormous majority, could of course do anything they wished. Free Trade was now doomed. Its undertaker was Neville Chamberlain, who introduced the important Import Duties Bill early in February 1932. This comprehensively and deliberately reversed the policy of Free Trade which had comprised the central foundation of Britain's economic ideology since 1846, and initiated in its place a form of Imperial Preference, hopefully leading to Empire Unity, advanced by Neville's father Joseph Chamberlain in 1903 and advocated by most of the Tory right ever since. (The deep symbolism of this moment was lost on no one. Joseph Chamberlain's widow and all of his children were in the Parliamentary audience for Neville's speech, and Neville Chamberlain, usually glacial in emotionless demeanour, was said to have had tears in his eyes.) From 1 March 1932, a general customs duty of 10 per cent was imposed on all imports. Exempted from this general duty, however, were all imports from the Empire, pending the convening of a major Imperial Economic Conference to be held in Ottawa in July, and certain other imported goods placed on a tariff-free list. A new Import Duties Advisory Committee was created to advise the Treasury on tariff policy. Significantly, the tariff-free list included most foodstuffs, raw cotton, many raw minerals, and other substances. These exclusions were designed to meet the most persistent charge which made Tariff Reform so unpopular in the past, that they entailed a food tax, as well as objections by manufacturers that they raised the price of raw materials. Although obviously welcomed enthusiastically by committed tariff reformers, they were not wholly satisfactory, failing to grant concessions to the Empire in a 'scientific' way which might foster imperial unity. To die-hard Free Traders tariffs remained anathema, even in the circumstances of the Depression, and their enactment now split the Liberal party, with the Simonites supporting tariffs and the government and the Samuelites opposing them. The Import Duties Bill passed in the Commons by the resounding vote of 454 to 78, with the entire Labour party voting against (arguing that the rich should be more heavily taxed, not, as opponents of the tariff argued, the poor), as well as Herbert Samuel, David Lloyd George, and their Liberal followers. Within a few years the Liberal Nationals, as Simon and his pro-tariff Liberal followers were known, became virtually indistinguishable from the Tories and were seldom opposed by Conservative candidates at any elections, although the party, rather remarkably, retained a tenuous separate existence until 1966 (when the four remaining Liberal Nationals formally merged with the Conservatives). They never rejoined the Liberals.

The Import Duties Committee was intended as an active mechanism for arriving at a 'scientific' tariff, based upon the needs of each industry. It was headed by Sir George May, whose recommendations for far-reaching expenditure cuts led to the formation of the National government. Its report, published in April 1932, recommended even higher rates of tariff protection, ranging from

20 per cent as a norm on manufactured goods to 33.3 per cent on some luxury goods. Some raw materials (but not foods) were to be subject to tariffs as well. The government quickly adopted all of its proposals, giving comprehensive tariff protection to the whole of British industry. May's Committee continued in existence until the war, making a wide range of tariff recommendations.

The next step on the new economic road was the convening of the Imperial Economic Conference, held in Ottawa in July and August 1932. The Conference proved to be a stormy one, and came close to breaking down. Most of the Commonwealth, with their own industries to worry about, found it difficult to offer any special status to imported British goods; for its part the British delegation (headed by Baldwin and Chamberlain) would not harm British agriculture by giving special status to Empire foodstuffs. An agreement between Britain and the other Dominions (except the Irish Free State) did produce a last-minute tariff accord, chiefly by charging lower rates of duties on Empire products rather than none at all. The period of nearly 30 years which intervened between Joseph Chamberlain's original proposals and the 1932 Conference saw most of the Dominions develop an industrial infrastructure of their own, making accommodation with the 'Mother Country' increasingly difficult. Nevertheless, the Ottawa Conference, especially when taken with the Statute of Westminster of November 1931 was universally seen at the time as marking a milestone in the evolution of the British Empire, which remained a coherent and, despite the bitterness of the Ottawa Conference, relatively unified geopolitical unit through the Second World War.

The Ottawa Conference also signalled the end of the broadly based coalition government which had taken office the previous year. In spite of MacDonald's protests, Snowden resigned, as did two Liberal Cabinet ministers, Herbert Samuel and Archibald Sinclair, none of whom could stomach the dramatic change in tariff policy. MacDonald remained, of course, as did J.H. Thomas (Dominions Secretary) and Lord Sankey (Lord Chancellor) among the Coalition Labourites and Sir John Simon (Foreign Secretary) and his contingent of National Liberals. Nevertheless, the government now became increasingly undisguisedly Tory (though headed by Ramsay MacDonald) in everything but name. When Sir Donald Maclean (1864–1932; a Welsh solicitor; he was the father of Donald Maclean (1913–83) of the Cambridge spy ring) died in June 1932, he was replaced as Education Secretary by Lord Irwin (Edward Wood, later Lord Halifax), the former Viceroy, a right-wing Conservative. Most of the new entries into the Cabinet at this time also came from the Conservative ranks, such as Walter Elliot (1888–1958), appointed Agriculture Secretary in September 1932, and Sir Kingsley Wood (1881–1943), who became Postmaster General in December 1933. With their enormous majority, the Conservatives could demand virtually anything, and it became apparent to many coalition Liberals and Labourites that they had materially helped to put what for all practical purposes was a right-wing Conservative government in power with an unprecedented majority. The notion of a government of national unity to meet the economic crisis, difficult to achieve in the best of circumstances, was largely a sham.

There is general agreement that the National government's economic policies were reasonably successful during the decade of the 1930s, although full employment simply did not return until the Second World War. Apart from its tariffs, the government also pursued a policy of low interest rates (with the bank rate dropping from 6 per cent to only 2 per cent in 1932), a low exchange rate, and the creation of a Sterling Bloc with the Commonwealth. Economic growth rates increased, with gross domestic product growing by 4 per cent per annum between 1932 and 1937, much above previous levels. The middle classes, especially in the south of England and the Midlands, did especially well in this period. By and large little affected by the era's mass unemployment, they benefited from low inflation, low interest rates, and a general expansion of the service sector. Labour productivity, as measured by output per man year, increased by 50 per cent in the 1930s, one of the few positive effects of the high unemployment rates in the old staple industries. The tariff probably directly benefited such industries as iron and steel, which no longer had to fear foreign competition to the same extent as before 1932. As a result, considerable investment did occur in new plants and equipment, even in areas of high unemployment like South Wales. Housebuilding boomed in this period, especially in metropolitan London, fanned by low interest rates and middle-class prosperity. Between 1934 and 1939 over 350 000 new homes were built every year, the majority by private builders. This was a greater total than in any five-year period in British history with the exception of the late 1960s. Nevertheless, as noted, unemployment remained stubbornly high, declining from 2 955 000 at its peak in January 1932 (about 22 per cent of the workforce) to 1 888 000 in December 1935, but never dropping below 1 373 000 (in September 1937), about 11 per cent of the workforce. Unemployment, the great problem of the interwar period, was never successfully conquered until the war.

The government also intervened directly in economic matters and the organisation of industry in other ways. By the North Atlantic Shipping Act, 1934, government loans were made available for the construction of ships on the North Atlantic route. This was instrumental in restarting construction on the liner known to us as the *Queen Mary*, the flagship of the Cunard Line, which was sitting half-built on the Clydeside drydocks (where it was known as 'Number 534'). In agriculture, the National government continued the marketing board schemes of the previous Labour government, in produce like milk, potatoes, and hops, which established intermediary board that purchased the produce of farmers and sold them to wholesalers. Rather remarkably, in 1933 the National government nationalised London's passenger rail and bus system by enacting the London Passenger Transport Act of 1933. The previous Labour government had almost succeeded in enacting a somewhat similar but actually more moderate measure, creating a consolidated but privately owned monopoly under a public corporation. This was the brainchild of Herbert Morrison, who, many years later, used it as a model for nationalised industries in the 1945–51 Labour government. The chief argument used by the National government in continuing and extending Morrison's proposal was that such an act was necessary for the coordination of transport in London and the extension of the tube system to outer London (which was carried out). Lord Ashfield, the famous American head of the London underground system, became chairman of the new Board, which was established as a separate and independent body from the Ministry of Transport. Although the London Board was a success, it nevertheless seems extraordinary that a government with a huge Tory majority would enact such a measure.

The government responded to the considerable publicity given to the most serious single economic problem of the 1930s, astronomical, persistent unemployment rates in the 'distressed areas' of the north, by enacting a Depressed Areas (Development and Improvement) Bill, later renamed the 'Special Areas Bill'. This act created the unpaid commissioners for the areas of highest unemployment and authorised small grants for local improvements. The Act was pitifully small in its scope, authorising the ridiculous sum of only £2 million for assistance, and was, by general admission, a near-complete failure. Although unemployment in the 'special areas' did indeed fall in the later 1930s, it still remained more than twice the national average.

As a decade the 1930s are remembered for two things, the Great Depression and the rise of fascism leading to the Second World War. Indeed, the later part of the decade was dominated by the issues of Appeasement and rearmament, and, in particular, by the effects of the coming to total power of the madman Adolf Hitler in Germany. That the 1930s were to be dominated by the threat of another world war would have seemed, in 1929, to be astonishing and incomprehensible, and one of the main reasons why the response of the democracies to the threat of aggressive fascism was so supine was that this seemingly unimaginable challenge loomed up almost out of nowhere. By 1935, however, war had become a growing possibility which came to dominate a great part of public debate in Britain. The difficulties presented to the British government in responding to the rise of aggressive fascism were compounded by the multiple international sources from which it emerged. In September 1931, Japan occupied three important Manchurian towns, thus beginning a period of Japanese aggression against China, and in February 1932 proclaimed Manchuria (the northeastern portion of China) as an 'independent' Protectorate with Henry Pu-Yi, the former Emperor of China, as 'Regent'. (In 1934 he was proclaimed Emperor of Manchukuo, as the new Japanese territory was named. Henry Pu-yi's story is well known to many in the West through the famous film *The Last Emperor*.) This began a decade of aggression by Japan against China, as the Japanese government came to be dominated by extreme nationalists and militarists.

The Depression, which forced most countries to erect high tariff barriers, itself had a negative effect upon international cooperation. In 1932–33 occurred three notable international conferences aimed at reducing international tensions and the likelihood of war, the Disarmament Conference at Geneva (February–July 1932), the Lausanne Conference on reparations (June–July 1932) and the second meeting of the Disarmament Conference at Geneva (February–October 1933), held after Hitler came to power. The first of these conferences, the first at which both the Soviet Union and the United States were represented, failed because of French objections. The second conference, aimed at reducing war reparations, failed due to objections by the American Congress. The third failed because of German objections, after the Nazis had come to power. The spirit of international cooperation which prevailed during the 1920s was now obviously over.

In January 1933, Adolf Hitler and the National Socialist party came to power in Germany on a platform of extreme nationalism, biological racism, anti-semitism, and anti-Communism. Hitler regarded the loss of the First World War by Germany in 1918 and the subsequent Versailles Treaty as national humiliations of incalculable dimensions which he lived to reverse. Hitler's long-term aims were at this point unclear, but apparently included the creation of a Greater Germany in central Europe embracing all of the German-speaking areas, including places outside of Germany like Austria. This necessarily entailed the grossest violations of the Versailles Treaty and possible German aggression. The entire ideology of Nazism was diametrically opposed to the spirit of international reconciliation of the 1920s, and the road to eventual war now began. In October 1933, Germany withdrew from the Disarmament Conference and resigned from the League of Nations. From June 1934 Hitler developed closer ties with Mussolini, his fellow fascist dictator. In January 1935, Germany reintegrated the Saar area into the *Reich*, an area under the League of Nations administration since the war. (This was done after a plebiscite which was probably fairly conducted.) In March 1935, Hitler denounced the clauses of the Versailles Treaty providing for German disarmament. As of the General Election held in November 1935 there was thus ample reason to fear the intentions of the new German regime, apart from its totalitarian dictatorship and persecution of Jews, socialists, and political opponents. As well, another source of international fascist aggression was also emerging, Mussolini's Italy, which initiated an invasion of Ethiopia, one of the few independent African states, in October 1935. International tension was reaching a high level, although Britain's response was still confused and muted.

Germany was itself still sending out mixed signals. In January 1934, Germany reached a 10-year non-aggression pact with Poland (whom she invaded five years later). In June 1934, probably because Hitler had, at this point, no real desire or intention of alienating Britain, an Anglo-German Naval agreement was reached, which seemed to bring German acquiescence in a lesser, untroublesome role *vis-à-vis* Britain's primary defence arm.

In Britain itself, there was intense opposition to anything which seemed to smack of encouraging rearmament in preparation for another war; this remained a genuinely appalling prospect, to be avoided at virtually any cost, until the time of Munich or later. Most imagined that another world war, if it ever came, would be indescribably destructive, with air power and modern armaments causing destruction to civilians on an unimaginable scale. Stanley Baldwin, not the most imaginative of men, put this sentiment memorably in a speech to the House of Commons in November 1932 (before, it should be noted, Hitler came to power) when he stated, 'I think it is well also for the man in the street to realise that there is no power on earth that can protect him from being bombed. Whatever people may tell him, the bomber will always get through.' Early in 1933 came two of the most celebrated indicators of this mood. On 9 February 1933 the Oxford Union, the famous debating society at the university renowned for producing most of Britain's political leaders, debated the resolution that 'this House will in no circumstances fight for King and Country'. The resolution was passed by 275 votes to 175, the vote receiving worldwide publicity as a sign of young England's degeneracy. (Most of those who took part in this debate certainly fought for King and Country seven years later.) In October 1933, a by-election was held at East Fulham, a Conservative seat though with a strong Labour challenge in the 1920s. The Conservative candidate, W.J. Waldron, a local alderman who was unpopular in the district and at Tory Central office, made a point of attacking the League of Nations and advocating an increase in the strength of the military. To us, this was a remarkably prescient and far-sighted view, but it was vigorously attacked by the Labour candidate, John Wilmot, a dynamic younger man who enjoyed considerable support from the Liberals (who did not adopt a candidate). Wilmot attacked Waldron as a warmonger, making this, most unusually, the central theme of his campaign. To intense publicity, Wilmot won easily, defeating the Tory by nearly 5000 votes. The East Fulham by-election caused enormous consternation to the government and has been credited, by Winston Churchill and others, with hampering rearmament. In November 1936, three years later, Stanley Baldwin, then Prime Minister, gave what is often described as one of the most notorious speeches of the decade, telling the House of Commons 'with appalling frankness' that because of the East Fulham result that if he had contested the 1935 General Election by telling the electorate that massive rearmament was necessary, 'I cannot think of anything that would have made the loss of the election from my point of view more certain.' Churchill's memoirs, *The Gathering Storm*, written after the War, contained the celebrated index entry about this incident, 'Baldwin, Stanley: confesses placing party before country.' To most Englishmen, the prospect before them, should war break out again, was most vividly illustrated in the famous classic film *Things to Come* (1936), which depicted a 30-year struggle in which the few survivors of the conflict revert to savagery.

During this period, such political opposition as was possible to the overwhelming strength of the National government was provided by the Labour party. With only 52 MPs, clearly its ability to stymie the government was almost non-existent. Yet this is generally admitted to have been a period of creative growth for the Labour party. Its leader during this period, George Lansbury, a Christian socialist, was rather effective as an opposition leader and helped to groom the new generation of Labour leaders who came to the fore in the later 1930s. The Labour party scored a very considerable victory in the London County Council (LCC) elections of 1934, turning a large Conservative majority into a Labour one for the first time. Herbert Morrison became leader of the LCC, employing his brand of 'municipal socialism'. The Conservatives never regained control of the LCC until it was abolished in 1964, although they achieved a tie with Labour in 1949. Labour also won control of many other municipal councils in 1934.

Labour was faced with a variety of challenges to it from the political left, and lost the support of most of the Independent Labour Party. It rebuffed all attempts by the Communist party to form a 'United Front'. Nevertheless, Labour's official policies during these years, at least as adopted at its annual conferences, were very radical, advocating widespread and immediate nationalisation. Many left-wing intellectuals and radicals in the party demanded the enactment of emergency powers legislation whenever Labour came to power again in order to forestall measures by 'capitalism' to block its programme. Behind the scenes, however, more moderate social democratic forces in the party were formulating a realistic programme of legislation very similar to the measures actually enacted by Labour in 1945. These would become an official part of Labour's policies after 1935.

Labour was at this time dominated by pacifists or near-pacifists, and an important reason for the failure of Britain to rearm was the fear by the Tories that Labour might be swept to power at a General Election on a popular anti-war tide. At the time of the East Fulham by-election, Labour's leader George Lansbury enunciated a policy of something like unilateral disarmament. 'I would close every recruiting station, disband the Army and disarm the Air Force', he stated. 'I would abolish the whole dreadful equipment of war and say to the world, "Do your worst." ' Many leaders of the Labour party simply had no understanding of the nature of international power politics and absolutely none of the true nature of Hitler's diabolical, menacing evil. Conditioned to rationalism and progress as the driving forces of modern society, and viewing the world in economic deterministic terms, they could not comprehend sheer evil and had not the slightest notion of how to stop it. But here, too, there were counterveiling trends within the Labour party, which would also come to the fore from 1935 on.

Only one significant change of a constitutional nature was made in this period, the passage of the Statute of Westminster in November 1931, which formally recognised the legislative independence of the parliaments of the Dominions and formally removed any question of British control of their legislation. Its preamble recognised the British Sovereign as 'the symbol of the free association of the members of the British Commonwealth of Nations', as the self-governing portions of the Empire were now officially known. The effects of the Statute were, in practice, very small, as, indeed, were the new freedoms it gave to the Dominions. There was, for instance, no formal right to secede from the Commonwealth while, in practice, the overriding foreign policy of the Dominions continued to be determined in Whitehall. There was still, however, a genuine and near-universal sense of loyalty to Britain among all of the Dominions except the Irish Free State, a sense of loyalty probably greater in the 1930s than in the past. Britain was to have very considerable trouble from nationalist movements in the Empire in the 1930s, especially from Egypt, Palestine, Ireland, and, above all, India, but the loyalties of the old Dominions were never in doubt.

8

The National Government from Recovery to War, 1935–39

For Britain, the second half of the 1930s started quietly enough, with a celebration of the Silver Jubilee of King George V. Nevertheless, the next five years were to prove both as controversial and eventful as any in British history, as the policies of the Appeasement of fascism were formulated and then collapsed under the pressure of Nazi expansion. By the middle of 1940 Winston Churchill was Prime Minister, Labour leader Clement Attlee Deputy Prime Minister, and Britain was at war, fighting alone and for its very existence as a nation.

The spring of 1935 saw the celebrations for the twenty-fifth anniversary of the reign of George V, the first occasion a royal jubilee celebration had occurred after only a quarter-century. While many saw this as a government stunt, it quickly and perhaps surprisingly became clear that the king was extraordinarily popular, and a genuine national mood of celebration was evident, especially in working-class areas. There, buntings and street parties, often spontaneous, were the rule. Given the cataclysm that had overtaken Europe in the Great War, by 1935 George V was virtually the only head of state of a major country who had been in place before 1914. Britain's stable constitutional rule obviously contrasted with the murderous thugs who now dominated central and eastern Europe, a contrast lost on few. The very colourlessness and bourgeois predictability of the king was now widely perceived as a great virtue, a sign of the superiority of Britain's institutions.

The Jubilee celebrations in May led to a significant Cabinet reshuffle in early June. Baldwin, the Lord President of the Council, and MacDonald, the Prime Minister, changed places. MacDonald was showing signs of confusion, even mental instability, while Baldwin, rather like the king, was increasingly seen as a rock of stability and wisdom and was earning renewed respect. The end of MacDonald's premiership (on 7 June 1935) removed any remaining pretence that the government was anything but an almost purely Tory one. Neville Chamberlain continued as Chancellor of the Exchequer and was clearly the heir apparent to Baldwin. Lord Hailsham, an arch-Tory, replaced Lord Sankey as Lord Chancellor. Sir Samuel Hoare, another lifelong Tory, replaced Sir John Simon, a former Liberal, at the Foreign Office, while Simon became Home Secretary. Simon was widely seen as an incompetent Foreign Secretary, and was even more widely distrusted. Only a few new faces entered the Cabinet; the most notable was Anthony Eden (1897–1977; later first earl of Avon), aged only 37, seen as the coming man of the Conservative party, who became Minister Without Portfolio with responsibility for League of Nations Affairs, and Malcolm MacDonald (1901–81), Ramsay's son, who became Colonial Secretary. The two MacDonalds and J.H. Thomas, the Dominions Secretary, were the only National Labour ministers left in the Cabinet.

The most immediate issue faced by the reconstructed government concerned the situation in remote Ethiopia; the first occasion when Britain came into something like potential conflict with the fascist dictatorships. Italy long held part of the Horn of Africa, Eritrea and Italian Somaliland, as colonies, but Mussolini badly wanted to extend his African empire as a kind of reincarnation of the Romans. Ethiopia (Abyssinia), adjacent to both colonies, was one of only two independent black African states, ruled by a feudal Christian monarchy. A clash of Italian and Ethiopian troops on the disputed Somaliland border in December 1934 was seized upon as the pretence for what was widely seen as the annexation of Ethiopia by Italy. Ethiopia was a member of the League of Nations and appealed to that body for assistance. France and Britain prevaricated, France because it needed Italy as a potential ally against Nazi Germany (Mussolini was not yet entirely in Hitler's orbit), Britain because it wished to avoid war. Anthony Eden, later famous as an anti-Appeaser, was sent to Rome in June 1935, offering Mussolini substantial concessions to avoid war, including parts of British Somaliland, Britain's own territory in the region, situated between Italy's two colonies. Mussolini rejected these offers, as well as all attempts at mediation, and in October 1935 invaded Ethiopia. By May 1936 Italy had occupied Addis Ababa, Ethiopia's capital.

Most British policy-makers wished to penalise Italy in some way for its aggression, with the majority favouring economic and military sanctions against Mussolini's regime. In 1934–35, as the crisis developed, the League of Nations Union, an influential society which supported internationalism, conducted a 'Peace Ballot', a nationwide questionnaire answered by 11.5 million people. About 90 per cent favoured economic sanctions and 70 per cent military sanctions against aggression, organised by the League. The government took this as indicating general support for an international effort to halt aggression, rather than support for unilateral British action. This became a live issue in the later half of 1935, as Mussolini prepared to invade Ethiopia. Sir Samuel Hoare, the Foreign Minister, endorsed collective action in a speech at the League of Nations in September 1935, but only if the 'burden' were 'borne collectively'. In October, the League of Nations applied sanctions against Italy, arguably the first time in history that international sanctions were aimed at an aggressor nation. These were well intentioned and, in their way, fairly comprehensive, but simply failed to deter Mussolini, who responded with rigid controls of the Italian economy. Relations between Britain and Italy deteriorated, with Britain concentrating a huge naval force at Alexandria. Cracks in the international alliance soon appeared, especially a failure, in early 1936, to agree on oil sanctions. France, in particular, opposed all-out hostilities against Italy, and in late 1935, Hoare and Foreign Minister Pierre Laval put forward a proposal for ending the Abyssinian crisis, the Hoare–Laval Plan, which involved far-reaching territorial concessions by Ethiopia to Italy. (It was on the occasion of Hoare's visit to Paris to negotiate with Laval that the phrase became current that 'sending a Hoare to Paris was like carrying coals to Newcastle'.) Put forward as an effort to head off conflict, it was one of the first egregious examples of Appeasement, that is, of trying to buy off the European dictators in order to avoid open warfare with them. Initially, the public response to the Hoare–Laval proposals was generally negative, with the *Times*, on 16 December, publishing a famous editorial entitled 'A Corridor for Camels', its term for the strip of land which, under the proposal, Ethiopia was to receive. Public confidence in the League and the efficacy of international sanctions was severely shaken, and the Government, despite its recent election success, was in deep trouble. Hoare resigned on 18 December 1935, to be replaced by the young and popular Anthony Eden. Mussolini proceeded to conquer Ethiopia, with Emperor Haile Selassie fleeing to London. The failure of sanctions to stop Mussolini doomed any realistic hope that the League of Nations could halt aggression through collective action. It began the pattern by which Britain and France would attempt to act together, but French supineness would encourage British Appeasement. It also showed deep discord between Anthony Eden, an anti-Appeaser, and Neville Chamberlain, the heir apparent to MacDonald and Baldwin, who in June 1935 termed sanctions against Italy 'the very midsummer of madness'. Right-wing Tories had generally been very cool to the internationalism of the League of Nations, and the failure over Ethiopia gave them the chance to act alone. 'Splendid isolation' by Britain generally entailed 'gunboat diplomacy' and military action, but in this case it presaged, rather paradoxically, the exact opposite, acquiescence in threatening aggression. For the time being, only a small minority in the Conservative party saw through these contradictions.

Despite what would soon prove to be a terrible failure, on 14 November 1935 the National Government held a General Election, nearly a year earlier than necessary. Labour had some reasons to be optimistic, despite the fact that it still numbered only 62 MPs. It had won ten by-election seats from the other parties, six since 1934. There was still mass unemployment, and a real fear of war. As things turned out, however, Labour had been over-optimistic. Although it did increase its numbers in the Commons by nearly one hundred, the National Government won another commanding victory.

	Total votes	MPs elected	% of total vote
Conservative	11 810 158	432	53.7
Liberal	1 422 116	20	6.4
Labour	8 325 491	154	37.9
Independent Labour Party	139 577	4	0.7
Communist	27 117	1	0.1
Others	272 595	4	1.2
Total	21 997 054	615	100.0

In some respects the results at this election were even more striking than those at the highly abnormal 1931 election, for it showed the division of the vote in more or less normal circumstances. The Conservatives remained in a remarkable ascendancy, winning more seats than in 1900 or 1924, their previous high-water marks in normal twentieth-century elections, and more seats than the Liberals had won in 1906. In some respects their popular vote – 53.7 per cent – was even more significant. It was barely lower than their share of the vote in 1931 (55.2 per cent), and the highest share of the vote that any single party has won in the twentieth century, 1931 alone excepted. Again excepting 1931, it was the only time since 1918 that any party has won more than one-half of the total vote, something which did not occur even in the landslide years of 1945, 1983, or 1997. The Liberal vote almost entirely collapsed, and the Tories had now categorically completed their evolution into the normal party of government and of the 'Establishment'. Virtually Tory to a man and woman, rather than divided between Tories and Liberals, the British 'Establishment' was now arguably stronger than at any time since before 1832. It had triumphed over the Labour threat, ruled over the world's largest Empire, and, Britain's institutions largely intact, was at the head of a nation of moderates and constitutional democrats. Traditionally, Stanley Baldwin is seen as having the major role in this state of affairs, and in 1935 he achieved what was arguably his greatest electoral triumph. As usual, in 1935, the Tories were strongest in their heartland areas, winning 147 seats in the south of England outside London, compared with only 21 for all other parties. But they remained surprisingly strong even in the north of England (106 Tory seats; 60 Labour; 5 Liberals) and in Scotland (43 Tory seats; 20 Labour; 3 Liberals; 5 others), and were the 'national party' in a realistic sense.

Labour won 154 seats, about the same number (151) as it had won in 1924, but far fewer than its high-water mark in 1929, when it secured 288 MPs. Nevertheless, its share of the total vote – 37.9 per cent – was far more satisfactory. Indeed, it was the highest share of the total vote ever won by Labour up to that point, achieved largely through the collapse of the Liberals. Labour did respectably in London, winning 22 seats, compared with 39 for the Tories, in the north of England and Scotland, and actually (as always) won a majority of seats in Wales, 18 compared with 11 Tories and 6 Liberals. It achieved a number of gloatful triumphs, especially the defeat of Ramsay MacDonald at Seaham by Emanuel Shinwell, and saw many of its leading figures, defeated in 1931, return to Parliament, including Hugh Dalton and Herbert Morrison. There were several reasons why Labour did not march fully ahead, despite the continuing Depression. The government still looked something like a national one, and despite the loss of his seat, MacDonald's name probably counted for something in many quarters. George Lansbury, Labour's old-fashioned Leader, did not strike many as an alternative Prime Minister, while its Deputy-Leader, Clement Attlee, was at the time virtually unknown. The party itself still appeared to have extremist policies, while the Abyssinian crisis exposed the party's deep divisions, especially between pacifists and interventionists. By (at this point) falsely espousing the League of Nations and calling the election a year early, it has been claimed that Baldwin 'stole' the election. Of course this is untrue, and at this point Mussolini rather than the much more dangerous Hitler appeared to be the prime aggressor. In Britain, too, elections are almost invariably won on domestic issues. Baldwin made few dramatic changes as a result of the election. Lord Halifax became Lord Privy Seal, and Alfred Duff Cooper became War Minister. A combative and hedonistic Tory, married to the Society beauty Lady Diana Manners, his anti-Appeasement stance nearly wrecked his career. A month later Eden became Foreign Minister, as a result of Hoare's resignation. Churchill still remained very much outside the Cabinet, now a right-wing Cassandra with a small personal following.

The year 1936 saw the further relentless deterioration of the situation in Europe, chiefly because of the rise of Adolf Hitler to the position of arch-aggressor. Yet 1936 is perhaps best remembered for an event utterly unexpected and without precedent, but which would temporarily put everything else in the shade. On 20 January 1936 King George V died at Sandringham, shortly after his physicians issued the famous bulletin that 'the King's life is moving peace-fully to its close'. (It is now known that the king's physician, Lord Dawson of Penn, in effect killed him a few hours earlier than nature would have done, in order to make the timing of his death easier for newspapers to report.) The new king was his 41-year-old eldest son, the former Prince of Wales, Edward VIII (1894–1972; created duke of Windsor in 1936), an extraordinarily glamorous bachelor who seemed to symbolise the new, post-Victorian age. Edward had led a playboy lifestyle, and had had a string of mistresses, generally older married women, but had never married or seriously contemplated marriage. He was determined to appear the modern 'People's King', and had, for instance, flown from Sandringham to London to attend his Accession Council. He was idolised by millions of people, in particular as a fantasy prince charming among millions of women. The new king's heart was certainly in the right place and he spoke his mind openly, most famously when visiting south Wales in November 1936, just before the Abdication, when he told the impoverished unemployed that 'something ought to be done to find these people employment...something will be done'. The new king, however, had many serious character faults, espe-cially an inability to work hard, and an inability to judge character. 'He would start things, and not see them through. He didn't know...right people from wrong "uns"', Attlee concisely summarised the situation decades later. From 1934 Edward's latest and closest paramour was Mrs Wallis Warfield Simpson (1896–1986; later duchess of Windsor), an elegant, sophisticated, divorced, and remarried American lady, who increasingly aroused fury in the British 'Establishment'. Mrs Simpson appeared to hold Edward in the palm of her hand, and was greatly feared as an adventuress who would prey upon the king's weak character. As their relationship deepened in 1935–36, it became increasingly clear that Edward meant to marry Mrs Simpson, who was in the process of obtaining a divorce from her American second husband, making her queen of the United Kingdom. The majority of the British 'Establishment' regarded her as an unsuit-able queen, centrally because she was twice divorced. After 20 years of revolt from Victorian values, Britain's religious leaders were simply not prepared to accept a divorced lady as queen, while the heavily Nonconformist Commonwealth states felt even less enthusiasm. (That Mrs Simpson was an American and a commoner was not relevant to this general feeling; nor did Edward yet have a reputation as a pro-Nazi: this only followed his Abdication.) Throughout 1936, Prime Minister Baldwin attempted to dissuade Edward from marrying her, without success, and (in common with the majority of influential people) rejected any compromise solution, such as a morganatic marriage whereby Mrs Simpson would become a duchess but not officially the queen. Of all this the British people knew nothing, with the British press and media engaged in a conspiracy of silence, although the foreign press had a field day reporting all the details. (Mrs Simpson's divorce, in Ipswich, was reported in one New York tabloid as 'King's Moll Reno'd in Wolsey's Home Town', Reno, Nevada, being the site of America's 'quickie' divorces; the reference to Cardinal Wolsey assumed a degree of erudition among its readers which surely few possessed.) As is well known, the storm broke suddenly and by accident. In late November 1936, the Bishop of Bradford, Alfred Blunt, gave a sermon calling upon the king to give evidence of a more Christian lifestyle. The Bishop knew nothing of Mrs Simpson, and was not referring to her, but Britain's press took the sermon as the signal to make the whole business public. A crisis point was now reached. It was made increasingly clear to Edward that, to marry Mrs Simpson, he must abdicate. His hopes for a 'King's Party', organised by Churchill and Beaverbrook, came to nothing. In early December, it appeared that a major constitutional crisis was about to begin; this continued until 10 December, when Baldwin announced that Edward would indeed abdicate, which he did immediately. That evening, Edward broadcast a renowned speech on the radio stating that he gave up the throne 'for the woman I love', and left for France. His brother succeeded as George VI. A modest and honourable man with a speech impediment, George VI (1895–1952; reigned 1936–52) was much more in the mould of his father, and more suitable, but less glamorous, as the British Sovereign. The new queen, Elizabeth (1900–2002; later Queen Elizabeth and still later Queen Elizabeth the Queen Mother), was among the most popular of royals, as was the new heir, Princess Elizabeth. Edward married Wallis Simpson in June 1937, and lived in semi-obscurity in France and North America, his only public role that of Governor of the Bahamas from 1941–45. The decision of the new king not to allow Wallis Simpson to be known as 'Her Royal Highness' caused a lasting breach, while the poorly considered visit by the Duke and Duchess of Windsor to see Hitler in October 1937 began a slide in popular esteem, one which accelerated as reports and rumours of the Duke's intrigues with Germany to regain the throne, possibly treasonous, became known. Had Edward remained on the throne, it is likely that he would have been as good a king as anyone else, but it was fortuitous that he abdicated in place of a more suitable monarch. The Abdication Crisis was one of the greatest sensations of the twentieth century, yet did no lasting harm to the institution of the monarchy and had few lasting consequences. When James Maxton, a far-left MP, proposed an amendment to the Abdication Bill abolishing the monarchy, it was defeated by 403 votes to 5, and perhaps the most notable feature of the Crisis was that it did nothing whatever to undermine the monarchy.

That the Abdication Crisis did not hopelessly split public opinion was a sign that, whatever the case elsewhere, an extraordinary degree of stability reigned in Britain. This was due to many causes, but perhaps first and foremost was the relative growth in the British economy at this time. The term 'relative' must be stressed, for of course this was still the Great Depression and unemployment remained stubbornly at very high levels in the north and Celtic areas. Nevertheless, there was now a sustained recovery, with the Index of Industrial Production rising by about 12 per cent between 1935 and 1938, and Net National Income increasing from £3 881 000 000 in 1934 to £4 671 000 000 in 1938. Real gross domestic product per head increased by about 16 per cent in the same period, one of the highest recorded increases in British history. As before, these gains were largely manifested in the south of England and the Midlands, and unemployment remained stubbornly high, never falling below 1 373 000 (in September 1937) during the latter part of the 1930s, about 11.3 per cent of all employed workers. Nevertheless, the overall trend in unemployment was down, with the percentage of the unemployed among all insured workers declining steadily. While the Depression was an unremitting horror story for hundreds of thousands of workers and their families, for those in the middle classes it later became, in retrospect, something like the 'good old days', the last prosperous period before bombings and socialism. This was a major reason so many were reluctant to go to war if this could possibly be avoided.

The coronation of George VI occurred on 12 May 1937. Taking place with the usual pageantry, George VI's coronation was an event of some historical importance. It was the first British coronation to take place after most of the European monarchies had been swept away (Italy was the only important European state to remain a monarchy, but, under Mussolini, its existence was purely nominal) and, as it turned out, the last coronation of a British monarch who was also Emperor of India and head of the British Empire. Despite the troubled world situation and the Abdication Crisis, it was highly successful, what the British do best, and a sign of reassurance. Two weeks later, on 28 May 1937, Baldwin resigned and retired. Poorly regarded and underrated in his time, in retrospect he is universally seen as one of the most dominant politicians of the twentieth century, probably the chief architect in the twentieth century of the emergence of the Conservatives as the normal majority party. In retirement, he devoted himself, rather unexpectedly, to heading the Lord Baldwin Fund, which raised large sums of money for German refugees. When the war came, Baldwin was chiefly blamed for Britain's unpreparedness, and it is probably fair to say that during the last years of his life he was reviled and derided to a remarkable extent, not least of all by Winston Churchill. He had more or less faded into complete obscurity when he died in 1947.

Baldwin's successor as Prime Minister was Neville Chamberlain, who took office on 28 May 1937. There was no election or opposition. Chamberlain was simply selected by the king on the advice of Baldwin, and he was officially elected Leader of the Conservative party a few days later. Ramsay MacDonald retired from the Cabinet and Parliament at the same time as Baldwin; Chamberlain's government was thus almost purely Tory and, in a sense, a new departure, although Chamberlain himself was 68 years old, while most of the faces in the Cabinet were, of course, already well known. Eden remained at the Foreign Office and Duff Cooper at the Admiralty, while Leslie Hore-Belisha (1893–1957), a popular, successful National Liberal who had been a Transport Minister (where he introduced the Belisha Beacon), became War Minister. The 'old gang' remained strong with Sir John Simon replacing Chamberlain at the Exchequer, and Sir Samuel Hoare becoming Home Secretary, where he proved to be a prison reformer, introducing an important Criminal Justice Bill which would have abolished corporal punishment; the start of the war forced its abandonment. Lord Halifax, increasingly influential with Chamberlain, took the senior non-departmental post of Lord President. Chamberlain's Cabinet of 21 included six peers and four baronets and knights, probably not dissimilar to what a Conservative Cabinet might have looked like had the First World War not occurred. Looking at it from another sociological perspective, 17 of its members had attended a public school (81 per cent), of whom eight were at Eton and two at Harrow. Eighteen had attended a university, with 12 at Oxford and three at Cambridge (71 per cent at Oxbridge). Although some of the Cabinet's minor and ex-Liberal members such as Ernest Brown (1881–1962; Minister of Labour) and Leslie Burgin (1887–1945; Minister of Transport) came from relatively humble backgrounds, and Malcolm MacDonald (Dominions Secretary) was Ramsay's son, eight men in the Cabinet came from families which were wealthy or aristocratic before the industrial revolution began, and might have sat in an eighteenth-century Tory Cabinet.

Neville Chamberlain was, of course, the son of the great Joe and the younger half-brother of Sir Austen Chamberlain, who had briefly led the Conservative party, served with distinction as Foreign Minister, and died shortly before Neville's accession to Number 10. It has been widely remarked that while Austen was intended as his father's political successor, and raised accordingly, Neville was supposed to be his father's successor in business, and his life had indeed revolved around the west Midlands business community and Birmingham local politics. While Neville Chamberlain is probably the most controversial modern Prime Minster, and perhaps the easiest to deride, he had many virtues, including a high degree of intelligence, insufficiently credited shrewdness, and much more experience in 'ordinary' life than most senior politicians. Since so much has been written about him and Appeasement, his faults are equally well known, especially an unattractive and foolish rigidity, self-confidence running to recklessness, and the misfortune to find his government centrally obsessed with foreign policy and war, subjects of which he knew virtually nothing. Chamberlain also had the habit of using unofficial, somewhat sinister figures as sources of information and backstairs dealings, for instance Sir Joseph Ball (1885–1961) of the Conservative Research Department. His main failing, however, lay in his misreading of the intentions of Adolf Hitler. In this he was, needless to say, not alone. After a spate of denunciations of Chamberlain and the Tory 'guilty men' during and just after the war, from both the left and Churchillian right, a virtual consensus has emerged among historians that, notwithstanding what can be seen as the fundamental weaknesses in Chamberlain's Appeasement policies, they were both rational and defensible, although the reasons that they are defensible and logical have often been obscured.

By May 1937, it was apparent that a far greater threat to Britain and to European stability was posed by Hitler's Germany than by Mussolini's Italy. Adolf Hitler (1889–1945) came to power in January 1933 on a policy, or rather an ideology, of extreme German racial-nationalism, expansionism, anti-socialism, anti-semitism and anti-Slavism. Hitler's unremitting hatred of Jews, for which he is now chiefly remembered, was then seen as only a small part of an overall picture. After banning all opposition forces, establishing concentration camps for his opponents, centralising all power in the Nazi party with himself as supreme head, accountable to no one, and removing Jews from the civil service and the universities, from 1934 Hitler moved to threaten European stability. In October 1934 Germany withdrew from the international Disarmament Conference and the League of Nations. In January 1935 the Saar (a coal-rich border area between Germany and France) voted overwhelmingly for reunification with Germany. In March 1936 Germany re-occupied the Rhineland areas which had been demilitarised by the post-1918 treaties, and in October 1936 moved closer to fascist Italy by forming the Rome–Berlin Axis; a month later, moves to bring Japan into treaty alliance began. As well, in November 1936 Germany recognised the right-wing insurgent government of General Francisco Franco in Spain, supplying it with armaments, experts, and troops. In March 1938, Germany annexed the independent German-speaking republic of Austria, adding over six million inhabitants to the German Reich. From May 1938 came the Czechoslovak crisis, leading to the annexation of the Sudetenland at the end of September 1938. The Sudetenland was chiefly inhabited by Germans, and Hitler seemed intent on redrawing the boundaries of Europe to bring about a larger German realm which would comprise all the German-speaking areas of central Europe. This enlarged *Reich* would be made purely 'Aryan' by expelling all or virtually all Jews. Hitler pursued this goal while increasingly in alliance with Italy and Japan, also expansionist powers.

The great question which Britain had to answer was at what point, if any, was Germany's expansionist policies to be resisted. Until early 1939 Britain always and invariably took a course of action which avoided war, even at the cost (as in the Czechoslovakian crisis) of permitting Germany to conquer additional lands. This policy, known as 'Appeasement', has given rise to endless debate then and since, especially after the outbreak of the Second World War in September 1939 made it appear particularly futile, while the relevations of the Nazis' wartime Holocaust against the Jews and other unparalleled enormities made Appeasement appear to be an unethical acquiescence in the advance of absolute evil.

British policy-makers at the time, however, could not see the unfolding situation with the eyes of a later generation, only with considerations which appeared fundamental at the time. Although Britain did indeed fight Nazi Germany alone between June 1940 and June 1941, during the 1930s it seemed to be folly to try to resist Hitler's advance unilaterally. Any British action against Germany had necessarily to be taken in conjunction with France, hopefully with Russia, and arguably with Italy, and each case presented great difficulties. France's military posture was oriented in a defensive direction towards stemming any German thrust into France, and while France was poorly equipped for an invasion of Germany. Even more than was the case in Britain, France's governments wished to avoid another war. Since France was adjacent to Germany, while Britain had no troops on the continent, France's attitude was crucial to any Anglo-French military resistance to Hitler, and France's attitude for the most part was hostile to military resistance. While an alliance between Britain,

France, and the Soviet Union might conceivably have stopped German expansion, there were many reasons why an all-out Britain alliance with Russia was also very difficult. The period of Hitler's expansionism, 1937–39, coincided with the height of Stalin's Great Purges, when millions were killed and Stalin was shooting his generals by the gross. Soviet policy, never straightforward, appeared to veer unpredictably from regarding the 'bourgeois' countries of the West as little better than the Nazis to seeking an alliance with them. Most Tories deeply mistrusted Stalin (who had, at this time, certainly killed vastly more people than Hitler) and regarded the prospect of a Soviet-dominated eastern Europe as, if anything, worse than a Nazi-dominated central Europe. In addition, it has to be realised that the Soviet Union had, in 1938, no common border with either Czechoslovakia or Germany, and, if its troops were to be sent into central Europe, had to be given permission to cross through Poland or Romania, both of which were dominated by ferociously anti-Communist right-wing governments.

Some in Britain, including Winston Churchill, continued to hope that Mussolini's Italy might be detached from its growing alliance with Nazi Germany and might even join in an anti-German alliance with Britain and France. Increasingly, however, it became clear that Mussolini had, for ideological reasons, aligned Italy with Germany, and that any price demanded by Italy for an alliance, especially its colonial expansion, would have been too high. The other great power – potentially, the greatest power – the United States, continued to be dominated by isolationism, the feeling that America should stay out of Europe's wars, although American President Franklin Roosevelt was clearly an arch-enemy of Hitler and of fascism.

After the Abyssinian fiasco, Britain did little or nothing to resist Germany's advances into the Rhineland or the annexation of Austria, other than to increase spending on the military (expenditure on the Army rose from £38 million in 1934 to £78 million in 1938, and on the Navy from £54 million to £102 million in the same period). Conscription, a sure sign that war was considered likely, and an obvious necessity in an age of mass armies, was not introduced until 26 April 1939, the first time that peacetime conscription was enacted in modern Britain. As in the rest of the world, Britain's leaders were mesmerised by Hitler, wondering where he would strike next. From May 1938 it became clear that Hitler's next target would be the Sudetenland, the border area of Czechoslovakia where Germans were in a majority. The 'failure of Appeasement' has meant, most fundamentally, the failure of Britain (and France) during the Sudeten Crisis of 1938. Before considering this, it might be in order to look at the rationale behind Appeasement, and the reasons why so many sensible people believed in a policy which must strike us today as utterly futile. Today, we inevitably think of Adolf Hitler as a monster in human form, perhaps uniquely evil, who had to be resisted by any means; the extermination camps are, today, never far from anyone's image of Hitler and his regime. In the 1930s virtually everyone knew of Hitler, from newsreels of his rallies and speeches, as a ranting hysterical demagogue, probably insane, and everyone knew that he had abolished democracy and persecuted the Jews and other groups. Nevertheless, it is important to keep in mind that Hitler did not kill any Jew or others until the invasion of the Soviet Union in June 1941, his aim being to expel most or all Jews from Germany. Nor was it clear that Hitler wished to become master of the whole of Europe, and it is this point which is crucial to understanding Appeasement. Until 1939 it appeared that Hitler's aim was the creation of a German-speaking realm in central Europe, which was to include Germany in its 1933 boundaries, to which would be added only other German-speaking areas, such as the Sudetenland. To many in Britain, Hitler's aims did not appear unreasonable and, indeed, seemed to correct a historical injustice, the fact that the principle of the redrawing of Europe's boundaries according to nationalities had not been applied, in 1918–19, by the victorious Allies to Germany. Hitler's aims thus appeared to be limited and manageable, and there was no reason to suppose that once they were achieved Germany could not be brought to within the behavioural norms of any European state. Indeed, for Hitler to wish to conquer all of Europe, thereby absorbing the tens of millions of 'inferior' Slavs and Jews, as he did after 1939, appeared to be a direct contradiction of the central Nazi policy of creating a pure 'Aryan' state. Many reasonable people thus believed that Hitler would stop after consolidating all the German-speaking areas into the German Reich. *Had* Hitler stopped after the Sudetenland, Appeasement would, indeed, have seemed a wise policy which averted war. As we know, however, Hitler did not stop, and by mid-1942 ruled over an empire from the Pyrenees to the gates of Moscow.

To the apparent reasonableness of Appeasement there was added the other central concern of its proponents, the fear of another world war. The horror of the trenches, and of 720 000 British soldiers killed – the 'lost generation' – was central to all policy-makers, as was the realisation that the next war, fought with bomber aircraft and tanks, would probably end civilised life. To many, almost any price was worth paying to avoid another war, especially as Britain, in the later 1930s, appeared to be emerging from its economic and political travails into stability and prosperity. Some on the right-wing of the Conservative party admired Hitler and other fascist leaders as bulwarks against Communism, but very few indeed admired his totalitarianism or all-consuming anti-semitism. While the generosity or otherwise of British policy towards Jewish and other refugees from Nazi Germany has been widely debated by historians, it is a fact that between 55 000 and 75 000 German and other *Reich* Jews were allowed to enter Britain, almost all after the Austrian *Anschluss* in March 1938 and *Kristallnacht* (when Germany's synagogues were destroyed) in November 1938. Additionally, about 90 000 *Reich* Jews emigrated to Palestine (despite immigration restrictions) and other parts of the Commonwealth, often because of British government pressure to admit more. This probably represented the highest total of German Jewish refugees taken by any country or political unit.

The Sudetenland crisis emerged in early 1938, after the Czech central government had attempted to suppress Nazi-backed moves for autonomy or independence by the Sudeten Germans, who were in a majority in the area of Czechoslovakia bordering Germany. The Czechoslovak government attempted to give greater autonomy, within Czechoslovakia, to the Sudetens, moves which were thwarted by the increasing extremism of Sudeten demands backed by Hitler. Britain at this stage (March–May 1938) attempted to prove an honest broker, urging the Czech central government to make concessions. As the crisis deepened, both Germany and France began to mobilise for war, with Germany fortifying the frontier against a possible French invasion, and France increasing its army to 1.7 million men. A second, even greater crisis, emerged in September 1938, when Sudeten German leaders broke off negotiations with the Czech central government, and Hitler, on 12 September, demanded that the Sudeten Germans be given the right of self-determination. Civil unrest broke out in the Sudeten areas. On 15 September, Chamberlain met with Hitler at Berchtesgaden, in remote southern Germany. Chamberlain (who regarded Hitler with contempt) believed that he had averted war by somewhat delaying and moderating German demands. After a good deal of pressure, the Prague government finally agreed (21 September) to the German annexation of the Sudeten areas. Chamberlain then (22–23 September) flew to Godesberg on the Rhine, to negotiate again on Hitler's demands for immediate surrender of the German-speaking areas. Chamberlain regarded Hitler's new demands as unacceptable, and a war appeared imminent, although Hitler told Chamberlain that this was the last territorial demand he would make in Europe, and that an alliance between Germany and Britain was possible: 'you take the sea and we the land'. Czechoslovakia now mobilised, and negotiations began (for the first time) between Britain, France, and Russia. Chamberlain appealed to Hitler for a further conference. In a famous and dramatic moment, when Chamberlain was addressing the House of Commons (28 September) on the extreme gravity of the situation, he was handed a note by his Parliamentary Private Secretary, Lord Dunglass (later Sir Alec Douglas-Home, Prime Minister 1963–64) announcing that Hitler had agreed to another international conference. This was the celebrated Munich Conference (29 September 1938), the meeting in southern Germany between Hitler, Chamberlain, Mussolini, and French Prime Minister Edouard Daladier. Czechoslovakia, despite being the subject of the Conference, was unrepresented. At Munich, Hitler got all that he wanted, especially the almost immediate evacuation of the Sudetenland by the Czechs. The new boundaries of Czechoslovakia were guaranteed by Britain and France, although it lacked a defensible border. Smaller portions of Czechoslovakia were also grabbed by Poland and Hungary, and, within ten days, Slovakia and Ruthenia (the eastern portions of the state) were given full autonomy.

Munich represented a catastrophic loss by the forces of democracy. Despite this, Chamberlain was almost universally hailed, on his return to London, as the saviour of world peace. Chamberlain is remembered today chiefly for the Munich debacle, and for two remarks he made at this time. Broadcasting on 27 September on the Czech crisis, Chamberlain stated 'How horrible, fantastic, incredible it is that we should be digging trenches and trying on gas-masks here because of a quarrel in a faraway country between people of whom we know nothing.' Three days later, on his return, he made a speech from the window of 10 Downing Street in which he echoed Disraeli's comments on returning from the Congress of Berlin in 1878, 'This is the second time in history that there has come back from Germany to Downing Street, peace with honour. I believe that it is peace for our time.' This claim, that Munich would bring 'peace for our time', would haunt Chamberlain, although the irony that by stabbing a peaceful democracy in the back he was bringing 'peace with honour' was apparently lost on him. Chamberlain, to reiterate, apparently detested Hitler, but honestly believed that with Hitler's acquisition of the Sudetenland, a *modus vivendi* with the Nazis was possible.

Chamberlain had moved to a pro-Appeasement policy in part by ridding the Cabinet of those who might have disagreed with it and promoting those who supported it. In February 1938, Anthony Eden had resigned as Foreign Minister, exasperated at Chamberlain's increasingly independent conduct of foreign policy. Eden was widely seen as the greatest exponent in the Cabinet of collective security. Recent historians have tended to downplay the differences between the two men (Eden was also, at this stage, a considerable Appeaser), but his resignation was commonly viewed as removing an obstacle to Chamberlain's policies. Eden resigned in protest against Chamberlain's determination to seek an agreement with Italy before the Spanish situation was resolved. In his place, Chamberlain appointed Lord Halifax, previously Viceroy of India and holder of a variety of other senior offices. Halifax, a committed High Church Anglican, had worked for reconciliation with Indian nationalists. Halifax is widely seen as the arch-Appeaser, a man whose Christian principles were utterly inappropriate at the time. Although this is arguably true, Halifax was also a considerable realist whose opposition to military force in the Sudeten Crisis was that it would have been ineffective in helping the Czechs. Halifax appears to have changed his views of Hitler almost completely during the Munich Crisis, and thereafter strongly supported rearmament. During the year after the outbreak of the war, he was probably the most popular choice (even in Labour circles) to succeed Chamberlain as Prime Minister, and probably only his membership in the Lords, and the view that Churchill was the only man for the grave crisis of war, prevented his coming to power. Appeasement in the form it took was, to a large extent, the product of Chamberlain alone, although almost no one at the time could see any truly realistic alternative policy against Hitler. Halifax appeared to shift his stance earlier and more forcibly than most, but without ever joining the small group of anti-Appeasers.

Chamberlain expected that a working agreement with Hitler would follow the Munich accords. Needless to say, it did not. Although there was, initially, near-unanimous support for Munich, dissent began quickly. Duff Cooper resigned as First Lord of the Admiralty (the only government minister to do so), and the anti-Appeasement forces in the Tory party, headed by Churchill, were slowly but surely strengthened. The agreement was forthrightly attacked by Clement Attlee, leader of the Opposition, and by Churchill, who claimed (3 October) that 'We have sustained a total and unmitigated defeat.' During the winter of 1938–39, it became clear that Czechoslovakia, with its industrial resources, had been sacrificed for nothing and, moreover, that guarantees by Germany to respect the new boundaries of the Czech state were worthless. Chamberlain attempted to draw Mussolini away from Germany, an effort which totally failed. Chamberlain did greatly speed up military production, especially in the Air Force, as well as civil defence measures, particularly in London. As late as 10 March 1939, however, Chamberlain told the press that 'Europe was settling down to a period of tranquillity'.

On the same day, however, Hitler occupied the remainder of the Czech state, declaring it to be a Protectorate of Germany as 'Bohemia-Moravia'. This was the first time that Nazi Germany took over a non-German-speaking area of

Europe, and a portent that Germany meant, in all likelihood, to conquer much of Europe. Most of British public opinion was outraged by this blatant example of Nazi treachery, and most former strong supporters of Appeasement now radically altered their positions. At first Chamberlain did nothing, apparently unable to admit that the entire basis of his foreign policy had been utterly wrong. On Halifax's urging, on 17 March 1939 he finally denounced Hitler, now promising that Britain would be 'resisting... to the uttermost of its power' any Nazi attempt 'to dominate the world'. Chamberlain's policies were now confused and contradictory. He pointedly refused to consider an international meeting of anti-Nazi powers proposed by the Soviet Union. Yet in late March 1939, when Germany made a series of demands against Poland, specifically concerning the Polish Corridor between Germany and Danzig, Chamberlain announced that Britain and France would come to Poland's aid if it were attacked by the Nazis. This was indeed a remarkable change in policy, for Britain and France were only marginally better able to help Poland against attack than assist Czechoslovakia. Poland was a much larger nation, with over 30 million people, but it was just as remote from Britain's military support, and Chamberlain gave this guarantee without consulting the Soviet Union, Poland's other great power neighbour. A treaty between Britain and Poland was formally entered into on 6 April, and similar promises were given to Romania, Greece, and Turkey. In late April, the British government introduced conscription for all males aged 20 and 21, in the teeth of bitter opposition from Labour and the Liberals. By the summer of 1939 it became virtually certain that a war would break out at any time. Perhaps the most notable international development of this period was that Stalin dismissed Maxim Litvinov, the Soviet Foreign Minister known for his backing of collective security against Hitler, and replaced him with V.M. Molotov, Stalin's robot-like stooge, who began to woo Hitler with the aim of securing a non-aggression pact. Chamberlain's behaviour towards Stalin in this desperate hour continued to be unforgivably offhanded, leading Stalin to give up on the prospect of reaching an agreement with Britain and France, and to seek a wholly unexpected accommodation with Nazi Germany. On 23 August 1939 came one of the greatest international bombshells of the twentieth century, the Nazi–Soviet Non-aggression Pact, whereby the two great totalitarian powers, seemingly at opposite and utterly irreconcilable ends of the political spectrum, became allies. Hitler entered into this strange pact purely in order to be free to attack Poland without fear of a two-front war; Stalin, by secret protocols of the Pact, gained hegemony in eastern Poland, the Baltic, Bessarabia, and other areas. To most leftists in Britain and around the world, the Soviet treaty with Nazi Germany was met with utter disbelief, and many quickly dropped their support for Stalin. Despite last-minute attempts at yet another compromise peace, war now drew nearer as it became clear that Hitler meant to take over much or all of Poland. On 1 September 1939 Hitler invaded Poland; two days later Britain and France declared war on Germany, and the Second World War had begun. In the debate in Parliament on 2 September, in the absence of Attlee, the Deputy Leader of the Opposition, Arthur Greenwood, rose to speak on behalf of the Labour Party. 'Speak for England', he was memorably urged by either Leo Amery or Robert Boothby (it was not clear which), prominent anti-Appeasement Tory MPs. Increasingly, they were indeed 'speaking for England'. While Chamberlain's Appeasement policies up to March 1939 seem reasonable if judged by the knowledge and beliefs which the British government had at the time, his behaviour thereafter seems far less rational, especially his failure to move with alacrity to woo the Soviet Union into a genuine and viable anti-Nazi pact, which alone might have saved Europe from another world war.

On the same day that war was declared, Chamberlain formed a small War Cabinet consisting of only nine men. By far its most notable innovation was that Winston Churchill, out of office for ten years, now returned as First Lord of the Admiralty, a post he had previously held in 1911–15. There was already a general sense that the brilliant but unstable Churchill might well emerge as the ideal wartime leader if war broke out and went badly, rather as Lloyd George had done nearly a quarter-century earlier. As events unfolded, Churchill was more and more often seen not as a pessimistic Cassandra on the fringes of political life but as a prophet who was uncannily and unfortunately prescient. During the later 1930s, Churchill had been the leader of a small group of Tory anti-Appeasers, a personal following not really connected closely with a similar group which had formed around Anthony Eden. As well as including Churchill in the War Cabinet, Chamberlain also brought Sir Maurice Hankey, the former Secretary of the War Cabinet in the Great War as Minister Without Portfolio, and Anthony Eden as Dominions Secretary, but outside the Cabinet. Chamberlain had also offered places to the leaders of the Labour and Liberal parties, who refused to join a government he headed. Thus the British war effort was led, from September 1939 until May 1940, by a purely Conservative government, just as the British war effort in the First World War had been led initially by a purely Liberal government.

The latter 1930s also saw very great changes in the Labour party, the official Opposition. In many respects, the years between 1935 and 1939 marked a coming-of-age of the Labour party, and by 1939 it seemed much like a party which could head a government with a large parliamentary majority than even a few years earlier, despite its two spells in government in 1924 and 1929–31. In December 1935, shortly after the General Election, Clement Attlee was elected leader of the Parliamentary Labour Party, winning 58 votes on the first ballot compared with 44 for Herbert Morrison and 33 for Arthur Greenwood, the other candidates, and then defeating Morrison by 88-48 in the second ballot. As Deputy Leader Attlee was a known item and was supported in his leadership bid by most Labour MPs who had sat in the 1931–35 Parliament, especially trade union leaders. In sociological terms, Clement Attlee was one of the most unlikely of Labour leaders, especially at the time, having the social profile of a typical Tory. His father was a leading City of London solicitor who had been president of the Law Society, the solicitor's professional society. Attlee attended Haileybury and Oxford, was a practising barrister and had served as a major in the Great War (for most of his early career he was known as 'Major Attlee'). He had an encyclopedic knowledge of cricket, did the *Times* crossword puzzle daily as a hobby, and remained a sceptical but, in the final analysis, loyal Anglican. In all respects, including appearance, he looked like every upper-middle-class Tory commuter on the 8:07 from Tunbridge Wells – except that he was a fairly radical member of the Labour party, who had worked for years in a settlement house in the East End and first rose to fame as Mayor of Stepney. Practical and competent, and famed for being laconic, but utterly without charisma, he was widely viewed as a man who had risen far above his level of ability and had reached a senior position because so few were left in the Parliamentary Labour Party after the slaughter of 1931. Few knew precisely what to make of him, and fewer believed that he would last very long as Labour leader, let alone 20 years, as he actually did. Hugh Dalton called Attlee's election 'a wretched disheartening result!' and said 'And a little mouse shall lead them.' Attlee was thus consistently underestimated, sharing that perception with many other notable British political leaders, such as Bonar Law and Baldwin.

To be a credible alternative party of government, Labour had to evolve a plausible set of policies on the international situation and on its management of the economy. Despite two terms of government, labour's actual programme, were it to be returned to power with a majority, remained remarkably woolly. On paper it was committed to a rather extreme socialism, but few knew just what that would mean in practice. In international affairs, its image was one of remarkable naiveté, a commitment to disarmament and internationalism which was obviously inappropriate in the emerging European situation; Labourites were also fond of attacking armaments manufacturers as 'merchants of death' and the cause of wars, rather than the governments which actually used their weapons.

Under Attlee, this greatly changed. Most Labourites knew nothing about defence matters, and Attlee established a Labour Party Defence Committee which made a careful and detailed study of military matters, such that frontbench Labour parliamentary speeches on defence matters were actually praised for their cogency by Tories. Attlee strongly backed measures of collective security and, from 1938, moved to a strong anti-Appeasement line, supporting increased military estimates to meet the fascist threat. His criticisms of the Chamberlain government were increasingly similar to those made by Churchill and other Tory anti-Appeasers. Labour also moved to clarify its domestic policies if it were elected to office, particularly in *Labour's Immediate Programme*, its manifesto put forward in October 1937. The *Programme* strongly presaged Labour's actual policies in 1945–51, including nationalisation of the Bank of England, public utilities, and railways. Only on the nationalisation of land (which was not carried out by the post-war Labour government) was the *Programme* much more radical than what actually occurred, while it was notable for its explicit failure to promise the earth by 'the nationalisation of the means of production, distribution and exchange' to which the party was nominally committed. This relative moderation was not lost on the British far left. Communists and fellow-travellers repeatedly called for the formation of a broad Popular Front of all left-wing forces in Britain, and were repeatedly rebuffed. Attlee also strongly supported Baldwin over his handling of the Abdication crisis. By 1939, Attlee had helped to transform the Labour party into a true Opposition party. It is improbable that Labour would have won a General Election at this time – one would normally have been held no later than November 1940, but was repeatedly postponed by Parliament after the declaration of war – and it continued to trail the Tories in the few early opinion polls which were conducted in 1939–40. Nevertheless, Labour looked much more like a credible alternative party of government than it had ever done before.

The 1930s were the decade of 'taking sides', when perhaps the clearest dichotomy between the political Left and Right in Britain in modern times emerged as the basis for debate and action. An important ideological left grew in size in Britain, especially among the middle classes, who had been largely immune to the growth of socialism just after the First World War. This occurred, in particular, among university students, which had perhaps never before been politicised in quite the same way. Within a year of its foundation in 1931 the Oxford University October Club (its Communist society) had 300 members; the Cambridge Socialist Club had 1000 members by 1938, in a student body of perhaps 5000. Nationally, the Left Book Club, founded by the publisher Victor Gollancz in 1936 to distribute socialist and anti-fascist tracts to the reading public, had 50 000 subscribers a year later. It had become arguably the largest vehicle for the serious public discussion of current politics in twentieth-century Britain, holding seminars up and down the country. While dues-paying membership of the British Communist party never rose above about 18 000 in mid-1939, sales of the *Daily Worker* the party's newspaper, reached 80 000 on weekends, suggesting a penumbra group of sympathisers reaching perhaps several hundred thousands. Notoriously, Soviet agents had little trouble recruiting the 'Cambridge spy ring' as subversive agents; its members honestly believed they were acting in the interests of mankind's future. Most younger intellectual voices in England, like W.H. Auden and Stephen Spender, were clearly on the Left. The British left became a major force, of course, as a response to mass unemployment and the seemingly irresistible march of European fascism. Many on the Left regarded the Soviet Union as a potential (or actual) earthly paradise, accepting the Communist party's propaganda at face value and dismissing criticism of Stalin and his regime as right-wing fabrications. Many others respected the positive achievements of the Soviet Union, particularly in the economy and education, while realising that its government was, in essence, another form of totalitarianism. In some sense there was an equivalent growth of the extreme right in Britain during this period, although in a different and limited way. Sir Oswald Mosley's British Union of Fascists (BUF) was, fitfully, actually larger than the Communist party, reaching a membership of about 50 000 in July 1934 before collapsing to only 5000 in October 1935. At its subsequent peak in September 1939, it had about 22 500 members. There were other small anti-semitic and pro-Nazi groupings as well, such as Arnold Leese's Imperial Fascist League. Many notable intellectuals and writers were at least vaguely, or often emphatically, on the political right, including, for instance, Britain's most famous poet and public intellectual T.S. Eliot, and there occurred in this period the growth of a Catholic and Anglo-Catholic right-wing intelligentsia which has received less attention from historians than the growth of the intellectual left. Yet university students generally eschewed the extreme right, while the British 'Establishment' had little or no truck with it. With the Conservative party in power with huge majorities, the middle classes relatively prosperous, and Britain's Empire and institutions more or less intact, right-wing adversial politics simply failed to develop to the same extent as did the adversarial left. Right-wing dissent by 'die-hard' Tories, for instance over India, stayed within the confines of the Conservative party. Conflict in Britain between Right and Left remained largely shadow-boxing, except for such incidents as the so-called 'Battle of Cable Street' of 4 October 1936. Cable Street, at the edge of the East End, was the location of violent scenes when Mosley's BUF attempted to march in force through heavily Jewish Whitechapel, and was prevented from doing so by a coalition of Communists, Jews, workers, and dockers: the 'battle' mainly occurred between the anti-fascists and the police. The 'Battle of Cable Street' has become legendary because it was one of the few places in Europe in the 1930s when the Left and Right came into direct conflict, and the Left won. By and large, the extreme Right gained victory after victory with ease.

Probably the most important scene on the European continent of conflict between the Right and Left was in Spain, where the Spanish Civil War raged destructively between July 1936 and March 1939. There, the authority of a popularly elected government composed of left-wing parties, similar to the Popular Front in France, was violently challenged by a revolt of right-wing army officers, beginning in Spanish Morocco and then spreading to the garrison towns of Spain. Led by Generals Francisco Franco and Emilio Mola, it was supported by the army and conservative forces in Spain, especially the Catholic Church. (Franco became supreme leader of the insurgents in October 1936.) The rival great powers began to intervene, turning the conflict into a battle-ground of right and left ideologies. In November 1936, Germany and Italy recognised Franco's insurgent government, pouring in arms and troops. Leftist forces, including the Soviet Union, supported the republican government, with Britain and France attempting to remain neutral. There was continuing conflict between the pro-republican forces in Spain, which included socialists, Stalinists, Trotskyites, anarchists, and others. In March 1939, Franco's forces captured Madrid after a civil war in which 700 000 persons had been killed. The British left strongly supported the republicans, with the British Communist party organ-ising volunteers for the pro-republican International Brigade. Over 2000 British men and women fought for the Spanish republic, including George Orwell (whose *Homage to Catalonia* is a classic of reportage) and young left-wing intel-lectuals such as John Cornford, one of 500 British volunteers killed there. Most Tories were at least friendly to Franco, but increasing numbers deplored the fact that his victory was a proxy for Hitler and Mussolini. The affairs of Spain came briefly to dominate British ideological politics, although paradoxically the con-flict there contained few of the elements now associated with the struggle against Nazism (for instance, anti-semitism and the Jewish question played no role there), while Franco kept Spain neutral in the war, remained in power for 30 years after the demise of Hitler and Mussolini, and at his death transferred the Spanish government to a stable, democratic constitutional monarchy.

During the years 1935–39, relatively little occurred in the status of the coun-tries in the British Commonwealth, which for the most part remained loyal to the Crown, arguably more loyal than earlier in the century. The greatest exception was Ireland, where Eamon de Valera moved, as before, towards total independence from Britain. De Valera, an extreme nationalist, became President of Eire (as the Irish Free State became known) in March 1932. His government abolished the oath of loyalty and the powers of the Governor-General; it pursued a tariff war with Britain until 1936. In 1936 the Senate, Eire's upper house, was abolished.

In 1936 a new Constitution was introduced which simply ignored the relationship of Eire with Britain. Two years later, an agreement between Britain and Eire seemingly settled affairs amicably, but Eire pointedly remained neutral during the Second World War, refusing to allow Britain to use the Irish naval bases to which, by treaty, it was entitled. Under de Valera, Eire moved to become perhaps the closest approximation to a clericalist, authoritarian state ever known in the English-speaking world, its deliberate encouragement of a small-holding peasantry reminiscent of backward regimes in eastern Europe at that time.

As always, India seemed on the borderline of semi-revolt, although perhaps less so in this period than just before. In August 1935, the Government of India Act was passed by Parliament, in the face of bitter hostility from Tory right-wingers. British India was divided into 11 provinces, with elected legislatures; these (but not the princely states) were collectively represented in a central legislature in Delhi. India was thus clearly on the road to eventual dominion status. The All-India Congress Party won the first elections, in early 1937, although its moderate wing gained the upper hand. Chiefly Hindu, the victory of the Congress Party alienated Muslims, while the issue of the princely states also remained unresolved. The Government of India Act also separated Burma, chiefly Buddhist in religion, and Aden from India, becoming separate crown colonies. In 1939, India was marginally more placid than it had been five or ten years earlier.

In contrast, affairs in Palestine degenerated, as the conflict between Arabs, Jews, and Britain became almost irreconcilable. The 'Arab Revolt' began in 1936, aimed at both the Zionists and the British. In July 1937 the Peel Commission recommended the partition of the Mandate into Jewish, Arab, and British states in a manner not dissimilar to what actually occurred 11 years later. Many Zionists opposed it, chiefly because the Jewish state would be tiny in size, while the Arabs rejected it in toto. Conferences in London in 1939 made no progress. Colonial Secretary Malcolm MacDonald, who made no secret of the fact that, if war came, the Jews would by definition be anti-Nazi but the Arabs could well prove strongly anti-British, issued a White Paper (the 'MacDonald White Paper') heavily restricting Jewish immigration and virtually abandoning Britain's commitment to the Balfour Declaration. The White Paper had profoundly negative effects, greatly strengthening the Zionist movement in the Jewish world, especially in America. Ironically, MacDonald's proposals were also rejected by the Arabs. The Palestine question continued to fester unresolved, with most Jews harbouring a sense of betrayal during their hour of greatest need. Despite this brief account of Britain's difficulties, it must be reiterated that the Commonwealth and Empire remained almost wholly loyal to Britain, all self-governing states (Eire being the only exception) declaring war against Germany immediately after Britain's declaration of war. 'Great Britain has declared war upon Germany, and consequently Australia is also at war', Australian Prime Minister Robert Menzies announced on the same day as the Second World War began. The British Commonwealth had thus retained a real, not a nominal existence in the later 1930s, and added considerably to Britain's overall geopolitical strength, although it added just as considerably to its defensive burdens.

9
The Second World War, 1939–45

The British declaration of war on 3 September 1939 led to an immediate reorganisation of the government, with Chamberlain forming a small War Cabinet of nine men. This was not the innovation that it seemed, for most, including especially Halifax at the Foreign Office, were holdovers from Chamberlain's previous Cabinet, while arch-Appeasers like Simon (Chancellor of the Exchequer) and Hoare (Lord Privy Seal) were well represented. Some faces were new, above all the appointment of Winston Churchill as First Lord of the Admiralty. After ten years in the political wilderness, the prime anti-Appeaser was now back in a position of leadership. As noted, Churchill had been First Lord of the Admiralty in 1911–15, and held that post at the outbreak of the First World War. 'Winston is back' was the famous Naval signal; there is an equally famous story that Churchill went to the offices of the Admiralty and found the maps on the wall exactly as he had left them in 1915.

Chamberlain's War Cabinet also included a number of other unusual appointments. Lord Hankey, the long-serving Cabinet Secretary and 'man of secrets', was brought directly into the Cabinet as Minister Without Portfolio. Below Cabinet level, Chamberlain also brought back Anthony Eden as Dominions Secretary and, within the Cabinet, retained the flamboyant War Minister Leslie Hore-Belisha, who was relentless in reforming the Army, to his eventual political detriment. Nevertheless, Chamberlain's new government was not a national wartime Cabinet in the sense that Churchill's government was to be after May 1940. As noted, Labour and the Liberals pointedly refused to serve under Chamberlain, and Britain entered the Second World War with a highly partisan government strongly reminiscent of Asquith's purely Liberal government that entered the First World War in 1914.

The first seven or eight months after the British declaration of war were and are known as the 'Phoney War', when little or no British fighting occurred, certainly compared with later. After invading Poland, Germany conquered the country in only three weeks, with the Soviet Union, under the provision of its Non-Aggression Pact with the Nazis, seizing the eastern half of Poland at the same time. Two months later, the Soviet Union alone attacked Finland, initiating the Russo-Finnish War of 1939–40. Meeting unexpectedly strong resistance from the Finns, the Soviet invasion of Finland led to near-universal condemnation and made an alliance with Britain, France, and Russia even more unlikely; indeed,

Britain seriously considered declaring war against Russia at this time. Russia's inept showing in this war (Finland finally capitulated on 12 March 1940, yielding territory to the Soviet Union; Russia is estimated to have lost 200 000 men killed, compared with only 25 000 Finns) convinced Hitler that any invasion against Russia would be a pushover for Germany. In the West, however, Germany did nothing, and the initial phases of the war were largely confined to the naval war, where *HMS Royal Oak* was sunk by a German U-boat (with a loss of 786 crew) at Scapa Flow in October 1939, while the Royal Navy disabled the German pocket battleship the *Graf Spee* off the River Plate in South America so seriously in December 1939 that it was blown up by its captain.

The Chamberlain government also took the time of the 'Phoney War' to bring about a transition from civilian life. Tens of thousands of children and their mothers were evacuated from London (many subsequently returned); a blackout was enforced; spending on defence rose from £254 million in 1938 to £626 million in 1939, and then to no less than £3 228 000 000 in 1940. As a result, taxes rose sharply, even on the rich. In 1937, a bachelor earning £10 000 (an enormous income, worth perhaps £250 000 today) retained £6222 after paying taxes. In 1939 he retained only £5897, and, in 1940, only £4965. The government, in other words, meant business about war, even before Churchill came to power. Nevertheless, because of its previous unpreparedness, Britain was initially much less ready to fight than Germany. Even in August 1940, at the Battle of Britain, the RAF Fighter Command consisted only 650 operational fighter aircraft, compared with Germany's 900 fighters and 1300 bombers.

This relatively quiescent phase of the war came to an abrupt end in the spring of 1940. In early April 1940, Germany invaded and conquered Denmark and then Norway, capturing Oslo on 10 April. Germany's takeover of Norway was regarded as vital to bring Sweden's iron ore to the Reich, and its possession of Norway's ports were seen as an important step for aerial attacks against Britain. Britain and France attempted to dislodge the Germans from Norway; they sent 25 000 men to Narvik, the chief Norwegian coastal port. Initially successful (the famous Parliamentary debate of 7–8 May occurred at this time), the Allies did capture Narvik in May 1940. However, the Allies were forced to evacuate the port, while its withdrawing troops suffered further losses at sea from German battle cruisers. By early May, as well, Nazi Germany moved against Belgium and the Netherlands, with a German invasion beginning on 10 May 1940. The Netherlands (like Switzerland, neutral in the First World War) fell to Nazi Germany on 14 May 1940 and Belgium the following day. Nazi Germany then pushed further on, attacking and invading France with an army of 2.5 million men and nearly 2600 tanks. Most of central Europe was now in the hands of Nazi Germany, with France tottering and the Soviet Union neutral. It seemed inevitable that a hegemonic Nazi Germany would quickly turn on Britain.

It was in this atmosphere of military disaster and near despair that the most famous and momentous debate in Parliament during the twentieth century occurred, the debate over the Norwegian campaign on 7–8 May 1940 which led to Chamberlain's resignation and Winston Churchill's elevation to the Prime Ministership at the head of a coalition government. The initial disasters in Norway had had a traumatic effect on British public opinion, moving the Labour party and much moderate opinion, including many Tories, against the Government. The Norwegian debate of May 1940 brought about a virtual revolution in British politics, Parliament turning strongly (but not decisively) on a serving Prime Minister who still commanded a large parliamentary majority. The debate was ironical, too, because its chief beneficiary, Winston Churchill, as First Lord of the Admiralty, fully shared in the responsibility for the Norwegian debacle. The debate in Parliament included almost all of the political notables of the day, and was marked by a number of renowned Parliamentary speeches. Admiral Sir Roger Keyes (MP for Portsmouth) addressed the house in full dress admiral's uniform, denouncing the Government for failing to attack the Norwegian port of Trondheim. Leo Amery, for some years a leading anti-Appeaser, attacked the Government in a speech whose celebrated conclusion quoted Cromwell's words to the Long Parliament, 'You have sat too long here for any good you have been doing. Depart, I say, and let us have done with you. In the name of God, go.' Lloyd George, still a respected figure at the age of 77, called upon Chamberlain to 'give us an example of sacrifice, because there is nothing which can contribute more to victory in this war than that he should sacrifice the seals of office'. When the vote was taken on the Government's conduct of the Norwegian campaign, 40 Tories voted with the Opposition, and 80 abstained, so that Chamberlain's majority was only 81 (281:200) instead of its normal 200 or more.

Chamberlain had tried to hang on, and, during the debate, made an ill-considered speech welcoming the 'challenge' of the vote. 'At least we shall see who is with us and who is against us, and I call upon my friends to support us in the Lobby tonight.' After the vote, Chamberlain tried to broaden the Government to include Labour and the Liberals. Labour, however, refused to support any Government with Chamberlain at its head. Chamberlain then decided, on 9 May 1940, to resign. At a celebrated meeting at Number 10 Downing Street between Chamberlain, Halifax, and Churchill, it was decided that Winston Churchill would succeed Chamberlain. Much about this famous meeting has been the subject of endless dispute, including its date (9 not 10 May 1940), and, in particular, the 'silence' of Churchill in conversation when Chamberlain allegedly tried to gain agreement that Halifax would be his successor. (As a peer, the succession of Halifax would have been difficult, but special provision could well have been made, in wartime, to allow him to address the Commons or perhaps disclaim his peerage.) The attitude of the Labour party has also given rise to much dispute. It is now difficult to make a fully accurate assessment of the actual course of these events. Nevertheless, one point which is often overlooked is that Chamberlain had at the very least to acquiesce in Churchill's ascent to power. Most of Chamberlain's actions over the year since the German invasion of Bohemia-Moravia could well be read as assisting Churchill not Halifax. Chamberlain brought Churchill back from the wilderness, and pursued a strongly anti-Appeasement and then anti-Nazi policy throughout. Although Halifax may indeed have been the initially favoured 'Establishment' choice, the possibility should not be dismissed that it was, effectively, Chamberlain who crucially engineered Churchill's elevation at Britain's hour of grave national peril.

Whatever the truth of the matter, it is indisputable that on 10 May 1940, Winston Churchill became Prime Minister of Britain. At the age of 65, he was one of the oldest men to become Prime Minister for the first time. He had also held more senior offices before becoming Prime Minister than almost anyone, including the senior posts of Home Secretary and Chancellor of the Exchequer, among others. He had sat in Parliament for nearly forty years, and had switched parties twice, moving from the Right to nearly the extreme Left, to the extreme Right, and then to a position as national leader at a time of grave peril acceptable to the entire political spectrum. More biographical works have been written on Churchill than on any other figure in twentieth-century British politics, yet there is a consensus that his character remains ultimately opaque and the consistency of his beliefs is both real and yet surprisingly difficult to chart with accuracy. At almost every turn in his career, Churchill did something unaccountable and unpredictable. Joseph Chamberlain's tariff reform campaign in 1903 seemed designed to attract supporters with Churchill's imperialist views, yet it specifically drove him out of the Conservative party into the Liberals. By 1930, Churchill had moved to the extreme right of politics, yet was an adamant opponent of Nazism. Always a kind of outsider and a rebel, Churchill was right more often than not, and was proven right by history. He was, too, an historian and biographer of great skill, at a time when few at the top of British politics had more than a schoolboy's knowledge of history. As well, he was the best orator and speech-maker of his time (the only man to win the Nobel Prize in Literature for his oratory), and one whose most sublime speeches, delivered shortly after he became Prime Minister, rank with those of Burke and Lincoln as the finest in the English language. Since his death, something of a reaction has set in among some (but of course not all) historians towards Churchill's reputation. From the Left, his often anti-democratic and 'reactionary' views have been emphasised, as well as his pledge to continue the British Empire; from the Right, rather the opposite claims are made, that Churchill could have secured a peace with Hitler in 1940 which preserved the Empire; instead, by fighting on Britain found itself subordinated to the United States, while Stalin emerged as the conqueror of half of Europe. All such critiques, although they may contain elements of the truth, invariably miss the point and will always rebound against those who make them. By saving democracy and British freedom, and by leading the alliance which wiped Nazism off the face of the earth, Churchill placed himself among a handful of persons in any sphere of life who are legendary and virtually beyond criticism, because criticism is simply pointless: William Shakespeare and Abraham Lincoln are the two closest parallels, although there may be others. The man and the hour indeed had met.

Churchill saw the leaders of the Labour party immediately after becoming Prime Minister on 10 May 1940, and formed an inner War Cabinet of five: himself as Prime Minister and also Minister of Defence; Chamberlain (still the leader of the Conservative party until his death five months later) as Lord President of the Council; Halifax as Foreign Secretary, and, from Labour, Clement Attlee as Lord Privy Seal and Deputy Leader of the House of Commons, and Arthur Greenwood (1880–1954), since 1935 Labour's rather less than celebrated Deputy Leader, as Minister Without Portfolio. This was the inner War Cabinet;

but there was also formally a large normal Cabinet of 27, of whom four were Labourites: Ernest Bevin the great and memorable Secretary of the Transport and General Workers' Union, as Minister of Labour and National Service; A.V. Alexander as First Lord of the Admiralty; Hugh Dalton (1887–1962), a notable Labour intellectual (and political intriguer) as Minister of Economic Warfare; and Herbert Morrison, Labour's great political organiser, as Minister of Supply. Besides the Labour ministers, the leader of the Liberals, Sir Archibald Sinclair (1890–1970) was included as Air Minister. Most of the others were Tories, but with several ministers brought in who had played no role in the National government. Lord Beaverbrook, the press lord and an old friend of Churchill's, achieved office as Minister of Aircraft Production. Leopold Amery, out of office since 1929, but one of the leading anti-Appeasers, returned as Secretary of State for India; so, too, did other leading anti-Appeasers, like Duff Cooper as Minister of Information, and Anthony Eden, now War Minister. Some pro-Appeasement figures remained, most notably Sir John Simon, given a viscountcy and made Lord Chancellor, but in general the centre of gravity of the Tory component of the Coalition government had moved to the Left. Below Cabinet level, the Coalition's ministers and junior ministers ranged genuinely across the whole political spectrum, from Sir Henry Page Croft, often regarded as the most right-wing member of the House of Commons, made Under-Secretary of War (as Lord Croft), to left-wing Labourites such as the fiery Ellen Wilkinson (1891–1947), made Parliamentary Secretary for Pensions. It was the closest approach to a genuine national government ever seen in modern Britain.

The new government did not, however, include everyone. Lloyd George declined to serve on health grounds; additionally, the former war leader apparently thought Britain would lose the war, and that he might become head of a future government. Sir Samuel Hoare, one of the most prominent pro-Appeasers, was sent to Spain as ambassador, where he did an effective and crucial job of keeping Franco neutral. Leslie Hore-Belisha had become embroiled in much controversy as War Minister, alienating Duncan Sandys (1908–87), Churchill's son-in-law; Lord Gort, the Chief of the Imperial General Staff, and Churchill himself, among others, and was removed from office by Chamberlain in January 1940, amidst claims of anti-semitism (Hore-Belisha was Jewish). Churchill gave no further office to this talented man during the war, although he did include him in his 'Caretaker' government in mid-1945. Churchill also brought with him a number of acolytes and loyalists. Brendan Bracken (1901–58), a strange, widely mistrusted Irish-Australian who had attached himself to Churchill since the 1920s, became Churchill's Parliamentary Private Secretary, while Frederick Lindemann (1886–1957; later first Viscount Cherwell), a German-born Oxford physicist known as 'the prof', was made Churchill's prime scientific adviser. Some of Churchill's hard-core supporters, however, fared less well, most notably Robert Boothby (1900–86), a fierce Churchillian anti-Appeaser who briefly became a junior minister under Churchill but who, a few months later, was forced to resign over alleged improprieties in securing the transfer of gold of a Czech acquaintance. For reasons which have never been fully explained, Churchill showed Boothby no mercy over a complex affair, and he never held office again.

There remained a very considerable body of Tory MPs who opposed this sudden turn of events, and who mistrusted Churchill and deplored his arrival in the new government of Labour. It has often been noted that, upon entering the Commons soon after the Coalition government was formed, Chamberlain was enthusiastically cheered but Churchill was received by his own party in near-silence. Although the wartime Coalition is now regarded as one of the ablest governments in history, many Tories (and others) were initially scathing about the new ministers. Loyalist Tories described Eden as 'a poor feeble little pansy', Attlee as 'feeble, inaudible, ineffective', Beaverbrook as 'a crook', Bracken's appointment as 'little short of a scandal'. It was, indeed, a government the likes of which had seldom been seen before, ranging over the whole political spectrum for one common purpose.

Churchill's emergence as Prime Minister put paid to any remaining hopes that there would yet be a negotiated settlement with Nazi Germany. Three days after taking over Churchill told the Commons that 'I have nothing to offer but blood, toil, tears, and sweat', and that the new government's 'policy' would be 'to wage war against a monstrous tyranny, never surpassed in the dark, lamentable catalogue of human crime. That is our policy. You ask, what is our aim? I can answer in one word: It is victory, victory at all costs, victory in spite of all terror, victory, however long and hard the road may be; for without victory, there is no survival.' Nevertheless, British victory was, in May 1940 and beyond, an extraordinarily unlikely hope. Hitler's triumphant march throughout Europe continued unabated. In June 1940 came the Nazi conquest of France, wherein Hitler accomplished in a few weeks, with minimal casualties, what the Kaiser's army failed to do in four years. On 21 June France capitulated. Its government fled and a fascist regime, under Marshal Pétain, took the place of the Third Republic. Britain had had over 200 000 soldiers in France; from 18 May through 4 June 1940 came the celebrated evacuation from Dunkirk, wherein the British contingent, together with over 100 000 French and Belgian soldiers, were removed to Britain, a total of 338 000 men, taken in a flotilla of 850 British ships. 'Wars are not won by evacuation', was Churchill's comment. With the fall of France, Britain now stood literally alone, apart from the Commonwealth and a few minor allies. It was then, in late May, that Halifax tried to convince the War Cabinet to use Italy (which remained neutral until 11 June) to negotiate a peace with Hitler which would leave Britain autonomous. After a protracted discussion, coincidental with the Dunkirk evacuation, it was resolved to 'fight to the death', thanks to the adamancy of the Labour ministers and Chamberlain's support for his successor. Halifax remained Foreign Minister until 22 December 1940, when he was then given the curious post of Ambassador to the United States, where his supercilious arch-Toryness was, at first, regarded with mockery, even hostility, by most Americans, although he there later proved himself an able diplomat.

How, in mid-1940, did Churchill plan to defeat Hitler? In reality, it is difficult, with the best will in the world, and with all of our hindsight, to see how this could be done, given that Hitler was triumphant across the continent, Italy was in the war as his ally, France had fallen, and the Soviet Union was neutral. (During the period until the German invasion of Russia in June 1941, the British Communist party denounced the war as an 'imperialist struggle' until it was driven underground as a potential security threat.) Churchill's long-term strategy was to bring the United States into the war, first as a provider of armaments and money to Britain, then as an active belligerent; to destroy Germany's military capacity through air attacks and bombings; eventually, to launch a cross-Channel invasion; and to stir up trouble wherever possible for Germany through Resistance fighters against Nazi occupation. Not even Churchill's warmest supporters could say, in the latter half of 1940, that this programme seemed remotely plausible. It would, in fact, have been far more sensible for Britain to come to some accommodation with Hitler, and the position espoused by Halifax would have had wider support, except for the fact that Hitler was utterly untrustworthy, operating from a position of military hegemony, and widely seen to be a brutal tyrant whose like had never been seen in modern times. (Although Jews and others were appallingly brutalised by Hitler, with Jews in Poland and elsewhere now often imprisoned in ghettos, the mass murder of European Jewry did not begin until Hitler's invasion of Russia in June 1941. Other captive peoples, especially the Poles and Czechs, now also suffered extraordinarily under Nazi rule.) In these circumstances, Britain had no choice but to fight on.

The immediate and most critical threat faced by Britain was that it was about to be invaded. From August through October 1940 came the so-called 'Battle of Britain', the beginnings of the Nazi invasion of Britain. This began with an attempt by the Luftwaffe (the German Air Force) to defeat the Royal Air Force and neutralise the Royal Navy. London became the target for incessant German bombardment – the 'Blitz' – which caused the British, in retaliation, to bomb Berlin. By May 1941, 43 000 British civilians had been killed by German bombing. To meet the Luftwaffe, the RAF mustered only 650 operational fighters, far fewer than those available to Herman Goering's Luftwaffe. Nevertheless, Britain won, thanks to 'the Few', the remarkable pilots of the RAF. They were crucially aided by Britain's monopoly of radar, a British discovery, and by many tactical mistakes on the German side, the first of a long series of military blunders made by the 'invincible' Nazis. It was at this time that Churchill made his most memorable speeches, words which inspired Britain and will live forever: 'We shall fight on the beaches, we shall fight on the landing grounds, we shall fight in the fields and in the streets, we shall fight in the hills; we shall never surrender.' (To the House of Commons, 4 June 1940); 'The battle of France is over. I expect that the battle of Britain is about to begin... Let us therefore brace ourselves to do our duty and so bear ourselves that if the British Commonwealth and Empire lasts for a thousand years, men will still say, "This was their finest hour".' (Broadcast on 18 June 1940); 'Never in the field of human conflict was so much owed by so many to so few.' (Of the RAF at the Battle of Britain, to the House of Commons, 20 August 1940.)

In reality, apart from staving off a German invasion, not much could be done. In July 1940 the British seized some of France's warships at Oran, Algeria, and a 'Free French' government-in-exile under Charles de Gaulle was established in London. Churchill now began to cultivate an extraordinary personal relationship with American President Franklin D. Roosevelt (a very distant relative), who strongly favoured Britain and did everything he could to assist Britain, although at the time America could not enter the war directly due to isolationist pressures. In March 1941, the American Congress passed the Lend–Lease Act, which allowed America to provide war materiel to Britain on a massive scale in exchange for the use of Britain's Caribbean islands to defend the United States. Nevertheless, the next year or so was a period of virtually unrelieved gloom for Britain, marked by heavy losses of shipping to German U-boats in the Atlantic, the German invasion of Yugoslavia (April 1941), the Nazi invasion and conquest of Greece (also April 1941), and of Crete (May 1941). In North Africa, after British successes against Italian troops, German tank forces headed by Erwin Rommel drove Britain back to near the Suez Canal, an offensive prevented only by General Claude Auchinleck's counter offensive in late November. Germany, Italy, and, in the Pacific, Japan, were now formally allied in a seemingly irresistible military coalition. By mid-1941, things were as black for Britain as they had ever been in modern history, with Britain seemingly only spared outright invasion by Hitler's forces. Historians have long disputed why the Nazis drew back from an invasion of Britain. Hitler had great respect for Britain's fighting abilities and still, it seemed, thought that Britain might agree to a peace treaty on German terms. He was not deterred from this view by the mysterious, much-debated flight of the number two man in the Nazi hierarchy, Rudolf Hess, to Scotland on 10 May 1941. Without Hitler's knowledge, Hess apparently was trying to make contact with the Duke of Hamilton in order to negotiate a peace treaty between Britain and Germany. Virtually everything about Hess and his mission, up to the time of his death as late as 1987, has become the subject of intense speculation, often of a highly imaginative kind.

At base, it seems clear that Hitler resisted invading Britain because he had already decided to invade and conquer the Soviet Union, despite Germany's non-aggression pact of 1939. As the centre of 'Judeo-Bolshevism', the home of millions of Slavs and Jews and the centre of international Communism, in ideological terms to Hitler an alliance between Nazi Germany and the USSR was highly anomalous if not anathematical. German conquest of Russia, with its *lebensraum* ('living space') for Germany's excess population and its boundless agricultural and mineral resources, had always been an aim of German ultra-nationalists, and was highlighted as a goal by Hitler in *Mein Kampf*. From mid-1940, it seems clear that Hitler began to prepare for an attack on the Soviet Union. Hitler expected a quick and decisive victory, similar to those he had achieved so often in the past, and, apparently, genuinely expected the 'rotten' Bolshevik system to collapse as soon as the Germans invaded. Stalin half-expected such an attack, and was repeatedly warned of its imminence by anti-Nazi agents. Because of Stalin's Purges against the Soviet military in the late 1930s, it was also very arguable whether the Red Army could effectively resist a German attack. Nevertheless, the Soviet Union was obviously no pushover for Germany, possessing a population of over 180 million, compared with Germany's 90 million or so, even in its expanded form. Stalin was every bit as ruthless as Hitler. The Soviet Union's centralised command economy revolved around an efficient heavy industry. Russia's vast spaces allowed defence in depth, while all previous invaders had been defeated by Russia's greatest military victor, 'General Winter'.

On 22 June 1941 Germany, suddenly and without warning, attacked the Soviet Union over a 2000-mile front in 'Operation Barbarossa', employing 3.6 million men and 3600 tanks. Britain, naturally, was delighted, with

Churchill, previously a fierce anti-Communist, promising to 'unsay no word' that he had spoken about Bolshevism. 'But all that fades away before the spectacle that is now unfolding…we shall give whatever help we can to Russia and the Russian people.' It quickly became clear that the military situation for Russia was grim, with the German Army Centre group reaching the outskirts of Moscow by October 1941. The Soviets suffered unprecedented casualties, and Barbarossa saw the beginnings of the Holocaust, the deliberate extermination of all Jews in German-occupied Europe; hundreds of thousands of others were also deliberately killed by the Nazi barbarians. It also became clear, however, that Germany could not take either Moscow or Leningrad (surrounded by German troops and subject to a siege of nearly three years in which at least 600 000 people died). Stalin managed to find an excellent set of military leaders, especially Marshal Georgi K. Zhukov, who saved Moscow, while by November 1941 German troops found themselves facing a Russian winter for which they were almost totally unprepared. By dividing the German army into three army groups (North, Centre, and South), instead of concentrating on seizing Moscow and thus splitting the Soviet Union, Hitler had made one of the greatest blunders of the war.

As the battle for Moscow was being hamstrung by the onset of winter, an even more decisive event was occurring on the other side of the world. On 7 December 1941 the Japanese, without warning, bombed the American base at Pearl Harbor in Hawaii, destroying much of the American fleet and killing over 3000 Americans, but also bringing the United States into the war. Three days later, Germany and Italy declared war on the United States (and not the other way round). Many historians regard Hitler's totally unnecessary declaration of war against America as his greatest single blunder. Some historians have seen Hitler's move as being intended to draw Japan into the war with Russia (in fact, Japan never declared war on the Soviet Union), or to permit all-out German U-boat attacks on American shipping while there was still time to defeat Britain and Russia. Others have been frankly mystified by Hitler's move, seeing in it further evidence of his irrationality and insane megalomania. At the same time as Japan attacked Pearl Harbor, it also attacked Britain's possessions in Hong Kong and Malaya, thus bringing Britain to war with Japan. This 'forgotten' theatre of the war was extremely serious, stretching British military prowess to the limits, and threatening a Japanese invasion, even conquest, of India and Australia. In fact, for the next year or more the situation in the Far East was as grim as in Europe, with Japanese planes sinking the battleship *Prince of Wales* and the cruiser *Repulse* on 10 December 1941, and then conquering Malaya in January 1942 and, with potent symbolism, taking Singapore in February 1942. Japanese conquest of Burma, the Philippines, and part of the Dutch East Indias and New Guinea followed, with Allied prisoners in Japanese camps being subjected to inhuman brutality by the Japanese military.

Although by this time, early 1942, and for some time to come, things for Britain were as bad as they could be, there nevertheless was now a sense that the war would be won. With America's untouchable military-industrial might and Russia's vast population, it seemed merely a matter of time before a victorious force could be amassed to defeat the Axis powers. Little or nothing, however, happened until early November 1942 when, within a few days, British forces under Sir Bernard L. Montgomery (1887–1976; later first Viscount Montgomery of Alamein) defeated the Germans under Rommel at El Alamein in Egypt, thus finally preventing German conquest of the Suez Canal, Palestine, and the Middle East. This was immediately recognised as a turning-point in the war, the first decisive British victory. A few days later the Allies invaded and seized North Africa, held by Vichy France and Italy. Mid-1942 brought the first great Soviet victories in Russia, including the Battle of Stalingrad (August–December 1942), and planning for an eventual Allied invasion of western Europe.

The Second World War also became a time of frequent meetings between Churchill and the other major Allied leaders, cementing, in particular, relations between Churchill and Roosevelt. Even before Pearl Harbor, in August 1941, the two men met at Placenta Bay, Newfoundland, where they issued the famous 'Atlantic Charter', pledging Britain and America to democracy and self-government, which became the basis for the United Nations Declaration a few years later. Just after Pearl Harbor, Churchill visited Roosevelt in Washington, staying in America for three weeks, and addressing the Canadian Parliament. Through Churchill's urging, America formally decided that Nazi Germany had to be defeated first, ahead of Japan, although most Americans probably viewed the Japanese as the principal enemy. The vision for a post-war United Nations organisation also began to take shape at this time. The Soviet Union was also represented at these meetings and brought into the coordination of the war effort, despite the mutual antagonism of Russia and the Western allies. In January 1943 came the Casablanca Conference, attended by Churchill and Roosevelt, which set back the cross-Channel invasion of Europe to 1944. It was here that Roosevelt, almost offhandedly, proclaimed the Allied goal as 'unconditional surrender' (a phrase first used by General Grant in the American Civil War), rather than mere Armistice as in the First World War. While this goal has been viewed as counterproductive by some historians, inducing (in their view) Germany to fight harder, no other goal was appropriate in dealing with the hellish regimes of Germany and Japan, and nor would Stalin have agreed to a less extreme goal, given the magnitude of Soviet casualties. Further conferences followed between Churchill and Roosevelt at Washington (May 1943), where the strategic bombing offensive against Germany was intensified and the date for the invasion of Europe (D-Day) set for 1 May 1944, at Quebec (August 1943), and at Cairo (November–December 1943), where Chiang Kai-Shek, China's leader, was brought into the discussion. At Teheran (November 1943) Churchill and Roosevelt at last met face-to-face with Stalin, the first time the three great Allied leaders, so different in ideology, had met. Thereafter the pace of meetings fell off, with only a second Quebec conference (September 1944) between Churchill and Roosevelt, and the very important Yalta conference (February 1945), only the second time, and the last, that Churchill, Roosevelt, and Stalin met together. At Yalta, the future of eastern Europe was decided in Russia's favour, as was the shape of the United Nations. Increasingly, Churchill's relations with Roosevelt proved difficult, with Churchill believing that the Americans were conceding far too much to Stalin. By early 1945 it had become clear that Britain was the least important of the three great powers, and faced bankruptcy unless assisted by the all-important United States. Roosevelt, obviously very ill at Yalta, died only two months later, while Churchill himself fell from power in July 1945. Relations between Churchill and Roosevelt had, in fact, deteriorated so markedly that (unaccountably, to most observers) Churchill did not attend the funeral of his comrade-in-arms in April 1945.

The year 1943 was also notable, for Britain, by the removal of the U-boat threat to shipping which had plagued the Anglo-American war effort. The shipping of men and materiel across the Atlantic was a *sine qua non* for winning the war. Hitler (like the Kaiser's military in the First World War) gambled on sinking enough Atlantic shipping to impede an American build-up in Britain. Sinkings of merchant shipping peaked in late 1942, with over 1.5 million tons of vessels sunk in each of the last three quarters of 1942. Thereafter, an improved convoy system, and the aerial destruction of German submarine plants, brought these totals steadily down. The year 1943 also saw the institution of a round-the-clock bombing campaign against Germany by the US Eighth Army Air Force and the British Bomber Command. The British, under Air Chief Marshal Sir Arthur Harris (1892–1984), controversially specialised in nightly raids to destroy Germany's cities and demoralise its civilian population, while the American forces specialised in daylight raids (at much higher altitudes) to destroy Germany's military infrastructure on a planned, pinpoint basis. Much about these raids was controversial, and Harris' attacks on civilian centres was openly attacked by George Bell, Bishop of Chichester (1883–1958), an influential Anglican clergyman. Some military historians have questioned the utility of Harris' indiscriminate raid. Nevertheless, once under way the combined bomber offensive greatly diminished Germany's war-making powers. Hitler retaliated with new formidable weapons, advanced rockets launched at London, the V-1s (in June–December 1944) and the even more advanced V-2s (September 1944–March 1945), whose devastation might have been far greater without the relentless destruction of Germany's war industries.

The Western Allies invaded Italy in early 1944, capturing Rome after a tremendous fight in June. This was, however, but a prelude to the main game, the opening of a Second Front in Europe which would lead on to Berlin. The Americans thought that an Allied invasion of Europe could be mounted in 1943; Churchill and the British, remembering the horrors of trench warfare, wished to put off the actual full-scale invasion as long as possible. Churchill also favoured, as in the previous war, a 'sideshow' invasion through the Balkans. It was absolutely clear, however, that only a full-scale invasion of Western Europe, closing in on Berlin from the west as the Soviets were doing from the east, could destroy the Nazi regime. Millions of American and Canadian soldiers and thousands of tons of materiel were shipped to southern England, under the supreme command of the little-known American general Dwight D. Eisenhower, with Montgomery, Admiral Sir Bertram Ramsay (1883–1945), and Chief Air Marshal Sir Trafford Leigh-Mallory (1892–1944) the senior British military leaders. Cloaked in secrecy, Operation Overlord resulted in the great Allied invasion of Normandy on D-Day, 6 June 1944, when 75 000 British and Canadian troops and 58 000 Americans were landed in 4000 ships. By the end of June 1944, 850 000 men, 150 000 vehicles, and 570 000 tons of supplies had been landed. Paris was liberated on 25 August 1944, with Charles de Gaulle becoming head of the provisional government, and the German border reached by November. After a setback in the Ardennes campaign (December 1944), the Allies began an all-out assault on Germany under Montgomery and American generals George S. Patton and Omar N. Bradley, coincidental with Russia's drive from the east. The Rhine was crossed in March 1945; Hitler committed suicide on 30 April, two days after Mussolini was shot by partisans. The Soviets took Berlin in early May and Admiral Karl Doenitz, Hitler's chosen successor, formally surrendered on 8 May 1945. In March and April 1945 the Allied troops liberated the western German concentration camps, Belsen, Buchenwald, Dachau, and the others, discovering horrors unknown before in modern history and altering forever our perceptions of 'civilised man'. These German camps were by no means the worst: Auschwitz, Treblinka and the other extermination camps, where millions perished, were all in Poland, and were liberated by the Soviets.

In the meantime, the war continued in the Pacific theatre, with the mainly American-led forces grimly liberating Japanese-held islands and territories, and bombing Japan on a daily basis. British forces finally retook Rangoon in April 1945. Most expected the war against Japan to drag on for several more years, with a full-scale invasion necessary by the Allies which might, when met by suicidal Japanese resistance, entail a million or more casualties. In the end, Japanese surrender came swiftly and by the most surprising of sources, the dropping of atomic bombs on Hiroshima (6 August 1945) and Nagasaki (9 August 1945). Developed at a phenomenal cost and in complete secrecy by Allied scientists, these resulted in Japan's official surrender on 2 September 1945, and changed the nature of war and international relations as fundamentally as gunpowder. Churchill's vision for victory over Germany had, most surprisingly perhaps, been realised in approximately the manner he foresaw. Given its initial disadvantages, Britain acquitted itself rather well in the Second World War, especially compared with the pointless bloodbath of the Great War. Britain mobilised approximately six million men for the Second World War, compared with 25 million mobilised by the Soviet Union, 15 million by the United States and, on the other side, 12.5 million by Germany and 7.4 million by Japan. Another 2.5 million or more were mobilised by the Commonwealth, 1.1 million by Canada, and 990 000 by Australia. Despite this, casualties were actually much lighter than in the Great War, with only 398 000 British military dead – about 55 per cent of the 1914–18 British total – and 65 000 civilian dead, almost all in bombing attacks. While the destructiveness of war had increased enormously, direct British engagement with the enemy was much more limited, with trench war-like murderous stalemate unknown except for a few unrepresentative phases of the war. The development of penicillin and other new forms of medical treatment also reduced casualties. During the war, British scientists also invented or perfected radar, jet propulsion, the first modern computer (ENIGMA, the top secret, now celebrated code-breaking machine at Bletchley Park, Buckinghamshire), and were a significant element in the development, in America, of the atomic bomb. British military production also grew enormously, although it was outpaced by the vastly larger capacity of the United States and, to a lesser extent, of the Soviet Union. During the Second World War, for instance, the number of aircraft of all kinds produced in Great Britain totalled 119 876, compared with 283 760 produced in America,

146445 in the Soviet Union, 107245 in Germany, and 6573 in Italy. British generalship in the Second World War was, by any reasonable standards, much higher than in the Great War. Most of the senior commanders and service chiefs of the Second World War, men like Sir Alan Brooke (1883–1963; later first Viscount Alanbrooke), Sir Harold Alexander (1891–1969; later first earl Alexander of Tunis); Sir Charles Portal (1893–1971; later first Viscount Portal), the Marshal of the RAF, described by Eisenhower as 'the greatest British war leader'; and Sir Arthur Tedder (1890–1967; later first baron Tedder), among many others, were men of considerable ability, even military brilliance, and there was a distinct absence in commentary on the war, then or since, of any sense that Britain's military leadership was utterly incompetent or out of its depth, as is the mainstream view, so often and regularly reiterated, of Britain's military leadership in the First World War. In some measure this view may be illusory: the type of fighting pursued in the two wars was completely different, as the casualty figures clearly show, while Britain's two great allies, America and Russia, probably carried the war to a successful conclusion to a much greater extent, *vis-à-vis* Britain, than did even France in the Great War. (Certainly the Soviet Union took, and gave, a far greater number of casualties.) Nevertheless, there are good reasons for believing that Britain had learned from its mistakes of a quarter-century before. Britain had a remarkably high 'learning curve' in military matters. During the Second World War, too, a feeling grew that Britain was experiencing a sense of national unity never seen before, and far more genuine in its quiet determination than the hysterical xenophobia of the Great War. While some historians have questioned the reality of this mood, there are reasons for believing that a sense of genuine national unity of a kind did exist, especially compared with the First World War, and a comparison of the two wars is instructive. In the 1939–45 war, Britain was indeed fighting for its existence, against a power of unmatched evil and inhumanity, and actually faced invasion; its cities were bombed and thousands died. None of these conditions existed in the Great War (although there were some German sea and air raids against British civilian targets). As a result, the British people had no need to resort to the hysterical super-patriotism of the Great War, and, whatever the intrusions into civil liberties, especially early in the conflict, the second war produced no Horatio Bottomleys or their ilk. Strikingly, there were few or no 'war profiteers' in the Second World War; no Honours Scandal, and no sense that Churchill's coalition was an unnatural, hothouse one whose ending was a precondition for the return of normality. Indeed, it was somewhat surprising, certainly to Churchill, that Labour gratuitously ended the coalition in May 1945, before the war with Japan had ended: many would have hoped, even expected, the coalition to continue into peacetime.

The war moved the centre of political gravity in Britain emphatically to the Left, setting the stage for Labour's great triumph in 1945. (This, too, was an obvious difference between the effects of the two wars.) The political far right in Britain was ostracised and marginalised, with out-and-out pro-fascists like Sir Oswald Mosley and A.R.D. Ramsay placed in jail for the duration. (In 1940, too, when invasion appeared imminent, tens of thousands of 'enemy aliens' were jailed, with most sent to Canada or Australia. Many of these were actually Jewish or anti-fascist refugees. This is widely regarded as one of the most shameful and mistaken incidents of the war.) More broadly, there was a sense, on the Tory side of politics, that things would never go back to 'normal', and that the post-war world would inevitably set a shift to the Left even if the Conservatives remained in power. Taxes reached levels unknown before in British history, and it seems likely that fewer among the well-off avoided paying them than ever before. Conscription meant the end of most servant-keeping; West End social life was suspended for the duration; many country homes were requisitioned by the government. There was little in the way of basic social legislation during the war, but in 1945, just before the General Election, Parliament enacted the Family Allowances Act, providing a sum of money (initially five shillings per week) for every child, to be paid to the mother rather than the father. This innovation was in part the brainchild of Eleanor Rathbone (1872–1945), an influential Independent MP and radical campaigner. Late in the war came the great Education Act of 1944, which initiated the '11-plus' system and divided secondary education into grammar, technical, and modern schools. Some comprehensive schools were initiated as a result, but provision for compulsory part-time education between the school leaving age (which remained at 14 until 1947, when it was raised to 15) and 18 in county colleges was not implemented. Most military officers – but not all – were products of the public schools and universities, and notwithstanding the wartime mood, there was still an expectation that a young public school or university graduate would inevitably become an officer rather than an enlistee. Nevertheless, the class-based nature of the British military had certainly lessened since the Great War. Alliance to democratic America (whose soldiers were notoriously 'over-paid, over-sexed, and over here') with its core value of universal democratic triumphalism, and, even more emphatically, to Bolshevist Russia, also assisted these trends.

The war also assisted the triumph of Labour in many other ways. Rationing was first introduced in January 1940 and, within two years, had spread to almost all basic foodstuff, commodities, and clothing. The British people had thus had a continuing experience of this type of 'socialism' for more than five years when Labour was elected. Virtually all aspects of British society (including information) and the economy were centrally controlled or administered in a total war exceeding in breadth anything known in the Great War. Intellectuals were not slow to see either the novelty or the dangers for the liberal tradition of this state of affairs, and it is noteworthy that two of the greatest (perhaps the two greatest) libertarian tracts of the time, *The Road to Serfdom* (1944) by Friedrich von Hayek (1899–1992), a naturalised Austrian, and *Animal Farm* (1945) by George Orwell (*né* Eric Blair, 1903–50), were products of the late stages of the war, not of the post-war Labour government (Orwell's *1984* was published a few years later, in 1949).

The forced equalitarianism and quasi-socialism of the war years plainly benefited the ideals of the Labour party, as did the fact that the Second World War was a 'people's war' against fascism. The general movement of the centre of political gravity to the Left temporarily gave legitimacy to the previously ostracised Communist Party of Great Britain, which briefly appeared to be little more than the local cheering-squad of Britain's 'gallant Soviet allies' rather than a sinister, subversive force. (It was in this period, too, that the Soviet penetration among young idealists in the 'Establishment' in the 1930s, particularly at Cambridge University, gave impetus to the activities of the notorious 'Cambridge Spy Ring' – Burgess, Maclean, Philby, Blunt, and an alleged 'fifth man' whose existence and identity continued to be matters of press speculation for more than half a century.) During the Second World War, even the Church of England temporarily moved to the Left. Between 1942 and 1944 the head of the Church of England was Archbishop William Temple (1881–1944), a longstanding and avowed Christian socialist who, in 1942, produced a tract on the just society in Britain, *Christianity and Social Order*, which advocated an extraordinarily radical programme of socialism. Temple's sudden death, after only two years as archbishop, was widely regarded as a national catastrophe, perhaps the last time that the death of a church leader in Britain would be so regarded. Temple's successor as archbishop, Geoffrey Fisher (1887–1972, Archbishop of Canterbury 1945–61) was in a much more conventional mould and certainly no political radical. The most famous artefact of this wartime mood of radicalism was the Beveridge Report (the popular name of a Treasury White Paper of 1942, 'Social Insurance and Allied Services'). Written by Sir William Beveridge (1879–1963), the report urged the replacement of all state income-maintenance services by a universal, comprehensive form of social insurance, funded by the state. Unemployment, sickness, and workmen's compensation were to be made universal, while maternity and death benefits were to be added, family allowances (government grants paid directly to the mothers of children) introduced to alleviate child poverty, and a comprehensive national health service devised to replace the hodgepodge of inadequate forms of voluntary medical insurance. All this was to be paid for from a commitment to full employment and economic growth. While Beveridge was certainly instrumental in producing his celebrated Report, many of these ideas were already widely discussed. Beveridge's ideas, though seemingly revolutionary, were, in some respects, quite limited, and had nothing to say about such subjects as family expenditure or rent, education, or nationalisation. The report was first received with enthusiastic praise from the press, even from right-wing sources, and seemed to herald a new attitude towards the responsibility of society to those in need. Soon, however, conservative fears of a full-blown welfare state being enacted in wartime, by, as it were, the backdoor, led to a significant Tory revolt against it when debated in the Commons in February 1943, and the Churchill government declined to commit itself to implementing the report, thus opening a major area of policy disagreement between the Tories and Labour. (Beveridge himself was a Liberal, not a Labourite.) Beveridge continued to outline his vision in works like *Full Employment in a Free Society*, published in 1944. Although many historians have questioned the direct links between the Beveridge Report and the welfare measures enacted by the 1945–51 Labour government, there does seem to have been a direct link between the Report's recommendations and actual legislation.

The Report was notable for its optimism for a better, fairer world after the war, and virtually everything that occurred during the war seemed to strengthen and encourage the notion that a triumphant left would, with peace, remake the world to usher in a new age of democracy and equality. In Britain, the national mood which unquestionably existed had something in common with the

Resistance on the European continent, which, in its Communist, socialist, or Christian democratic forms, produced an existentialist sense that fighting and destroying absolute evil, represented by Nazism, would prepare the way for a new world of hope. Nevertheless, there were, of course, distinct limits to what the Left could accomplish in wartime. During the first few years of the war, there continued to be an undercurrent of unrest towards Churchill and his government, even after the Battle of Britain, the Left deploring the fact that the war was still going badly and was apparently reluctant to open a Second Front against the Nazis, which of course did not come until D-Day. In 1942, two 'no confidence' motions were actually debated in the House of Commons attacking the government. The second, in early July 1942, just after Rommel recaptured Tobruk in North Africa, was of some importance, being supported by Sir Roger Keyes (who had helped bring down the Chamberlain government), Leslie Hore-Belisha, and Aneurin Bevan, one of the leaders of the Labour party's left-wing. Bevan attacked the allegedly class-ridden nature of the British military, which, he claimed, worked against the war effort. The government won the vote by the lopsided margin of 475-25, but many felt that the criticism of the government's lacklustre record were valid. A steady stream of criticism continued, and there was even talk, in the summer of 1942, of replacing Churchill with someone else, such as Lord Beaverbrook, Sir Stafford Cripps, or Australia's former Prime Minister, Robert Menzies, as extraordinary as this now seems. Mainstream Labour continued to support Churchill, while, after El Alamein, the tide slowly but surely turned, but much frustration remained, and Churchill faced a great deal of hostility from the extraparliamentary British Left until virtually the end of the war.

It would be reading history backwards, however, to claim that anyone could have predicted in advance the political earthquake which was about to unfold. Churchill wanted the coalition with Labour and the Liberals to continue until the end of the war with Japan which, before the atomic bombs were dropped, was not expected to occur until perhaps 1947. By the spring of 1945, however, with victory at hand, both Churchill and Labour became more blatantly partisan. In March 1945, for instance, Churchill refused to amend the Trade Disputes Act to allow greater financial support for the unions. Labour, too, came more and more to the view that an early election was desirable. Attlee wanted the coalition to continue, but found, at the party's May 1945 conference at Blackpool, that Labour now wished the coalition to end and an early election to be called. Thus, on 23 May 1945, Labour and the Liberals left the coalition, and Churchill formed a purely Conservative 'Caretaker' government, which held office until 26 July 1945. This two-month period was necessary because the disruption caused by the war, and the location of hundreds of thousands of British troops around the world, meant that polling could not take place until 5 July, while the results were not declared until 26 July 1945, after all ballots were in and counted. Churchill's Caretaker government generally, but not invariably, kept those leading Tories from the wartime Coalition in an equivalent position: Sir John Anderson (1882–1958; later first Viscount Waverley), Chancellor of the Exchequer in the Coalition, continued as before, as did Anthony Eden in the Foreign Office, as did most others. Where a Labourite or Liberal had held a post, they were, of course, replaced by Tories, as, for example, with the barrister,

Sir Donald Somervell (1889–1960), who shifted from Attorney-General to Home Secretary. Because of the political cataclysm shortly to occur, it is impossible to say what a Churchill government would have done had it remained in power, but some relatively liberal figures were given Cabinet posts, for instance Harold Macmillan (1894–1986; later first earl of Stockton), the new Air Minister, and R.A. Butler (1902–82; later baron Butler of Saffron Walden), now Minister of Labour. While containing few former Appeasers, the government also did not look too different from any pre-1940 Tory government. It would certainly not have enacted a Welfare State as Labour did, and would have come under great left-wing and trade union pressure over many issues.

The war brought about a political truce so that, in by-elections, only the major party which previously held the seat was allowed to contest it. This did not prevent independents or minor parties from contesting by-elections and, during the war, there was a perceptible drift to the Left, with the Tories losing 12 by-elections to other parties after Churchill became Prime Minister. Most were to independents, but three by-elections were won by candidates of the Common Wealth Party, formed in 1942 by Sir Richard Acland, a former Liberal MP, as a radical alternative to Labour which vowed to oppose all 'reactionary' candidates. There were no public opinion polls between February 1940 and February 1945, but those taken in the months before the July 1945 General Election were indeed striking: in February 1945 Labour led the Tories by 47 per cent to 27 per cent among respondents in a Gallup Poll asked to state their voting intention 'if there were a General Election tomorrow'. Two months later, in April 1945, the results were almost identical: Labour 47; Tories 28, while in June 1945, the breakdown was: Labour 45, Tories 32 (with the Liberals at 15 per cent; this underestimated the actual vote of both the Labour and the Conservatives). Nevertheless, it is easy to be wise after the event, and the advantages enjoyed by the Conservatives should not be minimised. At the dissolution of Parliament in 1945, the Conservatives still enjoyed an enormous majority, holding 398 seats in the Commons to only 166 for Labour, 18 for the Liberals, and 33 for others and independents. Winston Churchill was regarded everywhere, at home and abroad, as a heroic, almost superhuman figure, who had brought Great Britain through its darkest hour, while the Tories enjoyed all the advantages of incumbency.

The campaign conducted by the parties during the 1945 General Election has become notorious for Churchill's mishandling of his election broadcasts. Radio was the chief medium in which the campaign was conducted, with the Conservatives and Labour each allotted 10 half-hour political broadcasts on the BBC (the only broadcaster), the Liberals four, and the Communists and Commonwealth one each. Churchill delivered four of them; in one he claimed that 'No Socialist government conducting the entire life and industry of the country could afford to allow free, sharp, or violently worded expressions of political discontent. They would have to fall back on some sort of Gestapo, no doubt very humanely directed in the first instance.' Churchill's likening of Labour – which had until a few weeks earlier, shared with him the governing of Britain – to the Nazis did immense harm, and has been widely contrasted with Labour's moderate, effective campaign.

The results of the election were finally announced in late July 1945. They were, in the words of King George VI, 'a great surprise to one and all'.

The seemingly impossible had happened: Churchill, the world statesman, had been swept aside by a remarkable Labour landslide. The final results were as follows:

	Total votes	MPs elected	% share of the total vote
Conservatives	9 988 306	213	39.8
Liberal	2 248 226	12	9.0
Labour	11 995 152	393	47.8
Communist	102 780	2	0.4
Common Wealth	110 634	1	0.4
Others	640 880	19	2.0
Total	25 085 978	640	100.0

Labour thus had a majority of 146 seats over all other parties. The number of Tory MPs had been reduced by 176, from 398 at the Dissolution to only 213, while the number of Labour MPs had risen by no less than 227, more than doubling in size. The Liberals, despite high hopes of some gains because Beveridge was a Liberal, did very poorly, losing six out of 18 seats, while, similarly, the extreme Left gained only a derisory number of seats. Labour was almost completely dominant everywhere, even in previously impregnable areas like Birmingham. Even in the south of England outside London, the Tories' safest stronghold, Labour held 91 seats compared with only 88 for the Conservatives and three for the Liberals. Tory minister after minister went down to defeat. As always, it was possible for Tories to take an optimistic view of the situation. Labour had only won 47.8 per cent of the vote, and the anti-socialist Tory and Liberal vote was actually slightly greater than the vote polled by the Left. Britain's electoral system, as was always the case, magnified the winning party's MPs. There was a relatively low turnout, 72.7 per cent (compared with 76.3 per cent in 1931) on an old voters' register. There were many more Tory MPs in 1945 (213) than in 1906 (157); within four years the Tories had bounced back while, this time, there was no longer an Irish contingent to pad the Left's numbers. While all this was doubtless true, 1945 was, nonetheless, a stunning victory for British socialism, unquestionably its greatest hour. The entire political right, in Britain and Europe, appeared discredited by the Depression and fascism, and many observers did not expect the Conservatives to mount a serious challenge to Labour for the next generation.

Political historians have always been somewhat puzzled by just why Labour won so comprehensively. There is a general feeling that the Tories (as opposed to Churchill himself) were strongly associated with high unemployment during the Depression and with Appeasement, and were being punished for these associations. It is also thought that many soldiers assumed they would be demobilised more quickly if Labour won. The Tories' political machine was more heavily hit by the disruptions of the war than was Labour's, which had been strengthened by the sharp growth in trade union numbers during the war (the total number of persons affiliated with the Trades Union Congress had risen from 4 669 000 in 1939 to 6 576 000 in 1945). Perhaps most importantly, the war had itself created what might be termed a kind of socialist society, with the British people already used to thoroughgoing rationing, central planning, forced egalitarisation of a kind, and the unity of society's actions for the common good. While most people obviously longed for normality to return, for many, the war had, at home, in a sense, brought distinct improvements in living standards, with an end to unemployment and a much greater feeling that old-established class barriers and inequalities could be ameliorated under state direction. Also crucial was the fact that Labour had already been in government for five years, something which is often forgotten in considering its triumph in 1945. Labour's leaders, such as Attlee, Bevin, and Morrison, were already well-known, respected, and trusted national figures who had just conducted a victorious war. On no account could they reasonably be described as potential totalitarians or revolutionaries, and for this reason Churchill's attempts to portray them in this light utterly backfired. Without the mood of national unity and the state controls put in place by the war, and without Labour's long experience in government, it is unlikely (though not, of course, impossible) that Labour could have won decisively at this time. Indeed, it is quite conceivable that without the war they might have been doomed to permanent opposition status. The war, especially a war fought against fascism, had changed everything.

10
The Labour Government of 1945–51

By common consent, the Labour government which held power between July 1945 and October 1951 was one of the ablest of the twentieth century, quite possibly the very best, and the government with the most achievements to its credit, at least in peacetime. It set the parameters of the role and dimensions of what the British government, in modern times, could and should do, in a way which remained unchallenged for over thirty years and which, despite modifications, still remains partially in place. It accomplished more than any other peacetime government, arguably before or since, and in many respects represented the culmination of the entire tradition of Britain's reform movement since the Great Reform Act if not before. As well, despite its great achievements, it was an honourable government, composed of honourable men who rarely deceived or dissimulated.

Clement Attlee, Deputy Prime Minister from 1940 until May 1945, officially became Prime Minister and Defence Minister on 26 July 1945, and formed a Cabinet of 20. Attlee's succession to the premiership was, remarkably, not unchallenged, and a number of prominent Labourites thought that someone else, particularly Herbert Morrison, ought to become Prime Minister. Much of this short-lived campaign was spearheaded by Harold Laski (1893–1950), professor at the London School of Economics and chairman of the Labour party in 1944–45 (but not an MP) who had been lecturing the Labour party's leadership on how it ought to conduct itself during the campaign, attracting much attention to his extra-parliamentary role. Morrison himself was also active on his own behalf. But with the help of Ernest Bevin, the most powerful trade union leader, Attlee quickly formed a government. When Laski, as party chairman, continued to hector Attlee over foreign policy, Attlee sent him a celebrated letter (on 20 August 1945) stating that he had no right to interfere and that 'a period of silence on your part would be welcome'. Nothing more was heard of any challenge to Attlee's leadership, except briefly in 1946 when affairs were going very badly. He remained leader of the Labour party for ten more years.

Attlee's Cabinet was often viewed by observers, at least initially, as being divided into an inner circle of the 'big five' and the others. The number two man in the Cabinet, if not in Attlee's estimation, was Herbert Morrison, who became Deputy Prime Minister, Lord President of the Council, and Leader of the House of Commons. Morrison's role was to coordinate all significant domestic legislation and see its passage through Parliament. This he did extraordinarily well for the first two years of the Parliament, until he suffered a mild thrombosis in 1947. Morrison had strong ambitions, never fulfilled, of becoming Prime Minister, and was both widely admired and distrusted. Although Attlee appointed Ernest Bevin Foreign Minister, he was given *carte blanche* by Attlee at Cabinet meetings to sum up most discussions and say what he liked; like Morrison, Bevin enjoyed extra-departmental authority, in Bevin's case because of his unique importance in the trade union movement. Bevin's appointment was a remarkable one, for he had no foreign policy experience and had been a poorly educated (and illegitimate) van driver and carter before becoming the leading trade union figure in Britain, and then appointed to a position normally reserved for old Etonians of ancient lineage. There has been a good deal of speculation as to whether King George VI influenced Attlee's decision, with the aim of preventing the appointment of Hugh Dalton (whom the king was said to have detested) as Foreign Minister. Most historians now doubt that the king played a role: possibly Attlee needed a strong working-class leader as Foreign Minister to counter left-wing criticism of British foreign policy; possibly Attlee, who had originally intended him to be Chancellor of the Exchequer, foresaw difficulties in his working with Morrison, whom Bevin disliked. In the event, Bevin proved to be one of the greatest Foreign Ministers in British history and was regularly compared to Lord Palmerston in his vehement assertion of British power, especially against the growing Soviet threat. The other two members of the 'big five' were drawn from the conventional upper or upper middle classes and (like Attlee, the son of a wealthy solicitor) were sociologically indistinguishable from their Tory counterparts. These were Hugh Dalton and Sir Stafford Cripps. Dalton, the son of a Church of England canon who had been tutor to Edward VIII and George VI and a product of Eton and Cambridge, was a talented economist, a long-standing advocate of practical socialism, and an early anti-Appeaser. Holding the post of President of the Board of Trade from 1942–45, it was not surprising that he became Chancellor of the Exchequer, a post for which he was as well qualified as any other Labourite. He was better qualified to be Chancellor than to be Foreign Secretary, the post he was allegedly first offered. Dalton befriended many younger figures in the Labour party, although he also made many enemies with his bombastic, sarcastic style and his constant intriguing. Stafford Cripps was educated at Winchester and then, somewhat oddly, read chemistry at the University of London, but then became a barrister and QC. Cripps was a Christian socialist of often extreme and puritanical views, and found himself one of the few Labourites to survive the 1931 electoral disaster. His left-wing and unconventional views (he favoured the establishment of a Popular Front with the Communists) led to his expulsion from Labour between 1939 and 1945. Despite this setback, Cripps was appointed Ambassador to the Soviet Union in 1940 and served in the Cabinet (with special responsibility for securing Indian support in the war) in 1942. Attlee appointed this extremely unorthodox figure President of the Board of Trade in 1945, with an important brief – in effect, the recovery of British industry – which he handled very well, and became increasingly influential.

Below the 'big five' were another four or five Cabinet ministers of more than average influence. The best-known of these, of course, was Aneurin 'Nye'

Bevan (1897–1960), acknowledged leader of Labour's left-wing, a fiery, charismatic former coalminer from South Wales who had been expelled from the Labour party in 1939–40 and remained a thorn in the government's side during the war, being described by Churchill as 'a squalid nuisance' for his constant criticism of the government. Bevan became Minister of Health in 1945, proving to be one of the most constructive and successful ministers of the century. Attlee's Cabinet also included several elder statesmen of the party, such as Christopher Addison, Viscount Addison (1869–1951), a direct link with the Asquith-Lloyd George era (as, ironically, was Leader of the Opposition, Winston Churchill), appointed leader of the House of Lords, where he proved surprisingly influential, and William Wedgwood Benn, Viscount Stansgate (1877–1960; he was the father of Tony Benn) another direct link with the old days, serving as Liberal junior whip in Asquith's government in 1910–15 and then as a Labour minister from 1929–31. Stansgate became Air Minister. Apart from Nye Bevan and Ellen Wilkinsons, the only person of the Left in the new Cabinet was Emanuel Shinwell, a former 'Red Clydesider' (although born in the East End to Jewish immigrants), who became Minister for Fuel and Power with responsibility for nationalising the coal industry, an absolutely fundamental component of the Labour programme. Ellen Wilkinson was the only woman in the Cabinet, another passionate and outspoken leftist who became renowned in the 1930s for championing the Jarrow hunger marchers. Wilkinson became Minister of Education, but served only a short time, dying of an accidental overdose of drugs (prescribed for asthma) in February 1947. While many in the Cabinet remained household names to anyone interested in British political history, several have sunk into something like oblivion. The Home Secretary, normally a very senior figure, was Chuter Ede (1882–1965), a former teacher who had helped to enact the 1944 Education Act. As Home Secretary he was completely overshadowed by his more famous colleagues, although he is regarded as competent and respected. Arthur Greenwood the Deputy Leader of the Labour party from 1935–45, was made Lord Privy Seal by Attlee, playing a major role behind the scenes, but ruining himself, it is said, through alcoholism. Several members of Attlee's Cabinet, especially trade unionists in lesser roles – such as James Westwood (1884–1948), the Scottish Secretary, and Jack Lawson (1881–1965), the War Minister – similarly remain virtually unknown, even to historians.

There were several reasons why the post-war Labour government was so successful. Most obviously, it had an unquestioned majority in Parliament, making it impossible for right-wing sources to claim that it lacked a mandate. Just as important, from a practical viewpoint, was the fact that most of its senior members had held ministerial office during the war, that is, until only a few months before it won the 1945 General Election. Only six of Labour's Cabinet ministers had not held office in the wartime coalition; but of these, four had held a government office of some kind before 1940. Nye Bevan and George Isaacs (1883–1979; Minister of Labour and National Service) were the only members of the new Cabinet who had never held an office of any kind. This was a unique circumstance for a left-wing government coming to power with a radical programme: the Liberals in 1905, and Labour in 1964 and 1997 came to power after long periods in the wilderness. In contrast Labour's leaders – such as Attlee and Morrison – were intimately acquainted with the levers of government, and with the senior civil service, when they took office. Closely associated with this was the fact that, as noted, an infrastructure of unprecedently high taxation and far-reaching government controls over all aspects of the economy and national life already existed, and did not either require a revolution or a basic readjustment in lifestyle by the middle classes or others. It seems unlikely that Labour would have dared to raise taxes to the levels attained after the war, or attempted to control the economy in as thorough a way, had the war not already given to the British state a quasi-socialist system. The government also handled its backbenchers, and core supporters in the country, fairly well. It immediately delivered on its promises to nationalise coal and other basic industries, and instituted a welfare state which (in its view) quickly benefited the average person. In the Commons, backbenchers were kept busy with an endless stream of new legislation, and 17 separate policy groups were formed, allegedly in order to facilitate backbench contribution to policy formation. The parliamentary Labour party elected in 1945 had changed beyond recognition from previous Labour contingents. It contained no fewer than 259 new MPs, the majority of whom were at least broadly drawn from the middle classes: 49 per cent of Labour MPs were professionals and another 10 per cent (remarkably) businessmen, with only 41 per cent workers and trade union officials. The 1945 Labour intake included 44 lawyers, 49 lecturers and teachers, and 15 doctors. Twenty-three per cent were products of public schools, and 32 per cent were university educated. Many of these middle-class converts to Labour were ideological leftists, and a solid core of backbench MPs, estimated at between 30 and 80, could be relied to oppose the government, from a left-wing position, on many issues, especially foreign policy. Labour's left, however, was itself divided into a mainstream group, headed by MPs such as Michael Foot (b.1913) and Richard Crossman (1907–74), and a smaller, more extreme group, numbering no more than a dozen or so, of overt fellow travellers and pro-Stalinists. The mainstream group had a voice in the Cabinet through Nye Bevan and, collectively, the vocal Left was always outnumbered by the ranks of the loyal and quiescent MPs, especially former trade unionists, who were largely a force on the Labour right in this period. As always, most new and younger MPs hoped for promotion to the ministry; as always, this acted as a severe deterrent to disloyalty. The Cabinet itself did suffer from some initial disadvantages, especially its age structure: Cripps, at 56, was the youngest of the 'big five', while Attlee and Bevan were over 60 and others were older still. On balance, however, the experience and nous of the Labour Cabinet proved more valuable than the disadvantages of age.

The radical achievements of the Labour government came in three general areas, in nationalisation of industries, the creation of a welfare state, and its role in transforming the British Empire into a Commonwealth. Nationalisation came in the form of seven basic pieces of legislation between 1946 and 1949. From 1 January 1946 the Bank of England (which set interest rates) was nationalised, at Dalton's behest. In the same year the Coal Industry Nationalisation Act took the coal industry into public ownership from 1 January 1947. Also in 1946, civil aviation was nationalised and reorganised by the Civil Aviation Act, 1946;

for over 40 years, the bulk of Britain's aviation industry was owned by the State. The following year, the Electricity Act of 1947 nationalised Britain's electricity industry, and established the British Electricity Authority. The turn of the railways was next, with the Transport Act 1947 (operative from 1948), which nationalised Britain's railways, as well as canals, the buses and, perhaps anomalously, long-distance road haulage. In 1948 came the Gas Act, 1948, which established 12 Area Gas Boards and the Gas Council. The last and most controversial of these measures was the Iron and Steel Act, 1949, which nationalised (from early 1951) most of Britain's iron and steel industry.

Many of these measures found little opposition and appeared to be inevitable. The United States Federal Reserve, the equivalent of the Bank of England, had been established by the American government in 1913; it was obviously anomalous that the Bank of England, which set interest rates, should be in private ownership. It was absolutely inevitable that, under a Labour government with a large majority, coal would be nationalised, and as a result safety and conditions in the hellish coal mines plainly improved beyond recognition. Similarly, a rationalisation of the divided British electricity industry (power points had run on different systems, depending upon where one lived) was clearly desirable. Shareholders in all of these industries received very favourable terms, and had little to complain about. Throughout Europe and elsewhere, most of these industries had long been nationalised, and there was obviously a strong case for having Britain's natural monopolies under public control, especially after a devastating war. With its huge parliamentary majority, the government had the authority to push all of its measures through. Labour was generally careful to nationalise mainly natural monopolies and basic industries; it left finance and commerce alone (apart from the Bank of England), as well as the rest of Britain's industrial infrastructure.

The campaign against nationalisation mounted by the Tories focused on a few aspects of Labour's proposals which were more dubious. Road haulage – an industry with many small operators and low barriers to entry – was not a monopoly, and the government was forced to exclude very small carriers entirely from nationalisation. Steel was an efficient industry, included in Labour's programme chiefly to satisfy the left. The Tories mounted a great campaign against steel nationalisation, which was, in fact, privatised by the Conservatives in 1953. Labour's plans to nationalise the sugar industry ran into the famous 'Mr Cube' campaign mounted by Tate & Lyle, the major sugar company, and were never proceeded with. Apart from coal and the basic utilities, there is no evidence that nationalisation was popular with the public; nor did it invariably result in obvious benefits. Investment in industries such as the nationalised railways became wholly dependent upon the (seldom-glimpsed) largesse of the Treasury, and Britain's railways went into a 50-year decline, with half the system closed down in the mid-1960s. Few today, even in the Labour party, believe that nationalisation is appropriate for an advanced economy, except in some special cases. In the 1940s, however, it appeared to many to be the only way to deal with the failures of capitalism, shown most strikingly in the wastage of the Depression. The government adopted a particular model in designing the framework of nationalised industry which was not without controversy. With the precedent in mind of the BBC, established in 1926, and the London Passenger Transport Board, set up by Herbert Morrison in 1933, Labour – and especially Morrison, who put his stamp on Britain's public industries – enacted highly centralised public corporations or authorities to run all the nationalised industries, consisting of a chairman and a board of directors. The structure of these industries thus remained very similar to those of large private corporations although, of course, they were owned by the state and were technically responsible to a government minister. Workers in these industries had little or, more often, no share in their direction under nationalisation, and still negotiated pay and conditions in an adversarial fashion with the nationalised boards. Each nationalised industry was heavily centralised, normally with a headquarters in London, although there were usually regional divisions with some autonomy. The interests of the consumer were usually not represented at all in a direct way, and long-term planning was difficult because funding in the last resort was at the mercy of the Treasury. Unquestionably, however, many nationalised industries were an improvement to a greater or lesser degree on the previous private regimes, often marked in these areas by bitter owner–worker relations and long-term decline. On the other hand, affluence and full employment after the war meant that conditions in virtually all industries in Britain improved.

Although, in many respects, nationalisation marked Labour's clearest break with the past, to millions of ordinary persons it was the government's initiation of a full-scale welfare state which probably made the greatest impact. Labour's version of the welfare state had several main components, especially an overhaul and extension of national insurance, and, above all, the establishment of the National Health Service (NHS). The National Insurance Act 1946 replaced the patchwork of non-comprehensive insurance acts with a wide-ranging, universal scheme which covered everyone over school-leaving age (except certain married women) for unemployment, basic retirement pensions, maternity, health, widow's benefits, and death grants. The basic weekly rate for unemployment benefit was raised to 26 shillings, and an ancillary act provided benefits to persons injured at work. The National Assistance Act, 1948, introduced by Bevan, repealed all remaining provisions of the New Poor Law still in existence and established a comprehensive system of old-age benefits for the poor. The jewel in the crown of Labour's programme, the single act for which it is best remembered was, of course, the National Health Act, 1946. This transferred all hospitals under the auspices of local authorities and voluntary bodies to the state, to be administered through regional hospital boards, and provided free medical, hospital, dental services and pharmaceuticals for virtually all services provided. The NHS was a truly revolutionary initiative, since it did not require patients to be members of any insurance scheme to be treated (as was the case even in state-run European health schemes), but provided these services free to all. On the other hand, it did not establish 'socialised medicine', as its right-wing critics averred (and leftists hoped). Physicians were not strictly salaried employees of the state, but were paid according to the number of patients consulted, and could maintain private practices; indeed, there were private beds in many hospitals and the rich could still jump the queue. Nevertheless, the NHS removed the real fear of not being able to pay for medical treatment, or, still more, for hospitalisation and drugs, from the minds of millions of people. This was unquestionably the Attlee government's finest hour, and a lasting tribute to the creative abilities of Nye Bevan the Health Minister. It did seem to many to represent a humane and efficient 'third way' of social democracy midway between American laissez-faire and Soviet state socialism.

Labour also enacted a number of other notable measures. In 1946 it passed the New Town Act which created 14 new towns on either green sites or small towns within commuting distance of large old cities, but often with industries of their own. As the housing stock was new and jobs fairly plentiful, they became popular, with such 'new towns' as Milton Keynes, Harlow, and Telford becoming places of importance. While the architecture of these places might have been expected to be wretched, there is general agreement that they were surprisingly successful. In laws enacted in 1947 and 1949 it created rent tribunals to fix the rentals of furnished houses, then extended the act to unfurnished houses and flats. Labour did little in the area of law reform, but the Criminal Justice Act of 1948 restricted the imprisonment of juveniles and extended probation while abolishing the curious right of peers to be tried by their 'peers' in the House of Lords. The Legal Aid and Advice Act, 1949, extended the availability of legal aid in civil cases. A determined backbench-initiated attempt to abolish the death penalty passed the House of Commons in 1948 but was thrown out by the House of Lords and not proceeded with; the post-war Labour government thus allowed as many hangings for murder (and treason in wartime, in the case of William Joyce, 'Lord Haw Haw' and John Amery, hanged in 1945 for Nazi collaboration) as any Tory government. It passed only one significant piece of trade union legislation, the Trade Unions Act, 1946, which repealed the 1927 Act outlawing sympathetic strikers and, in particular, the necessity to raise funds only from workers who 'contracted in'. In the political and constitutional sphere, there were two laws, of limited importance. The Representation of the People Act 1948, abolished the university seats in Parliament, the right to vote more than once which had existed for owners of business premises in different constituencies, and also abolished the six-month residency requirement for voting. In 1949, the delaying powers of the House of Lords were reduced from two years to one, but no other changes were made to the composition or powers of the upper house. Although Labour's record of reform was certainly remarkable, it is also noteworthy that it had very distinct limits. Absolutely nothing was done by Labour, for instance, to advance women's rights or status (although the requirement that married women had to resign from the administrative civil service was abolished in 1946), and the social, sexual, and educational fields were left almost entirely alone. Constitutional changes were minimal, with Attlee and most of his ministers being distinctly conservative in their attitude towards the monarchy and other traditional institutions. Labour's reluctance to enact gratuitous changes in these areas, of the type likely to be desired by the left-wing intelligentsia but resented by the ordinary person, may well account in part for its continuing popularity during the whole of its term of office, especially when its forceful patriotism in foreign policy is also taken into account.

Labour's hopes for instituting a welfare state were always threatened by the grave difficulties faced by Britain's economy. Britain lost no less than one-quarter of its entire national wealth (about £7 billion, or about £200 billion in today's money) in the war, and had been forced to liquidate most of its assets overseas. As almost always, Britain imported more than it exported, and had very few means left to pay for imports. During the war, Britain had relied on extensive aid from the United States, but the Truman administration cut off this aid almost as soon as the conflict ended. A high-powered team led by Lord Keynes (John Maynard Keynes, 1883–1946), the world-famous economist, was sent to Washington to negotiate a loan on favourable terms. While he accomplished much, Britain continued to be close to bankruptcy until very extensive aid began to flow from America to all of western Europe from the Marshall Plan (named for America's Secretary of State, George C. Marshall, who proposed it), announced in June 1947. Between 1948 and 1951 (when the Plan ended), Britain received nearly £3 billion in aid under this scheme. In the meantime, Britain pursued a policy of severe economic restraint and rationing, which became possibly more severe than during the war itself, being extended in 1946–47 to bread and potatoes, food that had remained unrationed during the conflict. By late 1947 an enormous variety of goods were rationed, including virtually all foods and petrol (which at one point became unavailable to civilians). Rationing was a highlight of the 'Age of Austerity' which followed the war and became synonymous with the Labour government's post-war economic policies, to its political detriment. Domestically, Britain did initially pursue a low interest bank policy under Chancellor of the Exchequer Hugh Dalton, aimed at economic growth. As rationing and austerity bit hard, however, increased central control of the economy became necessary, especially after the appalling winter of 1946–47, which produced a fuel shortage that was arguably mishandled by Emanuel Shinwell, the Minister for Fuel and Power. All was, however, not gloomy: the government's single-minded concentration on production produced some dramatic results, with the index of industrial producing increasing by 31 per cent between 1946 and 1951, probably the highest rate of increase in British history. Labour was elected in 1945 in part because of widespread fears that, under the Tories, mass unemployment would return, and, except briefly during the winter of 1946–47, full employment became the rule. In 1948, for instance, no more than 359 000 persons were unemployed in any single month (with only 299 000 in the best month), compared with 1 912 000 unemployed in the worst month of 1938, and nearly three million unemployed in 1932. While (to the surprise of many) full employment became the rule around the Western world in the generation after 1945, this, together with the NHS, was probably Labour's greatest achievement, curtailing the human waste and despair of the 1930s. Although the number of strikes increased compared with the 1930s, and the government had to invoke the Emergency Powers Act twice, over the dock strikes of June 1948 and July 1949, in general there were few full-scale labour disputes. Britain's chronic balance of payments problem, the fact that it exported less than it imported, led, however, to perhaps the best-known single economic act of the Labour government, the devaluation of the pound by Sir Stafford Cripps as Chancellor of the Exchequer on 18 September 1949 from US$4.03 to $2.80. Today, when the pound 'floats', and has a different international value every day, it is hard to imagine the contention that this decision brought about, caused by the still-precarious state of the balance of payments and Britain's currency reserves in the face of a brief American recession, which diminished exports. The pound was kept at a high value to emphasise the central role of the City of London in attracting deposits from all over the world, its time-honoured role, and was a symbol of Britain's great power aspirations, but a high pound made British goods more expensive and obviously acted as an obstacle to exports. Devaluation cheapened the costs of Britain's exports (and raised the cost of imports), but also served as striking evidence that the City was not what it once was. It is generally agreed that the Cripps devaluation worked well, and that Britain's economy recovered, and was in very good shape, when blown off course again by the outbreak of the Korean War in June 1950, which led to a sharp escalation in military expenditure.

Apart from the far-reaching achievements of the Labour government in the domestic sphere, this period is remembered just as much for the turbulent events in Britain's foreign policy and the transformation of the Empire into the Commonwealth. Even before the war ended, it was clear that much of Europe would fall into Stalin's lap and become satellite regimes of the Soviet Union which, by V-E Day, occupied or controlled nearly half of Europe. As early as 1946 it was obvious that relations between Stalin and the West had deteriorated alarmingly, and that it was most unlikely that the wartime friendship between the great powers would continue. Winston Churchill, who had been powerless at Yalta and other wartime international conferences to halt the Soviet penetration of central Europe (in part because of the apparent unwillingness of President Roosevelt to take a firm stand) re-emerged in the world spotlight in March 1946 for the first time after his defeat with a famous speech at Westminster College in Fulton, Missouri, claiming that 'from Stettin in the Baltic to Trieste in the Adriatic, an iron curtain has descended across' Europe. Besides an 'iron curtain' separating east and west, it soon became clear that a 'cold war' had begun pitting Russia against the West. (This phrase was apparently coined by the American presidential advisor Bernard Baruch.) Opposition to the domination of Europe by any one great power had always been the central keystone of British policy in Europe; Britain had just fought a six-year war to prevent German domination and now, almost literally at once, found itself with the arguably equal danger of Russian domination. What could Britain do about it? As with so many other alarming problems facing the British government at this time, very little. America was rapidly withdrawing from Europe, perhaps motivated yet again by isolationism; Britain was virtually bankrupt and had worldwide imperial responsibilities. Britain might stem the threat posed by the vastly larger Soviet Union with the help of France and Germany, but France was demoralised, Germany divided and in ruin. America had, at this time, a monopoly of the atom bomb, but it could not be long before the Soviet Union produced its own. Within the Labour party, a small but vocal group of activists and backbenchers were pro-Soviet, although the Cabinet, and particularly Ernest Bevin the Foreign Secretary, were determinedly anti-Communist.

Stalin was arguably in a position to grab much of western Europe but failed to do so: Czechoslovakia, the democracy which in 1948 was once more conquered by totalitarianism, was the last European state to become part of the

Soviet bloc. In western Germany, Allied occupation forces prevented any direct Soviet military takeover. Both France and Italy were democracies with enormous local Communist parties. Although in both countries the local Communists briefly shared power with non-Communist parties in the early post-war years, neither ever became electorally strong enough to win absolute majorities in their own right. Countries such as Greece and Turkey, however, remained as possible targets for Soviet expansion.

By early 1947, however, it appeared that the United States, under President Truman, was determined to stop any further Soviet expansion and was not returning to pre-Second World War isolationism. Although America had never joined the League of Nations, the headquarters of the new United Nations organisation was placed in New York. In February 1947, Bevin told the Americans that Britain could simply not afford to defend Greece and Turkey, and that if America wished to prevent Communist takeovers, it would have to take over Britain's old role in the region. A month later, Truman agreed to do so, announcing the 'Truman Doctrine' (with bipartisan support) which proclaimed that as a matter of continuing policy America would henceforth stop Communist expansionism. This was, assuredly, one of the most important foreign policy shifts of any great power in modern history, a declaration that America would become, permanently, a super-power on the world stage. Britain would henceforth be relieved of the financial burden of its former role, but, in return, would inevitably play second-fiddle in most areas of defence to the United States.

Thus, by 1947 most of the main dimensions of the Cold War had become virtually set in the concrete they would retain for 40 years, at least in Europe: a divided Germany and a divided Berlin, eastern Europe under satellite Soviet regimes, but, on the other hand, no further Soviet expansion and western Europe permanently democratic. By 1948 or 1949 it became obvious that Germany could never be reunited as a Western-style democracy. The Soviet Union's satellites in eastern Europe became ever more repressive, and Stalin himself continued as unchallenged supreme ruler until his death in 1953.

There were a number of highlights in these years which illustrated the dimensions of the long-lasting conflict. In June 1948, the Soviets attempted to prevent the Western powers from resupplying the Western zone of Berlin. This led to the 11-month Berlin Airlift, in which essential supplies were flown into the isolated city. Eventually, the Russians called off the blockade. In April 1949, the North Atlantic Treaty Organisation (NATO) was established in Washington D.C., the most important and long-lasting international agreement of the post-war era, comprising the United States, Britain, Canada, France, Italy, and other western European democracies. Its headquarters was initially in Paris and Lord Ismay (Hastings Ismay, 1887–1965), a leading general and later a Conservative Cabinet Minister, became its first Secretary General. By NATO's charter, each member state pledged itself to come to the aid of any other which was attacked. This was obviously aimed at countering any new form of direct Soviet expansionism and, in effect, pledged the United States and Britain to defend western Europe if attacked by Russia.

By the later 1940s the Attlee government had thus entered the Cold War in a full-hearted way as America's closest ally, a situation which has, in effect, continued until the present. In the last years of the Attlee government it embarked on two more ventures which showed the seriousness of its commitment to repelling Communist expansionism. In late 1946 Britain decided to develop its own atomic bomb, a decision pushed through the Cabinet largely by Ernest Bevin against the opposition (chiefly on financial grounds) of Dalton and Cripps. Britain took six years to develop its own atomic bomb, which was finally tested (on an island off Australia) in late 1952. It also embarked on a programme of developing a hydrogen bomb of its own, a weapon which made even the atomic bomb look puny. In June 1950 Communist North Korea invaded South Korea, and America responded by going to war against North Korea. Britain immediately came in (without recorded Cabinet dissent) on America's side. The Korean War lasted, amid very bitter and brutal fighting, until July 1953, when, after a ceasefire, the partition of the two Koreas was permanently confirmed. Three brigades of British soldiers were sent to what was later known as the 'forgotten war', with 749 British soldiers killed. The Korean War had important political ramifications for Labour. After the war began, Hugh Gaitskell (1906–63), the newly appointed (in October 1950) Chancellor of the Exchequer, increased military expenditure substantially, from £777 million to £1110 million (with £4700 million over three years). Expenditure on health and related areas was cut slightly and in particular, the cost of spectacles, some optical services, and other minor items ceased to be free under the NHS. The Chancellor's new NHS charges led to an enormous fight between Gaitskell and Nye Bevan, for whom an absolutely free NHS was the cornerstone of his political commitment. As a result, Bevan, President of the Board of Trade, Harold Wilson (1916–95; later baron Wilson of Rievaulx, the future Prime Minister), and John Freeman, resigned from the government in protest (in April 1951), opening a split between Gaitskell and Bevan which never really healed, with deleterious consequences for the Labour party throughout the 1950s.

There were, however, significant differences between the approach of Britain and the United States towards the Cold War. When the Communists, under Mao Tse-Tung, gained control of the Chinese mainland in October 1949, Britain extended *de jure* recognition to the new regime a few months later, in January 1950. This was entirely at variance with the response of the United States, which regarded the new regime with utter horror and continued to recognise Chiang Kai-shek's Nationalist government on Formosa as China's legitimate government until the 1970s. During the decade after about 1948, the United States also experienced a controversial, far-reaching backlash against sympathy for the Soviet Union or membership in any Communist or pro-Communist group which is known as 'McCarthyism', named for Wisconsin Senator Joe McCarthy, who headed a crusade against alleged Communists in the American government and military. Britain did not experience anything like this, certainly not in a public way, and had nothing to compare with the so-called 'McCarthyite witch hunts' that hounded left-wing and controversial figures from many areas of life. Indeed, Britain might well be criticised for excessive softness against legitimate espionage and security threats, especially 'Establishment' figures who remained surprisingly immune to punishment. Some notable British spies were exposed during this period, however, such as Klaus Emil Fuchs, a top nuclear scientist who was arrested for spying in early 1950. The celebrated defection of Guy Burgess and Donald MacLean, top Soviet operatives in the Foreign Office, came in May 1951, but the other members of the so-called 'Cambridge spy ring', Kim Philby and Sir Anthony Blunt, were not exposed for many years. In general, then, Britain under Attlee did pursue a semi-independent line from the United States in foreign policy, generally more moderate and much less ideologically anti-Communist, while echoing it over the central principle of stopping Communist expansionism.

Arguably the most important international contribution of all made by the Attlee government was in giving independence to India and beginning the transformation of the Empire to the Commonwealth through decolonisation. Independence for India had long been a goal of Labour in opposition. Attlee himself showed an early, rather surprising interest in this question when he served, in 1927–29, on a major Commission of Enquiry, headed by Sir John Simon, to examine the political development of India; it entailed his making two extended visits to the subcontinent. Attlee visited India at a time when nationalist agitation for independence, headed by Mohandas Gandhi and Jawaharal Nehru, was becoming one of the major sources of controversy in Britain's colonial policies. Attlee gained a wide knowledge of India, but became well aware of how the different religious communities disliked each other. During the Second World War, the issue of independence for India obviously went on the backburner, although Britain was acutely aware of the destructive possibilities of an Indian nationalist uprising (which did not occur). Leopold Amery, the wartime Indian Secretary, had recommended immediate Dominion status for India, a proposal rejected by Churchill, and in 1942 Sir Stafford Cripps was sent to India to secure nationalist support for Britain in the war. It was clear that some large measure of Indian independence would have to be conceded, after the end of the war, even by a right-wing Tory government. Given all the problems it faced in 1945, Britain was simply too weak to keep India.

Labour found the Indian situation much more difficult than might be assumed. India was divided between Hindus and Muslims, who came increasingly to hate each other. There were other religious minorities like the Sikhs and Jains, and the Buddhist realms of Burma and Ceylon. Politically, India was divided between British India and the princely states, autocracies ruled by local maharajas. Most British opinion would, at independence, have strongly favoured a single Indian government for the whole of the subcontinent, but tensions between Hindus and Muslims was quickly becoming very violent indeed: on one day in August 1946 no fewer than 5000 persons were killed in Calcutta alone in intercommunal violence. At the end of 1946 Attlee decided to replace Lord Wavell, the Viceroy, who appeared to advocate a British military withdrawal from India, leaving the population to its own devices. In his stead he appointed Viscount Mountbatten (Admiral Louis Mountbatten, 1900–79, later earl Mountbatten of Burma), the Allied Supreme Commander in South-East Asia, a cousin of the king, who had been made acting Admiral and Supreme Commander while only a captain, aged 43. In one of the least-known and most depressing theatres of the war Mountbatten and his American, Australian, and British forces eventually got the upper hand. Politically, despite his background,

Mountbatten was a left-liberal, even a Labour supporter, who had no trouble working with Asian nationalist movements. He was also a skilled and charming negotiator. In India as Viceroy from March 1947, Mountbatten secured virtual carte blanche from the British government to complete the transition to independence by June 1948. It quickly emerged that the partition of the whole subcontinent into two states, one largely Hindu and the other largely Muslim state was the only realistic possibility. Plans to 'balkanise' India by allowing each province considerable autonomy was rejected by the Hindu-dominated Congress Party, headed by Jawaharlal Nehru (1889–1964), a socialist educated improbably at Harrow and Cambridge. Mountbatten and his wife, Lady Edwina, got on well with Nehru (who is rumoured to have had an affair with Lady Mountbatten), although much less successfully with the leader of the Indian Muslims, Mohammed Ali Jinnah (1876–1948), a notoriously difficult and truculent negotiator. By the terms of the final agreement, all the provinces of British India had to join either India or Pakistan, as the geographically divided Muslim component of India became known. Mountbatten advanced the date for independence to 15 August 1947, an incredibly short period of time to end an empire and create two large new states. There is much in Mountbatten's haste (fully backed, it seems, by Attlee) which might be severely criticised: the princely states, loyal allies of the British, were stabbed in the back; the Sikhs and other religious minorities were ignored; the boundaries of the two states (which had to be drawn from scratch) guaranteed communal violence. While Mountbatten hoped to become Governor-General of both India and Pakistan, and indeed became the first Governor-General of India upon independence (serving until June 1948), Jinnah insisted upon becoming Governor-General of Pakistan. Independence was indeed accomplished with considerable good will towards the British, and, in India, was made notable by Nehru's renowned 'freedom at midnight' speech. It was, however, accompanied by an orgy of communal violence, ironically without any precedent in the history of the British Empire: an estimated five million Hindus and Muslims were slaughtered by extremists from the other community. In early 1948, Gandhi was assassinated by a right-wing Hindu nationalist. Both India and Pakistan stayed in the Commonwealth, both remaining Dominions (rather than republics) for some years: India until 1950, Pakistan until 1956. Increasingly, however, their paths inevitably diverged from Britain's, while the intractable Kashmir dispute, dating from independence, still remains unresolved. Two Buddhist components of British India also achieved independence at this time as separate nations, Burma on 4 January 1948, and Ceylon (later renamed Sri Lanka) a month later. Ceylon (which remained a Dominion until 1972) stayed in the Commonwealth, but Burma, whose politics have always been opaque, quit the Commonwealth upon independence, one of the few newly independent components of the Empire to do so. With Indian independence, the Sovereign ceased to be the head of an Empire, and the designation 'Emperor of India' was dropped from the royal title. Attlee regarded the achievement of Indian independence as probably his greatest achievement, foreign or domestic. It began the process by which all Britain's colonies, even the most 'backward', would achieve full independence within a generation, something probably not foreseen by anyone in the late 1940s. It also raised very searching questions about Britain's relationship with the Commonwealth, and whether the Commonwealth could have anything more than a nominal existence. It raised as well the even more fundamental question of just what role Britain was to have in the post-war world. 'Britain has lost an empire but not found a role', American Secretary of State Dean Acheson's famous remark, applied not merely to its relationship with the old empire, but with the United States and also with Europe. Which of these would Britain regard as primary? Even early in the twenty-first century, this question has not been definitely answered.

Next to Indian independence, the most difficult and controversial question surrounding the fate of the Empire to arise at this time was certainly that of Palestine. Palestine had been acquired by Britain as a League of Nations Mandate in 1917–19, and had been, in effect, a British colony. Under the famous Balfour Declaration of November 1917, it had been promised to the Jewish people as their 'national home', but, despite extensive settlement by the Zionist movement, still had, in 1945, a Palestinian Arab majority. The history of Palestine after 1929 had been one of virtually continuous strife among the Arabs, Jews, and British. Although relatively quiet during the war, with the ending of the war turmoil quickly returned. The revelation of the Holocaust had made the Palestine question even more urgent than before: hundreds of thousands of Jewish survivors in Europe wanted a homeland of their own where they would be safe from anti-semitism, while Jewry, especially in the United States, which had previously been divided over Zionism, now moved decisively in the direction of establishing an independent Jewish state. Among the Arabs, rising nationalism wanted to establish an independent Arab state with, at most, a permanent Jewish minority. In opposition, Labour had strongly favoured a Jewish state in Palestine, and Jews expected it to be sympathetic to Zionism. This proved to be the opposite of its actual attitude. Bevin was deeply hostile to creating a Jewish state in Palestine, fearing an Arab backlash. He was arguably not free from anti-semitism, fanned by the Foreign Office's traditional Arabism. Britain's policies in Palestine – where, admittedly, it faced enormous difficulties – were particularly inglorious and left a continuing legacy of bitterness. Britain refused to allow in more than a handful of Jewish survivors, and cracked down hard on Zionists in Palestine. This led to a violent backlash from Zionist terrorist groups, resulting in several atrocities, such as the bombing of the King David Hotel in Jerusalem (July 1946) and the hanging of two British sergeants (July 1947), an incident which in turn led to an anti-semitic backlash in Britain. Arab terrorists were equally violent, while the United States, with its large Jewish community, was increasingly critical of British policy in Palestine, to the extent that American aid was endangered. Finding no way out, in April 1947, Britain turned the question of Palestine over to the United Nations; in November 1947, it recommended its partition into Jewish and Arab states, with an internationalised Jerusalem. The Zionist movement reluctantly accepted this compromise, while the Arab League, the body of the Arab states, continued to oppose partition and went on record (December 1947) as advocating the use of force to stop it. Britain's Mandate formally came to an end on 14 May 1948; the next day, an independent State of Israel was proclaimed. An independent

Palestinian state, which was supposed to come into existence at the same time, was, however, not created, the areas set aside for it taken over by Jordan and Egypt, with British connivance. A violent war between Israel and the Arabs ensued, the first of many, with a ceasefire finally reached in July 1949. Relations between Britain and Israel continued to be very cool for some years, and many Israelis continue, to this day, to regard 'Foreign Office Arabists' as behind Britain's Middle Eastern policies. Nor did Britain's stance invariably help its position in Arab eyes: over the next decade it became one of the chief public enemies of many nationalistic Arab regimes, especially Nasser's Egypt. Bevin's Middle Eastern policies proved to be among the least successful of those pursued by the Attlee government.

Relations with the older Commonwealth countries were, of course, much better. Canada, Australia, New Zealand, and South Africa comprised notable parts of the war effort, most declaring war in September 1939 for no reason but that Britain had done so. During the Second World War the Australian Prime Minister, John Curtin, pointedly announced that henceforth Australia would look to America rather than to Britain as its protective great power, but Australia continued to view Britain as the 'mother country' in every sense for another 20 years. There were only a few jarring notes in this picture. In 1948, the National party came to power in South Africa, representing hard-line advocates of racial segregation, a policy which became known as *Apartheid* ('separateness' in Afrikaaner). In 1949, the new government moved away from its British links by discontinuing the automatic granting of citizenship to British immigrants. Nevertheless, South Africa remained in the Commonwealth. More drastic was the action taken by Ireland, which, until 1949, still had a tenuous link with Britain, despite everything that had occurred. During the war, de Valera, the Irish Prime Minister, consistently rejected all British requests for assistance of any kind in the war against Nazi Germany. In April 1945, despite being begged, by advisors, literally on bended knee, not to do so, he signed the book of condolence at the German embassy in Dublin for the death of Adolf Hitler, using the argument that Hitler was the head of state of a country legally recognised by Ireland. In 1948 de Valera lost office, but his successor as Prime Minister, James A. Costello declared southern Ireland to be a republic (officially proclaimed 18 April 1949, the anniversary of the Easter uprising), outside of the Commonwealth. This ended the very last echoes of so many centuries of Britain's troubled official involvement with Catholic Ireland.

It seems clear that many within the Labour government thought that it would remain in power for decades to come, given the magnitude of their electoral victory in 1945 and the natural majority enjoyed by a successful working-class party. 'We are the masters at the moment and not only for the moment, but for a very long time to come' Sir Hartley Shawcross (b.1902), the Attorney-General, stated in Commons debate on the Trade Disputes Bill in April 1946. Some were even more contemptuous of those outside the movement, with Emanuel Shinwell claiming in May 1946 that 'we know that you, the organised workers of the country, are our friends … As for the rest, they do not matter a tinker's curse.' The most extreme (and counterproductive) exposition of this viewpoint came from Nye Bevan, at a speech in Manchester in July 1948, when he admitted that 'No attempt at ethical or social education can eradicate from my heart a deep burning hatred for the Tory party...So far as I am concerned they are lower than vermin.' 'Lower than vermin' became a rallying cry for the Tory party and the right-wing press. Churchill dubbed Bevan 'the Minister of Disease – is not morbid hatred a form of disease?', and the phrase continued to haunt him. (As a result of his speech, Bevan received large numbers of anonymous and obscene letters, as well as packages of excrement.) The Labour party did have some realistic grounds for belief in the likelihood of many years of power. It did not lose a single seat to the Tories (or any other party) at a by-election between 1945 and 1950, and held on to Hammersmith South, where the Tories had an excellent chance of winning, in February 1949. Yet its position was by no means as secure as it seemed. Gallup Polls showed that the Tories had caught up to Labour by early 1947, and then overtook them late that year, generally remaining five or more per cent ahead throughout the rest of its period of office. Labour made its share of mistakes – its handling of the coal crisis of 1947, especially the handling of the situation by Fuel Minister Emanuel Shinwell, who was forced to resign in October 1947 and was widely regarded as incompetent. Attlee mistakenly gave Nye Bevan responsibility for housing as well as health, leading to the neglect of this key area, which the Tories were able to exploit. Labour retained the reputation of being a rather doctrinaire and puritanical socialist party, retaining rationing and dampening consumer spending long after most voters would have preferred to see them ended, and despite the famous assurance, in November 1948, by Harold Wilson, President of the Board of Trade, that he had made a 'bonfire of controls'. Intellectually, the tide seemed to have turned against the wartime mood of social democracy, especially after the horrors of Stalinism became generally known, helped by the publication of such well-known works as Karl Popper's *Open Society and Its Enemies* (1945), George Orwell's *1984* (1949), and *The God That Failed* (1950), a collection of essays by disillusioned former Communists.

The Conservatives, too, did an excellent job of putting their house in order. Under R.A. Butler, Chairman of the Conservative Research Department, it modernised its organisation, especially to ensure that candidates for Parliament no longer needed to be wealthy enough to pay for their own expenses, and under Butler issued (1947) an Industrial Charter which committed the party to accepting Keynesian measures to produce full employment and most of the Welfare State. The party, however, also carved out a programme distinctive from Labour's, emphasising a much greater role for the private sector, especially in providing consumer durables and housing. This message was, it seems, especially effective with women voters, many of whom were deeply frustrated at the marginalisation of domestic spending and continued rationing. The wartime mood of national sacrifice in the interests of a social democratic future had, for many voters, clearly passed by the late 1940s.

The Labour party, too, was increasingly divided, often bitterly divided, over both personalities and policies. A Cabinet full of strong personalities, many of whom enjoyed independent reputations and followings, was bound to engender personal conflicts and rivalries. Many of these rivalries became well known at the time. Herbert Morrison thought that he should have been Prime Minister and should certainly have succeeded Attlee. Attlee, however, disliked him and did his best to prevent his succession to the leadership. The conflict between Nye Bevan and many of the Cabinet moderates was both widely known and reciprocated. At some stage, possibly before 1945 (the exact circumstances are clouded), Ernest Bevin was told that Nye Bevan was his own worst enemy, and, in response, made the most famous single one-liner of that time, 'Not so long as I'm alive he ain't.' Bevan's detestation for such Cabinet right-wingers as the rising Hugh Gaitskell was also evident. The government also suffered its share of regrettable incidents, especially, perhaps, the strange resignation of Hugh Dalton in November 1947 as Chancellor of the Exchequer over a minor budget leak, blurted out by Dalton in the Commons lobby on the way to delivering his budget speech, which managed to appear in some London afternoon newspapers. Dalton offered his resignation which, to considerable surprise, was accepted by Attlee. Sir Stafford Cripps became Chancellor, instituting a much tighter financial regimen associated with the central phase of 'Austerity'. In the last years of the Attlee Cabinet, several of its most prominent members died or retired, such as Ernest Bevin, who left the Foreign Office in March 1951 and the Cabinet a month later, and Sir Stafford Cripps, who resigned from the Exchequer through ill-health in October 1950.

The Cabinet was, by the late 1940s, also unusually old. By 1950, many of its members, including Attlee, had served (except for several months in 1945) continuously since May 1940. Attlee himself was 67 by 1950, and most of the senior members of the Cabinet were in their sixties or even older. (Bevan, aged 53 in 1950, was the youngest of Labour's leading figures.) Attlee tried to find a younger generation to move into leadership positions, but was only partially successful. Harold Wilson, later Prime Minister, was promoted to Cabinet rank in September 1947 as President of the Board of Trade at the spectacularly early age of only 31, and, by 1950, other figures such as Patrick Gordon-Walker (1907–80) and Alfred Robens (1910–99), influential in the party during the 1950s and 1960s, also achieved Cabinet rank. Attlee's most prominent younger appointees, however, was Hugh Gaitskell, who, after holding several junior positions, joined the Cabinet as successor to Cripps as Chancellor of the Exchequer in October 1950, thus making him by far the most senior younger Labourite. Like Attlee an upper-middle-class product of a major public school (Winchester) and Oxford, Gaitskell joined the Labour party through socialist conviction during the 1930s and entered Parliament with the 1945 intake. A right-winger within the context of the Labour party, he became the particular *bête-noire* of leftists such as Bevan, whose arch-rival he proved to be. After Ernest Bevin's resignation as Foreign Minister in March 1951, Attlee appointed Herbert Morrison in his place. Attlee regarded this as his worst appointment: Morrison, with his local government political skills, was ill-equipped, in Attlee's view, to negotiate on the international stage, lacking Bevin's expertise as a skilled negotiator acquired in the trade union movement.

The Labour party also suffered, during the latter phase, perhaps more fundamentally, from a lack of consensus on where it ought to go next. Leftists in the party wanted more nationalisation and socialism. It was genuinely unclear what policies the centre and right wings of the Labour party ought to have evolved once its 1945 agenda was enacted. In later years, Attlee stated that, had Labour won again in 1951, it would have placed greater emphasis on science and technology. The programme it actually presented in the General Election of February 1950 included a controversial miscellaneous 'shopping list' of industries included for further nationalisation, among them cement, industrial insurance, and, curiously, sugar-refining, which was dominated by one firm, Tate & Lyle. As noted, when the possibility of sugar nationalisation became real, Tate & Lyle initiated a famous anti-nationalisation campaign based around the character of 'Mr Cube', designed to be understood by housewives. Labour's 'shopping list' was widely admitted to be electorally disastrous, although it is not clear what policies a Labour party could have successfully offered.

Attlee decided to hold a General Election in February 1950. The campaign was fairly quiet, with Labour defending its record and the Tories, still led by the 76-year-old Winston Churchill, attacking further nationalisation, but also arguing that his world status would make it easier for him to negotiate with Stalin. In the end, the Tories made great gains, but not quite enough to overturn Labour.

	Total votes	MPs elected	% share of vote
Conservative	12 502 567	298	43.5
Liberal	2 621 548	9	9.1
Labour	13 266 592	315	46.1
Communist	91 746	0	0.3
Others	290 218	3	1.0
Total	28 772 671	625	100.0

The turnout was the highest in electoral history before or since 1918 at 84.0 per cent. Despite losing 78 seats compared with 1945, Labour did extremely well, actually polling about 1.3 million more votes than in 1945. The Tories, of course, bounced back almost entirely from the 1945 debacle, gaining over 2.5 million more votes and 85 more MPs, helped by a redistribution of seats in Parliament which favoured the suburbs. They returned to their normal position of hegemony in southern England apart from London, trouncing Labour there by electing 144 MPs to Labour's 54. But in most other areas of the country Labour gained a majority of seats, especially in big cities, Wales, and Scotland. The Liberal vote actually rose slightly compared with 1945, but the number of Liberal MPs declined further to only nine (five in Wales), and the party appeared to many to be on the road to extinction. Churchill had, in fact, with some success, tried to gain Liberal support in the election from its leader Clement Davies. No smaller party received more than an insignificant percentage of the vote, and Britain now emphatically had a two-party system in terms of parliamentary representation.

Labour emerged with a tiny majority of only five over all other parties. This is too small a majority to carry on for a full term, and another election was obviously not far off. The Korean War broke out in June 1950; severe budget cuts were made as a result and dissension within the party increased. As well, the cost of the Korean War badly affected Britain's fragile economy, while Bevin, Cripps, and (through resignation) Bevan and Wilson were gone from the Cabinet. Attlee himself was ill. The government also had to face a crisis in Iran, where the Anglo-Iranian Oil Company, one of Britain's major providers of petroleum, was taken under state control by Mohammed Mossadeq, Iran's new nationalist Prime Minister. Morrison, the Foreign Minister, decided to take a strong stand, but could do little or nothing until Mossadeq was forced from office by a CIA-inspired coup later that year. Attlee decided to hold another General Election in October 1951, in part because King George VI wished to make a six-month tour of Australia, New Zealand, and other Commonwealth territories in 1952.

The Tories were consistently ahead in the polls, particularly as the expenditure for the Korean War began to affect welfare spending. As in 1950, the General Election was fairly quiet, the chief excitement caused by an ill-considered front-page headline in the pro-Labour *Daily Mirror*, 'Whose finger on the [nuclear] trigger?', which seemed to accuse Churchill of irresponsible warmongering. Labour echoed this theme, but it had little electoral appeal. The Tory campaign was better organised and funded. The election was in many respects a copy of that fought 20 months earlier, but this time the Tories won, a narrow but sufficient victory.

	Total votes	MPs elected	% share of vote
Conservative	13 717 538	321	48.0
Liberal	730 556	6	2.5
Labour	13 948 605	295	48.8
Communist	21 640	0	0.1
Others	177 329	3	1.0
Total	28 595 668	625	100.0

Turnout was again high, at 82.5 per cent. Labour actually received about 230 000 more votes overall than the Tories, but these were often piled high in ultra-safe working-class seats while the Tories achieved more narrow wins, and increased its vote since 1950 by over 1.2 million, compared with less than 700 000 for Labour. The Liberal vote now completely collapsed, to only 2.5 per cent of the total. The Tories emerged with a majority of 17 over all other parties, and of 26 over Labour, probably sufficient for a full term of office, although obviously not a smashing victory. Labour still had a majority of seats in most regions of Britain apart from the south of England (where the Tories were ahead by 153-46), with the exception of Scotland where, curiously, the two parties each elected 35 MPs. Even in Wales the Liberals were reduced to three MPs.

Attlee immediately resigned, ceasing to be Prime Minister on 26 October 1951. This colourless and consistently underrated but exceptionally competent and cogently focused man had proved to be arguably Britain's greatest peacetime Prime Minister of the twentieth century, reshaping Britain's political and social foundations. Inevitably, both he and his movement had run out of steam, and there were serious and bitterly contested questions about what Labour should do next. At the remarkable age of 77 Winston Churchill now became Prime Minister for the second (or, technically, the third time, counting his Caretaker government of May–July 1945), the only occasion in his career when Churchill won a General Election as leader of a party. For the first time since May 1940 (again excepting mid-1945) the Tory party was back in power on its own, without coalition partners.

11
The Tories' Thirteen Years, 1951–64

Churchill back in power

Winston Churchill again became Prime Minister on 26 October 1951 and served for three and a half years, until April 1955. Churchill's peacetime government was a curious one: despite the world fame of the Prime Minister, it remains one of the most obscure administrations of the twentieth century. Apart from the Coronation of Queen Elizabeth II and the promulgation of 'Butskellism', in economic policy, even well-informed persons would be hard-pressed to name any major themes, events, or legislation associated with it. In retrospect, it seems to have been an unprecedented period of tranquillity, a safe haven at last after a long period of continuous strife and turmoil going back not merely to 1939, but, in some sense, to Joseph Chamberlain's famous Tariff Reform speech of 1903, after which British politics was perpetually in turmoil. It seems an 'era of good feelings', when, with Stalin's death and the end of the Korean War, the danger of nuclear war receded and a genuine consensus existed at home.

Churchill formed a rather unusual Cabinet of only 16 men (the most senior woman in the government, Florence Horsburgh (1889–1969), the Education Minister, held only ministerial rank until she was promoted to the Cabinet in September 1953). Six were members of the Lords, and three of them – Lord Leathers as Minister for Transport, Fuel, and Power, Lord Woolton as Lord President of the Council, and Lord Salisbury as Lord Privy Seal (Lord Woolton was chairman of Lewis's Ltd, the Liverpool retailer, before the war and was placed in charge of rationing by Neville Chamberlain in 1940) – had the job of coordinating overall domestic planning as 'super-ministers', popularly called 'overlords'. These seem perfectly reasonable appointments, although Labour quickly raised objections to their being in the Lords. Only ten Cabinet ministers were in the Commons, and many prominent Tories, such as Churchill's son-in-law Duncan Sandys (1908–87) had to be content with junior office or, like Walter Elliot, none at all. Only a handful of Cabinet ministers really mattered, fewer, perhaps, than in most governments. Apart from Churchill, the most important ministers were clearly Anthony Eden, the Foreign Minister, and R.A. Butler, Chancellor of the Exchequer, with Harold Macmillan, Minister for Housing and Local Government, and Sir David Maxwell-Fyfe (1900–67; later first earl of Kilmuir), the Home Secretary, closest to the inner circle, together with other ministers prominent in their day, such as Harry Crookshank (1893–1961), the Health Minister, and Sir Walter Monckton (1891–1965), the Minister for Labour, completing the team. Despite the fact that the more progressive elements in the Conservative party – such as Butler and Macmillan – now had the upper hand, in sociological terms it was a typical Tory government, with seven of the 16 Cabinet ministers the products of Eton, two of Harrow, and three of other major public schools; nine were graduates of Oxbridge and three of military academies such as Sandhurst. Most, however, had come from the upper or lower middle classes, despite their educational origins; five, including Churchill and Eden, came from the old landed aristocracy or gentry at one or two generations remove.

Churchill was now Prime Minister again and very much in charge of the government, combining the Prime Ministership with the Defence portfolio, an important post during the Korean War. For the first part of his term, at least, he was certainly still a vigorous leader in full command of affairs despite his years. At 77 in 1951, Churchill was far, far older than most of his ministers, especially the new figures who entered Parliament after the war. Edward Heath, later Prime Minister, for example, was elected to Parliament in 1950 and was appointed a Whip when the government was formed. Heath was born in 1916 – 11 years after Churchill first became a government minister in 1905. The early 1950s saw the completion of the process of apotheosis of Churchill as the greatest Englishman of the century. In 1952, just after King George VI's death, when Churchill suffered an arterial spasm, there was a serious move to convince him to go to the House of Lords with a dukedom, leaving Eden, the heir apparent, to lead in the Commons. No non-royal dukedom has been created during the twentieth century, but this seemed the only appropriate manner in which to honour Churchill. Churchill never accepted a peerage, although in 1953 he was made a Knight of the Garter (and was henceforth known as Sir Winston), and had already been given every other conceivable honour – the Order of Merit, the Companionship of Honour, innumerable honorary degrees and civic freedoms. In 1953, he was awarded the Nobel Prize for Literature, the only time it has been given, in part, for oratory, and, in part, for Churchill's very accomplished and distinguished historical writings. A decade later, in 1963, Churchill was made the second honorary citizen of the United States (the first was Lafayette, the French hero of the American Revolution). Normally, some of these honours are automatic – all Prime Ministers are offered peerages, for instance – but in Churchill's case they were quite sincerely meant, as the magnitude of what he had done to save Western democracy became clear. There was, too, a real sense among Conservatives that Churchill represented an authentic Western conservative hero of universal stature, a man whose anti-fascism gave legitimacy to his anti-Communism and anti-socialism.

Churchill's 1951–55 government was, of course, the first Conservative government to enter office finding a Welfare State and a considerable measure of state socialism in place. How it should deal with this reality naturally became the central *leitmotif* of the government's domestic policies, remaining so under all Tory governments until the Thatcher era. There was, in the early 1950s (and for decades to come) simply no question of the Tories overturning the achievements of the Attlee Labour government or of instituting a return to pre-war laissez-faire. The electoral risks, above all from the deliberate creation of greatly increased unemployment, were so immense, given the government's small majority, that it simply could not be tried. Nor could a frontal attack on the trade unions, although many Tories were keen to do so. As well, Keynesian and post-classical economic theory was now everywhere in the ascendancy if not hege-monic, and it appeared to many that a utopian situation had arrived wherein high unemployment need never again be known. The intellectual challenges to Keynesianism were seen as being mounted only from the fringes. Churchill's government, no less than Attlee's (and, indeed, more so), had to find the resources to remain a world-class military power with worldwide responsibilities. Under Churchill, defence spending rose from £1110 million in 1951 to £1436 million in 1954. There still remained a national debt of £26 billion, on which interest was perpetually due.

For these reasons, although Chancellor of the Exchequer R.A. Butler would have liked to cut government expenditure (and direct taxation) drastically, little could be done, and there could be no question of restoring the pre-1939 situation. The standard rate of income tax actually rose slightly, from nine shillings (i.e. 45 per cent) in the pound in 1951 to nine shillings and six pence in 1952–53; it was not cut below nine shillings until 1956, when it dropped to seven shillings and nine pence, or about 39 per cent. A bachelor earning £10 000 (still an enormous income) in 1951 retained only £3598 after paying his taxes; this at first declined still further under the Tories, to £3361 in 1952, while even in 1959 this bachelor retained only £4341. Due to the Korean War, the Tories entered office with a serious balance of trade situation, with a cur-rent accounts deficit of £369 million in 1951; this improved considerably the following year, but, throughout the 1950s and 1960s, balance of trade deficits threatened year after year, facing every Chancellor to embark on the so-called 'stop-go' path: giving something back to consumers through acquiescing in high trade union-induced wage settlements and minor tax cuts, and then see-ing this evaporate as inflation rose and imports increased, necessitating stringent economies (usually via high interest rates) in the short term. Thus was born, after Labour left office in 1951, the celebrated long-term malaise of the British economy which persisted for over forty years and was marked by the paradox of an ever more affluent home population, with full employment until the 1970s, simultaneous with an ever-diminishing role for Britain in the world economy, hallmarked by lost opportunities and disappointments as a manufacturing and exporting nation.

The Churchill government was thus forced into a policy of caution and con-tinuity, against the real wishes of many Tories – but certainly not all, for many well-placed 'One Nation' Tories such as Eden and Macmillan sincerely opposed any return to the 1930s. Virtually all nationalised industry was left in place, with only two instances of what would later be termed privatisation: the denational-isation of road haulage and of the iron and steel industry in 1953. Both repre-sented the most extreme fringes of Labour's nationalisation policies and had been opposed by many Labourites. The government actually extended nation-alisation, in a manner of speaking, when it established the UK Atomic Energy Commission the following year. Nothing drastic of any kind was done to tame the trade unions, and the Labour minister, the skilful, experienced fix-it

Sir Walter Monckton, preferred Commissions of Inquiry and backstairs negotiations to confrontation, generally with success. Prescription charges were
extended in the NHS: that was it. Everything else was more or less left alone.

That the Tories accepted the great bulk of Labour's reforms and, in many
cases, appeared fully to endorse them was not lost on the commentators in the
press. In February 1954 the *Economist* magazine coined the term 'Butskellism'
to refer to the similarity of agendas of the present and previous Chancellors of
the Exchequer. The word caught on, and has been used ever since to describe
the continuities between Labour and Tories at this time. Yet, as most historians
agree, there were differences: the Tories were certainly warmer to business and
opposed any extension of state power. Nevertheless, Churchill's government
evolved a distinctive programme, within the context of a broadly extended
Welfare State. It placed much greater emphasis on the consumer and on the provision, through the private sector, of consumer demand than did Labour.
Central to this approach was housing. Under Labour, housing had been relatively neglected, certainly compared with the export drive and creating a Welfare
State. In 1950 the Tories had pledged to build 300 000 houses a year through
the private and public sector. This pledge was of great importance to many hundreds of thousands of persons living, or often sharing, inadequate facilities.
Churchill gave Harold Macmillan the tasks of fulfilling the Tory pledge, one
which required the construction of new houses to increase by 50 per cent compared with the last years of Labour. In fact, assisted by his junior minister Ernest
Marples, Macmillan achieved this aim within two years, a total of 327 000
homes built in 1953 and 354 000 in 1954. This achievement was the making
of Harold Macmillan, and instrumental in his eventually becoming Prime
Minister. Most of the new homes were actually built by local authorities, not
the private sector, but this in itself was only accomplished by a deliberate redi-
rection of public funds. Many were built in housing estates at the edge of town,
and led to a minor scandal involving the use of agricultural land at Crichel
Downs, for which the Agriculture Minister Sir Thomas Dugdale was forced to
resign in July 1954. The housing programme entailed the removal of imposed
restrictions on house building. Removal of Labour-imposed restrictions was
another component of the Tory programme, which saw the abolition of whatever remained of rationing – on butter and meat in 1954 and on coal in 1958.

The 1950s saw the emergence of what became known as the 'affluent society', where, for the first time, millions of working-class people began to acquire
consumer durables and participate in what had been a middle-class lifestyle. The
Conservatives became strongly associated with the 'affluent society' as a successful counterpoise to Labour's Welfare State. Between 1950 and 1960 the
number of automobiles in Britain increased by nearly 145 per cent, from 3 million to 7.4 million, the number of telephones (a rarity outside the middle classes
before the Second World War) rose by 52 per cent, while the number of television licences increased from only 344 000 in 1950 to 10.5 million in 1960. An
industry of immense power and influence had thus been created from scratch.
In 1954 the Conservatives established a second, privately-owned television
broadcaster, the Independent Television (later Broadcasting) Authority (ITA).
Its creation was opposed by many, including old-line aristocratic conservatives
such as Lord Halifax, the pre-war Foreign Minister, a High Anglican who came

out of retirement to oppose the measure, as did many Anglican leaders, on the grounds that it would lower standards. (As a result, perhaps, the government appointed Sir Kenneth Clark, the distinguished art historian, as the ITA's first chairman.) Many leftists shared the same doubts as were held by arch-conservatives that a breach in the BBC's monopoly would inevitably enrich a few media moguls while lowering standards. (In the 1960s, the press baron Lord Thomson of Fleet immortally described the awarding of ITA's licence to Grenada Television as 'a license to print money'.) In many respects, Labour was far less ready to come to terms with the 'affluent society' than were Tories, especially with the hedonism seen as an inevitable consequence. The 1950s indeed seemed to provide evidence that the dire predictions made by some were coming true, with the growth, arguably for the first time in Britain, of a self-defined 'youth culture' in many respects deliberately adversarial to its elders and their values. Rock-'n-roll, gang violence, destructive and threatening modes of dress and behaviour, all made ultimately possible by the new affluence, even for school-leavers, was a feature of British society in the 1950s; it was new, or at least very different from anything seen earlier. While the Tories embraced the affluence brought about by the mixed system which had evolved since 1945, many traditionalists of course were disturbed by the evidence it gave of a decline in moral and cultural standards. Although far more Labourites opposed both unbridled capitalist affluence and the decline in standards, a minority regarded the subverting of these outworn values as a good thing, a liberating modern revolt. Both parties were thus split on the fruits of the 'affluent society', although the Tories, less puritanical and more pro-capitalist than Labour, were more sympathetic to it, especially as affluence seemed a certain vote winner.

Foreign policy naturally was of primary importance to the Churchill government, which was fortunate in its timing. In office, Churchill was no warmonger and made repeated overtures to the Russians for a summit conference. As the only major world leader in office who had had direct dealings with Stalin, Churchill could reasonably expect to achieve some results, but no meeting ever came about. Stalin in his last years was, in all likelihood, clinically insane and increasingly paranoid. Fortunately, he died in March 1953; after a power struggle, the much more moderate figure of Nikita Krushchev won out, while, almost immediately, the Soviets made gestures of conciliation to the West. In June 1953 an unsatisfactory, but lasting, armistice was reached ending the Korean War; a year later the defeated French evacuated Indo-China, leaving South Vietnam in anti-communist hands. While developing a British nuclear capacity and leaving conscription intact, Churchill's government gave the impression of flexibility, especially (at first) compared with the administration of the new American Republican president, Dwight Eisenhower, Churchill's old wartime colleague (whose mutual relations were, nevertheless, surprisingly cool). Britain also had its share of colonial and pseudo-colonial problems – in Kenya, where the terrorist Mau-Mau revolt began in the early 1950s; in Malaya, where a Communist insurrection broke out; in Cyprus, where virtual civil war took place between Greeks and Turks; above all in the Middle East, especially in relations with Egypt. Apart from the formation of the Federation of Rhodesia and Nyasaland in 1953, a white-dominated Southern African state given internal self-government, none of Britain's numerous remaining colonies gained independence during this period. Nevertheless, by 1955 the overall foreign policy situation, particularly *vis-à-vis* the Soviet bloc, was less threatening than since the end of the war.

Especially after Stalin's death, Britain had, as noted, seemed to many to have emerged, most surprisingly, into a new era of relative tranquillity and prosperity after decades of struggle and turmoil. This mood became most clear, perhaps, with the Coronation of Queen Elizabeth II in June 1953, the cause of genuine national celebration. In February 1952 her father King George VI died (of lung cancer) at the age of only 56. The new Queen, only 25 at the time, was attractive and happily married. Many thought that the accession to the throne of a female monarch heralded a new Elizabethan Age, harkening back to her namesake 350 years earlier, and newspapers drew up lists of who the achievers, gallants, and buccaneers of the new age were likely to be. Something of this mood was evident two years earlier, during the Festival of Britain of 1951, a world's fair on London's south bank, held a century after the Great Exhibition of 1851, but the 1953 Coronation, when the Affluent Society was beginning, was a clearer indication of the same mood. (It was also the earliest public event in Britain which millions watched on television.) The first successful ascent of Mount Everest, by New Zealand climber Edmund Hillary and Sherpa Tensing, word of which reached Britain a day before the Coronation, seemed to many to be another portent.

In opposition, even great political parties tend to self-destruct, or at least to look as if they are, and Labour in opposition was no exception. One of the worst examples of intraparty warfare in political history erupted almost as soon as Labour left office. It was led by Nye Bevan and his band of 46 supporters among backbench Labour MPs, especially by figures such as Michael Foot, Richard Crossman, Barbara Castle (1911–2002), and Ian Mikardo (1908–92), generally seen as the organiser of the 'Bevanites', Nye's loyalists. This body was first formed around 1946 as the 'Keep Left' group, opposing British participation in the anti-Soviet Cold War and advocating the formation of a 'third force' of European socialists. Naturally, they also favoured greater socialism at home. While Bevan was the hero of this group, and gave his name to it, he often acted independently, sometimes in a manner even more disruptive of the party's leadership. 'Bevanism' kept on surfacing during most of the 1950s, enjoying wide support from some constituency parties. It had its own weekly newspaper, *Tribune*, and conducted itself in a way which its enemies repeatedly described as 'a party within a party'. The Bevanites were most visible at Labour's annual conference at Morecambe in the autumn of 1952, often described as the most bitter and disruptive annual conference in the party's history, no mean achievement. There, six Bevanites were elected to Labour's Parliamentary Committee, and a variety of extremist measures were proposed by the grouping, although these were generally defeated. After assisting party unity during the next year or two, in 1954 Bevan himself again did his best to disrupt the party's unity, provocatively attacking the defence policy of Attlee (who was still the party's leader) in Parliament, and (in September 1954) famously attacking the 'right kind of political leader' currently favoured by Labour's frontbench as 'a desiccated calculating machine', without passionate concern for the poor. This was widely taken as a reference to Hugh Gaitskell, Bevan's right-wing arch rival, although it was apparently aimed as a criticism of Attlee himself.

The centre and right wings of the Labour were not slow to organise a counter movement aimed at marginalising the Bevanites (Bevan was nearly expelled from the party in 1954). Headed by Herbert Morrison and Hugh Gaitskell, it always enjoyed the support of a majority of Labour's MPs and trade union supporters, especially the most powerful trade union leaders who were, at this time, on the right of the party. Morrison and Gaitskell were rivals to succeed Attlee, who remained the party's leader until December 1955. Attlee was clearly a moderate in the party's range of views, although his performance at this time (he was 70 in 1953) was curiously muted, and he did little to restore the party's unity. Attlee liked Bevan, and (so he said) hoped he would eventually become leader. But he did everything possible to favour Hugh Gaitskell as his successor instead of the shopworn Herbert Morrison (or Bevan, who was increasingly seen as beyond the pale), remaining leader until the mid-1950s to give Gaitskell a chance to acquire more support than Morrison. The 'Gaitskellites', representing the moderate, social democratic wing of the party, were also increasingly well-organised. In 1956, one of the major Gaitskellites, Anthony Crosland (1918–77), published the most important theoretical work about their aims, *The Future of Socialism*, opposing further nationalisation, but advocating measures of Keynesian economic expansionism, an ill-defined commitment towards 'equality', and libertarianism in the cultural and social sphere. These views proved enormously influential, although his work was also criticised for its vagueness about the economic realities actually confronting Britain. The internecine conflict within the Labour party obviously did nothing to enhance its electoral prospects. It was also widely noted that virtually all of the Bevanites (with the exception of Bevan himself) and the Gaitskellites were middle-class intellectuals, educated at a public school and Oxbridge. Although Labour claimed to represent the working class, few of its representatives took part in the central debates of the time.

Churchill had suffered a stroke in June 1953; this fact was concealed from the public for many years. By late 1953 it was obvious to his colleagues that Churchill's powers were fading, and the business of the Cabinet gradually became more anarchic. Churchill's setpiece speeches, such as one at the Tories' Margate conference in October 1953, continued to be good, but his competence in private had obviously declined. Today, in the age of television and 'in your face' journalism, it is most unlikely that Churchill, who turned eighty in 1954, would continue in office. A number of factors made his retirement difficult. Because of the unique position he enjoyed, no one was game to tell him it was time to go. Churchill desperately wanted a summit conference between the new Soviet leaders and the main leaders of the West. This finally occurred in 1955, after Churchill left office, but not before. Churchill remained in office, too, in effect to spite those who wanted him to go. There was, finally, the problem of his successor. The anointed successor was Sir Anthony Eden (as he had been since 1945); there was no other candidate. But Eden himself was seriously ill, having had a gall bladder operation in April 1953, an operation which went badly wrong and led to a continuing bile duct ailment and two further, life-threatening operations. As well, there were increasing doubts in many quarters about Eden's competence apart from foreign policy.

Eden as Prime Minister and Suez, 1955–57

Winston Churchill finally retired in April 1955, but remained a member of the House of Commons for nearly ten more years. As noted, there was no question of his successor. Sir Anthony Eden became Prime Minister without a vote being taken or even soundings among senior Tories, the last time that this had happened. (Something of the kind arguably occurred in April 1976 when James Callaghan, the Deputy Prime Minister, succeeded Harold Wilson.) Even in the Conservative party in the twentieth century such automatic, unquestioned succession was rare, having previously occurred only with Arthur Balfour's succession in 1902 and Neville Chamberlain's in 1937.

Next to Churchill, Eden certainly enjoyed more prestige than anyone in the Cabinet. He had been Foreign Minister and a leading anti-Appeaser in the 1930s and was in the international spotlight ever since. He was, in sociological terms, from the primary 'Establishment', the son (unless rumours that he was actually the son of George Wyndham, a prominent Edwardian politician, were correct) of a landed baronet, an Etonian, an officer with a distinguished First World War record at young age (he was the youngest brigade major in the army), a First in Oriental Languages from Oxford. Despite this, he was seen as on the left of his party, at least in terms of principled opposition to Appeasement. Great things were truly expected of him; aged 57 when he became Prime Minister, he might well have continued in office for ten years.

Eden formed a traditional Cabinet of 18. Churchill's 'Overlords' concept had been quietly dropped within a year or two, and Churchill's Cabinet itself gradually became more traditional in appearance. A number of very promising younger men who entered Parliament in 1950 had been given junior office, such as Iain Macleod (1913–70), promoted to be junior health minister after a famous and successful attack in the Commons on Nye Bevan. Eden's Cabinet, however, was largely that left to him by Churchill. R.A. Butler, probably Eden's most likely successor at the time, remained at the Exchequer. To the Foreign Office Eden appointed Harold Macmillan, whose success at the Housing Ministry was probably the most notable domestic achievement of Churchill's premiership. Eden also decided on an immediate General Election, although he could have waited for more than a year. With his prestige and Labour's disunity, the outcome, if not exactly a foregone conclusion, was in little doubt. The election, held on 26 May 1955, produced a Conservative majority of 58, the first time in a century that an incumbent party had increased its majority.

	Total votes	MPs elected	% share of total vote
Conservative	13 286 569	344	49.7
Liberal	722 405	6	2.7
Labour	12 404 970	277	46.4
Communist	33 144	0	0.1
Others	313 410	3	1.1
Total	26 760 498	630	100.0

Turnout, at 77 per cent, was five per cent lower than in 1951, and about 1.8 million fewer persons actually voted. This decline affected Labour far more than the Tories: Labour's vote dropped by 1 544 000 compared with a decline of 431 000 for the Tories. The Conservatives, with 49.7 of the vote, very nearly gained an absolute majority, and actually polled 50.2 per cent if the handful of unopposed returns are excluded. Rather amazingly, this was the Conservatives' highest share of the overall vote between 1935 and 2001, the first election of the twenty-first century. In 1959 and 1983, years of sweeping Tory wins, because of the rise of the Liberals and other minor parties, the Conservative share of the vote was lower, although they won more seats. In 1955, the Tories produced their usual sweep in southern England outside London, winning 163 seats to 42 for Labour, but Labour remained ahead in other regions apart from Northern Ireland and, remarkably, Scotland, where, for the only time after 1935, the Conservatives won more seats (36) than did Labour (34). With six seats, the Liberals had now touched rock-bottom, although their share of the total vote marginally rose.

Even before Suez, some had had doubts about Eden's leadership ability. It soon became clear that (possibly because of his persistent health problems) he was a notoriously poor administrator, given to immature outbursts of temper tantrums against Cabinet ministers and civil servants and frequent, ham-fisted intervention in the day-to-day work of Cabinet ministers. By late 1955, many leading Tories were having second thoughts about his premiership. In December 1955, R.A. Butler was asked if Eden was 'the best Prime Minister we have', to which he replied, only 'yes'. Less than a month later, the *Daily Telegraph* proclaimed editorially, in an original but oft-repeated phrase, that Britain was 'waiting to feel the smack of firm government'. Eden had little interest in domestic affairs, and killed a proposal to limit New Commonwealth immigration, thus helping to create a race problem in Britain where none existed before. Eden gave technical education a boost, but left the flawed 'Eleven Plus' system in place. The Cabinet was deeply divided on retaining the death penalty, a bill to abolish it passing the Commons but rejected by the Lords. Eden agreed to a bill, passed in 1957, to limit the death penalty in effect to murders carried out with guns. Eden's instincts were probably on the liberal side of the conservative–liberal divide, but showed the major divisions which existed among the Tories on many social issues, and its refusal (unlike the Republican party in the United States after 1970) fully to capitalise on the popular support socially conservative policies obviously enjoyed with the electorate, especially among the working classes. The British economy continued the peculiar and in some respects unprecedented path it had taken during the decade, combining full employment and a rising standard of living with repeated balance-of-payments crises, 'stop-go' in budgeting, and a continuing highly frustrating loss of export markets, especially to Germany, France, and Italy, much remarked even at the time. The Eden government explored the possibility of becoming involved with the emerging concept of Western European economic integration, but withdrew Britain's observer from the Messina conference at which negotiations to form the European Economic Community (EEC) began. In general the Tory government remained very cool to Europe. It would have tolerated a Free Trade area with Europe, but not a formal customs union which imposed tariffs on Commonwealth goods. This remained the Conservative position for many years. In December 1955 Eden reshuffled his Cabinet, replacing R.A. Butler (who became Leader of the Commons and Lord Privy Seal) at the Exchequer with Harold Macmillan, and moving Selwyn Lloyd (1904–78), a little-known junior minister, to the Foreign Office, seeing in Lloyd a virtual cipher who would do whatever Eden wished. He also promoted a few talented younger men, especially Iain Macleod, who became Minister of Labour.

With an election won and a reshuffled team in place, it might have appeared that Eden's government would continue successfully for many years. The year 1956 would, however, of course prove the *annus horribilis* of Eden's premiership, leading to the catastrophic humiliation over Suez with which his name will forever be associated, Eden's own resignation early in 1957, and what many historians and commentators see as a fundamental climacteric in Britain's Great Power ambitions. In June 1956, Britain withdrew its remaining military forces from Egypt, whose government, formerly a pliant supporter of Britain, had, since 1952, fallen in to the hands of anti-Western ultra-nationalists, led by Colonel Gamal Abdal Nasser, who emerged in 1954 as Egypt's President. Nasser moved more and more to what seemed like open alignment with the Soviet Union, with ferocious anti-American, anti-British, and anti-Israeli propaganda being a highlight of the new regime. By mid-1956, the only remaining token of Britain's long period of dominance in Egypt was the Suez Canal, the key waterway still owned by an Anglo-French (and chiefly British) consortium. On 26 July 1956 Nasser seized control of the Canal and nationalised it, obviously in violation of international law. Britain feared that nationalisation was a prelude to the banning of British shipping from the Canal, crucial to the transport of oil from the Middle East.

While negotiations over the Canal between Britain, France, and Egypt dragged on, Britain and France (France clearly appears to have taken the lead) secretly arrived at one of the most extraordinary proposals in the whole history of international affairs. Under this plan Britain and France would secretly invite Israel to invade and conquer the Sinai, whose western boundary is the Suez Canal; pretending to a lack of foreknowledge of this attack, Britain and France would send a military force to keep the Egyptian and Israeli forces apart and, incidentally, take back the Suez Canal! The plan further envisioned the toppling of Nasser and his replacement by more moderate forces. The *chutzpah* of this remarkable scheme almost defies belief, and it seems incredible that sober-minded political leaders would consider it seriously. Yet, somehow Eden and a handful of his inner circle agreed to the scheme, chiefly at secret negotiations at Sèvres near Paris in mid-October 1956. By late October Israel's Prime Minister agreed to the scheme – by no means a foregone conclusion – and the Israeli military proceeded to invade the Sinai, conquering this largely desert area within a week (29 October–5 November). On 30 October, Britain and France issued a joint Ultimatum calling for the cessation of hostilities and, significantly, demanding a 'temporary' Anglo-French occupation of the Canal area to guarantee free passage. Anticipating Egyptian rejection of the Ultimatum, an Anglo-French invasion force left Malta. On 6 November the Anglo-French forces landed at Port Said, and were soon in control of about one-third of the Canal. At this stage, however, the Cabinet decided on a ceasefire. Why? The most important reason was unexpected American hostility to the venture, especially that emanating directly from President Eisenhower. America effectively threatened economic sanctions against Britain which, as Labour politician Denis Healey ironically noted, was probably the only time in history that economic sanctions have been used successfully in international affairs. Eisenhower was crucially motivated by a number of factors. He was running for re-election as president on a 'peace and prosperity' platform; the election took place at the very moment of Suez. The Suez campaign also coincided, through ill-fortune, with the Soviet Union's suppression (1–4 November 1956) of the anti-Communist revolt in Hungary, and Eisenhower was keen to contrast the tactics of the West with those of the Soviet Union. America was also fearful that Russia might intervene in the Middle East, quite conceivably starting a nuclear war. On 30 November, Britain and France announced an unconditional withdrawal, and the Suez campaign ended, costing Britain 21 dead (other sources say 16) and 96 injured. Britain was forced to acquiesce in Egyptian nationalisation of the Canal, and full diplomatic relations between Britain and Egypt were not restored until 1961. Late in November Eden told the House of Commons that 'there was not foreknowledge that Israel would attack Egypt'. This was plainly untrue.

Of course Eden was absolutely right to try to regain the Suez Canal: any great power would have done exactly the same thing. If a Panamanian dictator had seized control of the Panama Canal (then a United States possession) by force, half of America's entire military would have been dispatched, by any American president, within 24 hours; they would not have returned to America without the dictator's head as a trophy. Eden and many other Tory leaders often drew an analogy between appeasing Hitler and appeasing Nasser: what was the difference? Taking back the Suez Canal in 1956 would quite conceivably have effectively deterred Nasser's many imitators as ultra-nationalist Third World dictators, especially in the Middle East. His deposition would have prevented the 1967 Arab–Israeli war, the subsequent Palestinian problem, and innumerable acts of terrorism. What unfolded was the worst possible outcome for Britain. In significant part, the failure was Eden's own fault. There was no need for theatrical secrecy, collusion with Israel, or the misleading of the British politicians about foreknowledge. Winston Churchill wisely stated that if he had been in charge 'I would never have done it without squaring the Americans, and once I'd started I would never dare stop.' 'Squaring the Americans' was difficult, given Eisenhower's position and stance, but not impossible: the United States was having major difficulties with Nasser, while John Foster Dulles, American Secretary of State, was a ferocious anti-Communist who would literally do almost anything to stop the Russians. Eden was undermined, as well, by some within the Cabinet who were annoyed not to know the full details of the plan, or who, like Harold Macmillan, had been strong supporters of the scheme but then changed their minds once America's opposition (which they had underestimated) became clear.

The Suez debacle had a number of major consequences. Anthony Eden resigned as Prime Minister in early January 1957. There was no real reason for him to have done this. The campaign had harmed him and the Tories, but both could recover. Eden gave ill-health as his reason for going, which was certainly true (he was advised by his doctors to leave office), but it is difficult to imagine him resigning if Suez had been successful. Eden also resigned from Parliament. He was created an earl in 1961, wrote his multi-volumed memoirs, and died, if not forgotten, at least not well remembered, in 1977. He played little or no role in British politics after his resignation and, unlike many of his successors, offered no gratuitous advice to younger leaders.

Suez both electrified Britain and unified the Labour party. Most of the British people supported Suez, and would have been only too happy to see an Anglo-French triumph over Nasser. Indeed, Gallup polling suggests that Suez did remarkably little harm to the Tories: in terms of voting intention, Labour was narrowly ahead of the Tories (by 46-44 per cent) in February 1956, and had the same narrow lead (46-45) in December, when Eden's approval rating was still 56 per cent. As the campaign became central, it temporarily overshadowed everything, with the Prime Minister's wife, Lady Eden, telling Tories at the height of the conflict that she felt as if 'the Suez Canal was floating through my drawing-room'. Suez brought renewed unity to the Labour party, reuniting Gaitskell (who was, originally, not necessarily opposed to teaching Nasser a lesson, but felt personally betrayed by Eden's actions) and Bevan, as well as by the great bulk of Labour supporters. Labour was again emerging, in early 1957, as a unified force.

The most important result of Suez was its long-term cultural and political effect. Unfairly or not, 'Suez' has come to encapsulate a definite, clear turning-point in modern British history, when it ceased to be a great power. Curiously, no phrase associated with either World War signifies Britain's loss of world power, only a military campaign against a Third World state, fought jointly with another major power, which was highly successful until the very moment it was voluntarily called off. This is because 'Suez' has come to mean far more than the Egyptian adventure, encapsulating many of the trends of the 1950s, from the rise of the so-called 'Angry Young Men' among intellectuals such as John Osborne, John Braine, and Colin Wilson, to Britain's persistent balance-of-trade and export crises. Sociologically, Britain was changing, with the cultural unity engendered by the old 'Establishment' about to alter comprehensively. In 1955, Princess Margaret was dissuaded by the Archbishop of Canterbury from marrying a divorced man with whom she was in love. A generation later, most people would regard a repetition of this as almost inconceivable. In 1959, the custom of presenting debutantes to the Queen was abolished. The sixties were ready to begin. 'Suez' was a shorthand epitome of these tendencies, trends which were unrelated to the actual events of late 1956.

The Macmillan premiership, 1957–63

While Anthony Eden's succession to the premiership was undisputed, that of his successor, Harold Macmillan, was not. There were two declared candidates to follow Eden, Macmillan, and R.A. Butler. Although eight years younger than Macmillan, to that point Rab Butler had had much the more distinguished career, enacting the 1944 Education Act, reforming the Conservative party in opposition, and heading the Treasury as a reasonably successful Chancellor. He was much better known to the general public, and was widely expected to win. Nevertheless, he failed to win. There were also many counts against him, especially his pro-Appeasement stance in late 1930s, when he was Lord Halifax's junior minister in the Commons, his indecisive role over Suez, and the impression he gave of being too liberal over social policies and too starchy and academic in personality. The succession to the vacancy caused by Eden's resignation in early 1957 was famously decided by each member of the Cabinet being summoned before Lords Salisbury and Kilmuir, two senior ministers, with the former (who had a noticeable lisp) asking bluntly 'which is it to be, Wab or Hawold?' Most preferred Macmillan, as did Churchill, other notables in the party, and (it was reported) most Tory backbenchers and peers. This was reported to the Queen, who simply chose Macmillan. No vote was taken: Macmillan simply 'emerged' as an apparently consensual choice. Butler, in politics always a bridesmaid, was to suffer the same fate of being passed over again in 1963.

In upbringing and outlook, although not in social origins, Harold Macmillan was very similar to Anthony Eden. Macmillan's paternal great-grandfather had been a Scottish crofter; his grandfather founded the world-famous publishing house of Macmillans; the new Prime Minister's mother (oddly, like those of Churchill and Quintin Hogg, other leading Tory politicians) was an American, the daughter of a doctor in Indiana. In 1920 Macmillan married the daughter of the Duke of Devonshire, thus entering (in a sense) the high aristocracy; he was related – by marriage but not by blood – to nearly everyone in his government with aristocratic connections.

In most other respects, Macmillan and Eden had remarkably similar CVs. Like Eden, who was three years his junior, Macmillan was educated at Eton and Oxford, graduated with a first, and served as an officer in the First World War, when he was wounded three times. Entering Parliament in 1924 for the northern industrial seat of Stockton-on-Tees, during the 1930s Macmillan was one of the most left-wing members of the Conservative party, producing *The Middle Way* (1938) and other tracts which advocated, for a Tory, a remarkable degree of near-socialist planning. He was also a rebel over Appeasement, having actually lost the party whip in 1937. Churchill, whose views were similar, made him a junior and then a senior minister. In 1951 he became a notably successful Housing Minister and then, in rapid succession, Foreign Minister (April–December 1955) and Chancellor of the Exchequer. The most notable feature of his Chancellorship was the introduction of Premium Bonds, a successful form of quasi-lottery. Given their similarities in outlook, Macmillan and Eden should have been close, but they weren't. In character they were very different. Macmillan was a discursive, engaging intellectual, never happier than when discussing Trollope (his favourite writer) at a Pall Mall club. He was also, quite unexpectedly, an effective executive, coming, like Attlee, to quick and cogent decisions (Macmillan had been the active chairman of his family publishing firm for many years). Eden's character was the opposite: notably highly strung, and hypersensitive in private, and even more notably deficient as an executive. Attlee and Macmillan probably had the most balanced and sane private lives of postwar Prime Ministers, Attlee keenly interested in crosswords and cricket, Macmillan in the classic novels, and they were, not by coincidence, among the most competent. Macmillan's marriage to Lady Dorothy Cavendish, it should be said, was notably unhappy, and (as is well known) she had a long-standing affair with Robert Boothby, another progressive Tory MP. Macmillan, although pained, remarkably awarded a life peerage to Boothby in 1958. In his married life, Macmillan was also not dissimilar to Eden, whose troubled first marriage (almost uniquely for a major politician at the time) ended, in 1950, in divorce.

Because of Suez, Macmillan did not expect to remain Prime Minister for more than a few weeks. Instead, he stayed in office for over six and a half years, becoming the longest-serving Prime Minister since Asquith. Within two years he acquired a remarkable ascendancy, winning the 1959 General Election with a large majority and presiding over a period of prosperity. The last two years of his administration, however, were unusually troubled and divisive, and are best-remembered for the Profumo scandal. When he left office in October 1963 the Tories seemed very likely to lose the next General Election.

Like its predecessor, Macmillan's government was centred around foreign policy, especially relations with the Soviet Union. Despite Suez and Hungary, relations with the Soviet Union, headed by Khrushchev and committed to coexistence, improved. So, too, did relations with the United States, especially after a meeting in Bermuda between British and American leaders in March 1957. In October 1957, Russia startled the world by launching Sputnik I, the world's first earth satellite. It did this four months prior to America's first earth satellite, and also placed the first man in space in April 1961, ahead of the United States. A kind of panic set in over the Soviet Union's technological achievements throughout the Western world, leading everywhere to greater investment in higher education and a determination to 'modernise'. The Soviet Union also, in January 1960, tested an intercontinental ballistic missile, capable of delivering a nuclear bomb over an 8000-mile distance. In some respects, this period, roughly 1957–63, marked the height of the Cold War. It is best-remembered for such acts as the erection of the Berlin Wall (August 1961) and the Cuban Missile Crisis (October–November 1962), which brought the world to the very edge of nuclear war. Yet in many respects this impression is misleading. Nikita Khruschchev, Russia's leader, who held supreme power between March 1958 and October 1964, a vulgar and truculent Ukrainian peasant-turned-commissar, best-remembered, perhaps, for his threat 'We will bury you!', was no Stalin. He did not seek the expansion of the Soviet empire except, as with Castro's victory in Cuba early in 1959, when it fell into his lap; he was not paranoid and no more of a mass-murderer than he had to be, unlike Stalin, who was wedded to mass murder and terror as a way of life. Khrushchev's secret speech early in 1956, which became public knowledge soon after, denounced many of Stalin's crimes and did more than perhaps anything else to cause Communism to lose popularity among Western intellectuals. Khrushchev preferred *détente* to conflict and, during the Cuban Missile Crisis, was the first to 'blink'. Fitful progress, therefore, towards accommodation and avoiding a nuclear war was always possible with Khrushchev. In May 1960 a summit conference between Soviet and Western leaders was held in Paris, but quickly collapsed when the Soviet Union shot down a U-2 spy plane flying high over Russia. In the same year Khrushchev unforgettably banged his shoe on the podium at the United Nations to make a point. But progress was made, resulting, in July 1963, in the Nuclear Test Ban Treaty (NTBT) concluded between America, Britain, and the Soviet Union which prohibited testing in the atmosphere, with all its dangers of nuclear contamination. Macmillan was an active, important force for moderation and East–West progress during this period, always acting in concert with the United States, which, after about 1957, moved increasingly away from hard-line McCarthyist anti-Communism. Macmillan enjoyed much better relations with Eisenhower than did Eden, but came into full flower when John F. Kennedy became President in January 1961. Macmillan was, remarkably, a relative by marriage of the Irish Catholic president (Kennedy's sister had married the heir to the Duke of Devonshire; both died in air crashes during the war) and came from somewhat similar backgrounds in their respective intelligentsias. Macmillan was, of course, much older, by 23 years, but acted as a much-prized avuncular figure during Kennedy's brief term of office. The relationship between Britain and America during this period did seem to many to be (as was often said) that of Greece to Rome, and it is clear that this state of affairs was largely due to Macmillan's special relationship. Macmillan resigned six weeks before Kennedy was assassinated in Dallas; it fell to his successor, Sir Alec Douglas-Home, to represent the British government at his funeral.

The most significant contribution of Macmillan's government in international affairs was its granting of independence to many British colonies. Not a single British colony was granted full independence between 1948 and 1956. From 1957, however, the very nature of the Commonwealth was transformed, as independence came to Ghana (formerly the Gold Coast, 1957), Malaya (1957), the West Indies Federation (Jamaica, Trinidad, and other Caribbean states, 1958; the Federation was dissolved in 1962); Nigeria (1960), the largest British black African state; Cyprus (1961); Sierra Leone (1961); Tanganyika (1961); Uganda (1962), and Kenya (1963). Many more states gained independence over the next decade or two, so that by the end of the twentieth century Britain's remaining colonies consisted of a few odd rocks in the sea. Britain had taken the decision, at some point in the early-mid 1950s, that black Africa simply could not be held, and that more or less friendly local elites, ruling over independent states, were the best that could be hoped for. American hostility towards old-fashioned imperialism and the ability of the Soviet bloc to exploit colonialism were contributory factors, as was the fact that both France and Belgium, the greatest colonial powers in Africa, granted independence to most of their black colonies in 1958–60. After independence, however, the same depressing pattern appeared almost everywhere, of a 'democracy' established in a pre-literate tribal society being quickly replaced by a bloody dictatorship, generally following an army coup. Some, such as Ghana's Kwame Nkrumah, were elected rulers-turned-tyrants, while others, such as Idi Amin in Uganda, were psychopaths from the military. Nkrumah was an important factor, as well, in forging the Third World's 'anti-imperialist' alliance, initiated at the Bandung Conference of 1954, which included 'neutralist' countries such as India under Nehru, Indonesia under Sukarno, and Yugoslavia's Tito. In general, colonial self-government came with remarkably little opposition at home (although Lord Salisbury, a major Tory symbol and power-broker, resigned from the Cabinet over softness towards Archbishop Makarios of Cyprus in March 1957, only a short time after Macmillan came to power), even from Britain's elites. The major exception was over the treatment accorded to southern Africa, both to South Africa (which, of course, was an independent country) and to the east African colonies such as

Southern Rhodesia with a significant, powerful white population. In Cape Town, on a visit in February 1960, Macmillan delivered what was probably his most famous speech, to a Joint Assembly of the South African Parliament, where he proclaimed that 'the wind of change is blowing across the Continent, and, whether we like it or not, this growth of national consciousness is a political fact.' In fact, the South African pro-Apartheid government lasted for another 24 years, although in 1961 it voluntarily left the Commonwealth and became a Republic, due to the intense pressuring which was emerging against Apartheid. In Britain, a pro-white African lobby did emerge, but Macmillan's government, while understanding of its position, did little to assist it. Liberal Tory ministers, especially Iain Macleod, Colonial Secretary from 1959 to 1961, strongly supported colonial independence, with Macleod being denounced by Lord Salisbury in May 1961 as 'too clever by half' (apparently the origin of this common phrase) in his African policies. No one in Britain had the stomach for a fight to retain whatever remained of the colonies, and the full liquidation of the British colonial empire was now accepted by almost everyone.

The end of any realistic chance of Britain heading a world-empire raised the question of how Britain would, in future, avoid economic and political isolation. For many, the future lay with a united Europe. The democratic countries of western Europe had taken major steps towards unification with the Treaty of Rome of March 1957, which established the EEC – the Common Market – consisting of France, West Germany, Italy, and the Benelux countries. These countries had experienced high levels of post-war economic growth. Most people in France and Germany saw the EEC as a means for avoiding a future war. Macmillan was a fairly dedicated European, but he, and most other Tory ministers, were opposed to its implied limitations on British sovereignty. In its place, in 1959, Britain organised a rival Free Trade bloc, EFTA (the European Free Trade Association), consisting of Britain, Sweden, Norway, Denmark, Austria, Switzerland, and Portugal. The government was also inching towards a decision to join the EEC, a step which would still have had very wide opposition from many sources ranging from the Beaverbrook press to the old Commonwealth. President Kennedy was keen for Britain to join the EEC, and was an important factor in tilting Macmillan's stance. In July 1961 Macmillan announced that Britain would apply to join the EEC, and entrusted Edward Heath (b.1916), the increasingly influential Lord Privy Seal, with negotiating an agreement. In January 1962 the EEC decided on a Common Agricultural Policy which was disadvantageous to Britain; this was an obstacle to joining, as was the opposition of much of the old Commonwealth. In the meantime, as the decision to join increasingly became one of the central political issues of the time, the leader of the Labour party, Hugh Gaitskell, unequivocally opposing British entry, telling the Labour Party Conference in October 1962 that entry into the EEC would mean 'the end of a thousand years of history'. A few months later, in January 1963, the entire British project became temporarily redundant, when French President Charles de Gaulle vetoed Britain's proposed entry, apparently fearing Britain as a rival to France for the leadership of the EEC. Britain had no obvious fallback option (although many suggested a Commonwealth Free Trade association), and the French veto was an important factor in the decline of the Macmillan government.

It is not difficult to see why so many hopes were pinned on Britain's entry. By 1962, talk of Britain's long-term economic and political decline had become general, almost ubiquitous, with western Europe's success offering a striking alternative of success. For many, Europe also offered a replacement for the Commonwealth, now clearly outmoded as a vehicle for asserting British power. Additionally, for many the EEC represented the economic facet of European democracy's defence against Soviet Communism, the economic equivalent (without America) of NATO. Nevertheless, the EEC also represented an entirely new departure for Britain, which has remained extraordinarily controversial ever since, especially whenever British sovereignty was further threatened.

The Macmillan years saw a continuation of the familiar pattern of unprecedented increases in living standards side-by-side with repeated balance-of-payments crises, the latter caused by rising domestic demands fanning imports and inflation, and an inability of Britain successfully to compete in exports. Balance-of-payments 'crises', necessitating sharp increases in interest rates and restrictions on pay increases, occurred, in particular, in late 1957 and mid-1961, although they were an ever-present threat. Macmillan's four Chancellors of the Exchequer, Peter Thorneycroft (1909–94; later baron Thorneycroft), 1957–58; Derick Heathcoat Amory (1899–1981; later first Viscount Amory), 1958–60; Selwyn Lloyd (1904–78; later baron Selwyn-Lloyd), 1960–62; and Reginald Maudling (1917–79), 1962–63, had varying degrees of success in dealing with this constant threat, but could not come to terms with its underlying causes. Britain had some manufacturing and export successes in these years, for instance with the Mini, a £500 car launched in 1959 under both the Morris and Austin labels, which became world-famous and sold 5.3 million models by the early 1990s, but these were few and far between, and almost always dwarfed in success by foreign makes such as the Volkswagen 'Beetle'. The traditional remedy for Britain's manufacturing woes was the financial and commercial success of the City of London. The City remained strong, but could not at that time perform the role of world entrêpot it always had, hemmed in by all manner of overseas trading restrictions and overtaken by New York. The government did attempt some liberalisation here, however, announcing the convertibility of non-resident sterling on current accounts in late 1957, but many barriers remained. Britain's high tax rates also discouraged foreign investment, entrepreneurship, and thrift. As well, a nasty spate of strikes and industrial actions took place in these years, particularly in engineering, shipping, and transport, where newly elected left-wing union leaders such as Frank Cousins (1904–86) replaced former more moderate union leaders. Unemployment, though remarkably low by subsequent standards, began to inch up, reaching 621 000 in January 1959 and 878 000 in February 1963, compared with a high of only 298 000 in the two years 1955–56. The preferred response of the Macmillan government to these disturbing trends was to establish joint councils of various sorts, such as the Council on Prices, Productivity, and Income of August 1957 and the National Economic Development Council (NEDC or 'Neddy') of July 1961. 'Neddy' consisted of representatives of management, unions, and government which – in theory – were to arrive at a consensual programme for the country's economy. Of course this couldn't work, since no agreement could be legally enforced, while the government might, at any time, be forced by circumstances to shift economic gears dramatically. During the Macmillan years virtually no one, and certainly no one in the political mainstream, advocated a reduced role for government, privatisation, free exchange rates, or a deflationary, neo-laissez-faire agenda which would see unemployment temporarily rise. In particular, a return to anything like the unemployment rates seen before 1939 became the ultimate political taboo, one which Macmillan, an arch-opponent of the Tory laissez-faire policies of the 1930s, emphatically shared. Instead, a consensus increasingly emerged on the left and centre-left that Britain's poor economic performance could only be revived through 'modernisation', a catchcry which embraced everything from reform of the House of Lords to the creation of a National Enterprise Board to invest in long-term growth industries. It must be emphasised again that most British people at this time, including a large percentage of the working classes, continued to be more affluent than ever, buying their own homes and purchasing consumer goods from cars to televisions in a way never seen before. For this reason Macmillan could say, in July 1957, with much accuracy, that 'most of our people have never had it so good', a view shared by R.A. Butler in July 1960, who claimed that 'people are divided not so much between "haves" and "have-nots" as between "haves" and "have-mores".' This central paradox, ever-greater prosperity in an economy which was manifestly underperforming most of its rivals, was the chief theme of the Macmillan years and for a long time to come. It made finding a solution to Britain's economic underperformance much more difficult.

The Macmillan government grappled with many difficult social issues, not always with great success. The mid-late 1950s saw something of a considerable change in attitudes among the left-liberal metropolitan intelligentsia, towards greater liberalism in social behaviour and criminal matters. Most Conservatives emphatically detested these proposed changes, although an influential minority echoed them. In 1957 the death penalty was restricted, under the Homicide Act 1957, to murders committed with guns, and a defence of diminished responsibility in homicides was introduced. This change followed considerable public outcries over miscarriages, or alleged miscarriages, of justice, in such executions as those of Timothy Evans (1949), Derek Bentley (1952), and Ruth Ellis (1955). The restriction made little sense, since many of the most infamous and dangerous murderers did not use a gun ('Jack the Ripper', for example, used a knife), and, while it reflected public unease at the increased use of firearms, satisfied neither side in the debate. There cannot be the slightest doubt that the death penalty for the worst murders was (and is) supported by the great majority of the population, especially by Tories, and the Conservative government acted against the manifest wishes of the majority of its supporters in making this change, for no obvious reason. (The Home Secretary always had the power to reprieve convicted murderers.) Another social issue of similar controversy was homosexuality. Male homosexuality (though not lesbianism) had been a criminal offence, in all cases, since the 1890s. *De facto*, however, most upperclass homosexuals (of whom there were many) and their activities were simply ignored by the authorities unless blatantly offensive. In the early 1950s, however, a crackdown against homosexuals took place, in part because it was feared that those in government service could be blackmailed by Soviet agents. This in turn led to a reaction questioning the law itself. In 1957 a departmental committee, chaired by John Wolfenden, a prominent educator, recommended most controversially that homosexual acts between consenting adults should no longer be criminal offences. The Conservative government took no action on the Wolfenden Report, and male homosexuality remained a criminal offence until 1967.

Possibly the most controversial of these new social issues, however, concerned coloured immigration. Immigrants had always come to Britain, most famously the Huguenots, Catholic Irish (citizens of the United Kingdom, of course) to England and Scotland, and European Jews, especially after the Russian pogroms started in 1881. Their numbers, however, were relatively small (the total Jewish population of Britain in 1939, for instance, was only 350 000), and the migrants, being Caucasians, were indistinguishable from the rest of the population after a generation or two; indeed, there was among all such groups a general tendency towards assimilation and disappearance. Although small groups of West Indians had lived in such places as Liverpool and Cardiff, and Indians were long to be found at Oxbridge and the Inns of Court, from 1948 a massive, unprecedented wave of visibly, permanently distinctive New Commonwealth immigration became manifest in Britain. The Aliens Act of 1905 and subsequent Acts had given the Home Office the right to restrict immigration from outside the Commonwealth, but left immigration from the Commonwealth alone. As a result, tens of thousands of New Commonwealth immigrants began to arrive in Britain, although their numbers were not definitely known. In 1960, no less than 53 000 West Indians came to Britain, together with 9000 from the Indian sub-continent. Most settled (as all waves of immigrants do) in a handful of places such as the Notting Hill and Brixton areas of London and in Birmingham. In August 1958 there were serious race riots in Notting Hill, and intense pressure grew to restrict non-white immigration. The government, and most of the mainstream press, was surprisingly reluctant to do this but, in 1962, Macmillan was forced to pass the Commonwealth Immigrants Act which cut New Commonwealth immigration, although not to the extent which most Tories would have liked. Britain suddenly and gratuitously found itself with a race problem where none had existed before, and increasingly became prone to the politics of ethnicity, ethnic identity, and ethnic conflict, and their consequences in a way without previous precedent.

Macmillan's government also passed a number of other important reforms. Perhaps least noted, but affecting the largest number of people, was its abolition of military conscription. In April 1957, in the wake of a review of the British military after Suez, it announced that conscription would end in 1960, so that by the end of 1963 no conscripts would remain in the forces. (At the same time, the size of the British armed forces was greatly reduced.) Britain was the first major Western world to abolish the much-hated service requirement; America did not follow suit until 1973, after conscription made its Vietnam entanglement intensely unpopular. In 1963 the government replaced the London County Council (LCC), formed in 1888, with the Greater London Council (GLC), a greatly expanded area covering almost all of the Greater London area. Cynics noted that this gave the Tories a much better chance of gaining control of London local government, something which was almost impossible under the LCC. The GLC was itself abolished by the Thatcher government in 1985.

Not surprisingly, the Macmillan government made only minor changes to the British constitution. In 1958 it allowed the creation of life peers (barons and baronesses for life) in the House of Lords. This greatly expanded the type of person likely to be offered, or accept, a peerage, particularly among Labourites and those – such as trade union leaders or eminent scientists – for whom a hereditary peerage appeared absurd. It gave women the right to sit in the Lords for the first time, and probably preserved the House of Lords in its old form for several decades. In 1963 another minor reform of the Lords gave the right to sit there to all Scottish peers (rather than a small number of 'representative peers') and allowed any peer, or anyone who inherited a peerage, a six-month period in which to 'disclaim' his peerage for life, so that (if he wished) he could stand for Parliament. Passed to accommodate Tony Benn, who unwillingly inherited the viscountcy of Stansgate, its most important and immediate use was to allow Sir Alec Douglas-Home, the Earl of Home, to become Prime Minister.

For the first three of four years of his government, Macmillan could do no wrong, especially after the Suez disaster. He was dubbed 'Super-Mac' in a Vicky cartoon in the *Evening Standard* in November 1958, renowned for his 'unflappability'. His self-deprecatingly facetious yet incisive high Edwardian style, his intelligence, and his good luck endowed him with a reputation for success and a sure touch. Macmillan called a General Election for October 1959, with the Tories using the slogan on their advertising 'Life's better with the Conservatives – Don't let Labour ruin it.' Hugh Gaitskell, the Labour leader, had little to offer in return. Although he ran a good campaign, basically he was at a loss to find a successful theme to oppose the Tories' capitalisation on prosperity and peace. In the end the Conservatives picked up 21 seats, compared with 1955.

	Total votes	MPs elected	% share of total vote
Conservative	13 749 830	365	49.4
Liberal	1 638 571	6	5.0
Labour	12 215 538	258	43.8
Others	142 670	1	0.4
Total	27 859 241	630	100.0

Turnout was reasonably high at 78.8 per cent. The Tories gained over 450 000 votes compared with 1995, while Labour lost nearly 200 000. The main novelty of the election was the increase in the Liberal vote (but not in their seats), the party more than doubling its total from 722 000 to 1.6 million. (This was still lower than their total vote in 1950, however.) A new minor party of potential importance arose in the form of Plaid Cymru, the Welsh Nationalists, who received 77 521 votes. The Tories were dominant, as always, in the south of England outside London, winning 171 seats to Labour's 34, and also won a majority of seats in the Midlands, 49 to Labour's 47. Otherwise the old patterns remained.

From 1962 on, however, things began to go badly and progressively wrong for Macmillan and the Tories. At base, this was probably due to the increasing weakness of the economy, and to the measures the government was forced to take to deal with it, such as Selwyn Lloyd's 'pay pause' of mid-1961. In March 1962 the government lost a famous by-election to the Liberals at Orpington, in the heart of Tory country in suburban Kent. Although local factors were important, this was widely seen as marking a turning-point in the fortunes of both parties. A few months later Macmillan carried out the so-called 'July Massacre', sacking seven members of his Cabinet on Friday the 13th of July. The 'massacre' was oriented around getting rid of Selwyn Lloyd, the Chancellor of the Exchequer, whose deflationary policies were making the party electorally unpopular. As Macmillan himself noted, the 'massacre' was a serious.mistake. Most of the old steadying figures from earlier in the Tory government – such as Lord Kilmuir – were dismissed. Reginald Maudling became Chancellor of the Exchequer, and other younger men on the left of the party were brought into the Cabinet at this time, such as Henry Brooke (1903–84) and Sir Edward Boyle (1923–81). Enoch Powell (1912–98) also entered the Cabinet for the first time in this reshuffle, as Health Minister. Opinion on the reshuffle was scathing, the most common verdict being that 'Macmillan has sacked half the Cabinet – the wrong half.' Liberal MP Jeremy Thorpe commented, 'Greater love hath no man than this – that he laid down his friends for his life.'

Troubles, it has been widely noted, seldom came singly, and the latter phases of the Macmillan government were no exception. In January 1963 came de Gaulle's veto of Britain's EEC application, while six months later came the great Profumo affair. In September 1962 security forces exposed a Soviet spy at the Admiralty, J.A.C. Vassall, who had been Private Secretary to Sir Thomas Galbraith, a junior minister, who was forced to resign. Allegations against government ministers for negligence became common in the press, and in March 1963, two journalists who had refused to disclose the source of their information to Lord Radcliffe, a judge heading a Departmental Committee on security, were each jailed for contempt. (In fact, there was no 'source' to disclose; their stories had been invented.) This incident is widely seen as turning much of the press against the government, making it especially keen to harp on anything discreditable which might surface. They did not have long to wait. Early in 1963 stories began to circulate that John Profumo (b.1915), the Secretary for War, had become involved with a prostitute, Christine Keeler, whose associates also included Yevgeny Ivanov, a naval attaché at the Soviet embassy. Profumo first met Keeler while bathing naked at Cliveden, Lord Astor's famous mansion, and a network was revealed, highly unsavoury to many, of prostitution, drug dealing, immoral earnings, and the scandalous behaviour of the rich and powerful, with potentially dangerous national security overtones. The story thus had literally everything and was in any case the answer to a newspaper editor's prayer; given the media's relation with the government at the time the press was only too happy to give it full throttle. Because of the possible security implications of his associations, Profumo was extensively interviewed by a variety of government ministers, including the Solicitor-General Sir Peter Rawlinson. He denied everything to them, and then, to quell the tide of rumours, denied everything (22 March 1963) in a prepared statement made in the House of Commons. Early in June, however, Profumo admitted that he had lied to the House and was therefore forced to resign. The scandal, relatively minor except for Profumo's denial, rocked Britain, and became one of the most famous such affairs of the century. Needless to say, the press had a field-day, with the normally Tory-supporting *Times* heading its editorial (11 June 1963) 'It is a moral issue.' Confidence in the government, and in Macmillan's handling of the affair, was severely shaken, with Nigel Birch, a former minister, quoting Browning's line 'never glad, confident morning again'.

In the meantime, and despite the success of the Test Ban Treaty, Macmillan's health was rapidly declining (he was nearly 70), with a painful prostate condition making it difficult to stay on. Macmillan decided to resign. There was no clear-cut successor, and his decision came at the same time as the annual party conference at Blackpool, which allowed bandwagons for the leading candidates to develop. The most senior possible successor was R.A. Butler, but other possibilities had arisen, especially Quintin Hogg (Lord Hailsham), Iain Macleod, Reginald Maudling, and Lord Home, the Foreign Secretary. There was thus no chance of an assured succession to Macmillan. Nor was there any clear-cut method of choosing a successor. Moreover, Macmillan's decision to resign came at the Blackpool conference, where everything was televised and reported on; the succession could not be settled behind closed doors. Butler was the leading candidate, followed (according to opinion polls) by Hailsham and Maudling. Hailsham (and Home) was eligible to become leader as he was, during this period, able to disclaim his peerage if he wished and seek a seat in Parliament. Macmillan's initial preferred candidate was probably Hailsham, who disclaimed his peerage to become Quintin Hogg. Formal soundings were taken among many groups in the party. Remarkably, the dark horse Lord Home received surprisingly strong support (although far from a majority of any section of the party). After receiving soundings, Macmillan recommended to the Queen that Lord Home become Prime Minister. The Queen took his advice and Home formally became Prime Minister on 18 October 1963, five days after Macmillan's resignation. Home disclaimed his peerage, becoming Sir Alec Douglas-Home, the name by which he is known today. A revolt immediately brewed up among some of the younger members of the Cabinet. Iain Macleod and Enoch Powell refused to serve under Douglas-Home and were not appointed to his Cabinet. Some of the impetus for Home probably came from Macmillan himself who (rather like Clement Attlee and Herbert Morrison) would not have Butler as his successor; his preferred choice, Lord Hailsham, appeared to many to be too theatrical and to have an uncontrollable tongue. Apart from any other reason why the choice of Lord Home was curious, it seemed to fly in the face of the direction which Macmillan had taken fairly consistently during the previous 18 months, towards 'modernisation' and the promotion of middle-class men of obvious talent, such as Heath and Macleod. Ironically, too, Macmillan's illness proved to be not particularly serious, and there was no reason why he could not have led the party into the 1964 General Election. In fact, he lived for another 23 years, dying at the age of 92.

The events of the Eden and Macmillan government also had a considerable impact on the Labour party, generally enhancing its many internal divisions, which almost always exist among parties that have lost elections, but have been especially severe in the Labour party. The dichotomy between more moderate social democrats, represented by Hugh Gaitskell, and more extreme socialists, led, until his death in 1960 by Nye Bevan, erupted every few years, while new issues like nuclear disarmament also arose. Gaitskell became leader of the Labour party in December 1955 when Attlee finally retired, winning convincingly with 157 votes (among Labour MPs) to 70 for Nye Bevan, his arch-nemesis, and a humiliating 40 for Herbert Morrison, who was aged 67. In contrast, Gaitskell was only 49, the youngest man to head a major party in many years. Gaitskell was similar to Attlee in his social background, the son of an Indian civil servant and the product of Winchester (the famous public school, known for producing intellectuals as well as fox-hunters) and Oxford, where he received a first. Like Attlee, he was converted to socialism by experience, in this case by the 1926 General Strike. He was, however, also unlike Attlee in many respects. He was garrulous, articulate, intellectually flexible, and bohemian in his private life (he lived openly with his future wife before marriage, something rarely done at the time). He was also personally courageous, rescuing Jews and socialists from pre-war Vienna, a trait which featured in his whole career. He was a university lecturer in the 1930s and a civil servant rather than a soldier during the war, something held against him by many, especially on the left. Attlee marked him out for rapid promotion, and he became Chancellor of the Exchequer in October 1950 at the age of only 44, angering the left by Korea-induced budget cuts which fell in part on the NHS. Nevertheless, he was the darling of the still-dominant right and centre-right of the party, attracted great loyalty, and was not without considerable charisma. To the Left, he represented the pseudo-Tory face of Labour's middle-class supporters, a man who in effect had abandoned any commitment to real socialism in favour of a Keynesian managed economy. Although Gaitskell's personal followers mainly consisted of middle-class intellectuals, the left's critique was not entirely fair. The Gaitskellites' ideology centred around a commitment to 'equality', which could, potentially, have included such planks as much higher rates of death duties and an attack on the public schools, which were very radical indeed. The Gaitskellites were also much friendlier to social reforms such as the liberalisation of censorship and homosexuality than were many left-wing socialists. A clearer divide probably existed over foreign policy, where Gaitskell and his allies were generally strong, but not uncritical, supporters of the United States, although favouring a softer line towards the Communists than did America. Gaitskell, it should be noted, was very much in the ascendancy in the parliamentary Labour party for the first few years of his leadership, with the moderate trade unionist Jim Griffiths (1890–1975) being elected to Deputy Leader of the Labour party in February 1956 with 141 votes to Nye Bevan's 111 and the hapless Herbert Morrison's 40.

Nevertheless, for Labour to have any chance of success it was necessary for Gaitskell and Bevan to work together. Unexpectedly, by the 1959 election they forged a fairly satisfactory alliance. Gaitskell emerged as an outspoken and vehement opponent of Eden's Suez policy, thus diminishing the hostility towards him of the left. At Labour's Brighton conference in October 1957 Bevan (who was now Shadow Foreign Secretary) shocked his left wing supporters by opposing the growing movement for Britain unilaterally to renounce its nuclear arsenal, pointing out (with cogency) that, without nuclear weapons, Britain 'will send a Foreign Secretary, whoever he may be, naked into the conference chamber', unable to make deals with Russia; Bevan, moreover, condemned any passage of anti-nuclear resolutions by Labour as 'an emotional spasm'. Bevan greatly unified the Labour party, but alienated his core supporters, arguably making them, over the next few years, more extreme. In view of this new-found unity, it is somewhat surprising that Labour did so poorly at the 1959 General Election. Soon afterward, Bevan briefly became Deputy Leader of Labour, but died of cancer in July 1960, removing from the scene the British Left's most constructive, articulate, but also infuriating leader.

In Bevan's place the parliamentary Labour party chose as its Deputy Leader George Brown (1915–85; later baron George-Brown), a colourful right-winger, the son of a London van driver who had been a district organiser for the Transport Workers Union and an MP since 1945. Brown was best-known, perhaps, for a public slanging match he had in London with Nikita Khrushchev, the Soviet leader, in 1956. As an articulate right-wing trade unionist in the Ernest Bevin mould, Brown enjoyed considerable support in the party, beating off Frederick Lee (1906–84) and future Prime Minister James Callaghan for the Deputy's position after two ballots. Gaitskell and the right-wing of the party appeared to be riding high. Nevertheless, over the remaining three years of his life, Gaitskell continued to become involved in a remarkable number of bitter internal controversies within the Labour party. After the 1959 election, Gaitskell became convinced that the Labour party would remain unpopular so long as it was seen as formally wedded to doctrinaire socialism rather than to reformist Keynesianism; in particular he was convinced that Labour needed to abrogate the famous 'Clause Four' of its constitution, officially committing it to organise the economy by 'the common ownership of the means of production', that is, nationalisation. At Labour's Blackpool conference in November 1959, Gaitskell delivered a long attack on Clause Four. This produced fierce opposition, especially from the party's National Executive Committee, while Clause Four remained formally in place until the 1990s. Although everyone knew that no future Labour government would nationalise (at most) no more than a few other basic industries, it was widely considered impolitic and pointless to change Labour's sacred text, and generally concluded that Gaitskell, however honest, had made a great tactical mistake, alienating his core supporters.

Soon afterwards, an even more bitter row brewed up. From the mid-1950s a major new movement of the left had emerged, whose aim was to have Britain give up its nuclear weapons and to forbid the Americans to store nuclear weapons on British soil. The 'Ban the Bomb' movement, as it became known, received wide publicity from the Aldermaston marches, held annually from 1958 by the Campaign for Nuclear Disarmament (CND), organised that year when Britain tested its first H-bomb in the Pacific. The marches, from the site of Britain's main atomic research establishment in Berkshire to central London, attracted thousands of protesters among a coalition ranging from Christian pacifists to overt fellow-travellers. Many were convinced that an all-destructive nuclear holocaust was only a matter of time. The CND touched a familiar chord in traditional Labour (or, perhaps more accurately, liberal and radical) thought, although since the late 1930s the mainstream of the party had been wedded to the implementation of a credible British military force to deter aggression and were emphatically not pacifists, even if they were also not (usually) trigger-happy xenophobes. Almost overnight, however, the 'Ban the Bomb' movement became enormously strong in many sections of the Labour party, especially in constituency committees and among some trade unions. From the mid-1950s many trade unions came increasingly to be dominated by left-wingers, in a way which had seldom been the case in decades. Probably the best-known of these new radical trade union leaders was Frank Cousins, General Secretary of the Transport and General Workers Union from 1956 to 1969, who was a strong advocate of unilateral nuclear disarmament. The drive for unilateral nuclear disarmament – the Britain should renounce its nuclear weapons without waiting for a deal with the Soviet Union – became the aim of the 'ban the bombers', and was countered by moderates with multilateral nuclear disarmament, giving up these weapons by agreement. For Labour, things came to a head at the October 1960 Labour conference at Scarborough, where the unilateralists were expected to win a considerable victory, abetted by Bevan's demise. Here (just before the vote), Gaitskell gave one of his most famous and moving speeches, declaring that 'there are some of us...who will fight and fight and fight again to save the party we love.' The unilateralists won, but by much less than expected. Gaitskell's moderate supporters then itself organised a fairly effective group of moderate Labourites, the Campaign for Democratic Socialism, to gain control of the party.

Gaitskell's last big fight within the party took place in October 1962, and also centred around a Labour party conference, at Brighton. This time the issue was different, and Gaitskell took a stand which alienated many of his own supporters. Labour had evolved no strong views on entry into the Common Market. By and large (with many exceptions), moderates and pro-Gaitskellites favoured joining, while leftists opposed it, viewing the EEC as a 'bosses club' and fearing the growing influence of West Germany. Gaitskell might thus have been expected to favour British entry, which was being actively sought by the Tory government. To the astonishment of many, however, at Brighton Gaitskell firmly opposed British membership in Europe, arguing, in another famous speech, that entry 'does mean...the end of Britain as an independent European state...it means the end of a thousand years of history.' This speech won Gaitskell renewed popularity on the Labour Left (and perhaps on the Tory Right as well).

Gaitskell thus seemed fairly well-placed to lead Labour into the next election; his position would have been improved still further by the Profumo scandal and the other events of 1963–64. It was not to be. In December 1962 he became suddenly and critically ill, and died at the age of only 56 in January 1963. Gaitskell died under obscure circumstances, of a little-known disease called lupus erythematosus, which affects the immune system. Gaitskell's sudden death produced, over time, the usual raft of conspiracy theories, especially that he was poisoned by tea at the Soviet embassy, where he had applied for a visa. (Unfortunately for this theory, Gaitskell began to show the first symptoms of the disease before going to the embassy.)

The main beneficiary of Gaitskell's death was Harold Wilson, who succeeded Gaitskell as Labour's leader. Piqued by Gaitskell's style, Wilson had challenged him for the leadership in November 1960, losing by 148 votes to 81. Wilson was backed by most left-wing Labourites. At the time, Wilson had a reputation as a leftist, gained in 1951 when he resigned with Bevan from Attlee's government. He also had an even more widely-shared reputation for deviousness and opportunism. Wilson was the product of the Northern Nonconformist lower middle class; his father was a works chemist in Huddersfield. Wilson was unquestionably very clever, winning a scholarship to Oxford, where he gained a first and won many prizes. Although he took little part in politics at Oxford he had always been politically ambitious (he was photographed by his father at the age of seven outside Number 10). During the war he worked as a civil servant specialising in economics, and was elected to Parliament in the 1945 intake. Noticed and liked, he received rapid promotion and became a Cabinet minister at only 31. During the 1950s, his seeming Bevanism made him popular with the left, but he also worked as a consultant for a firm of international timber merchants. Gaitskell disliked Wilson as a bore and a Nonconformist puritan who was also exceptionally untrustworthy and ambitious, but valued his unquestioned economic expertise; during most of Gaitskell's leadership he was Shadow Chancellor, and then Shadow Foreign Secretary. Of all the men who have led a major party in modern Britain, Harold Wilson might well be the most difficult to characterise or summarise, and his ultimate political beliefs remain highly ambiguous.

George Brown, Labour's Deputy Leader, was widely expected to succeed Gaitskell, but his instability, fondness for alcohol, and lack of *gravitas* offended many. A third candidate from the party's centre, James Callaghan, was also nominated; it would seem Wilson's supporters convinced him to do so in order to take votes from Brown. Wilson was elected leader of the Labour party in February 1963 on the second ballot, receiving 115 votes to Brown's 88 and Callaghan's 41 on the first ballot, and then defeating Brown by 144 votes to 103. Brown remained Deputy Leader. The left naturally was exuberant while the Gaitskellite wing, hitherto in the majority, were shocked. Characteristically, Wilson took pains to emphasise that he stood in the centre of the Labour party and that his views were not dramatically different from Gaitskell's. Labour had enjoyed a considerable lead in the opinion polls since the end of 1961, and continued to do so throughout 1963, as the Profumo scandal and Home's elevation to the leadership dominated the Tory government.

These were also years when the Liberal party made a significant comeback, a trend associated in particular with Jo [Joseph] Grimond (1913–93), its leader from 1956 until 1967. Making good use of television, Grimond reoriented the Liberal party as a radical but non-socialist and anti-trade union alternative to the Tories; this had wide appeal for many, especially younger middle-class voters. Given up for dead in the 1950s, the Liberals rose consistently in opinion polls, receiving the support of as much as 25 per cent of those polled in mid-1962. The accession of Harold Wilson to the leadership of Labour resulted in a sharp decline in Liberal opinion poll support until the 1970s, although their votes at general and by-elections rose. The 1960s also saw much greater support for the Scottish National Party and for Plaid Cymru, the Welsh Nationalists, although a dramatic upturn in their fortunes did not occur until the later 1960s.

Sir Alec Douglas-Home as Prime Minister, 1963–64

Sir Alec Douglas-Home was Prime Minister for two days less than a year, from October 1963 until October 1964. When he accepted the Queen's commission to form a government, he was still, technically, an earl, and did not become a commoner again for a few days, the first peer since Lord Salisbury in 1902 to hold the premiership. More seriously, until elected to the Commons at a by-election, he was without a seat in either House of Parliament, the only Prime Minister in modern history to be in so unlikely a position. Douglas-Home's immediate need, therefore, was to find a seat in the Commons. Fortunately for him, a by-election was pending in the Scottish seat of Kinross and West Perthshire. In the full glare of publicity, Douglas-Home campaigned hard, making 48 speeches in a fortnight. Had he lost, his political career would probably have been over and the Tories would have been a laughing-stock, but he won with a reasonably good majority. He was then formally elected leader of the Conservative party. Labour and much of the press had a field-day in ridiculing the new Prime Minister. Harold Wilson lambasted the choice: 'after half a century of democratic advance, the whole process has ground to a halt with a fourteenth earl'. To this, Douglas-Home made one of the best rejoinders of modern politics: 'when you come to think of it, he is the fourteenth Mr. Wilson'. Although Douglas-Home obviously suffered from his background and the manner in which he was chosen, he also had many advantages as a leader. He was transparently honest and honourable, in contrast to the notoriously devious Harold Wilson. He had common sense, a quality prized by many above Wilson's cleverness. He enjoyed warm support from the Conservative's local associations and party members, certainly far more than many of the other candidates. At a time when the Cold War was still all-important, he had a notable record as Foreign Secretary. Much of Britain still loved a lord, so long as he was not impossibly supercilious or a half-wit and, despite the press's attempts to portray him as both, Douglas-Home was neither. Cartoonists depicted him with a hunting cap and half-spectacles, but it became increasingly difficult to make fun of him. On the other hand, Douglas-Home also had his share of deficiencies. His only experience in a domestic or spending portfolio was as a junior minister at the Scottish Office from 1951 until 1955; all the rest of his ministerial experience was in foreign affairs. While his Foreign Office experience was important, a few years at a major spending ministry would have been more valuable. He had not sat in the Commons since 1951, when he succeeded to the earldom, and his likely performance against the clever, relentless Harold Wilson remained untested; many feared the worst. The choice of Douglas-Home also contrasted with Macmillan's post-1962 aim of bringing in younger, self-made 'modernisers'.

Although Douglas-Home has often been harshly judged by some historians, this is unfair: he did a reasonably good, even very good, job in restoring the very dented fortunes of the Conservative party in a short time. Although at first he was bested by Harold Wilson in Commons exchanges, by the middle of 1964 he had greatly improved. So, too, did the standing of the Tories in public opinion surveys, although Labour retained a narrow lead in the monthly Gallup poll of voting intentions until the 1964 General Election. By his honesty and common sense, he overcame much of the odium of the Profumo scandal. There is general agreement, however, that Douglas-Home made one serious political mistake during his premiership, pushing through, in March 1964, the Resale Prices Bill. This act abolished resale price maintenance, the legal requirement that supermarket chains and other large shops not undercut the prices charged by small shops and traders. In theory, resale price maintenance was economically unjustifiable, creating artificially high prices by law and restricting competition. Nevertheless, most small shopkeepers regarded it as the only realistic way to compete against the large chain stores, and were dismayed by the Tories' policies. Small shopkeepers were part of the backbone of the Tories' supporters, almost their archetypal supporters. Despite intense opposition, Douglas-Home plowed on with the Resale Prices Bill. The Bill's second reading, in March 1964, saw 20 Tories vote in opposition and 20 more abstain. It won a vote excluding medicines from the scope of the Bill by only one vote. The government proceeded with the Bill in hopes that it would quickly produce lower prices for the consumer. Most observers now believe that the Bill's passage, just before an election which the government was expected to lose, alienated many of its natural supporters and was crucial to the Tories' defeat.

The economy continued to demonstrate the same paradox of greater affluence for most people side-by-side with an intractable balance-of-trade problem and a shrinking world role for British manufacturing and exports. In early 1962 serious strikes occurred in the engineering and shipbuilding industries, and a new spectre of rising unemployment appeared, with unemployment rising to 878 000 in early 1963, its highest level (except briefly in 1947) since before the war. Reginald Maudling, the Chancellor of the Exchequer, had to deal with yet another severe balance-of-trade crisis, the most serious in many years. The Tories were intent on creating a boom before the next election; this produced the normal response of rising imports, higher inflation, and significant wage demands.

There was, nevertheless, no reason to fault Douglas-Home during his year as Prime Minister: the government performed reasonably, if not spectacularly, well. Harold Wilson expected to lose the election, which was called for 15 October 1964, actually one week more than the legal maximum five-year interval since the previous General Election. In the end, Labour won, but very narrowly indeed. Many observers noted that the voters simply wanted a change after the 13 years of Tory rule. Labour's catchcry, 'thirteen wasted years', proved attractive, but not all that attractive.

	Total votes	MPs elected	% share of total vote
Conservative	12 001 396	304	43.4
Liberal	3 092 878	9	11.2
Labour	12 205 814	317	44.1
Communist	45 932	0	0.2
Plaid Cymru	69 507	0	0.3
Scottish Nationalists	64 044	0	0.2
Others	168 422	0	0.6
Total	27 655 374	630	100.0

Labour had a majority of only four seats over all other parties. It received only 204 000 more votes than did the Conservatives, and its share of the total vote, 44.1 per cent, was the lowest of any party with an overall majority in the Commons since 1922, when there were three major parties (indeed, four, since the Liberals were split). Labour actually polled 10 000 fewer votes overall than it had in 1959. Nevertheless, the Tories lost more heavily still, polling over 1.7 million fewer votes than in the previous elections. The Liberals were the chief gainers, doubling their votes but increasing their seats from six to only nine.

In so close an election, there were, for the Tories, an unusual number of 'what ifs?'. Would Butler have done better than Douglas-Home? Many thought so. Suppose Macmillan had remained healthy? Perhaps the most vexatious aspect of the Conservative's loss was that had the election been held 24 hours later, they would probably have won: on 15 October 1964 Khrushchev was unexpectedly deposed as Soviet leader, while on the same day Communist China exploded its first atomic bomb. Many believe that public fears for the future about these events would have produced more than enough votes for the Tories to have won. In any case, Labour was now in power after 13 years, but with such a narrow majority that another election was certain in the near future.

12
Reversing British Decline? Wilson, Heath, and Callaghan, 1964–79

Between 1964 and 1979 Britain had three Prime Ministers. Two were Labourites, Harold Wilson (1964–70; 1974–76) and James Callaghan (1976–79), while Edward Heath (1970–74) was a Conservative. Although Heath and the two Labourites were bitter political opponents, in many respects this 15-year period is best viewed as a consistent whole. All the governments of the period attempted, first and foremost, to reverse Britain's increasingly evident economic decline in what were, broadly, the same ways. This is not to say that their approaches were identical: the Heath government was, almost by definition, more hostile to the trade unions than were the governments of Wilson and Callaghan, but, basically, these administrations were recognisably similar in their presuppositions and formulae for improvement. These governments also existed at a time of rapid and, to many, disturbing social change, and against an often turbulent international background.

The Wilson government, 1964–70

Harold Wilson formed a Cabinet of 23. Since Labour had been out of power for so long, only three of these (Wilson himself, Lord Longford, and Jim Griffiths) had served as Cabinet ministers under Attlee, although ten others had held junior appointments in the Attlee government. Most of the Cabinet came from the centre and centre-right of the Labour party, with a predominance of moderates. Apart from the very arguable case of Wilson himself, it contained only four obvious leftists, Barbara Castle (Minister of Overseas Development), the Cabinet's only woman, Richard Crossman (Minister of Housing and Local Government), Anthony Greenwood (1911–82; Secretary for the Colonies), and Frank Cousins (Minister of Technology), brought in from the trade union movement. The other well-known Bevanites, such as Michael Foot and Ian Mikardo, were excluded, although Bevan's widow Jennie Lee (1904–88) was given the newly formed junior position of Minister for the Arts. The major positions were all held by moderates or right-wingers: Patrick Gordon Walker (1907–80) was given the Foreign Office; Attlee's former Attorney-General

Sir Frank Soskice (1902–79) the Home Office; and, most importantly, James Callaghan was made Chancellor of the Exchequer and George Brown appointed to the newly formed, highly anomalous post of First Secretary of State and Secretary of State for Economic Affairs. Sociologically, it was fairly representative of the Labour party as a whole, a mixture of the upper-middle-class public school and university-educated (11 had attended Oxford or Cambridge, compared with only five in Attlee's original Cabinet) and working-class trade unionists, now in a distinct minority (only eight members of the Cabinet sprang from the working classes). Unlike a Tory Cabinet, however, it contained no businessmen and only Lord Longford (Frank Pakenham, 1905–2001, seventh earl of Longford), the Lord Privy Seal, to remind anyone of the former governing classes drawn from the old aristocracy. One of Wilson's appointments immediately became a source of considerable trouble. Patrick Gordon Walker, the Foreign Minister, had actually been narrowly defeated at Smethwick at the General Election. The seat, in Birmingham, had a large influx of coloured immigrants and it was said that the Conservative winner, Peter Griffiths, had exploited the issue in his campaign. In the House of Commons a few weeks after the election, Wilson referred to Griffiths as a man who 'will serve his time here as a Parliamentary leper'. This foolish remark did Labour little good, for Gordon Walker proceeded, in January 1965, to lose a safe Labour seat (Leyton) to the Tories by a narrow majority. Britain's Foreign Secretary (who had held office without a seat) thus proved to be unelectable, and he was replaced at the Foreign Office by Michael Stewart (1906–90). Gordon Walker eventually found a seat and returned to the Cabinet in a lesser position two years later.

The major innovation in Wilson's Cabinet was its division of the major responsibility for economic management in two, with Callaghan at the Exchequer and Brown at the Department of Economic Affairs. George Brown had to be given a senior position, and this was one way of satisfying his restless energy while guarding against his notorious volatility. (In November 1963, Brown had been invited to the BBC to comment on the assassination of President Kennedy. Showing up the worse for drink, he managed to get into a fist fight with Eli Wallach, the American actor who, near tears, also appeared on the show.) Apart from giving an important but novel post to his arch-rival Brown, Wilson apparently divided responsibility for economics in order to devise a more innovative centre of policy formation than the famously conservative Treasury, giving Brown responsibility for taking a long-term view via what he termed 'creative tension' with the Treasury. The experiment was a failure, as anyone could foresee, and has never been repeated. The Treasury, with its authority, expertise, and continuing responsibility for day-to-day financial management and for the Budget, was self-evidently going to remain central to economic policy, and would win any contest with an upstart rival. Brown's Department of Economic Affairs was largely taken up with producing a National Plan for economic growth, after engaging in wide consultation with individual industries, the unions, and experts. This Plan provided a blueprint for four per cent growth per annum over the next five years, in large part by increasing exports. Brown might just as well have waved a magic wand and commanded the British economy to grow. The government of a largely capitalist economy in peacetime cannot 'plan'. Stalin could plan because he could shoot all opponents; Britain could plan in wartime because opposition is treason. No plan in the world, in Britain in the 1960s, could foresee such key variables as changes in interest rates, import and energy costs, or international crises a few years ahead, and nor can it accurately foresee consumer trends. No Labour 'plan' is likely to diminish the power of the trade unions or deliberately create high levels of unemployment in the interests of efficiency. Most importantly of all, whenever a short-term economic crisis occurred, dealing with it would automatically take precedence over long-term planning. The National Plan arugably came up with some useful ideas for increasing exports, but that is all. George Brown naturally became ever more fed up and embittered with Harold Wilson and British politics; this may well have been Wilson's intention.

While Wilson might have hoped to curb the powers of the Treasury and marginalise George Brown, the National Plan was also quite consistent with the Prime Minister's frequently-voiced rhetoric. In October 1963 he told the Labour conference at Scarborough that the 'white heat' of 'the scientific revolution' would not merely be among the central concerns of his government, but nothing less than the way in which 'we are redefining and … restating our socialism'. The appeal to science and technology struck powerful chords in the Labour party and beyond it. It seemed modern and progressive, in line with the leading trends in both America and the Soviet Union whose space successes caused universal amazement. It appealed to the strong puritan streak in the Labour party (and in Wilson himself) and to the central importance of education, and provided a contrast with the hedonism and amateurism of the Tories' 'thirteen wasted years'. It seemed as well to provide Britain with the only credible way out of its economic malaise. Yet, as either a strategic or tactical political weapon, it was also fraught with many dangers. Talk about the 'white heat' of a 'scientific revolution' raised expectations which proved impossible to fulfil. These unrealistic expectations were further increased by Wilson's appeals (echoing President Kennedy in America) about the crucial importance of 'the first hundred days' of his government (little actually happened) and his constant, absurdly inappropriate, appeals to the 'Dunkirk spirit' in sub-Churchillian rhetoric. With his inflated rhetoric on this and on many other issues, Wilson made his government a hostage to fortune and, indeed, Labour's 1964–70 government was probably the first to debase politics with hyperbolic, meaningless rhetorical promises which, advanced with ever-greater unreality by all parties thereafter, eventually threatened to undermine the political process through sheer cynicism. Nor was Wilson's appeal a particularly accurate description of either the cure for Britain's economic ailments or of science itself. For centuries, British prosperity depended in large measure on the 'gentlemanly capitalism' (as it has come to be known) of the City of London, headed by precisely the effete, antiquated social stratum which Labour attacked. (Ironically, in office the Labour government defended the City and its interests as vigorously as any other government; many argued this came at the cost of its own programmes.) In America and Russia, most spending on 'science' was actually for the military, closely followed, in the West, by the development of new consumer products (such as washing powder) in giant corporations, while pure scientific research, such as that carried out at major universities, often had no practical benefits whatever and no influence on economic growth.

The Wilson government's record in economic affairs proved, indeed, to be extremely disappointing. It provided the same dreary pattern of temporary prosperity, followed by a crisis and then by strong measures to control or diminish economic demand, as did most of its predecessors, but ratcheted up many notches in frequency and seriousness. Each crisis proved worse than the previous one, and its troubles multiplied with increased trade union militancy, the general anti-Establishment feeling of the 1960s, and the prospect (realised late in 1967) of devaluation. Government counter-measures proved generally effective in the short term but were inevitably succeeded by yet another crisis. While economic growth continued, it was nothing like the steady 4 per cent a year promised by the National Plan. When Labour entered office in October 1964 it found that Tory expenditure (largely to produce a pre-election spending boom) had produced a balance-of-payments deficit of £800 million, the largest in history. Labour responded by imposing a 15 per cent surcharge on nearly all imports and announced its intention to discuss with the TUC the initiation of an incomes policy, aimed at restricting the amount sought by unions in wage negotiations to non-inflationary levels. For the next 15 years pursuit of a viable incomes policy, agreed with the TUC, became the holy grail of all governments. The government also took the decision not to devalue sterling from its agreed rate of £1.00 = $2.80, which many believed was too high. There were several reasons why Labour did not devalue from its first days, a decision widely criticised ever since. Labour's previous devaluation, in 1949, caused turmoil, reduced confidence in Britain's economy, and made it seem to many as if devaluation (taken as a sign of Britain's declining economy) was an automatic accompaniment to any Labour government. Labour remained constantly in fear of currency speculation against sterling, speculation carried out by 'the gnomes of Zurich' (a phrase coined, rather remarkably, by Harold Wilson in 1956; Wilson, if nothing else, was one of the greatest coiners of familiar phrases of any British politician), speculation which might ruin Britain's export plans in an afternoon. Many nations, especially the old Commonwealth, still held sterling balances, and perceptions of Britain's financial strength depended, it was argued, on maintaining sterling at a high exchange rate. Devaluing the pound made exports cheaper, but also made imports dearer. For the next three years, devaluation remained Labour's primary economic taboo and avoiding it its main desideratum. Ironically, despite the 'white heat' rhetoric, the importance of the City remained paramount.

Chancellor James Callaghan, by nature more conservative and orthodox than either Wilson or Brown, also announced a package of deflationary measures in his first Budget, including a 2.5 per cent rise in income tax. A rise in the bank rate followed. The package did its job in the short term, stabilising the economy. In his second Budget (April 1965) Callaghan also made important changes in taxation policy, initiating a Capital Gains Tax and a separate Corporation Tax for the first time. Progress was also made with the TUC at the same time on an agreed incomes policy. These strong measures paid some dividends, and it appeared to many as if Labour had stabilised the economy.

Because of the extraordinarily fragile political situation, a General Election was certain to take place soon, and Wilson decided to call it for March 1966. At the time of the dissolution of Parliament, Labour had a majority of only one MP over the combined total of the Tories and the Liberals, and could easily lose even important Commons votes. The position of Sir Alec Douglas-Home as leader had also become progressively weaker, although the Tories did surprisingly well in local elections. Many Conservatives feared, however, that Douglas-Home would lose badly to Wilson at any General Election, despite the fact that opinion surveys showed them to be ahead of Labour. Home himself was psychologically dejected and, for no really obvious reason, decided in July 1965 to resign as leader of the Conservative party. Three candidates contested for his place, which was (for the first time) to be decided by a vote of Conservative MPs rather than a leader 'emerging' rather mysteriously as in the past. By all odds, Reginald Maudling should have won, a fairly successful former Chancellor of the Exchequer. But he didn't, and nor did the third contender, the then little-known intellectual right-winger Enoch Powell. Instead, the new leader of the Conservative party was Edward Heath (b.1916; later Sir Edward Heath), who received 150 votes to Maudling's 133 and Powell's 15. Heath's supporters fought a more professional and better-organised campaign. As a young (only 49) articulate grammar school and Oxford product who rose by his own merits (his father was a small independent builder), who had been an army major in the war, Heath was seen as a match for Wilson and evidence that the Tories had discarded their privileged image. Yet surprisingly little was known of Heath, beyond the fact that he was a strong supporter of entry into Europe and a favourite of Macmillan's. From 1951–59 Heath had been a government whip (and Chief Whip in 1955–59); by convention whips do not speak in parliamentary debates. Most of his time thereafter until 1964 was spent heading the Common Market negotiations. It was known that as President of the Board of Trade he strongly favoured the repeal of Resale Price Maintenance. Heath was a loner, a bachelor with few close friends who lived in Albany, one of the most exclusive addresses in London; his hobbies were classical music and yachting. The choice of Heath was seen to be an experiment. The right-wing and traditionalist elements in the party were very guarded about him, and he was seen by many as an inscrutable, humourless, rather mysterious character who utterly lacked the human touch, although an excellent debater. Over the next few months he relentlessly attacked Wilson in Parliament, appointing 'classless' centre-left Tories to the Shadow frontbench and purging many traditionalist Conservatives, with the notable exception of Sir Alec Douglas-Home, who became Shadow Foreign Secretary. It soon became clear that Heath was not popular with the voters, and Labour took a strong lead in opinion polls.

With signs of stability and growth in the economy, Wilson gambled that Labour's apparent reasonable success would be rewarded by the electorate, which was unfamiliar with Heath and didn't like what they saw. He was right; Labour ran an effective campaign, and easily won the election held in March 1966.

	Total votes	MPs elected	% share of total vote
Conservative	11 418 433	253	41.9
Liberal	2 327 533	12	8.5
Labour	13 064 951	363	47.9
Communist	62 112	0	0.1
Plaid Cymru	61 071	0	0.2
Scottish Nationals	128 474	0	0.5
Others	201 302	2	0.6
Total	27 263 606	630	100.0

Labour won a majority of 98 over all other parties, very similar to the 1959 outcome but in reverse. The total number of voters had declined, and was actually more than a million below the turnout in 1950 and 1951. Labour's share of the total vote was almost precisely the same as it had been in 1945, although the Tories' was higher. Labour was dominant in Scotland, Wales, London, and the north of England, and won a big majority in the Midlands. Only in the heartland of the south of England outside London did the Tories hold on, winning 134 seats to Labour's 67. The 1966 General Election would be Labour's high-water mark for 31 years. Labour's large majority was something of a mixed blessing, creating a substantial backbench, many of whom would never hold office and had few qualms about making trouble for the government. Many belonged to the 'new left', concerned with issues such as Vietnam, and were almost uncontrollable by the whips.

Over the next two or three years the Labour government experienced a decline in popularity and effectiveness arguably without parallel in modern British political history, and far more extreme than that suffered by the Tories after Profumo. Possibly the only parallel to this situation in the twentieth century (until the 1990s) occurred to Arthur Balfour's Tory government in 1903–05, when Joseph Chamberlain's proposals for tariff reform split the party. The central cause of the situation was, as usual, economic. In 1966 Chancellor Callaghan enacted, as a substitute for another rise in income tax, the Selective Employment Tax (SET), the brainchild of Nicholas Kaldor (1908–86; later baron Kaldor), one of two influential Hungarian-born advisers to Labour (Thomas Balogh, 1905–85, later baron Balogh, was the other). Kaldor's proposal was to tax employment in the service sector more heavily than that in manufacturing. This was a truly bizarre suggestion. Throughout modern history, there has inevitably been a drift of the work force from the primary (farming) to the secondary (manufacturing) to the tertiary (services) sectors. This tax proposed to reverse the order of nature. The problem with the British manufacturing industry was that it was overmanned and was not, in international terms, sufficiently productive on a *per capita* basis. A selective tax *on* manufacturing employment was thus sensible, not the opposite. The tax was also highly arbitrary: workers on a Ford assembly line were taxed more lightly, the men who brought parts to the factory in lorries (a service trade) were taxed more heavily. Even by the normal standards of the Wilson government, this tax was especially foolish. After a brief respite, yet another sterling crisis hit Britain in July 1966, forcing a rise in the Bank rate to 7 per cent, tax increases, and a prices and incomes 'stand still'. The government enacted a Prices and Incomes Bill in August 1966, just after the resignation from the Cabinet of left-wing trade union figure Frank Cousins. The government also endured a crippling seamen's strike, led by extremist trade unionists (and invoked a State of Emergency as a result). This led to a further run on the pound, which in turn made the government seek yet more American and international loans. In mid-1967 came the Six Day War between Israel and the Arabs, temporarily shutting off oil supplies. Another wildcat Dockers' strike ensued – and so on. It became obvious that major action was called for, and in November 1967 Britain devalued the pound, reducing the exchange rate from £1 = $2.80 to £1 = $2.40. This was not a drastic change, and the heavens did not fall in, but neither was there any immediate benefit, and devaluation was imposed at the same time as yet another package of spending cuts which fell, in particular, on defence. But Wilson greatly weakened his case in the broadcast speech he made on devaluation, remarkably telling the public that 'the pound in your pocket' had not been devalued. The phrase stuck, and was repeatedly used against the government. More strikes followed, in engineering and car plants. In 1968–69, the government then attempted to introduce legislation to curb strikes, producing (under the aegis of left-winger Barbara Castle) a White Paper, *In Place of Strife*. This proposed giving the government powers to call a 28-day 'conciliation pause' before a strike occurred, the establishment of an Industrial Board to impose fines on unruly unions, and other like measures. These proposals were extremely moderate, but they split the Cabinet and led to opposition from the TUC. A major revolt by backbench MPs ensued, with 55 Labour MPs voting against a motion approving the White Paper in March 1969, and another 40 abstaining. In June 1969, the government was forced to withdraw the bill altogether, in return for a 'solemn and binding undertaking' by the TUC to intervene in unofficial disputes (which had caused most of the trouble).

In the first few years of the Wilson government, foreign policy played a surprisingly large role in shaping attitudes to the government. Rhodesia, in southern Africa, had enjoyed internal self-government under a white settler government. As black African states gained their independence, the position of the Rhodesian government became increasingly untenable, and its premier, Ian Smith, threatened to declare 'UDI' – a unilateral declaration of independence – and in November 1965, actually did so. His actions were regarded as illegal by Britain and virtually all other countries. Wilson responded with the imposition of economic and oil sanctions, but was in a genuine quandary about what to do. Wilson met Ian Smith twice for extended talks, on *HMS Tiger* in December 1966 and on *HMS Fearless* in October 1967. Although in January 1966 Wilson declared that sanctions would bring down the Smith government in 'weeks rather than months', it was unable to bring Rhodesia to heel, and its white government continued to rule until 1979. Rhodesia enjoyed much support from the Tory right, but the left of the Labour party was increasingly exasperated by Wilson's stance. While Wilson had initially promised to continue a military role 'east of Suez' in a reduced way, from 1966 economic necessity forced a contraction of Britain's activities. In 1968 Britain formally announced a withdrawal of all military activities 'east of Suez' by 1971 (except in Hong Kong and similar areas) in order to concentrate solely on NATO and Europe. This reduction in Britain's role brought with it a reduction in Britain's influence: it was unable, for instance, to play a role in the disastrous Biafran conflict in Nigeria, and had ever-decreasing influence on the Cold War.

For opponents of Harold Wilson on the left, however, the great conflict of the 1960s was, paradoxically, in an area where Britain played no role whatever, Vietnam. From the early 1960s, but especially after Lyndon Johnson became President of the United States in 1963, America committed hundreds of thousands of troops and tens of billions of dollars to a poorly conceived, eventually unsuccessful, effort to prevent a Communist takeover in South Vietnam. Fighting with a conscript army at a time when the black ghettos of American cities became increasingly riotous, the American military action produced a widespread revolt among much of its youth, especially on university campuses. This youth revolt found an ever more enthusiastic echo in Britain, although Britain had no conscription and no troops in Vietnam. The Wilson government, which gave general verbal support to the United States and refused to condemn its Vietnam activities, bore the brunt of student and anti-war sentiment, chiefly from its own left-wing supporters, and also increasingly found itself suffering from the decade's general mood of youth revolt, rebelliousness, heightened radicalism, and a search for 'alternative lifestyles' symbolised by the Beatles and Mick Jagger.

Labour remained ahead of the Tories in opinion polls until early 1967, when these surveys turned drastically against the Wilson government. By December 1964 the Gallup poll of voting intentions found the Tories ahead of Labour by 49-32 and, by May 1968, by 56-28, results without precedent which, if reflected at a General Election, could have annihilated the Wilson government. Terribly poor showings in the opinion polls for Labour continued until just before the 1970 election. Labour did consistently badly in by-elections, losing 12 seats to the Tories and four to other parties between 1966 and 1970. Some of these losses were memorable. At Walthamstow West in September 1967 a Labour majority of 10 022 at the previous General Election was transformed into a Tory majority of 11 656, one of the greatest shifts in history. Labour lost Carmarthen in July 1966 to Plaid Cymru, Hamilton to the Scottish National Party in November 1967 (overturning a 16 576 majority), and Birmingham Ladywood to the Liberals in June 1969. Its results in local elections were, if anything, even worse. In 1968, only 450 Labour borough councillors remained in the whole of England and Wales, compared with 2184 Tories. In 1964 the Greater London Council election returned 82 Tories and only 18 Labourites, a previously unimaginable result. Wilson also now had extraordinary difficulties with the press. Since the early 1960s the press, with its new-found license and sarcasm, had lambasted the Tories. Increasingly, however, Wilson's cynicism, deviousness, and failure to deliver the goods was attacked in ever more vigorous terms. (One popular saying among Labour MPs about the Prime Minister at this time was that 'There are only two things I dislike about Harold Wilson: his face.') The turning point is often seen as the D-Notice affair of February

1967, a dispute which arose over the interpretation of the vetting, for security reasons, by the government's Defence, Press, and Broadcasting Committee, of incoming overseas cables before releasing them to the press. This custom existed for decades, but a major dispute suddenly erupted over the publication by a *Daily Express* columnist of material which the government argued it had warned against publishing. Although relatively trivial, the media made it, and Wilson's over-reaction to the affair, into a major dispute over press freedom. From then on, it has been noted, Wilson was increasingly treated with contempt by the press.

Wilson also had increasingly serious problems from other sources. He had long been the target of extremist and rogue elements within MI5, the security agency, which believed him, absurdly, to be a Soviet agent of influence. (Wilson did, however, have close links with shadowy businessmen who traded with the Soviet Union and he had visited Russia many times on trade missions during the 1950s.) Wilsons's personal entourage, especially his visible and powerful private secretary Marcia Williams (b.1932; later baroness Falkender), gave rise to both innuendo and speculation. His rather bizarre inner circle of advisers and confidants, a group which included the former army officer and intelligence officer MP George Wigg (1900–83), the prominent and ubiquitous solicitor Lord Goodman (Arnold Goodman, 1915–96), and a number of self-made businessmen, often immigrant Jews, such as the raincoat manufacturer Lord Kagan, strongly reminiscent of an offbeat Hollywood cult movie starring Peter Lorre, Sidney Greenstreet, and Humphrey Bogart, was tailor-made for press tittle tattle. For his part, Wilson became increasingly paranoid and frightened of covert attacks on him, routinely searching hotel bedrooms for hidden microphones. In May 1968 Cecil King, the powerful owner of the *Daily Mirror* and Lord Northcliffe's nephew, made an apparently serious effort to enlist Lord Mountbatten, Sir Solly Zuckerman (the government's scientific advisor), and Hugh Cudlipp, the paper's editor, in an attempt to stage a *coup d'état* against the Wilson government and establish a temporary dictatorship under Mountbatten. (No one there was having any part of this unconstitutional scheme.) Wilson also had an increasingly restless backbench; relations were not helped by the Prime Minister's 'dog license' speech of March 1967, when he warned Labour MPs that 'every dog is allowed one bite, but a different view is taken of a dog that goes on biting all the time. He may not get his license renewed.' By 1968–69, Wilson would almost certainly have been replaced as Prime Minister if there had been an obvious successor and an established method of challenging an incumbent leader. There was, however, no obvious challenger. George Brown, Foreign Secretary from August 1966, resigned from the government in March 1967. James Callaghan was moved to the Home Secretaryship in November 1967 and was too loyal; the other possibles, such as Tony Crosland, did not command wide support in the party. Wilson's effective policy was to have no clearcut successor, but to build up the positions of a number of contenders, each of whom jostled with his rivals, not with Wilson. From 1965 Wilson increasingly favoured Roy Jenkins (1920–2003; later baron Jenkins of Hillhead), a liberal intellectual Gaitskellite and an immensely talented and articulate historian and biographer, whose social liberalism and lack of socialist doctrine made him distrusted by the left. This 'divide and rule' policy saw Wilson through his darkest time.

Labour's record of social reform at home was wide-ranging and, to its supporters, highly impressive. The appointment of Roy Jenkins at the Home Office (December 1965–November 1967) was strongly associated with a raft of liberalising measures, many highly controversial. Labour often carried these out against public opinion. In 1965 the death penalty was suspended until 1970 by the Murder (Abolition of Death Penalty) Act, substituting a mandatory life sentence in its place. Without waiting for the five-year period to elapse, in December 1969 Parliament voted to continue the suspension indefinitely. The Criminal Justice Act 1967 allowed convictions by majority vote (10-2) in jury trials and suspended sentences. The Justices of the Peace Act 1968 abolished the age-old judicial functions of JPs. Even more as controversial was the Sexual Offences Act 1967, which legalised male homosexuality by decriminalising sexual acts in private places between consenting adults over 21. (It did not apply to Scotland or Northern Ireland.) The suspension of the death penalty was bitterly unpopular and it is inconceivable that it would have been approved at a public referendum. Logically, the Conservatives should have made this an election issue and promised to reinstate the death penalty. An imaginative right-wing Tory leader would have led a high-profile campaign on this issue. But the Conservatives never did, Edward Heath proving as much an abolitionist as any Labourite. The number of murders in England and Wales rose from 282 in 1960 to 393 in 1970, a 39 per cent increase. Another highly contentious area was abortion. Most churches, especially the Catholics, were bitterly opposed to its legalisation, although thousands were performed every year by 'back street' abortionists. The Abortion Act 1967 legalised abortion in cases where two doctors agreed that termination was justified if the physical or mental strength of the mother were threatened or if there was a substantial risk that the child would be seriously handicapped. Although drafted in fairly narrow terms, it soon became clear that the Act produced virtual abortion on demand, a situation feared by its opponents. There were only 22 000 abortions in England and Wales in 1968, but the number quickly rose to 109 000 by 1972, and kept rising, despite the ease of obtaining birth control devices. The majority of abortions were always performed on unmarried women. Labour also changed the basis of divorce law, in two important acts passed in 1964 and 1969. The latter, especially important, made the 'irredeemable breakdown of marriage' the sole grounds for divorce, sweeping away the contrived 'adulteries' and private detectives of the past. By the end of the twentieth century Britain had the highest divorce rate in Europe. A further act passed in 1970 recognised the contribution made to the joint home by women in awarding alimonial provisions. The government also abolished the censorship of plays by the Lord Chamberlain, and liberalised censorship laws.

Despite the Commonwealth Immigrants Act 1962, the number of 'New Commonwealth' immigrants into Britain did not fall during most of the 1960s, but actually rose from 56 000 in 1963 to 61 000 in 1967 before declining to 45 000 in 1969. The majority of these came from the Indian subcontinent, previously a minor source. Labour was under strong pressure from its constituents to limit further non-white immigrants, but under equal pressure from liberal groups to continue a flexible immigration policy and penalise racial discrimination. Labour passed two bills in this area, the Race Relations Acts of 1965 and 1968, which established a Race Relations Board to investigate unlawful discrimination and a Community Relations Council to work for harmonious race relations. The most celebrated event in this simmering minefield occurred in April 1968 when Enoch Powell, a member of the Shadow Cabinet, foresaw doom unless non-white immigration was halted. 'As I look ahead, I am filled with foreboding. Like the Roman, I "see the river Tiber, foaming with much blood".' (Powell had just returned from the United States, where he had seen the riotous, bitterly hostile state of race relations in America's big cities; his speech was a response to his American visit, not to any long-held ideological view.) Powell's outburst sparked demonstrations on his behalf by dockers and other ordinary workers and he received tens of thousands of congratulatory letters. A week later he was dismissed from the Shadow Cabinet (Heath and Powell never spoke again), despite the fact that Heath had committed a future Conservative government to 'drastic' curbs on immigration.

One area of increasing centrality was women's rights, virtually ignored by Attlee's government and, indeed, by all previous governments since the First World War. 'Women's liberation', or 'second wave feminism', as it became known (the 'first wave' were the suffragettes), became an increasingly visible and important movement in most Western countries from the mid-1960s on. While Labour was committed to empowering disadvantaged groups, its record on women's rights had been mediocre, and the trade unionist orientation of the party made it almost exclusively male dominated. Only a handful of women held significant roles in the 1964–70 government, with only Barbara Castle and Judith Hart (1924–91) holding cabinet rank (Hart in 1968–69) and fewer than a dozen women, notably Jennie Lee and Margaret Herbison, holding junior ministerial rank. (There were only 26 women MPs in the Parliament elected in 1966, of whom 19 were Labourites.) Only one piece of legislation directly affecting the status of women was passed by the Wilson government, the Equal Pay Act of 1970, which provided for equal pay for women carrying out comparable work and outlawed discrimination in employment; its full effect was delayed until 1975.

The government also made notable changes in education. The most contentious issue was that of comprehensive education. The 1944 system was, by the 1960s, widely opposed by most Labourites, who saw selection at 11 as unfair and utterly wasteful of talent. In 1965 the Department of Education asked all local authorities to submit plans for introducing comprehensive secondary education and ending the grammar schools. This was carried out in most, but not all, places by 1970 when its implementation was suspended by the Tories. In 1964, the government also announced plans to raise the school-leaving age to 16 by 1970; cost-cutting in 1968 caused a delay in the implementation of this measure until 1972 (the change was actually made in 1973). In the tertiary sector, Labour continued the previous government's policy of founding and funding many new universities. Probably its greatest innovation was the creation, in 1966–69, of the Open University, which offered part-time degrees, largely undertaken at home through correspondence, television, and cassettes, to anyone, without the need for previous qualification. Jennie Lee, Nye Bevan's widow, was given the job of establishing it, which she did, with Harold Wilson's backing, despite constant Treasury objections. The Open University was a great success, allowing tens of thousands to benefit from higher education denied, almost always for economic reasons, in younger life. The Open University was widely seen as the Wilson government's most constructive single act and was mentioned by most eulogists when Harold Wilson died in 1995.

These initiatives were new departures, initiating policies in areas largely left untouched by the Attlee government. There was also, however, some sops to the old left. The Wilson government carried out one piece of nationalisation in the old sense, renationalising most of the iron and steel industry in 1967. (This was not denationalised by the Tories until 1989.) It also abolished prescription charges in 1965, but proceeded to re-impose them in 1968 during a periodical financial crisis. Supplementary benefits for welfare recipients were also introduced, and pensions made easier to obtain. The re-imposition of prescription charges signalled a withdrawal from the old notion of the comprehensive Welfare State, or at least of its extension, and there are many signs of this withdrawal in other areas. In 1963, worried by continuous deficits in the publicly-owned railways, the Tory government commissioned Richard Beeching (1913–85; later baron Beeching), a leading industrialist, to investigate the railways and suggested reforms. This he did indeed do, recommending the shutting down of virtually half the system, including most rural lines (although almost none in London). The Tory government carried out most of these proposals in short order, but Labour followed suit, closing other lines, such as the direct route from Oxford to Cambridge, and re-opening very few. The 'Beeching axe' is now seen as one of the greatest acts of vandalism in recent history, condemning most of rural and small town Britain to the slower, more dangerous and uncomfortable public road traffic; Beeching was oblivious to the possibility of petrol costs rising (which they did) or to a return of passengers to a more efficient rail network. Probably the most famous tragedy to occur in Britain during the Wilson years was the Aberfan disaster of October 1966, when a giant slag heap collapsed onto the local village, killing 116 children and 28 adults. Aberfan represented the unacceptable face of nationalised industry: the National Coal Board had been warned for years of a possible disaster, and had done nothing. Over £2 million was subscribed by the public to a relief fund, little of which came to those affected. Similar tips were not cleared away for two years, and the Coal Board, under Lord Robens, did everything possible to avoid taking responsibility for its inaction.

The Wilson government also instituted a number of other very notable changes. In March 1966 it announced that decimal currency would be introduced in 1971, thus ending many centuries of the old irrational system of shillings and pence, dreaded by schoolchildren and incomprehensible to foreigners. In 1967 it appointed an Ombudsman (technically the Parliamentary Commissioner for Administration) to investigate complaints from members of the public about government bodies. In 1969 the voting age was lowered to 18; the following year the legal age of majority was also lowered from 21 to 18. Wilson created no hereditary titles, only life peerages (appointed, however, in record number) and knighthoods rather than baronetcies. An attempt to reform the House of Lords, announced by the government in 1967, was dropped in 1969 after a campaign in the Commons led by Enoch Powell and Michael Foot from the two extremes. Nothing was done to the Lords for another 30 years.

By the second half of the 1960s it was clear to most people that the Wilson government indeed marked a climacteric in modern British history, the end, perhaps, of the Victorian era, and of its final pretensions to great power status. For many the change was symbolised by the death and state funeral of Sir Winston Churchill in January 1965, only a few months after Wilson came to power. Many realised that they were burying an age as well as a man; London in the 1960s became 'swinging London', the visible face of a social revolution based on youth, sex, and rebellion.

The last year of Wilson's government, from 1969 to 1970, was marked by a distinct improvement in the economy, although at the usual cost. Roy Jenkins proved to a successful Chancellor of the Exchequer when he succeeded Callaghan in November 1967, while James Callaghan, a much more conservative figure than Jenkins, was a notably more moderate and orthodox Home Secretary than Jenkins had been, specifically rejecting 'the permissive society'. The economy picked up, helped by the government's prices and incomes policy and especially 'tight' budgets, with a surplus in the balance of payments finally materialising. Nevertheless currency trading against the pound continued, and inflation rose at an even higher level than before. For whatever reason, however, Labour's standing in the polls steadily increased, and, by May 1970, it had overtaken the Tories in the polls. The Conservative leader, Edward Heath, was consistently unpopular, and appeared unelectable. None of this surprised Wilson, who, apparently in late 1964, coined his most memorable phrase, that 'a week is a long time in politics'. Yet deep divisions remained: in May 1967 the government applied again to join the EEC, instigating perhaps the greatest line of internal division in the party's history, which would plague Labour for several decades. Yet despite the traumas of the previous few years, the government was reasonably confident of victory when it called a General Election for June 1970. Initially the campaign all appeared to be going well for Labour. A few days before the election, the trade figures for May showed an unexpected deficit of £31 million, the first for some time. Late polls picked up an unexpected swing to the Tories. The election produced the most surprising outcome since 1945, a swing of nearly 5 per cent to the Conservatives. The Tories won 67 seats more than in 1966, one of the largest swings since the war, while Labour elected 76 fewer MPs than in 1966, or 59 fewer seats than it held, after by-election losses, on election day. The results were rather mysterious, and there was no clear verdict among experts as to why the outcome occurred. While the Powellite race factor won seats for the Tories, it also produced a backlash among non-white and Irish voters. The Conservatives emerged with a majority of 30 seats.

	Total votes	MPs elected	% share of total vote
Conservative	13 145 123	330	46.4
Liberal	2 117 035	6	7.5
Labour	12 179 341	287	43.0
Communist	37 970	0	0.1
Plaid Cymru	175 016	0	0.6
Scottish Nationals	306 802	1	1.1
Others	383 511	6	1.4
Total	28 344 798	630	100.0

Turnout, at 72.0 per cent, was the lowest since 1935. The Tories were, as usual, dominant in the south of England outside London (169-34), and strong in the Midlands (51-45), probably because of Powell, but were behind Labour everywhere else outside Northern Ireland. Some Labour voters drained to the nationalist parties, while the Tory share (46.4 per cent) was less than it had been in previous post-war periods. Nevertheless, Harold Wilson was out of office and Edward Heath was in. The Wilson government of 1964–70 is among the most difficult of the twentieth century to judge. Its record of social reform was, for those who agreed with it, extremely impressive. Its economic record was poor, and was made worse by Wilson's own hyperbolic rhetoric, while the overall record of the government was diminished by the intrigues and failures of the 1966–69 period. For decades, few people could think of Harold Wilson without smirking, and he appeared to many to be a clever mountebank who could not be taken seriously as a major figure. Paradoxically, this image conceals a solid record of achievement in many areas, but was also evidence that 'modernisation' did not provide a panacea cure for Britain's deep-seated economic ailments, a lesson his successors were to learn as well.

The Heath government, 1970–74

Edward Heath entered office with very high hopes. In opposition, the Tories had done extensive research and preparation on its policies after taking office, and appeared to have re-invented itself, under Heath's leadership, as a modern, technocratic party of self-made younger men (and a few women) championing a dynamic capitalism, with the grouse moor, old Etonian image now confined to backbenchers. Nevertheless, although this new image seemed stark enough, it concealed deep ambiguities about what, over all, the Heath government's policies were likely to be. It was widely believed that Heath would pursue a policy of neo-laissez faire liberalism, rolling back the participation of government in the economy and definitively taming the trading unions, together with a renewed emphasis on law and order. In January 1970 the Shadow Cabinet held a policy meeting at Selsdon Park, a hotel in Croydon, where it attracted wide publicity in press reports that its priorities in office would be tax cuts, trade union reforms, higher pensions for those over 80, law and order and immigration control. Harold Wilson quickly seized on the Tories' policies, claiming that

'Selsdon Man is designing a system of society for the ruthless, and the pushing, the uncaring... His message to the rest is, you're out on your own.' 'Selsdon Man', and the manifesto it adopted for the 1970 election – *A Better Tomorrow* – clearly gave the impression, through intense free-market rhetoric, that its election would mark a decisive break with the Welfare State consensus. Like Wilson before him, Heath himself also created a number of other hostages to fortune in his rhetoric before the election. In May 1970 he promised that Britain would not join the EEC without 'the full-hearted consent of Parliament and [the] people', while the following month (in a press release) he promised to 'break the price/wage spiral...' by reducing certain taxes. 'This would, at a stroke, reduce the rise in prices, increase productivity, and reduce unemployment.' 'At a stroke', with its implication that prices would quickly fall (rather than rise more slowly) eventually became a catchcry used against the Tory leader.

There was, however, also another Edward Heath, whose policies and intentions were quite different. Far from being a laissez-faire anti-statist, this Edward Heath was a near-collectivist, emphatically a 'One Nation' Tory for whom the state played a primary role in moulding the economy and advancing the welfare of the people. To this Edward Heath, there might well be tax cuts and a trimming of 'socialist' programmes, but only if the central role of the state, especially in bringing about economic growth and keeping unemployment low, remained fully intact. Above all, this Edward Heath was whole-heartedly committed to Britain's entry into the EEC, which he envisaged as a super-collective economic entity, a replacement for the Empire, and a potential great power to rival America and Russia. Heath's commitment to the European venture probably exceeded that of any other mainstream British politician. The dichotomy between the two Edward Heaths continued across the range of issues. He was fiercely anti-Communist, but also the post-war Prime Minister most hostile to the United States; he drastically cut non-European immigration, but was a liberal on race; he was seen by many Protestants in Ulster as ready to sell them out, but was also the architect of Northern Ireland internment; trade unionists perceived him as an arch-opponent, but the Heath government regularly gave into trade union pressure, in part because it was not, at its heart, bitterly hostile to unions. This list could be multiplied many times. Of all the post-war Prime Ministers, Edward Heath was probably the most complex; he was, in fact, a bundle of contradictions, and this accounted in large measure for the failings of his government. As well, Heath's own personality contributed to the government's failings. He was utterly self-centred and oblivious to the feelings of others to an extent which many found repellent and abnormal, and always gave the impression of heroic solipsistic stubbornness to his supporters (but to few others), the 'captain who weathered the storm' (an appropriate metaphor in view of his love of sailing). Yet his government performed more 'u-turns' in policy than any other. Heath's performance was that of a weak, not a strong leader.

The Cabinet of 18 which the Tories formed also showed this mixture of old and new. The senior positions mainly went to well-known heavyweights – the Foreign Office to Douglas-Home, the Lord Chancellorship to Quintin Hogg, now re-elevated to the Lords as Lord Hailsham of St Marylebone, the Exchequer to Iain Macleod, the Home Office to Reginald Maudling.

Traditionalist Tories were represented: William Whitelaw (1918–99; later first Viscount Whitelaw) became Lord President of the Council and Lord Carrington (Peter Carrington, b.1919) became Defence Minister, both from traditionalist backgrounds, among others. The bulk of the day-to-day administration, however, was done by MPs allegedly in Heath's own lower middle class, upwardly mobile image, such as Peter Walker (b.1932) at Housing and Local Government (renamed the Environment Ministry later that year), Anthony Barber (b.1920; later baron Barber) at the Duchy of Lancaster, and – although few foresaw it then – Heath's most important appointment, Margaret Thatcher (*née* Roberts; b.1925; later baroness Thatcher) at Education, the Cabinet's only woman. Several of these figures attended a grammar school (like Heath) or very minor public schools and had superficially similar backgrounds. Nevertheless, the break between the Heath Cabinet and previous Tory ones should not be exaggerated. Eton was still represented by six Cabinet ministers, while six others attended another major public school. Eleven were alumni of Oxford, three of Cambridge, and one (Lord Carrington) of Sandhurst – 15 out of 18 – hardly evidence, by most analyses, of a social revolution. Only a few major Tory figures were left outside the ministry, most prominently, of course, Enoch Powell and also Edward Du Cann (b.1924; later Sir Edward), a prominent right-winger who had been Chairman of the Conservative Party in 1965–67.

The first blow to the new government came on 20 July 1970, less than a month after the election, when Iain Macleod suddenly died of a heart attack, aged only 57. Macleod's passing is often seen as a significant blow to the government's long-term success. A major figure, one of the few respected by Heath, it is often said that Macleod alone might both have been able to stand up to Heath and win support for the government among the public. In place of Macleod, Heath appointed Anthony Barber as Chancellor. Barber was widely seen as a political lightweight, Heath's yes-man. (After leaving politics in 1974, Barber disappeared into obscurity arguably more comprehensively than any other first-rank political figure of modern times.) Heath also made a few other important changes at the time, most notably bringing into the Cabinet John Davies (1916–79), a prominent industrialist and former Director-General of the Confederation of British Industries, as Minister of Technology. Soon after, Heath reorganised several smaller Cabinet departments into super-ministries, the Department of the Environment and of Trade and Industry, names which have largely continued. Heath (who is often described as would-be senior civil servant) paid great attention to organisational structures, and put in place a number of innovations which were potentially very far-sighted. Most significantly, he put in place the Central Policy Review Staff, quickly known as the 'Think Tank', to provide expert medium and long-term advice to the government. Rather strangely, nothing like this was known before in Britain. Heath's choice to head it, Victor, Lord Rothschild, is widely seen as highly successful. Rothschild, a successful scientist and enormously wealthy, but on the left politically (in the 1930s he had flirted with Communism, despite his family background), provided important, independent advice, especially over energy pricing. Nevertheless (and characteristically), Heath did little or nothing systematically to integrate the 'Think Tank' and other novelties into his approach to government.

The early days of the Heath government seemed to show that the first of the two Edward Heaths, the avid right-winger, was in the ascendant. The government announced plans to reform trade union power and curb immigration. In November 1970 John Davies announced that the government would support policies which did not shore up what he termed 'lame ducks' – in other words, that badly run companies would be allowed to fail, and could not look to the government for help. Barber's first budget, in October, cut income tax by 2.5 per cent and also cut corporation tax; this was paid for by increased prescription charges, museum admission charges, and the end of free school milk for children aged 8–11 (the last earning Mrs Thatcher, the Education Secretary, the title 'Thatcher – Milk Snatcher'). In October, Heath told the Tory party conference that he aimed at a 'quiet revolution' in attitudes towards industry. Things, however, proved not so simple. A dockers' strike in the summer of 1970 was settled when the government accepted a 7 per cent wage increase, and, in September, the government appeared to give in to terrorists when it released Palestinian airline hijacker Leila Khaled. In November, the government decided to loan Rolls-Royce aero-engineers £42 million to avoid bankruptcy pending a lost airline contract. In February 1971 it decided to nationalise Rolls-Royce (the airline engine builder), one of the few businesses ever nationalised by a Conservative government. This could be justified as in the national interest, but it seemed grossly inconsistent with the government's tough talk.

By the end of 1970 a pattern had thus already been established of tough right-wing talk, even policies, followed by climbdowns and 'u-turns' under pressure. As time went on, the Heath government came to discard more and more of its right-wing stance, favouring European-style economic *dirigism* ('direction') and seeing mass unemployment as the outcome to be avoided at all costs. Thus, in 1971 it passed its most important piece of legislation affecting labour affairs, the Industrial Relations Act, 1971. This was designed to modernise trade union law, to reduce the powers of militant trade unions, but also to bring the unions into a new, viable relationship with management and government. It gave workers protection from unfair dismissal, and introduced a concept of 'unfair industrial practice'. It established a new body, the National Industrial Relations Court, which was to hear complaints of unfair industrial practice. Crucially, it provided for a new system of registration for unions, removed many of their old, anomalous, legal immunities, and gave the government power to order a 'cooling off period' and ballots of members over strikes in major industries. The Act was vigorously opposed by Labour and virtually all trade unions, who saw it as an attempt to break the powers of the unions, although he government insisted its aim was to bring the unions into a working partnership.

Notwithstanding the Act, industrial relations under the Heath government proved to be lamentable. Time and again the unions emerged victorious from highly visible conflicts and the Act became a dead letter. A test of strength with the miners' union in 1973–74 eventually led to the end of the Heath government. Within a year of the government's formation, dockers, local authority dustmen and sewage workers, power station workers, postmen, and workers at the Ford car plane went on strike, the postmen for seven weeks early in 1971. States of Emergency were declared in July 1970 over the dock strike and in

December 1970 over electricity supplies. All these disputes were eventually ended, usually following a report of an independent commission, with massive pay increases, fuelling inflation and thus leading to further industrial unrest. More trouble than anywhere else, however, occurred with the coal miners. In January 1972 the miners began a strike in pursuit of a 47 per cent pay increase. This led to another state of emergency being declared, in February 1972. The following day travelling left-wing pickets, headed by radical union leader Arthur Scargill, forced the closure of the Saltley Gate cokeworks in Birmingham, the 'battle of Saltley Gate' becoming renowned in left-wing legend. An enquiry into the miners' case, chaired by Lord Wilberforce, came to the view that the miners had 'a just case for special treatment', and recommended huge increases. Even these, however, were not accepted by the National Union of Mineworkers, and the first of Heath's miners' strikes ended only after a further round of concessions by the government. The success enjoyed by the miners was rather surprising in that coal was shrinking fast as a major industry, the numbers employed in Britain in mining and quarrying declining from 841 000 in 1951 to 722 000 in 1961 to only 391 000 in 1971. The year 1972 saw further major strikes by workers in the construction industry and by dockers, a British Rail work-to-rule lasting nearly two months, and a one-day strike by engineers. The Industrial Relations Act, designed to improve labour relations, proved to be nearly hopeless. Unions refused to register under the Act; fines imposed on the unions led to further industrial action; court cases went against the government. In June 1972 the government was forced to use the Official Solicitor, a little-known legal officer, to quash contempt proceedings against three Transport and General Workers' Union members brought under the provisions of its own Act. The early 1970s saw one of the high water marks of industrial near-anarchy in Britain. It was fanned by continuing high levels of inflation – 10 per cent in 1971, 7 per cent in 1972, 9 per cent in 1973, 16 per cent in 1974 – by a new generation of militant, often overtly Marxist trade union leaders, and by Britain's anarchic trade union structure, marked by a plethora of small, incohesive unions and central leadership lacking true power.

The response of the Heath government to all this was centrally predicated upon its deep-seated fear of unemployment. Unemployment headed upward in 1969–72 and, around January 1972, briefly exceeded the one million mark for the first time since the pre-war dark ages (except for a short period in the winter of 1947). Although this was only 4 per cent of the work force, the one million mark was regarded as profound litmus test of unacceptability, a potential reversion to the terrible conditions of the Depression which was both socially unacceptable and politically suicidal. As a result, the Heath government ruled out, in so far as it could, deflating the economy through increased unemployment, and did everything it possibly could to diminish unemployment by every means. Unemployment fell fairly steadily after early 1972, declining to only 486 000 (less than 3 per cent of the work force) by December 1973. Given that high unemployment was an absolute taboo, the government's strategy took several separate paths. It cut and simplified many taxes, thus 'freeing up funds for investment', as it put it. In April 1973 it introduced the Value Added Tax (VAT), a far-ranging indirect tax on all transactions of goods and services, which replaced other taxes, such as the Selective Employment Tax. In May 1972 it introduced the Industry Bill, probably the government's greatest u-turn and most palpable rejection of economic neo-liberalism. Under the Industry Act, the government was allowed to spend up to £530 million over five years in whichever way it liked so long as it was 'in the national interest'. Up to £5 million could be given to any company without specific Parliamentary approval. Most of this money was to be channelled to rundown industrial areas. Many Tories and Labourites regarded this as a move towards socialism. A few weeks later, the government also announced that it was giving British Steel, a nationalised industry (which the government had no intention of privatising) a grant of £3 billion over ten years. In August 1971 the government also allowed sterling to float, rather than pegging it to a specific value against the dollar. This was widely regarded as necessary in the wake of the decision of the United States, the same month, to end dollar-gold convertibility, the basis of the post-war economic settlement. The pound floated downwards, in a way that helped exports, but which, of course, made imports more costly.

Edward Heath's greatest triumph was his achievement of entry into the European Economic Community, the central goal of his political career from the late 1950s on. Charles de Gaulle resigned as President of France in 1969; thereafter, the path to British entry was considerably eased, and, in fact, in June 1970 the EEC invited Britain to apply for membership. Heath faced considerable opposition from a relatively small number of anti-European Tories but, much more significantly, by a majority of Labourites. Through skill, in October 1971, after arduous negotiations, Heath was able to pilot entry into the EEC on the terms negotiated through the Commons by a vote of 356-244. Much opposition centred on the ending of most advantages previously enjoyed by the Commonwealth, and by the disadvantageous position of British agriculture. At this time, many on the British left saw the EEC as a 'capitalists' club' dominated by the old enemy, resurgent Germany; there was also an element of residual anti-Catholicism to joining a largely Catholic group. On the far right (led by Enoch Powell and his associates) there was a fear of surrendering British sovereignty, and of ditching the Commonwealth, including those countries which had fought for Britain in the wars. Most mainstream opinion, however, was strongly in favour of joining. Most Tories, including many right-wingers, nearly all Liberals, and most (but not all) former Gaitskellites in the Labour party, were strongly in favour of EEC membership, as were most mainstream newspapers. Given the amazing economic success enjoyed by the 'Six' (France, West Germany, Italy, and the Benelux countries), British membership was widely seen as a *deus ex machina* way out of Britain's economic malaise. As noted, many also viewed the EEC as the economic face of NATO, offering security through unity to Europe's democracies: this last point may explain, in part, the strong support given by most Tories to Europe at this time. The Treaty of Accession to the EEC was signed on 22 January 1972, but, given the great complexities of negotiation and piloting it through Parliament, Royal Assent to the formal bill establishing British membership, the European Communities Act, did not occur until 17 October 1972; Britain formally became a member on 1 January 1973.

Britain (and Denmark, which joined the EEC at the same time) left EFTA, the 'rival' Free Trade area it had established in 1960, upon formally joining the EEC. While many expected the question of British membership to have been settled forever in 1972, it has remained one of the most, if not the most, divisive issue in British politics ever since, deeply fragmenting the Labour party in the 1970s and the Conservative party in the 1990s. It also seems likely that many of the EEC's supporters in the early 1970s did not realise the extent to which membership would qualify and limit British sovereignty; none who supported it as an anti-Communist project could foresee that Communism would vanish from Europe while the European Community remained.

Probably the most traumatic issue faced by the Heath government, however, was one which would have been totally unsuspected even five years before it came to power. Seemingly from nowhere, the eternal vampire of modern British history, the Irish question, rose again from the dead in the most violent form imaginable. From the mid-1960s a strong civil rights movement arose among Catholics in the slums of Northern Ireland, drawing on American models, in order to alleviate the perceived discrimination against them in all walks of life exercised by the autonomous Northern Irish government. Although the IRA had never disappeared, and had engaged in violent acts on a regular basis after 1922, from the late 1960s a number of violent terrorist groups arose – the Provisional IRA (or 'Provos') and the Provisional Sinn Fein (the political arm of the IRA) – which engaged in killings, bombings, slaughter, intimidation, and mayhem as regular policy. Nothing like this had been seen in the United Kingdom in the twentieth century (with the exception of the Irish civil war of 1918–22), and Northern Ireland rapidly became the most violent place in Europe. Between 1969 (when there were 12 terrorist-related deaths in Northern Ireland) and 1977 (when there were 261 deaths), a total of 1582 violent deaths occurred in Northern Ireland (1178 of whom were civilians), with 449 in 1972 alone. There were also dozens of Irish-related murders, by bombings or shootings, on the British mainland. During the early 1970s, the constant threat of terrorism (from other groups besides the IRA, especially Middle East extremists) changed the lifestyle of the British people, instituting a regimen of constant searches and security checks. In Northern Ireland, extremist Protestants responded to the IRA by forming their own murderous paramilitaries, such as the Ulster Defence Association.

The Heath government attempted to deal with this intractable situation in the time-honoured way of British governments, a mixture of toughness and appeasement. From 1969, the Northern Irish government instituted a policy of internment without trial for suspected IRA terrorists, causing a backlash among the Catholics. By mid-1972 some 21 000 British troops had been sent to Northern Ireland, while the Royal Ulster Constabulary was also greatly expanded. The British government also welcomed the growth of more moderate Catholic elements, like the SDLP. But internal Irish violence always overtook these efforts, for example the 'Bloody Sunday' killings of January 1972, when thirteen Catholic men were shot dead by the army in Derry, under highly controversial circumstances. The Heath government also attempted to get an overall agreement with the Irish government towards a joint policy, reaching a degree of success with the 'Sunningdale Agreement' for a Council of Ireland

and 'power sharing' in December 1973. The most radical step taken by the Heath government occurred in March 1972, when Stormont (the Northern Irish Parliament) was prorogued and the powers of the Northern Irish government transferred to the Westminster government, with a new Northern Irish secretary exercising direct rule from Belfast. For this thankless and potentially dangerous post Heath chose William Whitelaw, a suave Establishment Tory. Levels of violence in Northern Ireland did begin to decline, although there was a heavy political price. After 1970, most Northern Irish Protestant MPs broke away from the Conservative (or 'Unionist') party to which they had given unquestioned support since 1886. In the 1970 election Rev. Ian Paisley (b.1926), a fiery Protestant populist leader standing as a 'Protestant Unionist', defeated the official Unionist candidate; at the February 1974 election 11 of the 12 Northern Irish seats were won by candidates of the United Ulster Unionist Council, who opposed the official Unionists. Had these MPs taken the Conservative Whip, the Tories would have maintained their position as the largest party in the Parliament elected in February 1974 (albeit in a minority position), and Heath might have clung to office. Any hint of a far-reaching agreement with Dublin alienated the Ulster Protestants, while Northern Catholics generally continued to regard the Westminster government as its bitter enemy. Heath's government, as so many British governments before and since, was in a classic 'no-win' situation over Ireland. Yet the terms of engagement between the two sides were not equal. The Ulster Protestants were loyalists whose primary desire was to remain British, in a United Kingdom, while the IRA consisted of terrorists and murderers, whose aim was to compel the Protestants of the North to accept the same subordinate position, against their will, in a united Ireland, from which Catholic Ireland has suffered for centuries during British rule. The British government had a primary obligation to support those loyal to it, who unquestionably represented the majority in Northern Ireland. (In a 58% turnout poll held in March 1973 – boycotted by many Catholics – 592 000 electors in Northern Ireland voted to remain part of the UK, and 6500 voted to be joined with the Republic of Ireland.) As before the First World War, although the Heath government recognised its primary obligation to support its loyalists, its policies, especially those entailing consultation by the Irish government in Northern Irish affairs, were regarded by most Protestants and many Tories on the mainland as appeasement. While levels of violence declined, the IRA and other Irish terrorist movements responded – just as one might predict – with contempt. Tory MP Airey Neave (in April 1979), Lord Mountbatten (in August 1979), Sir Anthony Berry (in October 1984 when the IRA planted a bomb at the Conservative Conference hotel in Brighton), and Tory MP Ian Gow (in July 1990) were assassinated by Irish terrorists, and dozens of innocent people in Birmingham, London, and elsewhere in Britain, were also murdered. With rising living standards and a decline in sectarian hostility, the Northern Irish situation gradually became more manageable. Yet at the end of the twentieth century it still festered unresolved, occasionally erupting into mass murder as at Omagh in 1999. The Heath government's time in office marked the most serious phase of the conflict. For the Heath government, Northern Ireland served as an insoluble nightmare which occupied the Cabinet night and day, distracting it from its more central business.

In many other of its policies the Heath government puzzled its Tory supporters, who saw it both pursuing and opposing established policy. The government quickly enacted the far-reaching Immigration Act, 1971, which placed Commonwealth citizens on the same basis as non-Commonwealth citizens in their right to settle in Britain, and provided for the issuance of temporary work permits, but also made it easier for Commonwealth citizens of British descent to settle in Britain. As a result the number of New Commonwealth citizens allowed to settle in Britain fell, from 61 000 in 1968 to 32 000 in 1973. On the other hand the government accepted for settlement in Britain tens of thousands of Kenyan Asians expelled by Idi Amin, although their claims for settlement were, in the views of many, rather weak. Through the 1971 Act Heath had hoped to end immigration as a major issue, but he failed to do this. In similar fashion the government did not restore the death penalty, and Heath was a consistent abolitionist; on the other hand the government toughened sentences against violent criminals and rationalised the court system.

Soon after coming to office, the government relaxed rules relating to credit. The aim of this change was to spark a boom, but its main result was that rampant property speculation ensued, although mortgage rates increased to the unheard of rate of 11 per cent. The average price of a house in Britain doubled in only three years, from £5000 in 1970 to £10 000 in 1973, while property values in London and the southeast soared. The government's attempts to make council house tenants pay a fairer rent, in its 1972 Housing Finance Act, led to massive resistance by Labour councils, symbolised by the non-compliance with the Act of the Clay Cross (Derbyshire) Council, which attracted national publicity. By 1973, many Tories admitted that its housing policies had failed. The government's byzantine attempts at reforming the structure of local government and the NHS were bureaucratic failures, the kind of reforms carried out by theorists with no experience of the actual practicalities of the systems they 'reformed'. Heath almost went out of his way to sneer at the 'special relationship' with the United States, and pointedly declined to go along with American initiatives. Heath, like Wilson, declined to create any hereditary titles, and further alienated his Tory supporters by recommending only very limited numbers of backbenchers for the knighthoods which had previously come almost automatically to long-serving backbench MPs. (On the other hand, he did recommend 'political honours' for party services, unlike Wilson.) Heath created only 34 life peerages in his time as Prime Minister, one of the lowest totals (9 per year) of recent times. In his personal dealings with backbench MPs Heath was renowned for his almost studied coldness and utter lack of friendliness or even basic courtesy. By 1974 he had pointlessly created a well-spring of disappointment and hostility among his own supporters which was in part responsible for his shock leadership defeat at the hands of Margaret Thatcher.

In other ways, too, the Heath government acted in a puzzling way. In opposition, the party had strongly backed a proposal to sell council houses to tenants. In office, however, it did virtually nothing to further council house sales. Yet one cannot imagine a policy more in keeping with virtually any modern conception of Conservatism. Instead of being wards of the state, with nothing to show for decades of council tenantry but a rent book, council tenants would become property owners with a stake in society and assets to leave behind. In 1980 the Thatcher government gave all council tenants the right to buy their homes at a discount; over the next 18 years nearly 1.5 million council houses were sold to their tenants. In his autobiography *The Course of My Life*, published in 1998, Edward Heath made a point of attacking this policy, despite its evident success. Similarly, the Heath government denationalised virtually nothing, although it 'hived off' some minor state-owned operations, such as the Thomas Cook travel agency (most peculiarly, a state-owned company) and the even more bizarre anomaly of the Carlisle state breweries, which had been nationalised during the First World War. Apart from a handful of such changes the entire infrastructure of nationalised industry was left intact. With the nationalisation of Rolls-Royce Ltd in 1971, the public sector was arguably larger under Heath than under Wilson, and the Heath government felt no impetus whatever to privatise.

One reason that the Heath government was able to avoid any really dramatic move to the right in the economy was that during these years the Labour party had shifted sharply to the left, in a way arguably not seen before in the British political mainstream. This did not occur at the parliamentary level so much as among the constituencies. In July 1970 Roy Jenkins, the articulate heir to the Gaitskellite legacy, was elected Deputy Leader of the party with 133 votes to 67 for left-winger Michael Foot and 48 for Fred Peart (1914–88). A year later, in November 1971, Jenkins was challenged again, chiefly in response to his strong support for British entry into the EEC, by left-winger Michael Foot and by Tony Benn, previously a moderate, but recently converted to an even more extreme left-wing stance; both were strong opponents of British entry. Jenkins received 140 votes on the first ballot, compared with 96 for Foot and 46 for Benn, and won on the second ballot by only 140 votes to 126. By this time British entry into the EEC had become the prime *bête noire* of Labour's left wing. In the constituencies, the hard left, largely composed of near-Marxist activists and militant trade unionists, increasingly gained control of many constituency associations. Apart from opposing EEC entry, the left increasingly demanded nationalisation on a scale not previously seen, particularly targeting the 25 largest companies and the banks. One left-wing resolution debated (and defeated) at the 1973 Labour conference called for the nationalisation of '250 major monopolies' as well as 'the land, banks, finance houses, insurance companies and building societies, with minimum compensation on the basis of proven need and the re-nationalization of all hived-off sections of publicly owned industries without compensation; all under democratic workers' control and management.' In this atmosphere the Gaitskellite tradition in the party became increasingly untenable, especially the standing of those like Jenkins who (unlike Gaitskell himself) strongly supported European entry. In April 1972, depressed by increasing anti-EEC and left-wing pressure within the Labour party, Jenkins resigned as Deputy Leader, ending any hope of becoming Prime Minister. Ironically he was replaced by a little-known moderate, Edward Short (b.1912; later baron Glenamara), who had served as Education Minister from 1968–70. Short, who did not arouse the hostility of the left as Jenkins had, received more votes than Michael Foot and Anthony Crosland in the first ballot for Deputy Leader, and then beat Foot by 145-116 in the second ballot.

Although the Left gained considerable strength in the constituencies at this time, it did not have it all its own way. In March 1973 Dick Taverne, a moderate Labour MP, stood down in his seat of Lincoln to recontest as a 'Democratic Labour' candidate against the party's Left, winning re-election in a seat which attracted national publicity. Labour's leaders promised re-negotiation of the terms of entry and a national referendum on European entry and Wilson, still leader and still popular, devised formulas for holding the party together. Despite its growing internal divisions, Labour did well in the opinion polls, and was consistently ahead of the Tories until just before the February 1974 election. Harold Wilson remained personally more popular than Edward Heath, who was, at best, more respected than admired.

During the Heath years, the Liberal party also gained greatly in popularity under Jeremy Thorpe (b.1929), leader of the party from 1967–76. The Liberals gained five seats at by-elections between the 1970 and 1974 General Elections, four from the Conservatives and one from Labour. The seat won from Labour, Rochdale, in October 1972, was taken by the ebullient heavyweight Cyril Smith, who symbolised a component of the Liberal's revival, its reignition of old, long-lost local traditions. Most of the Liberals' new support, however, seemingly came from disenchanted younger middle-class Tories and Labourites. At the peak of the party's poll revival in August 1973, 28 per cent of the electorate claimed that they intended to vote Liberal, compared with 38 per cent for Labour and 31 per cent for the Tories. Heath's unpopularity, and the failure of the Tories to deliver on issues such as housing (while Labour seemed to move to the left) led to the rise of the Liberals. Other minor parties also did well. The Scottish Nationalists (SNP) and Plaid Cymru both continued to gain support, with the SNP taking Glasgow Govan from Labour at a by-election in November 1973. Besides a resurgent far left, the Heath era also saw a revival of extreme Right, anti-immigrant, and ultra-patriotic groups. The National Front, which had fielded 10 candidates at the 1970 General Election, winning an average of 3.6 per cent of the vote, grew steadily in this period in areas of high immigration and growing unemployment. At the February 1974 election it would put up 54 candidates, who on average gained 3.3 per cent of the vote. Within the right wing of the Conservative party groups such as the Monday Club, hostile to further immigration, supportive of South Africa, and critical of Heath, became influential, although they remained fairly small. These years, in short, saw a growth in the minor parties, in the political extremes, and in nationalist movements, which worked against the domination of the two-party system. Their growth was constrained by Britain's 'first-past-the-post' electoral system and other factors, but they were far more visible than ten or fifteen years earlier.

By 1972 it was becoming clear that Heath's attempts to reduce wage settlements in the public sector (including nationalised industries) was in danger of failing. Heath had aimed for what was termed 'n-1', where an initially high wage settlement would be allowed in hopes that subsequent ones would be lower. This had some effect, but was not enforceable. Moreover, the government's own policies had often been anything but anti-inflationary. In 1972–73 the Chancellor initiated what became known as the 'Barber Boom', aimed at bringing about a 'dash for growth' before the next election. Its efforts probably had a positive effect on unemployment, but was obviously inconsistent with the drive to lower inflation. Heath next hoped for voluntary wage restraint by agreement with the TUC. This failed, too, and in November 1972 the government announced a 90-day freeze on wages, prices, rents, and dividends. In April 1973 came Phase Two of a comprehensive prices and incomes policy, limiting pay rises to £1 per week plus 4 per cent, to a maximum of £250 p.a. The Tory government thus abandoned any pretence at a marketplace solution to inflation, and turned to a statutory limitation on pay rises, enforceable by law. It was difficult enough to get the unions to agree to this in the best of circumstances, but in October 1973 came another blow, the Yom Kippur war between Israel and the Arabs, leading to an enormous increase in oil prices and heightened international tension. These oil price rises occurred during a period of particularly sharp commodity price rises for a wide variety of imported raw goods. The sharp inflation and more difficult economic circumstances around the world from 1973 are seen by many historians as a climacteric, the end of the long post-war boom and the beginning of a decade of 'stagflation' (inflation, low growth, and higher unemployment) throughout the Western world.

Amidst these difficulties Heath announced, in late October 1973, 'Phase Three' of a programme to control inflation, limiting wage rises to £2.25 per week, or 7 per cent. Heath strove long and hard to get general agreement with the unions on cooperating at controlling inflation, but would not agree to limit dividends, and negotiations proved unsuccessful. At this point, in November 1973, the National Union of Mineworkers announced another overtime ban in support of a substantial pay increase. Something like an atmosphere of economic apocalypse unknown perhaps since the formation of the 1931 National government became evident: food prices rose by 3.3 per cent in October 1973 alone (a 40 per cent annual rate); the balance of trade figures in the same month showed the worst-ever gap of £298 million; the bank rate rose to the extraordinary level of 13 per cent. Heath declared another State of Emergency as a result of the Miners' overtime ban, restricting heating and lighting, and ending television broadcasts at 10.30 pm. On 13 December came the 'three-day week', to take effect from 1 January, and also limitations on the openings of businesses before that date. Under the 'three-day week' rule, electricity for industry and commerce was allowed for only three days per week. Early in January came one-day rail strikes and an all-out miners' strike. The Governor of the Bank of England, Gordon Richardson, forecasted that 'years of economic austerity' lay ahead. The miners were, if anything, in a potentially stronger position this time than previously, given the sharp rise in oil prices.

Heath had no obvious way out but to dissolve Parliament and call a General Election on the single issue of 'who governs Britain?' This he did on 7 February 1974, with the election to be held on 28 February. The February 1974 general election was thus one of the very few in the twentieth century to be called ahead of time (no election was due before June 1975), and with the government still enjoying a working majority, on a specific issue. The only parallels were, seemingly, the December 1910 election, called by Asquith chiefly over House of Lords reform and the Budget, and the 1923 election, called by Baldwin in a bid to enact Tariff Reform.

Heath's decision was widely criticised at the time and since, but in many respects it was a clever one. Despite Heath's unpopularity, few Conservatives will fail to respond to an electoral appeal based on attacking trade union militancy and anarchy, and such a petition, 'the smack of firm government', will have great appeal to floating voters. With Labour bitterly divided, the Tories seemed certain to win; February 1974 seemed, to many, in fact, to be an unloseable election.

There were also reasons why this was too sanguine a view. The Heath government was, after all, the architect of much of its own misfortunes, especially by its incompetent trade union reform policies. More basically, it was unclear, on closer analysis, why the election was called at all: even if the Tories won a huge majority, the miners would still be on strike and inflation would still be very high. (The government's response to this was that it would have a clear mandate to govern.) Labour patched up its differences, calling for a 'social contract' with the TUC and strict price controls. (The phrase, dating back to Rousseau, was made familiar in a speech by James Callaghan in 1972.) Labour's manifesto was also one of the most radical on record, calling for 'a fundamental and irreversible shift in the balance of power and wealth in favour of the working people and their families' and a re-negotiation of the terms of entry to the EEC. Nevertheless, ironically it was Labour which appeared the more moderate of the two parties, compared with the combative, crisis-seeking Tories.

A number of things went wrong for the Tories during the campaign. Enoch Powell (who was not standing at this election) called, remarkably, for a Labour victory as the party more likely to take Britain out of the EEC. (Opposition to the EEC had become one of Powell's main concerns.) Powell's support for Labour was certainly important to the final result. The head of the Pay Board, the body dealing with wage rises, suggested midway in the campaign that the miners were about £3 per week worse off than the government claimed: to give the government its due, an extraordinary and improper intervention in the political process. Campbell Adamson, the head of the CBI, also did Heath no favour by calling, two days before the election, for repeal of the Industrial Relations Act. The monthly deficit announced during the election campaign was the largest ever recorded.

The election result was a strange one: no majority. The Tories gained more votes than Labour but, through the vagaries of the system, won slightly fewer seats.

	Total votes	MPs elected	% share of total vote
Conservative	11 868 906	297	37.9
Liberal	6 063 470	14	19.3
Labour	11 639 243	301	37.1
Communist	32 741	0	0.1
Plaid Cymru	171 364	2	0.6
Scottish Nationals	632 032	7	2.0
National Front	76 865	0	0.3
Others (G.B.)	131 059	2	0.4
Others (N.I.)	717 986	12	2.3
Total	31 333 226	635	100.0

Compared with 1970, the Tories lost 33 seats, and no less than 1 516 000 votes. Although Labour gained 14 more seats than in 1970 it, too, lost 540 000 votes. The biggest gainers were the Liberals, who nearly tripled their popular vote but, because of the British electoral system, elected only 14 MPs. Nationalist and independent parties in Wales, Scotland, and Northern Ireland also did well, polling no less than 1 532 000 votes and electing 21 MPs, including seven Scottish Nationalists. Labour made gains in London, the Midlands, and its traditional areas of strength, but looked unimpressive elsewhere: it had, for instance, seven fewer MPs in Wales and Scotland than in 1970.

There was no clear or obvious precedent about what Heath was now to do. Plainly, he had not received a mandate for his policies (only 37.9 per cent of the electorate had voted Conservative). Although Labour had more seats, it was still itself 17 MPs short of a majority. Had the Northern Irish Unionist MPs not broken away from the Tories, Heath would have had around 308 MPs compared with 301 for Labour, but this was itself not enough for a majority in the Commons. Heath spent the next six days trying to form a coalition with the Liberals, offering Liberal leader Jeremy Thorpe the Home Secretaryship. Thorpe might well have accepted, but the Liberals insisted on the enactment of proportional representation as its price, a price Heath would not pay and one his backbenchers would not have accepted. At his final Cabinet meeting he neither thanked his colleagues for their support nor did they pay any tribute to him.

The defeat of the Tories in February 1974 did not really mark the end of an era, except for the Tory party itself. Labour, now about to form a minority government, held to many if not most of the assumptions which underpinned Heath's policies, and approached the economic crisis in a way which was not wildly dissimilar. Edward Heath had more than his share of bad luck, especially the sharp rise in oil and commodity prices in 1973. On the other hand, both the assumptions of his government and the tactics it pursued were extremely dubious. His central concern was engendering economic growth, but his faith in growth was predicated upon a vision of the British economy which was in many respects unrealistic. His policy u-turns and his refusal to contemplate significantly increased unemployment worked against the success of his aims. The general approach pursued by the Heath government certainly had the approval of most mainstream informed opinion, and it might well be argued that Heath could not realistically have undertaken radically different policies. Yet in economic terms the Heath government was certainly a failure: prices and wages rose sharply but not (except in the first half of 1973) growth in Britain's GNP. Public expenditure, in the words of one leading economist, 'consistently outgrew the revenues available to finance it'; the balance of trade deficit remained a consistent problem. Heath's objective of breaking the power of the trade unions was plainly not achieved. The experience of the Heath government helped crucially to delegitimate 'One Nation Toryism' as an ideological stance for a Conservative government to pursue virtually without dissent.

Wilson, again, and James Callaghan, 1974–79

On taking office Harold Wilson formed a Cabinet of 21, chiefly consisting of holdovers from his previous government. The four most senior ministers were a particularly strong team, at least on paper – Wilson, Denis Healey at the Exchequer, James Callaghan at the Foreign Office, and Roy Jenkins as Home Secretary – especially in contrast to Edward Heath's appointments. Healey, from the centre of the party, was particularly difficult to describe in ideological terms. In opposition, he had made fiery speeches about how there would be 'howls of anguish from the 80 000 rich people' under a Labour government. Although he certainly increased taxes as Chancellor, Healey was not a leftist and began flirting with the 'monetarist' solution of increasing unemployment to fight inflation. Roy Jenkins, the hope of the pro-Europeans, was disappointed with the Home Office, and spent most of his time there preoccupied with Irish terrorism and, in the wider arena, with the Common Market referendum. Wilson also made a number of novel appointments. He brought in two avowed leftists, Michael Foot at Employment and Trade and Tony Benn at Industry. Foot had never held a government position of any kind before, but was renowned as the most vocal and influential Bevanite, a constant critic of right-wing Labour, while Benn, during the 1960s a party centrist, had moved steadily to the Left and was now the increasingly acknowledged leader of the 'hard left' which wanted a full-throated socialist labour party. In part to balance the Left, Wilson appointed some high-profile moderates, such as Anthony Crosland at the Environment and Harold Lever (1914–95), a millionaire financier, at the Duchy of Lancaster, where he became a key Wilson adviser. Wilson's 1974 Cabinet also included, for the first time, two women – Barbara Castle at Health and Social Security, and Shirley Williams (b.1930), a pro-European moderate, at the newly formed Department of Prices and Consumer Protection. Merlyn Rees (b.1920) was given the key Northern Irish ministry, Wilson also created a Policy Unit, working out of 10 Downing Street, consisting of pro-Labour experts, headed by Bernard Donoughue (b.1937), to offer ideas and advice. This built on a somewhat similar body, the Central Policy Review Staff, which Heath had instituted, although it was looser and less oriented towards the civil service. Wilson also continued to rely on his personal staff, entourage, and advisers such as Marcia Williams and Lord Goodman.

The new government immediately settled the miners' dispute, basically on their terms. The Industrial Relations Act was, of course, repealed. Labour had promised a 'social contract' with the unions, and immediately raised income and corporation taxes, and tightened price controls. The base rate of income tax rose to 33 per cent (up 3 per cent), while the highest rate of tax on earned income rose to 83 per cent, and to the extraordinary rate of 98 per cent on unearned incomes. A Capital Transfer Tax, to replace Death Duties, was introduced in 1974, making it more difficult to avoid estate duties. The government made it impossible for local authorities to sell council houses to tenants. On the other hand, the crisis mood of Heath's 'three-day week' quickly faded, and Wilson was widely hailed as a breath of fresh air who had learned common sense in opposition. Wilson had wished to call another General Election almost immediately, expecting to receive a substantial majority as he had, in roughly similar circumstances, in 1966. He was, however, forced to delay, largely because of the 'land deals affair', a property development scandal affecting Marcia Williams' brother. A number of other minor scandals, including the resignation of Lord Brayley, a junior minister, also caused Wilson to delay. In the end, a second General Election was held on 10 October 1974, just over seven months after the one called by Edward Heath. Wilson campaigned on an extension of the 'social contract', a voluntary (not statutory) range of agreements between the government and the unions. Labour also promised 're-negotiation' of the terms of entry into the EEC, thus managing to avoid a fierce internal dispute over a key subject on which the government was hopelessly divided. The Tories ran a surprisingly effective campaign, with Heath portraying Britain as 'poor, socialist, and alone' if Labour won. The outcome was only slightly less indecisive than in the February election.

	Total votes	MPs elected	% share of total vote
Conservative	10 464 817	277	35.8
Liberal	5 346 754	13	18.3
Labour	11 457 079	319	39.2
Communist	17 426	0	0.1
Plaid Cymru	166 321	3	0.6
Scottish Nationals	839 617	11	2.9
National Front	113 843	0	0.4
Others (G.B.)	81 227	0	0.3
Others (No.I.)	702 094	12	2.4
Total	29 189 178	635	100.0

Turnout was down markedly, with two million fewer votes than in the first 1974 election. The Tory vote fell by 1.4 million, Labour's by about 200 000, the Liberals' by 700 000. Labour picked up 18 seats, giving it a majority of three over all other parties, far from the huge majority it might have expected. Indeed, a majority of only three would normally have been quite insufficient to keep it in power for a full term, and yet another General Election might have been expected soon. Labour was, however, in a stronger position that it appeared, since many of the Celtic minor party MPs were on the Left, and preferred Labour to the Tories. In the event, the Parliament ran its full course.

Wilson continued as Prime Minister for two years, until April 1976, before retiring. In this time he was faced by two crucial issues, Britain's entry into Europe and the economy, as well as other important questions such as Northern Ireland and terrorism. There is general agreement that Wilson showed himself to be a master tactician during this time, skilfully leading a bitterly divided party. In terms of long-term economic strategy, however, the government's record was more mixed.

By late 1974, Labour had developed a deep and bitter internal feud over membership in the EEC. By and large, the centre and right wing of the Labour party were enthusiasts for Europe, with Roy Jenkins and the neo-Gaitskellites especially keen, while the left and most of the trade unions opposed entry and expected Labour to take Britain out. Wilson, keen to bury the issue, promised a national referendum on the subject in its manifesto for the October 1974 election. Wilson had been quietly moving to a strong pro-EEC position, and believed that the 're-negotiation' of some terms of British membership, especially over agriculture, allowed Britain to remain inside. A referendum on British membership in Europe, the only one in history, was then held on 5 June 1975. A 'yes' vote on the proposition 'Do you think that the United Kingdom should stay in the European Community (the Common Market)' was not a foregone conclusion, but it was certainly to be expected. Much of the Labour party, nearly all Tories and Liberals, and almost all of the press and mainstream informed opinion supported continued entry, while the 'no' vote was championed only by the left of British politics and a part of the Right, represented chiefly by Enoch Powell. In future decades, significant opposition to deeper involvement in Europe arose in the Conservative party and among much of the media, but at the time questions of diminished British sovereignty seemed only theoretical. Few could envision a time when Britain would outperform the Continent economically, when the Cold War would be over, or when a 'European super-state' would be feared by many. As a result, the Referendum was carried easily, with a 64.5 per cent 'yes' vote, on a turnout, coincidentally, of 64.5 per cent of the electorate (29.5 million out of 40.1 million). 68.7 per cent of voters in England voted 'yes', with the highest 'yes' vote in the Tory Home Counties. The vote was also 'yes', but by less, in Wales (64.8 per cent), Scotland (58.4 per cent), and Northern Ireland (a bare 52.1 per cent). This historic Referendum comprehensively settled the issue of British membership in the EEC and buried strong hostility to deeper involvement for a generation. In political terms, it was probably Harold Wilson's most accomplished manoeuvre, greatly diminishing the divisive effect of this issue within the Labour party. The near-unanimity of Tory support for the Referendum would certainly not have been repeated even 15 years later, while Labour became an increasingly warm supporter of British membership.

The Wilson government's handling of the economy faced all the difficulties of his recent predecessors; indeed, its record was worse than any of its predecessors. Inflation continued to be rampant, the retail price index reaching an incredible level of increase of 26.9 per cent a year in August 1975. The retail price index rose by 24 per cent in 1974–75 and by 16 per cent in 1975–76. Industrial production stagnated, being lower in 1976 than in 1973. The balance of payments deficit totalled £3.3 billion in 1974 and £1.5 billion in 1975. Unemployment rose steadily, and the previously 'taboo' level of one million unemployed was permanently exceeded after early 1975. Unemployment ran at 5.7 per cent at the time of Wilson's resignation, much higher than at any time since the war. The Wilson government was running out of options, and the trade unions, although pliant, responded to inflation and unemployment with further demands. In July 1975 the government abandoned voluntary pay restraint and published a White Paper, *The Attack on Inflation*, introducing a universal pay rise limit of £6 per week from 1 August 1975. This was generally accepted by unions, and had an effect in limiting inflation. The government then cut spending substantially in 1975–76 and, in April 1976, introduced Stage 2 of its pay policy, limiting pay increases to 4.5 per cent. There were few bright spots in this picture. In June 1975 North Sea oil began to come into production, with the British National Oil Corporation established in 1976 to coordinate this bonanza.

The post-war Keynesian, Butskellite settlement clearly was on its last legs by this stage. Internationally, the 1973 oil price rise had profoundly negative effects almost everywhere. For the Western world, the gloom was heightened by the victory of the Vietcong in South Vietnam in 1975 and the immediate loss of Laos and Cambodia to Communism (with Cambodia undergoing the Pol Pot genocide). Portugal, experiencing a revolution, nearly went Communist, and its former colonies in Africa were ruled by Marxist governments. In the UN and other international bodies, the Communist–Arab–Third World bloc railroaded through absurd anti-Western resolutions. Terrorism and hijacking were at their peak. America was temporarily paralysed by the Watergate Scandal and President Nixon's resignation. Countervailing tendencies, especially the coming to power of moderate elements in China after the death of Mao Tse-tung and further steps towards Soviet-Western *détente*, did little to lighten the gloom.

In this period the Labour party moved steadily to the left, seeing the rise of a new, powerful hard left well beyond the Bevanite movement of the 1950s. Calling for wideranging nationalisation and a range of other policy changes such as nuclear disarmament, it became dominant in the party's executive, in many constituency associations, and in many trade unions. The party also came under penetration by fringe Marxist groups, previously banned without question. In 1973 the 'proscribed list' of organisations Labour members were barred from joining was abolished. In November 1975 Labour's National Executive failed to take action on a report by the party's national agent on the extent of infiltration into the party by Militant, a Trotskyite group. The following year a Militant member, Andy Bevan, was appointed the party's National Youth Officer. At the same time, the old coalition of the party's senior leaders, trade union leaders, and backbench working-class MPs, increasingly weakened, while the pro-European liberal faction in the party was itself increasingly frustrated by Labour's leaders. The most prominent Cabinet leftist, Tony Benn, was given the Trade and Industry portfolio, where he tried to enact a National Enterprise Board (NEB) to acquire compulsorily the shares of private companies. Wilson, who was opposed to the dramatic left-wing measures but wanted to keep the party united, agreed to the creation of a watered-down NEB, but then, in June 1975, moved Benn sideways and downwards to the Energy ministry. Just before resigning, Wilson began to denounce attempts by the Left to 'deselect' sitting Labour MPs. Had Wilson not retired, an enormous row over the growing influence of the Left in the party might have taken place. In Parliament, issues such as women's rights began to take centre stage, with Labour passing the Sex Discrimination Act, 1975, that outlawed discrimination based on sex in employment and other spheres, and establishing the Equal Opportunities Commission.

Meanwhile, the Conservative party was also abandoning the Butskellite consensus in a way which was, in the long term, to prove decisive for British politics. Early in 1975 Edward Heath came under growing pressure to put his continuing leadership to the test. With bad grace, he agreed to allow a vote over his leadership. Although Heath's leadership was increasingly unpopular, there was no obvious successor. Only one MP was game to contest the leadership against Heath, Margaret Thatcher. While recently appointed assistant Shadow Chancellor, and winning considerable recognition in that role, she was a little-known middle-ranking former minister and, of course, handicapped by her gender. Most right-wingers in the party would have preferred Edward Du Cann or Sir Keith Joseph (1918–94) to contest the leadership, but neither did. Her campaign manager in the election by Tory MPs, Airey Neave (1916–79), ran a masterful leadership contest, telling her core supporters she was likely to win and waverers that she had no chance (and hence they could safely vote for her without defeating Heath). In contrast, Heath (unlike his leadership race in 1965) ran an incompetent contest. His contemptuous coldness and poor electoral record alienated so many MPs that the impossible occurred. On the first ballot, on 4 February 1975, Thatcher received 130 votes, Heath 119, and a third candidate, Hugh Fraser, only 16. Heath then withdrew from the race, throwing his weight behind William Whitelaw. The second ballot, held on 11 February 1975, saw Thatcher elected leader of the Conservative party with 140 votes to Whitelaw's 79, 19 votes each for Sir Geoffrey Howe and James Prior, and 11 for John Peyton. A right-wing woman had been elected leader of the Conservative party, certainly the most unlikely choice by the party since Disraeli. Edward Heath had just lost three elections out of four for his party and was notorious for his contemptuous treatment of backbench Tory MPs. His only reaction to Thatcher's win, recorded many years later in his autobiography *The Course of My Life* (p.535), is instructive: 'The media coverage was, on the whole, sympathetic about the shabby way in which I had been treated.' Heath was only 59, and few could predict that he would hold no position in any Tory Cabinet or Shadow Cabinet, although he would serve in the Commons for another 26 years. With Heath's defeat and Thatcher's election, the Conservatives abandoned their commitment to the quasi-corporatist Keynesian policies represented by Edward Heath.

Harold Wilson's second government also saw the peak of IRA terrorism in Britain, with murderous attacks in Birmingham, London, and elsewhere. A car bomb in Birmingham in November 1974 killed 21 persons. A total of 598 civilians were killed in Northern Ireland in 1974–76, in addition to nearly 100 soldiers and police. In July 1976 Christopher Ewart-Biggs, Britain's Ambassador to Ireland, was assassinated by the Provisional IRA. Guarding against terrorist attacks became a way of life, and the Labour government took drastic steps to deal with the threat, although it declined to re-enact the death penalty for terrorist murders. In Northern Ireland, a power-sharing Executive, consisting of all mainstream parties, took office on 1 January 1974 as a result of the Sunningdale Agreement. This Executive became the victim of a strike by the (Protestant) Ulster Workers' Council, beginning in May 1974, one of few instances in British history of a political strike achieving its ends. As a result, the power-sharing Executive resigned and direct rule from Westminster resumed. Abortive negotiations continued towards resuming local rule, but without result.

On 16 March 1976 Harold Wilson stunned the Cabinet by announcing that he intended to retire. While a few people had been let into the secret, and others guessed it, it came to most members of the Cabinet as a complete surprise. Wilson was only 60 and in good health; the reasons for his sudden voluntary retirement remain obscure. Seven other twentieth-century Prime Ministers voluntarily retired in office, but all were either old or ill. Mary Wilson, the premier's wife, is said to have detested public life; perhaps Harold Wilson had had enough of perennial crisis management and wished to go out while on top. Wilson's legacy is a mixed one, and there is general agreement that his genuine gifts as a tactician were not matched by success at transformative strategy, although his record was, in many respects, a notable one.

The choice of Wilson's successor was not straightforward. Wilson's preferred choice was James Callaghan, the ultimate winner, but he was not the anointed heir apparent. No successor to Wilson could be appointed by the Queen until an exhaustive ballot among Labour MPs took place, which took two weeks. There were six candidates: James Callaghan, Roy Jenkins, Denis Healey, and Anthony Crosland from the centre and right wing of the party, and Michael Foot and Tony Benn from the left. On the first ballot (held on 25 March 1976) Foot received 90 votes, Callaghan 84, Jenkins 56, Benn 37, Healey 30, and Crosland 17. It was clear that the centre and centre-right had more votes than the left, but not an enormous majority. It was also clear that Roy Jenkins, the preferred choice of the media and intelligentsia, could not be elected. Jenkins in fact withdrew. Some months later he left Parliament and took up the appointment of President of the European Economic Commission (he re-entered Parliament in 1982). On the second ballot (30 March), Benn having withdrawn and Crosland eliminated, Callaghan pulled ahead with 141 votes to Foot's 133 and Healey's 38. Finally, on 5 April, Callaghan was elected leader with 176 votes (about 56 per cent of the total) to Foot's 137. The growth of the Left within the Parliamentary Labour party can be gauged by comparing Nye Bevan's vote for leader in 1955 (70 votes of 267 cast, or 26 per cent) with Foot's 44 per cent in 1976. James Callaghan formally became Prime Minister on 5 April 1976, holding office until 4 May 1979.

James Callaghan (b.1912; later baron Callaghan of Cardiff) is a particularly difficult figure to slot into any well-known niche. His father was a Royal Navy chief petty officer who died when his son was nine, leaving the family poor. Born in Portsmouth, Callaghan did not attend a university but became, at 17, a tax inspector in the Inland Revenue and an official of the Association of Tax Officers, the tax inspectors' union. Callaghan thus belonged to neither the industrial working class nor the Oxbridge intelligentsia, the normal breeding grounds of Labour's leaders, but to the important, but seldom-noticed lower-middle class in public employment. Just as ambiguously, Callaghan sat for 42 years as MP for seats in Cardiff, and took the title 'Callaghan of Cardiff' when he entered the Lords. Yet Callaghan was not Welsh, was not perceived as Welsh, and did not speak for Wales; many people continued to be surprised when they learned of his Welsh links. Callaghan was an impressive man exuding avuncularity, confidence, and leadership ability, who seemed the image of a Stage ship's captain. Something of a social and even political conservative, it is likely that he would have been a fairly natural Tory but for the exclusionary rigours of the British class system of his youth. He was a competent and instinctive administrator but without a technical grasp of economics. Rather surprisingly, James Callaghan was the only man in modern history to hold all of the four senior Cabinet posts (Prime Minister, Chancellor of the Exchequer, Foreign Minister, Home Secretary); Churchill held only three, Lloyd George only two.

Callaghan's Cabinet of 22 initially continued with most of the members bequeathed by Wilson. Denis Healey continued as Chancellor as, initially, did Roy Jenkins at the Home Office. As Foreign Secretary Callaghan brought in the Gaitskellite intellectual Anthony Crosland. Michael Foot became Lord President of the Council and a number of older ministers, most notably Barbara Castle at Health, were retired. Callaghan brought in a number of his own appointments, such as Edmund Dell (1921–99), an economist from Manchester, at the Trade Ministry. A few months later, Jenkins left the Cabinet for his European appointment while, in February 1977, Crosland died suddenly, aged only 58. To replace him, Callaghan appointed the 38-year-old Dr David Owen (b.1938), an impressive (but also widely disliked) Cambridge-educated physician on the right of the party. Callaghan also made many other changes in his Cabinet, such figures as Merlyn Rees at the Home Office, Peter Shore (1924–2001) at Environment, Roy Hattersley (b.1932) at Prices, and, in 1978, John Smith (1938–94) at the Trade Ministry, Smith later becoming leader of the Labour party.

Callaghan's term as Prime Minister was marked by the well-rehearsed features common to all recent British governments, in an even more extreme and nearly desperate form. As inflation rose, even Labour, under Denis Healey, was forced to cut public expenditure by substantial amounts. The value of the floating pound compared to the American dollar fell relentlessly, dropping below $2.00 for the first time ever in March 1976 and reaching $1.57 in the October. At this time, the government approached the International Monetary Fund for a huge loan, $3.9 billion, to which conditions of spending cuts were attached. Unemployment continued to soar, reaching a new post-war peak of 1.6 million in August 1978 (about 6.2 per cent of the workforce). The government's main aim, however, was to cut inflation. Here, it gradually had some real success, bringing the annual increase in the retail price index down from 16 per cent in 1976–77 to 8 per cent in 1977–78, before rising slightly, to 11 per cent, in 1978–79. Callaghan's smooth style was also successful in obtaining union agreement to lower wage demands. The Labour government had, however, all but abandoned any pretence to achieving full employment. If a major part of 'Thatcherism' was to abandon the Keynesian goal of full employment in order to fight inflation, then Callaghan and Healey initiated an important component of 'Thatcherism', albeit without rolling back the state, cutting taxes, or privatising. Given its tiny majority (which technically disappeared in 1976) the Labour government could not embark on 'socialist' measures, and enacted only one piece of nationalisation: the Aircraft and Shipbuilding Industries Act, 1977, which took most of these industries into public ownership. Indeed, to raise money the government was forced, in 1977, to sell off 17 per cent of its holding in state-owned petroleum. Following the Kilbrandon Report on devolution in Scotland and Ireland, bills setting up Scottish and Welsh assemblies were passed by Parliament. The establishment of a Scottish Assembly was narrowly approved in a referendum, but a Welsh Assembly was rejected. Both acts were nullified when the Conservatives returned to power in 1979.

In 1976–77, Labour's by-election record was dismal. It lost a number of utterly safe seats – such as Walsall North and Ashfield (where, in April 1977, a Labour majority of 22 915 was transformed into a Tory majority of 264). The Tories were, moreover, ahead of Labour in most opinion polls after Margaret Thatcher became leader. Nevertheless, by mid-1978 Labour drew even. A factor in this gain might have been Queen Elizabeth's Silver Jubilee celebrations in 1977, which proved an unexpected popular success, marked by street parties and festivities. As well, the government concluded an agreement with the Liberal party which made an early General Election less likely. Had Callaghan gone to the polls on the government's record in 1978, it is possible, even likely, that he would have won. Callaghan, however, chose to soldier on, assuming that lower inflation and North Sea Oil revenues would ease the electoral situation still further in 1979.

Instead, however, things turned highly unpleasant for the Labour government in late 1978. The electoral deal with the Liberals was nullified by that party in November, and the unions were proving as recalcitrant as ever at moderating their demands. The government's proposal for a general maximum 5 per cent wage increase was rejected by the TUC, and a rash of high profile, damaging strikes began in October 1978 with Ford workers, spreading by February 1979 to include lorry drivers, public employees, and civil servants. The strike by public employees, affecting 1.5 million workers, signalled the 'winter of discontent', as it was soon dubbed, and led to massive layoffs as a result of a road haulage strike. By early 1979 unofficial strikes now erupted every week, suddenly bringing Britain to the point of chaos. The refusal of Liverpool grave-diggers to bury the dead was taken up as the visible symbol of this period, as was the contamination of the water supply in northwest England as a result of a water workers' strike and, above all, the piling up of trash in black plastic bags because of a strike by local manual workers, leading to an infestation of rats. The government now appeared to be on its last legs, its self-destruction encapsulated on 10 January 1979 by James Callaghan's alleged remark 'Crisis? What crisis?' on returning from a summit of major leaders in Guadeloupe. (Callaghan actually never said what was certainly his most famous 'remark'; he actually said 'I don't think that other people in the world would share the view that there is mounting chaos' when asked by a journalist about the 'mounting chaos' in Britain. 'Crisis? What crisis?' was invented in the *Sun* newspaper's headline the next morning.)

On 28 March 1979 a crucial vote of confidence, called by the Tories, took place. The government tried desperately to secure the support of the minor parties but lost by one vote, 311-310, one of the few occasions on which a Commons vote of confidence has brought down a government. Parliament was dissolved and a General Election called. The Tories ran an excellent, well-financed campaign centred around the slogan 'Labour isn't working', dreamed up by the pro-Tory advertising agents Saatchi and Saatchi.

In the end, the Conservatives won the election of 3 May 1979 easily, winning a majority of 43 over all other parties.

	Total votes	MPs elected	% share of total vote
Conservative	13 697 690	339	43.9
Liberal	4 313 811	11	13.8
Labour	11 532 148	269	36.9
Communist	15 938	0	0.1
Plaid Cymru	132 544	2	0.4
Scottish Nationals	504 259	2	1.6
National Front	190 742	0	0.6
Ecology	38 116	0	0.1
Workers Revolutionary Party	13 535	0	0.1
Others (G.B.)	85 338	0	0.3
Others (No.I.)	695 880	12	2.2
Total	31 220 010	635	100.0

The Tories gained 2.2 million votes compared with the October 1974 election. They obtained, surprisingly, many working-class votes, and also profited from its image of toughness on crime and immigration. Nevertheless, Labour did not disgrace itself, winning slightly more votes than five years earlier. The Liberals, who lost one million votes, were squeezed, despite gaining a new leader, David Steel (b.1938) in July 1976, replacing Jeremy Thorpe, who had resigned amidst mounting rumours of scandal. Labour still had enormous majorities among MPs in the north of England, Scotland, and Wales, but were trounced by the Tories in the south of England outside London, where the Conservatives held 146 seats to Labour's 13. James Callaghan, of course, resigned the next morning, and Margaret Thatcher became Britain's first woman Prime Minister. Callaghan had been an above-average Prime Minister, who was, until late 1978, effective at curbing inflation, and an excellent judge of talent. His government had been the first to break, however tentatively, with the post-war Keynesian consensus. Ultimately, however, his government was constrained by the unions and by the accumulated weight of accepted opinion, especially within the Labour party. Callaghan's government should, therefore, be seen as the last Butskellite administration which attempted to grapple with Britain's economic problems in the traditional way.

13
The Thatcher Era, 1979–90

What we mean by 'Thatcherism' combines several separate themes: 'rolling back' the scope of the state; abandoning Keynesian notions of full employment in order to tame inflation; refusing to accede to outrageous trade union demands; lowering taxes and privatising many state industries. The Thatcher era lasted for 11 years, and not all of these became government policy at the same time or at once. Many of Margaret Thatcher's Cabinet colleagues were not 'Thatcherites', and in many respects only her character and beliefs provided a unity to these themes.

It is also possible to trace the origins of aspects of 'Thatcherism' to the period before she came to power. Edward Heath is often depicted as a proto-Thatcherite who lacked the courage of his convictions, while Denis Healey, James Callaghan's Chancellor, experimented with 'monetarist' solutions to Britain's economic woes. Nevertheless, it is also quite wrong to underestimate the magnitude of the change that Thatcherism represented for British policy. 'Thatcherism' was not preordained to happen, and without her there is no reason to suppose that Britain would not have muddled along with some variant of the policies pursued by her predecessors. Why then did the Thatcher era occur? First and foremost, because everything else (with the exception of full-throated socialism) had been tried and failed. Had the 'modernisation' policies pursued by Wilson and Heath been successful or a fully workable 'social contract' set in place, it is very difficult to believe that the Thatcher era would have occurred. There were other reasons, as well. Thatcherites had a number of highly visible and palpable enemies – bloody-minded trade union bosses, effete Tory 'wets', woolly minded left-wing intellectuals, the Soviet 'empire of evil' in its decline phase – whom it was easy and popular to target. Thatcherism put in place the theories of right-wing economists and intellectuals such as Frederick von Hayek and Milton Friedman who moved from the periphery of intellectual debate to the centre with the collapse of Keynesianism. There was, as well, the crucial influence of Ronald Reagan in America: 'Reaganism', the American equivalent of Thatcherism, is often seen as having been centrally influenced by Margaret Thatcher, and Reagan was first elected in November 1980, a year and a half after Thatcher came to power. Nevertheless, the central themes of Reagan's policies, especially drastic cuts in personal taxes, significantly influenced the direction of Thatcherism after its initial phase, not the other way round. Thatcherism also represented a generational change. As Denis Healey once perceptively noted, Thatcherism was impossible before those with a direct adult memory of Britain's successful national planning during the Second World War passed from the scene. While there were plainly exceptions to this rule, it is nevertheless true that the gap in experiences between Edward Heath (b.1916), an officer during the war, and Margaret Thatcher (b.1925), a teenager during the war, was of great importance. Thatcherism also skilfully exploited quite contradictory desiderata: more authority, against the breakdown of authority and law and order, and less state control and less 'socialism', as perceived by much of the middle classes. But in the final analysis one comes back to the character and personality of Margaret Thatcher. Margaret Thatcher (*née* Roberts) was, of course, the daughter of a Methodist grocer in Grantham (who became Mayor of the town). She won a grammar school scholarship and, implausibly, read chemistry at Somerville College, Oxford, becoming a research chemist. She twice contested Dartford unsuccessfully before being adopted by Finchley, a safe Tory seat in north London, becoming a barrister, and marrying a successful businessman, Denis Thatcher. Promotion came easily to her, with appointment as a junior minister in 1961, just before her thirty-sixth birthday. The Education Minister was her first and only Cabinet position before her election to the leadership. She was regarded as very able, but few would have predicted her seminal role in British politics.

Thatcher formed a conventional Cabinet of 22, distinctly un-Thatcherite in composition. Twenty of its members had been to a public school, six to Eton, while 17 had attended Oxbridge. Only a few, however, were connected with the hereditary aristocracy; most came from the middle classes. All but two members of the Cabinet had served in Edward Heath's government, and Thatcher's Cabinet included such Heath associates and protégés as Lord Carrington at the Foreign Office, William Whitelaw at the Home Office, and Peter Walker anomalously at Agriculture. The most prominent active 'Heathman' excluded from the new Cabinet was Edward Heath himself (who had not been included in Thatcher's Shadow Cabinet). Mrs Thatcher did not know quite what to do with Heath, and finally made him the curious offer of Ambassador to the United States. Since Heath disliked America and had no diplomatic skills whatever, the offer was, not surprisingly, rejected, and Heath remained isolated from the Thatcher government and from Thatcherism as 'the incredible sulk' (as he became known), critical of the direction the Thatcher government took. Had Edward Heath been offered a Cabinet post, it seems highly likely that he would have acted as a central Cabinet opponent of 'Thatcherism', perhaps with great effect. While Mrs Thatcher's Cabinet included many 'One Nation' Tories such as Walker, Whitelaw, and James Prior (b.1927), and a good many men (Mrs Thatcher was the Cabinet's only woman) distinctly on the Left of the party, such as Sir Ian Gilmour (b.1926), the Lord Privy Seal, and Lord Soames (Sir Christopher Soames, 1920–87), Lord President of the Council, it actually encompassed only a handful of 'Thatcherites' besides the Prime Minister (although there were more at the junior level), chiefly Sir Keith Joseph (1918–94), Minister for Industry, and Angus Maude (1912–93), the Paymaster-General. Intellectually, Joseph was the most important right-wing force within the mainstream Conservative party. Joseph's conversion to monetarism in the 1970s is widely seen as a central event in legitimating dissent from Britskellism, and he was widely viewed as a possible Tory leader. His penchant for unfortunate remarks, especially one condemning the working classes for their high birth rate, and his lack of the common touch, had ruled him out from any realistic change of becoming leader. The most important proto-Thatcherite of all, Enoch Powell, had also written himself out of the picture by supporting Labour in the October 1974 election (because of its apparent opposition to the EEC) and then successfully standing as an Ulster Unionist candidate in a Northern Irish seat. One of the paradoxes of Thatcherism is that a majority of those in Mrs Thatcher's Cabinet were never full-blown Thatcherites.

Nevertheless, it was clear from the first that the new government dissented from the Gaitskellite consensus in many respects. Sir Geoffrey Howe, the Chancellor, immediately cut income tax, the basic rate decreasing from 33 to 30 per cent; the top rate on earned incomes from 83 to 60 per cent and on 'unearned' incomes from 98 to 75 per cent, raised VAT, and cut expenditure. It did, however, honour wage agreements promised by the previous government. Oil prices escalated again in 1980, producing one of the worst rounds of inflation in history, with the retail price index increasing by 18 per cent in 1979–80 and 12 per cent in 1980–81. This was accompanied by previously unknown levels of unemployment, which skyrocketed from 5.7 per cent in 1979 to 7.4 per cent in 1980, and then to 11.4 per cent in 1981, and 13.0 per cent in 1982, reaching 3 097 000 in December 1982 (and going still higher thereafter), levels unknown since the Great Depression. To this was added an increase in the bank lending rate to 17 per cent at its monthly peaks in 1979 and 1980, rates simply without any precedent. Most governments would have cracked under the strain, going into a u-turn, whatever its initial intentions, and seeking a 'social contract' with the unions or a statutory wage accord. Not so this government, despite widespread expectations, especially from 'One Nation' Tories in the Cabinet, of a Thatcherite u-turn. 'There is no alternative', Mrs Thatcher repeatedly stated, and then, famously at the Tory party conference of October 1980, 'The Lady's not for turning.'

The government thus carried on with its policies of abandoning any *dirigiste* attempt at controlling the economic situation, and proceeded with a programme of economic liberalism. Exchange controls on taking money overseas were abolished once the government came to power and, under the Housing Act, 1980, council house tenants were given the automatic right to buy their homes at substantial discounts. Over the next five years 623 000 council houses were sold off in this way, with a further 587 000 sold off between 1985 and 1989. This substantially raised the percentage of persons in Britain owning their own home, which increased from 53 per cent in 1975 to 67 per cent in 1990, one of the highest figures in the world. The trade unions were reformed, but only gradually and over a period of years, generally with the aim of enforcing ballots before strikes were called. The first of many waves of privatisation was begun in late 1975, with the sale of 5 per cent of British Petroleum (BP) and a variety of miscellaneous government holdings, totally £377 million, the Tories having pledged to 'roll back the frontiers of the state'. Really enormous sales, however, had to wait a few years. In 1983, 75 per cent of BP was sold for £543 million, while British Telecom was sold off in stages after 1983 for nearly

£4 billion, as well as, over the next 16 years, British Aerospace, British Gas, Rolls-Royce, the rest of BP, British Steel, the water companies, the electricity companies, British Coal, the nuclear industry, and all of Britain's railways, for the incredible sum, over the whole period, of £67 billion. By late 1981, Thatcher had also begun to purge the 'wettest' of wets in her Cabinet, dropping those – such as Lord Soames, Sir Ian Gilmour, and Norman St John-Stevas – with whom she was in sharp disagreement, and promoting 'Thatcherites' such as Nigel Lawson (b.1932; later baron Lawson of Blaby), who became Energy Minister in September 1981, and Chancellor of the Exchequer in June 1983, and Norman Tebbit (b.1931), probably the archetypal shoot-from-the-hip Thatcherite populist, who became Employment Minister at the same time. Tebbit, of course, became renowned for his remark, at the Tory party conference in October 1981, that his unemployed father in the 1930s 'didn't riot. He got on his bike and looked for work.'

Not everyone was pleased with this sudden and drastic change of policy, and, to many, British society was being destroyed by Thatcher's laissez-faire policies. The early Thatcher years also saw an outburst of civil unrest in Britain's inner cities, often (but not invariably) among ethnic minorities, which was without real precedent. Serious rioting occurred at St Paul's, Bristol (April 1980), Brixton (April and July 1981), and Toxteth, Liverpool (July 1981), the last a major civil disturbance, chiefly among the local black community. The Provisional IRA continued, as murderous as ever, assassinating Airey Neave (April 1979), the first major political assassination on British soil since Sir Henry Wilson was murdered by Sinn Fein in 1922, and then, in August 1979, killing Lord Mountbatten and his relatives in the Irish Republic. In October 1984, the IRA came close to killing off the entire government, planting a bomb at the Grand Hotel, Brighton, where the Tories were holding their annual conference, and killing Sir Anthony Berry, a junior minister, and others. Football hooliganism, both in Britain and by British fans abroad, escalated at this time, culminating in the drunken charge by Liverpool supporters at Heysel Stadium, Belgium in May 1985, in which 38 people were killed. Recorded crime escalated dramatically as well.

The response of the electorate to the initially poor economic conditions caused by Thatcherism was more muted than one might have assumed. Labour was ahead, fairly consistently, of the Tories in nearly all opinion polls held after the 1979 General Election until mid-1982, although Labour was never in anything like a commanding position. Nor did the Tories suffer undue by-election defeats as yet. Much of the reason for this lay in the steady, seemingly relentless growth of the hard Left within the Labour party at this time, which prevented it from capitalising on Thatcher's initial unpopularity; indeed, it was Labour which was increasingly seen by the media and most commentators as hopelessly divided and extremist-ridden. Just after the 1979 General Election, Tony Benn refused to stand for the Shadow Cabinet, going to the backbenchers to lead a left-wing campaign aimed at controlling the party. At the October 1979 Conference, the party adopted as policy the mandatory re-selection of sitting MPs in the life of each Parliament, a victory for far-left activists. In 1980, the party decided to select its leader and deputy leader by an elaborate electoral college composed of MPs, trade unions, constituency parties, and affiliated bodies, but delayed initiating it for a year. The party was now bitterly and publicly divided, with right-wingers such as Roy Jenkins and David Owen, under serious threat from the Left, now vocal in attacking James Callaghan and also the growing threat of the Left, and threatening ever more openly to leave the party. In October 1980, James Callaghan, then 68, suddenly announced his retirement, in order that the next leader be chosen under the old rules, by sitting MPs alone. The obvious successor to Callaghan was Denis Healey, a successful Chancellor, supported by the centre and right of the party, and popular with the public. He was, however, strongly opposed by the ascendant left within the party and among the trade unions. He was also disliked among some uncommitted MPs for his bullying and too-sharp tongue. After much soul-searching Michael Foot, the Bevanite leader, was persuaded to stand for the leadership, as were John Silkin (1923–87) and Peter Shore from the centre-left of the party. On the first ballot for leader (4 November 1980) Healey received 112 votes, to 83 for Foot, 38 for Silkin, and 32 for Shore. In the second ballot, however, Foot unexpectedly defeated Healey (the others having dropped out) by 139-129 votes. Healey (who was then unanimously elected Deputy Leader) was defeated chiefly by centrists who thought Foot more likely to unite the party than Healey, widely seen as abrasive and divisive. The leadership of the Labour party was thus in the hands of a man, whatever his undoubted intellectual gifts and eloquence, closely associated for decades with the extreme left of British politics, who was probably unelectable in the best of circumstances. In January 1981, at a special conference, the party decided that the leader and deputy leader of the party would be re-elected annually by the party's conference, with 40 per cent of the votes allocated to the trade unions, 30 per cent to sitting MPs, and 30 per cent to the constituency parties. This was the last straw for many Labour right-wingers, and a new centre-left party, the Social Democrats, was formed in March 1981, chiefly by the 'gang of four'. Roy Jenkins, David Owen, Bill Rodgers (b.1921) and Shirley Williams (*née* Brittain; b.1930), all well-known and respected moderate Labourites and former Cabinet ministers. Within a year, it had attracted twenty-five sitting Labourites and one Tory (Christopher Brocklebank-Fowler), with Shirley Williams and Roy Jenkins – who were out of Parliament – winning high-profile by-elections. Its aim was to form a pact with the Liberals (known as the 'Alliance'), with the goal (in Roy Jenkins' words) of 'breaking the mould of British politics'. Given the initial hostility to Thatcherism and the increasing extremism of Labour, it had every expectation of success, and did (when linked with the Liberals) remarkably well in opinion polls, consistently running neck-and-neck with the two older parties and emerging as the most popular single party in the voting intention surveys of November 1981–April 1982. The long-term effects of the Social Democrats' split from Labour was, however, arguably negative. Very few of the Tory 'wets' joined it, nearly all remaining loyal to Thatcher, while its existence gravely weakened the remaining moderates in the Labour party. In October 1981, with the new 'electoral college' in place, Denis Healey was challenged by Tony Benn and John Silkin for the party's deputy leadership. Healey received about 45.5 per cent of the vote on the first ballot, compared with about

36.6 per cent for Benn (who was victorious in the constituency party vote) and 18 per cent for Silkin. On the second ballot, Healey defeated Benn by the narrowest of margins, 50.4-49.6 per cent. Labour was by now hopelessly split on a range of issues. In 1981, the party conference voted overwhelmingly for unilateral nuclear disarmament, a policy opposed by most of the Shadow Cabinet; for a time, Labour officially adopted two contradictory policies on this issue. Given the apparent escalation of the Cold War at this time, unilateral nuclear disarmament became one of the main catchcries of the Left, with many Labour-controlled councils declaring themselves to be 'nuclear-free zones', and the Greenham Common protests by anti-nuclear women going on for a decade after 1991.

The most dramatic event of Thatcher's first term as Prime Minister, however, occurred in the most unlikely of places. In April 1982, the military junta ruling Argentina invaded the Falkland Islands, a British dependency in the South Atlantic, seizing control of them and also of South Georgia, another remote British outpost. Few people had ever heard of the Falklands, long claimed by Argentina but inhabited by British-descended sheep farmers. One immediate casualty of the Argentinian invasion was Lord Carrington, the Foreign Minister, who resigned from office (to be replaced by Francis Pym (b.1922)), taking responsibility for what he termed 'this very great national humiliation'. Responding Churchill-style to direct military aggression was Mrs Thatcher's *metier*, and for a time in the spring of 1982 it seemed as if the clock had been turned back a century or more. A flotilla of over 100 naval vessels (few in Britain realising that the Royal Navy had 100 ships left) was assembled to steam south and air attacks on the Argentinean positions on the Islands quickly begun. The Commonwealth, given up for dead, miraculously sprang back to life to support the Mother Country, and the United States, torn between Britain and a Western hemisphere power, generally supported Britain. The Falklands War, which lasted for two and a half months, was not without its tragedies, especially the torpedoing of the Argentinean cruiser *General Belgrano* and the loss of 20 men on *HMS Sheffield*, hit by an Argentinian missile, but overall Argentina proved no match for Britain even a quarter-century after Suez. Marine Commandos stormed the island and Argentina surrendered on 14 June 1982. Britain lost, in all, 254 men killed and 777 wounded. One immediate result was the overthrow of the barbaric military junta in Argentina. Margaret Thatcher emerged as, to many, a modern Boadicea or Elizabeth the Great, truly the 'Iron Lady', as she came to be known, 'the only man in the Cabinet'. Tory stocks in opinion surveys immediately rose, as well as Mrs Thatcher's own rating. 'GOTCHA' was the *Sun*'s famous headline after the sinking of the *Belgrano* in May 1982, and Thatcher's victory unquestionably fanned a populist wave of support. Labour was in a real quandary over the Falklands, forced between supporting overt aggression by a fascist military junta or an 'imperialist war' led by a right-wing Tory. Michael Foot unhesitatingly supported the British response, while suggesting that the ultimate fate of the Falklands might be negotiable.

The 'Falklands factor', as it became known, is widely seen as having transformed the political scene, paving the way for Thatcher's great win in the 1983 General Election. While this can certainly be cogently argued – as noted, the opinion polls showed a basic change of voting intention at the time – other important factors also existed. Most basically, Labour under Michael Foot was unelectable. Although unemployment was terrible, the economy was beginning to come around. Because of North Sea Oil, Britain was now running, most remarkably, a strong balance of trade surplus, which reached £7 billion in 1981, £4 billion in 1982, and £3 billion in 1983, despite the usual lamentable state of other British exports. Many upwardly mobile businessmen and professionals were benefiting from 'Thatcherism', and the age of the 'yuppies' and 'Sloane Rangers' was dawning. On the other hand, many middle-class employees in the public service were suffering greatly. The universities, for instance, were severely squeezed when Sir Keith Joseph was Education Secretary (1981–86). Mrs Thatcher was never forgiven (although by this time most Arts lecturers were anti-Tory in any case), with Oxford petulantly declining to give her an honorary degree, although she was the University's most successful graduate. In general, the Thatcher era opened or widened a growing rift between the middle classes in the private and public sectors, with the former gaining far more than the latter.

When it came, the General Election of June 1983 proved a walkover for the Tories, one of the great election triumphs of the century. The division in the left-of-centre vote between Labour and the Liberals had always been favourable to Tory electoral chances, and, with the Alliance now a major grouping, this factor was even more important than in the past (although the Alliance probably took votes from the Tories). Labour's enormously long and very radical manifesto *The New Hope for Britain* was a mixture of incoherence and blank cheques; it was quickly and famously dubbed 'the longest suicide note in history'. The Tory campaign was professional and well funded, and there was never any doubt of the outcome.

	Total votes	MPs elected	% share of total vote
Conservative	13012315	397	42.4
Liberal	4210115	17	13.7
Social Democrat	3570834	6	11.6
(Alliance Total)	(7780949)	(23)	(25.4)
Labour	8456934	209	27.6
Communist	11606	0	0.04
Plaid Cymru	125309	2	0.4
Scottish National Party	331975	2	1.1
National Front	27065	0	0.1
Others (G.B.)	193383	0	0.6
Others (No.I)	764925	17	3.1
Total	30671136	650	100.0

Turnout was down from 1979; indeed, the Tory vote was down by over 600000, and its percentage of the total vote also fell by 1.5 per cent. This decline, however, should be seen in the context of a genuinely popular third party, which contested nearly every seat and had been ahead in opinion polls only a year earlier. Because Labour still retained a vice-like grip on many industrial sears (hardly loosened by mass unemployment), the total number of Tory MPs elected did not really fall off the bell curve: the total of 397 Conservative MPs did not approach their numbers in the 1930s, nor the Labour totals in 1997–2001. Nevertheless, it was a great achievement, with the Tories gaining 58 seats compared with that in 1979. The Conservatives were virtually hegemonic in the south of England outside London, electing 168 MPs compared with the ridiculous total of only three Labourites and five Liberals. They had substantial majorities in London (56-26) and the Midlands (70-30) but Labour remained ahead in the north of England (89-68), Scotland and Wales. In Scotland, the Tories actually had one fewer MP than in 1979, continuing a long-term trend. No justice at all was done to the Alliance, which elected 186 fewer MPs than Labour, despite trailing them by only 27.6-25.4 per cent in votes cast. As usual, the 'first past the post' system penalised those parties without a firm and contiguous geographical base of support, which the Alliance lacked.

Mrs Thatcher was now all-dominant, and the next few years represented the zenith of 'Thatcherism'. Yet it is important to keep in mind the limitations which still existed on any truly sharp swing to the Right, or even an emphatic reversion to the circumstances of a generation before. Even with the Tories' enormous majority, attempts by backbenchers on a free vote to reintroduce the death penalty failed in 1983 and 1987. From 1983, Mrs Thatcher created a number of hereditary peerages for William Whitelaw (Viscount Whitelaw), George Thomas the Speaker of the House (Viscount Tonypandy), and Harold Macmillan (Earl of Stockton), but, for whatever reason, only a handful were created, and the overwhelming majority were non-hereditary. While the Tories gave a firm pledge that there would be no further large-scale New Commonwealth immigration, 25 000 such settlers were accepted every year during the Thatcher years, and, when the Hong Kong treaty was negotiated in 1984 with China, Britain gave a guarantee to accept 50 000 wealthy Hong Kong residents if they wished to come. While many Tories would have dearly loved to revoke all the 'permissive' changes since the 1960s, little or nothing could be done. The best-known piece of anti-permissive legislation of the Thatcher era was probably Section 28 of the Local Government Act, 1988, which prohibited the teaching of 'the acceptability of homosexuality as a pretended family relationship' and forbade local authorities to engage in 'the promotion of homosexuality'. On the other hand, the Thatcher government came more and more to drop any distinction (in benefits or the availability of mortgages) between married couples and those who were cohabiting. In 1980–82 it established Channel Four, an independent television channel which became well known for its unorthodox material. Certainly neither television, the theatre, the press, nor Britain's publishers were less frank or less oriented towards 'permissive' themes when Mrs Thatcher left office in 1990 than when she came to power in 1979. It should also be noted that, despite her enormous electoral wins, Thatcher was alienating some of the bedrock of traditional Tory support. During this period, for instance, the Church of England, formerly known as 'the Conservative party at prayer', became dominated, at least among its articulate spokesmen, by left-liberals who were sharply critical of Thatcherism in such reports that it issued as *The Church and the Bomb* (1982) and especially in *Faith in the City* (1985), which seemed to be an explicit attack on 'Thatcherism'. Certainly by 1990 only a minority of Anglican bishops were avowedly Tory, whereas in, say, 1938, a majority were certainly pro-Tory, albeit coexisting with a visible Christian socialist minority. Much of the ever-larger academic, educational, and welfare public sector middle class consisted of bitter opponents of Thatcherism, in contrast to the situation only a few decades earlier.

Thatcherism was most successful in limiting the welfare state, opening new opportunities for individual enterprise, and, above all, in taming the arrogance of the trade unions. Probably the archetypal example of this, and the best illustration of the contrast between Thatcher and her predecessors, came with the great miners' strike which began in March 1984. Less than ten years before, a miners' strike had brought about the political demise of Edward Heath, and Arthur Scargill (b.1938), the radical head of the NUM since 1981, who first attracted attention as the organiser of 'flying pickets' in 1972, was anxious to do the same to Thatcher. On the other hand, much had changed: membership in the NUM declined from 255 000 in 1974 to 200 000 in 1984 as coal pits relentlessly closed and coal was well and truly dethroned as 'king'. Flying pickets and 'militant shock troops' descended on coal mines after the NUM found a way to evade a national strike ballot. The strike was never general throughout Britain, and the government had stockpiled coal. The strike dragged on, becoming more violent (nearly 6000 arrests were made). It was revealed in October 1984 that Scargill had made (and probably received) a personal appeal to Libya's Col. Gadaffi for financial support, as well as support from Soviet sources, and the NUM's strike effort began to go very badly, especially after a strike-breaking miner was murdered in South Wales in November. NUM funds, though deposited abroad, were sequestered by the courts; more and more miners returned to work, and Scargill was forced to call off the strike on 3 March 1985. The miners' strike caused the loss of 26 million working days, the highest total of any industrial action since the General Strike. The NUM's key demand, that uneconomic pits be kept open, was of course not met, and these were systematically closed. By 1990, the NUM had only 53 000 members (compared with 90 000 in 1920 and 455 000 in 1948), and, remarkably, only 5000 left in 1997. The miners' strike of 1984–85 was unquestionably a turning-point in Britain's recent industrial history, showing that a determined government could take on a militant union and win; gaining the 'cooperation' of the unions was not necessary for a successful government, and it was not preordained that a strike in a major industry would result in a victory for the union. Thatcher emerged from the miners' strike with an almost legendary reputation on the Right and centre, while Labour's highly ambiguous position over the miners' strike did it little electoral good.

After the 1983 election Thatcher rearranged her Cabinet, making it still more in her image, although without shedding the Tory moderates. Nigel Lawson, a neo-liberal monetarist journalist, became Chancellor of the Exchequer. As Financial Treasurer to the Treasury he had been primarily responsible for the steadily falling growth in the money supply. Lawson's greatest achievement as Chancellor (a position he held until October 1989) was the drastic cuts in rates of income tax he made in successive budgets from 1986.

In March 1988, he reduced the standard rate of income tax to 25 per cent and the top marginal rate to 40 per cent, one of the lowest top rates in the world and a level not seen in Britain since 1930. It is no exaggeration to say that this was arguably the most important, and most far-sighted, taxation decision made by any Chancellor in modern times, one which helped significantly to regain, by the mid-1990s, something like British economic pre-eminence in Europe. This tax cut, it should be noted, was one about which Mrs Thatcher had considerable doubts, given its large size. Lawson also made significant changes to Corporation and other taxes, and introduced the tax-free PEPs (Personal Equity Plans), allowing millions to invest in a tax-efficient way. Lawson's period as Chancellor represented the fruition of Thatcherism. Thatcher was now fairly lucky in economic matters. In October 1986, the 'Big Bang' deregulated the Stock Exchange, modernising the City in an atmosphere of increasing 'globalisation' via computers and, later, the internet. Despite such setbacks as 'Black Monday' (the dramatic stock market crash of 19 October 1987), the City re-emerged into something like its pre-1939 or even pre-1914 guise, as one of the world's great entrepôts, a role which had, as much or more than the industrial revolution, been responsible for Britain's economic pre-eminence. The restrictions on international finance (as well as the replacement of the City by Wall Street) after 1914 and, still more, after 1939, were a significant element in Britain's economic 'decline', although one often overlooked by historians. A major component of Thatcherism was her wise decision not to 'modernise' British industry through direct intervention, as so many previous governments had tried to do, but to widen the scope of the City and await the boom which was sure to follow. Thatcherism was also associated – although it had no direct role – with the movement of Britain's newspapers from Fleet Street to Wapping in Docklands in 1986–87, a move undertaken (even by left-leaning papers) to be rid of the press unions and their particularly egregious 'old Spanish customs' in press industry overmanning and overpayments. In 1987, Thatcher commissioned a report into the Civil Service, 'Improving Management in Government: The Next Steps', which proposed that many functions of the civil service could be performed by semi-autonomous or even private bodies. Over the next few years such government organisations as Her Majesty's Stationery Office (HMSO), which prints all government documents, were privatised or re-established as autonomous, profit-seeking bodies. Like much of Thatcherism, these steps would have been inconceivable even ten years earlier.

Although Thatcher is often seen as a Cold War 'super-hawk' and linked to Ronald Reagan in an apocalyptic vision of Soviet–Western relations, in reality she was quite mainstream, and appeared aggressively right-wing only because the Left now advocated unilateral nuclear disarmament. In Cold War foreign policy, Thatcher was also extremely lucky. In 1982, Leonid Brezhnev, leader of the Soviet Union, died, and the ossified and incompetent Communist party turned to a number of geriatric stopgaps before, in March 1985, appointing Mikhail Gorbachev to lead the Soviet Union. Only 44, Gorbachev gave the Soviet Union's governing circles rather more than it bargained for, introducing 'peristroika' and 'glasnost' which meant nothing less than the transformation of the Soviet Union into a democracy, the end of the Cold War and, in 1991 (after Gorbachev had been removed from office by Boris Yeltsin), the disappearance of the Soviet Union itself. By the end of 1990, the Soviet satellites had become democracies, the Berlin Wall had come down, and Germany was unified. These almost miraculous events, utterly unpredictable a decade earlier, were accomplished with almost no bloodshed whatever. To some philosophers, the end of Communism meant 'the end of history'; it certainly suggested that the enormities brought about by the destruction of Europe's elite structure in the First World War had now been made good, and that (not quite the same thing) American liberalism and 'the end of ideology' were now ubiquitous in the Western world. Reagan, Thatcher, and other Cold War stalwarts were now widely seen as heroic figures who had been right all along and whose steadfastness was responsible for the miraculous events in eastern Europe. The ideological left had to deal with the reality that 'socialism' had both failed and disappeared, and attempted to reinvent itself around issues of gender and ethnicity.

In general, the record of Thatcher in foreign policy seldom deviated from the mainstream. In mid-1979 the Rhodesian crisis was finally settled, resulting in independence and a black majority government headed, after an election, by Robert Mugabe, a nationalist leader who become increasingly paranoid and dictatorial in the well-established African tradition. The Thatcher government thus settled the Rhodesian situation on the basis of majority rule, although many in the Tory party would have expected a right-wing Conservative government to be sympathetic to Ian Smith and the British settlers. Similarly in Northern Ireland the Thatcher government continued the broadly conciliatory and inclusive settlement, ignoring the desires of the fiercer Unionists. A new Northern Ireland Assembly was instituted in 1982 and, in November 1985, the Hillsborough accord between Britain and Ireland instituted regular conferences between the two countries over Northern Ireland, leading to the mass resignation of Unionist MPs. The Thatcher government put into place much of the groundwork which greatly diminished violence in Northern Ireland by the late 1990s.

Thatcher's relations with Europe were also surprisingly good, at least until her last years in office, and lacked the bitterness of the Major years. There were many reasonably successful European summits, and Thatcher's nominee as British European Commissioner, Lord Cockfield, was one of the main architects of the Single Market concept, a genuine free market of 350 million people. The latter years of the Thatcher period were, however, marked by much greater bitterness, with the Prime Minister increasingly opposed to a federalist conception of European integration, and to the 'harmonisation' of statutory arrangements through the EC, which she increasingly saw as the imposition of socialism by the back door. In September 1988, Mrs Thatcher criticised further European integration in a notable speech in Bruges. By October 1990 Britain was isolated in Europe over monetary union, and it was Mrs Thatcher's increasing opposition to further European integration that provoked Sir Geoffrey Howe, the Deputy Prime Minister, to resign from the Cabinet, setting in motion the train of events that led to Thatcher's downfall. At all times Mrs Thatcher's Cabinet included a majority of ministers who were pro-European. It could be argued that this was a fatal mistake, and that Thatcher's enormously powerful position should have enabled her to replace many of them with eurosceptics with whom she felt increasing sympathy.

Michael Foot resigned soon after the 1983 debacle. Denis Healey also declined to stand, and Labour's electoral college system was used for the first time to select both the leader and deputy leader. In October 1983, Neil Kinnock was elected with 71.3 per cent of the vote, defeating Roy Hattersley (19.3 per cent), Eric Heffer (1922–91) (6.3 per cent) and Peter Shore (3.1 per cent). Tony Benn, who lost his seat at the General Election, was unable to stand. For deputy leader the party elected Roy Hattersley (67.3 per cent), defeating Michael Meacher (b.1939) (27.9 per cent), and two trailing candidates. Kinnock (b.1942) was only 41 when selected. The son of a coalminer, of mixed Welsh and Scottish descent, he nevertheless grew up in post-Attlee Britain in circumstances which previous generations would have regarded as affluence, attending a grammar school and the University of Wales. He entered Parliament in 1970 for a Welsh mining seat, making a name as a left-winger who supported Michael Foot. He did not serve in Labour's 1974–79 government, but entered the Shadow Cabinet in 1979. Kinnock increasingly moved to the political centre, and became a determined opponent of the hard left and the Militants. While everyone admitted that Kinnock was able and articulate, he also developed a reputation as the 'Welsh windbag', known for long-winded vacuousness and lack of detail in the manner, perhaps, of Ramsay MacDonald. Roy Hattersley (b.1932) came from Yorkshire, attended Sheffield Grammar School and Hull University and became a journalist. He entered Parliament in 1964, and, unlike Kinnock, held a variety of posts, including Prices Minister in Callaghan's Cabinet. Hattersley was thought of as on the party's right wing, and wrote a work of 'revisionist' socialism, *Choose Freedom* (1987), regarded as important and in the tradition of Anthony Crosland.

Labour was still, however, beset by many difficulties. During this period the influence of the extreme left in the party was arguably at its very peak, and Labour was still mistrusted by the right-wing media and many moderates, despite its new and appealing leadership. In 1983, 18 sitting Labour MPs were deselected as candidates in the forthcoming election by left-wing constituency associations; several of these were, ironically, on the left of the party. Another seven sitting MPs were deselected even in 1987. In Liverpool, in 1983, militant tendency effectively controlled the City Council, adopting an illegal deficit budget as part of its policy of deliberate confrontation with the Tory government. Many other examples (e.g. 'Red' Ken Livingstone's term, 1981–86, as leader of the GLC) could be cited; they became the daily stuff of press headlines, but were as worrying to the new leadership of the party as to the right-wingers. Over the next few years Kinnock did his best to move the party to the political centre-left. Under his influence, the party abandoned unilateral nuclear disarmament, moderated its attitudes towards the EEC, and purged its militants; Kinnock often showed great personal courage in sticking to his guns in a very public way. Labour's standing in opinion polls rose perceptively – but not decisively – in 1985–86, and the party was ahead of the Tories until January 1987. Kinnock's personal rating was consistently good. By early 1987 there were reasonable hopes of winning the next election. Nevertheless, soon after the tide turned and the Tories pulled ahead. Kinnock ran a good, even inspirational campaign, and Labour's platform was much more moderate than in 1983, but this could not be transformed into a winning majority. In the General Election called for 11 June 1987, the Tories played effectively on remaining fears of trade union power and nuclear disarmament under Labour, and trumpeted Thatcher's strength: 'She's wrong but she's strong' became a catchcry. In the end, Thatcher won by a comfortable 101-seat majority, more than Macmillan's majority in his strong 1959 election victory.

	Total votes	MPs elected	% share of total vote
Conservative	13 763 066	376	42.3
Liberal	4 173 450	17	12.8
Social Democrat	3 168 183	5	9.7
(Alliance Total)	(7 341 633)	(22)	(22.5)
Labour	10 029 778	229	30.8
Plaid Cymru	123 599	3	0.3
Scottish National Party	416 473	3	1.3
Others (G.B.)	151 519	0	0.5
Others (No.I)	730 152	17	2.2
Total	32 529 568	650	100.0

Compared with 1983, the Tories wound up losing just 21 seats, and Labour gained just 20. Labour improved marginally on its 1983 showing, polling about 3 per cent more of the vote. The Alliance actually lost ground, polling 3 per cent less of the vote than in 1983 and losing one seat. In March 1988, the two components of the Alliance, the Liberals and Social Democrats, formally merged, becoming known officially as the Social and Liberal Democrats; in 1989 their title was shortened to Liberal Democrats. Paddy Ashdown (b.1941), a Liberal, became leader of the party in July 1988, holding this post till 1999.

After the 1987 election, the Thatcher era began to spiral downward to its conclusion in a manner which few could have foreseen. Like many strong leaders, Mrs Thatcher failed to groom an heir apparent. She would seemingly have preferred Cecil Parkinson (b.1931), the Transport Minister, but he became embroiled in a scandal over a mistress and an illegitimate daughter. There was thus no clear-cut route to retirement and an easy succession. Mrs Thatcher and her leading ministers, Nigel Lawson and Sir Geoffrey Howe, began to quarrel, and the government appeared to come apart. Many now questioned aspects of her judgment, especially after the retirement, in 1986, of Lord Whitelaw, a stabilising influence on the government. As noted, Mrs Thatcher had been, contrary to popular image, a relative moderate on issues like Europe, but she now emerged as emphatically on the anti-European wing of the party, although most of her senior ministers remained more or less keen Europeans.

A number of landmarks occurred on the way to Thatcher's political demise. In 1988–89 the government decided to reform the arbitrary system of local taxes, extending the payment of rates to all residents, not just homeowners.

Officially known as the Community Charge, the new system quickly became known as the 'poll tax', to be levied as a 'poll' on the total population. (Only about half of adults paid rates.) The new proposals were seemingly fair and an obvious improvement on the previous system, which encouraged Labour-dominated councils to overspend and tax the rate-paying minority for the privilege. Yet they provoked, especially in England and Wales, where they were introduced in 1990, mass unrest, boycotting, and even rioting. In part this occurred because of high levels of unemployment which still existed, in part because rate levels on private houses had been kept artificially low for many years. Michael Heseltine (b.1933), who emerged as Mrs Thatcher's greatest rival for the Prime Ministership, used the 'poll tax' issue to rally the anti-Thatcher forces.

Mrs Thatcher was first challenged for the leadership of the party by an unknown left-wing Tory MP, Sir Anthony Meyer, in December 1989. She easily defeated Meyer, 314 voted to 33 (with 27 abstentions). Over the next year a much more serious challenge emerged from Michael Heseltine (b.1933), a charismatic former Defence Minister. As Defence Minister from 1983–86, Heseltine had become embroiled with Thatcher in a bitter fight over the Westland helicopter affair. The financially shaky Westland company, which built some of Britain's military helicopters, needed rescue. Heseltine favoured a rescue bid by a British–European consortium. The Westland directors, and most of the Cabinet, favoured a rescue bid by an American firm, Sikorski. The dispute thus appeared to be one between the Cabinet's committed Europeanists (who were generally on the Left of the party) and the pro-American Thatcherites. This seemingly routine question escalated into an enormous and permanent quarrel between Thatcher and Heseltine, who resigned in the middle of a Cabinet meeting in January 1986, storming out of the room. The Sikorski bid was then accepted.

Several years later, Sir Geoffrey Howe, the former Chancellor and Foreign Secretary who, in July 1989, was made Lord President of the Council and Deputy Prime Minister, became enmeshed in an equally bitter row with Mrs Thatcher over Europe, especially over Thatcher's ever more visible stance against European integration. On 2 November 1990 Howe resigned from the Cabinet and on 10 November delivered a damaging and much-publicised speech in the Commons attacking Mrs Thatcher and her policies. Michael Heseltine then decided to challenge Mrs Thatcher for the leadership, building on discontent over high interest rates (caused in part by the boom created by the tax cuts of 1987), the poll tax, and Thatcher's increasing anti-euroscepticism. Mrs Thatcher, who was abroad at meetings much of the time, uncharacteristically chose as her campaign manager Peter Morrison MP, a hopeless incompetent at political arm twisting and hardball. Under the rules the Tories had adopted, Mrs Thatcher required a 15 per cent lead over the second place candidate to win outright, or 207 votes. She received 204, to Heseltine's 152. Thatcher's percentage of the votes cast, 57 per cent, was much higher than the percentage she had received against Edward Heath in 1975, or that which John Major would receive in the ballot for leader a week later. Yet it was just not enough. After boldly announcing that she would fight on, a great deal of pressure was brought to bear on her to resign, and key loyalists began to desert her. In the end she decided to go, and made the decision not to contest the second ballot.

Why did the Tories desert their most successful twentieth-century leader only two and a half years after winning an election with a majority of 101 seats? It is clear that many thought that the Tories were now so unpopular that they were certain to lose the next election, likely to be held in 1992, when Mrs Thatcher would be 67. Labour gained several key by-election wins in this period, especially one in Mid-Staffordshire in March 1990, and was now far ahead of the Tories in all polls, usually by ten or more points. Neil Kinnock's personal popularity rating was also consistently higher than Thatcher's, and there was a general expectation that Labour, with a centre-left orientation, was likely to win the next election. Most Tory MPs simply decided that Mrs Thatcher had to go sometime, and installing a new leader with over two years in hand gave them their only realistic chance of winning: the brutal but simple facts of political life. This must have been the case with a majority of backbenchers, or close to that number, since all or nearly all of the many dozen ministers and junior ministers in Thatcher's government presumably voted for her to continue, meaning that most backbenchers voted against her, including, presumably, some right-wing Tories.

It was also clear that Michael Heseltine could not be elected leader, and that the Thatcherite majority in the party would never vote for him. Since Mrs Thatcher had no real heir apparent, who was to succeed her? The choice fell on the unexpected figure of John Major (b.1943), a man almost literally unknown to the general public five years earlier. Major's curious life story soon became well known: the son of a 64-year-old ne'er-do-well music hall performer and garden gnome manufacturer, Abraham Thomas Ball ('Major' was a stage name he adopted); brought up in considerable poverty in south London, a school leaver from a local grammar school at 15, subsequently unemployed for 18 months, and casually employed before eventually joining a merchant bank in Nigeria (where he was nearly killed in a motor accident) in 1966. Major entered politics, slightly to the right of being a 'One Nation' Tory, as a member of the Lambeth Borough Council in 1968. In 1977 Major was, remarkably for a man of his background, chosen over blue-ribbon contenders to become the Tory candidate for Huntingdonshire, one of the safest seats in the country, and became an MP in 1979. First appointed to office in 1983, he was just another minor whip and junior minister, although one with a growing reputation for mastery of detail, until he was appointed Chief Secretary of the Treasury, with a place in the Cabinet, in June 1987. Even higher promotion followed with incredible speed: Foreign Secretary in July 1989 after Sir Geoffrey Howe's resignation, and then, only three months later, Chancellor of the Exchequer when Nigel Lawson resigned. Major stayed in even this position for just over a year before becoming Mrs Thatcher's successor. As Chancellor, Major presided over Britain's entry into the Exchange Rate Mechanism (ERM), in retrospect one of the most disastrous economic (and political) decisions ever taken by a twentieth-century Chancellor, although one widely praised at the time and made with Mrs Thatcher's approval.

John Major had his advantages: he appeared to be transparently honest and honourable – rather like Sir Alec Douglas-Home, whom he resembled in many respects apart from his social background – learned easily and quickly, knew first hand the daily struggle of the ordinary person and had not forgotten what he knew; he was totally lacking in 'side' and pretension. (In 2002, however, a sensation occurred when Edwina Currie, a highly visible former Tory minister, revealed that she had had a four-year affair with Major in the mid-1980s.) Of all modern Prime Ministers Major is possibly the one who would be most preferred as a next-door neighbour. (Who would be the least preferred? Probably Neville Chamberlain or Clement Attlee.) He seemed to be a charming family man with an all-consuming passion for cricket. On the other hand, he had many disadvantages as well: he simply did not look like a Prime Minister, and did not grow to look like one after six years in office. On the contrary, he had 'middle management' stamped all over him, and it perpetually seemed as if he would make a satisfactory Defence Secretary after three more years' ministerial experience. Major always seemed to be the archetypal example of someone who bore the stamp of the last man to sit on him. There were, as well, deep-seated ambiguities and uncertainties as to what he stood for. Selected as Thatcher's successor, he seemed more and more to be a liberal 'One Nation' Tory, with a liberal Tory inner circle of advisers, who nevertheless carried out many further instalments of privatisation and was a good social conservative. When Major resigned as leader in 1997, it was not really any clearer what he stood for than it had when he was first plucked from obscurity for senior office.

For whatever reason, John Major now became Mrs Thatcher's anointed, and she rallied the troops to support him in the second ballot (on 27 November 1990), when he contested the leadership against Michael Heseltine and Douglas Hurd (b.1930), the old Etonian diplomat and Foreign Secretary also on the left of the party. Major received 185 votes, the bulk of the Thatcherite bloc, to Heseltine's 131 and Hurd's 56. Although Major lacked the required majority, both men withdrew in his favour, and John Major became Prime Minister on 28 November 1990. And so it came to pass that the Conservative party replaced probably its greatest-ever peacetime leader with probably its worst, leading to the disaster of the 1997 General Election.

At the end of the twentieth century it was clear to all historians that Margaret Thatcher had been, with Clement Attlee, one of the two seminal figures in British politics since the Second World War. As with Attlee and his success, this could not have been predicted by anyone. Thatcher's success was, in particular, a personal *tour de force* carried out against what the majority in the Tory party would regard as their instincts and better judgment. Much in Thatcherism, too, simply put a stamp of approval on trends which had been gathering pace for decades, for instance the shift of the labour force from the manufacturing industry to the service sector, while much in 'Thatcherism' reflected policies put in place in the United States and reflective of post-1980 America. Yet 'Thatcherism' was emphatically not preordained to succeed, and many of its characteristic policies, especially privatisation and tax cuts, would almost certainly not have been enacted by any other Prime Minister. As a result, while the first half of Thatcher's term saw a continuation, in even more extreme form, of the effects of the 'British disease', especially massively high unemployment and inflation, the latter half of her term produced the beginnings of a 'British economic miracle' which left it, at the end of the century, with the strongest economy in Europe and an unemployment rate half that of most of her chief European rivals. There was, too, a cultural shift in attitudes towards capitalism, especially among the young, such that business life and entrepreneurship became popular career choices among those who would not previously have considered business careers; capitalism was looked upon as far less 'exploitative' than it had been a generation before, while the internet capitalism which emerged in the 1990s was often seen as genuinely empowering and popular. 'Thatcherism' may thus be fairly said to have gone a considerable way to restoring Britain to economic health and to bringing about a kind of cultural revolution. These achievements marked out Margaret Thatcher as plainly a greater and more imposing national leader than her immediate predecessors.

14

In Thatcher's Wake:
John Major and Tony Blair,
1990–2000

As Prime Minister, John Major had the difficult task of convincing the Conservative party and the wider electorate that he both was and was not Margaret Thatcher's 'son'. He had to show, as clearly as possible, both the continuities and innovations of his new administration. By and large, Major's Cabinet attempted to do both. Norman Lamont (b.1942), a Thatcherite and Major's deputy as Chief Secretary of the Treasury, 1989–90, who had been Major's campaign manager, became Chancellor of the Exchequer. A number of other keen Thatcherites were also appointed, for instance Michael Howard (b.1941) at Employment and the sharp-tongued and controversial David Mellor (b.1949) as Chief Secretary to the Treasury. Nevertheless, it was clear that Major had shifted the centre of gravity of the Cabinet to the Left, at least in Tory terms. Michael Heseltine had to be rewarded after his strong showing, and was made Environment minister, with responsibility for replacing the 'poll tax'. Chris Patten (b.1945), a decided liberal and centrist – a close associate of Major's – became Chancellor of the Duchy of Lancaster, Kenneth Baker (b.1934), another relative liberal, became Home Secretary, while Douglas Hurd remained as Foreign Minister. The rhetoric and emphasis of the new order also changed. For instance, Major deliberately invited Ian McKellen, the actor, a homosexual campaigner, to Number 10, and several years later (in February 1994) Parliament voted to lower the age of consent for homosexual acts from 21 to 18. (On a 'free vote'; but, as Major pointedly notes in his autobiography, 'free votes do not just happen'.) Major's rhetoric emphasised the creation of a 'classless' society which would have 'no artificial barriers of background, religion, or race', as he stated in his first speech to the Tories as Prime Minister. Returning Cabinet ministers also noted a dramatic difference in the tenor of Cabinet meetings, with the authoritarianism that had apparently marked the Thatcher Cabinet replaced by a new openness. Major's personal staff also differed from Thatcher's, with the appointment of the highly competent Sarah Hogg as Head of the Policy Unit of Number 10. Nor was there a place in the new Cabinet for Margaret Thatcher (who was still very much a member of the House of Commons). Major toyed with the idea of offering her either the

Exchequer or the Foreign Office but decided that her increasingly anti-European stance would be a liability, and that she would inevitably try to run the show. Thatcher had come to the same conclusion with Edward Heath.

Although Major had moved the party marginally to the centre-left, it was also clear that he was not abandoning 'Thatcherism'. Privatisation and most of the other policies associated with the former Prime Minister continued apace, while Major personally became the architect of much greater accountability throughout all public services, with explanations and guarantees being given to all persons using one of the public services for incompetent performance. Nothing like Major's 'Citizen's Charter' (as he termed it in March 1991) had been seen before, and to a large extent he helped to transform the culture of the public services, which previously had invariably been marked by Kafkaesque bureaucracy, red tape, and automatic stonewalling in virtually all of its dealings with the public. Much of what Major did strongly presaged (as he notes in his autobiography) the 'stakeholder' ideology which swept Tony Blair to power in 1997. Major's version of Conservatism has some parallels with the 'kinder, gentler' conservatism of President George Bush (1989–93) in the United States, who, like Major, succeeded a seminal conservative leader, Ronald Reagan. Major would probably never have spoken as Mrs Thatcher famously had in October 1987, when, ill-judgedly, she declared in an interview in a woman's magazine that 'there is no such thing as society, [only] individual men and women', even if the actual policies of the two Prime Ministers were not terribly different.

In the first instance, however, John Major found himself with a war to fight. On 2 August 1990 Saddam Hussein's regime in Iraq invaded and conquered Kuwait, an independent, pro-Western oil-rich coastal state that had strong British links, and declared it to be a province of Iraq. This was the first time since the Second World War that one sovereign state was invaded and conquered by another, and was as gross a violation of international law as could be imagined. The UN Security Council immediately condemned the move and applied sanctions. When Iraq's troops massed on the Saudi border, Western powers, including American and Britain, sent troops to Saudi Arabia, and it became clear a war was at hand unless Iraq withdrew. Saddam Hussein rounded up all the Westerners in Kuwait and held them hostage as human shields, eventually releasing them on 6 December 1990. As the UN deadline of 16 January 1991, given to Saddam to withdraw his forces from Kuwait, came and went, a vast international military force headed by the United States, but with an important British contingent, was assembled to liberate Kuwait, in 'Operation Desert Storm'. As Iraq was a Third World state of 18 million people, facing the might of American and dozens of other armies, the result could not be in much doubt. The Gulf War, which lasted from 16 January until 28 February 1991, was marked by guided missile attacks seen on television night after night. Iraq pumped vast quantities of Kuwaiti oil into the Persian Gulf to create an oil slick, and destroyed as much of Kuwait as it could. Kuwait was liberated on 26 February. Britain suffered 24 killed and 34 wounded.

In some respects the Gulf War was a rerun of the Falklands war nine years earlier, a quick and easy win against an aggressive dictatorship. Fighting and winning the war only three months after coming to office did John Major and his government no harm, and pictures of Major standing atop British tanks in the region became a familiar sight. The government moved ahead of Labour in opinion polls for the first time in several years, and Major's personal rating reached 60 per cent, a higher figure than Mrs Thatcher ever received in her eleven years. Yet the aftermath of the war was marked by much frustration. The Allies interpreted their UN remit narrowly, and did not move into Iraq to overthrow Saddam, who remained in power over a decade later, when the son of American President Bush was in the White House. The UN spent years attempting to get Iraq to comply with its requirement that it destroy its formidable war machine, and the Kurdish and Shi'ite minorities in Iraq were in constant danger of genocide.

In March 1991, the government also announced the end of the 'poll tax', eventually substituting a 'banded' property tax with relief for single-member households. In the meantime, since charges under the 'poll tax' were so high, the government raised VAT by 2.5 per cent to compensate for the loss of revenue. Major's most important venture during the first period of his administration, however, was the signing of the Maastricht Agreement in December 1991 (and more formally in February 1992). The Agreement, called from the city in the Netherlands where it was negotiated, was a general accord among the twelve EEC members to speed up the process of European integration. The Maastricht Treaty termed itself 'a new step in the process of creating an ever-closer union' in Europe. Major fought bitterly against the two most controversial features of the Agreement, plans to establish a common currency by 1999, and ratification of the Social Charter, a policy on employment conditions and the like which Tories regarded as socialistic. Major won the right to 'opt out' of these, but, to the fury of many Tory Europhobes, declined to rule out either on a permanent basis. Maastricht had to be ratified by each of the member states separately, and its enactment was thrown into considerable doubt by its defeat in a referendum in Denmark. Major delayed its passage through Parliament until after the 1992 General Election, which was imminent. Maastricht saw the emergence of a highly visible and virulent anti-European wing of the Conservative party, one whose importance would grow during the rest of Major's term of office.

The next General Election could not be delayed later than June 1992, and Major then decided to call it for 8 April 1992. Most pundits regarded his chance of winning as worse than even, with opinion polls showing the two parties neck and neck. Neil Kinnock had spent much of his time as leader moving the party to the centre and away from the extreme left, an effort which was largely successful. In October 1988, Tony Benn had challenged Kinnock for the leadership but received only 11 per cent of Labour's electoral college vote. The Tories concentrated on the alleged high taxing policies of Labour, claiming that the 'Alternative Budget' presented by Shadow Chancellor John Smith would cost every tax payer £1000 more a year. The tabloids and the right-wing press were fairly solidly against Labour. The end of the Cold War had removed nuclear disarmament as an issue, and Labour's position on Europe was fairly similar to the government's. The only event of interest in this unusually volatile election was the alleged exploitation of the tale of 'Jennifer', a sick child supposedly denied an NHS operation because of lack of funding, whose story Labour was accused of misusing. There was, apparently, a last minute switch back to the Tories, since all public opinion polls had underestimated the Conservative vote by about 4 per cent.

	Total votes	MPs elected	% share of total vote
Conservative	14 082 283	336	41.9
Liberal Democrat	5 999 384	20	17.8
Labour	11 559 735	271	34.4
Plaid Cymru	154 439	4	0.5
Scottish Nationalist Party	629 552	3	1.9
Others (G.B.)	436 207	0	1.0
Others (No.I.)	740 485	17	2.2
Total	33 612 693	651	100.0

The Tories lost 40 seats compared with 1987, while Labour gained 42, leaving Major with an overall majority of 21, and the likelihood – but not certainty – of remaining in office for four or five more years. All parties could claim some credit. In 1992, the Tories won a greater number of votes than any party in history, before or since, while their percentage of the vote (41.9) was only fractionally less than that polled in the banner year of 1983. Labour gained 1.5 million more votes than in 1987, and made good much of the loss in votes of their dark years. The Liberal Democrat vote was also up by one million. There was the usual geographical breakdown: the Tories were absolutely dominant in the south of England outside London (161 seats compared with 10 for Labour), but fair-to-poor elsewhere. In Scotland, the Tories won only 11 seats to Labour's 49. Since Labour was widely expected to win, however, John Major produced a remarkable victory, though a Pyrrhic one, since his margin in the House was insufficient to stop backbench rebels from making endless trouble. It is unclear, too, whether 1992 should be seen as John Major's first win or Margaret Thatcher's fourth, with her legacy carrying the Tories across the line.

Although events now seemed to have played into Major's hand, affairs were now to take a catastrophic turn, one which permanently derailed the government and had dire long-term consequences for the Conservative party. In October 1990, Britain had joined the Exchange Rate Mechanism (ERM), an international monetary device whereby sterling was valued for exchange purposes in terms of deutschmarks at a fixed rate. The rate chosen ($£1 = 2.95 \, Dm$) was a high one, making exports more expensive. Britain did this largely to curb inflation, which was dangerously high during the 'Lawson boom' of the 1980s. Proponents of the ERM, including John Major, credited it with decreasing Britain's inflation rate. The ERM might have helped, but such a claim seems dubious. Inflation was high everywhere in the world in the 1970s and 1980s, and then declined markedly in the 1990s, even in countries far removed from the ERM. In Canada, for instance, consumer prices increased by an average of 8.7 per cent in 1975–80, and then 7.4 per cent in 1980–85, but declined to only 1.5 per cent in 1991–92, 1.8 per cent in 1992–93, and 0.2 per cent in

1992–94. Similar declines occurred almost everywhere. Britain's inflation rate was actually lower after it left the ERM than when it was a member. In order to attract overseas investors to keep the pound high, however, the British government was obliged to maintain its interest rates above the German interest rate level, whatever that might be. The Bundesbank, the German central bank, in effect became the determinant of British interest rates. The Bundesbank was entirely independent of the German government and was notoriously concerned solely with German economic conditions, despite the fact that many European currencies had joined the ERM and were dependent upon its bank rate. This was an extraordinary and virtually insane arrangement; almost the exact equivalent of an agreement between Safeway and Tesco, its main competitor, whereby Tesco was somehow allowed to set Safeway's prices. Moreover, German reunification had forced the Bundesbank to raise its interest rate even higher and keep them there, while a tide of international currency dealing, carried on almost instantaneously on the internet, threatened to turn any run of bad news into a major panic. Britain, undergoing a recession in 1992, wished to lower its interest rates but was unable to because of the ERM. On 13 September 1992, Italy devalued its currency and left the ERM. International currency dealers started selling pounds in record numbers, convinced that Britain, too, would have to leave the ERM. The Bank of England and the Bundesbank were obliged to buy pounds to keep its price up.

The scene was now set for 'Black Wednesday', 16 September 1992, about which a great deal has already been written by its participants. Panic and chaos set in the currency market. The Chancellor, Norman Lamont, raised interest rates by an unbelievable 5 per cent in one day, without stopping the dumping of sterling by speculators, which was now in free fall. For reasons about which there is a basic dispute, Lamont and Major had trouble speaking to each other on that crucial day, and Major did nothing without consulting his inner circle of advisers, Douglas Hurd (the Foreign Minister), Kenneth Clarke (the Home Secretary), and Michael Heseltine (the Trade Minister), none of whom had any responsibility for interest rates or foreign exchange. Much of the chaotic handling of the crisis was virtually carried out in public. Before the day was over, Britain left the ERM, never to return, while within three weeks the pound was worth only 2.44 Dm, a 20 per cent devaluation from its peak level.

'Black Wednesday' was unquestionably the seminal event of British politics in the 1990s, one whose consequences lasted into the next Millennium. John Major and his Cabinet were immediately seen as incompetents, if not something like clowns. 'Black Wednesday' released an orgy of pent up Europhobia in the Conservative party and the Tory press which now became obsessive and powerful. Britain's post-Suez image as the economic 'sick man of Europe' now returned with a vengeance, paradoxically just when it was about to become the economic strong man of Europe. Neither Major nor his government ever recovered from 'Black Wednesday', and the goal of winning a fifth term later in the decade, never easy, became impossible. Labour took a 20-point lead in the opinion polls, and maintained an enormous lead consistently until the 1997 General Election.

In 1992–93, a further great series of Parliamentary battles took place when the Maastricht Treaty came up for formal approval. An intense, committed group of Tory Eurosceptics, numbering from 10 to 60, consistently voted with the Opposition parties against the Treaty, giving the government a knife-edge majority. On 4 November 1992, the government won the paving (preliminary) motion on the Maastricht Treaty by 319-316 votes. In March 1993, a minor Labour amendment on the composition of the European Committee of the Regions was carried by 22 votes, with 50 Tories voting against the government. Forty-six Tory MPs voted against the third reading of the Maastricht Bill in May 1993. Margaret Thatcher and many of her supporters now overtly or covertly supported the defeat of Maastricht and were avowedly opposed to any further increase in European integration. By 1993, hostility to Europe, and in particular to any further increases in the central power of the EC bureaucracy, became a fixation among most of the press and a wide variety of opinion-leaders. The press, in particular, deserted John Major in a manner without precedent for any modern Tory Prime Minister. While the left-liberal newspapers such as the *Guardian* and *Independent* inevitably detested any Tory government, Major also lost the support of Rupert Murdoch, the Australian-born media mogul, probably the most powerful press baron in the world, who owned the normally Tory *Times* and the tabloid *Sun*, and Canadian newspaper magnate Conrad Black, who owned the usually arch-Tory *Daily Telegraph*. By the mid-1990s a near-consensus had emerged in Fleet Street that Major was an inadequate mediocrity who would have to go. Hostility to further Europeanisation was at the root of this sense, hostility which was also fed by visible and wealthy anti-European activists such as Sir James Goldsmith. 'The bastards' – as Major termed the extreme anti-Europeanists in the Tory party (in an accidentally recorded interview with television reporter Michael Brunson in July 1993) – proved to be the bane of Major's government until its defeat. In April 1995, the Tories withdrew their Whip (i.e. temporarily expelled from the party) eight of the most extreme Euro-rebels.

In the meantime, Major ploughed on with governing the country. In May 1993, he rearranged his Cabinet quite radically. Norman Lamont went, a move almost inevitable after the ERM fiasco, and was replaced by Kenneth Clarke (b.1940), a heavyweight figure in the party who would probably have become Tory leader at some stage except for his notable warmth towards Europe. His appointment did not please the right wing of the party; perhaps to balance his appointment Major made Michael Howard (b.1941), a pro-'law and order' conservative, Home Secretary. Major also appointed John Redwood (b.1951) to the Welsh Office; two years later Redwood was to challenge Major for the Tory leadership.

Major's government was also distinguished for its genuinely innovative policies in a number of fields. In 1992, the government abolished the 'binary' system in tertiary education, turning Britain's polytechnics into universities. Whereas Britain had only about twenty universities in 1945, by the mid-1990s there were more than a hundred, in every part of the country. In late 1994, the government introduced the National Lottery (announced in 1992) which soon became a weekly ritual for millions of people. Britain's attitude towards gambling had long been notoriously hypocritical: government lotteries were outlawed in the 1820s, but vast numbers of people gambled regularly on and off the racetrack, via football pools, and in overseas sweepstakes. The National Lottery, with its truly vast prizes, normally created several millionaires every week, and was indicative of the change in morality and, in a sense, in the decline in socialistic objections to wealth accumulation. In 1994, the government also passed the Sunday Trading Act, which allowed most shops, including department stores and supermarkets, to open on Sunday. British Sundays remained days of suspended animation long after most people ceased to be strict Sabbath observers, and the government brushed aside objections by church groups to pass this Act. Both of these changes illustrated something of the surprisingly ambiguous nature of 'Thatcherism' – liberally subversive of long-standing restrictions but carried out in the interests of capitalism and wealth accumulation, not of 'progress' and left-wing ideologies.

By mid-1995, the tensions within the Tory party had reached such a level that Major decided to take the remarkable step of resigning the leadership, standing for re-election as leader of the party, and challenging anyone on the Eurosceptic wing of the Tories to stand against him. Nothing like this had ever happened before, and Major received may plaudits for his bold move. Major's apparent prevarication on the Single Currency – whether, when, or if Britain should ever join – led to ever-increasing hostility within the party and rumours of leadership challenges. Major had to secure 165 votes (a majority of Tory MPs) and a lead of 15 per cent over any other candidate to win. Major later said that he would resign if he received fewer than 215 votes. There were many potential rivals – Lamont, Heseltine, Michael Portillo (then a right-wing Thatcherite) – but in the end only John Redwood decided to challenge. There was little chance of his winning. Almost unknown, Redwood was often regarded as a rather tortured right-wing ideologue whom Major was probably going to sack. Major, oddly, used the leader of the House of Lords, Lord Cranborne (Robert Gascoyne-Cecil, b.1946) as his campaign manager (he was the heir to the famous Salisbury peerage and 'called up' to the Lords in his father's lifetime by a little-used law), a curious turn of events for the Cecil family. The vote took place on 4 July 1995, with Major winning 218 votes, Redwood 89, and 22 abstentions. Major's job was safe, although a 29 per cent vote – Redwood's share of those voting – for a virtually unknown challenger against a serving Prime Minister was not a ringing victory. Major received three more votes than his minimal survival figure, and hung on until the next election. Major made many changes after the leadership vote. Michael Heseltine became Deputy Prime Minister. This was interpreted as a reward for his support, and resented by the right wing of the party, but had actually been decided upon before the election. Malcolm Rifkind (b.1946) became Foreign Secretary, Michael Portillo Defence Minister. Naturally, Redwood was dropped at the Welsh Office, to be replaced by the youthful William Hague (b.1961). After April 1992, Major's Cabinet contained two women members, Virginia Bottomley (b.1948) and Gillian Shephard (b.1940), who were retained, and Ken Clarke remained Chancellor.

The last two years of Major's government brought no respite in its unpopularity, and there was never a single opinion poll in which it trailed Labour by less than 18 per cent. The government became unpopular among the middle classes, especially younger voters. Many home purchasers had experienced 'negative equity': they had purchased a house at a vastly inflated price during the housing boom of the 1980s and then found, in the recession of the early 1990s, that house prices collapsed, meaning that they could only sell their homes at a loss and, in the meantime, were repaying their mortgage at astronomical interest rates. This situation persisted in some cases until the late 1990s and caused enormous resentment. British membership in ERM had itself sparked an entirely unnecessary recession between about 1988 and 1994, with its nadir around 1992. As government revenues collapsed and welfare payments arose, the government could not pay higher pensions, alienating the elderly, or raise pay in the public sector, alienating the public sector middle class. Unemployment rose after 1990, peaking at 10.3 per cent in 1993; it still stood at 7.5 per cent in 1996. Many of the changes brought about by privatisation, for instance with the railways, were deeply unsettling. Major also did not do many of the things which might have helped him. London was almost completely neglected, its infrastructure falling to pieces. Unlike most Tories, he had no interest in strengthening the military, a natural Tory constituency, and it, too, was run down. Much of rural Britain was alienated by the 'beef war' and other aspects of the EEC's seeming hostility to Britain, and by the first glimmer of the BSC scare in 1996.

Another destructive element which marked the last part of Major's term was the media's all-consuming interest in 'sleaze', the discovery of chicanery by Tory MPs involving sexual or financial impropriety, or political favouritism. David Mellor and Neil Hamilton were probably the highest-profile subjects of media interest in 'sleaze', but such MPs as Alan Clark, Tim Yeo, and Michael Mates were also among those pilloried by the press on an almost daily basis. Major himself successfully sued the *New Statesman* when it claimed he had had an affair. While 'sleaze' had been 'exposed' by the media in nearly all post-war governments, these allegations reached epidemic proportions under Major, badly undermining the government's viability. It was also evidence of how far the press had turned against the Major government. The government routinely and almost automatically lost virtually every loseable by-election it contested, and was all but wiped out in most local elections.

A very bad situation for the Tories was made far worse by events in the Labour party. Kinnock and Hattersley resigned soon after the 1992 election, and in July 1992 the party chose John Smith (1938–94) as its leader and Margaret Beckett (b.1943) as Deputy Leader. Smith trounced the only other candidate for the leadership, Bryan Gould (b.1939) receiving 91 per cent of the electoral college vote. Beckett, the first woman elected to one of the senior positions in the party, defeated John Prescott (b.1938) and Gould. Smith, a clever Scottish QC, was determined to complete the party's move to the centre. In 1993, he managed the introduction of 'one member one vote', which meant the relinquishing of much of the block voting power of the trade unions, who were required to ballot their members individually before voting for the party's leadership. The 'electoral college' percentages were also altered to one-third each for MPs, trade unions, and constituency parties. Smith's long-term goal was to eliminate 'Clause Four', the party's contentious and unrealistic socialist objective. As Opposition leader, Smith rode high in the polls, consistently outdistancing the Tories.

On 12 May 1994, however, Smith suffered a fatal heart attack (he had had a history of heart illness) and died near Aberdeen, aged only 57. After the party's shock had worn off (or even before, as few wasted any time before speculating on a new leader) Labour chose Anthony (Tony) Blair (b.1953), truly a 'golden boy' of the media and politics, to succeed him. Although not of a wealthy family, Blair was educated at Fettes and Oxford, became a barrister, and entered Parliament in Labour's nadir year of 1983. Only 41 when chosen, Blair's Kennedyesque good looks, media presence, and pop star-like glamour made him a truly formidable opponent. On the fairly extreme right of the Labour party, he was determined to complete the reform of the party, turning it into a moderately social democratic entity which, like the Democratic party in the United States, fully accepted capitalism and, indeed, Thatcherism. Blair was easily elected in July 1994, defeating John Prescott and Margaret Beckett with 57 per cent of the electoral college vote. To balance him the party chose John Prescott, from the traditional northern working-class wing of the party, as Deputy Leader over Margaret Beckett. In October 1994, an attempt to revise Clause Four was defeated by 50.9-49.1 per cent of the Labour conference vote, but Blair's revision was finally accepted in April 1995 (with 65 per cent of the vote) at a special Labour conference. Labour had ceased, even nominally, to be a socialist party with full-scale nationalisation as its goal. Further reforms introduced by Blair loosened ties with the unions and reformed the party's internal structure.

Blair was an immediate master of relating to the media, and over the next three years won over much of the press, such that at the 1997 General Election newspapers with 61 per cent of the country's readership supported Labour's election, compared with the usual figure of 30 per cent or so. Blair also won over a surprising share of Britain's business leaders, convincing them that 'New Labour' – as he rebranded the party in October 1995 – was actually better for them than the disunited Tories. He held a massive lead among younger voters, but was, in his personal life, traditional enough to appeal to older ones as well, a surprisingly orthodox churchgoer and family man. While it was unlikely that the Conservatives, under John Major, could have won in 1997, Blair's ascendancy made it impossible.

Although the Major government was trailing Labour so badly in opinion polls that it was lapping the field, the British economy was arguably in the best shape it had been during the entire twentieth century. By 1997, there was full employment, low inflation, and continuous high growth rates; the City of London had been restored to its central international role, and Britain had the strongest economy in Europe. Overseas, too, the world appeared to be in better shape than in many decades, the end of the Cold War being swiftly followed by moves towards peace in the Middle East and the peaceful transition of South Africa with Nelson Mandela coming to power. In Northern Ireland, the IRA announced a ceasefire in August 1994 and was joined by a Loyalist ceasefire two months later. Using American Senator George Mitchell from 1995, a far-reaching accord, the 'Good Friday Agreement', was reached in early 1998 shortly after Labour came to office. During the 1990s the Provisional IRA was unusually quiet, with only an enormous bomb at Canary Wharf in

February 1996 breaking the tranquillity in a way which recalled its heyday, although civilian deaths in Northern Ireland still claimed 40–70 victims a year until 1994, when homicide levels declined. In 1997, Hong Kong reverted to the People's Republic of China, with Chris Patten memorably leaving the Colony as its last Governor. Despite widespread fears of the imposition of totalitarian rule, little changed except for the flag and emblems. Britain's only significant military involvement after the Gulf War was its role as part of the UN peacekeeping forces in former Yugoslavia from 1993, mainly in Bosnia–Herzegovina.

After mid-1995, the Tories awaited the next election, alternating between expecting the inevitable death sentence and hope that things could still go right at the last moment. Again, this universal mood of resigned despondency occurred despite the ostensible excellence of the government's economic performance. The General Election held on 1 May 1997 realised the very worst fears of the Tories. Not only did their vote drop disastrously, but a *de facto* tactical voting alliance between Labour and the Liberal Democrats did the maximum harm to the Tories in terms of the number of seats it won. So, too, did the intervention of Sir James Goldsmith's anti-European single issue Referendum party, which nominated 547 candidates and won 2.6 per cent of the total vote, and the even more extreme UK Independence Party. Whenever the Tories appeared to be creeping back up in the opinion polls, either Europe or 'sleaze' would surface again. Labour made sweeping but very vague promises about raising Britain's economic performance, promised an end to hospital waiting lists, and placed central emphasis on 'education, education, and education', as Blair put it in October 1996.

	Total votes	MPs elected	% share of total vote
Conservative	9 600 940	165	30.7
Liberal Democrat	5 243 440	46	16.8
Labour	13 517 911	419	43.2
Plaid Cymru	161 030	4	0.5
Scottish National Party	622 260	6	2.0
Referendum	811 827	0	2.6
Others (G.B.)	549 874	1	1.7
Others (No.I.)	790 778	18	2.5
Total	31 287 702	635	100.0

The election was, in Major's words, a 'comprehensive defeat' for the Conservatives, arguably the worst in its history. Labour won 26 more seats than in 1945, and only 11 fewer than the Liberals and the Labour associates had won in 1906, an election to which 1997 was quickly and often compared. Dozens of ministers and backbenchers bit the dust in a night that was quickly likened to going over the top at the Somme. Probably the most high profile losses of the election were those of Michael Portillo, seen as Major's most likely replacement, and Foreign Secretary Malcolm Rifkind. Outside the south-east of England the Tories lost disastrously everywhere. Most strikingly, they did not elect a single MP in either Scotland or Wales. The Scottish phalanx now consisted of 56 Labour MPs, 10 Liberals, 6 Scottish Nationalists, and no Tories. In the north of England, 13 Tories faced 139 Labourites. Even in the south-east outside London, while there were 95 Tories (compared with 161 in 1992), there were also 45 Labourites and 22 Liberal Democrats.

The vast Labour contingent was notably different from that elected before. Only 13 per cent of Labour's MPs were workers, compared with 29 per cent in 1987; while nearly a majority were professionals. Sixty-six per cent were university-educated, higher than the percentage of university-educated Tory MPs in 1970. Only a minority were Oxbridge (about 16 per cent had been to a public school, compared with 61 per cent of Tory MPs) and some cynics spoke of 'the triumph of the provincial lower second'. Most strikingly of all, there were now 120 women MPs, twice the number elected in 1992, and six times the number elected in 1979. No fewer than 102 of these were Labourites, compared with only 13 Tory and three Liberal Democrat women MPs. The Liberal Democrats elected a record number of MPs, 46, the highest total for the Liberals since 1929, although their percentage of the total vote actually declined.

As always in Britain, the 1997 election greatly exaggerated the actual vote of both the winner and loser, and Labour's victory was in many respects far less impressive than it seemed. Labour secured only 43.2 per cent of the total vote cast, about normal for any recent winning party, and a lower share than it obtained in 1964, when it won by only four seats. The Tory percentage of the total vote, 30.7 per cent, was by far its lowest in modern history, but almost identical to Labour's share of the total vote in 1987 (30.8 per cent), when it elected 64 more MPs. To the Tory vote, moreover, presumably must be added the 3 per cent or so cast for the anti-European parties. Similarly, the Liberal Democrat share of the vote (16.8 per cent) was nothing special, about what it always obtained since 1974. The overall number of votes cast, it should be noted, was 2.3 million less than in 1992, and widespread apathy among younger voters was a notable feature of the 1997 election. Labour actually received half a million fewer votes than the Tories had gained in 1992, difficult as that might seem to believe. Nevertheless, there was indeed a catastrophic decline in Tory votes, and the cost of John Major's leadership since the 1992 election, and of continuing civil war in the party over Europe, can be measured with some precision: 4.7 million votes and 171 MPs, more than half the total it elected five years earlier.

As 18 years had passed since the previous Labour government, Blair's Cabinet contained few survivors from the 1970s. Only four of 22 Cabinet ministers had held any ministerial posts before, even the most menial. The Cabinet contained five women, a record, among them the highly visible and popular Marjorie ('Mo') Mowlam (b.1949) at Northern Ireland. Like many other features of Blair's government, it was very difficult to classify. No one was drawn from the traditional aristocracy (although Harriet Harman (b.1950), Social Security secretary, was a relative of Lord Longford), but 15 were described as 'middle class', only seven 'working class'. Twenty-one had been to university, a record percentage, but only three to Oxbridge. The Cabinet included a blind man, David Blunkett (b.1947), Education minister, and at least one man, Chris Smith (b.1951), the National Heritage minister, who made no secret of his homosexuality. Several very visible ministers remained outside the Cabinet, most notably Blair's 'Svengali', Peter Mandelson (b.1953), Minister Without Portfolio, the grandson of Herbert Morrison. Apart from Blair, the most important ministers were Gordon Brown (b.1951), Chancellor of the Exchequer, Robin Cook (b.1946), the Foreign Minister, and Jack Straw (b.1946), Home Secretary. Brown soon became known as the 'Iron Chancellor', a successful administrator whose first important act was to give up the right to set interest rates, turning over the power to the Bank of England.

After some years in office, most observers remained extremely puzzled as to what the Blair government was about. Blair made great play with wanting to create a 'stakeholder' society and, in 1998, authored a Fabian pamphlet entitled *The Third Way: New Politics for the New Century*, another Blair mantra, drawn from the influential sociologist Anthony Giddens. (The 'third way' presumably runs between laissez-faire capitalism and socialism.) All these concepts remained highly ambiguous. It became absolutely clear that the Blair government accepted most, if not all, of the presuppositions of post-Thatcherite Britain: privatisation, lower direct taxes than in Europe, a tamed trade union movement kept at arm's length. The Blair government made absolutely no attempt to change any of these, let alone restore some kind of pre-1979 nationalised sector. Nor was there any talk of a 'social contract'. Blair had inherited an economy with uniquely good statistics, and did not rock the boat: unemployment continued to decline. Despite talk of 'public–private partnerships', there were none. At home, there was some minor liberalisation in areas such as homosexuality, where the age of consent was changed to 16, but, again, no wild innovations. The closest approach to one was the adoption of European human rights law as an adjunct to British law. Such other changes as there were were often not what one might expect a Labour government to do. For instance, in 1998, loans replaced maintenance grants for university students, something at which Thatcher herself had balked.

The major innovations came in the constitutional sphere. In 1999, all but 92 hereditary peers (out of 700 or so) were excluded from the House of Lords, and a more basic reform promised. Blair, however, made extraordinarily lavish use of patronage powers to create life peers, awarding no fewer than 153 in two years, 62 per annum, a rate that made Lloyd George's legendary peerage creations, at a rate of 16 per year, look like nothing. Many were Blair's friends or Labour party hacks, and were widely derided as 'Tony's cronies'. Constitutional change came to Scotland and Wales. In September 1997, a referendum on the establishment of a Scottish Parliament was carried by a 74 per cent majority. The resulting *Scotland Act 1998* set up a Scottish Parliament in Edinburgh of 129 members, elected by both first-past-the-post and proportional representation. In 1999, the first Scottish Executive was established, with Donald Dewar (1937–2000), the memorable Scottish Secretary, as its First Minister. Most major areas of governmental interest (including all but limited taxing power) were reserved to the Westminster Parliament. It remained to be seen whether the Scottish Parliament would see the end of demands for Scottish independence.

Labour secured 56 seats in the first Scottish Parliamentary election in May 1999, compared with 35 for the Scottish Nationalists, 18 for the Tories, and 17 for the Liberal Democrats. In September 1997, a similar referendum was held in Wales, which voted by only 50.3 per cent to establish a Welsh Assembly. This was set up in 1998, a body of 60 members in Cardiff with much more limited powers than in Scotland. Alun Michael became First Secretary of Wales in July 1999.

In April 1998, perhaps the beginning of the end came to the Northern Ireland conflict in the form of the 'Good Friday Agreement', which established a 108-seat assembly. The Agreement was supported by 71 per cent of the electorate. Ulster Unionist David Trimble (shortly to win the Nobel Peace Prize) became First Minister. A protracted struggle over the decommissioning of IRA weapons then ensued, with the British government eventually freeing all IRA and Unionist prisoners. The taste for extremism on both sides had clearly waned.

For his first three years of office and beyond, Blair and his government had a dream run. There seems little doubt that the media was vastly less critical of Blair than of Major, although their polices were either identical or even less to the liking of the mainstream press. There were several reasons for this. Blair made admittedly excellent use of 'spin doctors', government orderlies who dealt with the media and massaged the news. All post-war governments had dealt with the media in an attempt to gain an advantage, but none so comprehensively or professionally as Blair. With his unprecedented majority, Blair was absolutely in charge of his party and government, and there was no chance of a backbench revolt of importance. Disputes, if there were any, centred around the Cabinet, especially the long-standing rivalry between Blair and Brown. The quality of the Opposition, or rather the lack of it, was another fact. John Major resigned immediately after his defeat. The Tories then went through a three-ballot process of choosing a successor. On the first ballot, Kenneth Clarke led with 49 votes, followed by William Hague (41), John Redwood (27), Peter Lilley (b.1943) (24), and Michael Howard (23). Clarke represented the Europhile left of the party, with the others vaguely or clearly on the Right. Eventually, on the third ballot, William Hague defeated Ken Clarke, 92-70. Hague, born in 1961, was the youngest-ever Tory leader. Able, witty, and ambitious, he had the misfortune of looking like a schoolboy and leading a sadly depleted army against an enormously popular Prime Minister. He stood little or no chance of defeating Blair in the next election, but his selection showed the unpopularity of the pro-European wing of the party. Ken Clarke, a much more formidable figure, would probably have become Tory leader except for his pro-European views. For a year after June 1998, Peter Lilley was the Tory's Deputy Leader.

Ambiguity seemed on careful analysis to be at the heart of Blair and 'New Labour' and, indeed, Blair's Britain. Perhaps this was shown by the reaction to the shocking death in a car crash in Paris of Princess Diana on 30 August 1997, one of the few moments in modern history which everyone would remember how they heard the news. A spontaneous, unprecedented outpouring of grief overtook the nation, which briefly threatened to engulf the Queen and the Royal family. Blair, a royalist, headed the mourning and seemed to encapsulate, in a strange way, what Diana evidently meant to millions – although it was hard to put into words precisely what that was, a mixture of glamour and apparently genuine, but never far from media cameras, concern for the poor. To this millions responded. Some compared Diana to Evita Peron. The Australian historian Manning Clark, shortly before his death in 1991, said that the young of his country were 'the first generation of Australians to believe in nothing'. Was it 'nothing' in which the millions who turned out to mourn for Diana, so soon after Blair's triumphant election, believed? Was the grief for Diana the inadvertent but ultimate symbol of the Blair government? Or was it, perhaps, the Millennium Dome, the grandiose 'nothing' erected by Peter Mandelson to outdo his grandfather Herbert Morrison, the progenitor of the (in contrast, memorable) 1951 Festival of Britain? Whatever the case, sooner or later 'the people' (another 'New Labour' catchphrase) would eventually tire of Tony Blair, just as it had once tired of Balfour and Asquith, MacDonald and Baldwin, Eden and Wilson, Callaghan and Thatcher....

Index